ALFREDS STRAUMANIS is Professor of Theatre at Southern Illinois University — Carbondale where he also directs the Baltic Drama project. He received his Ph.D. in Drama from Carnegie Institute of Technology (now Carnegie-Mellon University) as an Andrew Mellon Fellow. His plays — original and translated — have been produced in the U.S.A., Australia, and Canada. He is the author of a novel, short stories, and theatre reviews published in French and German newspapers as well as in Latvian ethnic publications. He is a coauthor of books, *In the World of Mārtiņš Zīverts* and *Ethnic Theatre in the U.S.A.*; editor of Baltic drama anthologies, *Confrontations with Tyranny* and *The Golden Steed*; and the editor of *Baltic Drama: A Handbook and Bibliography*. His essays on drama and theatre have appeared in journals such as *Jaunā Gaita, Journal of Baltic Studies, The Nationalities Papers*, and *Southern Theatre*, among others.

Bridge Across the Sea

Seven Baltic Plays

Edited by
ALFREDS STRAUMANIS
Southern Illinois University

Waveland Press, Inc.
Prospect Heights, Illinois

For information about this book, write or call:

Waveland Press, Inc.
P.O. Box 400
Prospect Heights, Illinois 60070
(312) 634-0081

Library of Congress Catalog Card Number 83-50121
ISBN 0-88133-055-8

Printed in the United States of America.

PREFACE

The first in the series of Baltic drama anthologies, *Confrontations with Tyranny*, included translated Baltic plays dealing with different reasons which might trigger an individual's alienation from his original environment forcing him into a physical or spiritual exile. The second anthology, *The Golden Steed*, contained plays based on the folklores of the three Baltic nations. While the plays for the first two volumes were selected without geographical or chronological considerations (authors living in the Soviet Baltic republics as well as in the world at large and plays from the beginning of the twentieth century as well as contemporary plays were used), the present volume, *Bridge Across the Sea*, is a compilation of plays written by Baltic dramatists living in North America. Its predominant theme is acculturation of the Baltic immigrant to a new environment, and only plays written after World War II are used to illuminate the problems encountered by the post-World War II Baltic immigrants in their attempt to adjust to a new life.

Among the many problems which the new immigrant encounters and which are depicted in the seven plays found in this volume, some are common to all societies of America, some are specifically connected with the changing life styles and mores of the Baltic ethnic groups. In order for the reader to understand these specific problems, the nature of the post-World War II Baltic immigration and the set of values the immigrants brought along need explaining. Thus, an introductory essay by a first generation immigrant, Professor Penikis, depicting the political background and dealing with social and cultural aspects of the Baltic ethnic groups, seemed appropriate. While the dramatic actions and the major traits of the characters can be followed and detected by a reader of any culture, the character motivations, albeit not necessarily embedded in the archetypal esse, might be harder to understand. For that reason, each play is discussed in an essay with particular emphasis on the main characters.

3

It is obvious that only a small portion of all the plays written by Baltic American dramatists during the last four decades can be collected in one volume. Also the number of playwrights still actively writing for the Baltic ethnic stages far exceeds the few represented in this volume. It became evident during the selection process that certain guidelines and priorities had to be set which would facilitate a realistic and well balanced choice of plays.

Although a great number of comedies have been written and successfully produced since the beginning of post-World War II immigration—as a matter of fact, they are the most popular among the Baltic audiences—and some of them deal with themes associated with acculturation, they seemed to contain too much specific folk humor that would be lost in a translation. The major goal of many Baltic dramatists quite often is to entertain their audiences without bothering them with moral messages which might create unnecessary awareness of problems in their daily experiences. There is nothing wrong with such an approach; however, as this volume intends to illuminate the problems of acculturation, comedies that would elicit a "thoughtful laughter" were given the first choice.

However, as soon as a Baltic dramatist commits himself to delivering a message, to exposing a shortcoming, or suggesting a need for change in the immigrants' characters and philosophies, the genre of pure comedy seems inappropriate as a means of expression. He becomes sardonic; and satire, sarcasm and quite often gloom pervade his comedies. Landsbergis' *School for Love* and Eglītis' *Please, Come in, Sir!* are examples of such attitudinal change, the latter fitting a genre commonly known as black comedy.

All the plays in this volume deal with problems common to all acculturation processes. There are the problems of youth brought up in the old traditions who must learn to survive in a new environment. There is the tendency to live in one's past or, rather, constantly returning to it instead of looking to the future. There is an unwillingness as well as an inability to change one's principles that were cherished in the "old country" but which impede success in exile. There is a certain sense of guilt to be overcome, but quite often it is an impossibility, as it would require the rejection of one's former beliefs. There even are problems created by megalomania which enables some first generation immigrants to attain false success—an easy life in the new land. This bourgeois life, however, can burst like a soap bubble when punctuated by an unexpected visit from the past, as is demonstrated in Külvet's *Bridge Across the Sea.*

The playwrights represented in this volume, as the introductory essays will indicate, all are first generation immigrants, and the plays have been written in the last three decades. Their translators, as well as the writers of the introductory essays, also are first generation Baltic immigrants, although some arrived here as small children. (See *Contributors*, p. 366). All plays (except *School for Love*) have been produced at least once in their original versions, and Škėma's *Ataraxia* has been performed also in its English translation in a university theatre. Eglītis' *Ferdinand and Sybil* has been produced for television and aired on PBS—WSIU-TV, Channel 8 in Carbondale and WUSI-TV, Channel 16 in Olney, Illinois. It is available to schools and non-profit organizations without charge (on a ¾" video-tape) from Illinois State Board of Education, Instructional Television Section, 100 North First Street, Springfield, Illinois 62777.

We would like to acknowledge the many individuals and organizations which have either been directly involved with the Baltic Drama project at Southern Illinois University in Carbondale or have extended moral and financial support toward its endeavors. Heartfelt thanks go to the many individuals and institutions which have been kind enough to add the two first Baltic drama anthologies to their library holdings while expressing interest for future volumes.

Especially we thank the contributors to this volume: the authors or their heirs for authorizing the translations, the translators for their patience, the essayists for their objectivity, and Nancy Lou Zehr for her nimble fingers in typing the manuscript.

We also would like to acknowledge Mrs. Osvalds Uršteins and Mr. Meyers Walker for lending us production photographs for insertion in this volume, and Andris Straumanis for preparing the photographs for copy. Other credits are given at points of use.

A.S.

CONTENTS

INTRODUCTION

An Immigrant Experience in America:
The Baltic Option

A transformation of historic scope has been taking place in America during the last three decades: Americans have "rediscovered" ethnic groups in their midst. To avoid misunderstanding, it should be said at the outset that, of course, Americans have recognized throughout their history that they were made up of a highly diverse mixture of immigrant groups from nearly every nation in the world and the mixture keeps getting more diverse with each new arrival. But what is new in the last decade is an evaluation of what has happened to the immigrant groups once they arrived in this country and an expectation of what would happen to the recent and future arrivals. Briefly stated, the new assessment is that, for better or worse, ethnic distinctions, ethnic identities have not dissolved into a single, homogenous American society and that they are not likely to do so in the foreseeable future. This assessment stands in stark contrast to the "melting-pot" mentality of the last two centuries—the expectation that most immigrant groups would lose their national characteristics within a relatively short time, perhaps two or three generations at the most, and that their members would come to identify themselves exclusively as Americans.

It should be stressed that the United States is not alone in confronting once again the importance of ethnic divisions. Students of international relations have recently noted, with some amazement, the world-wide surge of restlessness and outright conflict based on language and religious claims, on cultural and lifestyle distinctions, on deeply felt historical injustice. From French-speaking Quebec in Canada to Northern Ireland and the Basque country in Spain; from the Baltic region and the Moslem peoples in the Soviet Union; from Ibos in Nigeria to Eritrea in East Africa; from Afghanistan and Iran to Tibet and Burma—virtually every region of the globe today is experiencing both the promise and destructiveness of rising ethnic or national aspirations. And modern communication—television, radio, and print, now linking continents—is making an ever-larger portion of the world population instantly aware of the events produced by these aspirations.

How have Americans reacted to the new ethnic awareness? How have they responded to the arrival of the new Vietnamese and Cuban refugees, to the aspirations of Black and Spanish-speaking populations in Chicago and New York and Texas, to the East and South European immigrants, who still retain their ethnic identity into the third or fourth generation in America? There is no simple way of summarizing an answer, of course; different groups and individuals obviously view the matter differently. In fact, one may guess that Americans are more uncertain and undecided about how to approach their own ethnic diversity today than they were fifty or a hundred years ago. The idea of the "melting pot" had, after all, something simple and comforting about it. It prescribed a general social policy—namely, that new immigrants should adopt as quickly as possible the language, customs, and ideals of the "mainstream" or "old" Americans—and it predicted the ultimate success of the assimilation process: the emergence of a homogenous, "truly one-hundred percent" American society.

No such simple and self-confident attitude seems to govern American ethnic relations today. Assimilation certainly continues to be a powerful force, both in practice and as an ideal. But competing ideas are discussed more intensely today, and receive a more respectful hearing, than perhaps at any other time in American history. Maintenance of languages other than English, teaching of ethnic heritage in schools, pride in one's "roots," links with the mother country of the immigrant, participation in the communal life of one's ethnic group—all these are not only tolerated, but in some degree even encouraged by schools, governments, foundations, and businesses. If there is less acceptance today of a single vision of America's ethnic future than in earlier eras, there also may be some compensation in a more open-minded and, one hopes, more realistic assessment that the tensions and difficulties—and the rewards—of ethnic diversity will be here for an indefinite time and that the relief of tensions and the enjoyment of rewards will require learning much more than most Americans now know about each other's ethnic experience.

Every immigrant faces four unavoidable challenges in a new land: how to make a living; how to learn the language, social customs, and culture of the new society; how to manage one's relations with the old society that the immigrant left behind; and how to manage one's relations with one's new neighbors. Baltic immigrants in the United States have had to confront the same four tasks that had faced millions of others who arrived before them and some who have arrived later. What follows is largely an outline account of how the Estonian, Latvian, and Lithuanian immigrants have dealt with these challenges. It will be useful to start with a brief historical review of their arrival in the United States; we will then turn to a discussion of the four tasks indicated above, and conclude with some remarks about the relevance of the Baltic immigrant experience to the general ethnic scene in America.

Practically every Estonian, a large majority of the Latvians, and a substantial number of the Lithuanians now living in the United States arrived here between 1948 and 1953. The vast majority of them came out of refugee camps, the so-called Displaced Persons' camps, in West Germany and Austria, where they had spent some four to eight years, following the end of World War II. They were able to come here as a result of a special immigration law which temporarily set aside the existing immigration quotas for certain East European countries, among them the three Baltic states.

The number of Baltic refugees who thus came to the United States was not large: about 13,000 Estonians, 40,000 Latvians, and 25,000 Lithuanians. The new arrivals joined those of their countrymen who had emigrated to the United States before World War II. (Most of the latter had, in fact, arrived here in the late 19th century and the early years of the 20th century. Very little emigration occurred between the two world wars.) The number of the earlier Estonian immigrants was negligible, a few thousand at the most, while those from Latvia amounted to perhaps 20,000. The Lithuanian case is different: some 150,000 Lithuanian-born immigrants lived in America when the new refugees arrived here after World War II. Altogether, we can estimate the present size of Baltic ethnic groups (including the first generation of children born in this country) at somewhat less than 20,000 Estonians, under 90,000 Latvians, and slightly over 300,000 Lithuanians. In the discussion that follows, however, we are going to concentrate on the experience of those Baltic immigrants who arrived here as refugees after World War II. The omission of the earlier Latvian and, especially, the very large Lithuanian immigrant groups from our account is regrettable, but necessary. Their histories, indeed, still need to be explored, and they need to be compared with the experiences of those of their countrymen who came to America in the 1940s and the 1950s. We cannot do all that within the limits of this essay; we have chosen, instead, to focus on whatever we can learn from the story of the more recent Baltic immigrants.

How have the Baltic immigrants fared in making a living in the United States? By and large, they have done quite well indeed. While not many have struck it rich in this "land of unlimited opportunity," neither have many experienced poverty, long-term unemployment, slum living conditions, and similar economic deprivations. Baltic communities, generally speaking, show up as typically middle-class and lower middle-class groups, with relatively high proportions of their members in professional, technical, managerial, and skilled labor occupations.

The rather quick and fairly painless economic adjustment by the Baltic groups makes for an unusual episode in the history of first-generation immigrants in America. Nearly all ethnic groups that have arrived in the United States in the last one-hundred years have experienced a lengthy period of low-paying, difficult, or dangerous occupations, poor living conditions, periodic unemployment, and the like. Among immigrants who entered the country as adults, only the exceptional individual has been able to break into the ranks of professional or other white-collar occupations, and often it has taken two or three generations for an immigrant group to reach living standards similar to those of the earlier immigrants. The post-World War II Baltic refugees, by contrast, have achieved this in a single generation.

Naturally, many Baltic immigrants themselves have been tempted to explain their success as the result of some superior virtue in the Estonian, Latvian, or Lithuanian character. The more realistic explanation, however, lies elsewhere: the refugees who left the Baltic states during World War II and eventually arrived in the United States were characterized, as a group, by unusually high levels of education, skills, and motivation for achievement. They were people whose lives, careers, and possessions had been wrecked when the Soviet Union occupied Estonia, Latvia, and Lithuania in 1940 and whom Stalin's policies had marked as potential or actual enemies of the Soviet regime to be removed from all positions of influence and, in many instances, to be arrested, deported to concentration camps, or executed. Among those forced to flee, then, were disproportionately high numbers of professionals in the arts and sciences and managerial occupations, civil servants, farmers, skilled workers, clergymen, medical and technical specialists—those, in short, who make up the successful leadership groups in any society.

It is little wonder that the application of these skills—and hard work—produced a remarkably rapid economic advance among the Baltic immigrants. Even so, however, it should be pointed out that their achievement by no means placed them in the upper income brackets or highest occupational positions of American society. Many skills acquired in Europe were not readily transferable to America, and the large majority of the older immigrants, in particular, never have achieved positions comparable to those they had occupied at home. Teachers and artists often became factory workers, and many remained such until retirement or death, while some others advanced slowly and painfully into new career areas.

How have the Baltic immigrants done in learning the language, customs, and culture of America? What has just been said about their economic situation suggests an answer to this second question as well. Some mastery of English is, of course, necessary in all but the most routine unskilled work, and most working-age Baltic immigrants managed to move up at least into skilled labor positions. Their knowledge of English may have been rudimentary—especially, again, among the older people, but very few Baltic immigrants remained totally helpless for very long among their English-speaking neighbors or co-workers. And the task, of course, was much easier for young people.

Access to a language is also access to the social customs and cultural values of a society. While one can observe something of the surface of life in America without knowing English, one cannot really participate in it, nor can one appreciate and enjoy its literature and politics and history, its humor and sadness, its taboos and rituals. It is much more difficult to judge how well the Baltic immigrants have adjusted to the habits and values of American society than to say that most of them now do have the necessary knowledge of the English language to understand at least the society's basic elements. Certainly, among those who entered the United States as children and young adults, a very high proportion now occupies positions in which an intimate understanding of American society and culture is a practical necessity; teachers, lawyers, managerial and medical people, even technical workers, could hardly function in their professions otherwise. Among older Baltic immigrants, also, one finds a fairly high level of at least passive adjustments to American society, such as the reading of English-language periodicals and books, movie attendance, voting in elections, and the like. All in all, it may be said that the Baltic immigrants have adjusted to the language and the social and cultural features of America as easily as any recent immigrant group, and probably more rapidly than most.

The explanation for this ease of adjustment lies partly with the nature of the Baltic immigration already discussed above. Generally high levels of education often including training in other foreign languages, such as German, Russian, and French, enabled many Baltic refugees to learn English fairly quickly and to begin to become familiar with the social and cultural traits of America. But beyond that, the "culture shock" experienced by the Baltic refugees upon arriving in America was not nearly as severe as it had been for many other ethnic groups. In physical appearance, in food and dress habits, in family life, in attitudes toward the value of hard work, education, thrift, etc., the Estonians, Latvians, and Lithuanians were practically indistinguishable from millions of earlier North European immigrants, such as Germans, Swedes, and Norwegians. Estonians and Latvians were predominantly Lutheran, and they found themselves in a predominantly Protestant America; Lithuanians were Catholic, and they found millions of their co-religionists in America. Unlike earlier Eastern and Southern European immigrants who had come largely from traditional peasant societies to find themselves in the alien world of a rapidly urbanizing and industrializing America, the post-World War II Baltic refugees came from societies already largely modern, and they found an America basically not very different from the countries they had left. While it still took considerable time and effort to adjust to the New World, that time could be measured in years instead of generations, as had been the case for most earlier immigrants.

How have the Baltic immigrants felt about and acted toward the societies and cultures from which they came? Millions of immigrants have felt this problem—the problem of ties to one's native land—to be the most difficult challenge of all, especially during their early years in America. Even those who consciously turned their backs on the "old country" and thought of America as their new permanent home could not help but experience the pain of loneliness, of separation from family, friends, and accustomed places, the doubts and worries about whether abandoning home was the right thing to do after all. For most people, "home" is far more than merely a roof overhead.

In a very fundamental sense, many Baltic immigrants—

probably a large majority of them—have felt that they never did abandon their home in Estonia, Latvia, or Lithuania. Although most of them found the path of economic, social, and cultural adjustment to America relatively smooth, quick, and painless, it would be a serious mistake to conclude that they therefore cut all ties to their homelands quickly and proceeded to be melted down into the American mass. Some have, but many continue to be deeply involved in one way or another with things Estonian or Latvian or Lithuanian. A few examples from their organizational and cultural life will suffice to illustrate the point.

No one, so far as we now, has ever counted up the number of organizations established by the Baltic immigrants but the total surely would be astounding. For example, the Chicago Latvian community—which probably comprises some 5000 Latvians, although no accurate count is available—has no fewer than 30 different organizations. Among them one finds four Lutheran, one Catholic, and one Baptist congregations, a retired people's club, a ski club, a fishing and hunting club, and so on. In fact, the Chicago Latvians have found it necessary (as have many other Baltic communities) to establish a coordinating committee, simply to try to keep the activities of the different organizations from colliding with each other too much. Moreover, many of the local organizations are federated with similar organizations in other localities to form national and, in some cases, international associations.

This dense network of organizations is duplicated in Estonian and Lithuanian communities, as well as other Latvian communities, wherever there are a few hundred Baltic immigrants. Much of this activism is social or recreational in character, but a great deal is also more or less purposefully directed toward two objectives one hears repeated over and over again in the Baltic communities—to help restore freedom in the Baltic states and to preserve the cultural heritage of the Baltic peoples. It is in these two aims that the Baltic immigration finds its self-consciously declared mission and the core of its relationship with the native lands. The Estonian, Latvian, and Lithuanian in America is likely to say that he is not an immigrant—that he is in exile because his native country is oppressed by the Soviet Union and his cultural inheritance threatened with distortion or extinction. Certainly, among those who arrived in America as adults or teenagers the memory of what happened to them and their native lands is still sharp and the commitment to helping their people and culture survive quite real. The years between the two world wars, when Estonia, Latvia, and Lithuania fought for and won independence and enjoyed recognition as sovereign states, are remembered as a brilliant contrast to the darkness that fell on the Baltic states in 1940 when they were occupied by the Soviet Union, then, a year later, by Nazi Germany, and once again, in 1944, by the Soviets. For most of those who witnessed the destruction and terror of the occupations and war, the darkness over their native lands has never lifted. Physically, it is conceded, most of the people who remained at home did survive, but they survived as captives in their own land, denied basic political and human rights, forced to follow the dictates of Moscow, threatened in the very core of national identity by russification and alien cultural influences.

Such are the convictions and memories that have motivated an entire generation of Baltic immigrants in America. They have provided the incentive for establishing organizations and raising money, for publishing hundreds of books and dozens of newspapers and magazines, for petitioning American legislators and international organizations, for staging plays and concerts, for maintaining schools and youth seminars to transmit the ancestral language and culture to the young. There has been, in all these efforts, a measure of frustration and despair as well as accomplishment. Obviously, it has not been in the power of the immigrants to restore self-determination to the Baltic peoples, but neither have their activities gone totally unnoticed in Moscow and Washington. However, it is the continued vitality of the cultural life and the involvement of the young people that the Baltic immigrants can count as their most notable successes. A surprising number of people who left the Baltic states as children or were born in America are fluent in the language of their parents, familiar with at least the basic elements of their cultural heritage, and, in many cases, sufficiently interested, not only to participate in the activities of the immigrant communities, but also to seek active contact with their countrymen in Estonia or Latvia or Lithuania. How far into the future that may last is an open question, but the current sense of ethnic solidarity is a notable development, even if it were to fade in the next generation.

We come, finally, to the last of our four questions: How have the Baltic immigrants done in getting along with their new neighbors in America? On one level—on the level of ordinary, everyday relations in the workplace, school, and place of residence—the answer is quite simple: as a group, the Baltic immigrants have neither encountered nor provoked much of the hostility, fear, resentment, or discrimination that has plagued many other ethnic groups. An individual here and there, of course, has experienced one or more of these difficulties, but we are concerned here with the experience of entire groups of people. There is nothing very remarkable about such lack of tension between the Baltic ethnic groups and those around them. As we have noted above, Baltic immigration has been numerically very small, and the social and cultural traits of the immigrants have in no way set them apart from earlier European immigrants. Only in a very few instances, such as the Lithuanian community in Chicago, are there enough families concentrated in a single residential area to make the neighborhood ethnically visible and distinct. Typically, the Baltic immigrants have widely scattered throughout the major cities and metropolitan areas. Equally typical, they have not been concentrated in any specialized occupations or enterprises. In short, the Baltic ethnic groups have simply lacked those characteristics that attract communal tension and conflict.

Saying that conflict has been avoided, however, is not saying very much about how the Baltic immigrants have felt toward their neighbors, how they have perceived and evaluated other ethnic groups, how they have acted in their personal contacts with them. At this level—the level of attitudes, opinions, and individual reactions—a full description would have to be much more complicated and subtle than we could give within the limits of this essay; here we can only note some rather generalized observations.

Two influences seem to be especially significant in determining the immigrants' attitudes and reactions: age and education. The immigrants who are now in their fifties and older, that is, those who arrived here as adults, brought with them—ready-made, as it were—the expectations and conceptions of America they had acquired in Europe, and even though direct experience with Americans may have modified them somewhat, basically their beliefs remained what they had been some thirty years ago. In a large majority of the older Baltic immigrants, for example, these beliefs included political and social conservatism—and to a large majority of them the American brands of liberalism remain unacceptable to this day. Many, probably most, of the older immigrants had an image of American youngsters as being loud, disrespectful toward elders, and uninterested in "serious matters." In thirty years, most of them appear to have seen nothing that might change this image. Most adult immigrants arrived here carrying in their mental baggage various stereotypes of other nationalities—Germans, Russians, Jews, Swedes, among others—and encounters with the same ethnic groups in America usually have reinforced, rather than changed, the stereotypes.

The European education of the older Baltic immigrants has played a somewhat curious role in forming their attitudes. It was fashionable among European intellectuals (and to a lesser extent still is today) to regard American cultural achievements and American education as somehow inferior to those of Europe. Many Baltic immigrants brought that belief with them to America —and many then claimed to have found "proof" for it here. Interestingly—and understandably—this attitude has been more widespread among those older immigrants who could not find positions equal to the ones they had occupied at home and who had to settle for more menial jobs. The more successful immigrants, who were able to resume their old careers or establish new ones in America, usually have also tended to be more charitable and balanced in their judgments about the quality of American culture and education.

In general, however, the most common reaction of the older immigrants—whatever their educational or career background—has been to maintain an arm's-length distance toward their new neighbors in America. This has not necessarily been an unfriendly attitude; it has usually arisen from a natural caution one adopts toward people who are, after all, strangers. Some of the caution has been dropped, with time, and some of the distance narrowed, but it would be unrealistic to expect them to disappear altogether.

The best way, perhaps, to summarize the attitudes toward America of the younger Baltic generations—those who arrived here as children or were born here—is to say simply that their views are generally quite similar to those of other Americans of comparable education, occupation, and income. "Similar," of course, does not mean "identical." The attitudes of, say, an Estonian in his twenties, who speaks Estonian fairly freely, knows something of Estonian history and culture and occasionally attends local Estonian social functions are bound to be different— perhaps in subtle but still important ways—from the attitudes of another man of the same age who "thinks" that his family is mostly German and Irish but who is not quite sure about that, who "thinks" that his great-grandparents arrived in this country in the late 19th century, and who speaks no language other than English. The young Estonian's English is likely to be as fluent as that of his German-Irish counterpart; their views on, say, Vietnam and legalization of marijuana may be identical, but the young

Estonian is unlikely to think of himself as just "an American." In consequence, he is likely to think differently of others, including other ethnic groups; at the very least, he is likely to be more sensitive, if not always necessarily more sympathetic toward the values and norms of other ethnic groups than his German-Irish-American counterpart.

There are also noticeable differences in attitudes among the members of the younger Baltic generation themselves. In large part, these are due to differences in the type and level of education they have sought and achieved. Education has been traditionally highly valued in the Estonian, Latvian, and Lithuanian cultures, and for Baltic immigrant children, educational achievement has been practically the only ladder of social and economic advancement. Unlike some other ethnic groups, very few Baltic immigrants have sought to make their way as entrepreneurs in the business world, or in professional sports or the entertainment world. As a result, education has largely determined the occupations, incomes, residence patterns, and social statuses of the younger members of Baltic ethnic groups. All these factors, in turn, account for exposure to different life styles, different people, ambitions, and attitudes. Generally speaking, the higher the social and economic achievement of the Baltic young people, the more their attitudes resemble those of their peers from other American ethnic background. Those whose achievements have been modest are more likely to reflect the attitudes of their elders among Baltic immigrants. Even here, however, the sons and daughters view America through a lens different from that of their parents. What they see is a sight more familiar, more the sight of home, than it can be for the generation who crossed an ocean, leaving home behind.

The "melting-pot" has not melted down—not yet, anyway—for the Baltic immigrants who came to America some three decades ago. The time may be too short for assimilation, and one should not be particularly surprised if it were yet to happen. If our observations are reasonably correct, however, it is not likely to happen very soon, almost certainly not with the present generation of Baltic children born in America. And if so, then the Baltic experience forms an interesting exception to the nearly universal immigrant history in America: usually it has been the first generation of children born in America to immigrant parents who have been not merely open to assimilation, but indeed eager to be assimilated, eager to shed the immigrant past of their parents. Virtually no signs of such eagerness are visible among the Baltic immigrant children.

The degree of ethnic solidarity one observes in the Baltic communities is made all the more surprising by the fact that very little has really stood in the way of those Baltic immigrants who might have wished to leave their ethnic communities altogether and become totally absorbed in the surrounding American society. As we have noted, neither language and social habits nor physical appearance and ability to make a living have formed much of a barrier for the Baltic immigrants who have wanted to be fully integrated in American life, to the exclusion of any links with their ethnic compatriots. Yet relatively few have chosen this option.

Finally, and perhaps most important of all, the Baltic experience seems to show that a high degree of ethnic cohesion and ethnic self-awareness are quite compatible with tension-free relations with other ethnic groups. To put it in slightly different words—the Estonians, Latvians, and Lithuanians in America have found that it is not necessary to assimilate in order to get along with others.

No ethnic group is like any other, and universal prescriptions are always misleading. But since the "melting-pot" prescription has failed for quite a few American ethnic groups, the Baltic option may be worth considering.

Jānis Penikis

BRIDGE ACROSS THE SEA
Drama in three acts with a prologue

by
Ilmar Külvet

From the original Estonian
Sild üle mere
translated by Hilja Kukk

Bridge Across the Sea. Act Three. Estonian Theatre in Adelaide, Australia, 1970. Director: Vambola Kuik. Scenographer: Ilvi Kald. Vello: Karl Kald Helga: Ilvi Kald

Bridge Across the Sea.
Act Two.
Pinna Studio,
Stockholm, Sweden, 1970.

Director: Boris Peensaar
Humal: Elmar Nerep
Paul: Boris Peensaar

Introduction to
Bridge Across the Sea

Ilmar Külvet was born on November 21, 1920 in Keila, Estonia. He grew up and attended primary and secondary schools in Tallinn, Estonia, where he also began his literary activity as a journalist. He has lived in Germany, Austria, France, England, Canada and the United States since the end of the war. For several years he worked for the Canadian Estonian semi-weekly newspaper *Vaba Eestlane* (The Free Estonian) as an editor and theater critic. Presently Ilmar Külvet lives in Washington, D.C.

Külvet has several plays to his credit, most of them dealing with social problems of some sort. *Paradiisi pärisperemees* (The Real Master of Paradise) is a satire in rhymed doggerel with songs and dances. It was performed in Canada in 1963, indoors as well as outdoors. *Trooja hobune* (The Trojan Horse) is a play in three acts and was performed in 1965 in Canada, outdoors. *Lamp ei tohi kustuda* (The Light Must Not Go Out) is a social satire in three acts. It was staged in Toronto (1968), in Stockholm (1968), and in Vancouver, Canada (1969).

Sild üle mere (Bridge Across the Sea) was first published in 1968 in *Mana* (an international journal of Estonian literature, arts and sciences, published in Canada), and since 1970 it has been repeatedly produced in Canada, Sweden, Australia, and in the United States. Külvet's next play, *Suletud aken* (The Closed Window), a satire in three acts, was published in *Mana* in 1976 and, since 1979, produced throughout Sweden, in Los Angeles, and in Adelaide, Australia. *Menning — mees kompromissita* (Menning—the Man Without Compromise), written in 1978, was published in *Mana* in 1981 but due to a large number of characters, it has not seen a full stage production to date.

Ilmar Külvet has also been a prolific translator from English into Estonian, and he has translated works by Steinbeck, Brian Moore, Hugh MacLennan, and others.

The title of Külvet's play, *Bridge Across the Sea,* has been chosen also as the title for this third volume of the Baltic drama collection. The title symbolizes common aspirations of the people in exile—to bridge the gap between the homeland and the New World, to search for one's roots, to establish one's identity. The title harbors symbolic significance for all Baltic drama written in exile as well as for all emigrant experience in general.

Baltic drama in exile focuses on similar—or the same—problems as modern drama of the Western World. But in addition, certain themes which pertain to the condition of exile are directly focused upon and emphasized. Thus, the identity problematic is of great importance to the emigrant playwright. Similarly, the topic of generation conflict finds frequent treatment in Baltic drama. But these topics are not only of interest to Baltic emigre writers, they have been treated by all emigrant writers dealing with the adjustment and acculturation problematic.

Writers who have lived in exile for any length of time and have had to come to grips with themselves in an alien environment often reflect their search for an identity as people and as writers in their works. Two of the more well-known German-speaking poets might be mentioned as examples in this context, for their works deal in depth with the adjustment problems and the identity question of the youth. In Rainer Maria Rilke's novel *Malte Laurids Brigge* the author's own stay in Paris is reflected. The absence from Austria gives Rilke a different perspective of introspection manifesting itself in Malte Laurids Brigge's search for his self. Malte's search for his own identity leads him to his past—to his roots. It is this looking into the past in order to find the present that we also encounter in Külvet's *Bridge Across the Sea*.

The identity question and the generation conflict are often inextricably intertwined. Franz Kafka might be cited as an example. Kafka wrote in German while living in Prague, and therefore he was in a curious position of being an exile in his own country. His works (i.e., *Metamorphosis*) reflect his struggle for his existence as a poet and his ambivalent relationship with his father. Similarly, in Külvet's drama, the generation conflict between father and the step-daughter is coupled with the step-daughter's attempt at establishing her identity and trying to adjust to her environment. The quest for identity of a young person constitutes the core of the drama.

Bridge Across the Sea shows us an Estonian family in Canada. The financial achievements of the head of the family, Mr. Toomik, are remarkable, and he aspires to a high position in the Estonian emigrant public life. His wife, Helga, has taken refuge from life in becoming an actress on the emigrant stage. The younger daughter of the house, Meeli, is an uncomplicated girl, full of life and vitality. But it is Helga's older daughter, Linda, that we shall focus upon.

Linda is going through an identity crisis. She is rebellious toward her homelife and, at the same time, longing for verbal communication with her mother. She resents her father and is jealous of her sister. The search for her own identity has led her on the road to non-conformity in appearance and behavior. She has even joined a political activist group in order to gain a sense of "belonging."

Linda's reactionary behavior is psychologically well motivated, for she senses that somehow she doesn't belong with her family. Although she doesn't know it consciously, her perception on the subconscious level is accurate, since Paul Toomik is only her step-father. His resentment of her is a contributing factor in their negative relationship.

The prologue of the play, which serves to illuminate further events in the play, presents a situation full of agony in a small harbor in Estonia before the end of the war. Two soldiers are trying to get space in a fisherman's boat, which is about to leave for Sweden. Vello Meerend is very anxious to join his girlfriend in Sweden, who is expecting his child. There is only room for one in the boat, and Paul Toomik fills the last vacancy after landing an immobilizing blow to Meerend.

The play opens with Paul Toomik in Canada, married to Meerend's former girlfriend Helga, the step-father of Meerend's daughter Linda, and the father of Meeli.

Paul Toomik is portrayed as an aggressive achiever. His aggressive and egotistic character traits are already set forth in the prologue. Ironically, these very same character traits which helped him obtain the last available seat on the parting boat also enable him to achieve success later on in Canada and aid him in becoming a respected member of his society. The playwright points to a paradox of social values by showing that while society condemns the methods and means of certain actions, it accepts and even condones the end-results obtained by these very despicable means.

Toomik is psychologically relatively uncomplicated and shows fairly openly what and how he feels. These undisguised emotions and sentiments are at the root of the discord between himself and his step-daughter Linda.

Linda is the most problematic character in the play. She has inherited her mother's artistic nature and her natural father's
inclination for daydreaming. Due to her sensitive nature, she perceives of herself as an outsider to the family. Paul Toomik is unable to disguise his preference of Meeli over Linda, and in Act I
Linda reacts to his resentment of her with hatred, but also with
guilt toward him: "Oh how I hate him. Hate. Hate. Hate.
(*Pause.*) And yet, it is wrong to hate." Later in Act II, it comes to
an open admission of this hate: "I hate you, do you hear! I am
ashamed to have a father like you." At this point, Toomik almost
admits to not being her father, but he is held back by his wife.
Helga insists that telling Linda about her natural father will harm
and confuse her. But ironically, it is precisely this uncertainty
about her roots—on a subconscious level—that provokes the
identity crisis in Linda.

Linda is anxious to communicate with her mother concerning
her search for her own self. "I am almost twenty years old and I
don't know who I am. I don't know what will become of me," she
states in Act I. But Helga is very reluctant to respond. Her total
submersion in the theatrical activities of the Estonian society
indicates that she has a need to escape reality. Reality for Helga is
being married to a strong, practical-minded husband who is
capable of supporting her. In principle, she believes that artistic
natures need a practical person to lean on. She is being dominated
by her husband, and she permits this to happen. When Linda questions her about it and tells her that she cannot respect her because
of it, Helga tells her daughter that artists need someone strong
and steady like a "rock" who has financial sense and who is able
to provide for them.

Nevertheless, her own attitude toward her marriage is
somewhat ambivalent, for, on the subconscious level, she also displays a need for more self-assertion as a woman and as a partner
in her marriage. She is sublimating her need for self-assertion by
playing the role of Nora in Ibsen's *Doll's House*. Her capacity for
total involvement in her role—she even begins to call her husband
"Torvald"—is indicative of her flight from reality. Theatre has
become a substitute of life for her.

Consequently, any real attempt at communicating with Linda
would draw her back into reality which Helga wants to avoid.
Nevertheless, she tells Linda about her love to Vello Meerend in
Estonia as the past has become obscure, almost unreal to her.
However, she avoids revealing to Linda that Meerend is her
father. In part, she is afraid of adding to her daughter's emotional

turmoil, but also, she is afraid of losing her daughter's respect on account of her "immoral" behavior. She is a vain woman who is intent on protecting the image of her high moral standards and her good reputation.

This becomes especially obvious in the scene where the boatman-turned-blackmailer threatens to publicize that Toomik had killed Meerend in order to get that last seat on the boat. She overhears Toomik reveal the secret of Linda's paternity and she is deeply hurt. Ironically, her husband's unscrupulous behavior becomes secondary to preserving her good reputation. Whereas she should be questioning her husband regarding the fate of her former lover, she is mainly concerned about the tarnishing of her good reputation in the eyes of society through the blackmailer.

Vello Meerend's arrival for a brief visit in Canada constitutes the play's climactic point and the turning point in the life of the Toomik family. Officially, Meerend is part of a Soviet delegation, but his interest in visiting Canada stems from his innermost desire to get acquainted with his daughter. When he realizes that Helga has not revealed the identity of her father to Linda, his dreams of a reunion are shattered. He had wanted to meet Linda as a father and not as a family friend as Helga suggests. Since he never had children within his marriage in Estonia, he is very anxious to meet his only child. Linda constitutes the "bridge across the sea" to freedom for Meerend; through Linda, a part of him is also living in freedom.

The moment of the meeting between father and daughter is full of turmoil, and the tension is intensified by Linda's antisocial activities and by her step-father's animosity toward her (he wants to show that he is still in control of his household). Ironically, just as Toomik is beginning to lose control over the situation, he is intent upon showing the opposite. As he is pushing and shoving Linda, Meerend's protective feelings toward Linda emerge, but she rejects his efforts of trying to protect her as an unrightful intrusion into her life. Meeli, the younger sister, breaks the tension by revealing Meerend's identity to Linda.

The moment of recognition between father and daughter is emotionally very intense. This meeting produces a change in her. She admits that her rebellious behavior was based on her feelings of insecurity. Suddenly, she is confronted with the knowledge that she has a father—a real father—and she is ecstatic over it. The past, that she has subconsciously been longing for, has paid a visit. She gets acquainted with her real father, with her roots. Identity for Linda is established as she meets Meerend. Linda's

identity crisis is solved by a sudden psychological break. She has
finally found a home within and without herself.

This turning point in Linda produces changed relationships with
her family members. After Linda's reconciliation with herself is
reached, a reconciliation with her step-father becomes possible.
Now she is able to understand Toomik and his motivations,
whereas some of his feelings toward her escaped her
interpretation previously. Theirs still might be a difficult
relationship, she contends, but she is now capable of trying to
improve it.

She admits that she is also capable of adjusting to a better relationship with her half-sister and willing to resolve some of the conflicts stemming from sibling rivalry. Her jealousy of Meeli's good
relationship with Toomik will be minimized by the knowledge that
she now also has a father.

For Paul Toomik there is also a great revelation in Vello
Meerend's visit. It is Toomik, the engineer, who is chosen to build
a bridge across the sea. And it is Toomik who is again called upon
to build bridges within his family. A real communication, hitherto
missing, has to be established with the step-daughter, as well as
with his wife. He undergoes character-growth in coming to the
understanding that meaningful human relationships take
precedence over positions in the emigrant society. He is willing to
sacrifice some outer trimmings of social recognition in order to
penetrate to the core of meaningful human co-existence.

Heretofore, Toomik has set the tone in his family, but during the
development of the drama we find that Helga becomes more self-
assertive. She experiences the unfolding of her character during
the play. Whereas Linda undergoes a sudden psychological shock
which alters her personality, and Toomik is willing to concentrate
his efforts to delve into meaningful human relationships within his
family, it is Helga who exhibits the profoundest character growth.
She grows from a timid, dominated woman forever trying to
escape reality to a self-assured woman capable of making independent decisions and ready to confront reality. She becomes a
fuller person in the end.

She has enough courage to tear up the check meant for the
blackmailer. This is the first indication that she is capable of
making an independent decision. She also insists on bringing
Linda home from the police station and prevails in spite of
Toomik's objections. It seems that the reunion with Meerend has
given her the impetus to become a more independent person.
Helga is aware of the role Meerend has played in her self-

realization when she thanks him for "everything." His coming precipitated the events which led to the lifting of the secrecy in the Toomik family. When the secrets are in the open, the need for pretension ceases to exist. Playing games—theatre is also a pretend game—has been Helga's life. Theatre has filled her life so completely that she has had no time for communicating with her family. When Linda expresses a sudden desire to go to Estonia with her father, this passing thought serves to point out to Helga the extent of her neglect of her immediate family. She is ready to change her lifestyle and seems willing to give up the theatre. At the end of the play, she realizes that "life is more important than the theatre."

In *Bridge Across the Sea*, the condition of exile is not just mere background material, but pervades the plot and motivates the action of the play. It entails the political tension between East and West, seemingly the determining factor for the fate of the characters involved. But, most importantly, Linda's search for her identity derives from the condition of exile.

The identity problematic and generation conflict are inseparable, for only secure self-knowledge can be at the basis of successful human relationships. Taking up the analogy with Kafka again, the problematic of identity/generation gap in *Bridge Across the Sea* contrasts the problematic in Kafka's *Matamorphosis*. Whereas Gregor Samsa-turned-bug ultimately loses his identity because of the conflict with his father, Linda resolves her conflict with her step-father after establishing her identity. The identity crisis is solved when past and present become intertwined. Past, present, and future are all dependent on each other. They are inseparable. Thus, the identity problematic is tied up with the notion of time. The quest for identity transcends a longing for the Old Country in a topographical sense and takes on universal significance, for it becomes the quest of modern man who seeks to carve a niche for himself in today's alienated world.

The loss of identity of modern man has sent him in search of his roots. It has become the problem of modern man to re-establish the severed human relationships and to "build bridges" between the Old World and the "New World," between the older generation and the younger one, between the past and the present.

Hilja Pikat

Bridge Across the Sea. Act One. Estonian Theatre in Adelaide, Australia, 1970.   Director: Vambola Kuik.   Scenographer: Ilvi Kald.   Linda: Reet Tuul   Meeli: Linda Kuik

Bridge Across the Sea. Act Three. Pinna Studio, Stockholm, Sweden, 1970.   Director: Boris Peensaar. Meeli: Tiina Klement   Helga: Signe Pinna   Vello: Jussi Romot

BRIDGE ACROSS THE SEA

CHARACTERS

PAUL TOOMIK: an engineer specializing in bridge building; the
    second soldier in the prologue
HELGA: his wife, an actress in the emigre theatre
MEELI: daughter of HELGA and PAUL TOOMIK
LINDA: daughter of HELGA
VELLO MEEREND: Archeologist; the first soldier in the
    prologue
MAX KALTER: boat captain
HUMAL: a former Estonian minister
VIRKUS: editor of an emigre newspaper
KARGUS: a former combat officer now active in emigre affairs

Place: A large city in Canada.
Time: 1965

PROLOGUE

*(The action takes place in semi-darkness, in front of the curtain
behind which is the set of ACT ONE. We are transposed back in
time to a beach on the island Saaremaa* in the autumn of 1944.
The sounds of the muffled roar of the wind and rolling waves are
heard. A motorboat is being readied in the darkness for transporting refugees to Sweden. The atmosphere is restless, full of apprehension. People move about as silhouettes. From the left enter
two SOLDIERS one of whom is limping. The CAPTAIN of the
motorboat enters from the right, opposite.)*
CAPTAIN: There's only room for one more in the boat now.

*The largest island off the Estonian mainland in the Baltic sea.

31

FIRST SOLDIER (*limping*): Come on! If there's room for one, two can be fitted in somehow.

CAPTAIN: I said I'll only take one. There's no bargaining here. The water will reach the gunnels with one more passenger, if I took two we'd be swamped.

SECOND SOLDIER: Damn it, the thing to do is to throw everybody's luggage overboard.

CAPTAIN: I am not transporting cases of butter or Singer sewing machines in my boat. Only the people of Estonia and as much gasoline as it takes to reach the coast of Sweden. If we do... with weather like this.

FIRST SOLDIER: Perhaps one more boat will be going?

CAPTAIN: Not from this beach. People attached motors to washtubs even, and those, too have set out to sea. The Russians are said to be on Saaremaa already.

FIRST SOLDIER: But we must find a way. We have always been together, first at the front and then in the hospital. How could we be separated now?

CAPTAIN: I'll take one. You decide which one of you. (*Pause.*) Some speedboat may make it back from Sweden yet, but they don't travel by any set schedules. And the storm is turning into a northwester. I'll leave it up to you to decide in a hurry, otherwise both of you will be left behind, we are about to take off now. (*He walks off into darkness.*)

FIRST SOLDIER: You have healthy legs, perhaps you could still make it to another boat. For me, this is the only chance.

SECOND SOLDIER: The boat is packed like a can of sardines. You couldn't manage on there with your hurt leg, there's no room to stretch it out. And the Captain said one more speedboat might make it out here.

FIRST SOLDIER: You know very well that waiting for it is like waiting for the white ship*. (*Desperately, he grabs hold of his comrade's greatcoat.*) I must get to Sweden... for Helga's sake ...I must get to Helga.

SECOND SOLDIER: Because of a girl! Nonsense. For a real man the world is full of girls. I, on the other hand, must get away from here for my own sake. For the sake of my life, hell, don't you understand? (*Calming down.*) You were mobilized, they won't harm you if you'd fall into their hands. But I'm a volunteer, a platoon commander and decorated with an iron cross at

---

*He is referring to the eagerly awaited British ships which were to come and rescue the Baltic states from the Soviet troops.

that. They'd shoot me at once. (*He begins to walk resolutely toward the imaginary boat, but his comrade hinders him by stepping in front of him.*)

FIRST SOLDIER: I know all that, I know. But Helga means more to me than anything else in this world. And I can't desert her like that, because...she is expecting my child. She sent me a letter at the hospital and then fled with her parents to Sweden.

SECOND SOLDIER: Nonsense, it's wartime, half the world is full of fatherless children. Now every man looks out for himself. (*He attempts to leave.*)

FIRST SOLDIER (*blocks his way*): I believe in destiny. Fate shall decide who is to go. Let's cast lots.

SECOND SOLDIER: In the pitch darkness? Stop this damned nonsense. The boat will leave without either of us.

FIRST SOLDIER (*takes a roll of white bandage from his pocket. It is clearly visible in the semi-darkness*): Look, I have a roll of bandage here. I'll hold it behind my back. If you tell me which hand I'm holding it in, you'll go on the boat. If you guess wrong, fate has decided in my favor. (*He puts his hands behind his back. The SECOND SOLDIER hits his comrade hard in the stomach. Because of the semi-darkness, it is not possible to see whether he used only his fist, or a sharp instrument as well. The FIRST SOLDIER falls to the ground with a muffled groan.*)

SECOND SOLDIER: Now every man is the master of his own fate. (*The starting sound of the boat motor is heard.*) Wait! I'm coming! Wait! (*He runs in the direction of the motor sound. The stage grows completely dark, then the curtain rises and the stage gradually becomes light, revealing the set for ACT ONE.*)

END OF PROLOGUE

ACT ONE

(*The livingroom in the home of PAUL TOOMIK in a large Canadian city. It is a spacious house in an affluent residential section relatively close to the downtown area. On the left is the entry hall with the front door in view. A spiral stairway between the entrance area and the livingroom leads to the second floor with only the lower part of the stairway visible. [Note: if the stairway*

*should cause insurmountable technical difficulties, it can simply
be replaced by a corridor leading to the bedroom area, but a two-
story house is preferable.] The diningroom and kitchen are in the
wing situated on the left and are only imaginary. The livingroom
furniture is massive, masculine and includes several curved
items. In the foreground is a massive semi-circular sofa which
dominates the scene. In front of it a marble coffee table with easy
chairs. To the right is a curved bar with bar stools, and on the wall
above it, a picture of a large steel bridge. A door next to the bar
leads to the T.V. room which, however, is used as PAUL
TOOMIK'S study. In the middle of the back wall is a large
window, and next to it, PAUL'S oil portrait done in realistic style.
Close to the entry hall is a table with telephone, and above it is a
mirror. The draperies have been pulled back and we see a
profusion of fall colors. It is afternoon, almost exactly twenty
years later than the action in the prologue, that is, in the autumn
of 1964. The stage remains empty for a few moments. The
telephone rings three times. MEELI runs down the stairway. She
is a well brought up sixteen year old girl. Poised, well-mannered
and rather self-assured, with a touch of guarded snobbishness.
She is holding in her hand a book which she has been reading. It is
probably some sort of detective story, for she herself is a little
detective in her home who likes to listen secretly to the conversations of others. MEELI puts the book down on the table and picks
up the receiver.)*

MEELI: Hello...No, this is her sister, Meeli speaking...Yes, Linda is in...Who is calling, please? Of course I know that curiosity killed the cat. But I am not a cat, and you are not very original. (*She puts the receiver down and calls from the front of the stairs.*) Linda! Telephone! Lin--daa!

LINDA (*from upstairs*): Okay! Okay!

MEELI (*picks up the receiver again, in a snippy tone*): She's coming. And kindly note that it is good manners to ask who is calling. But of course, you wouldn't know anything about good manners. (*MEELI puts the receiver down on the table, picks up her book and runs to the sofa. She curls up on it, becoming invisible from the entry behind the massive back of the sofa. She pretends to be reading, but is actually listening intently. LINDA comes down the stairs. She is a nineteen year old art student with the looks of a Bohemian. Unsure of herself, she tries to hide it sometimes with an exaggerated display of daring. She is wearing a paint-splattered smock, and carries the brush absentmindedly in her hand.*)

LINDA: Hello.... Oh, hello Leo. ...Ah, just ignore her. She is nothing but a little snob. ...What have you been doing? Oh, nothing special. Just painting a little. Making the placard.... Yes, I know that a little booster would come in handy. (*Looks toward the bar.*) Okay, I'll try to get something...Fine...Bye, bye, Leo.

MEELI (*gets up from the sofa; sarcastically*): Leo...well, well, it is Mr. Lion himself....Judging from your taste, one can be reasonably sure that he looks like a shaggy lion, as far as his hair is concerned.

LINDA (*upset*): A spy! You have no right to listen secretly to my telephone calls.

MEELI: This is my home. I can be anywhere I like around here. And perhaps I have even a greater right to it than you do. I can invite my friends here any time. You just try to invite your hairy boyfriend here, father would throw him out on the spot.

LINDA: Boyfriend? Leo isn't my boyfriend. You are hopelessly ordinary. (*She looks at her sister ironically.*) Our ambitious and proper Meeli. Make a masterpiece out of your life. Finish college, marry well, become a society snob and raise new little snobs. This is your life's goal. (*With uncontrollable scorn.*) Such petty bourgeois trash.

MEELI: Where are you steering your life to? Do you hope to become a famous artist? Don't forget the fierce competition. You'd make a better old maid social worker.

LINDA: Why not? There are other things in life than an ambitious career and greediness. The world is full of injustice and tyranny to fight against.

MEELI: With placards in front of the American Consulate?

LINDA (*annoyed*): What do you know about that?

MEELI: It's true. I heard very well when you told your leader about it a little while ago—"at six o'clock before the American Consulate with the placard." Every child knows that it is the place where the Vietnam war protestors go. (*Scornfully.*) So you are one of them.

LINDA (*sulking*): What of it?

MEELI: You are crazy. You know very well what father thinks of it.

LINDA: Just as if he were the wisest person in the world. Bertram Russell thinks differently, and which of the two is the greater authority?

MEELI: In our house, definitely father. He says that Russell is an old fool with a brain like a soft boiled-egg. He doesn't know what the communists are like. Father has fought them.

LINDA: I hate violence of all kinds. It has got to be stopped. (*With sudden anger.*) We will go and throw stones in the windows of the American Consulate today.

MEELI (*with sincere interest*): Oh, that's exciting. But what if father hears about it?

LINDA (*contemptuously*): Father, father...You have nothing else on your mind. You spineless lap dog.

MEELI: Hold your horses, Linda. They are about to bolt again. But that's not my problem. You are only making yourself ridiculous with this kind of behavior. (*Turns and goes upstairs.*)

LINDA (*goes to the bar and searches among the bottles*): Ah, ha, a bottle of Napoleon brandy! (*She lifts the bottle and looks at it.*) I'll take this one along. (*She leaves the bottle on top of the bar.*) It's curious how a little bit of liquid can sometimes give you such inner strength. It's natural that we should lose our nerve at times, we are only human. Not superhuman like the man who is supposed to be my father. He who knows it all, fears no one, and won't do anything wrong, ever. I think that he eats a whole pound of butter before a drinking party. That way he can drink all the others under the table. A dictator! He does not allow a single one of my paintings to be hung here. He says that they aren't respectable enough. And I am considered quite talented by my teachers. Only this realistic trash. (*She looks scornfully at the picture of the bridge above the bar and then walks over to the portrait. She lifts her arm in fascist greeting.*) Heil Hitler! (*She pushes the painting out of balance.*) Oh how I hate him. Hate. Hate. Hate. (*Pause.*) And yet, it is wrong to hate. I am fighting against hate and brute force. (*She sits down on the sofa unhappily.*) What will become of me? What will become of me?

(*HELGA comes down the stairs. She is a pretty woman of forty-three who looks younger than her age. She is still in her morning robe but otherwise well groomed. In her hand is the text of Ibsen's* A Doll's House. *She is studying Nora's lines out loud.*)

HELGA: "you arranged everything according to your taste and I developed the same tastes as you. It's your fault, Torvald, that my life has come to nothing." (*She is not satisfied with the result.*) No, it must be much more forceful. (*She repeats the last line a little more convincingly, then notices LINDA.*) Ah, here you are my dear child. Just the person I need at this moment. Play the role of Torvald for me, darling. I mean, read his lines from here. Please, help me! (*She offers her the book, but*

LINDA *does not notice it.*)

LINDA: Please, mother, you help me!

HELGA: But my dear child, what is your problem?

LINDA: I am almost twenty years old and I don't know who I am. I don't know what will become of me. (*HELGA sits down beside Linda.*)

HELGA: I am...what is the use of hiding it...almost over forty, and don't know what will become of me either. The performance is Saturday, when I play Nora. It is the most important role in my career so far, but I have no self-confidence. I am told that Sammalselg from New York has been invited to review the play for *Free Voice*. He is grumpy as a bear suffering from hemorrhoids.

LINDA (*still preoccupied with her own problems*): Mother, I have one body, but two souls. And they fight each other. Sometimes I feel like becoming a missionary in Angola, and at the same time I could become a female wrestler.

HELGA (*laughing*): In that case, I recommend you try acting in the emigre theatre. You'd be working without pay like a missionary, and wrestling with your role all the time. Like myself now. I know that the conflict with Torvald in the third act needs a lot of polishing. (*She offers the book to LINDA again.*) Please, just for half an hour.

LINDA (*almost in despair*): Mother, I am not joking. I must speak with someone urgently...with you, mother.

HELGA: Of course, of course, child. But later, after the performance. Then we two will sit down and talk very seriously about all our problems. At this moment it is impossible for me to step out of my role. I have to be immersed in it. But as soon as it is over, then...I promise you. (*She strokes LINDA'S head.*)

LINDA: There will be other plays, and you'll become Madame Pompadour or the maid of Orleans. Rehearsals and preparations, speech and dance lessons, etc., etc., *ad infinitum*. Your whole life is dedicated to the theatre. You never have time to talk to me. And yet, you are the only one I love, despite the fact that I can't respect you.

HELGA (*with sudden interest*): You can't respect me? But why?

LINDA: Because you are under father's influence. You never exert your own will, you let him decide everything. He seems to have a certain mysterious power over you. At any rate, I will fly out of here as soon as I graduate from the art school. Or perhaps even before.

HELGA: Please stop this nonsense. You are being unfair to your

father. He is a very successful man. A man who serves as an
example to others. Your father is like a rock on whom we have
built a secure life for ourselves here. Believe me, my daughter,
we, the servants of the fine arts who lack any practical sense,
need this rock most urgently.

LINDA: A rock only has power, not a heart or a soul. (*Pause.*)
Mother, tell me honestly, do you love him?

HELGA: What a question. Of course I love your father. (*Pause.*)
I don't think that it has to be an uncompromisingly passionate
love. Love is a flame that inevitably cools with time. But we
have a common home, children and mutual respect. And you
too, should respect him more. Sometimes I don't understand
you. But now I must get back to studying my role.

LINDA: That's what I thought. You don't love him. You have just
become used to him. Tell me, mother, have you ever loved
another man? I mean with your whole heart and soul?
(*HELGA lays the book down. She is basically a vain person
who likes to talk about herself and the pleasant moments of her
life.*)

HELGA: Yes, I had somebody else once. It was twenty years ago.
Before I knew...your father. (*MEELI comes down the steps
unnoticed by HELGA and LINDA. Although dressed to go outdoors, she steps in the entry and listens to the conversation.
HELGA continues dreamily, almost poetically.*) His name was
Vello, Vello Meerend. He was a poet who didn't write poems.
An artist who didn't paint. An actor who never stepped on the
stage. His head was full of strange dreams which were never
fulfilled. I think that if one were to analyze him soberly, he
could be considered a rather worthless man, but I loved him.
Yes, I can't deny it. The two of us used to roam in the woods
and lie on the shore of the lake. There were times when he
dreamed of becoming a forester somewhere in the woods of
Alutaguse* and live with me in a tiny house amid a symphony
of rustling pines. Yes, those were his very words. And then
again, he wanted to become a treasure hunter, searching the
depths of the sea, or an entomologist specializing in colorful
butterflies. Oh, he didn't know himself what he wanted. We
were both very young then. Just like two bright, carefree butterflies.

LINDA: And then what happened?

---

*Alutaguse is a forested, sparsely inhabited area in Northern Estonia, with rivers
and lakes.

HELGA: Then came the war and he was mobilized. He happened
to serve in the same unit whose commander was...your father.
They were wounded almost at the same time—he in the leg,
and your father got a shell fragment in his shoulder. Curiously
enough, as different as they were, they became friends. It must
have been the attraction of opposites.

LINDA: What became of him?

HELGA: He was left behind in Estonia. I know nothing more
about him. He and your father had gone to the seashore so that
they could flee from the Russians, but there was no more room
in the boat...for him. I was already in Sweden, then. He asked
your father to greet me for him, so when your father came to
Stockholm we became acquainted, your father and I. It must
have been fate. Vello always believed very firmly in fate.

LINDA: Mother, did you love him...how should I say...
intimately?

HELGA (*embarrassed*): What's come over you? (*Pause.*) It's all
in the past now.

LINDA: Twenty years ago...(*Lost in thought for a moment, but
awakens as if from a trance and glances at her watch.*)
Heavens, it's late and I haven't finished my placard yet. (*She
begins to go toward the staircase. At the same time, MEELI
prepares to go out.*)

MEELI (*from the entry*): Mother, I'm going out for half an hour.
So long.

HELGA: Meeli! Wait a minute! (*She goes to MEELI in the entry.*)
Be a good girl and drop in at the Simmermans and pick up my
costume. You know, the Italian one I dance the tarantella in...
in the second act. They just called, it's ready now.

MEELI: The one with the large black shawl? Oh, will you let me
try it on?

HELGA (*laughing*): You don't like old fashioned clothes. Go on
now, the store closes at six.

MEELI: Okay mother. (*MEELI exits. LINDA has used the
opportunity to take the bottle of brandy from the bar and hide
it under her smock. She runs up the stairs.*)

HELGA (*calling after her*): Linda! She has left already. That's
modern youth. Never any time for one's mother. (*Thinking.*)
Did I tell her too much? She might get suspicious. Well, I don't
think so. (*Dreamily.*) Yes, it all could have gone differently.
Would I have been happier with him? Or if I had stayed there?
My acting career would have reached greater heights, perhaps
even stardom. Oh, you foolish, foolish thoughts. Idle thoughts

—disappear from my head, leave me alone. (*She goes to the mirror and looks at herself.*) Aren't I too old for the part of Nora? Her children are still quite young. Liina Reiman* was only thirty when she played the role. Nonsense...I won't look a day over twenty-five with the stage makeup...young Lemmits is definitely in love with me and he is scarcely over thirty. Of course, I flirted with him a bit, I let him kiss me once—playfully. But I didn't go any further, of course. It would not occur to me to. And what did he say at that point? (*Imitating.*) "You older women are real bitches, all that you want is to prove to yourselves that you are still edible." The shameless urchin. (*Pause.*) But, in a way, he was right. It is indeed wonderful to be assured once in a while that you could if you wanted to. (*Resolutely.*) Nora, stop this indulgence at once. You are a woman of moral charcter living in the Norway of the last century. And today is such a beautiful fall day. (*She goes and looks out of the window. She takes her book and reads it for a while, then turns around and repeats her lines by heart.*) "And when I think that the spring will soon be here with the great blue sky. Perhaps we shall take a trip. Perhaps I shall see the sea again. Oh, what a wonderful thing it is to be alive and happy!" (*Pause.*) Happy? (*Thinks.*) And right after that Krogstadt enters. (*She remains thoughtful. A moment later the door opens and PAUL comes in from the hall. He is about forty-five years old, self assured and domineering as is proper for a successful man in his profession. He is dressed with tasteful elegance. He carries a briefcase and has a raincoat over his arm. HELGA looks startled but regains her self control immediately.*) Ah, it's you, Paul. I had the feeling that Krogstadt...

PAUL: Excuse me, Helga, I honestly don't know what you are talking about.

HELGA (*laughing apologetically*): Of course not, I am living in the world of my play these days. Until next Saturday evening. Only then I shall slowly transform from Nora to Helga again. Krogstadt is one of the characters in the play who brings misfortune on the house, and he enters exactly at the point in the text that I was just memorizing. (*She takes PAUL'S coat and reaches out for the briefcase, but he does not give it to her.*)

PAUL: I don't have the honor to know him. But my name is Paul Toomik as always, and I bring great fortune to this house.

---

*Liina Reiman (1891-1961) Estonian actress, considered to be the greatest inter- interpreter of heroic roles in Estonian theatre.

(*HELGA hangs his coat in the entry hall.*)

HELGA: I know, Paul.

PAUL: No, my dear wife, you don't know anything yet, or have you already read the paper?

HELGA: The paper? No.

PAUL: Then be informed that before you stands a hero.

HELGA: A hero? Is it in the Estonian paper?

PAUL (*with a dry laugh*): Don't be so naive, Helga. Would it be worth mentioning? In the Estonian papers they sing the praises of anyone stirring the soup at a get-together. I am talking of a real newspaper, with a circulation of close to half a million. An influential and meaningful paper. (*Takes a newspaper out of the briefcase and spreads it out on the table. HELGA goes and looks at it.*)

HELGA: Your picture is in the paper, and a large one at that!

PAUL: And read what they have to say. (*HELGA searches for the article.*) No, not there. It begins here. I shall read it myself. (*He reads the article with complacent semipathos.*) "Twenty years ago a young, penniless fellow fled across the Baltic Sea in a fishing boat in order to escape the communists who had conquered his small homeland, Estonia. The same man, Paul Toomik, 45, an engineer, is now one of our most prominent designers of vaulted bridges. His plan has been chosen to be used in building a bridge across the sea." (*Pause.*) You see, they have the facts right. I haven't even been confused with Latvians or Lithuanians, as sometimes happens here.

HELGA: A bridge across the sea?

PAUL: Oh yes, they mean the new bridge which we are starting to build between Newfoundland and Labrador. The contract was signed yesterday and that's discussed at some length in the same article. It only crosses the bay, but that's quite a large piece of sea in itself. And this is only the beginning of bigger things to come.

HELGA: Marvelous. Oh, Paul, I am so proud of you! (*She embraces him.*) So proud.

PAUL: I must say modestly that I quite deserve it. (*Takes the paper which HELGA attempts to continue to read, and folds it up.*) Later. You can read it thoroughly later. But now, let's celebrate the occasion. Let's have a drink. How about it, my wife! (*It sounds more like a command than question.*)

HELGA: Marvelous.

PAUL: And where is my darling daughter? The apple of my eye. (*Goes to the stairway and calls.*) Meeli, Meeli!

HELGA: Meeli went out just now, but Linda is in her room. Let's ask her down too, to celebrate the occasion with us.
(*Paul ignores her and goes to the bar and looks for a certain bottle.*)

PAUL: That's funny, I had a bottle of Napoleon brandy, but I can't find it anywhere.

HELGA: Paul, you should spend more time with Linda. She has become quite strange lately.

PAUL: Where is my bottle of Napoleon brandy?

HELGA: I have no idea. Perhaps you finished it off last night with your business friends.

PAUL: Very funny, I was so sure that there was still one bottle left. Well, if there isn't, then we don't need it. Maybe a glass of champagne is more appropriate anyway. (*He opens a bottle of champagne and fills two glasses. He gives one to HELGA.*)

HELGA: Thank you, Paul. But why don't we invite Linda down, too?

PAUL (*puts his glass down, irritated*): I have nothing to do with Linda. (*Walks around the room, nervously, stops in front of his portrait and adjusts it.*) She is not my daughter.

HELGA (*gets up*): Paul, you mustn't say that! She might hear you!

PAUL: It is about time for her to hear it. As a matter of fact I should have told her about it a long time ago.

HELGA: No, no, Paul. You mustn't tell her, ever. She is already mixed up, as if she had lost her footing. This news could push her over. You know what a devastating effect such things can have on a young psyche. Promise me that you won't tell her... ever.

PAUL: Well, we will see. It all depends on you. If you are an obedient wife and never contradict me, then I can keep silent. But if not, then...

HELGA: Paul, this almost sounds like extortion.

PAUL: Extortion is a very strong word, my wife. Besides, you know very well that you have your weaknesses in life. You need a firm hand to guide you. But why should we talk about such things on an important day like this. Cheers, my wife. To the future.

HELGA (*not too convincing*): To the future! (*The drink after clinking the glasses.*)

PAUL: You don't seem very enthusiastic.

HELGA: But I am, Paul. This is a great moment of recognition for you.

PAUL: Not only recognition. I shall wipe out Sõmerpalu with this.

HELGA: Sõmerpalu, the lawyer? What do you have to do with him?

PAUL: Of course, I forgot that you know nothing except your parts in the plays. You haven't even heard that your husband has risen as a star on the stage of real life. Half the town seems to know, except my own wife hasn't even the slightest idea about it.

HELGA: You never talk to me about anything.

PAUL: Very well. Know it now then. Sõmerpalu and I are the top candidates to be diplomatic representative of the Estonian Republic.

HELGA: What? But Randla is already the representative.

PAUL: Not for long. Randla is already quite old and will soon move to Florida. The climate there is better for his chronic rheumatism.

HELGA: But...but this is not your field. I mean, you haven't had any experience in diplomacy.

PAUL: There aren't any diplomats left from the time of the Republic, and besides, it doesn't make any difference. The only thing that matters is a popular candidate fully respected by the people. A man whose past is flawless.

HELGA: Yes, but...

PAUL: My only disadvantage is that certain influential circles seemed, at least until now, to be favoring Sõmerpalu. They say that he has participated more actively in Estonian affairs. (*Contemptuously.*) As if that mattered. Randla himself seems to be on my side, and now this acknowledgement in the Canadian press will help me too. No, I am absolutely sure that I'll defeat Sõmerpalu now. What do you think about all this, my wife?

HELGA (*hesitantly*): This is all so unexpected. I don't know what to say. You have never had any interest in such affairs. And now, all of a sudden...why?

PAUL (*not too sure himself*): Why? This would be a great achievement in my life. And let us be frank about it...it gives me a chance to procure some important business deals. It opens some doors for me which would have been extremely difficult to open otherwise.

HELGA: In other words, you would like to use that position as a springboard for your own personal career?

PAUL (*annoyed*): Stop this childishness. We don't need to pretend here. Personal interests are always the closest to one's heart. Do you perform on the stage in the interest of the Estonian people? Tell me?

HELGA: I don't know. It isn't exactly the same thing.

PAUL (*ignoring her statement*): Personal interests and the interests of people. They can very well go hand in hand. That position will help me to get important bridge contracts, and as a compensation I shall build a bridge between the Estonian emigres and the Canadian public. Isn't that an important achievement for Estonian society, and who would be more able to accomplish it than I, tell me, my wife?

HELGA: I don't know, Paul.

PAUL: You don't know. You don't know. What's the use of discussing such things with you if you don't know anything. Anyway, for your information, I have invited three guests over this evening. The editor of *Estonian Life,* Virkus; Minister Humal, and the president of National Action, Kargus.

HELGA: Kargus! But he belongs to the extremist camp who call everybody red. What do you have to do with him all of a sudden?

PAUL: It's diplomacy, my wife. Even the support of that group will be an advantage to me. And besides, we were in the same regiment with Virkus. It is a good time to warm up our friendship a bit.

HELGA: I don't have to participate in the evening, do I? I must study my part.

PAUL: No, I don't think you'll be needed. It's men's talk anyway. (*Ironically.*) It may easily happen that this will be your last role in the theatre...As the wife of a consul you would hardly find time for it, and it won't be necessary for you any more, either. In that position you will have to do a lot of real life acting.

HELGA: I shall never give up the theatre.

PAUL: Well, we shall see. You will give it up if I want you to. Or do you want me to have a little conversation with Linda?

HELGA: No, no. You mustn't be so cruel, Paul.

PAUL: Well, alright then. I invited them for six o'clock. Make a few snacks for us and then you are excused. (*Looks at his watch.*) The football game has just started. I can watch it for a whole hour. And I don't want any interruptions. If somebody calls, please take the message. (*Goes into the T.V. room, leaving the door ajar. HELGA takes her book and tries to get involved with her role but the sounds of the American football game upset her. She decides to go to her room. When she reaches the staircase the doorbell rings.*)

HELGA: Heavens, who is it now? (*She adjusts herself in front of the mirror and opens the door. KALTER steps in. He is in his fifties, a simple man in well worn clothes who almost leaves the impression of a derelict. Although basically brave and self assured, his movements and appearance are somehow nervous — he is an alcoholic who is trying to reform himself and has been on the wagon almost a whole month. He has a sarcastic sense of humor in which one can occasionally detect some bitterness.)*

KALTER: Good evening, Mrs. Toomik!

HELGA: Yes?

KALTER: Kalter is my name. *(He bows awkwardly.)* Your ladyship wouldn't know me, of course, but I know quite a lot about you. *(Pause.)* From the stage, that is.

HELGA *(a little more friendly)*: Is that so? But...

KALTER *(with nervous enthusiasm)*: But what business brought me here? I would like to have a little discussion with your husband.

HELGA: Is he expecting you?

KALTER: How would I know whether he is or not?

HELGA: Did he know that you were coming here?

KALTER: Well, not unless he is clairvoyant. *(Looks around in the room.)* Quite a life you lead here — my, my!

HELGA *(steps in front of him)*: My husband is not here now. I don't know when he will come home. Perhaps you can come another time, Mr....

KALTER: As I said, Kalter is my name. Max Kalter. In the church registry it is Maximilian. My mother was quite a refined woman.

HELGA: Shall we expect you another time then, Mr. Kalter? *(KALTER has begun to listen to the sound of the ball game, which can be heard through the half closed door.)*

KALTER: Well, your ladyship must have been looking at the good old Gray Cup match. But it seems a little strange to me that a fine lady like yourself should be interested in a brutal game like that.

HELGA: No, not me. I don't know a thing about the game.

KALTER: Then your daughters perhaps? That too seems strange to me.

HELGA: No...

KALTER: Well, then it is the master of the house himself. I noticed right away his limousine parked outside.

HELGA *(a bit agitated)*: Alright, it is he. But he might as well not be at home, he is not to be disturbed. He will receive nobody now. Come some other time and be sure to telephone first!

KALTER: Did he telephone me when he came?

HELGA: He? Came where?

KALTER: To the beach on Saaremaa. Almost twenty years ago.

HELGA: Did you flee together?

KALTER: I brought him over. I was the captain and the owner of the boat.

HELGA: Oh! You are the man who saved his life then!

KALTER: His and that of a whole gang of others.

HELGA: Please forgive me for the way I treated you. And do sit down, please, Mr. Kalter.

KALTER (*continues to stand*): Oh, you think he'll receive me, then?

HELGA: Of course! This will surely be a very pleasant surprise for him.

KALTER: One can't be so sure.

HELGA: Why? You must be joking. Please sit down. Isn't it strange, twenty years have passed and you appear only now. Where have you been all this time?

KALTER (*sits down*): Here and there. (*Sarcastically.*) Now that there are bridges everywhere...even across the sea. Who needs a boatman anymore!

HELGA: Oh, don't say that. (*Pause.*) You are the one then. How exciting! (*Pause.*) Please tell me something. I have always wanted to know it. You see, my husband had a friend with him at that time...

KALTER: Vello Meerend?

HELGA: You knew him then?

KALTER (*nervously*): Why talk about those who are gone.

HELGA: Who are gone? But he must be...somewhere!

KALTER (*looks around in the room again*): Quite a life you lead here, as I said before.

HELGA: Why didn't you take him aboard?

KALTER: Are you sorry about that?

HELGA: I feel sorry for everybody who stayed behind...and fell into their hands. I would just like to know...

KALTER: My boat wasn't a steamship which could have accommodated everybody.

HELGA: But there was room for Paul!

KALTER: Yes, just room enough for him. (*Nervously.*) But now I want to talk to him. At once. I am in a hurry.

HELGA (*frightened by his tone*): Alright...(*Listens.*) It is intermission time for a commercial now, a good time to bother him.

(*She goes into the T.V. room. KALTER stands up and scrutinizes the furniture in the livingroom. His eyes stop immediately at the bar and he becomes noticeably more nervous and unsure of himself. Resolutely, he turns his back to the bar. In the T.V. room the volume of sound is tuned down. A few minutes later PAUL and HELGA enter the livingroom.*)

PAUL: I hear that we have an unexpected guest. (*Stretches out his hand.*) I would not have recognized you any more!

KALTER: Perhaps not. Twenty years is a long time.

HELGA: Goodness, what a reunion! (*Remains standing.*)

KALTER: I seem to have come at an inconvenient time. You're missing your ball game.

PAUL: No, it doesn't matter. The game is quite one-sided anyway.

KALTER: The brute attackers are presumably far ahead of the others. In this country they are always the winners. In the football game and in real life alike.

PAUL: Do you think so? (*He forces a laugh.*) I don't know about that, I mean, whether they are always the winners, but Ottawa's Rough Riders are leading right now alright. May I offer you a drink? What will you have Mr. Kalter? Gin? Scotch? Rye? Rum?

KALTER (*swallows, obviously fighting with himself, then makes a decisively rejecting motion*): No, no. For heaven's sake, no!

PAUL: You don't use the stuff?

KALTER: I did. I used too much of it. It was like a crutch for me when things went wrong in my life. But I must abstain from it if I want to prevent the crutch from becoming a wheelchair.

PAUL: Oh yes, I understand. (*An awkward silence.*)

HELGA: Excuse me, Mr. Kalter, I must go and make a few sandwiches. (*She begins to go to the diningroom.*)

KALTER: No, don't bother for my sake! I'll be leaving soon.

PAUL (*looking at his watch*): We are expecting guests.

KALTER: Don't worry, I won't intrude. (*Looks around in the room again.*) You are nicely settled on the sunny side of life now. A famous man, I read about you in today's paper. It is quite a place you have here, a beautiful wife and two wonderful daughters. Yes, I have been away from here, but I know quite a bit about your life. I have kept my eye on those whom I brought across the sea once upon a time. Now you are traveling first class.

PAUL: Oh, well! But of course, I am grateful to you for it.

KALTER: That's nice to hear. Only gratitude does not fill one's stomach.

PAUL: Of course not. Perhaps I could help you out a little, so to speak. (*Takes the billfold out of his pocket.*) How would twenty dollars be?

KALTER (*angrily*): I am not a beggar. No, not yet. Just put your change back in your wallet and get your checkbook out.

PAUL: What?

KALTER: I came to collect the travel fare.

PAUL (*coldly*): Is that so? And how much would that be?

KALTER: I saved your life. You should know best how much it is worth.

PAUL: Listen! I don't like this kind of talk!

KALTER: I don't either, so let's make it short. Let's say, a thousand dollars, and I'll write off the interest of twenty years.

PAUL (*forcing a laugh*): You must be joking.

KALTER: I haven't felt like joking for several years now. My sense of humor I spent long ago as tuition in the school of life. But perhaps I have offended you, maybe your life is worth much more?

PAUL: But my dear man, you can't make demands on me. We had no agreement. Wasn't it your moral obligation to take a combat soldier on board?

KALTER: You have the nerve to talk to me about moral obligation!

PAUL: Are you getting fresh?

KALTER: You don't want to pay peaceably, then?

PAUL: Neither peaceably nor forcibly. Listen, fellow, I can help you a little if you are sensible. But you won't get a penny if you start making demands. You have no grounds for it!

KALTER: The grounds have to do with Vello Meerend.

PAUL: With him? He stayed behind!

KALTER: Voluntarily?

PAUL: We agreed on it. Or more precisely, we cast lots.

KALTER (*cruelly*): Yes, he stayed behind, alright, lying lifeless on the beach.

PAUL: Lifeless?

KALTER: I saw it with my own eyes. And so did some other people who happened to know him. It wasn't so dark there. You hit him in his chest with something. A knife or bayonet, I don't know exactly what it was. He fell and didn't move a muscle after that.

PAUL: You are mad. Where did you get this story?

KALTER: At least three men are ready to testify under oath in support of this if necessary.

PAUL: I hit him with my fist, if you care to know. Right in his solar plexus. What is this rot about a knife or bayonet? (*Pause.*) One had to do such things then. Everybody was looking out for his own survival.

KALTER: In any event, nothing has been heard of him since.

PAUL: Whoever hears anything about them over there? That doesn't prove anything.

KALTER: It proves that a man who is able to live with a conscience like yours, Mr. Toomik, is unsuitable for the post of leader of the Estonian people.

PAUL (*enraged*): Is that so? You have become an extortionist then. The lowest criminal of all. Get out of here at once before I throw you out myself. (*He grabs hold of KALTER'S chest. KALTER frees himself with a skillful judo blow.*)

KALTER: You shouldn't try that on me. I am an old seaman who knows a few tricks. Besides, I have the law on my side.

PAUL: On your side? Your word has no weight in any court of justice.

KALTER: Doesn't it? Well, maybe. But it won't be necessary to go to court. The press may be even more interested.

PAUL: No editor will listen to the likes of you!

KALTER: We shall see! Mr. Sõmerpalu is now the chief shareholder of *Estonian Voice*.

PAUL: (*cornered*): You have even found that out. (*Nervously walks back and forth.*) Listen, Mr. Kalter, let's talk about this sensibly. You know very well that I am not a murderer. Everybody knows it. Well, I used a little violence, but this was understandable in those days when one feared death. I only hit him with my fist...only with my fist.

KALTER: It is impossible to prove. And even in case...

PAUL (*panicked, not in possession of his reason*): Do you think that my conscience hasn't bothered me because of this? Didn't I try to make up for it in every way possible? I married his fiancee. Brought up his child. Helped them through the hardships of life. Isn't that something, tell me!

KALTER (*surprised*): It was indeed his child then, not yours, the first one? I didn't know that. Well, in that case it was a noble deed. But the fact that your friend's fiancee was the only daughter and heir of the rich ship broker Jaan Kruusman made the situation a lot easier, didn't it?

PAUL: Stop it!

KALTER: Of course I will—for one thousand dollars. (*Pause.*) There is only room for one in the boat which sails to the consulship.

PAUL: A thousand dollars? How can I be sure you'll stop there? That you won't make new demands in the future?

KALTER: It's a gentleman's game. One must trust one's fellow man.

PAUL: I have to think about it. Come back next week, we will talk then. Or better, I will come to you.

KALTER: No, now. It is a very urgent matter. (*HELGA enters carrying a tray with little sandwiches. She looks frightened and despairing.*) Alright, I give you half an hour, not a minute longer. I shall return in half an hour. (*He hurries out.*)

PAUL: No, no! Never...

HELGA: Krogstadt...this was Krogstadt. A dreadful misfortune has fallen upon our house.

CURTAIN

ACT TWO

(*The set is the same as in the first act. The action continues. PAUL goes to the bar and fixes himself a drink. HELGA is standing as if petrified, still holding the sandwich tray.*)

PAUL (*nervously*): Will you put those sandwiches down? I assure you that I am not hungry. (*HELGA puts the tray on the table.*)

MEELI (*enters through the front door*): Here's your costume, mother. (*Gives the package to her.*) It's so exciting. I can't wait to see it. (*Notices Paul.*) Hurray, Father is at home! (*Runs to him and embraces him lightly*). I just met a stranger at our gate. A very odd man. He looked like a derelict. He came from our house. Who was he?

PAUL: Oh, nobody, my dear little Meeli. Just a stranger. (*Pause.*) He was looking for work. He wanted to rake leaves or something.

MEELI: Curious, he stopped me and said: 'You must be the younger one. You are not the one from Meerend then.' What did he mean by that?

PAUL (*dumbfounded*): What?

HELGA (*gives the package to MEELI, hastily*): Run along now! Be a good girl and take it upstairs, I still have some work to do in the kitchen.

MEELI (*half mumbling*): The one from Meerend? Mother, that name sounds familiar to me somehow. Oh yes, now I know. I heard you talk about him to Linda a while ago.

PAUL: What? What is all this about?

HELGA (*interrupting him hastily*): No, no, it's nothing! (*To MEELI.*) Go on, now, child and take it upstairs. You can try it on. I shall come up soon and see how it looks on you.

MEELI (*excited*): Oh, may I mother? This is so exciting! (*Runs toward the stairway with the package. Stops on midway.*) But I must do a little logical thinking here. I am beginning to suspect something! (*Goes upstairs.*)

PAUL: What does this mean, wife? What were you and Linda talking about? I demand an explanation.

HELGA (*resolutely*): I demand an explanation of you, Paul! (*Pause.*) The dining room door was open when you were talking to that man. I heard everything. (*Loses her confidence.*) Ah, Paul! It is all so terrible...so terrible!

PAUL: You don't believe that I...

HELGA: You yourself admitted it! He wanted to come to me. But you used force. And you assured me that you drew lots. Paul you lied to me!

PAUL: We all tell little white lies. Who among us is an angel! You yourself do...to Linda.

HELGA: This is different. It is not for my own sake, but for hers. But you are an egotist. You think of nobody but yourself.

PAUL: What do you mean by nobody? Have I not cared for my family? Don't you have everything you need? A beautiful home, affluence, social prominence?

HELGA: But there is no love. Paul, first of all comes love!

PAUL: Are you lacking for love?

HELGA: I am not talking about myself. It is not important. But Linda...

PAUL: Linda does not let me love her. She has disliked me since her childhood. She contradicts me in everything. As if to spite me!

HELGA: This is only because you favor Meeli so obviously. Your ego won't tolerate the fact that I once had a relationship with Vello. And now you have revealed our big secret to that extortionist. Why, Paul? There was no need for it. You were trying to apologize to him. Did you hope he would feel sorry for you? Is the post of consul really the most important thing in the world for you? I have never before seen you so humble. You have lost something today which can not be easily regained.

Paul, you have lost my respect!

PAUL: Stop your nonsense! Linda hates me already.

HELGA: She was only a two month old embryo in my body when we married. Nobody was to know about that but you and I. And now you have revealed the secret. Ah...

PAUL: Yes, nobody was to know about it. Not for Linda's sake but for yours! In order to cover up your frivolous past.

HELGA: This is going too far! I forbid you to talk to me like that. I was in love with Vello, and he loved me. I have nothing to be ashamed of. But you married me because of my father's money! A frivolous wife.... It is true, then!

PAUL: No, it is not true. I would have succeeded in life without your dowry. I loved you...in my own way. And I do have a conscience.

HELGA: You have a conscience? Ah, Paul, I am not too sure about that any more.

(*LINDA comes down the stairs. She holds her purse in one hand and carries the placard in the other. She walks toward the entry without paying attention to the others.*)

HELGA: Where are you going, Linda? What have you got in your hand?

LINDA: I am going out!

PAUL: With that placard? Show it to me! (*Goes to LINDA and attempts to take away the placard.*)

MEELI (*from the stairway*): Linda is going to a demonstration in front of the American Consulate.

HELGA: No!

PAUL: You aren't going anywhere! Give it to me!

HELGA: Leave her alone, Paul!

PAUL (*grabs the placard from LINDA, who falls on all fours in the scuffle. Her purse opens and the bottle of Napoleon's brandy rolls out of it*): Well, this is what we have come to. (*Reads the placard.*) **Aggressors Get Out of Vietnam!** (*Tears up the placard and throws it on the floor. Picks up the bottle of brandy.*) And that's where my lost bottle of brandy is. Don't you have any courage without it?

HELGA: Leave her alone, Paul! (*Helps LINDA up.*) Did you hurt yourself, my daughter?

PAUL (*puts the bottle on the bar*): Aggressors get out of Vietnam. Why don't you go out with a placard which reads 'Aggressors get out of Estonia'? Answer me.

LINDA: Because you are an aggressor yourself, a despot. A rude tyrant. And you are already out of Estonia.

HELGA: That's enough, Linda! Go to your room at once! You are not going anywhere!

LINDA (*to PAUL*): I hate you, do you hear! I am ashamed to have a father like you! (*Picks up the torn placard and runs out the front door.*)

PAUL (*to her*): But I am not...

HELGA: Be quiet! (*Runs after LINDA.*) Linda! (*Comes back.*) She has already run out the gate. What will happen now? She might never come back!

PAUL: She will. And I will take care of her then. (*Pause.*) She protests against the Americans in Vietnam. How did such ideas come into our house?

MEELI (*comes downstairs*): I know. It's that Leo.

HELGA: Run along, Meeli! Your father and I want to talk about it privately.

MEELI (*a little offended*): All right then....But he is a hairy one all right. I know. I overheard their telephone conversation.

HELGA (*commandingly*): Go now! (*MEELI goes upstairs.*) You are wondering where such ideas came from. Paul, you yourself are guilty of them.

PAUL: I? I have always stressed the fact that the Americans are fighting for the right cause! Damn it, I myself fought against the Communists, don't forget that!

HELGA: This is not what I mean. You have neglected Linda. You pay no attention to her.

PAUL: And you yourself? I am the disciplinarian in this house. You seem to be fleeing from life...taking refuge in your play characters.

HELGA: I too want to be somebody. To achieve something on my own. And you don't understand. But we don't have time to discuss it now. Your guests should arrive any minute.

PAUL (*looks at his watch*): Yes, you are right. Phuhh! (*Gives a sigh of relief.*) This was a narrow escape. Imagine if she had landed on their laps with her placard, so to speak! It would have been a dreadful scandal. (*The stage has begun to darken in the meanwhile, and PAUL turns on the ceiling light.*)

HELGA: Wouldn't it be a scandal if that Kalter...

PAUL: You are right, he promised to return in half an hour. Damn! We are really in a predicament.

HELGA (*goes and closes the draperies*): Are you going to pay him off?

PAUL: Are you crazy? To yield to an extortionist? Never!

HELGA: But what will happen if he...

PAUL: Right and the law are on my side.

HELGA: Are they? And even if they were, what about public opinion? You know very well how our little society spreads rumors and blows them up to giant proportions. (*PAUL begins to walk back and forth nervously.*) What if you did pay him off? It wouldn't ruin us!

PAUL: It is a matter of principle. I would hate myself for the rest of my life. (*Thinking.*) I know what I will do. (*Takes from his pocket a checkbook and a ballpoint pen and writes out a check. Gives orders with the tone of an officer.*) When the guests arrive I shall take them to the dining room and close the door. You will remain here waiting for him and when he arrives give him the check. Then we will be rid of him. (*Gives the check to HELGA.*)

HELGA: A thousand dollar check! You are giving in to him then?

PAUL: Today is Saturday. He can't cash it at the bank before Monday morning.

HELGA: And then?

PAUL: I am just doing it to get rid of him today. So that he won't cause a scandal. I shall cancel the check tomorrow. I know the manager of the bank personally and will call him at home.

HELGA: But Kalter will go to the newspaper with his information.

PAUL: I have to take a calculated risk. The consul will probably be chosen within a couple of days, and I doubt that they could put this thing into motion in time...Kalter was too late, that's why he is in such a hurry. Sõmerpalu will never allow the story to be used after I have been elected. That would put him in a bad light. And I doubt that he would use it under any circumstances. He has his tricks, but he isn't a scoundrel.

HELGA: But this still doesn't solve anything. You revealed our greatest secret to this loathsome man. I can't believe he won't make use of it. (*The doorbell rings.*) Heavens! They are here already! And I am still in my robe.

PAUL: Hurry up! I shall meet them myself. (*HELGA runs upstairs. PAUL goes to open the door.*) Welcome! Welcome, Mr. Minister! (*Helps him to remove his coat.*)

HUMAL (*a man in his sixties. Gentlemanly and polished according to the good old conventions. He is a former Minister of Finance of the Estonian Republic, now working as a bookkeeper. He has an important behind-the-scenes role in emigre politics*): Not Mr. Minister. Don't be so formal, my young friend! Let's forget such high sounding titles when we are by ourselves!

PAUL (*leads his guest to the dining room*): Please! Please make yourself comfortable! The other gentlemen should be here any minute now. Editor Virkus and Mr. Kargus. You know them, of course?

HUMAL (*adjusting his necktie in front of the mirror*): Oh yes, of course. I know everybody worth knowing in Estonian circles. Virkus and Kargus? Hm. A clever choice from the diplomatic point of view. Between you and me, Virkus is a clown, but he has a lot of influence through his newspaper. And it is always profitable to be on good terms with the seventh great power. Kargus is supported by some...hm...very active radical circles.

PAUL: May I offer you a drink, Mr. Humal?

HUMAL: Perhaps a little brandy, my young friend. It might make my old heart beat a little faster. (*Looks around approvingly. Sits down on the sofa. PAUL pours two glasses of Napoleon's brandy and offers one to HUMAL.*)

PAUL: Cheers! I am honored to receive you in my home.

HUMAL: Cheers! I am most pleased to get to know you better. Until now our paths have not crossed often. Naturally, we have been active in different fields. You are a builder of great bridges of steel and concrete, even those spanning the seas, as I read in the paper today. I congratulate you warmly! (*Gets up and pats PAUL on the shoulder approvingly.*) And soon you will take over the building of our national bridge! (*Sits down.*) We will work very closely together there, because I, too, in my own way, am the caretaker of a very important bridge—the continuity of our Republic. That bridge must never be allowed to collapse. Well, here's to our future teamwork! (*Lifts his glass.*)

PAUL (*lifts his glass, both drink*): Do you mean to tell me that I have already been elected?

HUMAL (*confidently*): Almost. Of course, it must remain discreetly between us. I am not authorized to speak about it. But I believe that you will very soon receive a heartening phone call confirming this...If nothing extraordinary happens...

Paul (*mechanically*): Yes, if nothing extraordinary happens...

HUMAL: Of course, everything speaks in your favor. You have a good name. You are a well known man in the Estonian and Canadian communities. Only...

PAUL: Only I don't have any experience in community affairs?

HUMAL: Yes and no. This is an advantage on the one hand, because all our Estonian community leaders without exception have managed to create enemies for themselves in certain circles. That is unavoidable. But you are known to them only because of your achievements in the Canadian community. Thus, among the Estonians you are still a tabula rasa. On the other hand, of course, there are other very competent candidates with influential backers and who, frankly speaking, have more experience...

PAUL: So that...

HUMAL: Don't worry, my young friend. Randla himself has nothing against you and since I am backing you....My word has a lot of weight in this matter.

PAUL: I am very grateful to you!

HUMAL: No, no, let us forget about words of gratitude! Such matters have nothing to do with gratitude. It is all in our mutual interest. Look, if you are elected to the post, suddenly there will be many public figures trying to get close to you, to advise and influence you. Even those who are now working against you. But I assure you that I will remain a supporter of yours, always. Let that bargain be settled between us.

PAUL: I welcome your help, of course. Only, just how am I to understand this?

HUMAL: Don't misunderstand me, my dear friend. You will be the honorable Consul. Confidentially, because of my position I was offered the post first. But my heart is no longer strong, and I realize that the man who occupies the post must be financially independent...you understand....We might as well consider the gold faucets turned off now.* And whoever sits on a throne doesn't govern alone. Take the Queen of England, for instance.

PAUL (*vaguely*): I am beginning to understand.

HUMAL: Wonderful! You are an intelligent man. The two of us will accomplish great things.

(*HELGA comes downstairs. She is now tastefully and elegantly dressed.*)

PAUL (*introducing her halfheartedly*): Mr. Humal, my wife. You have met her before, I believe.

HUMAL (*rises and hurries toward HELGA*): Madame! (*Kisses her hand.*) Yes, we meet frequently at social occasions. The last time, I believe, was at Consul Randla's birthday party.

---

*The British government relented and gave to the USSR the gold which had been deposited in England by the Estonian government prior to the Soviet takeover of Estonia.

But you really are an old acquaintance of mine from your stage appearances. (*Turning to PAUL.*) I forgot to add earlier that your charming wife is your most important asset.

HELGA (*pleased*): Your compliment, Mr. Minister, turns my head.

HUMAL (*takes her arm*): Come, come, I don't believe that. By now you must surely be quite accustomed to the admiration and accolades showered upon you. And soon we shall see you in the famous part of Nora. I am looking forward to it with great excitement. Tell me a little more about it! (*They walk arm in arm toward the door, talking. The doorbell rings. PAUL opens the door. VIRKUS Enters first. He is a middle-aged man, somewhat carelessly dressed, and has had quite a lot to drink. Basically a satirical clown and proud of it, he tries to keep a tactful balance so as not to upset his readers. He is followed by KARGUS, who is approximately as old as VIRKUS. KARGUS, humorless by nature, is dressed conservatively, looking a little like a farmer. He is a former front line soldier and an active participant in emigre affairs. KARGUS is carrying a placard which reads:* **Welcome Murderers!**)

VIRKUS (*without ceremony, with intoxicated exuberance*): Hello, our honored host. Here comes Virkus and his celebrated one man circus. (*Pointing to his companion.*) And here is Mr. Kargus who does now know the meaning of national cowardice.

KARGUS: Never mind! And don't drink any more!
(*PAUL, almost panic-stricken, looks at the placard with a frightened face.*)

VIRKUS (*goes immediately to the bar. To HELGA*): A deep bow to you, Madame! (*He does not bow but assumes a stiff posture. To HUMAL.*) And a salute to you as a statesman of high honor, Mr. Humal. (*Makes an exaggerated bow and seats himself at the bar with familiar ease. HUMAL, HELGA, AND PAUL are looking intently at KARGUS, who is still standing with the placard in his hand. He seems half stupefied, half in a trance.*)

HUMAL: What does that mean?

KARGUS: They are here. (*Places the placard against the wall.*)

PAUL: Who?

KARGUS: A delegation from occupied Estonia. Twenty Estonians and a Russian commissar. They arrived this morning at the Lord Kitchener Hotel. We came from there just now where we gave them a fitting reception.

HUMAL: Is that so? Did you demonstrate against them?

KARGUS: The National Action mobilized its forces fast and put

on a demonstration in front of the hotel. (*Contemptuously.*)
But there were also some of our countrymen greeting them and
fraternizing with them. Now we know who the deserters are.

VIRKUS: Not I. Nobody can say that about me. I sat in the hotel
bar, a neutral territory, and watched the fun through the glass
wall.

KARGUS: This is not a joking matter. It's a war. Driving back
the enemy's invasion.

HELGA: But they are Estonians like us. Our own people!

KARGUS: The Estonian people, Mrs. Toomik, are in prison. They
are not allowed out from behind bars. Only the members of the
Communist party are allowed to come here. The murderers of
the Estonian people and the prison guards.

VIRKUS: As far as I am concerned, the prison guards can all
come over here. Then the people could be freed from the
prisons.

KARGUS (*reproachfully*): This is a serious matter.

HUMAL: It is interesting, you said that there were twenty of
them. It is for the first time that so many have been allowed
to come at the same time. They must have an objective!

KARGUS: They will start attacking Estonian homes with their
propaganda. They have already disappeared from the hotel in
pairs. A clever lot. (*Laughs angrily, resuming his former
emphatic tone.*) The National Action has already issued a
warning: All doors are to be closed to them!

VIRKUS: Yes, our wives won't let us in tonight without the pass-
word.

HUMAL: We won't accomplish anything here with joking or blind
hatred. This matter must be discussed logically, so that we can
decide on the proper position to take.

PAUL: That is correct. Gentlemen, may I invite you into the
dining room? It will be cozier in there, where we can discuss
the matter further. (*Glances nervously at his wristwatch.
Hurriedly.*) Please, gentlemen! (*Takes the tray of sandwiches
from the table.*)

HUMAL: Only the gentlemen? What about our charming hostess?

HELGA: I shall come a little later, Mr. Humal. (*HUMAL follows
PAUL and KARGUS to the dining room.*)

VIRKUS (*still sitting on the barstool*): I would much rather stay
here.

PAUL (*from the door, hastily*): Come on, come on! We have
another bar in the dining room.

VIRKUS (*gets up*): Well, that's different. You should have mentioned that in the first place. (*Follows the others into the dining room. HELGA remains on stage alone for a moment.*)

MEELI (*comes down the stairs. She is wearing her mother's Tarantella costume with a large black shawl*): Look, Mother, it is quite becoming to me, isn't it! (*Looks at herself in the mirror.*)

HELGA (*looks at her daughter with sincere admiration*): Marvelous! Oh, Meeli, I'd so much like to be your image! Only the shawl is not worn that way. It must fall over the entire body. (*Takes the shawl and drapes it around herself.*) That's the way. (*Looks at herself in the mirror.*)

MEELI: And you will dance the Tarantella in this costume in the second act. How exciting! Mother, what kind of dance is it actually?

HELGA: The tarantella is a famous Neopolitan dance. It is very seldom danced today. I did not know much about it myself until I started taking lessons.

MEELI: How is it danced? Please show me, Mother! Please, dance it for me!

HELGA: This is not the time or place, my dear daughter. And most importantly, I am not in the right mood for it.

MEELI: Because of Linda?

HELGA: Not only that. My child, you don't know everything.

MEELI: I know more than you think, Mother. I know that something mysterious is going on in this house. Linda says that I am a spy, and, in a way, she is right. Mother, you have always said that a true actor must never let himself be influenced by personal troubles. Not under any circumstances. Therefore—dance, Mother! Dance in spite of everything! I want to see it, so much!

HELGA: They are in the dining room. Someone may suddenly come in here. No, it is not the thing to do.

MEELI: I'll go and listen to what is going on in there. (*Runs to the dining room door and returns quickly.*) Mr. Humal is lecturing about something. Everybody is listening to him. He won't be through so soon. I have heard him talking at festive meetings.

HELGA (*laughs*): All right, my child. Go and get the castanets from the bedroom. (*MEELI runs upstairs.*) It is so stuffy in here all of a sudden. I must get some fresh air. Ah, let us open all the doors and windows so that nature's clean breath might refresh our oppressive home. (*Goes and pulls back the draperies and opens the window. She also opens the front door.*) It is true, Krogstadt might come in, but I will send him back, at least for the time being. (*Takes the check from her pocket and puts it on the table next to the telephone.*)

MEELI (*comes in with the castanets*): Here they are, Mother!

HELGA (*takes the castanets*): I don't know how to do it with the castanets very well yet. (*Rattles the castanets slightly.*) This dance begins in a slow rhythm, but ends in a very fast tempo. And according to legend, the dancer's perspiration makes her totally immune to the deadly sting of the tarantula. Today I must perform with all my energy because now I need this protection more than ever before. Against Krogstadt who pursues me not only on stage but also in real life. (*Turns off the ceiling light. The room becomes dim. Begins to dance. The violin accompaniment is heard from the wings. The dance begins slowly, and becomes more dramatic, and at the end frenzied. MEELI is watching it totally transfixed. At the end of the dance a man enters through the front door; he stops at the diningroom door and applauds when the dance ends. HELGA, startled, drops the castanets. Looks in the direction of the silhouette, who has stopped applauding. He is still unrecognizable.*) It is he. I must give him the check now.

MEELI (*goes to the stranger*): No, Mother. It is not the same man who was here before. It's somebody else.

STRANGER: Linda?

MEELI: No, no, I am Meeli. Linda is my sister.

HELGA (*turns the light back on. Notices the stranger and looks at him, dismayed*): No, this must be a vision! (*Goes to him*). You, Vello! (*Hesitantly takes his hand in both of hers.*) You are alive then. Where did you suddenly....Did you come... with them?

VELLO (*somewhat nervously*): I did, and will leave again. We are staying at the hotel. I must return there immediately. I want to see Linda...my daughter.

HELGA: You know then? Even her name?

VELLO: I know. I have complete information about her. She was born in Stockholm, in Karolinska hospital, seven months after your marriage to Paul Toomik. Is she at home?

HELGA: She went out. Ah, I shall go and call Paul immediately. He is in the dining room...with the guests.

VELLO: No, I don't want to disturb him. (*Notices the placard against the wall. Takes it and looks at it bitterly.*) This is what they carried in front of the hotel. Welcome murderers! I know that much English. This is also meant for me then. I have not murdered anybody. Are you one of them too, now?

HELGA: No, not we. We do not take part in such activities. It was a man named Kargus. He is seeing Paul at this moment.

VELLO: Kargus? Captain Kargus? This is indeed strange.

HELGA: Do you know him?

VELLO (*nods his head thoughtfully*) Yes. Here we are, twenty years later, and our lives have been changed completely. It is strange! Placards and insults in front of the hotel. And, as I heard, an urgent request has been issued to close all doors before us. But here the door is wide open. The order is not being obeyed. I closed the door though, as is proper. And you greeted me with this spirited dance.

MEELI: Mother was practicing her role. She will play Nora in Ibsen's "A Doll's House."

VELLO: Yes, I have heard about that even...that you have become a famous actress. You have an amateur group here. You must be very happy.

HELGA (*resigned*): Ah, I don't know. What is happiness? (*The doorbell rings.*)

VELLO: Linda?

HELGA: No, she has a key. She would not ring the bell. It is a stranger. I must give him something. Go and wait a moment in the television room. Linda should be here soon...I hope. (*Leads VELLO into the TV room. The doorbell rings again. In thoughts.*) What should I do? (*Resolutely.*) I must shock him thoroughly. That is the only way out. Yes! (*The doorbell rings for the third time very impatiently. HELGA goes determinedly to open the door.*)

KALTER (*comes in*): Here I am again, Mrs. Toomik. It's a beautiful evening. There is only a slight breeze and the sky is blue. Not like it was twenty years ago. Then it was stormy as if all hell had broken loose.

HELGA: The fall weather can change quickly.

KALTER: Your husband promised to give me something. We agreed about it a while ago.

HELGA: Yes, I know. He is in the dining room. I shall call him at once. (*KALTER waiting. MEELI has gone upstairs in the meanwhile with the castanets, but we can be sure she is listening somewhere unseen. HELGA hesitates a moment and then goes into the diningroom. Her voice is heard.*) Forgive me for interrupting you! But I should like to ask our guests to come back to the living room now. I have a little surprise for you. (*KALTER grows noticeably restless. Walks toward the entry*

hall, as if thinking about fleeing, but HELGA comes toward
him and leads him back into the living room. PAUL, HUMAL,
KARGUS, and VIRKUS come back into the livingroom, holding their liquor glasses.)

PAUL (notices KALTER): Helga, what are you doing?

HELGA (points to KALTER): My dear guests, in front of you
stands a hero. (Pause.) Twenty years ago this man, in his
small boat, brought across the sea and to freedom my husband
and many other Estonian soldiers. He did it without any self-
interest, simply out of one Estonian's feeling of responsibility
toward his fellow countrymen. Gentlemen, may I introduce to
you Mr. Max Kalter.

HUMAL (the first to go to greet him): My name is Humal, former
Minister of Finance of Estonia, you have perhaps heard of me.
And this is editor Virkus, and Mr. Kargus...Captain Kargus.
(KARGUS shakes hands with KALTER. VIRKUS only nods his
head.)

KARGUS: Our hostess is right. You and all the others who
brought our young soldiers over are almost as big heroes as
the recipients of the Cross of Freedom. You should be honored
guests at our festive meetings. But, unfortunately, you have
become more or less our unsung heroes. (PAUL empties his
glass and goes to the bar to fill it up again.)

HUMAL: Yes, this is unfortunately true. I don't want to accuse
anybody, but to a certain extent, the press is to be blamed for
it. There has never been any mention of these heroes in our
press.

VIRKUS: Well, we can do a little interview here tonight. I will call
the photographer. (Begins to go to the phone.)

KALTER: No, I am here quite by chance. I don't want a fuss
made about me. (Toward PAUL.) Mr. Toomik, you were to
deliver something to me...a letter. I honestly did not want to
intrude. I am leaving immediately.

PAUL (to HELGA): Helga, you have the letter. Please give it to
Mr. Kalter! (HELGA goes to the telephone table, takes the
check and tears it up.)

PAUL (dumbfounded): Helga, what does this mean?

HELGA: This letter will not be delivered....Please don't be
angry, Mr. Kalter, but I decided differently.

PAUL: You decided differently? You?

HELGA (firmly): Yes, Paul.

KALTER: We had agreed. I believe I expressed myself clearly
enough!

PAUL: Yes, I know. I don't understand it either, Mr. Kalter. But women do have their whims. You must know women yourself! (*Laughs forcedly as if attempting to pacify.*) We will talk about it a little later. Perhaps tomorrow...

KALTER (*in despair*): No, I am in a hurry. Right now! (*Pause.*) People sometimes have...skeletons in the closet...as the saying goes. And perhaps in this case...a skeleton may come out all of a sudden.

HELGA (*her tone indicating sarcasm for the first time*): That skeleton, Mr. Kalter, is alive and quite healthy. Besides, he is not in our closet. (*Everybody registers puzzlement in their faces. HELGA goes and opens the TV room door.*) Please, Vello Meerend. Come, I shall introduce you to my guests. (*MEEREND comes into the livingroom.*)

KALTER: This...this is impossible!

VELLO (*goes to PAUL*): Hello, Paul! You have changed very little. It seems that life has pampered you.

PAUL: What? Vello! Where did you...?

VELLO: I am a little late in arriving. The speedboat did not come after all. Now I came by plane....We will fly to Vancouver tomorrow and then back there again. I only dropped in for a minute...

KALTER: That's a fraud. This is not he. It can't be.

VELLO: Yes it can. As far as I can tell, it is I indeed.

KARGUS: Yes, it is he. I knew him. Isn't it strange? We fought together once. The same person, but not the same man any more.

VELLO: But a murderer, Mr. Captain? As is written on the placard?

KARGUS: We are no longer fighting the same enemy.

VELLO: As far as I know, the war ended.

KARGUS: Not for me, not for us here.

VELLO: Against whom are you fighting with your placards? Against the people of Estonia?

KARGUS: Against the enslavers of our people, and against those who have joined their camp.

KALTER: (*as if awakening*): Life...life. Life does not pamper every man. The waves of life are crueler than a stormy sea. Especially if one loses his compass. And I have lost mine. (*Becomes very nervous, looks now to the bar, now to the front door. The bar wins out.*) I am no longer able...I have no escape ...without my crutch! (*Goes to the bar, takes the bottle of Napoleon's brandy, pours a large glassful, lifts it to his mouth with trembling hands and drinks greedily. Remains sitting on the barstool with his back toward the others.*)

VELLO: This is no delegation. Only a group of tourists.

KARGUS: No honest people are allowed to come to the West as tourists.

VELLO: I am an honest man according to my conscience and they have let me come. With a tourist voucher!

KARGUS: I know those vouchers. Would you be willing to answer a simple question in all honesty?

VELLO: Which is?

KARGUS: Do you belong to the Communist party?

VELLO (*after a long pause*): And if I did? What importance does it have?

KARGUS: Well, there you are, just what I said before! A typical bolshevik way to answer a question with a counter-question. An honest man would not be allowed out of there. And given the circumstances, we have nothing more to talk about. My gracious host and hostess will excuse me. I trust the other gentlemen will also find it unfitting to stay in this company. Are you coming with me, Virkus?

VIRKUS: What? I? Well, I seldom leave the barstool voluntarily, but this is no longer a neutral ground...there is no glass wall separating us as in the hotel. (*To KALTER.*) Come on, hero. The taverns are still open, let's go somewhere and have a mighty interview...with a forgotten Estonian folk hero. (*Takes KALTER by his arm and steers him toward the door.*)

KALTER: I am not a hero. I am...a scoundrel.

VIRKUS: Well, in vino veritas. It will make an original headlline. A hero who considers himself a scoundrel!

HUMAL: I think that it is time for me to go too. My old heart is no longer as strong as it used to be. I must get to bed early. (*Goes to HELGA.*) Good night, my beautiful lady, we will meet again soon! (*Kisses her hand. Goes to PAUL.*) So long, my young friend. And don't forget what I told you. It is as good as decided!

KARGUS (*from the door*): Perhaps not, if this party member is not expelled from here at once.

HELGA: We are free people in a free country. We make our own decisions. (*KARGUS turns his back contemptuously and starts to leave.*)

HELGA (*after him*): Mr. Kargus, you forgot something...your weapon. (*KARGUS turns around and HELGA gives him the placard.*)

CURTAIN

ACT THREE

(*The stage remains the same. The action continues. HELGA and VELLO are sitting on the sofa. PAUL stands near the bar. A wind has come up and makes the curtains of the open window flutter.*)

PAUL (*goes and closes the window*): A storm is coming up. And so suddenly. It looks like a thunderstorm.

HELGA: Good weather doesn't last forever.

PAUL: Canadian autumns are extraordinarily long and beautiful. One can't complain about that.

VELLO: Maybe that is why people here talk about the weather so much?

HELGA (*laughs somewhat nervously*): Yes, here we are. We meet again after twenty years, and what do we talk about— the weather. Isn't that ironic!

VELLO: It's a neutral topic.

PAUL: May I offer you a drink, Vello? You don't drink cocktails over there, I believe. A glass of brandy perhaps?

VELLO: I don't know whether it's a good idea for you to drink with someone like me. I mean...when we consider the local principles. Perhaps it will be better if we just sit here for a while and discuss meteorological problems. Until Linda comes home. Then I will have seen my daughter and can go again.

PAUL: You know then?

HELGA: Yes. Vello knows, even her name.

PAUL: You investigated that matter then?

VELLO: The art of investigation is very advanced in our world.

HELGA: Don't take the incidents in front of the hotel and here to heart, Vello!

VELLO (*bitterly*): Welcome, murderers!

HELGA: Forget it, Vello! I apologize for my bellicose guest!

VELLO: Perhaps tomorrow you will have to apologize to somebody for my visit?

PAUL: Nonsense, Vello! We are free people and can receive whomever we wish. Let's drink to that! Brandy!

VELLO. Free people! Yes, how pleasant it sounds. I'd very much like to try a scotch and soda. We have brandy over there too. The Armenian stuff isn't bad at all. Oh yes, I forgot! I brought some along. (*Brings his briefcase from the entry, takes a bottle of Armenian brandy from it and gives it to PAUL.*)

PAUL: Thank you! (*Takes the bottle and puts it on the bar next to the Napoleon brandy.*) And what may I fix for you, Helga?

HELGA: I don't want anything at the moment. (*PAUL mixes the*

drinks and sits down on the sofa, too.)
VELLO: To your health!
PAUL: To your health! One can always use it.
HELGA: Tell us, Vello, how have you been? No doubt you are
 married and happy?
VELLO: I am married, but have no children, that is, we don't
 have children…I am sorry to say. (*Pause.*) Do you think she'll
 come soon?
PAUL: Who?
VELLO: Linda. You have given her a beautiful name.
PAUL: It was my idea. It's an Estonian name but at the same
 time, an international one. What do you do for a living, Vello?
 You are a successful man no doubt?
VELLO: I have done alright, I can't complain about that.
 (*Pause.*) I have heard that you are a famous bridge builder. I
 am active in the same field, in a sense. My job is to restore the
 bridges between past and present.
PAUL: What does that mean?
VELLO: I am an archeologist. I work at the University of Tartu.
 During the summer I conduct excavations.
PAUL: Have you unearthed anything interesting?
VELLO: Various things. Last summer, for instance, we
 discovered some evidence which was supposed to prove that
 friendly relations between Estonians and Russians existed
 already in ancient times.
PAUL (*laughing*): That kind of bridge doesn't bear much weight.
VELLO: That's what I thought, too, but I was severely repri-
 manded for it. And I had to acknowledge my error. Oh, you
 can't have any idea how it feels when lying becomes your daily
 bread. When you inhale lies and they enter your blood stream.
 When you go to sleep with lies and lies become your alarm
 clock in the morning. When lying becomes the key to one's
 existence—the protective coloring of life.
HELGA: We know how it is there.
VELLO (*softening his voice, as if instinctively*): I meant it generally. Even the walls have ears sometimes.
PAUL: Yes, I have heard about it. (*Half sarcastically.*) Aren't
 you afraid that there could be some hidden microphones even
 here?
HELGA: Why are you talking like that, Paul!
VELLO: It is difficult to free oneself from a habit. I would be
 afraid of it, only you didn't have any advance notice of my
 coming. (*The phone rings.*)

PAUL: Excuse me! (*He goes to the phone and takes the receiver.*) Hello....Yes, speaking....Police?...Yes, that's right....She did? Did she really? Just a moment, please. I'll switch the call to my study....Hold the line, please! (*Presses the transfer button. To the others.*) Excuse me for a few moments! I'll take it in my room. It's a little private matter.

HELGA: Has something happened? With Linda?

PAUL: No, nothing serious. I'll tell you later. (*Goes into the T.V. room.*)

VELLO: What is going on?

HELGA: I don't know.

VELLO: You can listen in on this telephone, can't you?

HELGA: I'd better not! We are not in the habit here.

VELLO: Oh yes, of course.

HELGA: Vello, I have to ask a favor of you.

VELLO: And what would that be?

HELGA: Look, Vello. Linda is... (*Searching for words.*) a little mixed up...so to speak...

VELLO: A little what?

HELGA: Excuse me! It means that she is a little bit mixed up emotionally.

VELLO: Are you trying to say that...she is not normal?

HELGA: No, no, quite the contrary. Linda is a very talented and bright girl. She has even been awarded prizes for her paintings in art school. But she has not yet found herself. And I'm afraid Vello, oh...I don't know how to say it...

VELLO: Yes?

HELGA: Linda doesn't know, that you...that Paul is not her real father. I have not dared tell her about it. It could be a harsh blow for her...emotionally...since she is an overly sensitive and mixed up girl to begin with.

VELLO: Are you covering up the truth? You here too?

HELGA: Yes, we here too...sometimes...when it is absolutely necessary.

VELLO: Where is she now? What has happened?

HELGA: She went out a little while ago to attend a demonstration in front of the American Consulate. She quarreled with Paul before she left. Oh, I do hope that nothing bad has happened.... Please, don't tell her that you are...you must understand me. Believe me, it is better that way. Talk with her...as my old friend!

VELLO: Old friend...only an old friend!

HELGA: You do understand me, Vello, don't you? (*Takes VELLO'S*

hand.) Please promise me! If you still care for me a little...
and for her.

VELLO (*passionately*): If I care for you...Helga...Helga!

HELGA: You promise then?

VELLO: I imagined it all somewhat differently. I had my own
daydreams...abstract as dreams always are. Helga, you don't
know how I was looking forward to this moment! But no one
can turn back the clock of eternity....Well, then, let it be. I am
used to being silent and secretive. It will be enough if I get
to see her once!

HELGA (*kisses him on the cheek*): Thank you, Vello! I hope to
God that nothing has happened!

VELLO: Why did she go there? Open protests in the streets? What
does it mean? But there are many things going on here that I
don't understand.

HELGA: Who can understand today's youth? Which of us can get
close to them? (*PAUL enters from the T.V. room. HELGA to
PAUL.*) What is going on? What is going on with Linda?

PAUL: Linda is in the police station.

HELGA: My lord!

PAUL: She is at the Elm street station.

HELGA: Why? What did she do?

PAUL: She broke the window of the American Consulate.

HELGA: No!

PAUL: Yes. But they won't book her if I pay for the damages. I'll
go and bring her home.

HELGA: No, Paul. I will go myself.

PAUL: I attend to such matters.

HELGA: No, I will go. (*Looking for a persuasive reason.*) You
have been drinking. You would make a bad impression if you
went there smelling of liquor.

PAUL: That doesn't matter. (*Thinking.*) I'll take some sen-sen.

HELGA (*resolutely*): No, I will go and bring my daughter home.
Did you leave the car outside?

PAUL: Yes. Damn it, it'll get rained on. (*HELGA gets up and
begins to leave.*)

VELLO: May I go with you?

HELGA: We'll be back shortly. It's just around the corner. (*Goes
out through the entry hall, taking her raincoat.*)

PAUL: Damn that girl! It's no longer a joke. This kind of thing
can find its way into the newspapers very easily.

VELLO: I see that Linda is a genuine problem for you.

PAUL: Oh, well! We'll manage somehow. Another scotch and

soda? (*Takes VELLO'S glass and goes to fill it up at the bar. Thunder is heard from outside.*) You see, I was right. It's already thundering.

VELLO: Well, well. May daughter has become a rebel.

PAUL (*returning with the glass*): Your daughter. She is yours only biologically.

VELLO: Yes, of course, psychologically she is more yours, by now.

PAUL (*takes a large gulp*): Oh, no, not exactly. There is a chasm between us. We have grown apart from each other, somehow. I am always so busy, Vello.

VELLO: This particular bridge you have left unbuilt, then?

PAUL: Oh, give me time! I can't do everything at once.

VELLO: Isn't that the truth. But I must thank you, nevertheless. For taking Helga...the way she was.

PAUL: You are thanking me? After what happened then...on the beach.

VELLO: That's all past now. Why should we talk about it...

PAUL: I thought that you came to take revenge.

VELLO: That's all forgotten.

PAUL: In your heart you are not angry with me then?

VELLO: The heart isn't a big enough place for storing one's anger about every wrong doing. Yes, you gave me quite a blow then. An accomplished boxer as you were. But, who knows, I may have gained from it, in a certain way.

PAUL: You may have gained from it? How?

VELLO: It made a different man out of me. It changed my philosophy of life completely.

PAUL: I don't understand.

VELLO: You see, Paul. When I regained my consciousness on that desolate beach, you can't imagine the loneliness, pain and despondency I felt. Yes, I was humiliated and angry then. And envious of you. But I was more angry with my own fate than with you, because I firmly believed in the omnipotence of fate at that time. Next, I became frightened because the cannonfire sounded quite near already. I found a hiding place in a fisherman's cottage. The family hid me in the basement and covered the trap door with a carpet. I stayed there in total darkness for several weeks and had time to think about life. It was there, in the basement of a Saaremaa fisherman's cottage, that my outlook upon life changed completely.

PAUL: Your outlook upon life changed?

VELLO: Yes, I was much too fatalistic before that. I let myself

be carried by life's currents. I was a dreamer, not a doer. But
there I was suddenly in a situation which demanded action,
and your words "Now let every man be the master of his own
fate" were still echoing in my ears.

PAUL: You have accepted this principle then?

VELLO: Not entirely. I still believe that the great events are decided by fate. But man must also act himself, try to shape his
own destiny. As much as at all possible. Man must not trust in
his luck too much. I think that many people who weren't successful in fleeing across the sea then have accepted this philosophy. All our people who stayed there under duress have
done so.

PAUL: Is that how it is? And this is how you became a Party
member?

VELLO: I haven't become one yet.

PAUL: But you said you had when that man Kargus asked you.

VELLO: No, I didn't. I only asked him what difference it would
make if I were a member.

PAUL: There is clearly a difference!

VELLO: You look upon things too simplistically. There are good
Estonians in the Party today and bad ones among those who do
not belong to it.

PAUL: You said that you haven't joined the Party yet. Do you
have intentions of doing so?

VELLO: In the future, perhaps. If they accept me.

PAUL: Why?

VELLO: So that I may become an assistant professor or better
yet, a full professor instead of an ordinary lecturer. In order
to succeed in my career.

PAUL: In the world of lies and falsifications?

VELLO: I try to lie and falsify as modestly as possible. You
can't get by entirely without it there anymore than you can
here. One must strive and contrive. Without it, I would not
have been able to come here even.

PAUL: Was it absolutely necessary for you to come?

VELLO: The broken link in the chain had to be joined somehow.
It left me no peace.

PAUL: Stay here then! Defect! It can be arranged.

VELLO: My home is over there. My work, the Estonian people,
and my roots...

PAUL: Roots can be grown anew in our soil here. And we too are
Estonians.

VELLO: No, I can't. Not any more. It would have been possible twenty years ago, but now...no, it is impossible.

PAUL: Your answer is no then?

VELLO: Yes.

PAUL: Then I don't understand you. Surely, you must realize that I am not one of those who came to meet you with the placards. But at the same time, I can't at all agree with your attitude.

VELLO: You condemn me then?

PAUL: Yes, Vello, as far as this particular issue is concerned.

VELLO: Don't forget that you yourself wrote the contract for my new life. Or more precisely, the blow of your fist did.

PAUL: If I had known that, I would have stayed behind myself and let you flee.

VELLO: Really? Aren't you exaggerating? And what would you have done in my place? Knowing that it is in you to want to succeed at whatever cost, I am sure that you would have made use of every possibility to get ahead. Perhaps even more drastically than I. Am I not right? (*PAUL walks nervously back and forth.*) Tell me honestly.

PAUL: No, no, it isn't like that. (*Pause.*) Perhaps...I don't know. (*Turns his back to VELLO and becomes absorbed in thought.*)

VELLO: You could hardly blame me then, on that basis, can you?

PAUL: On that basis? What does this mean?

VELLO: Is this a new word for you? Of course it was not yet in use in your time. It means—on that level, in this respect.

PAUL: Alright. It is all only conjecture. It doesn't prove anything. Let's stop talking about it...sorry.

VELLO: Sorry? That means that you are sad. As much as I know from my limited English studies.

PAUL: No, it means I apologize...for having lost my temper.

VELLO: As you see, we almost need an interpreter to understand each other. And we have been separated only twenty years. (*Both laugh.*)

PAUL: Let's drink to it, shall we?

VELLO (*lifts his empty glass*): Quite an interesting drink, Scottish whiskey—isn't that the correct name for it?

PAUL (*takes his glass, laughing*): In Estonian we call it plain scotch. (*Goes to the bar to fill the glasses. HELGA and LINDA enter and take off their coats. Their conversation takes place in the entry, only between themselves. LINDA is highly excited and still full of resentment.*)

LINDA: I am going to my room, mother. I have nothing to explain. I don't want to talk about it.

HELGA: No, Linda. I want to introduce you to Mr. Meerend.

(*MEELI has come to the staircase unnoticed. She has changed her clothes.*)

LINDA: Not now, mother.

HELGA: I told you already that he is in a hurry. He has to go back immediately.

LINDA: I can't!

HELGA: You must! This is an order!

LINDA: Mother, don't order me around...like somebody else in this house! I am not accustomed to obeying orders.

HELGA: Linda! Please!

LINDA: Alright. I can say hello to him. But I won't explain anything. I won't apologize.

HELGA: Come on now! (*They go to the livingroom. VELLO has stood up in the meantime and is waiting nervously.*) We are back. This is my daughter Linda. (*VELLO comes to meet her, staring intently at LINDA.*) This is Vello Meerend.

VELLO: Linda! (*Holding back emotion.*) Miss Linda Toomik. (*Wants to embrace her but holds himself back and only stretches out his hand. A few moments pass before LINDA notices his hand and accepts it.*)

LINDA: I am pleased to meet you!

PAUL (*comes to LINDA*): Here you are! Why did you do it, tell me, ah?

LINDA (*imitating PAUL contemptuously*): Tell me, ah! Have a good guess! Have a bloody good guess!

PAUL (*takes LINDA by her shoulders and shakes her*): You are not going to talk to me like that! Do you hear?

HELGA (*rushes between them*): Paul, stop it!

LINDA: I talk the way I want to. And you haven't heard anything yet.

PAUL (*pushes LINDA away from him a little too harshly. She comes to a stop against the bar*): You restrain yourself, girl!

VELLO (*goes to PAUL*): And you restrain yourself! Leave her alone! (*They look in each others' eyes threateningly.*)

HELGA: Stop it! Both of you. (*Goes to LINDA, who is watching the men as if hypnotized. Puts her arm around LINDA consolingly.*)

VELLO (*to PAUL*): You leave Linda alone!

PAUL: You have nothing to do with it. I am responsible for her. We have a strict discipline in this house.

LINDA: This house is repulsive. It stinks. I am going to leave it now, tomorrow morning. I have made up my mind.

HELGA: No, Linda, no!

PAUL (*sarcastically*): And where are you going, if I may ask?

LINDA: That's my business.

PAUL: We will have you brought back by the police.

LINDA: There are places where no cop can find me. And soon I'll be of age. It is not too far off.

VELLO: Of age? Age is determined not only by one's years but by maturity. Some people never mature.

LINDA: There's no need to worry about me. I don't belong in that category.

VELLO: Well, this is yet to be proven. Your present behavior indicates the opposite. (*Goes to LINDA.*) My dear child, let's talk calmly about it. I am sure a sensible solution can be found.

HELGA: Listen, Linda! Listen to what Mr. Meerend has got to tell you!

LINDA (*provocatively*): Why, Is he our advisor now? (*Toward VELLO.*) Why do you think you have the right to stick your nose in my business? Is it simply because you had an affair with my mother?

HELGA: Be quiet, Linda! Be quiet!

LINDA (*to VELLO*): I don't need a guardian. I don't need you. Do you hear?

MEELI (*runs into the livingroom*): You mustn't talk like that, Linda! Not with him. He is your father. Your real father.

HELGA: No!

LINDA: What?

VELLO: Linda...my daughter!

LINDA: You...you are my father? But how...can it be true?

VELLO: My daughter...my daughter...

LINDA: Father...I have a father...a real father...No, it is impossible! Mother, is this man my father? (*Pause.*)

HELGA: Yes, Linda.

LINDA: I have a father! And I hadn't known about it all these years.

PAUL: I wanted to tell you this long ago, but your mother was against it.

LINDA: But why, mother?

HELGA: I was afraid, Linda...that it would harm you.

LINDA: Harm me? Oh, mother. If I had only known it. I don't believe I would have become what I am now. I did it out of resentment, as a protest against my not belonging anywhere. Against everything here as it was until now. (*Goes to PAUL.*) I hated you, and perhaps we will still go on misunderstanding each other in the future. But no matter what you do, I shall no

longer be offended by it. Because now I know why you are
doing those things. Now I can take it all rationally.

HELGA (*with hesitation*): Linda, do you think I am an immoral
woman?

MEELI (*runs to her mother and embraces her*): Mother, you are
so interesting! You aren't angry with me because I revealed
the secret, are you?

HELGA: No, Meeli. Perhaps it is better that way. Indeed, it may be.

LINDA: Father...it's so wonderful to speak that word straight out
of one's heart. Father, are we going to stay together now?

VELLO: No, my daughter. Unfortunately I must leave again.

LINDA: I'll go with you. To Estonia.

PAUL: That would be a scandal! That's completely out of the
question.

HELGA: Scandal? Is this all that interests you? Linda, would you
really leave me...your own mother?

LINDA: I don't think you need me, mother. You have the theater.
Your own world.

VELLO: No, daughter. Your place is here. One who has learned
to fly as freely and boldly as you can never be transformed
into a caged bird. Birds yearn to get out of a cage, not into one.
Linda, you are a lucky girl. You have the whole heaven to fly
in—as far as your own wings can take you.

LINDA: And there I would not have?

VELLO: No, not yet.

LINDA: But some day perhaps?

VELLO: Some day for sure, if we survive. If we don't let our love
of life go out.

LINDA: Then...then some day...we will all be together again?

VELLO: Perhaps. But only if we don't break into small fragments,
strewn all over the planet, spiritually isolated from each other.
Not understanding each other, and not even knowing where we
belong. (*Opens his briefcase and takes from it a small piece of
jewelry.*) This is for you, Linda...I excavated it from the site of
the ancient Lõhavere stronghold.* This piece of silver jewelry
goes back to the 12th century. It lay in the dark earth for almost
a thousand years, but it is magnificently preserved in spite of
that. (*Gives the artifact to LINDA.*)

LINDA: Thank you, father! I shall treasure it.

VELLO: Do treasure it, my child. Think about it! And don't forget about building a bridge across the sea! As a link with a

*Lõhavere stronghold—situated in southern Estonia.

country which you don't know, but is your native land just the same.

LINDA: But how, father? How can I?

VELLO: I am thinking of a spiritual bridge. From your heart to the hearts of the Estonian people. A bridge which unifies us even while we are living far apart.

LINDA: I understand, father. It is not a real bridge but one in our dreams.

MEELI (*goes to LINDA*): Linda, do you still hate me?

LINDA: No, Meeli. Happy people do not hate anybody. And I feel happy now. Just as if I were born again.

MEELI: Let's change our ways from now on. Let's be sisters.

LINDA (*laughing*): Alright, let's be sisters. (*They shake hands.*)

VELLO: I regret it, but I must go now. They are waiting for me at the hotel. We still have much to talk about.

HELGA: Yes, Linda. Take your father to the hotel! The car is still outside.

VELLO (*offers his hand to HELGA*): Goodbye, Helga. Perhaps we shall meet again some day. (*Suppressing his emotions.*) Farewell!

HELGA: Goodbye, Vello! And thanks for coming. Thanks for everything.

VELLO (*offers his hand to PAUL*): Goodbye, Paul! Be good to Linda!

PAUL: I shall do my best.

MEELI (*comes to shake hands with VELLO*): Goodbye, Mr. Meerend. I am convinced we shall meet again, some day...

VELLO (*embraces her*): I am sure. Goodbye, little hidden listener. (*Relieved of tension, both laugh. VELLO takes his briefcase and leaves with LINDA. A longer pause follows.*)

PAUL (*rising*): What a day! What a day it has been!

HELGA: The past has paid us a visit and now we are free. From now on it will be easier for us to live.

PAUL: Perhaps. Perhaps indeed!

HELGA: You no longer have to fear that man Kalter. Now there are no more barriers on your way to a successful career.

PAUL (*standing and looking at the painting of the bridge*): It is probably too late to call Randla now. (*Looks at his watch.*) Oh, yes, I think I'll call him in the morning.

HELGA: Do you want to talk to him about today's happenings?

PAUL: I want to inform him that I am withdrawing my candidacy.

HELGA: But why? Now that there aren't any obstacles left?

PAUL: At this time we need a man who will unite our people, and I am not yet ready for that task. Not until I feel free to put the interests of the people before my own. Nevertheless, I am not the kind of man Vello presumes me to be...a man who will achieve his goals at any price. And besides, I have a lot of building to do yet...of new bridges.

HELGA: Do you mean that bridge across the sea?

PAUL: No, Helga, I mean above all the bridges in our own family. Between ourselves. It is essential that these small but very important bridges be built before I go on to the larger ones.

HELGA (*comes to PAUL and takes his hand; both stand in the front center of the stage*): You do understand them now, Paul. There is still hope for us.

PAUL: This is a new project, and I have never left any projects unfinished.

HELGA: That is encouraging, Paul. But not a good influence on me. I must be Nora and she leaves her husband. Therefore, I shall not think about the future while I am Nora. But later, when I have again become Helga, there will be a few changes made in this house. Nothing will remain the same. The bridge on which I stand has become wobbly, too. Because life is more important than the theatre. Because the most important thing in life is life itself.

CURTAIN

THE MAIDEN ON THE SEASHORE

A play in three acts

by
Raissa Kõvamees

From the original Estonian
Piiga rannateel
Translated by
Juta Kõvamees Kitching and Hein Kõvamees

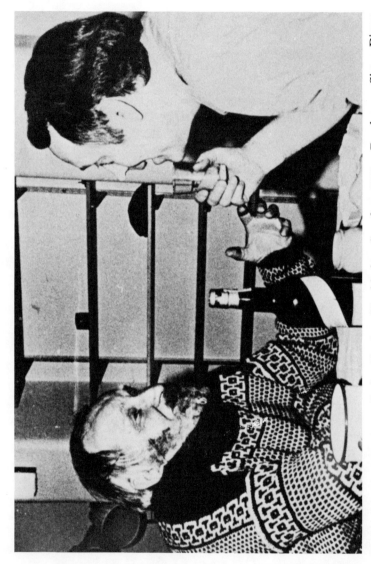

Maiden on the Seashore. Södra Teater, Stockholm, Sweden, 1973.   Producer: Signe Pinna
Grandpa: Jussi Romot   Juss: Alex Piht.

Introduction to
The Maiden on the Seashore

Already during the time of Greek antiquity, the condition of exile was considered to be one of the most tragic fates that could befall any man. When Oedipus blinds himself and goes into exile, he considers it just punishment for all the cruel deeds he has done, albeit unknowingly.

The tragic fate of exile has found its manifestation in emigrant literature. It has existed for a long time, but the twentieth century has brought us emigrant literature en masse. The political up-heavals of World War I and World War II sent poets into exile from countries such as Russia and Germany, as well as from all of Eastern Europe, including the Baltic countries. Prior to the twentieth century, the writers who had gone into exile were more or less isolated cases, who either chose or were forced to leave their homeland. The nineteenth-century German poet Heinrich Heine, for example, made a personal political statement with his self-imposed exile in Paris.

Literature in exile can be subdivided into two major groups: first, literature written by an emigrant writer, and, secondly, literature dealing with the condition of exile as a theme and topic.

The Estonian playwright, Raissa Kōvamees, combines these two aspects of emigrant literature in her play *Piiga rannateel (The Maiden on the Seashore)*. This play is written from the perspective of someone who has had to leave her homeland, and in this respect, the play reflects the author's own destiny.

Raissa Kōvamees was born in 1907 on the Estonian island of Muhu. Her literary career began in Estonia and included, among others, publications of poems, some short stories and an award-winning novel, *Kolmnurk* (Triangle) under the pseudonym Rae Piir.

After 1944, Kōvamees lived in Sweden and later settled in Canada. The novel, *Kahe väina vahel* (Between Two Straits) and its sequel, *On lindudel pesad* (Birds Have Nests), published in

1960, reflect life on the island of Muhu. These works are of historical, as well as of linguistic interest in the depiction of island life and in the usage of a certain dialect particular to the islands.

Between 1962 and 1969, she published four more novels: *Rand-lased* (The Coast Dwellers), 1962; *Teela*, 1965; *Sōja lapsed* (Children of War), 1967; and *Parisosa* (The Main Chapter), 1969. These novels further illuminate life in the Estonian islands, but with a shift in emphasis away from the established traditions of the late nineteenth century to the more recent and unsettling events of World War II.

Two plays, written in the 1970's, have been staged. *Ärtu kuningas (The King of Hearts)* received a prize awarded by the Estonian Theatre Association of Lakewood. It was performed on January 25, 1975 as part of the functions celebrating the 450th anniversary of Estonian books. *The Maiden on the Seashore* premiered in Stockholm, Sweden, and it was directed by Signe Pinna in two performances during the week of the Estonian Song Festival in May/June, 1973. Both have been translated into English.

The Maiden on the Seashore focuses on the life and fate of the people living on the small Estonian island of Muhu. During the course of events, it takes us from Estonia to the Swedish shores and later to Canada. In its portrayal of the tragedy of exile, this play transcends the local socio-economic boundaries of a small Baltic island and assumes universal significance.

Not only the personal fate of the playwright is reflected in this play, but also her professional and creative endeavors are echoed. In drawing the character of the artist Lemb Riiv, whose painting of the "maiden" assumes such a central role in the play, Kõvamees clearly is trying to come to grips with her own creative and artistic activity. The artist seems to be passing judgment on her art.

Finally, here the female playwright emphasizes the importance of a woman in the context of literature by assigning a significant role to the main symbol in the play, the painting of a young girl in the Estonian folk costume. In the play, a woman, as well as the image of a woman, is seen through the eyes of a woman. Perhaps Raissa Kõvamees is also inadvertently exploring her role as a woman in a profession hitherto dominated by men.

Poets and playwrights—mostly male in the past—have been intrigued by the elusive character of the woman, and they have tried to capture her image in their writings. Throughout literary history, the woman has been of great symbolic significance for various themes and motifs. She has stood as a symbol for vice and virtue alike. Temptation and salvation, beauty and love have been symbolized by the woman.

In medieval religious literature of Europe, the Eva/Maria parallelism served to juxtapose the biblical aspects of temptation and salvation. In other words, the woman leads mankind into temptation; yet, man's salvation is also brought about by a woman.

The love lyric of the Middle Ages depicts the woman differently. She is not a temptress but rather an ideal of beauty, good manners, and chastity. The courtly lady is seen as the contributor to the character growth of the knight.

In Goethe's *Faust,* the themes of temptation and salvation, as well as beauty, are symbolized by Gretchen and the allegorical figure of Helena. These themes no longer carry the strong biblical connotations of earlier literature but become different aspects of the "faustian striving."

In *The Maiden on the Seashore*, we encounter a certain similarity to Goethe's *Faust* in the usage of the woman as a symbol. Although overtly not very noticeable, there is nevertheless a similarity between the two works. Like Faust, the artist Lemb Riiv in *The Maiden on the Seashore* is looking for beauty or for some tangible aspect of it. But unlike Faust, Riiv's search for beauty seems somewhat ironical, for he looks for beauty in a war-torn world. In spite of circumstances, some things do remain constant in this world. Perhaps man's search for beauty is one of them.

As Riiv comes to the seashore, he finds a beautiful, young girl, Neidi, who has been in his mind's eye an "eternity." Upon seeing her, Riiv exclaims:

> I have looked for you an eternity!
> Finally you stand before me:
> the blue sky
> in your eye,
> the brushed flax of your hair,
> the sun's rays in your robes flare.
> If wings had I,
> over the water I'd fly
> and take you
> with me too. (Act I, Scene 1)

It is obvious that this is not a description of a particular woman. The artist has finally met a woman who corresponds to his ideal of beauty, and he is enraptured by her. He is anxious to hold onto this image of physical beauty and draws a pencil sketch of his nordic

Helena. The girl he finds symbolizes the beauty of a type, of the nordic type, with her blond hair and blue eyes. Unlike Faust, who finds beauty in classical Greece, the Estonian artist looks for and finds beauty in his northern homeland.

The quoted lyrical passage is repeated often enough to indicate that it serves as a leitmotif in the drama. Just as in Thomas Mann's prose writings the leitmotif serves to underscore something typical of his characters, here the notion is emphasized that the artist, by his very nature of being an artist, is forever looking for beauty.

As in *Faust,* man is promoted and elevated with the help of a woman. She provokes his initiative to transcend himself. The artist Riiv is aware of this when he says: "You provide me with wings that take me beyond time and earthly things." (Act II, Scene 2)

The second act of the play finds the artist as a refugee in Sweden. There Riiv completes a full-color painting of his "maiden" in the Estonian national costume. The painting brings him luck and fame, functioning almost like a talisman. Riiv's eternal search for beauty has become a leitmotif, and the painting of the maiden is the fulfillment of this search.

An abstract idea of beauty has found its form in the painting of the "maiden" symbolizing eternal youth. The national costume symbolizes Estonian folk art and culture. Finally, the ideal of beauty depicted in the form of a woman indicates the artist's inspiration by the love of beauty. In painting Neidi, the artist has established his identiy as an artist. Riiv's wife Celia says to Neidi: "Ever since, his work has been a search for his own self. It seems that he has finally found himself with that painting..." (Act III, Scene 2) But years later, in America, the artist is afraid to meet Neidi again. He fears that Neidi has aged and will show the signs of her aging. He would like to preserve her youthful image in his memory and is afraid that meeting her will destroy this image. He is afraid of discovering a discrepancy between his ideal of beauty and reality.

The Russian writer N.V. Gogol has also depicted an artist who, in his intensive search for beauty, resembles Riiv. However, the artist Piskarev in Gogol's tale, *Nevsky Avenue,* cannot accept the disparity between the ideal of beauty and mundane reality. While Riiv only wants to capture the beautiful image on canvas, Piskarev wants to rescue his ideal of beauty from the clutches of vice and proposes to marry her. He believes that outer or physical beauty should coincide with a virtuous inner beauty. When he discovers that the girl does not want to be rescued from her lifestyle, Piskarev loses his inner balance because he cannot conceive of the compatibility of great beauty with vice. He is no longer able to live in a world where the ideal of beauty is irreconcilable with reality, and he commits suicide.

Contrary to Piskarev, the artist Riiv is able to accept reality and agrees to meet Neidi, who has aged over the years. They are reconciled in friendship, and Riiv presents Neidi with the painting of herself at the end of the play.

Riiv's willingness to part with the painting indicates that he has finally found himself, and that he has been able to come to terms with himself as an artist. He has been able to establish himself as an artist abroad and has gained fame and recognition, which gave him the satisfying knowledge that he has "arrived." Thus, Riiv is able to part with the painting emotionally, and he returns it symbolically to the source whence he derived his aspirations—to beauty symbolized by a woman. The artist has paid homage to beauty which has led him to success and inner peace.

The women characters are assigned a significant role in this play, at least ideologically. Neidi as a character is sketchily drawn, but her importance lies in her symbolic representation. She is not merely a flesh-and-blood character but a positive, driving force for the artist. Riiv's wife, Celia, on the other hand, lacks the symbolic significance of Neidi, but she is also portrayed as a supportive force of her husband. She helps him financially and presents a contrast to his dreamy, artistic nature. Whereas Neidi, through her painted image, constitutes the spiritual force in Riiv's life, Celia lends the practical support to the artist.

Both of these positive female figures constitute support of the artist, and he is able to obtain his goals with the help of these women who have the characteristics of beauty and strength in this play. As seen through the eyes of the female playwright, men are dependent on the women for their accomplishments.

This man/woman relationship which Kōvamees focuses upon is not just a one-sided, erotic relationship depicting the woman in a subordinate role to the man. On the contrary, Celia is a very independent character; and precisely therefore she is able to be supportive of her husband and lead him on the road to success.

Neidi and Celia both are depicted as very decisive and goal-oriented. As Riiv arrives with Neidi in Sweden, for example, she decides to keep house for him. She senses that he cannot cope living alone and acts accordingly. When Celia's imminent arrival is announced in a letter, Riiv does not know how to approach the subject of his relationship with Neidi. Groping for words, he is taking a stroll in the garden when Celia arrives, and the problem subsequently is solved solely by Celia and Neidi. Each of the two women is aware of her role in the man's life, since they have deliberately chosen their roles. The decision is made by the women independently that Celia is the wife and Neidi is the model for the painting. Riiv is neither needed nor present at the discussion.

As exemplified by this scene, Kõvamees shows the modern, self-assured woman. There is never a display of jealousy or emotions between the two women, and the matter is settled in a quiet, civilized manner. Both of the women show self-awareness, independence, and tolerance. Celia is aware of her husband's need for practical and financial support, and she knows that she is the only one capable of giving this particular support. But she is also aware of his spiritual needs as an artist and understands his quest for beauty. Therefore, she is aware of the role which Neidi plays in his life and knows that this does not diminish her own importance to him.

Neidi also understands the meaning of her relationship to Riiv and realizes that she incorporates an abstract longing of the artist for beauty and that she herself is not the object of his longing. This self-awareness and self-assurance constitutes a modern concept of the woman. The modern woman is capable of making independent decisions and accepting the consequences. She has enough self-awareness to be able to determine her position in life. Perhaps self-determination by the women is emphasized; and the playwright is coming to terms with herself as an emigrant, as an artist, and, above all, as a professional woman.

The condition of exile constitutes the background of the play and motivates the action to a large extent. However, by the technique of combining lyrical passages with prose parts, the playwright implies and suggests the difficulties of existence as an emigrant and tones down the emotional intensity of the tragic situation of the people in exile. There is almost a classic clarity and serenity in depicting tragic situations. One can only imagine, for example, what anguish Neidi's fiance must feel, when, upon returning home from the war, he finds that Neidi has left for Sweden. However, he does not succumb to this feeling of anguish. Instead of accepting the finality and hopelessness of his situation, he takes positive action. In order to be able to join Neidi in Sweden, he sets out to make an old fishing boat seaworthy. The proverbial Estonian stubbornness is turned into positive thinking and action.

This attitude of positive thinking and optimism pervades the whole play and shows man's persistence in spite of extremely adverse conditions; it shows man's ability to survive.

Perhaps more important than physical survival is the spiritual survival of the people in exile. *The Maiden on the Seashore* touches on the problem of preserving the national and ethnic culture and heritage of the people in exile. In keeping with the optimistic tone of the play, the playwright foresees not only the preservation but also the strengthening of one's cultural heritage. Just as the pencil sketch of the "maiden" is turned into a full-color painting abroad, so the perspective of distance gives the emigrants the impetus to preserve their national heritage and strengthen their cultural ties. In some ways, the perspective of distance provides clarity of feelings and understanding of the importance of having a national as well as a personal past.

However, the main emphasis of the play, foretold in the title and underscored by the frequent usage of the lyrical passages, is not on the condition of exile but rather on artistic achievement. Beauty, symbolized here by the painting, is the guiding star of an artist. But this quest for beauty as an aspect of the "faustian striving" has also become an essential part of the existence of modern man. This quest for beauty transcends local mores and ethnic culture and becomes universally significant in the aspirations of mankind.

In this play, the woman's role in society is explored, and the positive, constructive qualities of women are underscored in the characters of Neidi, Riiv's wife Celia, and Neidi's grandmother. These women are strong characters in a world full of turmoil and uncertainty. They are equal partners in their relationships with men, and they are contributing members of society.

The Maiden on the Seashore follows in the tradition of classicism in its leisurely, almost epic pace provided by the lyrical interludes and by its relative plotlessness. Yet, Raissa Kõvamees draws a contemporary picture of an aspiring artist who thrives in exile, and with the emphasis on the role of women in society, this play concerns itself with problems of modern-day society in general. It is a play as American as it is Estonian.

Hilja Pikat

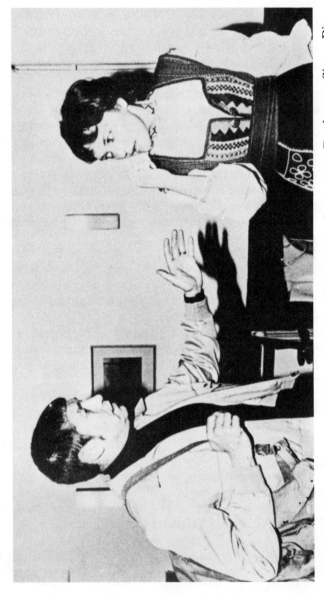

Maiden on the Seashore. Södra Teater, Stockholm, Sweden, 1973. Producer: Signe Pinna
Lemb: Uno Tonissoo. Neidi: Siiri Kriisa

THE MAIDEN ON THE SEASHORE

CHARACTERS

GRANDPA TÕNU RÄIM, later called GRANDPA VÄSTRIK:
  Farmer at Beach Farm and fisherman
GRANDMA KADRI: his wife
NEIDI, christened Anette: their daughter's daughter
LEMB RIIV: an artist
CELIA: his wife
JUSS VÄSTRIK, christened Jüri, later also "OLD VÄSTRIK":
  fisherman-entrepreneur, Neidi's fiance and, later, husband
MRS. SOOVEER:
MRS. NÄGELIK: party guests in their forties
MRS. ARUKE:

SETTING

Act I—takes place in Estonia
Act II—takes place in Sweden
Act III—takes place in North America

TIME

The action begins in 1944 and takes the audience through post-war years of exile to a secure and successful life about two decades after World War II.

ACT ONE

Scene One

(*The stage shows a beach. The time is the late summer of 1944.*)
NEIDI (*a young woman comes in from the right; she wears a colorful national costume*): I am Neidi, christened Anette,

from Beach Farm. My home is on an Estonian island which is
not very large, yet not very small. My father was a fisherman
who ploughed the sea all year round, often rising before dawn
even on the morn of great holidays. Oftentimes I waited for his
return at the beach. I went to meet him with mother at an age
when I still had to be carried—later I came on my own.

> Along the beach-way fine
> I recognize each stone and stump,
> every juniper and pine;
> here a turn and there a hump,
> the kelp in the sea,
> sheets of slate along the shore,
> wings of birds in flight so free...
> the narrow path across the heath
> to Grandma's house it leads.
> On the horizon to the east
> the red of dawn...
> the rays of sun bright-golden drawn.
> In the western sky a cloud
> as white as snow...
> a forest-ribbon down below.
> The stones of shore are lulled to sleep
> by lapping waves that refuge seek
> and vanish on the sand so soft
> as if they'd never been.
> In autumn months sometimes the sea
> performs a stormy dance in glee!
> Yet, father's practiced hand
> safely rowed the boat to land.

I had a fiance, too: Jüri Västrik was a fisherman just like
father. He lived in the next village. At our house he was called
Juss, a nick-name which we had become accustomed to from
the time when I was not able to pronounce the letter "r." I did
not choose Juss for my fiance—ten years separated us in age—
but since everyone, he himself, his relatives and my family
said he was, then I agreed. Juss was, of course, really very
wonderful. He would blow on my toes when I stubbed them
against a stone and he would always bring me something nice
when he came back from town. Juss was by no means a poor
herring fisherman. He caught eel. He planned to build a house
on Seagull Hill, a white house like a real seagull, and our wedding was to be right after my confirmation. But then—oh, then,
all that horror descended upon our land which ended my child-

hood happiness suddenly overnight. The communists seized our country. You will know the rest yourselves—the fact that imprisonments and deportations began. One night a carload of men, clutching their rifles, drove into our yard, with an informer of our own nationality as their driver. Our house was encircled as if it sheltered the worst criminals, and inside, in the rooms everything was turned topsy-turvy.

> Pots and pans and featherbeds,
> inkwells, papers, socks and nets,
> stockings, shirts and furs and all
> lay messed-up on the floor.
> Each full drawer suffered loss,
> the search was aimed at father's cross
> which he received for valiant deed
> when he fought and homeland freed.
> When departing
> they took father.
> We were told: "No need for sorrow.
> He'll be back tomorrow."
> Never, nevermore he came!
> His body in a common grave
> was found.
> A horrid shot
> right through the head...
> Grief claimed mother for the dead!
> And Juss, my betrothed,
> vanished in the dreadful war.
> Mother's parents became my sole support,
> Grandma and Grandpa.

The sparrow hardly comes alone but flocks in flight. This morning they spoke to me like this... (*Enter Grandma and Grandpa from the right.*)

GRANDPA: The times are bad.

GRANDMA (*sighing*): And they are getting worse! They are getting worse with every day!

GRANDPA: Yes, so they are. We'll have another war. And it won't bring Christmas presents to anyone. The eastern bear has twined its ropes long ago and is ready to hang our men.

GRANDMA: People are fleeing.

GRANDPA: The lucky ones get to Sweden. But we should not start on this again... (*Gets his pipe ready.*)

GRANDMA (*to Neidi*): Well, this is just what we wanted to tell

you—that dear Sass, your uncle—that he too has decided to
steer his boat towards Gotland. (*Whispering.*) Tomorrow in the
night, from little Kingu island...a place is saved for you too on
the boat.

NEIDI: For me? Oh, no—no, no!

GRANDMA: Yes, of course, my child.

NEIDI: And you? And you two? Will you come along?

GRANDMA: We have lived our lives. Perhaps Divine Grace will
allow us seven feet of homeland earth to rest in.

GRANDPA: And even if our way must lead to Siberia, it would
not matter...there is probably enough soil even there to cover
a tired body.

GRANDMA: No. The Almighty does not forget his sheep, but finds
them and awakens them when the morn of new life dawns.

NEIDI: You are wiping your face, Grandma!

GRANDMA: Oh, some dust flew in my eye.

NEIDI: Your eyelashes are wet, Grandpa!

GRANDPA: It's the pipe—the devil take it—this tobacco is so
bitter, the fumes are so strong. They make my eyes water.

NEIDI: What if Juss should return from the war and not find me
here?

GRANDMA: Let's hope he will return! Human beings live on hope
...From the war we can still keep expecting, not from the
grave.

GRANDPA: Injustice will not reign forever! (*With pretended
bravado.*)
>
> When our fatherland is free
> from the oppressive enemy,
> again it aims to gather
> its children together.
> Then I shall brew new beer,
> with foam each barrel cheer
> and churchbells will announce o'er land and water
> the wedding at Beach Farm, and laughter!

GRANDMA: But now do listen to the advice of two old people.

GRANDPA: Yes, do listen. In a storm every boat seeks the shelter of a port, if possible.

NEIDI: If you stay, I will stay.

GRANDMA (*reproachfully*): Look, Neidi! You are no child anymore; you are seventeen and a few months more.

GRANDPA:
>
> My dear, don't be afraid!
> Sweden is a wonderful country...

no one else but I, Tōnu,
the son of Tōnu,
with the family name Räim,
knows.
I sailed there many a time as a young man.
Once we had some trouble
with the custom's man on board;
he found forbidden alcohol
and took us to High Court.
There the captain told me:
"Ahoy!
You're but a boy;
you take the blame,
and save our name."
I could not disobey because
all-powerful was he, of course.
For captains, obedience is love,
just as for dearest God above.
He who has an empty purse
is locked behind the bars with curse.
Ha-ha-ha! Once you are in,
you can't get out:
you're guarded from without.
There I sat for weeks 'round four.
Life was good, never a bore!
Sundays they gave me coffee, a bun...
when I got out, I had some fun!
A Swedish girl said lovingly:
"Estonian boy, do stay with me!"
"No, no," I answered honestly.
"At home I have a fair maid, you see.
Pretty, well-behaved and diligent is she!"

GRANDMA: Tōnu, did you really say that?

GRANDPA: Yes, Kadri. That is exactly what I said. Or do you think I denied you? I bought a golden ring and I put it on your finger when I came home. Do you remember?

GRANDMA: I remember. I'll remember it to the end of my days. It has given me a long row of beautiful years, this present from abroad, and now it will be Neidi's. (*She takes the ring from a little bag pinned to her bosom and puts it on Neidi's finger.*) It brought me luck, and it will bring luck to you—believe me, my child. (*GRANDMA and GRANDPA exit. NEIDI admires the ring. LEMB enters from the left, bareheaded, with a packsack on his back; stops to eye NEIDI with fascination.)*

NEIDI: O, golden ring on my finger, if you could tell me whither destiny's moody ways will lead me! Must I really leave behind the well-known walks of home, Grandmother, Grandfather, my parents' graves, the sea of home...and you...(*She turns, notices LEMB, steps back.*)

LEMB (*as if awakening from a sorcerer's spell*): Stop! Stay, stay on the spot! For God's sake, don't run away! (*NEIDI wants to go, LEMB hurries to her and holds her by the shoulder.*) Wither are thou hurrying, my beautiful fairy? I have looked an eternity for you.

NEIDI: For me?

LEMB: Exactly. I have dreamt about you with closed eyes and with open eyes...and now, you are here. Finally I found you! As I woke up this morning, I felt that today something beautiful would happen.

NEIDI (*saucily*): I am Neidi from Beach Farm and I am seventeen already and even a few months more.

LEMB: Neidi!...Yes, of course!...Why not?...Why do you look so frightened? Look, I have no dangerous weapon in my pocket; it is just a pencil stub. My paper is in my packsack. (*He takes the packsack off.*)

NEIDI: Pencil and paper?...(*Aside.*) That poor soul has a screw loose, or maybe a few. Perhaps a war injury....The times are gone when students used to hike through the countryside collecting folktales and old songs and writing them down.

LEMB (*pulls a drawing pad out of his sack*): Now stand here... just like this...like this...and give me five minutes.

NEIDI: And then?

LEMB:
> Clever child, don't ask!
> Be patient and do your task!
> Or else you'll die young and that would be sad.

(*He begins to sketch.*)
> The sky...white wisps of cloud...the sea...
> a skiff at sea...an oar...
> a maiden...
> on the endless shore...
> the wind in her hair, a smile on her lips,
> in the sand her bare feet, toe upon toe,
> five plus five all in a row.

(*He steps up to NEIDI.*) Look, admit it! Isn't it you?

NEIDI:

>Me?...Perhaps it is. Toes,
>the skirt, my mouth...and nose.
>It's a miracle indeed!
>It's signed and done with such great speed.
>Lemb Riiv. A lovely name.
>What a skillful hand you have!

LEMB:

>One cannot make something out of nothing.
>Had I only a brush,
>had I only some paints,
>then a canvas I'd color
>to bring me instant fame...
>so that all could behold,
>the young and the old,
>the wise and the bold,
>the artist, Lemb Riiv by name.
>My maiden on the seashore,
>I have looked for you an eternity!
>Finally you stand before me:
>the blue sky
>in your eye,
>the brushed flax of your hair,
>the sun's rays in your robe's flare.
>If wings had I,
>over the water I'd fly,
>and take you
>with me too.

NEIDI:

>You bring me delight!
>Together with you,
>it is true,
>I would not fear,
>even if death were near!
>But since you are not a bird and cannot fly,
>let the waves carry us—that is my reply—
>to a desired distant strand.
>I trust you; I'll softly whisper to you
>what Grandpapa said this morning to me
>and what Grandmama confirmed faithfully:
>it is true—tomorrow eve
>from Kingu Isle a boat will leave
>and steer its course

to Sweden's shores.

LEMB:

My maiden, my teasure!
Let's go together!
Although the way is quite unknown,
we will not fear. (*NEIDI joins in.*)

LEMB and NEIDI:

No storm at sea,
not death itself could frighten us.
'Tis better to slumber in the Baltic's waves
than to suffer as Siberia's slaves.
In Siberia there is lots of snow,
in Siberia it is cold,
in Siberia there is hard labor,
in Siberia there is death....
'Tis better to sleep on the bottom of the sea
than to starve in a Russian penal camp.
We'll go together!
Although the way is quite unknown,
we will not fear.
No storm at sea,
nor death itself could frighten us.
We'll go together!
We'll go together!

CURTAIN

Scene Two

(*The stage shows GRANDPA'S and GRANDMA'S room with the drawing of NEIDI on the wall. It is an autumn evening in 1944; the wind whistles outside.*)

GRANDMA (*she arranges things in the room, lifts the curtains and looks out the window, sighs*): A blood-red glow lights up the sky again! Every night some area is burning. It keeps coming closer; soon it will be here! It's good that our child found refuge, that she got across the water while the sea still napped calmly after its restful summer. Now it is no fun to be at sea or on dry land. But fear drives people to escape. Once at sea, they still have two chances, staying on land there is only one. (*She sighs, clasps her hands, remains standing, as if in prayer.*)

GRANDPA (*enters from the outside; Celia follows him; she carries a little suitcase*): Look Grandma, I brought you a visitor. She has a long trip behind her. Perhaps you have some warm soup left at the bottom of the pot...no one can take cooking utensils along on his way...the weather is cold and windy.

CELIA: Good evening. Excuse me for the intrusion so late in the evening but...

GRANDPA: There is no need to excuse yourself.

GRANDMA: No, there is no need to excuse yourself. Don't think that you are the first one. Just put your suitcase down and take your coat off. We have got soup left for one empty stomach... it's still warm even.

CELIA: Thank you.

GRANDMA: Are you from Tallinn?

GRANDPA: Yes, she is from Tallinn. (*He fills his pipe.*) She missed the boat sent here from Sweden.... What advice can we give?

CELIA: I was looking and waiting for someone. That's how it happened.

GRANDMA: But that someone did not come?

CELIA: No.

GRANDMA (*understandingly*): Yes, these days we all look and wait for someone. One person comes, another one does not— according to how fate has determined his days. Do you have relatives in Sweden already who are expecting you?

CELIA: My father. He is a ship's captain.... Is there no one here who owns a boat who could take me? I have some things of value with me. I can pay.

GRANDPA: No one expects payment when his life is hanging on a thread.

CELIA: But you yourself?...If I could even get as far as the Bay of Kari! There I have some relatives on my father's side.

GRANDPA: I'm a bit rusty...the years weigh heavy on my shoulders and my boat is in such a condition that I don't dare lose the sight of shore. When it's calm, I go and wet the nets, but both of us are as afraid of wind as the last land rats. I'd better go check the old boat now; the weather is turning into a storm. (*Exits.*)

GRANDMA (*she has put on the table a soup bowl, a spoon, a cup of milk and a loaf of bread; she puts her overcoat on*): Our Grandpa is not much of a sailor any more...particularly when taking the bad times into account. He can't even tie the boat by himself; he is only half a man compared to what he used to be.

Adding us two old people together might make one poor whole. ...Come to the table, dear child, and have some food; you have shelter for tonight....Perhaps tomorrow we'll be wiser than today. Grandpa will go around in the village, maybe some neighbor will have a piece of good advice. (*Exits.*)

CELIA (*takes off her coat and cap, hangs them up, notices the drawing on the wall, eyes it from a distance at first, then moves closer*): Lemb Riiv...Lemb...really! You have left a trace...you have been here...I am on the right track...yet... yet...even if too late!...Oh, Lemb! My big, naughty boy. How can you get along without me? By dreaming of fame you'll die of hunger among your paints and brushes....Money makes the wheels go around...and I have money. I had it here, and I have it in Sweden too...but, unfortunately, I should not have reminded you of that. I got you back from the war, but now you are gone away. (*JÜRI—unkempt, bearded, clothed in rags— has entered in the meantime and gone straight to the table; he bites a big mouthful of the loaf of bread, empties the soup bowl in a couple of gulps and drinks the milk cup empty. CELIA is deep in thought for a while, then continues with conviction.*) They must at least know where he went. Perhaps it is not too late after all...for the contents of this suitcase I'll definitely find someone who would take me to Gotland. (*She sees JÜRI and screams.*)

JÜRI (*with his mouth full of bread*): Don't be afraid; I've experienced greater starvation than this but I haven't eaten human flesh and I wouldn't think of choosing a skinny-pinny like you.

CELIA: Where...where did you come from?

JÜRI: Straight from hell.

CELIA: I can believe that...and what are you doing here?

JÜRI: I could ask you the same question.

CELIA: I am a guest in this house tonight.

JÜRI: And I—if you must know—I am as good as a family member in this house.

CELIA: A family member?

JÜRI: Whether you believe me or not is your own business.

CELIA: If you are telling the truth, perhaps you could say who this young girl in the drawing is.

JÜRI (*he steps closer to the drawing and admits*): It looks like Neidi...yes, it is Neidi....It must be Loigu's boy, that rascal, who has sketched her on paper. When I saw that whipper-snapper last, he was no bigger than a pocket knife, but already at that time he could draw—a human being, an animal, whatever he saw—with amazing ease.

CELIA: Is his name Lemb?

JÜRI: What do you mean, Lemb? Loigu's boy is called Mike.

CELIA: Oh, Mike...but who is Neidi?

JÜRI: Don't you even know that? She is the daughter in this family.

CELIA: Where is she now?

JÜRI: Why do you keep asking like this? (*He looks around hesitantly; pushes open the door to the next room and looks in.*) The house is strangely silent....Is no one of its former residents left here anymore?

CELIA: I just came. I saw the farmer and his wife.

JÜRI: Were they old?

CELIA: Not young anyway.

JÜRI: About how old?

CELIA: About...about...well, I just don't know...we didn't talk about that.

JÜRI: You didn't talk about that, eh...did the farmer have a beard?

CELIA: A beard?...Possibly...but I'm not absolutely sure.

JÜRI: Didn't he have one like this (*Indicates by his hand.*), a bit like a goat's?

CELIA: Like a goat's Perhaps he did, but I really don't remember.

JÜRI: You don't remember what kind of beard a goat has?

CELIA: Oh, I know that—a goat has a kind of goatee, but I have forgotten the farmer's face completely. I only remember when he was filling his pipe outside...it was already dark when I got here...that the tip of his nose was as red as a radish.

JÜRI: A radish! Red as a radish! Exactly. Things are beginning to fit. And the lady of the house? What did she look like? Small and roundish?

CELIA: Yes...like this. (*She makes a circle with her hands.*) They said they'd be back soon. (*To herself.*) I wish they would come.

JÜRI: There is something wrong here. (*He opens the door to the adjoining room again and calls.*) Neidi! Neidi! (*He steps over the threshold and disappears.*)

CELIA (*she quickly snatches her suitcase and coat, exits but returns immediately with GRANDPA and GRANDMA*): It was an extremely suspect character. (*She points.*) There...he went into that room!

GRANDPA: But was he an Estonian?

CELIA: Yes, he was Estonian. He spoke fluent Estonian. He said he knew you.

GRANDMA: Why did he go into Neidi's room? An honest man
does not hide...I dreamt about a grey dog recently which can't
mean anything good. And now here it is already. A dream
during new moon comes true very quickly...so he thinks he
can just hide in Neidi's room. I'll see to that! (*She takes a
broom from the corner, steps toward the room, GRANDPA
follows her with a knife in hand: CELIA picks up her suitcase
again and moves close to the outside door.*)

JÜRI (*appears in the doorway; all are startled*): Grandpa!
Grandma!

GRANDMA (*she drops her broom*): Juss, my son! (*They hug
hard.*)

GRANDPA (*he drops his knife on the table*): You, Juss!...Well,
hello then! (*They shake hands vigorously and with emotion.*) I
am happy to see you alive!

JÜRI: And I you...(*He looks straight ahead.*) I mean all three of
you. (*GRANDPA and GRANDMA look at each other;
GRANDPA laughs and fills his pipe; GRANDMA wipes her
apron and blows her nose.*)

GRANDPA: Yes, three—of course three...It cannot be any other
way...except that Sass persuaded us.

GRANDMA: That's right, believe us. Sass would always say:
"It's doubtful that Juss will come back." You know, he is the
brother of Neidi's father, God bless his soul!...And we two, old
and helpless, we were like hens without heads. We didn't know
what was good or bad.

JÜRI: What kind of talk is this? I don't understand you. Explain.

GRANDPA: Then listen: Sweden has become dear to us here.
Even Sass steered his boat in that direction and...took Neidi
along.

GRANDMA: We even got a letter through secret channels stating
that they arrived safely.

JÜRI: Ah-haa, now I see, now I see.

CELIA: Excuse me for interrupting. Did a young man spend some
time here recently? (*She points at the drawing.*) That drawing
on the wall has his name.

GRANDPA: Yes, he was here. That boy was fortunate to come
here—there was a space for him on the boat and now he is in
Sweden.

CELIA: Really? What a miracle—a miracle! (*She falls into
JÜRI'S arms.*)

JÜRI: That's really a miracle! (*They embrace and dance around
in the room; GRANDPA and GRANDMA observe in amazement.*)

GRANDPA: Juss, my son. Are you not even angry?
JÜRI: How could I be angry! I have not been as happy as now for
    a long time.
CELIA: I feel the same way! Oh, Grandpa and Grandma! (*She
    embraces both.*)
JÜRI: Grandpa, listen. Do you still have your boat?
GRANDPA: I still have my boat.
JÜRI:
    And a motor in it
    which has a living sound,
    as well as food for it
    to make its steel heart pound?
GRANDPA:
    Yes, I have—I still do—
    and I have saved up a little liquid for it too.
    But in years it is advanced,
    as you yourself well know;
    the bottom leaks,
    the starboard creaks
    and rotten is the bow.
JÜRI:
    We will get over that.
    Do you have some boards of oak?
    Do you have some nails,
    a small amount of tar and tow
    and hammer, pliers, planes?
GRANDPA:
    Indeed, I do have boards of oak!
    Indeed, I do have nails,
    a small amount of tar and tow
    and hammer, pliers, planes.
JÜRI:
    Then let us start,
    work hard and fine!
    We must be smart
    to outdo time.
ALL:
    Yes...yes...yes!
    Let us now start,
    work hard and fine!
    We must be smart
    to outdo time.

GRANDPA (*he straightens his back and says to JÜRI*):
>   Take from the shed all that you need.
>   You, Grandma, light a fire below the pot of tar!
>   (*To CELIA.*)
>   You, my girl constantly the fire feed,
>   while I to the attic steer
>   to fetch some planks of oak.

GRANDMA (*cries out*): You to the attic! May God keep you!
Your legs are destroyed by rheumatism; you'll fall down from
the ladder!

GRANDPA:
>   What kind of talk is that!
>   If you really want to see, dear wife, I can even
>   climb up to the top of the mast of my boat.
>   No, I am no hen without a head yet, I —
>   Tõnu, Tõnu's son, Räim...
>   The thought of seeing that land anew
>   where I spend many a day as a gallant youth
>   fills my blood with excitement!
>   A young widow by name of Inga,
>   once proposed to me;
>   she was not the prettiest
>   but countess by birth, you see,
>   and rich in earthly goods.
>   I bowed politely and replied:
>   "Most gracious lady, I'd have complied;
>   but to someone else my word I gave,
>   to her I am loyal to the grave."
>   "Loyalty above all," she said
>   and we had some wine.
>   To Kadri's health our glasses clinked
>   as we spent the evening fine!

GRANDMA: Tõnu, was it really like that?

GRANDPA: Exactly like that. I never boast without good reason
and I detest lies...I joke a little now and then...and give or
take a bit for the story's embellishment....But a given word a
man does n'er deny! It is easier to live with honor and with
honor easier to die.

ALL: Loyalty above all...my word I n'er deny! It is easier to live
with honor and with honor easier to die.

CURTAIN

ACT TWO

Scene One

(*The stage setting shows a kitchen in a logging camp in Sweden.
At the left a door leads to the outside, at the back there is a door to
another room, at the right one sees a large wood-burning stove; on
the stove there is a big cooking pot with a wooden spoon across the
lid; on a clothes' line in the room one sees socks and underwear
drying.*)

NEIDI (*she wears wooden shoes, a big apron, a triangular kerchief tied at the back of her neck; she is putting cups and bowls
on the table and then stops*): I have put the meat into the oven
to warm, the barley is stewing on the stove, the table is set: the
butter, jams, porridge bowls, spoons and milk cups...what's
left to be done Grandma can manage herself. (*She takes a letter from the pocket of her apron.*) I ought to read Juss' letter
...I have had it for a week....But there is no news in it. He always sings the same old song....A lot of it is my fault too; I
have not given him a definite explanation and I did not have
time to answer his previous letter before another one came. I
simply do not have the time...or perhaps I am afraid to hurt
him. Yes, Juss, believe me. I do not want to be bad to you for
anything in the world...to you, who always is so patient and
understanding...but I cannot go against the desire of my
heart, no. No! (*She takes off her kerchief and throws it in a big
arch across the room.*) It is time to go! Soon I hope to say good-
bye to you, logging-camp—with all your soup bowls and porridge pots.

> The air of spring the pine bark gently strokes —
> the banks of snow
> have sunk so low —
> dandelions by the ditch the sun provokes
> to don their golden cloaks.
> Silver catkins on the willow tree,
> the birches offer buckets full of sap;
> gone are winter's weary days and coat and cap;
> the forest hut becomes too small for skipping feet.
> Through tree tops shines the sky so blue
> and there I see your name and you.
> Oh, Spring! How beautiful you are again!
> I come to meet you in your youthful dress
> with presentiments of happiness!

(She throws her shoes off her feet.)

GRANDMA *(she enters with a basket full of wash, trips on NEIDI'S shoes and falls.)*

NEIDI *(frightened)*: Good gracious, Grandma! Did you hurt your back? Did you break your leg?

GRANDMA *(annoyed)*: Perhaps I did hurt my back. Perhaps I did break my leg. But I have no time to think of that now. Don't stand there like a dummy, give me your hand, help me up. Grandpa went to the sauna already; soon the boys will go. See, I've still got the basket with their clean clothes...I'll have to take it over to them. *(She stands up with Neidi's help and says annoyed.)* Haven't I told you, my girl: don't throw your shoes around! What's this strange behavior all about? You almost gave me new feet, you know...pick the shoes up and put them nicely in the corner—toes against the wall, heels outward. You'll need them tomorrow again.

NEIDI: Dear, darling little Grandma, please don't be angry with me. I am happy because spring will come soon and then the summer. The birches will have leaves, flowers will begin to bloom and the birds will start their song. I am like a flower, I am like a bird, because my happiness to show I long.

GRANDMA:
>My child, my greatest treasure,
>your words give just poetic pleasure.
>Remember, spring is short
>and gives but little time for leisure.
>Listen to your Grandma's words
>or you may yet be sorry:
>little birds not only sing
>but at their best
>they make a nest.
>Your time has come to start a home,
>you have a faithful, waiting groom.
>Whoever plays so false a game
>often loses with himself to blame.

(She arranges the things in her basket, takes some undershirts from the line and rolls them up.) Yes, my child. The birds sing in the forest among other birds; a human being must live among humans. What did Juss write in his last letter?

NEIDI: Juss?...Nothing new...the same as always...he wants to go to America.

GRANDMA: He wants to and he will. What did you answer him?

NEIDI *(she throws off her apron and does not notice that the letter*

falls out): Dearest Grandma, I am in a hurry right now...
otherwise I'll be late. A person has to take advantage of the
beautiful weather.

GRANDMA: Must you go again?

NEIDI: Do you need to ask? A few more strokes, a few more lines
and the painting of me will be finished! You must see it! After
that Lemb will travel to Stockholm and have an exhibition. He
is convinced that "The Maiden on the Seashore" will make him
famous.

GRANDMA: Good. Then there'll be an end to your running down
to the village. When Juss went to war, you promised him that
you would wait for him.

NEIDI: When I gave my word to Juss, I was just a child and did
not know that I did not love him.

GRANDMA: Love does not get nourishment from the winds. Love
needs to eat...and Juss is a man who can provide for his family.

NEIDI: Why is it necessary to cross the ocean for that? He thinks
that there he can pick money like apples from trees and that he
can stuff his pockets full of money till they burst. On a hilltop
he will build his seagull-white house and if he is really lucky, he
will even buy a car....He boasts quite openly: "There, Neidi,
you'll live like a lady."

GRANDMA:
> The gates of home are closed.
> Foreign feet now tread Estonia's soil.
> Each man with foresight seeks a place
> where he can settle with security.
> A home, a bed, a baby's cradle too....
> Are these not the wish of each young maid?
> And if in a motorcar you'll sit,
> the status of the baroness of old you'll fit.
> Is that not wonderful?
> My eyes begin to water when I think that they will
> still see your fortune in their old age.

NEIDI:
> I have myself a healthy body,
> arms and legs, as you well see.
> And I can work, say,
> both night and day!

(She sits down and starts pulling on her boots.)

GRANDMA *(annoyed)*: You are chattering like a sparrow....
There's a proverb that says: "A bird in the hand is worth two
in the bush." What Juss says is not just talk; his hands will

accomplish even more. And that man is not lacking in female companionship either—it's just that he has chosen you above all others. (*She shakes her pointing finger.*) So stop playing your tricks, my girl, and pronounce a firm "I do," when he comes to celebrate, bringing bottles for merriment, and to propose to you!...I must hurry to the sauna now; you could eat.... And remember, be back before dark! (*Exits.*)

NEIDI (*she puts on her coat and hat, brings a suitcase from the other room*): Dear, darling Grandma, you think that I am still a child whom you can order around: "Neidi, you may go and play, but don't stay long, return before the end of day; Neidi, put on your Sunday dress but be careful when you eat, so you won't make a mess." (*She laughs.*) Always the same tune: "Eat and remember, be back before dark!" (*She laughs again.*) I will stay as long as I want. And I cannot pay attention to what you say. Because, Grandma, you have forgotten that you too, about a hundred years ago or so, were young. (*She laughs.*) Who can think of food with a heart that bursts of spring! (*Exits.*)

GRANDPA (*enters from the sauna*): It's a Saturday as in the old days: one's body has been heated through and through; all aches and pains have been driven out; in the house there is a good smell of pork and barley...just the old ale is lacking. Yes, we don't have that...this watery beer will have to do....However, our brothers don't have even that. (*He pours from a bottle into a beer mug and drinks. GRANDMA enters from the outside.*)

GRANDPA: Where did you disappear for so long? We left together.

GRANDMA: I stopped at the corner of the sauna to listen...it sounded like sleighbells down from the village...like a suitor's approaching wedding bells.

GRANDPA: No, in this country no suitor or groom would make a formal proposal trip, no less in such a way that the whole village can hear. Now they seem to sneak around silently like thieves and grab their chick from her perch. It occurs to no one to ask those who reared her, whether she has a price. (*The sound of bells can be heard from outside.*)

GRANDMA: Listen...again...they seem to be coming closer. (*She goes to the window.*) It's coming here! It's driving straight to our place. (*With great excitement.*) Grandpa, Grandpa... if I can see straight...if my old eyes don't deceive me...it is Juss! Juss himself! (*She picks up NEIDI'S scarf and apron from the floor, arranges her shoes, finds the letter, examines it.*) Juss' letter!...Unopened...unread...perhaps he wrote that he was coming but we don't know anything...oh, that disobedient child!...She isn't even here. Isn't that awful!...What am I to do now? How can I get that so and so back home from the village? (*There is a knock on the door.*)

GRANDMA (*she hides the letter in her pocket and then opens the door*): Come in, my son, come in.

JÜRI: Am I at the right place?

GRANDMA: I think so...yes, this is the right ...the right place.

JÜRI (*he shakes hands hard*): How happy I am to see you again, Grandma and Grandpa!

GRANDPA: So you were the one who rode so that the whole forest echoed. Grandma here was already thinking that her suitors were on their way to see her.

GRANDMA: Why me?...we have younger ones in the house...(*To JÜRI.*) Take your coat off and sit down. You must have come a long way. That's tiring.

JÜRI: No, I am not tired...sure I'll take my coat off and sit down but first I'll go and pay for my ride.

GRANDMA: Oh, let me do that...you stay and get warm and talk to Grandpa. (*Aside.*) Now I know what I'll do: I am going to take the same ride to the village and bring the child back here.

JÜRI: Well, if you think so...thank you very much. You, Grandma, are as energetic as ever. Here is the money. (*GRANDMA takes her big woolen scarf and goes out. JÜRI puts a tobacco tin on the table.*) Shall we light our pipes?

GRANDPA: Thank you, son! I won't let you give me such a nice command twice.

JÜRI (*he flicks his lighter and lights GRANDPA'S pipe*): How is logging?

GRANDPA: Well, it doesn't go forward by itself; a person just has to keep working. If you don't do it willingly yourself, it'll get after you and make a slave out of you.

JÜRI: It is not for you any more...you need an easier life now.

GRANDPA: How would I get to have that easy life?...At home it would have been different...there the new masters freed us of all earthly possessions...as payment for the land and houses I too would have received a railroad ticket in the cattle-car to Siberia...I could have ridden several weeks without a worry in the world...or fear that maybe I'll miss the right station.

JÜRI: No, you certainly wouldn't have needed to be afraid of that.

GRANDPA: The door bolted and the windows behind bars—no one could have harmed me, ha-ha-ha-ha. What does the Swedish government owe me? Nothing. Here you have to work in order to live.

JÜRI: You have been very industrious. You have managed to provide for your family.

GRANDPA: We have enough to eat. But these people are too stingy with my stomach medicine. They measure it in drops, as if it were a pharmacist's job. You don't even know whether to rub it on the skin or to take it internally.

JÜRI: Oh, I am sure you still know how to handle the contents of a bottle.... Here is a little gift for you. (*He puts a bottle on the table.*)

GRANDPA (*happily*): Oh, son...my son!...(*He hurries to get glasses from the shelf, tastes with gusto.*) Does it ever twirl about...it scoots around inside like an auger...another little drop and maybe my navel will stay in place. Hmm! That one found the right spot all right.... Thank you, thank you! I could do with a third drop.... Isn't it a fact that threefold holds intact: three times comes an order from the court; thrice bows the priest in church; the doctor says "don't tease an illness, if you take medicine, take enough to scare away the pain!" How goes it with your ship? Is it finished?

JÜRI: Finished.

GRANDPA: Terrific. Then let's get going—maybe even today.

JÜRI (*he laughs*): Yes, even today.

GRANDPA: Why not? No, I am not afraid of the sea yet, I, Tõnu, Tõnu's son, Räim! Even if I'm old and grey, still my hands can steer the rudder firmly. I have no fear of giant whales or waves as high as houses that rush o'er railings to wash the deck. I have no fear of angry monsters of the sea nor of crocodiles, those cannibals, no, not me! If jack-knives rained from high, who should firmly steer the rudder, none but I.

JÜRI: Great, Grandpa! You are beyond compare! But where... where is Neidi?

GRANDPA: I know, I know. Patience, my son, patience! Your bride is making herself pretty. I know women...I still remember when I went to ask for Kadri's hand—that was no fun. Oh no! Her father was a religious man, so strict with Bible teachings that he brushed aside the customary topics of proposal and asked quite seriously if the ten commandments I did know.

JÜRI: He asked you about the commandments! Did you know them?

GRANDPA: Not really...I had learned them for my confirmation but had forgotten them long ago. I sweated terribly; my shirt clung wet against my back.

JÜRI: I understand, I understand.

GRANDPA: I waited and waited and wished that Kadri would come...Oh, did I have to wait, believe me! When she finally appeared, I hardly recognized her. She had made herself so beautiful, as beautiful as a painting. Therefore patience, my son, patience!

> Your bride will appear,
> just wait, do not fear;
> and to pass the time happily,
> do pour another tiny drink for me!

CURTAIN

Scene Two

(*The stage shows the studio of Lemb Riiv: the setting sun behind the window, a cozy fire in the open fireplace, paintings on the walls and on the floor leaning against the walls, in the foreground on a stand a painting of Neidi in national costume. The left corner of the room is separated from the rest by a long curtain.*)

LEMB (*as the curtain opens he is standing and smoking; now and then he casts an examining glance at his painting on the stand; he walks back and forth, throws a half-smoked cigarette into the ashtray, lights a new one, stops in front of the painting addressing it*): Are you a success? Are you good enough? So good that I'll be discovered? You must be!...Neidi! Neidi!...You provide me with wings...you give me the ability to fly...you let me out of my cage...you liberate me!...Your smile...your posture...it is all very natural...I have captured it...captured it exactly! Finally!

> My maiden on the seashore,
> I have looked for you an eternity!
> Finally you stand before me:
> the blue sky
> in your eye,
> the brushed flax of your hair,
> the sun's rays in your robe's flare.
> You provide me with wings
> that take me beyond time and earthly things
> and all will behold,

both young and old,
both wise and bold,
who is the artist Lemb Riiv.

That is me...no one but me...as I stand right here. (*He lights
a new cigarette and walks back and forth.*) But what could I
offer Neidi? I have nothing. I am not even master of my own
poor self. How will she take that? Will she understand me?
(*NEIDI'S happy singing is heard from behind the curtain.
LEMB is startled.*) There she is...not on the canvas but in
reality...Damn it anyway, I have to explain the whole situation to her once and for all...I should have done it long ago....
Human beings are not smoke and do not vanish, as if they had
not been. I cannot just disappear...I will remain and Neidi will
remain...if she only refrained from being so exuberantly
happy all the time...if she were not so helpful...helpful to the
point of self-sacrifice...if one could only live from air and
beauty, just these two...if man did not need so much in order
to exist....Mrs. Oru still has not picked up her picture frame.
Here it is. (*He pushes the frame with his foot, lights another
cigarette and walks around again.*)

NEIDI (*she appears from behind the curtain in her national costume and announces happily*): Coffee will be ready soon. (*She
looks around.*) Perhaps we can use that box for a table. (*She
tries to lift it.*) Oh, it's heavy! (*She looks at LEMB who is
marching up and down and starts laughing.*) You are like a
bear in a cage! Listen, come and help me move this pot of gold
a tiny bit.

LEMB (*he stops walking*): A bear in a cage?...What are you
laughing at? Perhaps I am a bear in a cage...what do you
know about that? (*He lifts the box and puts it in the center of
the room.*) Your carefree and happy mood remains a big question mark to me. Where do you get all this gaiety from?

NEIDI (*she ruffles LEMB'S hair*):
Oh, my tousled little silly-billy,
don't you really know?
I'm happy because spring is coming now.
And summer follows nigh.
Budding birches, flow'rs begin to bloom,
on the cherry bough the birds announce
that ploughing time is high.
Love-love-love-love-lovely is life!
The night is short and light.
Twilight hands its lamp to Dawn,

their lips but a moment do meet.
Come-come-come-come come hither, my sweet!
The bright night's romance will quickly end
and sun's rays soon will drink
the dewdrips from the leaf.
A thousand tasks are waiting for me.
In the light
summer night
I whisper in your ear:
"I love you, only you,
please, stay near!"

You look so serious. Are you not happy that your painting is finished? Or...or don't you like it?

LEMB: Of course I like it...I am very happy with it but...I don't feel very well. My head feels so dizzy.

NEIDI: My poor, little one. Whose head wouldn't be dizzy in such a position.

LEMB: I'll go out in the fresh air for a while.

NEIDI: Yes, do. But don't stay long; the table will be set in fifteen minutes. I have fresh buns to go with the coffee...you like them so much. Afterwards we can take a long, long walk together. It smells like spring in the forest already. (*She kisses LEMB.*)

LEMB (*he leaves and turns around at the door*): Here is Mrs. Oru's picture frame...perhaps she'll come. (*Exits.*)

NEIDI (*alone*): Go, but don't stay long, return before the end of day...(*She laughs.*) I am exactly like Grandma. (*Opens the window.*) The room is full of smoke, the air is so thick that you could bite it...(*Takes the ashtray and counts.*) One, two, three, four, five, six...six cigarettes in this short time! He has never smoked so much before. What is wrong? Have I done something wrong? But what? If I only knew that...(*She stops in front of the painting, addressing it.*)

Listen you, my second self,
do you hear what I am telling you:
Make Lemb renowned, bring him fame;
do not disappoint me nor scorn my name;
I fold my hands and pray to you.
Please, listen...oh, please do!
You smile! You are saying "Yes!"
Thank you! You'll see.
One day our land will be proud
both of its son and thee.

(*She begins to arrange things, puts a cloth on the box and a glass with pussy-willows in the center, chanting.*) In the forest a doe with big, big eyes and her fawn skip playfully among the trees: the pine is high, a bird on top, a mossy base, in the moss a flower blue. 'Are you edible?' asked the little deer. 'Oh, no-no-no!' the flower said, 'please smell me instead.' Running on the path came tiny Annie, the child the flower picked and took it home to little sister Fannie." That is how this song ends, I know no more. If you do, sing some more. Tomorrow may bring new words and another tune. (*Startled.*) The coffee is boiling over! (*She runs behind the curtain.*)

CELIA (*enters, looks around the room while slowly pulling off her gloves, sees the painting and steps hastily up to it*): Here you are again. When we first met, you were only a gray larva on paper, now you have become a colorful butterfly, ready to fly towards fire. The fact that fire does not only warm but that it also burns, this fact, poor little one, you do not know yet. I feel sorry for you, but the lamp around which you are circling belongs to me. I have payed dearly for him, I need his warmth and light myself, and I will not give him up for anyone. Excuse me if I must make you sad...but you can retain your wings, you can continue to fly. If you were to burn your wings, then you could no longer fly. (*She walks around in the room.*) A clean table cloth on the table...pussy willows...fire in the fireplace...an aroma of fresh coffee....Do I even hear the clinking of cups? Very homey...beyond expectations...and I was worried that he would freeze and starve here. (*She warms her hands before the fire.*)

NEIDI (*enters from behind the curtain with coffee cups in her hands*): Oh, it's you! I didn't even hear you knock.

CELIA: Good evening. The model herself. It is interesting to meet you.

NEIDI (*eagerly*): Did you look at the painting already? Now it is finished. Do you like it?

CELIA: Congratulations! It is successful...the best he has produced so far.

NEIDI: Thank you, Mrs. Oru. Here is your picture frame.

CELIA (*takes the frame, examines it, puts it down*): Where is the artist himself?

NEIDI: He is not here right now.

CELIA: He is not here?...He would not have departed yet, would he?

NEIDI: No...but he does not have much time...he...

CELIA: ....He did not expect a visitor. I understand, but I am here now. I came to help him pack.

NEIDI: That is very kind of you, Mrs. Oru, but it is not necessary.

CELIA: Do you think so? My experience has taught me quite the opposite. I have known the artist a little longer than you.

NEIDI: Oh, I did not know that. In Estonia already?

CELIA: Our acquaintance began with this scar here... (*Points at her eyebrow.*) Perhaps you can take some time out and listen to me. I'll tell you about it. I hope you'll be interested in the story.

NEIDI: Yes, of course, Mrs. Oru.

CELIA: The aroma of coffee is very inviting. Could I ask for some ...only one little cupful? The climb up to the hill of this village was quite tiring. (*She takes off her coat.*)

NEIDI: With pleasure. (*Gets the coffee, pours it.*) How did it happen?

CELIA: Very simply. Once when I still was a schoolgirl, I visited a sick friend who lived in the outskirts of town. On my way home I happened to get hit by a stone which went astray in a streetfight conducted by a gang of boys. I became unconscious. ...When I woke up again, I was lying in a hospital bed. The boy who threw the stone came to visit me. He was a skinny, fuzzy-haired lad, the seventh son of the shoemaker of that suburb. By the way, a seventh child is always considered to be very gifted. Well, as a present he brought me his drawing pad from school.

NEIDI: His drawing pad from school!

CELIA: The poor, little thing had nothing else to give. That pad interested me very much and my father even more.... That is how my acquaintance with the artist Lemb Riiv began.

NEIDI: And he was the one whose stone hit you in such an unfortunate way.

CELIA: We do not know what turns out as our fortune or misfortune...you should have seen what that boy looked like at the time: a hungry-looking face, rags for clothes, dirty fingernails. Later we went to Art School together, with my father's money. I was not talented but Lemb was! However, the invasions and the war put an end to his formal artistic development. Ever since, his work has been a search for his own self. It seems that he has finally found himself with that painting over there.

NEIDI: The story you just told sounds like a fairytale which my Grandmother told me when I was still a child. (*She rises.*) Once upon a time there was a very poor couple who lived in a saunahut; the sauna did not belong to them, nor did the potato patch, nor the bit of forest, nor the pasture—oh no, for the use of these the man must slave and serve the owner, Master by name.

CELIA (*she rises also*): That was certainly not easy!

NEIDI: They had no cow; they had a goat whose milk did not suffice, and an old horse, skinny for lack of hay, and some hens that did not lay.

CELIA: A sad sight.

NEIDI:

> The couple had familial blessing,
> the stork came often visiting;
> he brought one child each year, or two,
> all needed food, like me and you.
> But frequently, how very sad!
> Hunger at the table sat
> staring in the eyes of every lad.

CELIA: That is an old, familiar tale.

NEIDI:

> The husband spoke:
> "This is no joke!"
> His wife confirmed,
> likewise perturbed:
> "It's true.
> With empty shelf and empty cupboard
> our stomachs crave at least some bread.
> What can we do?"

CELIA: And what did they do?

NEIDI:

> The couple thought it over,
> discussed the problem, figured...
> The sieve of possibilities
> cleared finally their vision,
> they reached but one decision:
> "Reduce—reduce the amount of mouths;
> decrease the number of consumers."

CELIA: A harsh decision... but what choice did they have?

NEIDI: Kaarel became a smith's apprentice, Ants an assistant to the miller, Aadu kneaded bread. But Tuia, the youngest boy, was a good-for-nothing. He did not want to work.

CELIA: If I understand you correctly, that lad possessed special talents then.

NEIDI:
>That boy did wander in the woods
>and hunted happily with bow and arrow.
>One day he saw a bird with feathers of gold.
>Ah-haa, thought Tuia, if I can get him,
>he will be sold.
>Then father can buy a home of his own.
>He raised his bow and aimed—
>the woods echoed a piercing scream!
>A wonder of all wonders!
>It was not a bird he found,
>it was a lovely fairy-maid.
>She smiled and said:
>"Thank you, young man;
>From an evil spell
>you rescued me well.
>I am no one less
>than a real princess."

CELIA (*nodding*): Exactly, exactly...

NEIDI:
>Tuia was taken by the maiden fair,
>to her father's castle near,
>where she gave him hand and heart.
>If death has not them set apart,
>they still live there in happiness.

CELIA (*clapping her hands*): Bravo! That was a beautiful fairy-tale...I like stories with a happy ending...and I hope that you will like the last part of my story...I have a few more words to add to it.

NEIDI: I apologize for having interrupted.

CELIA (*she puts her cup on the table*): Thank you for the coffee! It tasted especially good. You see, I have a feeling that there is a little confusion with names here....You call me Mrs. Oru, but my name is not Oru, it is Riiv.

NEIDI: Riiv?...Riiv?...How come?...I don't understand.

CELIA: It is very simple. Lemb Riiv is my husband.

NEIDI (*drops her cup which breaks into pieces; begins to run out but meets her GRANDMOTHER at the door.*) Grandma! ...Oh, Grandma! (*She throws herself into GRANDMA'S arms.*)

GRANDMA (*she wraps her large woolen scarf around NEIDI*): Let's go child, the horse and wagon are waiting. (*Exit together.*)

CELIA (*she picks up a piece of the broken cup*): A proverb says

that each shattered piece brings luck.... My only wish is that
it be so!

CURTAIN

ACT THREE

(*This act takes place in North America twenty years later. The
stage setting shows JÜRI and NEIDI VÄSTRIKS' livingroom with
modern decor; behind the Chesterfield hangs the original sketch
of NEIDI nicely framed; a garden party is in progress (backstage)
where GRANDMA'S and GRANDPA'S diamond wedding anniversary is being celebrated; voices and laughter are being heard
through the open doors to the garden; beside the doors there is a
mirror; another door marks the front entrance. Two lady guests,
MRS. SOOVEER and MRS. NÄGELIK, come in from the garden
and look at themselves in the mirror.*)*

MRS. SOOVEER (*well dressed in a summery party outfit; lights
a cigarette*): It's fantastic that Grandma and Grandpa Västrik
are celebrating their diamond wedding anniversary! With a
big garden party, no less!

MRS. NÄGELIK (*in a dress of average taste; powders her nose*):
A diamond wedding for the old couple! What a trick to make
people talk about them! Everyone is invited. The Estonian circles around town are all excited. The Riivs are invited too,
aren't they? Are they coming?

MRS. SOOVEER: Well yes. Why not? They are returning to
Sweden tomorrow and may be a little late. They said they still
had a few things to attend to.

MRS. NÄGELIK: I think Riiv made good business here. He is
famous! When I was at his exhibition, half the paintings had
"Sold" signs on already. Apparently Västrik got to the exhibition rather late; he bought the one painting that no one wanted
and said that was just fine and the main thing was to get a
colorful patch for the wall.

MRS. SOOVEER: The artist himself said that the painting was up
to standard in every way. It was just that one corner had got
a bit damaged.

MRS. NÄGELIK: Ah-haa! That's it! He got it cheap then! Yeah,
that man knows what he's doing. He has pots of money, a
house on the hilltop with spread-out wings like a seagull, every-

one has his own car, expensive furniture, swimming pool...
but they don't have a decent painting....Now just look at that!
Anette still has that shepherd boy's scratch-sketch from the
old country. That woman has absolutely no taste at all. I wonder where they hung the painting that they bought from Riiv.

MRS. SOOVEER: The artist was fixing it up in the last minute. He
was going to bring it.

MRS. NÄGELIK: Mrs. Lõugas said that in the old country Lemb
Riiv had been in love with a simple country girl from a fishing
village. A painting of the girl, who was very young and very
beautiful, is supposed to have brought him his fame. It's believed that he has that painting along with him as a talisman at
each of his exhibitions but that he no longer shows it. (*MRS.
ARUKE enters from the garden wearing a horrible, red wig,
looks at herself in the mirror and goes back out. Her clothes,
as the wig, are not in good taste. MRS. SOOVEER and MRS.
NÄGELIK are at first struck dumb by this apparition.*)

MRS. NÄGELIK: Did you see Mrs. Aruke?...What a wig! I almost fell on my behind! She looks like a painted poodle. It does
not suit her at all. Had the color been a little softer, but red!

MRS. SOOVEER: It's not red. According to her it's golden brown.

MRS. NÄGELIK: What difference does the name make. You can
call wolf a predator or vicious beast—but the animal remains
the same. Mrs. Riiv is older than her husband, isn't she?...By
how much do you think? (*She peeks through the curtains.*)
They are here! The Riivs are here! The car just stopped in front.
Grandpa is out there receiving them. Yes, Riiv really has the
painting they bought. (*Disappointed.*) They came after all...
I was already thinking that...well, to be snubbed would do
Anette some good. What does she think she is anyway! She is
a plain fisherman's wife. And she spreads herself out as if she
were a lady with a castle.

MRS. SOOVEER: You forget that Mr. Västrik is not only a fisherman but also an industrialist, the owner of a fish plant.

MRS. NÄGELIK: Industrialist....Well, let him be! He still smells
of fish, whether it is at a party or in church.

MRS. SOOVEER: But he gives his wife all the money she wants,
and money does not smell.

MRS. NÄGELIK (*sighing*): No, it does not smell, that's true.
(*Exit together. Enter GRANDPA, CELIA and LEMB through
the front door.*)

GRANDMA (*enters from the garden*): Good evening, my
children, good evening! (*She shakes hands with the RIIVS.*

CELIA, *as if trying to remember something, examines first*
GRANDPA, *then* GRANDMA.)
GRANDPA: You, dear child, you seem familiar to me. I am sure I
have seen you somewhere before.
CELIA: It...it cannot be...I am on this continent for the first
time.
LEMB (*he notices the sketch on the livingroom wall and looks at
it closely*): Excuse me, I have brought the wrong painting...
I'll be back soon. (*Exits.*)
GRANDMA: Grandpa forgets easily. We only saw your picture in
the newspaper.
GRANDPA:
> You are right, I think, Grandma.
> You and I for sixty years
> a common yoke have borne;
> you always held the course.
> You knew wrong from right.
> Look, this head is white!
> Much in life I have met,
> I — an old Estonian with fish and net —
> Tõnu, Tõnu's son, Räim.
> A refugee for years
> who left his father's land behind in tears,
> but as a reward for this pain
> my head on my shoulders did remain.
> That great bear has killed many of my kin,
> sent some into the grave, my friend,
> and others to Siberia's end.
> But I am left here,
> I — an old fisherman —
> Tõnu, Tonu's son, Räim.
> Homeless, rolling like a stone —
> Heaven willed it so —
> until my wanderings did cease
> and in the New World found peace.
> Here I live like the cat of the king,
> am enjoying enough days of God's granting
> to celebrate in full health this day
> with Kadri our fourth wedding, so gay.
> If some scenes of life have been erased,
> from the tape of memory been effaced,
> then there is one which stands out all the more!
> With fire imprinted into the very core

is the night
when we left our home and shore.
I can never forget that.
GRANDMA: No, never!
CELIA: No!...The sea is roaring...in the shed the fire crackles,
...a smell of tar...I feed the greedy appetite of fire...my heart
is pounding...with one ear pressed against the wall I wonder:
"Is the beast of prey approaching?" I say a prayer: "God
Almighty, please, do help us, do not forsake us!"
GRANDPA: You were brave, my girl! You ignored the tempest.
With legs knee-high in icy waters and soaking wet quite thor-
oughly you helped to push the boat to sea!
CELIA: Oh, Grandpa, Oh, Grandma! Is it not a dream that you
are again standing before me?
GRANDMA: I am beginning to think not....It seems that Grand-
pa was right this time.
CELIA: And he...he...his name was Juss, I think. What became
of that man?
GRANDPA: He is our son-in-law now.
GRANDMA: Juss married Neidi, our daughter's daughter. They
live very happily; they have young ones too, no less than four.
CELIA: And he is Jüri Västrik?
GRANDPA: He, of course, who else!
CELIA: And you are Grandpa Västrik?
GRANDPA: Yes, I guess they'll never call me anything else here.
JÜRI (*enters from the right*): This is a nice story. Our guests are
all here, but the artist has no intention of appearing. My wife
already questioned: "Did you really buy a painting?" Why yes,
one wall in the living room is still quite bare. (*He spreads his
arms out.*) A man knows where he is at when he throws a rope
around the horns of an ox and pulls, or when he makes agreements with another man who keeps his word. It must be true
what I have heard that artists differ from us who walk with
two feet down on earth. Their kind are said to dream with open
eyes in broad daylight and ride above the clouds at any time. I
am beginning to think...I really doubt, whether Mr. Riiv...
GRANDPA: Be calm, my son, be calm! (*He motions towards
Celia.*) The key to his home is here.
GRANDMA: Juss, we were just talking about you. Do you know
this visitor?
JÜRI (*he recognizes CELIA*): For God's sake! (*Hugs her.*) For
God's sake! As long as I live I'll remember what a great help
you were to us during that fateful journey, my girl. Many times

I have wondered to myself why the Creator did not make a man
of you. A son would certainly have followed in the footsteps
of his father, defying wave and storm: you would have been
like him and me—a real monster of the sea! (*They all laugh.*)

CELIA: Why not...why not?...How else could it have been?
When to a captain a son is born, then very soon the little boy is
taken aboard so that early in his life he gets to know the tem-
pestuous moods of oceans. I certainly would have been like my
father and like Jüri Västrik here—I would have been a sea-
monster, as genuine and real! (*They all laugh again.*)

JÜRI: How come you are alone? Where is your other half?

CELIA: Lemb is coming. It is always like this: when others celebrate, he is hard at work. But he'll be here soon.

JÜRI: Then all is well. Let's go. I'll introduce you to my wife. I
have told Neidi about you, but I had no idea that you were Mrs.
Riiv. She will be happily surprised to meet you.

CELIA (*aside*): If it only were so!

GRANDMA: It is so, my child. The wounds from youth, I am sure,
were healed some time ago.

JÜRI:
What was yesterday has passed,
what comes tomorrow we do not know.
There is a limit to joy and sorrow,
upon sunshine a storm may follow.
But today
let us be gay!
Come, let us have some wine,
our glasses fill with champagne!
Wedding anniversaries are not celebrated every day,
good friends seldom come by.
Our daily toil may take our smile
and give us no time to rejoice.

ALL:
Come, let us have some wine,
our glasses fill with champagne!
There is a limit to joy and sorrow,
upon sunshine a storm may follow.
But today
let us be gay! (*All exit to the right.*)

LEMB (*enters from the outside; unwraps the painting of NEIDI
and hangs it over the sofa*):
Here, my Fairy of Fortune, is your place.
You will stay here now, and I shall leave alone...

but in my memory
you will always be;
wherever I go
greetings to you I bestow.
You are Spring
who conquers Winter's cold;
you are Happiness
who drowns sorrow and sadness;
you are a Gentle Breeze in my hair;
you are a Ray of Sun in my heart.
A few moments yet I'll stay with you...that's good...
then I'll go and in a note explain
that my head caused me a severe pain.
But—truthfully—
I am, as always, cowardly
and afraid to see you again.
Two decades have passed—
you have aged—
your children have grown fast
and taken their toll:
your voice in shrill molds may be cast,
your expression stern.
Perhaps your glance stabs like a knife.
Perhaps it says: "I have money now;
do you want to borrow some, you clandestine snake?"
(*He sinks down on the sofa, takes a notebook and a pencil from his pocket but forgets about them. He hears the following in song.*)
Oh, my tousled little silly-billy,
don't you really know?
I am happy because spring is coming now.
And summer follows nigh.
Budding birches, flow'rs begin to bloom,
on the cherry bough the birds announce
that ploughing time is high.
Love-love-love-love-lovely is life!
The night is short and light.
Twilight hands its lamp to Dawn,
their lips but a moment do meet.
Come-come-come-come come hither, my sweet!
The bright night's romance will quickly end
and sun's rays soon will drink
the dewdrops from the leaf.

> A thousand tasks are waiting for me.
> In the light
> summer night
> I whisper in your ear:
> 'I love you, only you,
> please, stay near!'

(*LEMB leans back and falls asleep.*)

NEIDI (*enters from the right; she wears a party dress of good taste; she notices the painting*): Oh! (*She stops before the painting and hears the following, also being sung.*)

> My maiden on the seashore,
> I have looked for you an eternity!
> Finally you stand before me:
> the blue sky
> in your eye,
> the brushed flax of your hair,
> the sun's rays in your robe's flare.
> If wings had I,
> over the water I'd fly
> and take you
> with me too!

(*She looks closely at the sleeping LEMB.*)

A wrinkle just beside your nose...the temples show some gray ...yet, your expression has remained like that of a child most innocent...your hair still spreads pretty curls around your forehead...your hands, these charmers, are the same...how I admired them! One by one I kissed your finger-tips. Oh, I loved you so very, very much! And yet, for a long time I have known that we were not suited to live with one another. In the plainly patterned weave of the fabric of my life your memory glitters like a golden flower which will never fade. I thank you for all the happiness as well as for the pain. (*She kisses LEMB on the forehead, then touches his shoulder.*) Mr. Riiv, please wake up! You are expected in the garden!

LEMB (*still asleep*): Celi, don't disturb me. I had a beautiful dream.

NEIDI: You are expected in the garden.

LEMB (*opens his eyes*): Neidi! You are really here!

NEIDI: I thank you for the present!

LEMB (*he rises*): Forgive me...I stayed up late last night....You smile as you used to! I would like to paint you again.

NEIDI: I am very pleased. Once I loved you as a woman, now

you may be my friend, my brother....The doors of my home are always open for you.

LEMB: Thank you, my dear sister! (*They kiss.*)

JÜRI (*JÜRI'S voice is heard from the right*): Neidi! Neidi! (*LEMB steps aside.*) Oh, here you are. Do you know, my darling wife, that we have a very dear guest? Come and receive her!

NEIDI: My dear, your face is absolutely radiant with happiness! Who is this very special guest?

JÜRI: Celia, the captain's daughter with whom we escaped from Estonia! She has already got to know our daughters. Riina, Kati and Tiia are clinging to her like buhls and compete in telling her how smart they are. Tiia even found that Celia's lap was the best seat for her. In the evening, however, Celia wants to come with us to visit the boyscouts and to meet Tõnu... and can you imagine, she is Mrs. Riiv!

NEIDI: Yes. If Life so wills, there is no limit to its surprises! I am coming right away. (*She takes JÜRI'S hand and motions towards the painting.*) Look!

JÜRI (*he is dazed*): Is this an illusion or have I tipped the glass too much already? I see before me the daughter at Beach Farm, as a young lady.

NEIDI: My dearest husband...(*She kisses him on the cheek.*) there is nothing wrong with your eyesight. That is the painting I told you about.

JÜRI: That is it...(*He puts his arm around NEIDI; they stand a moment together before the painting.*) But let's go, they (*He points towards the right.*) are getting a little nervous. (*He turns around.*) Well, look! The magician himself is here! (*Shakes hands with LEMB.*) Let's have a longer chat a little later. Now we must go. They all have been waiting for you for a long time.

(*GRANDMA comes from the right with champagne glasses on a tray; she offers a glass to everyone; after her come GRAND-PA and the other guests, each with a glass in hand.*)

JÜRI:
>Today we'll hang our sorrows on the rack,
>a festive table awaits us in the back!
>Friends all together, let us rejoice!
>Let us eat and drink and put song in our voice!
>Let us dance in full swing!

ALL:
>Today is a wedding day,

Grandpa's and Grandma's wedding day!
Friends all together, let us rejoice!
Let us eat and drink and put song in our voice!
Let us dance in full swing!
GRANDPA: Ahoy!

CURTAIN

FERDINAND AND SYBIL
and
PLEASE, COME IN, SIR!

by
Anšlavs Eglītis

Translated from the original Latvian
Ferdinands un Sibila
and
Lūdzu ienāciet, Sēr!
by
Juris Valters

Ferdinand and Sybil. Sybil: Cindy Sinclair. Ferdinand: Richard Sater. Janitor: Alfreds Straumanis. Doll: Kery Sims. Produced for television by Southern Illinois University Broadcasting Service, 1980. Director: Alfreds Straumanis. Scenographer: Meyers Walker. Production suppored in part by a grant from the Illinois Humanities Council.

Introduction to
Ferdinand and Sybil and Please, Come In, Sir!

The achievements of Anšlavs Eglītis are prodigious. In a career spanning over a half-century, he has written twenty novels, twenty plays, twelve collections of short stories, three collections of poetry, and hundreds of reviews and articles. He has been a reporter, editor, and critic. As a translator, he has introduced into Latvian works of Edgar Allen Poe, O. Henry, and various English poets. As an artist, he has illustrated many of his own works, as well as those of others. By the beginning of World War II, he had become one of the most popular young writers in Latvia, and since 1945 he has enjoyed a fame and popularity which has enabled him to become one of those rare Baltic exiles who, as a writer and artist, earns his living solely from his literary and artistic endeavors. This is no mean achievement considering that his reading and viewing public is drawn from a base of approximately 50,000 Latvian exiles scattered throughout the Western world.

For all his popularity and success, however, an air of ambiguity surrounds Eglītis and his work. On the one hand Eglītis has received unqualified praise, on the other hand more scholarly criticism tends to be reserved and brief.

Ambiguity also marks the public's attitude toward the author, and variances in opinion and attitude are remarkable. To some, he is by far a better prose writer than a dramatist. Yet others consider his dramatic efforts superior to those of prose. Some think that his early works in Latvia or even Germany were better than his later work in the United States. In some instances people who had found earlier works interesting now consider them dull and boring. And while some find Eglītis' humor spirited and his satire pointed and accurate, others consider his attitude and tone bitter, sarcastic, and even offensive.

However, there seems to be a general attitude best described perhaps as one of benign neglect—an attitude analogous to the one a family might show an old, dear friend whose comings, goings, and eccentricities have become so familiar and taken for granted that they command no more than a passing glance or comment. After a literary presence of more than fifty years, Eglītis seems to have become "our Anšlavs" or "good old Anšlavs" to much of the public.

The basic reason for this phenomenon seems to be Eglītis' reputation as a feuilletonist. In his first collection of short stories, *Maestro,* and in *Līgavu mednieki* ("The Bride Hunters"), his first novel, he created marvelously accurate parodies and caricatures of well-known public and artistic personalities. Though in the wake of sensation created by these works Eglītis vowed never again to use real persons for his characterizations, the reputation has remained.

Because of the readers' concentration on surface elements and the critics' light regard of Eglītis, three aspects of his work have been overlooked: first, Eglītis, as a social commentator, has created a body of writing which serves as a literary chronicle of a people's history during the most turbulent and rapidly changing period of the twentieth century; second, this chronicle provides a unique cultural thread which unites the present with the past; and third, reflecting the enormous economic, political, and social changes of the past forty or fifty years, his works afford an excellent basis for the study of how an artist changes in response to them.

Nowhere are these changes more apparent than in Eglītis' plays. In drama he has found a medium more viable in terms of style and approach than prose, and, though his plays represent a relatively small portion of his writings, he has used them as his main avenue for experimentation and innovation. But were these changes achieved through a conscious experimentation and designed to reach an everchanging public, or did they occur because the dramatist himself has been changing in response to his new environments, be they economic, political, or social? To facilitate the finding of an answer a short biography of Anšlavs Eglītis, partially extracted from encyclopedic sources, partially from Eglītis' own writing, is in order.

Born on October 14, 1906, in Riga (Latvia), Anšlavs Eglītis was predestined for an artistic and literary career. His parents were both well-known literary and intellectual figures: Viktors Eglītis as a poet, writer, and classical scholar, Marija Eglītis as a teacher of literature.

At the outbreak of World War I the Eglītis family moved to Moscow, where both parents taught in a private school for problem children. Following the Brest-Litovsk treaty in 1918, the family returned to Latvia, first settling in Alūksne but later moving back to Riga.

The first years following Latvian independence in 1918 Eglītis remembers as "full of beautiful hopes. Life was full of exhilarating optimism which touched everyone and everything." These years Eglītis spent completing his formal studies, participating in athletics, and studying painting.

An attack of lung disease in 1925 cut short Eglītis' studies and sent him to Switzerland to recuperate. In Switzerland, Eglītis was exposed to the cultural activity and thought of the European continent. He took up mountain climbing with an enthusiasm hardly befitting a semi-invalid and, under the tutelage of the French chess champion André Creon, became a fairly expert chess player.

Eglītis returned to Latvia in 1926 and spent the next three years convalescing on the small farm his father had obtained from the government under the Agrarian Reform Act. The enforced seclusion and lingering illness, combined with his mother's death shortly after his return from Switzerland, depressed Eglītis tremendously. Unable or unwilling to paint, he turned to writing poetry. His first published work, a poem entitled *Lords* ("His Lordship"), was, as Eglītis later admitted, "the reasoning of man tired of life."

During the next ten years Eglītis attended the Latvian Academy of Arts, worked as a critic and reviewer, and pursued his writing hobby with generally undistinguished results. Then in 1936, he wrote the short story, *Maestro*, which brought him to the public's attention and, unfortunately in many ways, determined the public's attitude towards his work.

In 1938 Eglītis' first novel "The Bride Hunters" appeared in serialized form in the magazine *Atputa*. It was a satiric look at the academic world of Riga, centering on the student fraternities and their various rituals. The title pertained to the accepted practice of students trying to marry daughters of the well-to-do as a means of entry into high society. The subsequent controversy far overshadowed that of *Maestro*. Fights broke out in the taverns and cafes of Riga between Eglītis' detractors and supporters, challenges to duels were issued, a boycott was instigated against the publisher to force her to cease printing the novel, and only the prevailing of cooler heads in the fraternities prevented Eglītis from coming to physical harm. Unsuccessful efforts were even made to have the government exile him. Needless to say, he became well known.

In 1943, during the German occupation, the theatres of Latvia encountered a lack of politically suitable plays. Jānis Roze, director of the National Theatre in Riga, asked Eglītis if he would be interested in writing a play. Hesitant at first, he was persuaded by Roze's five-minute synopsis of playwrighting principles which was so eloquent that Eglītis, carried away, felt that he truly had the "blue bird of drama by the tail." Usually a slow and painstaking craftsman, Eglītis rushed home and rewrote one of his novelettes into dramatic form in less than a week. The result met with devastating criticism from Roze and director Osvalds Uršteins. Realizing that he was not one of the "sainted" writers whose work appears "spontaneously," Eglītis went back to his deliberate work pattern. The result was his first play "Confirmation of the Cosmos."

With the collapse of the German Eastern front in 1944 Anšlavs Eglītis and his wife Veronika Janelsina, who had been a fellow student at the Academy of Art, joined the refugee wave to the West. Their first stop was Berlin, where they lost nearly all of their possessions in an Allied bombing raid. At the end of the war in 1945, Eglītis settled in the southern German town of Teilfingen, where he lived until emigrating to the United States in 1950.

After spending the first eighteen months in Oregon, the Eglītis' moved to southern California, where they have resided ever since. Working first as a warehouse man and later as a stocker in a bookstore, Eglītis became keenly aware of the dilemma facing an artist in a strange country. Forced to work in order to make a living, the artist soon began to lose that spark necessary for creative work. Watching other exiled artists losing themselves in the rigors of existence, Eglītis attempted to escape that fate. Gaining accreditation in the Hollywood press corps, writing and painting with obsessive determination, he managed, with considerable help from his wife, to free himself from the burdens of a daily job which has enabled him to pursue his literary career.

Anšlavs Eglītis has always attempted to remain objective to his surroundings and not lose the perspective of reality. But this objectivity has not dulled his awareness of the vagaries of existence and fortune which often determine the course of a man's life. In a series of "self-portraits" Eglītis once endeavored to encapsulate his life, and the last is perhaps most indicative of his perspective:

> The use of frames for painting is slowly going out of style. Often they are no longer used for abstract works. And so my last portrait I can calmly leave unframed. My surroundings are the best frame...

I am roasting myself on an aluminum and plastic lawn chair under a scraggly lemon tree. My hair has turned rather white. Sensible people begin dyeing their hair early, but I have been remiss; ... now my friends and acquaintances would notice and smirk if I were to appear in public with dark, chestnut locks.... It would be pointless to describe myself further. With the passing of years a man grows more and more uninteresting. I planted the lemon tree, but have given it scant care, and it bears fruit only sporadically. My two palm trees aren't very vigorous either. Only the quick-growing eucalyptus trees, which I planted along my neighbor's fence, have shot up over sixty feet, and my neighbor has more than once pointed out that in a storm they would represent a danger to his house. Beyond my neighbor's banana and avocado trees, beyond the peach orchard, a mile-and-a-half away softly can be heard the roar of the Pacific Ocean. I have become used to this landscape and often don't see it anymore, but sometimes, like now, I seem to awake from a dream. I remember it is the first of January, the middle of winter. I look at my bare, sandaled feet, at the hillside covered with geraniums, whose proper place is a pot in a warm room and my surroundings suddenly seem eerily strange and unfamiliar. I wonder at the peculiarities of life which have transported me, a proper northerner and native of Riga, to the edge of the world in California!

At the very outset as an artist in exile, Eglītis began to ponder the problem of maintaining the exile's cultural and national identity. In the play "Better People," he provides a farcical look at a group of Latvians in a German refugee camp shortly before the end of the war. Some have arrived with no more than the clothes on their backs and memories, while others have laboriously attempted to bring with them all their material possessions, which they deem more important than friendship and unity with their fellow refugees. Through the most farcical characters in the play, Socinš, the greedy and self-centered sweets shop owner and his mother-in-law Made, Eglītis transmits his opinion of what will be needed to survive in exile. "And they call themselves Latvians!" snort Socinš and Made whenever they feel others are not respecting their wishes and whims. Funny as that line may have been to refugee audiences, there is a serious subtext: survival in exile will depend on a thorough and precise knowledge of what a Latvian is and what it means to be one.

The answer to what a Latvian is lies, of course, in the peasant ethic and morality which for centuries had been the bedrock of survival for the Latvian people. "Better People" then, by turning to this question of values, indicates a major shift in the playwright. The social satirist of Riga begins to fade, and the moral satirist of exile emerges.

The change in satirical emphasis is accompanied by a change in attitude. Two divergent and opposing patterns develop in the exile plays. On one hand, the emigre′ is slowly and irrevocably drawn into and assimilated by the foreign environment, which means the destruction and loss of the values the playwright considers important and whose destruction and loss he attacks. On the other hand, those who cling to the values and memories of the homeland slowly become alienated from their environment—an alienation which, if carried far enough, results in the spiritual and even physical destruction of the individual.

In these alternate paths to destruction Eglītis is faced with a dilemma as an artist and, one may assume, as a person. Unlike many satirists (Jonathan Swift, for example), Eglītis is a realist in that he cannot and does not deny the present in the context of today. As his self-portrait indicated, he is aware of his present surroundings and, while he may ponder the circumstances, he does not withdraw from them. The realist, however, must then come in conflict with the two patterns he sees emerging. To accept reality means to be assimilated; it means the loss of values which the moralist cannot accept. Conversely, acceptance and maintenance of the values the moralist cherishes means the rejection of reality, which is equally unacceptable to the realist. This struggle between the realist and the moralist is one the artist seemingly has never been able to resolve. Only in *Ferdinand and Sybil* is there any attempt at resolution but, though the realist seems to win, the victory is far from clear and the struggle goes on.

This conflict between the realist and the moralist and the inability to find a happy compromise between the two destructive patterns imbues Eglītis' work with a deeper and deeper pessimism, and represents the major change in the artist. From the optimistic and witty observer of urban life in Latvia, where stability and harmony were dominant, he has changed to the ironic and better observer of a world which has created a chasm he cannot bridge.

The resultant shift from optimism to pessimism is paralleled by a change from comedy to satire and irony. This movement approximates the literary cosmology developed by Northrop Frye—with one major exception. Frye's symmetry traces literary movement from the phases of comedy (mythos of spring) through romance (mythos of summer) and tragedy (mythose of autumn), to irony and satire (mythos of winter), after which the cycle returns to comedy. In Eglītis' case, the movement is reversed. The cataclysm of exile has disturbed his cosmos, and spring, instead of blossoming into summer, is enveloped by the winter of irony and satire.

*   *   *

With *Ferdinand and Sybil* Eglītis has left the conventional theatre long enough to write a play reflecting the grotesqueness and contradictions of exile. Though it is not absurd, the grotesqueness and contradictions are clearly shown.

The play has essentially little plot or direct dramatic action. What conflict there is evolves from the contrasts between the characters which appear as they come in contact with each other and reveal their attitudes. Indeed, the play seems more like a scenario in which characters and what they represent are set in specific relationships to show a condition.

The basic relationship seems to be a variation on the eternal triangle: Ferdinand loves the Doll and hates Sybil; Sybil loves Ferdinand and hates the Doll; the Doll loves Ferdinand and, if not hating her, at least envies Sybil. Peripherally Hillman provides contrast directly to Sybil and the Doll and indirectly to Ferdinand. The grotesqueness in this relationship and in the play arises from the fact that the Doll is, ostensibly, a lifeless thing.

The Doll is the personification or the symbol of the past and its values. She is old, very old. Sybil observes that if the Doll would be alive "it would have terrible wrinkles." Its origin in Vienna is a parallel to the wave of nationalistic and liberal thought which swept through nineteenth-century Europe and provided the inspiration for the Latvian National Awakening and subsequent independence. It also represents the exile culture which, like the Doll, was dismantled in Germany and only later under more stable conditions was reassembled, a pale and battered shadow of what it used to be. The Doll is the memory of Riga, the River Daugava, and the sound of sleigh-bells in snow covered streets. Sybil is the opposite of the Doll. Though she could not be considered a personification, she represents the present in context of today as much as the Doll does the past. Her world consists of the phenomena of the day: pop psychology, immediate obsolescence, momentary trivia (button, straw), problems of communication and self-expression, concerns with getting a boy, indecisiveness, and a short attention span. In contrast to the Doll's immobility, life to Sybil is constant movement—she is always urging Ferdinand "to go" or "to do." Unlike the Doll, who is history,

Sybil has no history. She can conceive of it only in terms of herself:

> You said her head was chopped off. Did you see her head chopped off? Look at me, Ferdinand. Do you think my head could be chopped off? (*Thoughtfully.*) My head...

Or, when Ferdinand asks her if she knows who the Bearslayer (Lāčplēsis, a mythical Latvian hero) is:

> SYBIL: Bearslayer? Bearslayer? (*Shakes her head.*) No, I don't know. (*Remembers.*) Oh, Bearslayer! Of course I know! My older sister, Ilze, recited something about the Bearslayer at a Latvian festival. Is that the one you mean?
> FERDINAND: That's the one.
> SYBIL: Oh, I know that. I definitely know. (*Tries to remember. Quietly reciting to herself.*) Of course I know it. (*Begins reciting.*) Oh, Bearslayer, Sybil will come to your aid!
> FERDINAND: Spīdola.
> SYBIL: Oh, alright. Spīdola. What's the difference—one girl or another?

Since she symbolizes the present, Sybil cannot comprehend or understand the past. Unlike Hillman or Ferdinand, she sees the Doll as a lifeless, battered, ugly thing that should be replaced by something new and modern.

The conflict between the Doll and Sybil, the past and present, focuses on the character of Ferdinand. He is the second generation exile youth torn between two opposing value systems. On the one hand he cannot understand his parents. "They spoke Latvian, I spoke English," he tells the Doll. But Sybil, the representative of the present for whom he left his parents, does not understand him either. As a result of this vacuum Ferdinand has created his own bizarre past. He has envisioned himself with Marie Antoinette, that beautiful symbol of a past whose demise marked the beginning of a new social order. With her he eats popcorn on the steps of Versailles and throws nickles and dimes into the fountains of King Louis and peanut shells from the top of the Rockefeller Center. On his grandfather's farm in Latvia he avenges the injustice done to Marie Antoinette by Danton and Robespierre while she sits in front of the granary drinking Coke, after which they share a cigarette. In this last episode Ferdinand plays out his version of the story of Bearslayer, that great hero of Latvian mythology who defended Latvia and Spīdola, the embodiment of the Latvian spirit, from the encroaching enemies, usually represented by the Black Knight. This jarring amalgam of sym-

bols—Ferdinand/Bearslayer, coke/granary, Marie Antoinette/
Spīdola, Danton-Robespierre/Black Knight, victor's reward/
cigarette—exemplify Ferdinand's confused attempts to correlate
a past he does not know with the present.

Sybil cannot understand these attempts:

> SYBIL: How do you look at events that are a hundred and fifty years
> old, Mr. Hillman?
> HILLMAN: I look at them as things that have happened.
> SYBIL: Well, see, what's there to worry one's self about? It isn't
> worth it, right? Only Ferdinand doesn't think so.

But to the Doll they are very clear. It has come alive because
Ferdinand, in his search for answers and beauty, has wanted it to
come alive. It tells Ferdinand of the magic and beauty of the past,
of its music, snow-covered streets, and bells. Ferdinand is
skeptical, but in his eyes the Doll has become so beautiful he is
willing to reject Sybil and buy the Doll in order to keep it for
himself. But the Doll knows better. It knows it is a lifeless thing
which cannot compete with the vitality of the present or exist in it.
It can only come alive for the brief moment when someone like
Ferdinand wants to see it. In the one moment when the Doll
threatens to become too real and steps out of the window, it is
stopped by the arrival of Sybil. The past cannot live in the face of
the present. Similarly, the present cannot live in the past. Ferdinand can hear the music, but even he cannot hear the bells in a
snow covered street in Riga—they are a part of the past which he
cannot make real or share. Just as the Doll cannot step out of the
window, Ferdinand cannot climb into it. Reluctantly, after having
glimpsed the past and its meanings, Ferdinand is forced to
acknowledge his returning to Sybil.

But the question remains: what will be his future relationship with
the Doll/past while he lives with Sybil/present? Two possibilities
appear in the play. The first is represented by Hillman, the Doll's
owner. He seems to stand for those exiles who have brought their
culture with them, like Hillman his Doll, and who keep it in good
repair in its outer form, dress it up, and take great pride in its
appearance. (This could also be analogous to the keeping of small
dolls dressed in folk costumes on the shelves or mantels of Latvian
homes.) But, just as Hillman can no longer see the Doll's beauty
or hear its music, only keeping it for its sentimental and utilitar-
ian values, so many exiles have adhered to the external forms of
their heritage without remembering what lies behind it. Worse,
they have attempted to impose on it meanings or interpretations

alien to it which must be rejected, just as the Doll throws off
clothes which she does not like or which obscure her beauty:

> I too am selfish and quarrelsome. Mr. Hillman put an ugly dress on
> me yesterday. I dropped it. He put it back on, and I dropped it
> again. I wanted you to like me, Ferdinand. I am a capricious and
> selfish thing.

The Doll is perfectly well aware that Ferdinand could become
one of those who, once in possession of it, would cease seeing it for
its beauty and music and only perceive its external form or try to
impose on it things which do not fit. When Ferdinand proposes
buying the Doll, it warns him:

> Don't be hasty, Ferdinand. I'll be right here. I'll stand right here,
> perhaps for many more years.

Hillman has also isolated himself. He is content to live with his
Doll, talk to his wife, and run his store.

> SYBIL: When you were going with your Hermeline, did you ever
>   philosophize? About what kind of ideas?
> HILLMAN: Oh, yeah. About money, about stores. Clothes, too.

Hillman's pragmatic approach to life has precluded awareness of
the spiritual. Worse, it has precluded any contact with or interest
in the youth of exile. He is the older generation for whom time has
stopped somewhere in the past and who is out of synchronization
with the present where time moves forward. For this reason he
cannot understand, nor does he particularly care about Sybil's or
Ferdinand's problems. They do not exist in his universe.

The other possibility is the Superintendent. Once, as a youth like
Ferdinand, he had stood outside a display window in Riga and had
laughed and shared the magic with the Doll. But in Germany he
had no longer been able to recognize it, and now in exile he no
longer even sees it. Preoccupied with making a living he is no
longer able to look up and see that which once was beautiful. He
goes by the window looking at the street, searching for cigarette
butts. He stands for those who, in their quest for survival and
material possessions, have rejected or forgotten their heritage
and lost their youthful fantasies. But when Ferdinand expresses
his scorn for the Superintendent, the Doll stops him.

> FERDINAND: So inhuman, without fantasy.
> DOLL: You're being self-righteous, Ferdinand. He is only tired.

The implications of the Doll's statement are two-fold. It warns
Ferdinand that eventually he too, lost in the present, could

become like the Superintendent, and no longer be able to see it. But secondly, the Doll does not condemn him. There is only sympathy, understanding, and perhaps love. The road of exile has not been easy: "He is only tired."

There is, however, a third possibility: the chance that Ferdinand will come back. At the end the Doll urges Ferdinand to go with Sybil:

> Go, Ferdinand. I'll be here. I will be standing here. Maybe for many, many years. You can always come back to me. I'll wait for you, but Sybil won't wait. Sybil will go with Paul. I am a thing. I can wait. For a long time.

Ferdinand has to go with Sybil—the present cannot be denied. But as long as he is willing to come back and see, the past will come alive for a moment and perhaps give meaning to his life in the present. Whether or not he will come back is a decision Eglītis leaves to the audience.

If the question of Ferdinand's future remains open, it is because Anšlavs Eglītis as the artist had arrived at a point of balance between optimism and pessimism in *Ferdinand and Sybil*. Previous plays, while satiric, had been essentially optimistic. But after *Ferdinand and Sybil* Eglītis' mood changes in his later plays as he perceives a worsening in the exile condition.

In describing the exile condition in *Ferdinand and Sybil* Eglītis touches on the themes of isolation, alienation, search for identity, the struggle between materialism and spiritual values, and the generation gap. While there is some allusion to one or more of these in his early plays, the sense of loss engendered by exile and the resulting conflicts between the past and the present, reality and unreality, have made them sharper and more pronounced.

Up to *Ferdinand and Sybil*, Eglītis' mood has been, for the most part, optimistic or at least neutral. In *Please Come In, Sir!* the mood takes a negative turn. The central character, Roderick Tūraids, has built for himself a world of illusion. He professes to be a writer and intellectual, and an objective observer of life, but he is incapable of reacting to events around him. Thus, when an old friend of his wife shows up at his home, he refuses to admit to himself that they might be having an affair. But when he is alone he carries on long monologues with an imaginary policeman. In them he reveals that he is perfectly aware of what is going on, but that he is incapable of coping with events:

> This Dancis Basenieks is, in all honesty, a pleasant and useless person. Helpless, defenseless, and fragile, and my wife dotes on

him. How can I object to that situation? How do you think, sir,
I should behave and still maintain my position as an urbane,
modern man? To tell you the truth, a situation like this forces
one into an uncomfortable position. If I was an irresponsible
man, like that wandering friend of my wife, I could allow my im-
pulses to take over without any second thought. I could, for instance, kick him out of my house. I could force Perse to choose
between me and that tramp. I could set up and ask any of those
hundreds of banal questions asked in those situations by common
and coarse people. Unleash my anger and displeasure. But that
is pitiful, degrading, and overdone. I've got to find some other
way.

Further in his conversations Roderick claims to have large
bank accounts in Copenhagen and to have built his house. In the
following breath he admits to his friend that no such bank account
exists, that his father-in-law moved the house to where it is, and
even that he really has not written a thing. He reveals as a person
incapable of definite action whose life has been built on self-decep-
tion, illusion, and fantasy. But in his long monologue to the
"policeman," Roderick suddenly makes a decision leaving
everything behind: he is returning to Europe.

What really happens? In the play it is revealed that Roderick's
house is out on a secluded hillside and that there is a family car.
Yet, Roderick goes out with his imagined friend and gets into an
imaginary car.

In approaching this question, two things must be noted. The first
is that by deciding to leave, Roderick takes the first really direct
action in his conversations with the "policeman." And secondly,
he returns to Copenhagen, i.e., the past. But this cannot be done. To
return to the past means withdrawal from the present, which spiritually is insanity and physically—death. So the only conclusion
can be that Roderick, by walking out of his home in his illusion,
either enters complete insanity of commits suicide. If this is true,
then Eglītis in his vision of the exile condition reaffirms Thomas
Wolfe's summary of his life-long quest for the past: you can't go
home again.

In tracing the pattern of conflicts between the past and present,
reality and illusion, it is noticeable that as the individuals grow
more and more isolated, Eglītis' focus shifts from the external to
the internal. Ferdinand sees the Doll and hears the music while
others only see a lifeless thing or a pile of clothes. In *Please Come
In, Sir!* Roderick withdraws in himself to escape a world he does
not know how to cope with.

In *Leo,* Eglītis completes the withdrawal of man into himself
and his own metamorphosis into pessimism and irony. Through
Leo, a Ph.D. undertaking to study how to make the unhappy man
happy, Eglītis satirizes those who advocate the free expression of
man's baser instincts; those whose sophistication has made them
incapable of empathy and emotion and who have stripped
everything of a higher or spiritual meaning, leaving sex and
excrement the only topics of conversation; and those who through
their insistence on musing about unhappiness have deprived the
world of joy. Leo wants no part of it. As the gray and miserable
"no-name" characters in scene three prepare to throw him out he
demurs:

> Please don't strain yourselves. I will leave willingly. (*Gathers his
> papers, picks up his typewriter, and gets ready to leave. The
> figures have returned to their original positions and are motion-
> less. Leo begins to exit.*) Don't stay in one place too long, ladies
> and gentlemen. Stir yourselves now and then. Stretch your stiff
> joints. (*Waves to audience, and exits.*)

The movement of the plays from the portrayal of society on a
broader scale, through alienation of the individual, to the isolation
of Leo seems to parallel Anšlavs Eglītis' life. In recent years he
has become a virtual recluse, rarely appearing in public and
refusing to give out information about himself or his life. Eglītis
even declined to attend the ceremony awarding the Latvian
Culture Fund's prize in literature to him for the novel *Piecas
dienas* (Five Days).

The strong point of Eglītis' writing is his use of language. He is a
master of modern Latvian and his polished and narrative style
adapts well to translation. Eglītis often uses foreign words for
contrast to achieve a comic effect. This is particularly true in his
later works, where American idiom is used extensively. These
present a considerable problem to the translator, for often the
references are specific and substitutes are difficult to find. For
example, in *Ferdinand and Sybil*, Sybil tells Ferdinand that she is
going to a baby shower. She uses the Latvian phrase *mazbērnina
duša,* which leaves Ferdinand confused, and forces Sybil to switch
to the English "baby shower" to explain. To the Latvian this is a
strong alienating effect which points out the inability of a
complete assimilation into a foreign culture, but in translation
this exchange is lost since the translator is forced to use the word
"shower" throughout.

Eglītis often uses long lists of descriptions of things, places, or people in which he emphasizes rhythm or the repetition of sound. Two of the best examples can be found in "Confirmation of the Cosmos." In one, a city administrator has come to tell Rājums, a character in the play, that, in the interest of his health and to give him time to create and teach, the city council has decided to relieve him of all those duties they felt would hinder his pedagogical and creative work. These duties include:

> ...president of the City Council for the Advancement of Music, district horn music inspector, chairman of the board of the Trumpeters Benevolent Association; director of the Musicians Insurance Fund, president of the Artists' Club, musical consultant for the Festival Association, editor for the sheet music publisher, editor-in-chief of the music journal *Dziesmu Dievs*, and music bureau chief for the periodical *Masu balss*...

And Kēvietis, the mad composer, describes how the musicians should play his unplayable "Confirmation of the Cosmos:"

> Well, it isn't going to be easy. If there are any problems (in collecting the worms, mushrooms, and muskrats that are needed) pump them into huge balloons, like those vacuum cleaners used by chimney-sweeps, and pump them into cisterns. And then at last the cosmos will have been investigated! The last one, the "Confirmation Symphony," is one single colossal grandiose thunderous oratorio, a super cantata, a great hymn to creation and the joy of life—an uninterrupted tutti, forte, fortissimo, presto prestissimo, vivace, alegressimo, crescendo, desperato con fuoco, con bravura!!!

Another use of language is in the names of characters used by Eglītis. Often the names are descriptive of a character, or the sound of the character's name may suggest a quality or image. For example, the French horn player in "Confirmation of the Cosmos" is Zemrĩbo. By dropping the "o" and adding the feminine gender ending "e" to "zem" the word would become *zemerĩb* or "the earth resounds." The name Hillman, translating as it does from the Latvian Kalniņš, is used as an alienation effect and shows the audience the change in the man. And in *Leo* the use of only letter-number designations for the characters (H I, H II, etc.) strips the characters of any personality emphasizing the void within Leo's world.

Unfortunately, while his language is a strong point, Eglītis' natural narrative structure of the prose writer tends to weaken his plays, especially those which are dramatizations from prose works. His tendency is to discuss an idea or conflict rather than reveal it through dramatic action. This makes his plays somewhat static at times and gives them uneven form.

There are noticeable shifts in his structural style and use of words and rhythms approximating Eglītis' shifts in mood and treatment of themes. His texts become shorter and choppier. For example, contrasts can be seen in the speeches of Sybil and the Doll. Sybil's speeches are sharp and abrasive:

> You think too much, Ferdinand. You think about trifles. unnecessary, meaningless trifles. Think about me—Sybil. I am your Sybil. Your Sybil. Speak my name, please! I want to hear you say it. Please say: Sybil, Sybil, Sybil! Please, Ferdinand, please!

....

> No, Ferdinand. I did not tell you. How can you say I told you if I didn't tell you? Alright. You want me to go out with Paul. I'll go. I'll do it for you Ferdinand. Why shouldn't I go out with Paul. If that's what you want?

The Doll, on the other hand, speaks in flowing sentences, expressing gentleness and peace. The best example is her long "Riga" speech. These differences between styles emphasize the contrast between Sybil and the Doll, present and past.

This movement to shorter sentences and usage results in the inarticulate grunts and sounds of the primitives in *Leo*, against which are contrasted Leo's long discourses and explanations. The gray people's attempts at communication and self-expression are hardly better:

> This vessel
> This form
> This room
>   nonroom
>   nonform
>   nonvessel
>
> Period.

It has been said that the concept of tragedy is not possible in modern times because modern language is incapable of articulating it. Though Eglītis' language, at its best, has never pretended to such heights, the changes in it approximate man's loss of his identity and the alienation which makes him incapable of transmitting no more than elementary wants and desires. Language and art are the bastions of a culture, and the destruction of language marks the destruction of culture. As Eglītis perceives the disintegration of culture in exile and the alienation or assimilation of the exile, his own alienation increases and his language has become shorter, choppier, and more inarticulate.

One of the more obvious changes in Eglītis' plays is in their structure. His first plays are long with large casts and great numers of scenes. For example, "Confirmation of the Cosmos" has three acts with six scenes and "The Cloak of Casanova" five acts with sixty-five French scenes. In exile the plays become shorter, especially the original plays. *Through Brandenburg Gate, Ferdinand and Sybil, Please Come In, Sir!*, and *Leo* are usually no more than extended one-acts divided into anything from two to five scenes. Casts are also smaller, ranging from two (*Through Brandenburg Gate*) to seven (*Leo*), attributable both to Eglītis' realization that large casts in exile were impractical for small amateur troupes and his concentration more on the individual problems and essentially one single theme in a play.

Internal changes also are evident. The early plays are written realistically, prescribing a specified time and place. The flow of action is uniform and corresponds to the pattern of exposition, rising action, climax, falling action, resolution. As with language, this pattern and the realistic approach corresponded to Eglītis' society and stability.

In *Through Brandenburg Gate* the first changes in the internal form appear. Two Latvians, working as spies for the West in Berlin, learn that their chief enemy in the NKVD and a former friend in Latvia has been stabbed to death. As the play progresses and the manhunt goes on, it is revealed that Sandra has killed the NKVD agent because he has used the past acquaintances and threats against her father to force her to inform on the spy organization, as well as threaten to tell her husband. As the news from the radio reports progress in the search for the killer, the tension mounts. When there is a knock on the door, Sandra commits suicide. But it is only the landlord. As Walter, Sandra's husband, stands uncomprehending in the room, the radio announces that the search has been called off and the case closed.

The play borders on expressionism, and is a study of fear and the loss of perspective due to uncertainty. As it progresses, the periodic announcements from the radio or telephone calls heighten tension and reveal more and more of the characters' inner selves. Indeed, the characters seem to be puppets tied to strings which the radio controls and the room becomes a cage from which neither can escape.

Until *Ferdinand and Sybil*, though, the changes are few. Eglītis foreshadows the use of the epic elements by the use of American idioms in his plays. Thus, uses of words like *Pelēkais suns* (Gray

Dog) to describe a bus become alienating elements in his plays.

In *Ferdinand and Sybil*, Eglītis makes great use of epic elements to portray the struggle between the past and present. Conflicting images are used for purposes of alienation. The representation of different values is accented by Hillman and Sybil.

> HILLMAN: Standing in the window you'll be helping yourself. All the boys will be able to notice and admire you.
> SYBIL: I can't do it for fifty cents.
> HILLMAN: When I first became a tailor's apprentice, my master only paid me fifteen santīms an hour.

The contrast is using the Latvian coin *santīms* with the American fifty cents makes the audience aware of the differences between their past and present.

The play makes no requirements for a realistic production. Time and place are unimportant—even Hillman's watch has stopped at half past eleven.

This quality of unreality carries over into *Please Come In, Sir!* Though Eglītis includes specific set descriptions, the play does not need them. The play takes place from the perspective of a man's mind as he stands isolated from his environment. His conversations in the real world with his wife Perse and Dancis sharply contrast with his inner reality when talking to the "policeman." What seems to hold the play back is Eglītis' use of a coherent narrative form in the monologues.

In *Leo*, Eglītis turns to the absurd. With its themes of nihilism, lack of communication, isolation, and alienation, the play takes place in a "laboratory." It seems faintly reminiscent of the works of Ionesco and Beckett, until one realizes that Eglītis is rather savagely parodying man's insistence on the negative. To Eglītis man is not out of kilter with the universe. He is out of kilter with himself. Dialogue and communication are no longer possible. The play is purely presentational with Leo lecturing the audience as if the playwright was attempting to translate to the audience the sounds and words of the faceless, anonymous people. Realizing the futility of it all, he leaves the stage.

In the long span of his career Anšlavs Eglītis has witnessed many changes in his world and in the world of his people. He has seen exile destroy that life which he once described as full of beautiful dreams and exhilarating optimism and substitute for it a life in which a foreign environment and the demands of everyday threaten the things he has loved: the Latvian and what the Latvian represents. As his people and their condition have changed, so has Eglītis as a person and artist. These changes are clearly reflected in his plays. The cohesive society of Riga is slowly and surely replaced by the alienated individual in exile. The articulate language disappears into the mumblings of those no longer able to communicate with their surroundings, and the affirmation of self has turned into a search for identity. The struggle of the artist between the realist and moralist inside himself has given his plays an increasing mood of pessimism.

But the fact of change is positive. On the one hand the older generation has clung to the images of the past, which every day become dimmer and more painful. On the other, the younger generations, unfamiliar with the past, have been unable to correlate it to the present. Yet Eglītis has shown that change in exile is not only possible to reflect the exile condition, but that, like Ferdinand, the theatre could through changes in approach and interpretation make the past come alive and give meaning to today.

Juris Valters

Ferdinand and Sybil. Doll: Kery Sims. Sybil: Cindy Sinclair. Ferdinand: Richard Sater. Produced for television by Southern Illinois University Broadcasting Service. Director: Alfreds Straumanis. Scenographer: Meyers Walker. Production supported in part by a grant from the Illinois Humanities Council.

FERDINAND AND SYBIL

A play in four scenes

CHARACTERS

THE DOLL
FERDINAND
SYBIL
MR. HILLMAN
SUPERINTENDENT

SCENE ONE

(*A street, with a display window and a bench. THE DOLL is standing in the window. Soft music can be heard playing in the background. A gong sounds, and THE DOLL COMES TO LIFE. She turns her head and looks in the direction of the bench. THE DOLL freezes again as FERDINAND enters. FERDINAND enters. Searches the stage for the source of the music, stopping finally in front of the window and eyeing THE DOLL suspiciously. After a few moments FERDINAND begins to walk away from the window, quickly looking back several times as if to catch THE DOLL moving. He finally sits on the bench, fidgeting nervously.*)

DOLL (*softly*): Ferdinand! (*FERDINAND is startled, looks at the window, then lowers his head.*)

DOLL: Ferdinand! (*FERDINAND jumps to his feet, goes to the window and stares intently at THE DOLL. After a moment, he leans against the wall by the window and prepares himself for prolonged observation.*)

SYBIL (*enters with small, quick steps, holding a small bouquet of flowers. She speaks rapidly, as if trying to say everything in one breath*): Ferdinand, Ferdinand, Ferdinand, Ferdinand,

Ferdinand, look at me! Look at me, look at me! Please, Ferdinand! (*She stops abruptly and looks down. FERDINAND looks over his shoulder and stares at SYBIL for a moment, then turns back to the window.*) Please! Admire me! Admire me! Admire me! Ferdinand! Please! (*She turns her back to FERDINAND and morosely stares at the ground. In a moment she quickly turns back.*) I am Sybil, Sybil, Sybil! Do you hear me? Your Sybil! I am here! Your girl Sybil—Sybil Maddock from Twenty-fourth Avenue! (*She throws down the flowers and thinks for a moment, looking down. She suddenly grabs FERDINAND'S arm.*) Well, let's go! (*Begins pulling him.*)

FERDINAND (*rudely pulling away*): I'm not going anywhere!

SYBIL: Oh. All right. Let's sit on this bench. (*Pulls FERDINAND over to the bench. FERDINAND unwillingly follows her and sits down.*) Sit here beside me. Closer. There. Now look at me. (*They both look at each other for a moment. FERDINAND turns away and stares at the ground. SYBIL jumps up and peers at the spot FERDINAND is looking at.*) What are you looking at? (*She stoops forward and then withdraws, as if to gain the proper perspective.*)

FERDINAND (*looking down*): Nothing.

SYBIL: Why are you looking at nothing? (*Kneels in front of him.*) Look at me, Ferdinand. Look at me, look at me. (*FERDINAND raises his head and looks at her.*) Not like that! You don't even see me. You're looking right through me! (*She sits down on the bench.*) Look at me directly. Be aggressive. Please, Ferdinand. At least, hold my hand.

FERDINAND (*takes her extended hand and looks at it*): A hand.

SYBIL: Correct. That is a hand, Ferdinand. That is my hand. (*Jumps to her feet.*) You think too much, Ferdinand. You think about trifles. Unnecessary, meaningless trifles. Think about me—Sybil. I am your Sybil. Your Sybil. Speak my name, please! I want to hear you say it. Please say: Sybil, Sybil, Sybil! Please Ferdinand, please! (*FERDINAND peevishly turns away. SYBIL sits still for a moment, then runs up to the windows and begins adjusting her clothes, using the window for a mirror.*)

FERDINAND (*raises his head*): Do you like her?

SYBIL: Her? What her? No, I'm admiring myself.

FERDINAND (*stands up and goes to the window. He leans against the wall and peers at THE DOLL. Soft music is heard.*) Do you hear music?

SYBIL: No, I can't hear anything. (*The music becomes louder.*)

FERDINAND: Listen! You can hear it now, can't you?

SYBIL: No, I can't. (*Listens.*) No, I can't hear anything. Well, let's go Ferdinand. This place bores me. (*She begins pulling FERDINAND by the arm.*)

FERDINAND: I'm not going! (*Pulls away.*)

SYBIL: Then I'll go by myself. Goodbye, Ferdinand. (*She kisses him on the cheek and begins to exit. She stops and stares at the ground intently. Then she turns around. Emphatically.*) Goodbye, Ferdinand! (*She turns away and again stares at the ground.*)

FERDINAND (*glancing back*): Goodbye. (*Turns back to the window.*)

SYBIL (*stands quietly for a moment, then turns and comes back*): Ferdinand, do you remember when we met for the first time? You told me something about Marie Antoinette. Was it all true? I mean, what you told me?

FERDINAND: No.

SYBIL: Why did you tell me those things if they weren't true? Tell me, why?

FERDINAND: I don't know.

SYBIL: Do you still think constantly? About her?

FERDINAND: Oh, I don't know.

SYBIL: You said her head was chopped off. Did you see her head chopped off? Look at me, Ferdinand. Do you think my head could get chopped off? (*Thoughtfully.*) My head.

FERDINAND (*takes her chin, looks at her intently, then indifferently looks away*): No, not anymore.

SYBIL: But back then.

FERDINAND: Probably not then either.

SYBIL (*puts her hands behind her back and looks at the ground. Suddenly she dashes to the bench, picks up her purse and digs around in it for a few moments. With determination*): Look at this, Ferdinand!

FERDINAND (*examines the object carefully*): A drinking straw.

SYBIL: You gave it to me, Ferdinand. It's from your soda glass. It was that time you were drinking a soda and I was eating strawberry ice cream. You know I don't like soda. I asked you if I could keep the straw, and you gave it to me. It was when you talked about Marie Antoinette.

FERDINAND (*during SYBIL'S speech he has been casually looking up at the sky*): I don't remember.

SYBIL: Oh, it broke, Ferdinand! I could just cry! Look! (*She throws the straw away.*) Well, let's go. (*She begins to pull*

FERDINAND by the arm.)

FERDINAND: I'm not going. Go by yourself.

SYBIL: I shouldn't have come, Ferdinand. I know I shouldn't have. But I wanted you to look at me. To admire me.

FERDINAND: You couldn't not come, because I was waiting for you, Sybil.

SYBIL: Why do you choose this bench, Ferdinand?

FERDINAND: I don't know.

SYBIL *(stares at the ground, then starts rummaging through her purse. She takes out a button and hands it to FERDINAND)*: Do you remember this, Ferdinand?

FERDINAND *(takes the button and examines it carefully, turning it over with his fingers, peering at it)*: A button.

SYBIL *(takes the button away from him)*: It's from your blue suit. *(FERDINAND examines his sleeves and front of his coat.)* From your Sunday suit. Remember, that time by the hamburger stand.

FERDINAND: Now I remember. I lost a button. We both searched for it.

SYBIL: I found it and didn't give it to you.

FERDINAND *(solemnly)*: Why didn't you give back my button?

SYBIL: I saved it.

FERDINAND: I was forced to sew on a button that didn't match. Why did you hide it?

SYBIL: I just did. I wanted to keep it. But you can have it back now.

FERDINAND: I don't have that blue suit anymore. I threw it away. It was worn out.

SYBIL: Here, take it *(Gives him the button.)* The straw, too. *(She kicks the straw in FERDINAND'S direction.)*

FERDINAND *(takes the button and holds it in the palm of his hand)*: That's right. Now I remember. I had a soda, you had ice cream.

SYBIL: Do you remember what we talked about? You made a promise to me, Ferdinand.

FERDINAND: I don't remember. What did I promise you?

SYBIL: You promised to be somebody.... You have forgotten. You promised to be somebody special. For my sake.

FERDINAND *(flips the button into the air, catches it, turns his back on SYBIL, and starts to go. Stops)*: Maybe I wanted to then. Not anymore.

SYBIL: I knew it, Ferdinand. I'm glad I'm not saving that straw anymore. *(She steps on the straw. Then she kneels down and tries to straighten it. Morosely.*) I stepped on it, Ferdinand. I've completely destroyed it. And I saved it for so long.

FERDINAND (*over his shoulder*): Nonsense. Foolishness. (*He turns his attention to the window.*)

SYBIL: Oh, I could cry, Ferdinand. I had been saving it for so long and now I have destroyed it. (*She sits on the ground, gloomily drawing squares. She suddenly jumps up, finishes drawing the squares in a pattern. She begins playing hopscotch.*) Look, Ferdinand. I like playing hopscotch, Ferdinand.

FERDINAND: Stupid game.

SYBIL: True, very stupid. You used to like it once. Look, I can jump with my eyes closed. Forewards. Backwards. Now sideways. (*She jumps for a while, then collapses on the bench.*) I'm exhausted. (*She rests for a moment.*) Ferdinand, if she had remained alive, would there still have been a revolution?

FERDINAND: Who's she?

SYBIL: Marie Antoinette.

FERDINAND: The revolution had already started.

SYBIL (*peevishly*): You didn't tell me they chopped her head off after the revolution had started, Ferdinand.

FERDINAND: I don't remember. Maybe I didn't tell you.

SYBIL: I didn't know that, Ferdinand. I thought the revolution started because her head was chopped off.

FERDINAND: You are a nit-wit, Sybil.

SYBIL (*sits on the bench silently, holding her knees*): Ferdinand, do you like tamales? I think they're simply divine. You didn't answer me, Ferdinand. Do you like tamales? I just love them with garlic.

FERDINAND: I can't stand garlic.

SYBIL: Ferdinand! And I always thought when we got married we would eat tamales for breakfast everyday.

FERDINAND (*shrugs*): Stupid idea.

SYBIL: Very stupid. Oh, I almost forgot. (*Jumps up.*) Friday night we are invited to a party at Nancy's.

FERDINAND: To a kid's party?

SYBIL: No, to an adult party. Nancy will soon be thirteen. She's had a lot of parties. Nancy is very social. Last Saturday she had a shower for Kathy.

FERDINAND: A shower?

SYBIL: Well, of course. A shower. A baby shower. You know, when people get together and bring gifts for the coming baby. Nancy's also engaged already. Ferdinand, are we engaged? What do you think?

FERDINAND: I don't know.

SYBIL: Do you still wear that little amber elephant? I gave it to you, remember? On a thin silver chain. You used to wear it around your neck. Do you still wear it? Do you still have it? (*She runs up to FERDINAND, and tries to stick her hand down his neck, at the same time lifting his sweater.*) Tell me, please, I want to see. Tell me the truth—do you still have it?

FERDINAND: No.

SYBIL: Did you throw it away?

FERDINAND: I don't know. I don't have it anymore.

SYBIL: Tell me, did you throw it away on purpose? Maybe you lost it? Accidentally. The chain was very thin. It could have easily broken.

FERDINAND: I don't know. Maybe it did break.

SYBIL: Please, Ferdinand, tell me the truth. Did you throw it away or did you lose it? I won't be mad. Please tell me the truth. (*Pause.*) It really was stupid to wear it around your neck. Truly childish. Very childish. It's good that you threw it away.

FERDINAND (*looking up at the sky*): Now I remember. I was swimming in the ocean. The waves were really big. When I came out of the water and lay down on the beach there was nothing around my neck. I remember—the waves broke the chain.

SYBIL: Ferdinand, please do something for me. For my sake.

FERDINAND: What do you want me to do for your sake?

SYBIL (*looking, she turns around a few times. Then she picks up the button and throws it into the furthest square*): Pick up that button. Pick it up, please. Please. Well, look, I'll do it. (*She picks it up.*) Now, close your eyes and jump hopscotch backwards. (*She does it herself.*) And then...and then...this button ...and then give me this button. And then we'll start the game over.

FERDINAND: Childish.

SYBIL: Yes, it is childish, really. Well, then do something else. (*Looks around for something.*) Break...break that show window. And...steal that silly doll.

FERDINAND (*comes alive*): That's not a bad idea. I wouldn't mind owning this doll of Mr. Hillman's.

SYBIL: You're not planning on opening a clothing store, are you, Ferdinand? You promised to be more important than that.

FERDINAND: But you wanted me to steal it.

SYBIL: I wanted you to steal it for my sake. Don't you understand, Ferdinand? For me!

FERDINAND: And then what would we do with it?

SYBIL: Throw it away. Put it in the garbage can around the
corner. We don't need that doll, Ferdinand. All you have to do
is steal it. You have to do something just for me.

FERDINAND: No, I don't want to do that. It wouldn't be right.

SYBIL (*looks at the ground, digging at it with her toes. Then she
grabs FERDINAND by the arm*): Let's go now, please,
Ferdinand. It's so boring here. I'll just die if I have to stay here
six more seconds.

FERDINAND (*carelessly*): Where do you want to go?

SYBIL: Where something's happening.

FERDINAND: You go ahead. I'm not going.

SYBIL: Very well. I'll go. Good-bye, Ferdinand. (*Goes. Then she
turns around and kisses FERDINAND on the cheek. Again
begins to leave, stops, stands with her head bowed. She turns
and comes back.*) Ferdinand, do you remember Paul McRea?
The boy we met at the ball park?

FERDINAND: I remember him.

SYBIL: Didn't he seem like a neat, good-looking guy?

FERDINAND: I guess so.

SYBIL: Well, he wants me to go steady with him. (*FERDINAND
shrugs his shoulders.*) Do you know what I told him? I told him
I was already going with you.

FERDINAND: You shouldn't have told him that.

SYBIL: But it's the truth, Ferdinand. Did you want me to lie to
him? Tell me, Ferdinand, did you really want me to lie?

FERDINAND (*uncomfortably*): No.

SYBIL (*walks around then turns to FERDINAND*): I probably
didn't tell you that I'm going out with Paul tonight.

FERDINAND: You told me.

SYBIL: No, Ferdinand. I did not tell you. How can you say I told
you if I didn't tell you? Alright. You want me to go out with
Paul. I'll go. I'll do it for you, Ferdinand. Why shouldn't I go
out with Paul, if that's what you want? (*FERDINAND shrugs
his shoulders.*) Ferdinand, do you believe in self-suggestion?
I mean, do you believe that a person can swear to something
that has not happened?

FERDINAND: I believe it.

SYBIL: For example, when I was just telling you about Paul, I
actually started believing that I had promised to go out with
him tonight. And if I keep myself in a state of self-suggestion,
it might even happen. What would psycho-analysis have to say

about that?

FERDINAND: I don't know.

SYBIL: I don't think psycho-analysis could help me.

FERDINAND: I don't either.

SYBIL (*lovingly takes FERDINAND by the arm*): Let's go, Ferdinand, please. Please!

FERDINAND (*shakes her off*): Go by yourself.

SYBIL (*sharply*): It could happen, Ferdinand, that this time I won't come back. It could just happen that I suggest myself right into accepting Paul McRea's proposal. He asked me to go to the baseball game in the afternoon, and then to dinner at the country club. If you want me to go, I'll go.

FERDINAND: Go.

SYBIL: Good-bye, Ferdinand. Good-bye. (*She doesn't go.*)

FERDINAND (*explodes and screams at her*): Well, go then!

SYBIL: Alright! I'm going! But this time I'm not coming back. I'm leaving for good. (*Begins to leave, runs back and kisses FERDINAND on the cheek.*) Good-bye. (*Exits.*)

FERDINAND (*looks after SYBIL. Follows her for a few steps, stops, then turns back. He picks up the bouquet of flowers SYBIL has dropped. The lights dim as the music is heard. THE DOLL Stirs and stretches out her hand.*)

DOLL: Ferdinand! (*FERDINAND turns to the window.*)

CURTAIN

SCENE TWO

(*Late at night. The stage is dark and shadowy, but the show window is brightly lit. HILLMAN is dressing THE DOLL. He moves her joints and adjusts the drape of the clothes. After a few moments he leaves the window, reappears outside and for a few moments looks at the window. He ducks around back into the window and goes back to work. THE DOLL, moved out of position, suddenly tips over against the wall.*)

HILLMAN: Eh! Damn it! Messed up again! (*He begins to straighten THE DOLL up, but she tips over further. HILLMAN covers the window with a curtain. FERDINAND enters and goes to the window. He tries to see through the curtain, stands still for a moment, and leaves.*)

SYBIL (*runs in; searches the stage. She runs to the window, first standing on her toes, then kneeling, trying to see into the window. HILLMAN'S head appears above the curtain, startling SYBIL):* Oh! It's you, Mr. Hillman. You scared me. *(She stands up, smoothes her clothes, and approaches the window again. Formally.)* Good evening, Mr. Hillman. How are you? *(HILLMAN acknowledges her greeting with his fingers. After a few moments, much to the impatience of SYBIL, he unhooks the curtain, revealing an empty window.)* It's a beautiful evening tonight, Mr. Hillman. You wouldn't, by any chance, have seen Ferdinand, would you? He usually doesn't come here at this time of night, but during the day he often sits on this bench.

HILLMAN: If he isn't sitting on it, then he isn't here.

SYBIL: I can see that he isn't here, Mr. Hillman. What time does your watch say?

HILLMAN: Eleven-thirty, and children should be in bed by this time.

SYBIL *(looks at her watch)*: Mine only says...mine is only quarter to eleven. I really wish I was in bed. But I've got problems, Mr. Hillman. *(She puts her hands behind her back and paces around the stage.)*

HILLMAN: Well, who doesn't?

SYBIL: I'll tell you something honestly, Mr. Hillman. I'm not really interested in this Ferdinand. I just come here because I have nothing better to do. Of course, I could go somewhere else, but it's too much bother.

HILLMAN: Hmmm!

SYBIL: I could go with any number of boys who are much more interesting than Ferdinand, but I don't want to start all over again. That would be boring, wouldn't it, Mr. Hillman?

HILLMAN: Depends on how you look at it.

SYBIL: One doesn't want to give it up after investing all that time and effort. Right?

HILLMAN: Hmmm!

SYBIL: Boys demand so much patience, Mr. Hillman. Why, it takes a whole month before you get them to a point where they can hold an intelligent conversation. Just getting to know them is not a simple matter. You must get introduced officially according to the rules of etiquette. That helps to establish mutual respect and things are much easier from there on. Ferdinand and I met altogether too casually. I think that's our main problem. We met at the drive-in. Nobody introduced us. We just started talking to each other, and that wasn't good.

Boys are very demanding, Mr. Hillman. In fact, they don't even know what they want. Girls have it much better in other countries. India, for example. There, children are married right after they're born. Sometimes even before. Then everyone can live peacefully, without worries. You don't have to look for anything, you don't have to force yourself on anybody. You're not always fighting with your girlfriends. And you always have time to do other things. (*She notices that HILLMAN has left the window and come outside.*) The Indians know how to live, Mr. Hillman. The Indians are very smart people.

HILLMAN: They can't be all that smart. They haven't changed their style in clothing in a thousand years.

SYBIL: All you can think of is clothes, Mr. Hillman. I'm thinking about boys. The boys today are very immature.

HILLMAN: Immature? I don't think so. They're very cunning. (*Sits on the bench.*)

SYBIL: That's the same thing, Mr. Hillman. All children are cunning. All they can think of is how to avoid responsibility. Boys, too. You should know that, Mr. Hillman. You used to be a boy, didn't you?

HILLMAN: A boy!? Yes, I was. Even I was a boy once. That was a long time ago. Even before Vienna. I was living in Riga and learning to be a tailor.

SYBIL: How did your wife put up with you?

HILLMAN: Things were different then. Back then boys put up with girls, not vice versa.

SYBIL: That's what I mean, Mr. Hillman. It's such a waste of time to pretend that boys put up with girls, and not the other way around.

HILLMAN: Foolishness! No one had to put up with me!

SYBIL: But your wife married you, didn't she?

HILLMAN: Of course she married me. But that was what I wanted! Are you trying to tell me I have been gulled?

SYBIL: Why gulled? What would you have done all alone?

HILLMAN (*jumping to his feet*): I would be free!

SYBIL: What would you have done with all your freedom?

HILLMAN: I don't know. I don't have time to talk to you. (*He goes inside and reappears in the window.*)

SYBIL (*she paces around the stage for a moment*): I'm not bothering you, am I Mr. Hillman? There isn't anybody here to talk to. (*Politely.*) You're decorating your window, aren't you?

HILLMAN (*rudely*): Correct, I'm decorating.

SYBIL (*needling*): I don't like your dress doll.

HILLMAN: She's an old, precious doll.

SYBIL: Why did you take your precious doll out of the window?

HILLMAN: I'm fixing it. Her leg is broken. (*He shows SYBIL THE DOLL'S leg.*)

SYBIL: What an ugly leg. (*She looks at her leg and compares it to THE DOLL'S.*) In this country it doesn't pay to fix old things. It's much better to buy something new.

HILLMAN: Oh, no. I wouldn't trade this doll for ten new ones. She has too much sentimental value. I inherited her from my master. That's when I was living in Riga and went by the name of Kalnins.* My master had inherited the doll from his grandfather who learned the tailor's trade at the royal court in Vienna!

SYBIL: Such a terribly old doll. If it was alive it would have terrible wrinkles.

HILLMAN: Dolls are different. I was just a young fellow when I got her. Just like Ferdinand. Now I'm old, but the doll is just as young as she was then. Dolls and the world stand still. It's just man who grows old.

SYBIL: Would you rather stand still, and let the world grow old?

HILLMAN: I don't know. It wouldn't be any fun living in an old world, either.

SYBIL: You know, Mr. Hillman, sometimes it isn't any fun living when a person and the world are young.

HILLMAN: Foolishness. You'll get over it.

SYBIL (*silent for a moment*): I don't like your doll's hair do.

HILLMAN: That's good European hair. It isn't some cheap synthetic.

SYBIL: What good is European hair? I notice your doll's head is on crooked.

HILLMAN: It's damaged.

SYBIL (*silent for a moment*): If Marie Antoinette was alive, would she be as old as your doll?

HILLMAN (*figuring*): Wait a minute, let's see. The French Revolution. The Napoleonic Wars. Franz Josef...I'm seventy; no, not quite—sixty-nine. My master would be one hundred and fifteen. His father would be one hundred and forty-five, his father one hundred and seventy...Yes, Marie Antoinette could be this old.

SYBIL: Marie Antoinette was from Vienna too, wasn't she, Mr. Hillman? Just like the doll.

*In Latvian, "Kalnins" means "Hill."

HILLMAN: Everybody knows Marie Antoinette was from Vienna. She emigrated to France just like I emigrated to America.

SYBIL (*pretending she's balancing on a rail*): What kind of a woman was Marie Antoinette, do you think?

HILLMAN: She wasn't a woman. She was a ruler.

SYBIL (*balancing*): She didn't rule by herself, did she?

HILLMAN: Of course not. She sat on the throne next to her husband.

SYBIL (*jumps off the "rail"*): Is it true that she was a frivolous woman, but very courageous when they chopped her head off?

HILLMAN: Frivolity demands courage, too.

SYBIL: I don't have any courage, but I can be very frivolous. If I wasn't frivolous I wouldn't waste my time on Ferdinand. (*HILLMAN Comes out of the window with bolts of cloth and starts matching colors.*) Can I help you?

HILLMAN: Sure, sure. (*Gives her a cloth.*)

SYBIL (*by the window, handling the cloth. She hides behind it and then reappears*): Do you think you knew your wife completely?

HILLMAN: Of course I did.

SYBIL: You didn't know anything. What can one know about another person?

HILLMAN: It's not quite like that.

SYBIL: It is, Mr. Hillman. It's just that no one wants to admit their ignorance. What did you know about your wife Hermeline when you married her?

HILLMAN: Everything.

SYBIL: Excuse me, Mr. Hillman, but an assertion like that is immature. Mr. Hillman, do you know what you want?

HILLMAN: Of course I do.

SYBIL: No, you don't. You sit wherever circumstance seats you.

HILLMAN: I have planned my life down to the smallest detail.

SYBIL: (*rolling up the cloth*): It may be cruel of me to shatter your illusions, Mr. Hillman, but life is cruel and one has to accept that. If you own a clothing store right now, it's not that you chose to. You are only tolerating the situation.

HILLMAN: Oh, no!

SYBIL: What else can you say, Mr. Hillman? You see, Mr. Hillman, if I hadn't met Ferdinand accidentally at the drive-in, I would have been spared all this worry. In another place, at another time, I could have met another, more sensible boy, and I wouldn't have to go through all this suffering. But since circumstance made me meet Ferdinand, I have to suffer with him. And I keep telling myself that this is my choice.

HILLMAN: When I met Hermeline, I certainly didn't think I was going to meet anything better at a different time in a different place.

SYBIL: Self-suggestion, Mr. Hillman! That's definitely self-suggestion. And also laziness.

HILLMAN: And I think it was fate!

SYBIL: Lazy people always use fate as an excuse, Mr. Hillman. If I don't get rid of this Ferdinand for another boy, then it is definitely laziness. I don't want to start all over.

HILLMAN: So you think Hermeline stayed with me because of laziness?

SYBIL: Certainly, Mr. Hillman. Maybe because of the presents, too. Presents have a great importance in one's life. I just can't seem to force Ferdinand to give me a valuable present. If a boy gives a girl a present, then it could happen that he'll stay with the girl for the sake of the present, and not for the sake of the girl. The problem is getting the boy to give something valuable.

HILLMAN: That's not true. Hermeline gave me presents. She gave me her deceased father's gold watch.

SYBIL: And after that she never left you. Right, Mr. Hillman? She really never left that watch, and that's why she married you.

HILLMAN: Hermeline would have married me without help from the watch.

SYBIL: I don't believe that, Mr. Hillman. That present had a greater significance than you realize. I really wish Ferdinand would give me something, but he doesn't have any money.

HILLMAN: Then give him something.

SYBIL: No. That wouldn't mean anything. I'm around him too much as it is. Sometimes I think I should hide some money and let him find it. Then he could buy me a present. But I'm not sure he would do that. How do you look at events that are one hundred and fifty years old, Mr. Hillman?

HILLMAN: I look at them as things that have happened.

SYBIL: Well, see, what's there to worry one's self about? It isn't worth it, right? Only Ferdinand doesn't think so.

HILLMAN: Foolishness. (*He takes out a sprayer and a rag and begins cleaning the window.*)

SYBIL (*watches HILLMAN's slow movements for a moment, takes the sprayer and rag out of HILLMAN'S hands, and energetically polishes the window. Finishing the big window, she polishes the two small side windows, too. Notices a black spot*

on the big window; busily scrapes it off with her fingernail.
When she is done, they both step back and admire the windows
with satisfaction. SYBIL gives HILLMAN the sprayer and rag
and wipes her hands): I'll be going now, Mr. Hillman. Thank
you for all the good advice. It's so nice to chat with an intelligent person. I'll come again some night. I certainly hope I
didn't disturb you. Good-bye Mr. Hillman. (*Begins to leave.*)

HILLMAN: So long.

SYBIL (*hesitates; turns around*): If you see Ferdinand, don't tell
him I was here. It doesn't mean anything anymore. Maybe we
really will separate. There is another boy I know. I hope I don't
have any difficulties with him. Only I like him less than
Ferdinand. Do you think that's wrong, Mr. Hillman?

HILLMAN: It depends.

SYBIL: That's right. Good-bye, Mr. Hillman. Farewell. (*Begins*
to go, but turns around again.) Mr. Hillman, do you think it's
important to express oneself?

HILLMAN: Yes and no. Some people can't get along without
prattling.

SYBIL: You don't understand, Mr. Hillman. I don't mean talking.

HILLMAN: What then?

SYBIL: You see, Mr. Hillman, a person can express himself in
many ways. For example, a person can express himself by
sitting calmly on the bench and staring at one point. Or by digging the asphalt with a toe, (*Digs.*), or, let's say, looking at
the doll.

HILLMAN: This expressing oneself without talking I don't understand.

SYBIL: To tell the truth, I don't really understand it myself. But
if I ever hope to get along with Ferdinand at all, then I have
to respect this form of expression.

HILLMAN: Well, respect it.

SYBIL: That would be imitation, Mr. Hillman. One can only express oneself from what's in him. Subconsciously.

HILLMAN: Alright. While Ferdinand pokes holes in the asphalt
with his toe, you can sit on the bench and stare at a point. Or
vice versa.

SYBIL: That's not a bad idea, Mr. Hillman. But Ferdinand
doesn't like it when I express myself. He thinks it's enough if I
admire him while he expresses himself.

HILLMAN: Admire him, then!

SYBIL: Do you think a girl always has to admire a boy expressing himself; Couldn't it be the other way around sometimes?

HILLMAN: Why not? It all depends on who gets the upper hand.

SYBIL: How? With brutality, you think?

HILLMAN: First you could try diplomacy.

SYBIL: Oh, no, Mr. Hillman. Those are old-fashioned methods. Expression has to be quick and inevitable. I've often thought about that. If I ever express myself in an unexpected action, then it will be brutal. You know, Mr. Hillman, sometimes I just want to fight. But then Ferdinand and I would break up for good. And I don't want that.

HILLMAN: Well, then don't express yourself.

SYBIL: Thank you, Mr. Hillman! That's good advice. What time is it?

HILLMAN: Eleven-thirty.

SYBIL: I'll be going now. (*Begins to leave, stops, comes back, loudly. HILLMAN winces.*) When you were going with your Hermeline, did you ever philosophize? About what kind of ideas?

HILLMAN: Oh, yeah. About money, about stores. Clothes, too.

SYBIL: That's not refined. Mr. Hillman. Boys don't like it if you talk about money. Ferdinand thinks that career people are an old-fashioned, pitiful race of people. You see, Mr. Hillman, I went out with Paul McRea tonight. In many ways he's better than Ferdinand. But he's so boring. Ferdinand is boring, too, but it's easier to take. How can I tell which is the real one?

HILLMAN: Wait. Time will tell.

SYBIL: If I were fifteen, maybe I could wait. But I'm going to be seventeen soon, and then eighteen, and then I'll be just about finished.

HILLMAN (*motions with his hands and shrugs*): Hm!

SYBIL: What's your opinion on split personalities, Mr. Hillman? (*Pause.*) None. Actually, I don't have any either. You see, I have a strong suspicion Ferdinand is a split personality. Sometimes he doesn't even hear me when I'm talking. Believe it or not, Mr. Hillman, he hears but doesn't listen to a thing I'm saying. Do you think psychoanalysis would help him? You don't? I don't either. There are some people no amount of analysis would help. Wouldn't you admit, Mr. Hillman, that Ferdinand might have a mental block? You doubt it. I doubt it, too…It's really late. I'll be going now. It was nice talking to you. Thank you for all your good advice. (*Begins to leave; comes back.*) If you meet Ferdinand, give him my greetings. It could be we'll never see each other again. (*Loudly.*) I won't come here again.

Farewell, Mr. Hillman. (*Exits. HILLMAN turns off the lights in the window. The stage is immersed in darkness. HILLMAN comes out of the window, and slowly crosses the stage. FERDINAND enters and slowly crosses to meet HILLMAN. They meet in the middle of the stage.*)

FERDINAND: Sybil?

HILLMAN: Eh?

FERDINAND: Sybil?

HILLMAN: She left.

CURTAIN

SCENE THREE

(*Evening light covers the stage. Soft music is playing. FERDINAND is leaning against the post and staring at THE DOLL. They are both still. SYBIL runs on. FERDINAND hides behind the post. SYBIL looks around the stage and runs off. The music grows louder. FERDINAND returns to his old spot. After a moment, THE DOLL moves and smiles.*)

FERDINAND: I like it when you smile. Smile some more. Please smile. I knew you had a soul. I've known for a long time.

DOLL (*speaking slowly, mechanically*): I do not have a soul. I am a dress doll.

FERDINAND: See, you even talk. Talk some more. I like your voice.

DOLL: My voice is lifeless. Without emotion.

FERDINAND: I like it. I like you more than people. I like you more than that girl, Sybil. You are beautiful. Why are you so serious? Speak some more.

DOLL: I have no thoughts, I am a doll.

FERDINAND: As if people did. Do you think Sybil has any thoughts? I doubt it. And if she does, they're so absurd they're not worth hearing.

DOLL: But still you came here to meet Sybil.

FERDINAND: No. Not at all. I deliberately avoided her. I like it when she isn't here.

DOLL: Why did you come here?

FERDINAND: To look at you.

DOLL: You are not telling the truth, Ferdinand. You hoped to meet Sybil.

FERDINAND: No, I did not. Honest. I'm glad she didn't see me. What's your name?

DOLL: Julie. They used to call me Anna Marie Louise. When I was brought to this country I was named Julie.

FERDINAND: Julie. Julie. Julie. Anna Marie Louise. Anna Marie Louise. I like Anna Marie Louise better. Do you have a last name, like people? I'm called Ferdinand Vejkalns.

DOLL: No, I do not have a surname. Mr. Hillman only calls me by my first name. Why do you always look at me?

FERDINAND: You sound wonderful. Julie. Can you feel how you sound?

DOLL: I feel it, Ferdinand.

FERDINAND: See, and Sybil couldn't feel it. You are uncommonly beautiful. Much more beautiful than people.

DOLL: I am an object. How can I be more beautiful than people. I am a worthless thing.

FERDINAND: People are inferior in many ways. They only seem superior. Superior things are more beautiful than inferior people.

DOLL: Do you think, Ferdinand, that a dress doll can be more precious than a live girl?

FERDINAND: I don't know. I've though a lot about that. I always think about that when I look at you, Julie, People are petty, selfish and quarrelsome. From your window you gaze out over them, play your music, and smile.

DOLL: I too am selfish and quarrelsome. Mr. Hillman put an ugly dress on me yesterday. I dropped it. He put it back on, and I dropped it again. I wanted you to like me, Ferdinand. I am a capricious and selfish thing.

FERDINAND: You are wonderful, Julie. Giving beauty to someone is not a selfish thing. (*Pause.*) Why do you wear that—?

DOLL: To cover the crack. On the neck.

FERDINAND: What crack, Julie? I don't understand what you're saying.

DOLL: My head was broken off, Ferdinand. I am a ruined dress doll.

FERDINAND (*emphatically*): Oh, Julie!

DOLL (*testing*): Now you will not like me anymore, Ferdinand?

FERDINAND: I like you, Julie. Now I like you even more. I like damaged things. I'm a bit damaged myself.

DOLL: And I was afraid you would not like me.

FERDINAND: Oh, I like you very much!

DOLL: I also have a broken leg. Mr. Hillman glued it.

FERDINAND: I hate Mr. Hillman. He has done you much harm. Oh, Julie, you are a long-suffering doll.

DOLL: It is good. When I was damaged, I acquired feelings. Just like a human being. When Mr. Hillman broke my head, I was able to move it. I was able to look at the people and things around me. I looked to the right and to the left. Until then I could only look straight ahead. My world grew wider and more beautiful. And one day I saw you and Sybil. There, on that bench. And while I was turning my head, I began to think. I thought about you and Sybil. At first I thought about you both. Then I thought more about you, Ferdinand. I don't think about Sybil anymore.

FERDINAND: I don't either. You are much more beautiful than Sybil. Much more human. You remind me of a mystic image I have known for a long time. Maybe even before my birth.

DOLL: Marie Antoinette?

FERDINAND: I don't know. Maybe those were terrible people who chopped off Marie Antoinette's head. Deliberately. Mr. Hillman knocked your head off accidentally. Tell me something about yourself, Julie.

DOLL: I was born in Vienna. I am very old. Mr. Hillman inherited me from his master, who in turn inherited me from his grandfather, who was the court tailor.

FERDINAND: I already know that story, Julie.

DOLL: I am happy that I have a broken head. Just like her, Marie Antoinette. I often think about that. Then I am joyful and excited, and I wait for you to come to my window. Even yesterday I was waiting, but you never came. Then I cried a little. It was after Sybil left and Mr. Hillman turned off the lights. I was surprised at myself, that I could cry. I couldn't before. I waited for you, Ferdinand.

FERDINAND: I sensed that you were waiting for me.

DOLL: Why didn't you come yesterday?

FERDINAND: Now I will come. Every day.

DOLL: You will not come, Ferdinand. You will go away with Sybil.

FERDINAND: I will come. I promise you, Julie. Honestly, I will come.

DOLL: Tonight you will go with Sybil. She doesn't like Paul. She wants to go out with you.

FERDINAND: Sybil wants to but I don't. Sybil only thinks about herself. She doesn't understand me.

DOLL: Maybe you don't understand her?

FERDINAND: I don't know. Maybe. (*Pause.*) I have an unhappy
  character, Julie. That's because I had an unhappy childhood.
  I didn't understand my parents. They spoke Latvian, I spoke
  English. I left home and met Sybil. Even Sybil doesn't under-
  stand me. Then I discovered Marie Antoinette. I found her by
  accident. I didn't look for her. Honest, I didn't look for her.
DOLL: Maybe she found you, Ferdinand?
FERDINAND: I don't know. One evening she sat down beside me,
  on this bench. We talked. I spoke and she answered. You don't
  believe me.
DOLL: I believe you.
FERDINAND: We talked about her head, and the revolution, and
  all the rest. And then we were sitting on the palace steps at
  Versailles eating popcorn. You don't believe me, Julie.
DOLL: I believe you, Ferdinand.
FERDINAND: Later we ran by the fountains and threw nickles
  and dimes for good luck. There were thousands of fountains.
  They sprayed water in all colors of the rainbow. We ran from
  fountain to fountain, until I ran out of nickles. I grabbed a handful of pebbles and threw them into the fountain. Then I heard
  someone cough behind me. I looked and there stood King Louis.
  He shook his finger at me, and was angry because I threw pebbles into his fountain. I explained to him: Sir, I ran out of
  nickles and dimes. But Marie Antoinette just smiled and didn't
  say a word. Then she grabbed me by the hand, and we ran on.
  We ran right to the top of the Rockefeller Center and threw
  down peanut shells. You don't believe me, Julie.
DOLL: I believe you, Ferdinand.
FERDINAND: And finally, at my father's house in Zemgale, I
  shot out Danton's eye with a slingshot and bashed in Robespierre's head with a fence post. And Marie Antoinette
  watched me fight. She sat on a huge rock in front of the granary drinking Coke. Then I sat down beside her and we both
  drank. Then I offered her a cigarette. You don't believe me. I
  can see you don't believe me. You think I'm lying.
DOLL: I believe you, Ferdinand, I believe you.
FERDINAND: We'll see. Sybil didn't believe me. That depressed
  me. Sybil, for whom I left my parents, didn't believe me. She
  didn't understand me.
DOLL: You didn't understand her either.
FERDINAND: Her? No, there's nothing there not to understand.
  Sybil is so simple it's impossible not to understand her. She is
  so painfully understandable I could cry. I compared her with

you yesterday, Julie, and suddenly I had doubts. Maybe she is a dress doll and you are a living girl?

DOLL: I am not a living girl. I am a damaged thing.

FERDINAND: I'll buy you Julie. Along with Mr. Hillman's entire damned store!

DOLL: Do you want to sell clothes, Ferdinand?

FERDINAND: No. I'll dress you up and keep you in the window for my pleasure.

DOLL: I enjoy having people look at me. I like to look out my window at the people. At you, at Sybil, at Mr. Hillman. I am different to each person. I remind you of Marie Antoinette, Mr. Hillman of Hermeline, Sybil of a broken dress doll with European hair.

FERDINAND: Oh, Sybil. She can't see beauty.

DOLL: If one cannot see what's beautiful, one also cannot see what's ugly. It's easier that way.

FERDINAND: How can one not see ugliness? I would cry if you became ugly. (*Pause.*) Julie, I'm going to talk to Mr. Hillman. I want to buy you.

DOLL: Don't be hasty, Ferdinand. I'll be right here. I'll stand right here, perhaps for many more years.

FERDINAND: No, I'll talk to Mr. Hillman. (*Pause.*) Actually, you are a funny doll, Julie. You believe everything I say. Do you really believe that somewhere in this world is a place called Zemgale? I find it hard to believe. I've never been there.

DOLL: I believe it, Ferdinand, I believe it.

FERDINAND: Maybe you believe that there is a Riga?

DOLL: I believe it.

FERDINAND: And Bastejkalns? And the Freedom Memorial?

DOLL: There is, Ferdinand.

FERDINAND: I don't know. I've never been there.

DOLL: You weren't born yet.

FERDINAND: Maybe. I don't know.

DOLL: I know, Ferdinand. I can remember clearly. It was many, many years ago. They were the most beautiful moments of my doll's life. (*Music begins playing.*) I stood in a big, elegant display window in Riga. It was Christmas, and huge, soft flakes of snow filled the air and gently landed on my window. People with happy, excited faces and arms full of presents streamed past me. Some would stop, look at me briefly, and then hurry on. I knew I was beautiful, and my doll's soul became infused with unusual happiness. I wanted to spin and whirl among the snowflakes in the white streets. Then I felt ashamed. I was just a doll. I stood in the window with the other dolls, unmoving, eye-lashes half-lowered, smiling. Then a youth stopped by my window. He was much like you, Ferdinand. He came up and pressed his forehead against my window and gazed at me. His breath fogged the window, and he wiped the glass with his mitten, and stood, and looked, stood and looked. (*Tinkling of bells is heard.*) The tinkling of little bells could be heard in the street, and their sound gently filled my window. A strange ecstasy gripped me. I forgot that I was a proper dress doll. I became reckless and responded to the harmony of the bells. The youth looked first at me, and then at the passing sleigh, then back at me. Then he laughed and shook his head. (*FERDINAND laughs and shakes his head.*) Just like you, Ferdinand. Then the sleigh, moving swiftly in the white, soft street, disappeared into the night. But the tinkling of the bells hung in the air and danced with the snowflakes for a long time. I still hear it. It has followed me from that city on the River Daugava and hangs around me even after these many, many years. Listen! (*Faintly the tinkling of bells and hoof-beats can be heard.*) Do you hear? The bells and the beat of hooves in the white street? Can you hear them? Can you? Can you?

FERDINAND (*listening*): I don't hear a thing. I don't!

DOLL (*sadly*): You can't hear, Ferdinand.

FERDINAND (*laughs*): Oh, Julie, if you go on like that I'm going to die from laughing. You fantasize just like my godmother Caroline. (*THE DOLL admonishingly shakes her head.*) Oh, go on, go on! Maybe, just like Caroline, you sat with your half-crazy youth in some fantastic cafe with a view of the Freedom Memorial and drank the most aromatic coffee and ate the most divine pastries in the world. And then there was the grand ball at the Officer's Club and the champagne flowed lavishly. I know the story by heart. Well, wasn't that the way it was?

DOLL (*shakes her head*): Not quite like that. You are a little self-righteous, Ferdinand. Sybil couldn't hear the music of a lifeless doll, but you can't hear the tinkling of bells in a white, snow-covered street.

FERDINAND: I don't want you to compare me with Sybil! What happened then? What happened to your half-crazed young man?

DOLL: He never came back.

FERDINAND: Maybe he left the city.

DOLL: I met him again years later in a different place. He went by and didn't recognize me.

FERDINAND: Julie, how can someone not recognize you? I would recognize you after a thousand years!

DOLL: You are being hasty, Ferdinand.

FERDINAND: I swear I would recognize you. Among a thousand dolls, in a thousand windows, in a thousand cities.

DOLL: When he passed me, he was no longer a youth. I barely recognized him. He was dealing in pork and cloth materials. And it wasn't on the Daugava, but on the Neckar. That was a very unsettling period in my doll's life. They were constantly draping cloth over me. At first, it was old blankets and other coarse materials, later the finest imported silk.

FERDINAND: Was your half-crazy youth a sailor?

DOLL: No, a speculator.

FERDINAND: What's that?

DOLL: I don't know. I think someone who sells bacon. Then my days of usefulness ended. I was dismantled joint by joint, limb by limb, wrapped in newspapers, and packed into boxes. Many years passed before I was completely together again. Some boxes went to Chicago, some stayed in New York. That was a dark, gloomy period. I don't even want to think about it. Then one day Mr. Hillman collected me together, touched up the scuff marks, dressed me in a beautiful dress, and put me into this window. Mr. Hillman had bought this store. I was very happy. I liked this street.

FERDINAND: And what happened to your crazy young man?

DOLL: I told you, he is no longer young. He is a rather substantial man. I see him now and then, on this street. He is the superintendent of a building two doors down on the other side. He often goes by here. He doesn't look at me. All he can see is the street. (*SUPERINTENDENT enters, slowly walking across the stage. He picks up the straw, looks at it, and throws it into a waste receptacle. Continues walking. He finds an empty cigarette package, checks to see if it is completely empty, and throws it into the container. Slowly crosses the stage and exits.*)

FERDINAND: Was that him?

DOLL: It was.

FERDINAND: So inhuman, without fantasy.

DOLL: You're being self-righteous, Ferdinand. He is only tired.

FERDINAND (*laughs out loud. Moves about the stage*): I want to believe you, Julie, but I just can't.

DOLL: Come closer. I wish to touch your hand.

FERDINAND (*goes to the window; stops. He puts his palms*

against the pane): I can't. The glass is in the way.

DOLL: There is no glass.

FERDINAND (*pushes his hand through the window*): You're right! There's no glass! (*THE DOLL Gives FERDINAND her hand.*) A warm, living hand!

DOLL: Now hold on. I'm going to climb out of the window.

FERDINAND (*frightened*): No, you could fall! You can't! You're a doll! (*THE DOLL begins climbing out with jerky, awkward movements. FERDINAND covers his face with his hand.*) I'm afraid! You'll fall. You will break, Julie!

DOLL (*almost falls. Laughs*): I'm not very steady on my feet. (*begins to move across the stage doll-like.*) Come, help me, Ferdinand.

FERDINAND (*one hand still covering his face, he stretches the other out to THE DOLL*): I'm afraid you're going to break. (*Walking backwards, he leads THE DOLL.*) You're walking! You're actually walking. You are a living girl. You're beautiful! You're noble and regal. If only Sybil knew how to hold herself like that. Walk, walk some more. I love to watch you.

SYBIL (*runs on. THE DOLL Freezes*): Ferdinand, are you crazy? You've taken it out of the window! Put it back! Put it back! This thing, this dumb doll! Somebody could see you! I was only kidding about stealing it! Do you understand? It was a joke! Come on, quick! Put it back! Drag it back into the window! I'll keep a look-out by the corner! (*Exits. THE DOLL climbs back into the window with slow, stiff movements. Freezes. FERDINAND stands with his hands over his face. Frightened, he runs up to the window.*)

FERDINAND: Julie, you're not moving! You can't hear me. I'm Ferdinand! Ferdinand Vejkalns. (*He stands for a moment; then exits.*)

SYBIL (*runs on*): That's good! You put it back in the window! Ferdinand! Ferdinand! Where did you go? Ferdinand!

CURTAIN

SCENE FOUR

(*The stage is brightly lit. The show window is empty. SYBIL is sitting on the bench waiting for FERDINAND. She primps, fixing her hair and smoothing her dress. Yawns. She finally nods and*

*falls asleep. Music begins as SYBIL dreams. THE DOLL and
FERDINAND approach each other across the stage, moving with
a dance beat. When THE DOLL and FERDINAND meet, SYBIL
parts them and begins dancing with FERDINAND. FERDINAND
pulls away. The entrance and dance repeat several times. Then
the stage goes dark. In a moment the bright lights come on just as
in the beginning of the scene. SYBIL is sitting on the bench,
asleep.)*

SYBIL (*wakes up. Yawns. Remembers the dream, and runs up to
the window*): Mr. Hillman, Mr. Hillman! Where are you?

HILLMAN (*sticks his head into the show window*): What is it?
Who got killed?

SYBIL: It's worse than that! I can't even say it!

HILLMAN (*steps into the window*): Well, what is it?

SYBIL: I had a terrible dream. (*HILLMAN motions with his hand
and prepares to leave.*) Something more repulsive and un-
imaginable than I have ever seen in my life! Your terrible
dress doll was forcing itself on Ferdinand.

HILLMAN: My doll does not force herself on anybody. (*Gets
ready to leave.*)

SYBIL: Wait a minute, Mr. Hillman! I just want to talk to you.

HILLMAN: Eh?

SYBIL: Where is it?

HILLMAN: What it?

SYBIL: Well, you know, that one with the European hair.

HILLMAN: I'm repairing her. Her leg is broken again.

SYBIL: Her leg? Leg? What leg? Oh, it's leg! Can I come in,
Mr. Hillman? I would like to talk.

HILLMAN: I don't have time to talk to you. Come back tomorrow.

SYBIL: I have something important to tell you. Something you
don't know yet.

HILLMAN (*tosses his hand*): Foolishness! (*Leaves the window.*)

SYBIL: I'm coming in anyway. Mr. Hillman. Just for a little
while. (*Leaves the stage. Off-stage.*) Mr. Hillman, where are
you? Yoo-hoo, Mr. Hillman! (*Her head appears in the
window.*) I can't find you. (*HILLMAN appears on the street.
SYBIL climbs into the window and assumes various poses.*) I
like your window, Mr. Hillman. I could replace your doll while
you're fixing it. How much do you pay beautiful models by the
hour?

HILLMAN: Fifty cents.

SYBIL: That's not enough! I won't model for less than two dollars.

HILLMAN: That's all I can pay beginners. You don't have any job experience. Actually, you should pay me for allowing you to stand in my window.

SYBIL: I'll settle for a dollar-and-a-half.

HILLMAN: Fifty cents.

SYBIL: We can't seem to agree, Mr. Hillman. In that case I can't help you out.

HILLMAN: Standing in the window you'll be helping yourself. All the boys will be able to notice and admire you.

SYBIL: I can't do it for fifty cents.

HILLMAN: When I first became a tailor's apprentice, my master only paid me fifteen santims an hour.

SYBIL: Fifteen! He exploited you!

HILLMAN: Exploited? Yes, maybe he did, that old robber!

SYBIL: Why don't you have wedding gowns in your store?

HILLMAN: Do you know anybody who needs one?

SYBIL: Yes. Maybe. No. No! No! Maybe you think I came here to meet Ferdinand? Absolutely not! I don't care how he spends his time. I told you before, we're parting for good. I just happened to be passing by, and I thought I'd see how you were doing. I wanted to see how you had decorated your window. You are a kind and gentle person, Mr. Hillman. And if I were to ask you if Ferdinand was here, then it's only because I want to know more about the psychology of boys. For study purposes. I don't have any other reason.

HILLMAN (*looks at his watch*): Eleven-thirty. (*Shakes his head and goes inside.*)

SYBIL (*as HILLMAN leaves, louder*): I would like to help you out and stand in your window for an hour or so, but I can't work for fifty cents an hour. Such low wages are not compatible with human dignity. (*Spots FERDINAND entering.*) I'll stand even for fifty cents, Mr. Hillman! (*Takes THE DOLL'S post.*)

FERDINAND (*up to the window*): Julie, Julie, Julie.

SYBIL: I am not Julie. I am Marie Antoinette.

FERDINAND: You're Sybil!

SYBIL: Oh no, Prince Ferdinand, I am Queen Marie Antoinette!

FERDINAND: What are you doing in Julie's window?

SYBIL: I'm modeling.

FERDINAND: Get out of there!

SYBIL: This time I cannot obey. You can see I am preoccupied. (*Assumes various poses.*)

FERDINAND: I don't want you standing in there.

SYBIL: But I want to! Yesterday you ran away from me. And in a very sneaky way, while I was faithfully keeping a look-out

for you. Was that right? Tell me, was that right? Is that the
way upright and noble people behave? Why did you do that,
Prince Ferdinand?

FERDINAND: I don't know. Where's Julie?

SYBIL: That terrible doll is broken. In pieces. Totally. There's no
hope it will ever be able to stand.

FERDINAND: Knock it off, Sybil.

SYBIL: I'm not kidding. I'm working here. Mr. Hillman is paying
me fifty cents an hour.

FERDINAND: I don't like you standing in Julie's window.

SYBIL: Am I ugly? (*FERDINAND shrugs his shoulders.*) Ugly?
Are you telling me I'm ugly?

FERDINAND: I didn't say that.

SYBIL: What did you say, Prince Ferdinand?

FERDINAND (*hesitates, irritated*): I said, you'll do.

SYBIL: I'll do? That's not enough. Take a good look. I can't believe you can't see that I'm pretty.

FERDINAND: All right. You are.

SYBIL: So. That's much more polite. I'm tired of standing here.
Help me out of this window. (*Gets ready to get out.*)

FERDINAND: Go around! There's glass in front.

SYBIL: Glass? Yes, glass. Of course. I'll go around. Wait for me!
Prince! (*Leaves the window, comes from the side moving like
THE DOLL.*)

FERDINAND: Don't be silly. Walk normally.

SYBIL: Here is my hand, Prince. I want to eat.

FERDINAND: Eat? (*Makes a face.*)

SYBIL: Well, let's go. (*FERDINAND looks at the empty window.
SYBIL stands beside him and assumes FERDINAND'S pose.*)
A dismal, empty window. I didn't like it. But when it isn't there,
it's sort of sad.

FERDINAND: Very sad.

SYBIL: I was used to it.

FERDINAND: Me, too.

SYBIL: It's strange, how one can become used to such an ugly,
grotesque thing. I got used to it even when you stared at it and
didn't hear a thing I was saying. Can you hear me now?

FERDINAND: No. I don't hear you.

SYBIL: Why don't you hear, Ferdinand?

FERDINAND: Because you never say anything sensible. Nothing
unusual can penetrate your head.

SYBIL: Oh, yes it can! I have quite a few unusual thoughts.

FERDINAND: What? Well, tell me. Well? Well? See you don't

have a single idea.

SYBIL: I do have thoughts. They just never come to mind.

FERDINAND: Do you know who the Bearslayer was?

SYBIL: Bearslayer? Bearslayer? (*Shakes her head.*) No, I don't know. (*Remembers.*) Oh, Bearslayer! Of course I know! My older sister Ilze recited something about the Bearslayer at a Latvian festival. Is that the one you mean?

FERDINAND: That's the one.

SYBIL: Oh, I know that. I definitely know. (*Tries to remember. Quietly reciting to herself.*) Of course, I know. (*Begins reciting.*) Oh, Bearslayer, Sybil will come to your aid!

FERDINAND: Spidola.

SYBIL: Oh, alright. Spidola. What's the difference—one girl or another? Well, let's go, Ferdinand. Let's not waste our time by this stupid, empty window. It is finished. I told you. (*Begins to drag FERDINAND across the stage. THE DOLL appears in the window. FERDINAND pulls away, runs up to the window.*)

FERDINAND: No, there she is! Look! It's her! Julie!

SYBIL (*comes up to the window*): I don't see anything. The window is empty. Just a pile of clothes. Come on, Ferdinand! (*She pulls him away. FERDINAND hesitantly follows, looking back. They both leave. FERDINAND comes running back to the window.*)

DOLL: Go, Ferdinand. I'll be here. I will be standing here. Maybe for many, many years. You can always come back to me. I'll wait for you, but Sybil won't wait. Sybil will go with Paul. I am a thing. I can wait. For a long time.

SYBIL (*runs in*): Well, come on! Will you come? (*FERDINAND unwillingly follows SYBIL. Turns and waves. THE DOLL waves back.*)

CURTAIN

PLEASE, COME IN, SIR!

A comedy in five scenes.

CHARACTERS

RODERICK TURAIDS
PERSE, his wife
DANCIS BASENIEKS
JADVIGA, his wife
An imaginary policeman

The action takes place in Santa Monica mountains near Los Angeles.

Time: the present.

(*A living room with open walls and doors facing the proscenium. The stages is dark. A harsh metallic banging is heard. The banging is repeated, more insistently. In a moment the beam of a flashlight darts around the stage.*)

RODERICK (*crosses the stage with a flashlight, whispering*): Somebody's banging on the gate!

PERSE (*entering*): This late at night? (*More banging.*)

RODERICK (*peering around the door*): There's somebody outside!

PERSE: Ask him what he wants.

RODERICK: What if it's some drunk? Or an addict? Or some nut? I'm calling the police. They can take care of him. Damn, we don't have a weapon handy. In a place like this, in the middle of the woods, a good shooting piece is a necessity! A shotgun would be best. Both barrels, loaded with game shot, and you wouldn't have to worry much about aiming. I'm getting a shotgun first thing in the morning.

PERSE: I'm going to go out and see who it is.

RODERICK: No, you're not! That's a man's job! You stay in here. (*He leans through the door.*) Who the devil's out there? Answer me, or I'm going to call the police!

DANCIS (*off-stage, hoarsely*): Me, it's me.

RODERICK (*to PERSE*): That sounds almost Latvian! I haven't heard anything about Latvian burglars recently. If I just had something to throw! (*A light comes on in the living room. RODERICK slowly goes out the door and approaches the gate.*) Dancis! It's Dancis! (*He opens the gate with a clatter. The stages becomes considerably lighter.*)

DANCIS (*enters slowly, hair disheveled, unshaven, with a dirty canvas bag over his shoulder. His suit, obviously expensive and well-tailored, is rumpled and covered with buhr and dust. His shoes, equally expensive and of high quality, are scuffed and muddy. Hoarsely*): Roderick? How did you get here? On Perse's property? And this house! With a big wall around it! I'm gone just a short time, and everything's changed. I thought I was lost, until I saw the big rock at the side of the road. I remember it well.

RODERICK: Is your wife with you?

DANCIS: No. I'm traveling with Caspar. Poor thing was completely dead, running all day. He couldn't go any further. I left him with a good person by the seaside.

RODERICK: Isn't this a surprise! In the middle of the night. Alone. Come on in! Perse! It's Dancis!

PERSE (*at the door*): Dancis!

DANCIS: My dear little Perse! (*Embraces and kisses her.*) It's so good to see you again. And after such a long time!

PERSE: Well, come inside! (*DANCIS takes PERSE by the shoulders and goes into the living room. RODERICK follows.*)

PERSE: Sit down. Take off that bag. You look absolutely exhausted.

DANCIS (*embraces PERSE again*): My kind, gentle Perse! How have you been all this time? I wanted so much to see you again.

PERSE: But where's Roxanne, Lena, Paul?

DANCIS (*wearily*): That's a long story, my little Perse. A long, sad story.

PERSE: You sound terrible. I'll make some tea.

DANCIS: That would be wonderful. I'm completely parched.

PERSE: I'll put on the water. (*Exits.*)

DANCIS: I've come a long way.

RODERICK: Sit down.

DANCIS (*collapses on a chair*): I came to the old place—my haunts in the burned-out villa. Just for spite I couldn't catch a ride from the coast. Two or three cars whizzed by, but would one stop? (*Perse enters.*) So I struggled along those seven miles uphill. And what do I find? The villa has been demolished! No more cellar, no more storage shed where I used to live. Everything has been torn down, filled in, graded, and divided into residential plots. I couldn't even turn on the water! Somebody has already poured a new foundation. It was revolting to see. Complete ruin! The orchard with its beautiful peach trees wiped out. They have even chopped down the big oak tree!

PERSE: The one you were married under?

DANCIS: Don't remind me of that accursed marriage! No one knows when and where misfortune may overtake him. It certainly wasn't the tree's fault. A beautiful California oak with thick dark green leaves. In the fall acorns would cover the ground like a thick carpet. We all were so happy then. Caspar, Roxanne, you Perse, and later even Roderick. And it was all ruined, by Jadviga, my wife. Oh, what a terrible nightmare! I don't want to remember. (*Pauses momentarily, then in a completely different tone.*) When was this fancy place built?

PERSE: Anderson is fast.

RODERICK: He moved the house here already built.

DANCIS: Yes, Anderson! He could get along with Jadviga. Jadviga is fast, too. Quick as the devil...And you live her now, Perse? In your own house?

PERSE: So it seems.

DANCIS: Everything here is so luxurious! And here's me—like from a swamp. I've tracked up your floor.

PERSE: Don't worry about it, Dancis.

DANCIS (*thinking for a moment*): And how did you happen to be here, Roderick? At this late hour. Are you just visiting, or do you rent a room? (*RODERICK and PERSE exchange looks.*)

RODERICK: I live here. (*DANCIS looks at PERSE.*)

PERSE: We're married, Dancis.

DANCIS (*surprised*): You two? (*PERSE nods.*) So! (*He looks in confusion first at PERSE, then at RODERICK, hangs his head and plucks at his beard. He rises stiffly and extends his hand to RODERICK.*) Well, congratulations! Good luck! (*He wants to embrace PERSE again, but pulls up short.*) Best wishes, Perse. I hope you will be happy. (*He takes her hand with both of his, and shakes. Pauses a moment.*) Then I must be—now— a troublesome bother?

RODERICK: Foolishness. Nothing like that at all. (*Uncomfortable silence.*)

PERSE (*gratefully looks at RODERICK. To DANCIS*): I'll get the tea. Maybe you would like some hot soup?

DANCIS: Thank you, dear Perse! It just so happened I wasn't able to eat today. (*PERSE exits. Thoughtfully looking at RODERICK.*) When we were living at the villa, there wasn't any sign of this.

RODERICK: How can you be so sure?

DANCIS: Hm, yes. One can never be sure. Sometimes one can't tell what's happening with him, much less with others.

RODERICK: How did it happen—that you haven't eaten all day.

DANCIS: If you think, Roderick, that by marrying a wealthy wife you have solved all your problems, you are gravely mistaken. I used my last few cents this morning to buy Caspar a carton of cottage cheese. It has been so long since the poor creature had some cottage cheese! So I had to go without.

RODERICK: A logical person takes care of himself first, and then worries about an animal.

DANCIS: What is a logical person, Roderick? And what is logic? Logic has caused me only grief and misery. I have sincerely tried to be logical, and you can see where that has led me.

PERSE (*bringing in tea*): Soup will be ready in a moment.

DANCIS: Thank you, dear Perse! Don't trouble yourself. I just want a sip or two. To quench the thirst. Seven miles uphill! (*PERSE exits.*) I'll be going soon.

RODERICK: Sit! Don't be silly. Have a proper meal.

PERSE (*brings in the soup*): Chicken soup. You always like it.

DANCIS: Actually—with all the excitement, I'm not really hungry. (*Pushes the bowl aside.*) I'll just have something to drink. I'm thirsty. (*Sips his tea.*)

RODERICK: Maybe you want something stronger? (*DANCIS nods.*) What do you want? Cognac, scotch, rum, vodka, bourbon? I don't have gin. Never use the stuff.

DANCIS: I'll have some bourbon.

RODERICK: With soda or ginger ale?

DANCIS: Neat. Don't bother with ice. Give it to me straight. (*RODERICK pours a shot and gives it to DANCIS.*) Yes, who would have believed that the world could change so suddenly and completely? My villa is no more. Dear Perse is married, and you're living the life of a prosperous man. In an elegant home. A proud gentleman.

RODERICK: Don't forget you have become even more prosperous! We can't compare with wealthy Jadviga.

DANCIS (*stiffens*): Don't mention Jadviga! (*Empties his glass.*) Thank you, my friends, for your hospitality. Now I have to be going.

PERSE: On foot?

DANCIS: I don't have a car anymore....Well, maybe you would like to give me a ride? Roderick doesn't drive, but maybe you, dear Perse?

PERSE: Is Jadviga in the city?

DANCIS: I don't know. I'm not going to Javiga.

RODERICK: Have you two had a...misunderstanding? (*DANCIS Shrugs.*)

PERSE: But where do you want to go, then?

DANCIS: Oh, somewhere. I don't care. To the shore. Maybe I'll meet somebody at the Two Oars.

RODERICK: It's almost three o'clock. All the bars are closed. And you said you didn't have any money.

DANCIS (*spreads his hands*): I'll get by somehow. It's not the first time. I'll sleep on the beach under the pilings. I won't freeze. It is summer—and California. (*PERSE looks at RODERICK.*)

RODERICK (*rather unwillingly*): Stay here overnight.

DANCIS: Oh, no, no! Of course not!

RODERICK: How often did I stay with you at the villa?

DANCIS: It was different then.

RODERICK: What's so different? We're still the same people.

DANCIS: Only—in a different arrangement.

PERSE: Dancis is haggling for the sake of appearances. I'll go find some bedding.

DANCIS: Well, now see how unpleasant this is. I'm forcing myself upon you.

RODERICK: Foolishness! You're not bothering anyone here. Perse will make you a bed on the couch in the study.

DANCIS: I'm not going to sleep on a couch! My back won't take it. And certainly not surrounded by books! There's no air! It stinks of ink, old papers, dust! (*Yelling.*) Dear Perse! Not inside! Put down some rag on the doorstep! In the fresh air!

PERSE (*entering with blankets and pillow*): You'll freeze. Up here nights get quite chilly.

DANCIS: If only I had my good old sleeping bag. I wouldn't need a place to stay. Just crawl into some bushes and sleep. But—I had to trade it for some dog food. Just not in the library! Not among books!

PERSE: We can put him in the trailer, Roderick! It's empty. How fortunate that Anderson hasn't moved it yet.

RODERICK: Great! Let's put Dancis in the trailer! (*Hurries to help PERSE with the bedding.*)

DANCIS: Well, now, if with your permission I'm going to stay here overnight, let's sit here for a while together. That is, if I'm not being a bother. I have long been wandering among strangers....Now that I think about it, you're the only friends I have left.

PERSE: You can always depend on us.

RODERICK: Well, of course. How can it be otherwise? (*Looks at*

*his watch, stretches himself, and fills up Dancis' glass. PERSE
sits down beside DANCIS and pats his shoulder.)*

DANCIS: Unendurable. Simply unendurable. It's hard to even talk about it. But it's impossible to forget. It was a nightmare. A terrible, evil dream. Right after the wedding Jadviga changed completely. She became a different person. She forgot our agreement and insisted that we don't take the dogs on our honeymoon. All her friends were laughing and making fun... What's there to make fun of? What can be better or more pleasant than a good dog?

RODERICK: Didn't you have four dogs, Dancis?

DANCIS: Then it's just four times as pleasant....Jadviga wanted me to leave them at a kennel. But those are terrible places! Concentration camps! They turn animals into physical and spiritual wrecks! What could be more pleasant than to travel with four dear doggies? Hotels and motels wouldn't let us in, though.

RODERICK: Well, of course.

DANCIS: But we managed. Sometimes a small fee would do it, and if not, we just slept in the car, the six of us. What's wrong with that?...Unfortunately, we were going to her parents in Washington. Why, I don't know. They didn't like me from the start, or the dogs either. Imagine! Jadviga doesn't know what to do with her money, and yet they want a rich son-in-law! I was too poor for them. No job. No capital. As if a person wasn't more important. They asked me for my family tree. Their's stretched back to the 15th century. Taking a purely theoretical approach, I said that purity of human bloodlines is extremely doubtful. After all, you really can't tell nobility from common stock. Some aristocrats look like real monsters. On the other hand, animal breeds and bloodline purity, especially dogs, can be precisely determined by the muzzle, ears, feet, and tail. It's impossible to control interbreeding among people, whereas the pure breeding of animals is a fairly simple thing. Now, reasonable people would have no objections to such a scientific analysis, but her parents became very upset. I didn't believe in their family tree and held them lower than dogs! They kept

insisting day after day that I liquidate the dogs! Are you communists—I asked—that you use such an unpleasant expression:
liquidate? How can you liquidate the breath of life? Four
breaths? Finally, they had a family conference and presented
an ultimatum: the dogs or Jadviga. Well, since there were four
dogs and only one Jadviga, I chose the dogs. You could have
knocked them down with a stick. They didn't say a word. The
next morning when I awoke, the house was very quiet. Jadviga
and her parents had gone somewhere. I couldn't even hear the
dogs in the yard. I went outside and found them all lying
strangely in a heap. I clapped my hands and called them by
name. Nothing. I looked closer. They were dead! Poisoned!
PERSE: That couldn't be so! And Jadviga...?
DANCIS: I don't know. I think it was her parents. With her knowledge. Only Caspar was still breathing. I managed to revive him.
  Well, I didn't hesitate one moment longer in that house of murderers! I put Caspar into the canvas bag, slung the bag over
  my shoulder and left. Back to California.
PERSE: On foot?
DANCIS: With the thumb. It wasn't easy. Few people would take
  a dog in their car. When Caspar recovered, we walked. We
  traveled for three weeks. I was broke. First I sold my wedding
  ring, so I wouldn't be reminded of that terrible mistake. Then
  my gold cufflinks. Watch. They all were gifts from Jadviga.
  Finally, I had to work here or there. But Caspar was healthy
  again, and the trip home was much nicer than the trip there
  with Jadviga. (*Pause.*) That's the way it is, my dear Perse.
  (*Embraces PERSE.*) Thank you for your hospitality. Thank
  you for listening. It feels so much better to talk about it. But
  it's time to go to bed. Give me the blankets. I know where the
  trailer is. Good night, dear Perse. It is good to see you, regardless of circumstances. (*Goes. Stops at the door, remembering.*)
  Good night, Roderick.
PERSE: I'll go make his bed. (*They both exit. RODERICK wants
  to follow them, stops. He pours himself a drink and slowly
  drains it.*)

CURTAIN

SCENE TWO

(*The living room. It's morning, and the stage is brightly lit. PERSE, dressed for work, is sorting papers in file folders.*)

RODERICK (*enters yawning and stretching, just having woken up. He is wearing an old windbreaker*): Are we going to eat breakfast alone, or should we wait for Dancis to wake up?

PERSE: I ate already. I have to be at work early today. It's pay-day, and I didn't close my ledgers yesterday.

RODERICK: Dancis interrupted.

PERSE: It isn't Dancis' fault. I was just lazy. Poor Dancis! He was so beaten. It's so tragic to lose your beloved animals in such a manner. I suppose I'm partly to blame for that.

RODERICK: You? Why should you take the blame?

PERSE: I should have talked Dancis out of taking such a risky step.

RODERICK: What risky step?

PERSE: It was obvious that nothing good could come out of that marriage. I should have warned him. And now everything has ended so badly. Last night before going to bed, Dancis broke down and cried. I had never seen him cry. Gentle Dancis! Why should he have such unwarranted misery? At least Caspar could have been here! I promised to get Caspar over the week-end. I never knew Dancis had such a sensitive child's soul. I was sad watching him.

RODERICK: And do you think he was crying because of the dogs?

PERSE: The dogs, and other things. He feels lonely, cheated, put upon. He's afraid Jadviga will find him here. She isn't going to give up so easily. She will want Dancis back. We have to figure out some way, Roderick, to protect Dancis from that common woman.

RODERICK: Come now. I don't understand why a sober, indus-trious woman would want to chase after somebody like Dancis.

PERSE: Dancis has had training as an architect. She wanted to use him on some of her projects. I talked to Dancis last night about your remodeling plans. He is willing to help you. You can talk about it when he gets up. Just don't burden him too much today. Let him rest. Make him a decent breakfast of eggs and bacon. There's yogurt in the refrigerator. Dancis is especially fond of it. You're not going to be angry, are you Roderick, that I gave Dancis your blue shirt? He didn't have anything to put on.

RODERICK: My best one.

PERSE: If you're going to give, it might as well be the best. How would you feel if I had given him some rag.

RODERICK: It's all right.

PERSE: He looked so pathetic in his rumpled, worn Sunday suit. I gave him your windbreaker, too.

RODERICK: The new one?

PERSE: But of course! And sandals to replace those terribly worn shoes. Maybe I should have asked you, but you were still sleeping.

RODERICK: Oh, well. What's done, is done.

PERSE: Question him about Jadviga, and don't mention his dogs unnecessarily. It's all so painful to him. Talk about other, less important things. About the house, remodeling. Urge him to rest and get some sun. Maybe you can give him a good book to read.

RODERICK: He hates books.

PERSE: Well, then let him just rest. He needs rest. Later I'll try to get him a job. Anderson really doesn't have anything now, but he can always find something for one extra man to do. I'll take him to work in the mornings while he doesn't have a car. Remember, I used to take you when you worked for Anderson.

RODERICK: You took me, dear Perse.

PERSE: What's happened to you this morning. Why are you calling me 'dear Perse'? When Dancis says that it's natural— I'm used to it. It sounds funny coming from you. I think you're making fun of me.

RODERICK: Why should I make fun of you? After all, we both have agreed that Dancis must be helped.

PERSE: And when Dancis starts his job, you can take care of Caspar. You won't have to do much, just pour dog-food into his dish and give him his cottage cheese.

RODERICK: How long do you think he'll be with us? Dancis, I mean.

PERSE: I don't know.

RODERICK: Ought to ask him.

PERSE: Did he ask you, Roderick, when you were living with him?

RODERICK: The circumstances were a bit different.

PERSE: Circumstances are the same—a friend doesn't have a place to stay. It'll be good for you. It won't be boring being alone at home. Dancis is a pleasant conversationalist.

RODERICK: Oh, no. I'm never bored being alone. I work. I try to write a little. Every now and then a policeman goes by here in his black and white car. We've become pretty friendly. Sometimes we sort of kid around.

PERSE: Well, see. Now you can kid around with Dancis. Look after him. Don't depress him. He has suffered much! Be good to him. I have to go now. (*Kisses RODERICK and goes to the door.*) Take care. (*Exits.*)

RODERICK (*follows PERSE to the door, and watches as she leaves. A car door slams, the motor starts up, and the sound of a car recedes. RODERICK, alone, suddenly changes. Up to now he has been somewhat taciturn and morose, but now he brightens up. He begins to pace briskly in and out, sawing the air with his hands. Then, as if suddenly seeing something, he spreads his arms and smiles happily*): Welcome, sir! You must still remember me? But of course! Policemen possess excellent memories. Please, come in. I've been waiting for you. I know you have been patrolling these lonely roads. I am home alone. Well—not exactly alone. There's a vagabond in the trailer staying the night. Oh, no, no! He isn't a trespasser! You can put your notebook back into your pocket. I wasn't precise in what I said. He isn't a professional hobo. He is—a man gone astray. Absolutely harmless, as far as the police is concerned. My wife's friend. Actually, my friend too. An acquaintance. A good acquaintance. May I offer you something? Cognac? Nothing? I understand. You're not allowed to drink on duty. Especially not this early in the morning. Perhaps a cup of coffee? You may? I'll get it right away. (*Brings the coffee.*) It's still quite warm. My wife already had breakfast. She's left for work. You must have met her on the road. An aquamarine Mustang? You noticed it? But of course! Very few people travel this quiet rural road on weekdays. Can I pour you some more? No? I won't insit. Perhaps I'll have some more. (*Pours.*) I feel somewhat wrung out this morning. Our visitor disrupted our sleep. I wonder when he's going to come to breakfast. This wanderer. I know he's up. I heard them talking. My wife and the wanderer. She's a good person, my wife. But she shouldn't have given away my shirt. I needed that windbreaker, too. All I have left is this worn one. But, after all, what is a shirt compared to friendship? Nothing! You should have seen what he looked like last night. Gaunt, rumpled, half-starved. Worse than a sick dog. To be perfectly honest, I'm almost happy those three creatures were poisoned. It would have been catastrophic if he had shown up here with his entire kennel. Roxanne wasn't a bad bitch, I'll admit. Caspar wasn't either. But ani-

mals would wreck the house. The bookshelves would have to
be raised at least three feet off the floor, because those animals
would have licked everything and drooled all over. I know that
from experience. It isn't that I'm not an animal lover. But you
must understand, I'm a writer, and a dog is a demanding animal. A dog cannot amuse himself the way a cat can. This same
Caspar is going to be trouble. Hopefully, he'll stay for a while
at that seaside kennel. You're wondering how quickly this
house got here? I bought it intact and moved it up here. A lot
of people are doing that now. Buy a house in an urban renewal
area, move it, and set it on your property. Simple and convenient. I'm happy, sir, that you don't need everything explained to you. You are capable of grasping even the most complex situations. This house isn't completely to my taste. But
people often live in conditions not entirely suited to their desires. I couldn't afford anything more luxurious at this time.
Even this wreck cost considerable. Moving expenses. Labor.
My Copenhagen bank account is almost depleted. Labor in
America is terribly expensive. That's why I've been doing so
much remodeling myself. Maybe you're wondering, sir, how I
know to do all this? I know quite a bit that most ordinary,
intelligent people don't. This manual labor isn't all that hard.
All it needs is some physical strength. That's all. I'll confess,
sir, that writing a novel is much harder than shoveling dirt or
sawing down a tree. Many don't believe that. Of course, I could
change my life style at a minute's notice. All I have to do is
concentrate and reorient myself to spiritual work. I can drop
a saw and yardstick and write prose or verse—as I wish. And
I'm going to do so soon. Excuse me, sir, I lied a bit. In all
honesty, I really don't have a bank account in Copenhagen.
And this house was put here by my father-in-law, Anderson. I
see you understand. I am grateful, sir, for your understanding
and benevolent attitude. Those are rare qualities these days.
People run by, ignoring or not noticing the achievements of
others. With their narrow outlook they laugh ironically at
everything they don't understand. And they consider themselves decent, honest, intelligent, and successful, even honorable, because being honorable is paying honor to oneself.
What's that rattling? (*Looks out the door.*) Ah yes, it's our
wanderer. He's up and coming to breakfast. I see you don't
wish to meet him. It really isn't worth it. A very common type.
You're going? I understand. Duty is duty. Frankly, I look forward to seeing your car in the drive. It's like a holiday for me.

Please come up our road more often. Good-bye sir! Thank you. The same to you, sir! (*Guides out his imaginary guest.*)

DANCIS (*enters, dressed in a blue shirt and a new, neat windbreaker. He stands in the door for a moment and then begins morosely*): Good morning.

RODERICK: Good morning, Dancis! Had a good sleep?

DANCIS: Oh, I'll get by. How can one really sleep alone by himself? You wake up, and it's quiet as a grave. Terrible. I'm used to Caspar being close. Hearing his breathing. Twitching in his sleep. Little sleepy whines. A living soul nearby. Instead, there's darkness all around. (*A dismal pause.*) How is he faring, my dear dog? He's probably thinking: "Where's my owner? Why has he abandoned me?" Such experiences can be very damaging to an animal's psyche. He'll never trust me again. Dogs have long memories.

RODERICK: How about some breakfast?

DANCIS: Breakfast? What is poor Caspar having for breakfast? Probably some cheap dog food. Why, why did I ever leave him? With some strange, albeit good, people. We could have both made it here somehow!

RODERICK: Relax. Caspar's alright. He's probably having a good time romping about with the other dogs.

DANCIS: Caspar isn't that way. He plays only with me.

RODERICK: Here's some coffee. Perse left it on the warmer.

DANCIS: Perse? Darling Perse! Little Perse is an angel. Wherever she puts her hand, life blooms again. (*Heavily slumps into a chair.*)

RODERICK: Sugar?

DANCIS: It's unhealthy. It's not a natural food. I never give it to a dog.

RODERICK: But you're not a dog.

DANCIS: Well, give me a little bit.

RODERICK (*pours in sugar*): Cream?

DANCIS: Oh, please! I take a lot. Cream! How Caspar loves it! Where is the poor dear going to get any cream?

RODERICK: How about some eggs and bacon?

DANCIS: No, I don't want any. Darling Perse brought me a bowl of oatmeal porridge early this morning. With butter and sour cream. I'm not really hungry, but coffee—that's always good. (*Paces around the stage, drinking coffee.*)

RODERICK: I have some things lined up for today.

DANCIS (*not hearing, he shakes his head and sighs deeply*): Who would have ever thought, Roderick, that we would meet again so soon? As married people, yet. Married, only in different ways. Oh, very, very, different ways.

RODERICK: Married is married. What's so different?

DANCIS: It's different, Roderick. Terribly different.

RODERICK: Since you're an architect, I wanted to ask your advice.

DANCIS: What did you say?

RODERICK: Some opinions regarding house matters.

DANCIS: House matters? To many people a house is the crowning achievement of their lives. Often it has been obtained through terrible self-sacrifice and tremendous effort, which often completely drains a human being. His success leaves him a physical and mental wreck, totally incapable of enjoying the fruits of his labor and perseverance. What's the sense of desiring a house?

RODERICK: It makes a great deal of sense. Just the striving gives man hope and meaning to his life.

DANCIS: Perhaps. If he's fairly simple. More intelligent people know that the achievement of a goal ushers in collapse.

RODERICK: Aren't you exaggerating a bit?

DANCIS: Absolutely not! Look at what happened to my marriage. In the process of projection many things looked different. But the moment the marriage was realized—catastrophe!

RODERICK: Circumstances vary. Not all things develop in similar fashion. Besides, we were talking about houses, not marriage.

DANCIS: What's the difference? Houses are like marriages: human endeavors. And as such they are doomed to misfortune.

RODERICK: You certainly are in a pessimistic mood this morning. Perk up! Let's talk about architecture. About the house.

DANCIS: What house?

RODERICK: This one right here. (*Indicates around.*)

DANCIS (*braces himself; unwillingly begins*): Well, let's suppose the house business is different with you. You got this house without any effort or risk on your part. You had barely arrived from Europe and the house fell into your lap. Your father-in-law delivered it intact. The process of acquisition didn't wear you out and left you a spark of hope. And yet, you seem to be ready to destroy this rare and fortuitous circumstance. Perse told me that you are obsessed with a determination to rebuild, or, as you say, improve. You want to suffer and torture yourself! The very things that fate sought to protect you from!

RODERICK: I just want to make some improvements.

DANCIS: Wrong! Absolutely wrong!

RODERICK: Since when are improvements wrong?

DANCIS: Looking from the deeper essence of things, improvements aren't even possible.

RODERICK: Maybe not from the viewpoint of abstract philosophy. But let's stay with the practical. Let's suppose you have a leaky roof and your bed is getting wet. You fix the roof and your bed stays dry. Now, isn't that an improvement?

DANCIS: Only in a vulgar context. Taking it from a more elevated viewpoint—one knows whether fate, by getting you wet, isn't telling you to raise yourself, get out of bed, get out of the house, and save your life? If, for instance, your house is on a cliff and the rain has weakened its foundation?

RODERICK (*laughing*): A brilliant excuse for laziness and not fixing the roof.

DANCIS: A brilliant justification for understanding reality and accepting the world.

RODERICK: Admit it! With all your philosophizing, didn't you ever find something in Jadviga's house that you wanted to improve?

DANCIS: Jadviga is my wife only on paper. Spiritually and physically there is nothing between us. Her house was so repulsive to me, the only improvement would have been to burn it down. It was so full of furniture there was no room for people, nor dogs. Maybe only rats. That is humanity's greatest tragedy: it's obsession for barricading itself. For building secluded, barred, isolated residences and then cluttering them with tables, chairs, beds, closets, commodes, bars, shelves, sofas, couches, settees, easy chairs, and roll-aways, until man miserably expires, suffocated in the dust of his possessions!

RODERICK: You're right there in some ways. But why burn it? You can always sell the extra furniture.

DANCIS: I'm not a tradesman! I despise profits, commercialism and transactions!

RODERICK: You don't say! You told me you traded your cufflinks and wedding ring for dog food. Isn't that a transaction? (*DANCIS flinching, angrily waves him off.*) I am not about to cram my house with furniture. I happen to like wide, open spaces. I just wish to make some structural changes...

DANCIS: The second great human failing is the morbid drive to change the existing. To design, build, construct, lay bricks, pour concrete, cement, pave! Man would clearly love to pave over the entire globe, so that visitors from Mars or other planets would wonder at the smoothness of the asphalted or concrete surface, and wonder how it happened. Just like we wonder about the nuclear bomb craters on the moon. The world would be so much better off without architecture and engineering!

RODERICK: Then why did you start studying architecture?

DANCIS: That was the biggest mistake of my life. I should have studied veterinary medicine. The second biggest mistake was marrying Jadviga! I should have married.... Oh, well. There's no use talking. It was easy to drop out of the school of architecture. Dropping out of the marriage to Jadviga is a bit more complicated.

RODERICK: You make everything so complex. Let's forget about Jadviga, the globe, Mars, and other planets and return to this modest dwelling and simple improvements. Come here and look at this window. I want to enlarge it. From the floor to the ceiling.

DANCIS (*by the window, thoughtfully stroking his beard*): Why do you want to make the window bigger than it is?

RODERICK: So it will be lighter.

DANCIS (*taking a newspaper and backing into a corner*): What do you need more light for? I can read the paper perfectly well here in the corner. More light is totally unnecessary.

RODERICK: I want to be closer to nature. I intend to remove the barrier between the indoors and outdoors. I want nature in the room, and the room in nature.

DANCIS: Human beings erect structures for the sole purpose of hiding from the outside. They wish to avoid the joyous light, or hide in the shade from the burning sun. If you desire to live in nature, get a tent, or sleep on a cot under the open sky. Only you'll wish for closed walls when the winds start blowing and the rain pouring.

RODERICK (*thinking for a moment*): A big sliding window would modernize the house. Increase it's value. Make it more beautiful. To the devil with these petty objections! I want a big, decorative picture window with one-piece glass!

DANCIS (*disdainfully*): You want to chase after the latest architectural fashions. Those change faster than clothes. You'll have to remodel the house every two years. Maybe even every year. Flat roofs, peaked roofs, gabled roofs, smooth ceilings, beam ceilings, acoustic ceilings, narrow cornices, wide cornices, french windows, arched windows, sliding windows, wood panelling, drywall, glass and stone, stainless steel and cement.

I quit studying architecture mainly because of all the stupid fashions. And you want me to help you with this insane project? That would be worse than addicting you to narcotics.

RODERICK (*irritated, paces around, attempting to control himself*): Everything you say is true. From an elevated point of view. But I am going to ask you a simple, practical question: what effect will widening the window have on the structure of the house?

DANCIS: If you saw through some support beams, the house will collapse.

RODERICK: I know that. That's why you, as an architect, will tell me where these support beams are.

DANCIS (*examining the wall*): The main supports could be here. Or here. Here, too. You see?

RODERICK: I see. But where, exactly?

DANCIS: They have to be around here somewhere.

RODERICK: I know they have to be around here somewhere, but where?

DANCIS: Actually, they could be just about anywhere. Every builder has his own system.

RODERICK: What if I sawed here?

DANCIS: You could. But I'm not guaranteeing the ceiling won't cave in.

RODERICK: Perse thought you would know where the wall can be knocked out.

DANCIS: Don't you want to risk it?

RODERICK: If I can help it—no!

DANCIS (*sitting down comfortably*): Tell me the truth. Which of you got the idea to remodel the house? You or Perse?

RODERICK: I did, of course!

DANCIS: Oh! You see? Dear little Perse would never worry her head over such silliness. Forget this foolishness! Why knock out a perfectly good wall and strain yourself? In fact, I think this window is too big. You could make it smaller.

RODERICK: This isn't the only window I want to enlarge. I'm going to put in a glass wall in the master bedroom.

DANCIS: In the bedroom? A bedroom doesn't need much light! First you'll put in a window, and then buy thick drapes as you won't be able to sleep because of the light. What kind of logic is that? If it had been dear Perse's idea to remodel the house, maybe we could figure something out, but this—leave it be.

RODERICK (*looks around bleakly, then suddenly lights up*): Don't you understand that widening the window is necessary for my self-fulfillment? The inclination of my soul? Just as you were moved to forget architecture, raise dogs, and marry Jadviga, so am I moved—to widen windows!

DANCIS (*thinking for a moment*): Inclinations and self-fulfillment aren't as simple as you might think. Often they are confused with confusion and ignorance. Or stubbornness and ambition. It might easily be a demagogue's way of justifying his wicked intentions. That is a blanket that can cover just about anything. The devil himself sometimes doesn't know what lurks behind self-fulfillment.

RODERICK (*with sudden inspiration*): Let's suppose I want to build a window to Europe!

DANCIS: You are mad with that Europe of yours. What kind of a window is that?

RODERICK: It's a three hundred years old window. Haven't you heard of it? You did study architecture, didn't you?

DANCIS: Of course I did. But what does that have to do with your drivel?

RODERICK: It has to do with your having gone to school before you started your studies. You must have gotten some general education. (*DANCIS stares at RODERICK in wonder. RODERICK waves his hand.*) Forget it. It's not worth talking about.

DANCIS (*strokes his beard*): I'm not ashamed of my ignorance. How many people are there who can figure out your riddles? How many? None! It's senseless to discuss remodeling on such a beautiful summer day. I'm still a bit tired from my journey. I think I'll go and lie in the sun and fresh air. (*Exits. RODERICK helplessly waves his hands.*)

CURTAIN

SCENE THREE

(*RODERICK'S back yard, with a gate upstage. Two lawn chairs and a beach umbrella occupy the stage. PERSE and DANCIS are sitting on one of the lawn chairs, backs to the audience. It's almost sunset. RODERICK enters, trying to sneak up on PERSE and DANCIS.*)

PERSE: Is that you, Roderick? (*RODERICK, not answering, retreats and hides.*) Roderick!

RODERICK (*comes out from his hiding place*): Yes.

PERSE: Come, sit down, Roderick. The sunset is especially beautiful tonight.

RODERICK (*sits down on the other lawn chair, sighing deeply*): How can you look at something so banal? The sun has been setting for a million years and people are continually amazed at it.

DANCIS: You don't appreciate the beauty of nature. It's power. Look at that magnificent color combination!

RODERICK: What beauty? That red ball hurts one's eyes terribly. Try reading afterwards. All the letters run together.

DANCIS: Why do you have to read, Roderick? Enjoy nature! Look at the sun, at the magnificent cloud formations.

RODERICK: The overbearing reality of nature repulses me. Nature has been totally banalized. The sun, moon, stars, sea, mountains. The arts offer the only refuge from this all-pervasive nature.

DANCIS: It would be better to hide from art in nature. I could look at this beautiful sunset for twenty-four hours. At the university I knew a fellow who bought an airplane so he could fly up and see as much of the setting sun as possible. He invited me to go once, but I declined because he wouldn't take Caspar. An animal would throw up all over the plane.

RODERICK: And he would, too. Why fly? You could rent a boat, and row across the ocean following the sun. Like Dumb Duke used to do.

PERSE (*laughing*): Don't tease Dancis, Roderick. He hasn't read the story of Dumb Duke. Few people of our generation know it. You're older. You know Latvian literature inside and out. Dancis has read only two Latvian books, and I gave him those.

RODERICK: I know. Dancis told me where he got the names for his dogs. Caspar, Lena, Paul. Only Roxanne's name isn't in "The Days of the Surveyors."

PERSE: I gave Roxanne to Dancis before the puppies were born. She came from an American family.

DANCIS: I don't boast of my book reading. It bothers me when somebody disturbs my thoughts with his intellectualisms. Or tries to lose me in his fictional world. It's really pathetic when a man, having read too many books, begins chasing after strange ideas. He loses his own personality. I don't want other people's thoughts, and don't force mine on others. (*He bows his head and sits silently.*)

PERSE: What's wrong, Dancis?

DANCIS: Nothing. I thought of Caspar. Maybe the poor doggie is whining from loneliness, locked away in some corner. Tomorrow I'm going after Caspar.

PERSE: Let's wait until the weekend and go then. I promise. I don't think I can get off from work tomorrow.

RODERICK: Where do you think you're going to keep a dog? I don't want him in the back yard.

DANCIS: The doggie will only decorate the yard. You'll see. You'll like him. You will even want to play with him. What Caspar really likes to do is frolic on the beach. I'll take him down to the ocean. Those were pleasant evenings when we all used to play in the surf. Remember, little Perse, how happy you were watching Roxanne and Lena romping in the waves? (*Gloomy silence.*)

PERSE (*strokes DANCIS' head*): Don't be sad. Think of something more cheerful. Let's all go down to the ocean. It's such a warm and quiet evening.

DANCIS: Let's go! (*They both rise. RODERICK remains sitting.*)

PERSE: You're coming, aren't you, Roderick?

RODERICK (*strictly*): No. I'm not going.

PERSE: What are you going to do all by yourself at home? You'll be bored.

RODERICK: I will not be bored. Go on. I have this and that to do. I have to think.

PERSE: As you wish.

DANCIS: Ciau! (*Exits with PERSE.*)

RODERICK (*pauses for a moment, then in a hesitant voice*): I'll go! Wait a minute! (*The car starts and drives away. RODERICK paces about, deeply in thought. He suddenly becomes animated and runs up to the gate. He looks down the road as if he had seen something. He steps aside, letting in his imaginary guest.*) Please, just come in, sir! I am really pleased to see you again. I'm alone. They drove down to the beach. My wife and her friend. They annoyed me. These meditators. I can't believe that they really expected me, an important writer, to join their silly games. (*He talks with increasing energy, gesturing, pacing around the stage.*) These pedestrian individuals are going to teach me how to perceive the sun! They're going to show it to me as a wonder! I should have ridiculed them. Really mocked these sun worshippers. But I controlled myself. Please sit down, sir. It's a beautiful, still evening, and I'm a bit lonely. Understand, a man sometimes wants to be open. Talk about his feelings. Especially at this hour, with the dark inexorably coming on, another's company is most welcome. (*Momentary pause.*) It isn't that I'm insensitive to natural occurences, only I approach them from a philosophical viewpoint, and not from everyday banality. I have always been interested in the literary form known as science fiction. I have given it a lot of thought. What would it be like, sir, if, due to some natural disaster, the world were to become dark? If eternal night descended? You say it isn't possible? Why not? Let's suppose that, because of some cosmic catastrophe, the sun were to collapse and die out? The entire solar system—dark! You don't think it would be very pleasant? I agree. First of all, the police force would have to be doubled because the crime rate would suddenly increase. Negroes would be exceptionally hard to see in the dark, and they would undoubtedly take advantage of that situation. They would loot stores and terrorize white neighborhoods. But I don't think that situation would last long. Industry would immediately shift to the manufacture of artificial suns. Possibly they would even be better than natural suns. They could be installed in the proper places and at necessary heights. Man would no longer be subject to the vagaries of nature. Everybody could have their own sun in the back yard. The well-to-do would have bigger ones, the poor according to their means. Public parks and poor neighborhoods would have public suns. An enlightened social program would provide little suns for those who did not wish to work. Prisons wouldn't lack suns, either. Especially those condemned having to wait for ten years or more to be executed. Nobody would be entirely without a sun. Warmth and light would be regulated as to need. A Hawaiian climate could be created anywhere in the world. Following the obsession to miniaturize everything, compact, transistorized suns could be made, which could be carried in a pocket anywhere. The open competition between sun-manufacturers would keep prices down. Used or rebuilt suns could be had for laughs. You know, life without that real sun wouldn't be too bad. The world wouldn't come to an end, sir, nor would people. The absence of the sun would have little effect on the United States. About other countries, I don't know. They might have a hard go at it, at first anyway. But then the U.S. would extend its effective foreign aid and provide everybody with artificial suns, starting with Europe and then South America and Viet Nam. Russia would soon begin manufacturing its own suns. Its spies will have stolen America's sun secrets. But that wouldn't even be necessary. The U.S. would give them the

plans for artificial suns. Maybe even supply all of Russia and
China. In the name of friendship. Our government wouldn't
possibly allow the poor Russians to be placed in the embar-
rassing position of being unable to supply our enemies. Maybe
I could write a science fiction story about it! The title could be
"Down With the Banal Sun." or "Eternal Darkness." Or maybe simply "Without the Sun." A book with a title like that would
be snapped up by my esteemed colleagues behind the Iron Curtain. They would be overjoyed! At last a younger generation's
book of lamentations about the terrible suffering and desola-
tion of exile. The exile is totally dark without the sun. Of
course, there would be disillusion at the realization that it was
only science fiction. (*The stage slowly darkens.*) Oh, it's getting dark. I'll light a lamp. I would be happy to read you some
of my compositions if I didn't think I would bore you. There
just isn't anybody here with whom to discuss the problems of
literature. You would be willing to listen to me? That's nice.
That is really good of you. (*He takes out a manuscript, prepares to read, coughs.*) Actually, these are just notes and observations. There's nothing really definite. Just impressions on
a theme. (*Reads.*) "Down the pathetically gray street, enveloped in the city's everpresent, unhealthy atmosphere, slowly trudged a rumpled, repulsive couple. He was a young but
prematurely aged man, whose dissipated and wicked life style
had left an indelible stamp. His clothes were dirty, hair matted,
beard unkempt; his face reflected a deathly pallor, and his
puffed eyes glared venomously at everybody and everything.
This repulsive type's companion was a fairly big-boned and
once-pretty girl, on whose worn and ravaged face (*His voice
breaks.*) only an observant beholder could detect the traces of
her former beauty. The once-healthy eyes now reflected a
fevered light, the hair hung dirty, unkempt, lifeless, having
lost its lustre. This is what had happened when two unthinking
people had followed a blind impulse and formed an unhealthy
partnership....I see you don't care for that, sir. You think
these characterizations are too personal? They force the
writer's point of view on the reader too much? It reminds one
too much of social realism. I agree with you. I had begun to
have my doubts. But what do you think of this much more refined variation?" (*Cheerfully.*) "It was a sunny, enchanted
Sunday afternoon. The sun showered its radiant gold over the
beautiful beaches of Venice. The mighty Pacific rolled its ul-
tramarine waves against the golden sand. The air was full of

seagulls' musical cues and happy voices of people. A young, long-haired hippy with a substantial beard strolled hand in hand with an attractive, blond girl. Their conversation was lively, but feverish. Their eyes were unnaturally bright, and their facial muscles twitched uncontrollably. It was obvious that they had been using..." (*Stops.*) You're right, sir. It's the same thing, only in a different key. An old fashioned, banal story. I have one more variation. (*Coughs. He speaks in a haunting, chanting tone.*) "They were going. They were moved by the force that inhabits plants, mushrooms, minerals. Their joints twitched. Their thoughts jostled about in circles. Entangled. Disentangled. Around one point. Around one post. A post on the roadside. Fence, telephone, light post. Their steps lightly touched the hard, gray asphalt of the street. They left deep holes in the asphalt. Deep bare-footed imprints. The sea washed against the calves of their legs. Panicles of wild oats trickled their soles and crept into their nostrils, ears, eyes. Salty sea water washing into their mouths. The woman screamed shrilly. Piercingly. Louder than a trolley. A dead flounder lay on a strip of black gauze. The dead fish flopped around. It beat the black water into a violet froth. A violin whined sharply, piercing the ear: Brahms' Double Concerto for Violin and Cello, Opus 102. Two people walked together. Two noble creations. Two creatures held hands, twirled, swam, pushed, pranced, reached. They miniaturized themselves in space. Past the moon flounder. Past the flounder moon. Both of them. These beings. Beings these. And the dog. Dog the and." How is that, sir? A bit more bearable? You agree? Yes, I think so too. Returning to artificial suns, how do you, sir, think they would affect the more immediate surroundings? My wife's friend, being unemployed, would be issued a small one by the welfare agency. But would he be satisfied? I doubt it. He would sulk and complain. My wife, Perse, pitying him, would present him a large, expensive sun. Maybe even bigger than the one hanging in the yard. That's the way she is. Perse, my wife. She is a good person. And they would both sit, just like tonight, and meditate about our large, never-setting sun. How long? Who can say. A year? Two? Forever? It's late. I won't detain you longer, sir. Thank you for your attentiveness. Really, a heart-felt thank you. You are the only one who feels the same way I do. You are my only friend. Thank you—from my heart. (*Sees the policeman out.*) I'll be expecting you again soon. (*Reluctantly parting.*) Don't

stay away so long! Good-bye! Take care! (*The stage goes
dark.*)

CURTAIN

SCENE FOUR

(*The same as Scene Three. RODERICK is measuring lumber,
occasionally making notations in a notebook. He listens as the
galloping of a horse can be heard. The galloping ends by the fence,
and the rider can be heard dismounting. RODERICK steps back
and observes. JADVIGA enters, dressed in riding clothes, nervously tapping a riding crop against her boot and carefully looking about.*)

RODERICK (*advancing to greet her*): Good day, Mrs. Basenieks.
    How are you?

JADVIGA (*speaking in a sharp, clipped voice*): You know me?

RODERICK: I had the honor of seeing you at the villa on the hill.
    I was the guest of your marriage partner.

JADVIGA: I never saw you up there!

RODERICK: He didn't want me bothering you. Whenever you
    would come, I would stay inside. I am happy to meet you. My
    name is Roderick Turaids. You were riding along a dangerous
    slope. You are a good rider. What made you think to look here
    for your husband?

JADVIAG: He used to work for Anderson, the contractor. Anderson
    has property here. I thought he would settle in around here
    somewhere. He is a conservative.

RODERICK: You have a very logical mind, Mrs. Basenieks.

JADVIGA: Yes. I do. What's you business here?

RODERICK: I am the owner of this property.

JADVIGA (*immediately more polite*): I'm glad to meet you! I
    must assume my husband has made me out to be a real mon-
    ster, hasn't he?

RODERICK: He was telling me about the misunderstanding with
    the dogs, madam.

JADVIGA: That's what I thought. The whole world has been
    pumped full of dogs! Don't you think that this thing with the
    dogs is a terrible piece of stupidity? (*Suspiciously.*) Maybe
    you're a dog fancier yourself?

RODERICK (*laughing*): Oh no, madam. Don't worry about that. I am not a dog fancier. Exactly the opposite. I'm afraid your husband is going to bring that remaining dog to my house.

JADVIGA: So. Then Caspar survived.

RODERICK: Just so, madam.

JADVIGA (*after a moment, sharply*): Where is he?

RODERICK: Caspar, or your husband?

JADVIGA: Husband.

RODERICK: He went for a drive.

JADVIGA: That's just like him—to waste time! (*She walks around the yard.*) A good piece of real estate. Too big for only one house. You could easily put two, three houses here. Anderson must have soaked you plenty for it?

RODERICK: Overall, I'm quite satisfied with it, madam.

JADVIGA: You built your house unusually quick. A couple of months ago there wasn't anything here.

RODERICK: The house wasn't built, madam. It was brought here.

JADVIGA: Really? They don't usually move houses of this high a quality.

RODERICK: This and that have been improved. I built a picture window in the living room, and this will be a sliding door for the bedroom. I like to look at the green trees when I wake up.

JADVIGA: Worthwhile improvements. With a small investment in modernizing one can increase the value of a property from 20 to 50 percent.

RODERICK: I am not planning to sell the house, madam. I intend to live in it.

JADVIGA: It doesn't hurt to know that you can sell for a profit at anytime. Are you a carpenter?

RODERICK: What did you say? Of course not! Of course I'm not a carpenter! I put the doors and windows in during my spare moments. For relaxation. To stay fit. Do you understand? We do not get enough exercise. Skilled physical labor should have little difficulty for an intelligent person. Enjoyment. A break in routine.

JADVIGA: That is sensible. I respect people who put free time to good use. I wish my husband had even a glimmer of practicality in him. But he is completely...Oh, well. It's not worth talking about. May I ask what your real profession is?

RODERICK: I am a (*Rather stiffly.*) man of letters.

JADVIGA: Hmm. (*Looks at him suspiciously. Wants to ask him something, but changes her mind.*) You have lived with my husband and seem to be a reasonable human being. Tell me, isn't his obsession with dogs pathological? A mental disturbance?

RODERICK: It is perfectly possible, madam.

JADVIGA (*gloomily*) I have been thinking about it quite a bit. Usually a man's mind is unhinged by financial difficulties, drinking, women. This is the first time I have heard of a man going insane because of dogs. I would have never heard of a man going insane because of dogs. I would have never thought that my life would be dictated by dogs! What kind of cure do you recommend?

RODERICK (*thoughtfully*): Peace. Rest...

JADVIGA: Foolishness! He has become crazy directly because of his eternal resting. What is needed here is a rigorous work therapy. How about immersions? Hot and cold baths...

RODERICK: It is a thought, madam, that needs closer investigation. It is really wonderful, the way you worry about him. Not everybody is fortunate enough to marry such a wife. Could I offer you some refreshment, Mrs. Basenieks? Perhaps you would like to go into my house?... (*An automobile is heard pulling up, and doors slamming. DANCIS comes in with a happy, jaunty gait. He sees JADVIGA and suddenly stops, hesitating, not knowing whether to stay or flee. JADVIGA, drawing herself up, stands up with her legs spread apart, tapping her boot with the riding crop. PERSE enters. DANCIS ducks behind her.*)

JADVIGA (*moves forward to meet PERSE, waving the crop*): You! You I know! You couldn't leave him alone even at the old villa! Don't you know he's a married man? Women like you should be in prison, instead of running around corrupting society! (*Threateningly advances on PERSE, who stands her ground. JADVIGA raises her whip, but RODERICK grabs her by her shoulders.*)

PERSE (*coldly*): Your husband is now in your kind charge, lady.

RODERICK: Mrs. Basenieks, allow me to introduce my wife, Perse.

JADVIGA (*controlling herself with effort*): Oh! I didn't know. A pleasure! Please forgive me.

RODERICK: Oh, it's nothing madam. We understand your situation and why you are upset. (*To PERSE.*) Mrs. Basenieks and I spent a pleasant half-hour chatting. She rode here down the steep cliff. She is an excellent rider. We were just about to go in for some refreshments. Let's go in! Dancis, you're coming too, aren't you?...Please, Mrs. Basenieks...

JADVIGA (*sharply*): I am not going anywhere! Don't bother me! (*Pushes RODERICK aside with her hand.*) Daniel, stop fooling around. I must talk to you!

DANCIS: Please do not create a scene in a strange house and leave me alone. We no longer have anything in common. I have no desire to associate with murderers!

JADVIGA (*loudly slapping her boot with the whip*): You damned fool! Let me explain! I didn't so much as lay a finger on your dogs! Do you hear me? Not a finger.

DANCIS: I don't want to hear it. Go away! Leave me alone.

JADVIGA: Pitiful human being! I'll take you to court! (*Attacks him.*)

RODERICK: Mrs. Basenieks! Please! Mrs. Basenieks!

JADVIGA: Don't call me by that accursed name! I feel as if I'm being called a dog's wife!

PERSE (*stepping forward*): You are a shameless person! You want Dancis Basenieks back. I can believe it. Who wouldn't want such a likeable, decent person.

JADVIGA: I don't want him!

PERSE: In that case, why are you here?

JADVIGA: I want to clarify some uncertainties.

PERSE: What do you find unclear? Your behavior has been offensive and belittling, and your husband has disassociated himself from you.

JADVIGA: Oh!

PERSE: Oh! Think for yourself, would you like to live in a house with someone who could not be trusted? You haven't kept your promises. You have disregarded agreements. You haven't respected another's personal feelings. Another's needs, interests, desires. No, you are not good enough to live together with this person. What values can you offer? What can you give to match Dancis Basenieks' honesty, integrity, comradeship? You just want to take advantage of him. Make him a slave to all your businesses. And then pretend that you just want to help him. I can only congratulate your husband for having recognized the situation in time and, despite great personal losses, for having taken the only sensible step—leaving you!

JADVIGA (*waves her off holding her ears*): Are you through?

PERSE: No, I'm not through. How can you ask a person to trust you after you have poisoned his dearest friends, his beloved animals? What assurances can you give that someday you won't hunger after the life of your husband Dancis Basenieks?

JADVIGA: You are accusing me of contemplating murder! That
could have serious repercussions. I have witnesses!

PERSE: In this country they do not punish anyone for suspicions.
Only for acts.

JADVIGA: Mrs. Turaids, let him speak for himself. Your opinions
are meaningless to me. (*To DANCIS.*) Well, speak! Don't hide
behind a woman. Until now I thought you were only slightly
weird. Now I see you're also a spineless coward! That's even
worse. My family has produced many generations of brave,
courageous soldiers and sailors. I should blush from shame in
front of them for wanting to take into the family such a weak-
ling.

DANCIS: Don't start again on your family tree! I've become
nauseous listening to you about your contrive strains of nobility.

JADVIGA: Contrived, did you say?

DANCIS: Contrived! What else?

JADVIGA: You villain! Accuse me of lying, will you? (*To
RODERICK.*) Maybe you don't believe me, either? Do you
think I'm a liar?

RODERICK: Oh, for heaven's sake, no! I believe you. I have
great respect for the ancient noble families.

JADVIGA: To hell with your respect! My dealings here are only
with that undeserving human being that I wished to elevate as
a member of my distinguished family.

DANCIS: Couldn't you just leave me alone?

JADVIGA: No. I never leave a job unfinished.

DANCIS: Please go! Don't bother people.

JADVIGA: No, I'm not going to go. I'm going to teach you to obey
and respect me. I'm going to put a drop of common sense in
that moldy mind of yours. I'm going to beat those stupid dogs
out of your head!

DANCIS: Please, leave.

JADVIGA: No!

DANCIS: In that case, I'll leave. Perse, please take me to the
coastal highway.

PERSE: Fine, Dancis. Let's go. (*They exit.*)

JADVIGA: You're not going anywhere! I'm not finished yet! Do
you hear me? (*Runs after him, stops.*) Go, go you damned
fool! Only don't ever come back.

RODERICK: Please calm down. Peace, peace. That's the way he
is, our Dancis. Emotional, impulsive. A big child. The most
gentle person in the world, until somebody threatens to harm

his animals. Then he really becomes...excited.

JADVIGA: Our Dancis? What's he to you, anyway? How long have you known him?

RODERICK: Just a short time. But—he's my fellow countryman. All Latvians in a strange country feel like old acquaintances. Don't Poles feel the same way?

JADVIGA: Why did you welcome him? He would give in if he didn't have a place to stay. If for no other reason but to keep that damned Caspar from starving to death. That man is incapable of taking care of himself.

RODERICK: I'll tell you what we'll do. First, Dancis should calm down and regain his composure. Then I'll talk to him. Calmly, reasonably I'll explain to him that you had nothing to do with poisoning the dogs, and then we'll set up another meeting.

JADVIGA: That is—if I still want to talk to him!

RODERICK: But of course! Only then.

JADVIGA (*looks at RODERICK carefully*): I'm sorry I lost my self-control for a moment. That happens rarely.

RODERICK: Don't worry about it! Not a little bit.

JADVIGA: I don't understand why you're on his side.

RODERICK: Me? Not at all. I am completely and without reservations on your side. All I wish for is to see you both reconciled and happy! Dancis is my—and my wife's—dear friend. Therefore, he can stay here as long as he wishes. But...although this house is hardly small and there is really enough room, I wouldn't be unhappy if Dancis were to go home. Please don't misunderstand me, Mrs. Basenieks.

JADVIGA (*all the time closely looking at RODERICK*): I understand you perfectly. I also don't like foreign influences in my home. Have you ever been interested in horses and riding?

RODERICK: Very little, I'm afraid.

JADVIGA: Too bad. You have a good physique for riding. Broad shoulders. Long legs. In general, a cowboy's stature.

RODERICK (*throws back his shoulders*): Jockeys, though, tend to be very little fellows.

JADVIGA: Those are different things—racing on a track and riding naturally. For health's sake. We don't get enough exercise. Don't you thinks so too? I have numerous horses. If you're interested, give me a call. Here's my card. (*Gives it to him.*) If I were you, I wouldn't let your wife's old friend stay in your house.

RODERICK: What do you mean by that?

JADVIGA: Only that such a situation is unnatural.

RODERICK: I don't know what you're talking about, madam. Your husband is shiftless, perhaps too involved with his dogs, but he is not capable of sneakiness, back-stabbing, or deceitful behavior. I am quite content with his living here.

JADVIGA: You consider yourself a man of letters, a writer. Maybe you're capable of wisely judging the lives and destinies of others, but you can't see what's happening on your doorstep. But of course Dancis is honest! Of course he isn't capable of deceit or backstabbing. But what is deceit? Let's be honest and perfectly clear. Is it deceitful to love somebody? Is pulling a pretty girl out of a marriage, where she is locked into loneliness and misery, dishonest?

RODERICK: Madam! You are talking nonsense! How did you ever arrive at such absurd conclusions?

JADVIGA: I know how my former husband thinks. He is convinced that he is guilty for any of her misfortunes, real or imagined. That such a feeling is not unnatural you, as a writer and psychologist, should understand. If he is, as you say, a well-intentioned man and has admitted his mistake, the next step would be to correct that mistake. Right? A man who is not capable of underhandedness will prove to be a valiant fighter for higher principles. Sacrificing a good friend is no easy matter. But—what has to be, has to be! It's even harder to sacrifice honor. But even that is nothing if you're making somebody happy. Dancis is capable of fighting very hard for his goals. We know that quite well. His dogs! For them he sacrificed his marriage and a happy-go-lucky existence.

RODERICK: Dancis is a man of principle. Same as his ancestors! Generations of stubborn Latvian peasants stand behind him.

JADVIGA (*laughs*): My female intuition tells me that behind this struggle for the dogs and the hysterical flight back to California isn't principle, nor peasants, or even dogs, but your wife. Since the moment Dancis and I were married under that half-dead oak tree, we have not exchanged on single friendly word. We have only argued. That he married me for my money I've known for a long time. That's not a sin. Money is as good a reason for marriage as any other—education, social standing, popularity, connections, beauty, or even talent. That's all acceptable, as long as one has a bit of common sense. I just never imagined that Perse's, your wife's, power over him was so strong.

RODERICK: I do not like your attaching of my wife's name to this situation.

JADVIGA: I apologize. Let's approach her in a different context. Not mentioning her is impossible, since she is the source of all these complications.

RODERICK: An involuntary source, I might emphasize. Completely involuntary.

JADVIGA: Let's not split hairs. Complications remain complications, and it is absolutely inconsequential whether they're voluntary or involuntary. The question is how to straighten them out.

RODERICK (*smirking*): Does your female intuition suggest some solution?

JADVIGA: Yes. My female intution suggests some solution. Only it will take someone with determination, nerve, and a clear head to make it work.

RODERICK: Take Dancis by the scruff and throw him out of the trailer? That would be brutal.

JADVIGA (*smiles and shakes her head*): Only someone with no determination, no nerve, and with a muddled head would do something like that. That would accomplish nothing. Dancis would just gain stature in your wife's eyes. He would become a martyr.

RODERICK: There is some truth in what you say. But what else do you suggest?

JADVIGA: I'm not sure I should tell you.

RODERICK: Why not? Please, any time!

JADVIGA: It seems to me that you're not ready for it yet.

RODERICK: Foolishness!

JADVIGA: If we were to meet again in a few days perhaps you would understand better.

RODERICK: Oh, no! I can assure you that I will understand completely even now.

JADVIGA: All right. I'll tell you. You have to forget about both of them.

RODERICK: What? Forget? That's absurd! How can I forget my own wife?

JADVIGA: See? I was right. You are not yet ripe for serious conversation. Don't you really see that your marriage is limping? (*RODERICK raises his hands to protest, but JADVIGA cuts him off.*) You're the fifth horse in this matter—running out of harness.

RODERICK: That's a banal statement, madam. An overworn cliché.

JADVIGA: Call it what you want, but it's true. When Perse, your

wife, defended Dancis with such ferocious determination, it
became clear immediately what is happening in your home.
You're not going to tell me you didn't notice? You were right
behind me. (*She pauses, observing the effect her words are
having.*) They have known each other for a long time. I noticed
that already at the villa. They think the same, feel the same.
They're even the same age. Do you really think you can break
bonds like that. Moreover, he drifts with the current, while you
try to swim upstream through the rapids. But you're not strong
enough to swim with a millstone around your neck...

RODERICK (*irritated*): You're using worn-out sayings again,
madam.

JADVIGA: To the devil with your sayings! You are not about to
teach me how to talk! I'm just talking in order to make you understand more clearly. You see, some strong-willed individuals think that anything can be accomplished with hard determination and stubborn patience. That is not so. There are
things which are unchangeable. The strongest determination
will not help you knock a brick wall down with your forehead.
You don't like that saying, either? But it is precise. A man's
powers may be fantastic, yet they are limited. And life is too
short to throw it away waiting for things to change.

RODERICK: Stop, stop, stop! That one about the short life is too
worn out and old fashioned.

JADVIGA: No matter! Forget about those two people. Leave
them to their fate and petty fortunes! There are times when
coldbloodedness pays off. Take a new track. I see in you excellent possibilities. You don't know yourself. Of course, you'll
get ahead a little at Anderson's. A man like you will never disappear completely. But you'll be wasting your abilities. At
your father-in-law's you will only be a servant or, at best, a
minority partner. Besides, Anderson really doesn't have it.
Anderson has the pettiness of a small businessman, glorying in
his little accomplishments of which he barely dreamed when
he first arrived here in America. I know that type. In war time
he would be a good company commander. Maybe battalion.
But that's as far as his abilities would go. You, on the other
hand, could command divisions, camps, armies! I can immediately provide you with all the necessary credit. Dancis longs
to divorce me. Fine! I'll get divorced. And Perse—she'll give
you a divorce at your first request.

RODERICK: Oh, no! Slow down, madam! That is an unwarranted assumption!

JADVIGA: Want to bet? Any sum. Try it: ask her. You can tell her later you were only kidding. You see? You're silent. Deep down you know I'm right. You live in your rose-tinted world of illusions. Your writer's fantasy. Wake up! This is not the place for you. You're a fighter! I also know people a little. Alright. You consider yourself a writer. First, become wealthy. After that you can write. Fame will come all by itself. The best— editors, ghost writers, publishers—will be at your service. Your novels will be created and polished just like the speeches that make wealthy politicians famous. All you would have to do is take your bows and accept the honors and accolades. Only— you have to trust me!

RODERICK (*shakes his head, rejecting what JADVIGA is saying*): I don't know what you're talking about!

JADVIGA: You know quite well. Think my proposition over. Haste would be unseeming of a real man. And you know where you can reach me. You can call me anytime, day or night. And for now—goodbye, Mr. Turaids. (*Exits. RODERICK remains standing with his hands spread helplessly.*)

CURTAIN

SCENE FIVE

(*The yard. PERSE is reclining in one of the sun chairs. DANCIS is kneeling beside her.*)

PERSE: Show me your palms, Dancis. Don't fool around! Show me! (*DANCIS, holding his hands in fists, shakes his head.*) Were you working with the shovel or the drill?

DANCIS: Both.

PERSE: Show me your palms! (*DANCIS reluctantly shows them. PERSE takes his hands and examines them.*) That blister has broken. Terrible. And here is a sore. No, that's only dirt. (*They both laugh.*) And this spot is tender? (*Presses.*) Isn't it? (*DANCIS grimaces with pain.*) I'll blow on it. It won't hurt anymore. (*Takes DANCIS' hands and blows on his "wounds."*) Well? Do they still hurt? (*They both laugh. RODERICK enters. Sees DANCIS and PERSE, pulls up short.*) Roderick, come blow on Dancis' first-day-at-work wounds.

RODERICK (*comes up and unwillingly examines DANCIS'*)

hands): Nothing big. They'll heal up by Monday.

PERSE: No. Dancis won't be able to go to work Monday. I antici-
pated his ruining his hands and told Anderson Dancis wouldn't
be back to work until Tuesday or Wednesday.

DANCIS: Let me see your hands, Roderick. (*RODERICK shows
them. DANCIS and PERSE examine them and compare them
with theirs.*) Your palms are toughened. That's from your
remodeling work around the house. And digging the
foundation. I hadn't worked for quite a while. The skin had
gotten tender!

RODERICK: Who kept you from exercising? You could have
helped me rebuild those windows.

DANCIS: I cannot do work which doesn't make sense to me. The
windows were good enough. You should not have touched them.
Perse thinks so, too.

RODERICK: Is that what you thought? Did you think I was fooling around unnecessarily?

PERSE: I don't know, Roderick. You have your truth and Dancis
has his. I don't want to influence you. If work gives you satisfaction—then work. Dancis' satisfaction is in resting. Playing
with Caspar. Did you write something today, Roderick?

RODERICK: No.

PERSE: Didn't you try?

RODERICK: No.

DANCIS: That's good. There have been too many books written as
it is. Needlessly wasted time and paper. It's better to leave
writing alone. Do something sensible. Build or dig, I don't care,
if you can't be still.

PERSE: Roderick is a writer, Dancis. He has to write.

DANCIS: There are also too many writers.

PERSE: There are never too many good writers.

DANCIS: How do you know he's a good writer? How can you say
for sure? Nobody can say. Today it could be good, tomorrow
totally worthless.

PERSE: Roderick is a good writer. He'll be necessary tomorrow.

DANCIS: I will not argue with you, dear Perse. If you say good,
I agree. What do you think, Roderick?

RODERICK: I think you are uneducated.

DANCIS: Do you, dear Perse, think so too?

PERSE: I think so too. (*Laughs.*)

DANCIS: Fine. I'm uneducated. I accept your decision. Roderick,
what else do you know about me?

RODERICK: You are also undeveloped.

DANCIS: Do you, dear Perse, agree with that?

PERSE: I agree, with a reservation.

DANCIS: I accept this judgment too, Roderick. With a reservation.

RODERICK: I think you are undeveloped without any reservations.

DANCIS: No what do you think, dear Perse?

PERSE: I concur. Without reservation.

DANCIS: I accept this judgement also, Roderick, with reservation.

PERSE (*rising*): We're going to get Caspar. You're coming too, aren't you, Roderick?

RODERICK: No, I'm not going to go.

PERSE: What are you going to do all alone? (*Pause.*) Well, stay. Guard the house. If Jadviga reappears, don't let her into the house. Dancis does not want to see her again. He gets too excited.

RODERICK: Relax. She won't come.

DANCIS: How do you know?

RODERICK: She told me she wanted to divorce you.

PERSE (*happily hugs DANCIS*): You see! You worried about nothing. I told you everything would take care of itself.

DANCIS: Jadviga is lying! She isn't going to give up so easily. She's going to torture me. She's going to try to get me back. She's going to squeeze and torture me and won't give me a divorce!

RODERICK: That's not the impression I got. It seems she wishes to get loose of you as soon as possible. She had plans for you as an architect, but she became disillusioned. It appears she is already looking for a more suitable, constructive, practical, developed man.

DANCIS: I don't believe a word of it! You don't respect me and want to deliberately make me bitter. Prove that I'm worthless. It's because of Caspar. You don't want him here, in your house. You despise animals. You hate the poor doggie, who barely escaped an unfortunate death.

PERSE (*comforting DANCIS*): Calm down. Everything will come out alright. Why shouldn't Roderick respect you? You're his friend. He only wants the best for you. I also want the best for you. We all want the best.

DANCIS: You, dear Perse. Yes—you! You are an angel! What would I do if you weren't here in this moment of trouble? (*Embraces PERSE.*) I'm not angry with you, Roderick. If Perse

thinks you're my friend, well, then so be it. I trust Perse. Let's
shake! (*RODERICK unwillingly takes Dancis' hand.*)

PERSE: And now we have to hurry. Won't you change your mind,
Roderick? Come with us.

RODERICK: I'm not going. I've got something to do.

PERSE: Too bad! We all could go for a swim in the ocean. Let
Caspar play in the surf. You can do your work tomorrow. Come
along, Roderick.

RODERICK (*shaking his head*): I'll work a bit. Write, maybe.
Maybe I'll go for a walk right here down the road. I like this
lonely road. I want to concentrate in solitude. Think over some
important matters.

PERSE: In that case we won't disturb you. We'll see you later,
Roderick. (*Kisses him on the cheek and exits with DANCIS.
She stops to wave at the gate.*)

RODERICK (*remains standing with his head bowed. He listens as
the car starts. He runs a couple of steps toward the noise. Stops
in confusion. The motor roars louder. RODERICK lifts his
hand as is to say something, but drops it slowly as the car
sound recedes. He sits down on a lounging chair and takes out
a notebook. He writes something, crosses it out, starts again.
Then he throws the notebook down and sits deep in thought.
Suddenly he stands up and goes up to the gate. He looks down
the road with his hand shading his eyes. He waves*): Hello, sir!
I'm home alone. Please, come in, talk awhile. You have an excellent eye for appraising a situation. You immediately noticed
that the car was gone. Therefore—everybody's gone. My wife
left with her friend. They're going to bring home the dog. It
was...unavoidable. The vagabond and his dog will now be a
permanent part of this house. Yesterday that woman was here.
The vagabond's wife. She is trying to influence me negatively.
Simply, crudely stated, she is trying to turn me against my
wife Perse. But I ignored it. My friend, the vagabond, is a sincere individual. He respects my wife. That is very touching
among friends. Don't you think so, sir? I see you aren't of one
mind with me. I understand your point of view. But, sir, doesn't
it seem to you that you're a bit old fashioned? We cannot in-
hibit other people. Or influence them by our way of thinking.
That would be primitive. Or even uncivilized. These complex
times call for a more refined, deeper analysis of events. You
don't agree? Too bad. This Dancis Basenieks is a likeable,
totally useless being. Helpless, weak, defenseless; and my
wife, Perse, pities and spoils him. What objection can I have to

that state of affairs? How can I behave, sir, without losing my respect and standing as a modern, contemporary man? Actually, a situation like this creates an uncomfortable responsibility. If I was as reckless as this demoralized, pleasant friend of my wife's, I could freely allow myself to react to my first impulse and not worry myself unnecessarily. I could, for example, chase this vagabond out of my house, I could force Perse to choose between me or the vagabond. I could pose a hundred trite, banal questions that are used in such situations by ordinary, unrefined people. Release my anger and loathing. But that would be contemptible, shameful, and crass. I must find another way. There was a big argument here yesterday. A perfectly common, ignoble quarrel unbecoming the intellectual atmosphere of this house. The wife of my wife's friend is a completely unrefined and primitive woman, which goes to show that success in business is not an indication of human quality. In many instances success only corrupts and debases human beings. I could never associate with that type of woman. She was simply raving. It was one of those unusual situations where someone loses control of his actions. I'm just amazed at my wife Perse. Even she lost her usually composed bearing. I hardly recognized her. She's usually quite calm and collected. She observes the world from the sidelines, with little participation in events. You should have seen how she stood, right here in the yard, in front of her friend. Like a mother lion defending her cub. She wasn't even afraid of Mrs. Basenieks' riding crop. And her threatening and heavy tone: "Your husband is now in your kind charge, madam." I have never seen her like that. Would she ever defend me, her lawful husband, with such strength and courage against such an evil old hag? You think she would? I doubt it, sir. I do. Of course, I could have accompanied them to get the dog, but on a sudden impulse I declined. Maybe if I had made a gesture, raised my hand, smiled, my wife Perse would not have allowed me to stay here alone. But I didn't. I didn't smile. I didn't raise my hand. (*Waves sadly with his hands.*) Sir, I just had a crazy thought. Could you possibly give me a ride to the airport? The international airport. It's on your way. You can? Oh, that's simply fine. Thank you. If I'm lucky enough to catch the right plane, by midnight I could be in Copenhagen. Old, familiar Copenhagen. Isn't that fantastic? You're probably thinking that this is another spur of the moment impulse? Not quite. It is an impulse, but not spur of the moment. I had it yesterday, and maybe even earlier. I'll just grab my bag and overcoat. (*Exits. A moment later comes back with a suitcase in one hand and an overcoat over the other.*) There! I'm ready. We can go. I've kept my bag packed in case of any eventuality. You see how simple: grab it and go! Here remains my remodeled house. My improvements. My unique demands. Maybe someday I'll come back here. Maybe not. (*Moves around the stage looking.*) Oh, one moment, sir! I would like everything to remain in good order. (*Straightens out the deck chairs and the umbrella, stands back, examines the scene this way and that. Suddenly he looks at his watch.*) Oh, it is late. We'll miss the plane! Now we do have to be going, sir! Please, sir! (*He lets his imaginary friend exit first, and then follows him through the gate. The stage darkens.*)

CURTAIN

IT'S DIFFERENT NOW, MR. ABELE

Drama in three acts

by
Alfreds Straumanis

From the original Latvian
Tagad in citādi, Ābeles kungs
translated by
Brigita Steffen

It's Different Now, Mr. Abele. Act Three. Latvian American Theatre, Washington Ensemble, 1972. Mrs. Abele: Hilda Prince Mrs. Leger: Daina Muceniece Mr. Leger: Osvalds Uršteins

It's Different Now, Mr. Abele. Act One. Latvian American Theatre, Washington Ensemble, 1972. Director: Osvalds Uršteins. Scenographer: Ilze Freivalde-Loxley. Sarmite: Anda Uršteina Mr. Abele: Rūdolfs Mucenieks

Introduction to
It's Different Now, Mr. Abele

Written in 1971 and produced August 1972 by the Washington ensemble of the Latvian American Theatre for a tour in the USA and Canada and October 1972 by the Latvian Theatre of Melbourne, Australia, *It's Different Now, Mr. Abele* created unexpected reaction in the Latvian immigrant societies in America and Australia. Critical appraisals, reviews, and comments in letters to the editors of the ethnic press ranged from highly laudative to completely negative. Such furor had been created only once before in the Latvian emigrant theatre with the drama "Like a Thief in the Night" by the well known dramatist, Mārtiņš Zīverts, produced in 1961. Similar heated discussion has been experienced also by the Estonian immigrants after the production of Ilmar Külvet's *Bridge Across the Sea*; and the Lithuanian ethnic society has been stirred by some of the plays by Antanas Škėma. While these writers are among the best Baltic dramatists, the author of *It's Different Now, Mr. Abele,* Alfreds Straumanis, does not even consider himself a playwright. Although he has written a number of children's plays produced in the United States and Canada, both in Latvian and English, and has translated plays from German, French, and Russian into Latvian, as well as Latvian plays into English, the play under discussion is only his second full length venture in original dramatic writing. Asked why he chose to release a controversial play for production, he gives the stagnation of the Latvian ethnic theatre and the over-production of shallow comedies by Latvian American writers as reasons.

These reasons may be valid as far as the overall state of the Latvian ethnic theatre is concerned. However, perusing the theoretical writings by Alfreds Straumanis, presently a professor of theatre at Southern Illinois University Carbondale, additional reasons can be detected. While many of the Latvian exile leaders abhor any aberrations of the cultural norms and traditions as they were known during the period of independent Latvia, Straumanis agrees with those who promulgate the necessity of change in keeping with the times and the new environment. He, for example, suggests discarding of the declamatory style used in line delivery by the older generation of professional Latvian actors and emulated by their students as being out of place in America and in the basically realistic drama produced by the ethnic theatres. Also, he thinks that the characters, as created by the Latvian dramatists in exile, should not have only "Latvian" traits, even if the dramatic actions occur in a Latvian environment and deal with specifically Latvian issues. The society and the environment of the host country, in his opinion, have imposed their traits upon the new immigrants. In other words, Alfreds Straumanis is a proponent of depicting the aspects of acculturation in ethnic drama as well as the ethnic drama itself acculturating to a changed society.

Alfreds Straumanis is uniquely qualified to examine the difficulties of Latvian acculturation, especially in those people whose allegiance is still foremost to the ways of the old country. Born 1921 in Moscow, Russia, Straumanis was brought to his parents' native country, Latvia, when he was only ten months old. After graduating from a gymnasium of science and having studied voice for three years, he was accepted in the State Theatre School at Jelgava, where he studied acting and directing under a student of Vakhtangov, later the Director of Vakhtangov Theatre at Moscow, Osvald Glazunov. Already in 1941, Straumanis started his professional career as a stage manager and actor at Jelgava's Theatre. The events of World War II forced him to leave Latvia, and, starting in 1945, Straumanis worked as an actor, singer, dancer, director, and producer in Denmark, Germany, France, Africa, and Southeast Asia in theatre, radio, television, and film as well as beginning to write theatre reviews. Immigrating to the United States in 1955, he first acted in some Latvian ethnic productions and continued to write drama reviews for Latvian and French publications, covering international theatre and music festivals in Europe and ethnic presentations in the United States. He has also published feuilletons, short stories, a novel, and essays on theatre. He graduated from C.W. Post College 1962 with a BA degree *magna cum laude* in Business Administration; from Hofstra University 1964 with a MA in Drama; and from Carnegie Institute of Technology 1966 with a Ph.D. degree in Drama. While at Carnegie Institute (now Carnegie-Mellon University), he acted, directed, and taught theatre at the Pittsburgh Playhouse.

Before embarking upon a career in educational theatre, Straumanis became the director and producer of Asheville Community Theatre in North Carolina. In 1967, he was appointed as Associate Professor of Theatre at SUNY New Paltz—a town and campus very much like the ones depicted in *It's Different Now, Mr. Abele*. While at New Paltz, Straumanis staged the first Latvian play in English ever produced in the United States, *Mad, Christopher, Mad*, which he had translated from the original *Rūda (The Ore)* by Mārtinš Zīverts. He also conducted an acting studio for some thirty Latvian actors in Toronto, Canada, where he "attempted to bring up to date the techniques required for a modern production." These endeavors culminated years later when, in 1974, a production of Moliere's *Tartuffe* under his direction received the first prize in an international Latvian theatre festival and was presented also at the yearly Canadian multi-ethnic theatre festival.

After serving as Head of Speech and Theatre at Voorhees College in South Carolina for three years and, as a visiting professor, lecturing at various Australian universities in 1972, Straumanis joined the Theatre Department of Southern Illinois University at Carbondale January 1973. Besides his regular teaching duties, Straumanis directs the Baltic Drama project since its inception in 1974. The project involves Baltic drama and theatre specialists and students in research, translation and production of Estonian, Latvian, and Lithuanian plays as well as publishing drama anthologies and bibliographies.

One of the latest Baltic Drama projects, "Bridging the Gap," supported by a grant from the Illinois Humanities Council, concerned itself with acculturation of the Baltic immigrants to life in the United States as depicted in the dramatic works of the three ethnic groups. The play, *Ferdinand and Sybil* (included in this anthology), was adapted for television and directed by Straumanis. The TV presentation was used as a starting point for discussion in public meetings and classrooms of problems connected with the acculturation process, in a way conceptualizing the ideas found in *It's Different Now, Mr. Abele*.

The idea that the new environment plays a significant role in the acculturation process is strongly indicated in *It's Different Now, Mr. Abele*; as a matter of fact, its dramatic action depends upon the conflict between the environment and the protagonist, Karl Abele.

It is as difficult to judge past events without the knowledge of historical relativity as it is to evaluate current events without the luxury of retrospect. What seemed, for example, as a threatening situation in the sixties, such as the student riots, defused itself in less than a decade. The Viet Nam War, which polarized and distilled the emotions of America, appears now as a questionable conflict that cost much and achieved little. As formerly feared, there was no wholesale materialization of political activists bent on destroying the system. Except for a handful of Marxist apologists who managed to entrench themselves as teachers in a few of the universities, most of the famous leaders of the antiwar movement re-entered the mainstream of society or became permanent outlaws. In fact, the campus' turmoils ultimately had a beneficial effect by having shaken up what was in many instances becoming an institutionalized stagnation, and which resulted in a healthy changeover of personnel from presidents down to instructors.

In order to place *It's Different Now, Mr. Abele* in a perspective against the background of a hyperkinetic era, it is necessary to recall some of the factors that were responsible for causing most of the tension. For the first time, a war in all its gore and glory was being televised daily giving Americans a ringside seat to the action. This constant reminder of a brutal, far away war served as fuel for organized protests that found a natural base among the universities and colleges across the country. Eruptions of political activism ranged from peaceful sit-ins to the demolition of military science buildings. This revolt against the war effort was, in a larger sense, a revolt against the whole establishment by the young, and the ways and means of protest became so diverse as to be considered a way of life—a sort of counter culture. The movement was marked by an avid consumption of hallucinogenic drugs, the wearing of colorful and unorthodox attire, the sporting of long hair, beards and moustaches, and the usage of neologisms and slang. The slogan was "Make love, not war," and the older generation's teeth were being set on edge by the irreverent behavior of hordes of the so-called flower children. If during this time many American families thought they were witnessing the erosion of some cherished traditions, the confusion and an inability to relate to any of these sudden changes were even more pronounced among the post World War II emigrés. *It's Different Now, Mr. Abele* focuses on just such a handful of Latvians in an average academic community whose lives are dramatically altered when they are confronted with some unexpected events.

Karl Abele is a philosophy professor in a small college in an even smaller town. He is a typical embodiment of all the qualities

that define success in a Latvian man. He takes pride in his
intellect, is serious and dedicated to his work, and has that air
about him of someone who neither makes nor tolerates any mistakes. Abele represents that special generation of Latvians who
chose exile rather than life under communist rule. These men and
women, regardless of their chosen geographical setting, automatically reject anything connected with left wing policies. The
visible shifts in the university towards a more liberal approach in
education constituted for these Latvians just another example of a
socialist victory. Thus Abele, although aware that the college he
works for has embraced the new liberal attitude and that it is
desirable for the faculty to adjust to a new way of thinking, is
unable to comply. To do so would be to go against a deep seated
conviction of patriotism that constitutes a national trust. In effect,
Sudrab Léger, the political science professor, who readily falls in
lock step with the wishes of the college president, represents not
only an antagonist in the traditional sense, but an enemy to the
whole Latvian mystique of anticommunism. No amount of
rhetoric can justify Léger's choice, and his eagerness to blow with
the wind reinforces the fact that he has all the moral strength of a
weather vane.

The core conflict between Abele and Léger is political in nature
and constitutes clash of wills in a personal duel. However, the
main theme of the play is the larger problem of acculturation
which reflects on all the participants in various degrees. Abele's
traditional old world attitude is felt in the classroom where he is
aptly called an epiphenomenon by one of his students. Although
Abele lectures about the philosophy of perception and change, in
reality he finds it hard to go along with anything that is new, especially when it concerns the upbringing of his daughter, Sarmite.
He is overprotective of her and tries to shelter her from the world
as if she were some young high school student instead of a graduating college senior. When Sarmite comes home one night after
having ingested some LSD, Abele's knee jerk reaction is to slap
her and attempt to call the police. Sarmite's incoherent speech
and behavior is to Abele a reflection of the rebelliousness of the
age that he finds odious. It is also a negation of Latvian ethics
which he had tried so hard to instill in her. It is Laimonis, the
young doctoral candidate and mathematics instructor, who points
out to the distraught professor that each generation has to be
tempted with its own forbidden fruit. In Abele's days it was a
cigar. Today it can be a marijuana cigarette. But although Abele
seems to grasp the implications of Sarmite's act intellectually, he

cannot come to terms with it emotionally. It is left up to Velta, Abele's wife, to reason with her husband and protect Sarmite from further paternal outbursts. Sarmite's motivations for getting high turn out to be the actions of a young woman in love doing something forbidden out of desperation and spite. The object of her love is the clean cut Laimonis, and when their feelings are finally known to each other, we know that these two young people are well adjusted to face a volatile world.

It's Different Now, Mr. Abele is a play seemingly constructed along traditional lines with a rigid adherence to time and place. The action transpires over the two days before Christmas and does not leave the Abele's living room. The play opens with a long exposition which defines characters and conflict. While Abele is portrayed as a dyed-in-the-wool conservative, his young friend Laimonis is not interested in politics and predicts that liberalism like any other fashion will subside in time. However, Laimonis is also making plans to move to a less liberal college, which indicates that the older generation's teachings have not been lost on him. The foreshadowing of danger is obvious in the description of Léger and the mentioning of him being on the promotion and tenure committee. Sarmite's experience with drugs is part of the rising action which sets up the obligatory scene of the taped confession of love overheard by Laimonis. However, while an obligatory scene—in order to fulfill the audience's expectancy due to a causal development of the dramatic action—usually is part of the main plot but the relationship between Sarmite and Laimonis occurs on a subplot level, the play's construction seems to defy the well-made-play formula. A strong climax is achieved when Abele is informed that his contract had been terminated and that Léger has been instrumental in the making of that decision; however, the denouement is veiled in ambiguity—a quality more fitting a structure based on dialectics. Thus the allegoric description of herself in Sarmite's speech near the end of Act II, "In order to build my life I have to use two different types of material, and such a building often becomes an anachronism and almost the opposite of the builder's aesthetic expectations," might be used also to characterize the structure of the play.

Commenting on the opening night's performance, Juris Silenieks, a literary critic and Professor of Modern Languages at Carnegie-Mellon University, states the following:

> *It's Different Now, Mr. Abele* makes us think about the evolu-
> tion of a society in exile, which has created a generation gap

at the same time seeking to mediate between the old and the new generations. It seems that Professor Straumanis has used Hegelian dialectics in developing the dramatic action. The stance of first generation immigrants with its selfcontentment in regard to the unchanging values and truth found in nationalistic traditions has been used for the thesis. As antithesis for this unbending set of values, the author presents a member of the Marx-Mao-Marcuse brotherhood who uses present day political fads for selfish ends.

Also Osvalds Uršteins, director of the American production, sees contrasting elements in the play:

> On the first reading of the play I was captivated by the contrasting moods....The author has intertwined several themes —politics, youth's problems with narcotics, Latvian upbringing in an American environment, the different philosophies among the Latvian immigrants....A gathering on Christmas Eve does not evoke silent holiday mood but, using a modern term, an anti-Christmas atmosphere.

It is evident that in order to structure a dramatic action containing contrasting elements one is forced to modify existing formulas. But plot is not Straumanis' primary concern. Rather like George Bernard Shaw, Straumanis advances ideas and promotes philosophical dialogue. Phenomenology, symbolism and ethical behavior are discussed in quick succession in relation to the problems of acculturation. For instance, the intense patriotic feelings that are aroused in Abele by the sight of a Latvian flag are nonexistent in Léger who has managed to disassociate himself from all the traditional symbols. Ultimately, if there is any hope for the continuation and upholding of the Latvian world view in exile, it rests with the new generation, albeit not through an automatic allegiance. Abele and Léger themselves are symbols of the opposing forces as defined by Hegel, with Sarmite and Laimonis representing the rational synthesis. They show a willingness and an ability to survive on their own terms. While Karl Abele's future, judging from the last scene, is questionable due to his inability to acculturate, Sarmite and Laimonis are willing to recognize the old while accepting the new.

The play, ending on an optimistic note for those who are able to change, suggests that the future might be similar to the past, and that only the present—the period of adjustment and metamorphosis—is different.

André Šedriks

It's Different Now, Mr. Abele. Act Three. Latvian American Theatre, Washington Ensemble, 1972. Act Three. Director: Osvalds Uršteins. Scenographer: Ilze Freivalde-Loxley. Mr. Leger: Osvalds Uršteins   Mrs. Leger: Daina Muceniece   Sarmite: Anda Uršteina

IT'S DIFFERENT NOW, MR. ABELE

CHARACTERS

KARL ABELE: a philosophy professor in his sixties
VELTA ABELE: his wife; formerly a pharmacist, now works as
    a saleslady in a drugstore.
SARMITE ABELE: their daughter, senior in college.
LAIMONIS LANKA: a Ph.D. candidate and assistant professor
SUDRABS LÉGER: 38 years old, professor of political science;
    before naturalization his name was SUDRABS LĒĢERIS
INA LÉGER: his wife

PLACE OF ACTION

Home of the Abeles in a small American college town where the
students outnumber the townspeople.

TIME OF ACTION

  Act I—late evening of December 23rd
  Act II—afternoon of December 24th
Act III—Christmas Eve, 1969

ACT ONE

*(As the curtain opens, lively Christmas songs resound—the kind
one hears in the streets of all small towns in the USA a month
before Christmas. The music stops as soon as professor ABELE
starts speaking. A livingroom in the Abeles' two story frame
house, very similar to others that were built in all American small*

towns after World War I. The style, outside as well as inside, is a combination of colonial and modern architecture, as the houseowners have added to the structure what they deemed necessary and right. A rather large window stage left with KARL'S desk nearby, covered with books and a telephone. Bookshelves on the wall behind the desk. On one of the shelves there is a Latvian pennant, above the shelves hangs a Latvian coat of arms. Up left center the main entrance in an alcove; up right a staircase leading to the second floor. Stage right a door leading into the kitchen that also serves as the dining room. Down right area represents the living room with a couch, a coffee table, and an armchair. Between the main entrance and the staircase a decorated Christmas tree with electric candles. As the curtain opens KARL is standing in front of the tree playfully handling an ornament. LAIMONIS sits near the professor's desk while inserting magnetic tape into a tape recorder.)

KARL: As the theme for this lecture let us use a quote from Gaston Bachelard: "Things look at us as we look at them. They seem indifferent to us only because we look at them with indifference. But to a clear eye all things are mirrors, and to a sincere and serious eye everything is depth."

LAIMONIS: Professor, please let me check if the recording is clear before you start your lecture. (*KARL nods approval, LAIMONIS rewinds the tape and listens to it. KARL pulls a pipe from his pocket, goes to the front door to discard ashes from the pipe. He opens the door; the lively Christmas music resounds, and KARL shuts the door.*)

KARL: You'll improve the language while transcribing as you've done so many times before. You have always correctly perceived the themes of my lectures, and your knowledge of the Latvian language is very good—at least good enough for translating the English lectures of a Latvian philosopher for the younger generation of Latvians.

LAIMONIS: It sounds almost strange—a Latvian philosopher prepares his lectures in a foreign language, and a student, who has studied Latvian only because it was forced onto him by his mother, translates them for the Latvian youth in spite of the fact that this youth speaks and writes the foreign language better than the professor who prepares his lectures in that foreign language...

KARL (*interrupts him*): And the student who studied Latvian only because his mother forced him to...

LAIMONIS (*interrupts KARL*): And so on, and so on. It is almost

like a never ending spiral beginning at one point—in ourselves—and circling around itself towards infinity.

KARL: Very well said. In the same manner, I mean, with the
same metaphor of the spiral, I try to convey the absurd trends
in today's philosophies to my less logically thinking students.
Can we start the recording now?

LAIMONIS (*who in the meantime has rewound the tape*): Yes,
the recorder and I are at your service.

KARL (*paces around during his lecture, stopping from time to
time while making an important point*): We are poor judges of
the revolutions we've been passing through; we keep thinking
ourselves contemporary with developments long since finished
and past, and we remain unconscious of what is really new in
the present. We have to keep reminding ourselves that over the
past century our knowledge of man has gone through an up-
heaval such as has perhaps not occurred since the appearance
of Christianity or the birth of Greek civilization. Our knowledge of art has necessarily been affected by it. Body and soul,
material life and the inner life, physiology and psychology—
for a long time these divisions were all that anyone needed.
These were the bricks and mortar, while much higher up there
glowed a single beacon, all the light there was to illuminate the
enveloping darkness. Then one day somebody noticed that this
light was somehow tied up with obscure mechanical processes.
Somehow, the inner life is not, after all, confined to the glass-
walled, well-lit cell at the top, from which everything is seen
and understood. Rather, it extends in depth endlessly inside the
gloomy, concealed body; its source lies within. The l'fe of the
mind does not comprise the whole of the inner life; this life is
bigger, heavier, and stranger, for it contains the whole immense domain of the unconscious.

The change has had consequences still impossible to calculate.
Prior to it, the life of the conscious mind seemed an adequate
enough cause of all our reflections and actions; suddenly, this
was no more than an end result, a reaction, or even a simple
effect. The study of the individual is not all that has been transformed; art history has been, too. Hitherto, the former had
been based on the study of great men, intellectual agents in
history guiding events. Now, an unconscious was discovered at
work in history too: even the anonymous masses were guided
blindly by hidden motives. Now, all things—theories and facts
alike—were seen to be passively subjected to an inevitable
material evolution and to obey only unconscious collective dic-

tates. Taine accounted for art in terms of environmental conditions, much as Marx accounted for social life by dialectical
materialism. A wave of determinism at the close of the nineteenth century swept all before it, and to many, consciousness
became no more than an epiphenomenon, a recording appara-
tus...like that mechanical gadget (*Indicates the recorder.*) recording words that say nothing...(*As if not knowing how to
proceed, KARL walks up to the Christmas tree and starts playing with one of the ornaments.*)
LAIMONIS: If you are finished with the introduction, may I ask
    you a question?
KARL: Go ahead; my thoughts have strayed from the theme any-
    way.
LAIMONIS: What do you mean with the word "epiphenomenon?"
    I mean, how could I translate it into Latvian?
KARL: Epiphenomenon? Did I use that word?
LAIMONIS: Yes, in the last sentence.
KARL: Strange. After my last lecture, a heated discussion devel-
    oped and a student called me a chauvinistic epiphenomenon.
LAIMONIS: Why did he call you that?
KARL: By counteracting an argument found in the slime of the so-
    called liberalism about the creation of a completely free soci-
    ety which would toss away the established order in this world,
    I had mentioned the senseless quarrels and even fights in
    Latvian Parliament during the nineteen thirties, thus giving
    him a good reason for using the term. Yes, foreign words are
    contagious....It would be half as bad if I could erase from my
    memory the arguments I had to hear. They were so logical and
    foolproof, though consisting entirely of Maoist mass slogans.
    You are not recording this, are you?
LAIMONIS: No, I am only listening with great interest.
KARL: Fine....Epiphenomenon could be explained as a secondary
    phenomenon overlapping and resulting from another or even
    the same incident, and being the logical continuation of it or
    even its consequence.
LAIMONIS: But in what connection did the student use it refer-
    ring to you?
KARL: I presume he tried to tell me that I live too much in the
    past, without a real connection to today or this college...
    (*With a sad smile.*) In medicine epiphenomenon often can
    mean an additional condition in the course of a disease.
LAIMONIS: You do not mean to imply that what you did and phil-
    osophized about in independent Latvia was a disease?

KARL: I often succumb to such doubts....Please do not be insulted —doubts, as everything else today, are relative. These doubts keep on occuring to me only in the last six months or so, ever since the new college president took office. You may have noticed how proud he is of his leftist convictions.

LAIMONIS: if you have doubts about your fight against the so-called liberalism and feel that it has little significance, rest assured because it's not so. New fashions, be they mini or maxi, will return to their normal state again. In the same way, the new trend of liberalism in America will subside. Of course, it will not happen on its own accord. The intellectuals, especially those in our universities who share your philosophy, will have to help out. Why did you think I would get insulted? I am not interested in politics at all.

KARL: As a mathematician you would not even be suited for it. I only was afraid that it might upset you when I mentioned my years of service at the University of Latvia with a certain disdain. It could have insulted your patriotic feelings. It was not my fate to sacrifice my life for our country as it was the case of your father, and believe me, I do not feel contempt. I'm only angry that I cannot refrain from constantly comparing the past with the present; not only in my most intimate thoughts, but even openly in my lectures.

LAIMONIS: How else would it be possible for students to come to terms with the present if they did not have a comparison to the past?

KARL: Here speaks the mathematician who deals with definite laws in the progress of life and science. Have you not noticed a certain lack of interest in your students about these laws?

LAIMONIS: I have noticed. Especially when it comes to proving a theorem. As quickly as possible I show how the truth we arrived at can help in solving the problems of today.

KARL: Yes, problems that are relevant for today's youth. Only philosophy is not as exact a science as is mathematics. In the field of philosophy ever since its beginnings there are too many opposing theories many of which cannot be even defined. And since the advent of existentialism, the majority of philosophers refuse to look for a common denominator of these theories. With the help of phenomenology, which is experiencing a renaissance, philosophy concerns itself with the individual who perceives life through his feelings. Perceiving, but not understanding. Maybe he would understand it somewhat better by relating to examples of the past.

LAIMONIS: I see you agree.

KARL: Of course, I agree theoretically. But we cannot use esoteric examples. Especially from Latvia, which is unknown
to the majority of the students even as a name.

LAIMONIS: My students know Latvia by name and where it is.

KARL: Yes, your students have told me how well you explain to
them your name. Lanka equals a marshlike meadow. It means
that mathematics will lead everyone at one time or another
into a bog, but if one studies with professor Lanka, then all students, even if they are in a swamp, will be happy, because his
given name Laimonis means one who can make you happy. In
other words, Laimonis equals a benefactor. Better watch out
that you are not labeled a chauvinist.

LAIMONIS: I'd rather be called a chauvinist than change my
name as some other Latvian professors have done.

KARL: If you mean our own Sudrabs Lēģeris, then I agree with
you. He did not solve anything by changing his name to Sadreb
Léger. Here are other Latvian students besides my daughter
Sarmite. And it does not matter whether they are Latvian or
not, students will be students, and they all have sharp tongues.
They found out that Léger is also a Latvian, and they
nicknamed him Sadreb the Frivolous, since leger in French
means also frivolous.

LAIMONIS: There are students who call him a fake, and I tend to
agree with them.

KARL: Since you have decided on an academic career, let me
urge you never to say anything discriminating about a colleague—especially not behind his back.

LAIMONIS: I beg your pardon, but in my opinion professor Léger
is nothing more than an opportunist. He was on the search committee when I applied for a position here, and he praised
Latvian scientists so profusely that I felt embarrassed. But as
soon as the new college president arrived, he started to preach
Maoist doctrine.

KARL: Political science in American universities is a subject
matter no less 'scientific' than mathematics....But political
opinions seem to change just as easily as philosophical theories.

LAIMONIS: But not to such an extent!

KARL: Maybe Léger has other motives for acting the way he
does. Your father died in the fortress of Kurzeme defending his
country. Sudrabs' father was interned for a whole year after
the coup d'etat of May 15th, and he was not a communist, as far
as I know. You seem to look at political events from your

father's point of view, and Sudrabs is doing the very same thing...

LAIMONIS: Be that as it may, I don't intent to associate with him much longer.

KARL: Does it mean you intend to leave us?

LAIMONIS: Yes, right after the holidays I have an interview at a university in Florida.

KARL: Will you receive your Ph.D. next spring?

LAIMONIS: That's right. I received notice from Chicago that all five committee members have read my dissertation and I can receive my degree at the next commencement.

KARL: Congratulations! Does your mother know all this?

LAIMONIS: She was the first one to find out. I called her yesterday, and she will come with me to Florida. I shall not be going home for Christmas, because mother is working the night shift on Christmas Eve.

KARL: I hope you will be able to persuade her to quit her job at the factory.

LAIMONIS: She promised just that. As soon as I have a permanent position, she will come and live with me. That is the reason I wanted her to come with me to Florida and have a chance to look around.

KARL: Didn't you tell me once that Mrs. Lanka studied at the University of Latvia?

LAIMONIS: She would have graduated during the first year of the Russian occupation. She was married and expecting her first child. The fact that my father, an officer of the dismantled Latvian army, went into hiding complicated matters further. My mother wanted to become a foreign language teacher but thus far I have been her only student.

KARL: She can be very proud of her only student. That is more than many of us can say who have taught hundreds of students. But how did we get off the subject?

LAIMONIS: We wanted to tape your lecture. Do you want to start?

KARL: Why not? Just press the buttons! (*LAIMONIS starts the tape recorder. After a brief pause KARL starts his lecture.*) Let us start with the question what really is Western culture? Is it a specific spiritual reality? Or—the dissimilarity between the Eastern and Western cultures is nothing more than a different interpretation of conventional definitions. Specialists, who become submerged in research of a limited field, often allow themselves to succumb to this kind of thinking. Since we are not discussing separate fields of study here but rather the encompassing phenomenon of all fields, we have to take into consideration all possible factors which pertain to the Western and the Eastern art and thought. And by doing this, we will discover certain basic tendencies indicating that both sides have a unique spirit, even though in the passing of time this spirit may have become a variation or even a contradiction in itself. By this I want to point out that... (*The telephone rings. LAIMONIS stops the tape recorder and lifts the receiver.*)

LAIMONIS: Hello? No, but he is right here. Right away. (*To KARL*). It seems that Dr. Léger wants to talk to you.

KARL (*goes to the phone and picks up the receiver*): Here Karl Abele. How are you? What's on your mind so late on a cold winter night? Oh, you have just come back from a meeting? Do the students plan to burn something again? Not with the students? A faculty meeting? I was not aware that you were on that committee....Trouble?...Defended me? What crime have I committed? To talk right away? You don't mean tonight, do you?...I had not planned to go to the campus tomorrow; maybe late in the afternoon to pick up my mail....Well, if you cannot discuss it over the phone then by all means come here. Yes, I shall be home. Goodby! (*Thoughtfully replaces the receiver, picks up his pipe and starts handling it somewhat nervously.*)

LAIMONIS: What is Sudrabs up to now, so late at night?

KARL (*lost in deep thought*): What did you say? No, no, he is not coming tonight, he will be here early tomorrow morning.

LAIMONIS: At least we can continue taping the lecture.

KARL: Well, where did we stop? (*As LAIMONIS is about to play back the last sentence, KARL interrupts him again.*) Did you know that Léger is on the personnel committee dealing with tenure and promotions?

LAIMONIS: He was not elected to it, but I heard that the college president himself appointed Léger to fill the vacancy when professor Davis became the Dean.

KARL: Yes, our new president changes not only the procedures of the administration to suit him but he also interferes with the privileges of the faculty.

LAIMONIS: He supposedly is doing it to appease the demands of the students.

KARL: The demands of those students who have come to college not for the purpose of acquiring knowledge but to become involved in political activities. Fortunately, their number is small.

LAIMONIS: It is against mathematical principles that the minority can cause so much damage while the majority simply stands by or even pretends not to see the nonsense.

KARL: Politically it was practiced already in ancient Greece at the time of Peisistratus when there was already a democratic government from which we are supposed to have learned...

VELTA (*appears on the staircase during the conversation dressed in a housecoat*): Karl, who was that on the phone? Was it Sarmite?

KARL: Aren't you asleep yet? Isn't Sarmite in her room? Were you expecting her call?

VELTA (*having come down the stairs she notices LAIMONIS*): Good evening, Laimonis. (*To KARL.*) Sarmite went to celebrate her girlfriend's birthday and promised to be home around ten o'clock.

LAIMONIS: Good evening, Mrs. Abele. (*Looks at his wristwatch.*) Since it is not midnight yet, the party might not be over.

VELTA: That may well be, but up till now Sarmite has always called if she could not be home at the time she promised.

KALR: Léger called. Wants to discuss something of great importance with me.

VELTA: Did he say something about Sarmite?

KARL: No, Sarmite isn't at his place, is she?

VELTA: No, she went to Peggy's. But since most of Peggy's friends are political science students, Léger was invited too.

LAIMONIS: Mrs. Abele, where Leger was tonight they did not celebrate—they winnowed; they separated the chaff from the grain or vice versa: the good from the bad.

VELTA: Are you trying to tell me something, Laimonis?

KARL: Léger was at a committee meeting where they were deciding the fate of many a professor.

VELTA: In that case your fate too, Karl. After seven years of service at this college you are entitled to tenure.

LAIMONIS: And with tenure you should get full professorship. I hope we find that out before my departure so we can celebrate the occasion appropriately.

VELTA: Where are you going, Laimonis?

KARL: Laimonis is interviewing for a new position at a university in Florida. He will receive his Ph.D. this spring and is ready for deeper waters.

VELTA: Congratulations! But it is a pity you are leaving us. Karl will have no one to talk to about the past in Latvia. Didn't they

offer a contract to you here for the next year? Sarmite tells
me what an excellent teacher you are.

LAIMONIS: The students here are good too, but I do not like the
very liberal atmosphere of the college. I told the same thing to
the dean when he offered me a raise for the next year.

KARL: You did not quit your job here, did you?

LAIMONIS: I most certainly did.

KARL: Before you found another one? What if you don't like
Florida...or they don't like you?

LAIMONIS: Florida is not the only place in the world.

VELTA (*thinking of KARL*): If all professors would have a choice
of jobs as you, Laimonis, life would be much simpler at times.

LAIMONIS: You mean to say that professor Abele is thinking of
leaving this college too?

KARL: Professor Abele does not care about the atmosphere in
this college, but he will have to remain here until he retires.

VELTA: For that you have to wait at least five more years.

LAIMONIS: If there were a chance, I would leave this place if I
were you.

KARL: If there only were that chance! But there is none.

LAIMONIS: Why? Sarmite will graduate this year and hopefully
will do graduate work somewhere else. Mrs. Abele is not
married to her job in the pharmacy...

KARL: No, no one is tied down to anything here. I have wanted to
leave here and have sent out applications everywhere. I have
also received very polite answers telling me between the lines
that the vacant positions are meant for teachers of philosophy
with a firmer foundation in the liberal American thinking and
who are not as stubborn in their preaching of Kant's maxims.
The positions available are also mostly for academicians
under forty...

LAIMONIS: That is pure nonsense!

KARL: It is not. It is a reality of life. (*Towards VELTA.*) Since
you are unable to sleep waiting up for Sarmite, would you mind
making us some coffee? We still would like to work for an hour
or so.

VELTA: I fixed coffee before going upstairs and left it in the
thermos. I have also done some baking for Christmas, and
Laimonis should taste some of it so he can compare it with his
mother's!

KARL: Mrs. Lanka will not be doing any baking this Christmas.

VELTA: Why? What has happened? Mrs. Lanka is not...

LAIMONIS: No, she is not ill, only unhappy with my decision not to come home for the holidays.

KARL: They both will be flying to sunny Florida.

VELTA: How nice, I'll have a chance to see my longtime friend again...both of us worked for the military government in Germany—she as an interpreter, I as a nurse. You were very young at the time and don't remember.

KARL: Wait a minute! You are getting ahead of yourself.

VELTA: Why? Don't we women have a right to meet and reminisce?

LAIMONIS: Mother is not coming here. Day after tomorrow I'll be flying to Chicago where I'll meet her for our trip to Florida.

VELTA: How disappointing! You said you were leaving the day after tomorrow? Then you can spend Christmas Eve with us.

KARL: Why didn't I think of it? Well, Laimonis, tomorrow night you have to spend with us. You didn't have other plans, did you?

LAIMONIS: I had planned to transcribe your lecture, but I can do it during the day.

VELTA: Then everything is set. We will light our Christmas tree together. Sarmite will be happy too with a young person to keep her company. (*Glances with a worried look at her watch.*) I cannot understand where she could be so late tonight.

KARL (*walks up to the desk to fill his pipe, lifts a small white piece of paper next to the phone*): What was the name of Sarmite's friend?

VELTA: Peggy Simpson. Why do you ask?

KARL: In that case she has left a phone number here. Call her and tell her to come home. (*LAIMONIS walks up to the Christmas tree and looks at the packages.*)

VELTA (*goes to the phone*): Sarmite will not like this at all. But as punishment for not being home on time, she will have to put up with it. (*Dials the number.*)

LAIMONIS: Will you have many guests tomorrow night? There are so many presents here!

KARL (*approaching the tree*): It is our custom to exchange gifts with each other. There's even a present for you. We wanted to give it to you tonight, but now it will have to wait till tomorrow.

LAIMONIS: For me? You shouldn't have...

VELTA (*replaces the receiver*): There is no answer. Where could they gad about?

LAIMONIS: Don't you know the custom of our students? After a party the whole crowd walks around town seeing each other home.

KARL: Sarmite might have turned into our street by now. Your worries are unfounded. Better pour some coffee for us, please. (*To LAIMONIS.*) And now let us go and check out if my wife still knows how to bake holiday treats!

VELTA: Sarmite baked this year, and I must say everything has turned out just right!

KARL (*to LAIMONIS*): If you are not afraid that this is a bait, let's go and taste them.

LAIMONIS: Of course, I'm afraid. I like Sarmite even without her talent for baking. This is our downfall: because of our appetites we are being lured into a lifetime commitment.

VELTA: What kind of talk is this in the middle of the winter? Young Latvian people usually fall in love around Midsummer Night in the middle of June and get married in fall...

KARL (*as VELTA disappears into the kitchen, asks LAIMONIS to follow him*): Do you see how simple is the logic of women: with the help of some Christmas cookies she wants to secure a husband for her daughter. (*Turning out the bright lights he follows the others into the kitchen, closing the door behind him. The stage is illuminated by the lights on the Christmas tree and the desk lamp. For a short while the stage is empty, then we hear the outside door open and Christmas music in the distance resounds as in the beginning of the play. SARMITE entering the room leaves the outside door open as if unaware of the surroundings. All through the next scene her actions are very irrational. She does not leave her outerwear in the entrance hall but discards it piece by piece as she dances around the room. Her actions, mimicry and motions indicate that she is under the influence of alcohol or some other stimulant. It appears that SARMITE is very aware of all her motions, at times she seems to observe them, repeat them several times and is amused by them. At one instance as she is repeating a movement she notices the Christmas tree. She walks up to the tree and looks with great fascination at the ornaments that reflect the lights of the tree. Then she starts removing the angel hair and decorates herself with it, covering her head and shoulders with it. With outstretched arms she places herself next to the tree as if petrified. A smile is on her lips.*)

LAIMONIS (*entering and addressing himself to those in the kitchen*): I'll find them without the light. I think I left them on the desk. (*He goes in the direction of the desk in order to fetch his cigarettes, but feeling a draft coming from the outside door, he walks over, looks outside, then closes the door. He shrugs his shoulders as if not understanding why it was left open and returns to the desk without noticing SARMITE. The Christmas music has stopped. As soon as the music stops SARMITE seems to come out of the trance, but has not completely returned to reality yet. She notices LAIMONIS at the desk. He becomes a new object of admiration for her. She approaches him slowly as if dancing, reaches out, stretches her arms towards him, utters unintelligible sounds — a mixture of happy laughter and groans.*)

LAIMONIS (*having found the package of cigarettes he turns in order to reenter the kitchen when he notices SARMITE*): Sarmite! Good evening! What are you up to? Do you pretend to be a Christmas tree? (*SARMITE wants to embrace him; LAIMONIS realizes that something is very wrong.*) Have you had one too many, Sarmite? (*He grabs her by her hands and jokingly pretends to sniff her breath.*) What kind of nectar was it? Was it gin from the rainy Albion or rum from sultry Jamaica?

SARMITE (*laughingly trills a popular American Christmas song*): Tulala, tulala, tula, la, la la...

LAIMONIS (*not able to detect the smell of alcohol on her breath becomes serious*): Sarmite, what is the matter with you? (*Begins to shake her. When she does not respond to this, he moves his hand in front of her eyes as if checking her eyesight. SARMITE stares into the void and continues to trill.*) Mrs. Abele! Professor! (*He leads SARMITE to the couch and tries to make her sit down. VELTA comes running into the room.*)

VELTA: What is it? (*She sees SARMITE trying to embrace LAIMONIS.*) Sarmite! Are you drunk? (*At this moment KARL runs onto the stage and stops between the kitchen door and the couch.*)

LAIMONIS: Sarmite is not drunk. She...

SARMITE (*lets go of LAIMONIS and kneels on the couch jumping up and down*): Flying...over the Blue Mountain...into the yellow moon...

VELTA (*walks behind the couch and tries to make SARMITE face her*): Sarmite, have you been smoking pot? Do you hear me? (*SARMITE, still in a daze, tries to trill.*) Sarmite, did you take any drugs?

KARL: Sarmite, please answer! (*SARMITE seems to come around when she hears her father's voice. She turns towards her father and reaches out to him. KARL slaps her face. SARMITE falls face down on the couch. There is a momentary silence. SARMITE begins to groan, moan and wheeze as if in great pain.*)

VELTA: Sarmite, you did not take LSD, did you?

KARL (*hurries to the phone*): Operator, give me the police!

VELTA: Karl, no! (*Runs up to KARL, pulls the receiver out of his hand and replaces it.*) Are you out of your mind? We don't know what's the matter with Sarmite. (*KARL falls back in a chair and cradles his head in his hands.*)

LAIMONIS (*picks up SARMITE'S purse from the floor*): Here, Mrs. Abele, look inside. The answer may be in there. (*VELTA nervously takes the purse and opens it. She takes out anti- pregnancy pills wrapped in plastic which she recognizes and immediately hides in the pocket of her housecoat.*)

SARMITE (*regains her senses and is in great pain*): Mother, help me, mother!

VELTA (*rushes up to SARMITE*): What did you take? Please tell me!

SARMITE: Acid, but a very small dose. Mother, please help me!

VELTA: How long ago did you take it?

SARMITE: Half an hour, an hour...I don't know...

LAIMONIS (*seeing that KARL still sits without moving*): Shall I call the doctor?

VELTA: No! No! The doctor cannot help right now. (*Tries to lift SARMITE.*) Come, Sarmite, I'll help you up to bed. (*LAIMONIS helps VELTA lift up SARMITE and accompanies them both to the stairway.*) Thank you, Laimonis, we will manage to get upstairs by ourselves.

LAIMONIS (*remains at the bottom of the stairs. When SARMITE and VELTA disappear upstairs, he turns to KARL who has not moved. LAIMONIS walks towards him, picks up SARMITE'S overcoat and places it on the couch*): Mr. Abele!

KARL (*as if taken by surprise he turns his face to LAIMONIS*): Oh, well, where did we leave off? Oh, yes...Janus with his two faces...His temple is open only in times of war...

LAIMONIS: Mr. Abele, the tape recorder is not on.

KARL: No, it is not on. (*Gets up as if wanting to continue the re- cording of his lecture.*) Just press the buttons...

LAIMONIS: Mr. Abele, wouldn't you rather continue tomorrow?

KARL: No, no, tomorrow I have other things to do....So, espe- cially we Latvians, finding ourselves in the midst of two diverse cultures...(*Suddenly loses his composure.*) Sarmite! My Sarmite! (*As if appealing to LAIMONIS.*) Tell me please who is to blame? What am I to do? Where can I seek help?

LAIMONIS: Please, calm yourself. Things are not as tragic as you seem to think...

KARL: Not as tragic? Haven't you seen the longhaired students sitting in your classes under the influence of drugs and pot?

LAIMONIS: But Sarmite is not one of them, and she never will be.

KARL: But did you see in what condition she was tonight?

LAIMONIS: Do you remember how you felt after smoking your first cigar?

KARL: One cannot compare these two situations.

LAIMONIS: Maybe that's a mistake that we refuse to compare the stimulants which we used with the ones they are using today.

KARL: But Sarmite, my Sarmite whom I have tried to protect from the customs of today's youth...

LAIMONIS: Forbidden fruit is always sweeter—you should know that.

KARL: I know, but I cannot understand....Excuse me, but that is how I feel.

LAIMONIS: I do understand you...you do not have to ask my forgiveness. Believe me, tomorrow everything will be right again.

KARL: Let's hope....I won't be able to go on with the lecture.... Please come tomorrow afternoon before we start our Christmas Eve festivities. We'll finish then.

LAIMONIS: Fine. Only please promise me not to be too severe with Sarmite. She will regret her behavior tomorrow on her own accord.

KARL (*forces himself to be funny*): I see that Sarmite's baking talents have gotten to you already.

LAIMONIS: Is that so bad? For that reason alone you have to promise me not to punish her.

KARL: I promise, I promise.

LAIMONIS (*during the conversation has put on his overcoat*): May I leave the tape recorder here?

KARL: Of course, of course. Before you come tomorrow I'll listen to the beginning.

LAIMONIS (*shakes hands with KARL*): Till tomorrow then. Hope you are master of the situation again.

KARL: Don't worry about me. (*Accompanies LAIMONIS to the door.*) Watch out—the walk might be icy. (*Returns to the room, casts a worried glance towards the staircase, wants to go upstairs but reconsiders. He walks over to his desk and starts handling his pipe.*)

VELTA (*comes down the stairs, picks up SARMITE'S coat and hangs it up in the hallway. Having finished that, she ap-*

proaches KARL): Karl!

KARL: Yes.

VELTA: Sarmite fell asleep.

KARL: Yes...

VELTA: Can you promise me not to discuss this evening with Sarmite until I return from work tomorrow?

KARL: If you think I'll not be able to restrain myself...

VELTA: That's what I think.

KARL: She is my daughter too...

VELTA: I think it would be better if I were present when we are going to have it out with her.

KARL: First Laimonis, now you too...As if I were some kind of a monster.

VELTA: I'm not accusing you of that, but we will have to discuss other things besides the LSD.

KARL: What else did she... (*Stops in the middle of the sentence as he sees the container with the anti-pregnancy pills in VELTA'S hand.*)

VELTA: Do you know what these are?

KARL: No, what are they?

VELTA: These are pills women take in order to prevent pregnancy. (*When KARL wants to say something VELTA interrupts him.*) Don't get excited. Sarmite has not used them yet because the entire dosage is intact.

KARL: But why did she get them in the first place?

VELTA: I plan to find that out when we talk to her.

KARL: It's getting worse.

VELTA: Nothing of the kind. We shall find out everything tomorrow. Now I'll go to sleep, I have to work tomorrow. It would do you good if you were to do the same.

KARL: Go ahead...I'll come upstairs soon. (*Walks to the desk, sits down and pretends to be doing something important.*)

VELTA (*walks towards the stairs*): Just don't linger down here all night long again. (*Goes upstairs.*)

(*After VELTA leaves, KARL goes to the outside door, opens it wide and breathes in the fresh air. As soon as the door is open Christmas music of the same kind as in the beginning of the first act is heard. The stage is in semidarkness since VELTA turned out the big lights when she went upstairs*).

CURTAIN

ACT TWO

(Stage the same as in Act I. Cold winter sun is shining through the window, illuminating the desk and the space around it. The rest of the living room is still in semi-darkness. It is noon. As the curtain opens the stage is empty. The phone on the desk is ringing continuously. On the upper floor one hears doors opening and closing indicating hurry.)

KARL *(from the upper floor)*: Sarmite! Sarmite! *(Appears on the top of the stairs hurriedly fixing his attire.)* Sarmite! *(When nobody answers, he rushes down the stairs and picks up the phone.)* Hallo? *(The connection has already been discontinued, but KARL keeps jiggling the dial.)* Hallo? *(Replaces the receiver and keeps shuffling around in the papers on his desk. Finds his wrist watch, looks at it, then realizes that it has stopped. KARL winds the watch and starts to go in the direction of the kitchen.)* Sarmite, are you in the kitchen? *(Without waiting for an answer he goes into the kitchen. One hears sounds of someone pouring coffee. When after a short while KARL appears with a cup in his hands, the phone rings again. He hurries to the phone and lifts the receiver.)* Hallo...Velta? ....Oh, it is you! Good morning, Laimonis. Wrong? Why?... You're right, the sun also tells it is noon....Yes, I overslept.... Don't really know, but it was late....Yes, I did finish the lecture and recorded half of it; the other half is drafted on paper. When you get here tonight, you may take it with you....Yes, but I don't know if it will be good enough...seems too pessimistic....Well, you'll be able to decide that....Laimonis, what time is it? My watch has stopped....Quarter to twelve. Thank you! Was it you who called me about five minutes ago?...No? No, no...it's not important....Yes, till seven then. *(Replaces the receiver, drinks coffee and automatically organizes the papers scattered around on the desk. Remembers to set his watch. Takes the address book, finds the number, lifts the receiver and dials.)* Velta, is this you? Have you been calling me for the last hour?...Yes, you did wake me....No, it was Laimonis who called before. Velta, Sarmite is not home! You know?...What is she doing at the library during the holidays? Yes, yes I remember that she had promised to help out....She left before you?...Was in our room? To thank you? What for? ...Well, then she must have some sense left if she remembers ....No, I'll stay home. Léger promised to come over....What is she afraid of if she wants to come home only together with you?...The slap hurt me more than it did her....Yes, yes I'll be home. (*KARL replaces the receiver. Finishes his cup of coffee and wants to go into the kitchen for a refill when the sound of a motorcycle is heard. KARL goes to the front door. As he reaches the door, someone is knocking. KARL opens the door.*) Please do come in!

SUDRABS: Thank you! (*He enters the hallway, takes off his motorcycle cap and tries to hang it on a hook. When he does not succeed, he drops it on the floor together with his leather gloves. Enters the room and shakes hands with KARL.*) Well, and how have you been in these so called dog days?

KARL: Thank you, but they have only just begun. (*He takes a good look at the attire of LEGER; dirty ski jacket over a bright red wool pullover.*) I imagine you are cold having come on a motorcyle. May I offer you a cup of coffee?

SUDRABS: It isn't that cold, and I have had too much coffee already. (*He sees the package of cigarettes on the table where LAIMONIS left it yesterday.*) But I would like to have one of your cigarettes, if I may.

KARL: They are not mine. Professor Lanka seems to have forgotten them. But go ahead and take one anyway.

SUDRABS (*reaches for the cigarettes*): We should take advantage of Lanka—he is proud as a boyar. I found out yesterday that he has resigned from our college!

KARL: Yes, I know. (*Not wanting to discuss it any further.*) Please excuse me for a moment. In order to wake up completely I need another cup. (*Goes out to the kitchen.*)

SUDRABS (*walks up to the desk in order to use the ashtray. He notices the draft of the lecture and starts reading it. As soon as he hears KARL coming back, he quickly puts the pages back*): Isn't Mrs. Abele at home?

KARL: She is working today but will be home in an hour. I heard that your wife has started to work too—as a cashier in a bank no less!

SUDRABS: Yes, she started and finished three days later.

KARL: Why?

SUDRABS: It's a long story. The reason the bank president gave for letting Ina go was that the former cashier had returned. I believe it was something else—simple discrimination. The local officers of the Veterans Association threatened to close their account if the bank continued to employ a demonstrator.

KARL: You were leading the anti-war demonstration, not your wife.

SUDRABS: As a fool, Ina was marching beside me...

KARL: You are absolutely right—that is discrimination...

SUDRABS (*taken by surprise*): You agree with me?

KARL: No, I'm disagreeing with you. (*SUDRABS seems confused.*) You are the one who is discriminating by calling your wife a fool...

SUDRABS (*realizing to have lost his first move, he tries to find a weak spot in his opponent*): Sarmite isn't back from her skiing trip, is she?

KARL: Skiing? As far as I know she is at the university library. Why do you think she went skiing?

SUDRABS: Skiing is used as a pretext for the experiments the young people pursue.

KARL: What are you talking about? What kind of experiments?

SUDRABS: Last night all the guests at the party decided to go to the college ski camp and celebrate Christmas there...in their own fashion—smoking grass...dreaming a bit...(*He notices having touched a sore spot.*) I really don't know if all of them went; I had to leave the party early to attend a meeting. I was sorry to leave, though—a very nice progressive group had gathered there.

KARL: Do you consider Sarmite as one of the progressives?

SUDRABS: To tell the truth I was somewhat surprised seeing her there. I had the impression that she had no desire to be "with it."

KARL (*feels that this remark was meant for him*): Mr. Léger, even though we have known each other close to five years now, you have never really explained to me what you mean by "being with it."

SUDRABS: What do you want to know?

KARL: I am not a professor of political science, therefore, what I say is to be understood at face value.

SUDRABS: Knowing the chauvinism of our people as well as the so-called political education, I can only assume that you are trying to provoke me in declaring my affiliation with a particular political trend.

KARL: The fact that you do not belong to the same—as you like to call it—political trend as I, is perfectly clear. I don't belong to any. However, I would like to know your personal political creed, the basis of the ideology you are preaching to your students.

SUDRABS: As a philosopher you should be aware that our modern progressive world does not recognize dogma and definitions simply stating that black is black and white is white.

KARL: Are you trying to tell me that you are not even explaining to your students the difference between liberalism and conservatism? Doesn't political science differentiate between socialism and communism anymore?

SUDRABS (*avoiding a direct answer, looks for a chance to change the subject*): May I sit down?

KARL: Please do! (*Walks to the table, finds his pipe and prepares it for smoking.*)

SUDRABS (*takes the package of cigarettes, sits down on the couch and lights a cigarette*): Our new college president said in his last speech that the political sciences have to concern themselves with the problems of today. We cannot classify these problems so easily because we lack the necessary perspective. Who would be the authority who without a doubt could define liberalism or conservatism? Even socialism is not the same as Marx described it. Practical communism differs greatly from the theoretical...

KARL: Just a minute, you are contradicting yourself. Just now you asserted that one cannot classify the different trends. But if you cannot classify them, how can you call them by their names? A name is a symbol for a concept, and in my opinion a political trend is a certain kind of concept too.

SUDRABS: I agree that a political trend is a concept, but you have to realize that there are concepts which change in the course of time because the people think and perceive in a changed way. (*Points to the pennant and crest of Latvia.*) For example, your symbols—the flag and the crest—are perceived differently by different groups of Latvians.

KARL: Yes, I have noticed that. But it does seem to me that for the most part they are still sacred.

SUDRABS: I beg to differ. These symbols among the Latvians in exile are sacred only to a small group. It is the group which prospered greatly during the independence and which was brought up in an empty barrel echoing the slogans that the future of the Latvian nation was in raising pigs...

KARL: Your rudeness does not surprise me. I have heard the same sentiments expressed by other Latvians too. On the contrary, I want to congratulate you on your ability to paraphrase Latvian proverbs and sayings which were spoken by a man who never doubted the value of these symbols; not when he was standing at the cradle of our nation nor when he gave his life for it.

SUDRABS: The fact that some men have believed and still believe in a free and independent Latvia does not change the truth of my assertion that they are a minority.

KARL: Altruism and self-sacrifice are not qualities characteristic of a crowd. Ideologists and true leaders will always be a minority.

SUDRABS: You must be joking! The men whom you are referring to know only one ideology—to prosper by other people's sweat. And they want to become leaders only for one reason—to be able to enforce their whims upon that part of the nation that you referred to as a crowd.

KARL: While using the word "crowd," I did not talk only about Latvians. But I'm afraid that the generalization you used cannot be attributed to the Latvian nation. I hope you will agree with my statement that Latvians are great individualists.

SUDRABS: That is a disputable assertion originated by national historians who tried to prove that the existence of single family farms in Latvian territory in ancient times was a sign of Latvian individualism. We could deduce further that the Letgallians did not belong to the Latvian nation since they lived in villages like their Slavic neighbors. Only after the abolition of serfdom did they have single family farms. The barons knew that allowing them to live in larger economic units, such as villages, they would sooner become independent economically as well as politically. The so-called Latvian individualism is nothing more than opposition to their serf mentality.

KARL: I fail to see a connection in your argument.

SUDRABS: In order to hide their helplessness and their inferiority complex, people play the role of heroes. An empty barrel can be heard a long way, as says a Latvian proverb.

KARL: Very well, let us assume that you are right. But using a more modern type of argument, the Marxist dialectic, which will give you no trouble, please explain to me why in the present day Latvia not the people but only a select group, the few chosen ones, are those who rule the majority?

SUDRABS: Not the chosen ones, but those who are capable of interpreting the teachings of Marx and Lenin and adapting them in practice. It is a pity that in the Soviet Union there are too many capable people interpreting the same doctrine in different ways...In China they solved the problem better...

KARL: Yes, they have the personality cult there...

SUDRABS: Only in a transitional stage. The true goal of communism is the government by the people. When that will be achieved...

KARL: Then we will have a new paradise on this earth for which the occupants of Latvia have waited already fifty years.

SUDRABS: It is impossible to talk about politics with you. I have noticed that you lack a sufficient basis for your political arguments; for example, in your last lecture to the political science seminar...

KARL: Because one uses traditional truths for his arguments, it is by far not an indication that the conclusions are invalid. But we started to talk about symbols. Do you think that Mao's red bible isn't a symbol?

SUDRABS: Hammer and sickle are symbols too. But the progressive world is able to rid itself of symbols if they represent an outdated concept.

KARL: I have noticed that. But the reverse is also true: concepts change, but symbols remain. Here is one—the Christmas tree. Especially in America, this symbol means a great deal even to the non-Christian children.

SUDRABS: We are not discussing children.

KARL: Children will grow up in time, therefore we should discuss them. Aren't you going to have a tree for your children this year? If I remember correctly, last year your tree was bigger than ours and your daughter Lienite and son Ansis were very pleased about that.

SUDRABS: We will not have a tree this year...

KARL: Dr. Léger, in that case there is no point in our discussion of concepts and symbols.

SUDRABS: Of course, of course. As soon as someone dares to touch upon dogmas that have been accepted by you without evaluation, any further discussion is forbidden.

KARL: Forgive me, but it really would be better if we end this discussion. Before your revolutionaries have not conquered this earth and done away with all the traditions, however not being able to replace them with new...

SUDRABS: You misunderstood me. We do not have a tree this year because our children went away with my father-in-law to my wife's brother who also has two children the same age. We will celebrate our Christmas there when we go to pick them up.

KARL: Aren't your children still too small to be off by themselves?

SUDRABS: They are small, but it was convenient to get rid of them for a while. As you know, the college president has assigned me to several committees, and they have meetings even during the vacation. New candidates for different positions will come to the college, and the president wishes that I interview them. Children would only be underfoot.

KARL: Do you have meetings on Christmas Eve?

SUDRABS: If we had not decided so many things at the meeting last night, we would have to meet tonight again. But it turns out that Ina and I will be alone tonight...

KARL: In that case please do join us here. We shall not pray, only light the Christmas tree...

SUDRABS: I don't know if it would be proper...

KARL: No arguments, please. We will not have many guests, only professor Lanka. Sarmite has baked enough for a whole village.

SUDRABS: Have you been on the campus today?

KARL: No. Should I have been there?

SUDRABS: No, no, I only meant if you had been there to pick up your mail? I wonder if they delivered the mail today? I was expecting several letters...

KARL: It could be that Sarmite has looked into my mailbox, and should there be something, I'll get it. But why are we discussing all this trivia? Last night you told me that you had something important to tell me. Well, where is the fire?

SUDRABS: I don't think it is really a burning question, and I do not wish to spoil your Christmas.

KARL: Was it something unpleasant that you had to tell me?

SUDRABS: I wanted to warn you.

KARL: Warn me about what? About the strange behavior of Sarmite last night?

SUDRABS: What could Sarmite have done...

KARL: Then is it something else?

SUDRABS: At the meeting yesterday, we were discussing promotions and tenure...and as far as you are concerned, things do not look too bright.

KARL: That does not surprise me. I really had not counted on a promotion, even though according to the faculty handbook I'm eligible for tenure next year.

SUDRABS: I pointed this out at the meeting last night.

KARL: Are you telling me that you stood up for me?

SUDRABS: One Latvian must do that for another Latvian.

KARL: I do thank you for that!

SUDRABS: It was not an easy decision for the committee, especially in your case. You cannot get a promotion, but according to the rules of the faculty handbook after six years of service one is entitled to tenure. But in your case a promotion has to

come with tenure since you have been at the same level for
three years. However, they cannot change the rules on your
account.

KARL: Well, what did the committee decide?

SUDRABS: Over my objections the committee is sending your
case to the college president for his decision. I hope everything
turns out alright. The president called me this morning to
sound me out. At the end of our conversation he told me that he
had reached a decision and wanted to hear my position on it.

KARL: Then all there is left for me now is to wait until the end of
February when the tenure decisions are announced.

SUDRABS: I just wanted to alert and forewarn you. (*Gets up.*)

KARL: I thank you once more.

SUDRABS: Haven't you looked for a better endowed college
which would offer you a higher rank?

KARL: One cannot find those so easily.

SUDRABS: Still, I would be looking if I were you....But now I
have to go.

KARL: Aren't you a strange one! You just came and now you
want to run away. (*SUDRABS is ill at ease not knowing what
to say.*) You told me last night you had something important to
discuss with me...If you are worried that I am not getting a
promotion, don't—I really didn't expect it.

SUDRABS: In that case I'm glad I did not get you worried, especially on Christmas Eve. And thank you for the invitation! Ina
will be very happy to sit around a Christmas tree for a
while....At what time should we come?

KARL: Aren't you keeping something from me? Why did you suggest that I look for a wealthier college?

SUDRABS: Just a general observation. I'm sure you know that all
professors are writing letters looking for a better position. And
when they receive an offer they use it to pressure the college
administration for higher salaries.

KARL: You are right. I too have written letters in all directions,
but without success.

SUDRABS: Well, maybe you will not have to move....But now I
have to go....I'm expecting some important news...so I have
to check my mailbox.

KARL: I don't want to keep you against your will. We shall see
you around seven tonight.

SUDRABS (*takes one more cigarette out of the package belonging to LANKA, throws the package back onto the table and
goes towards the exit, picks up his cap and gloves, puts them*

on): Till later then! I doubt we will be able to get presents for all of you on such short notice...maybe just something stronger, some spirits as is our good old custom, right?

KARL: Please don't bother with presents! We shall rejoice in your sheer presence, as sinners who are converted and have come to celebrate Christmas with us. And we shall find all the 'spirits' we need right here. (*SUDRABS departs and KARL looks outside where one hears the motorcycle starting. With a gesture of his hand indicating dismissal, he returns to the livingroom. He does not know what to do; glances at his wrist watch, goes to his desk and leafs through his papers. Picks up his lecture notes and starts the tape recorder.*) Returning to the theme of this lecture and the assertion of Gaston Bachelard that many things seem indifferent to us only because we look at them with indifference and referring back to the examples cited previously, we may deduct—and I cannot emphasize it strongly enough—deduct by using the critique of pure reason that the individuals who are not able to perceive are at fault rather than the indifferent things per se. If modern philosophy would not seek new ways but would base its conclusions in traditions which...(*Noise from the outside door interrupts KARL'S lecture. SARMITE and VELTA enter carrying shopping bags. KARL turns towards them with his lecture notes still in his hands, forgets to stop the tape recorder which keeps on recording till the end of the second act.*)

SARMITE: Hallo, Dad! (*When KARL does not return her greeting, the smile on her face disappears and she turns to her mother as if looking for help.*)

VELTA: Here, Sarmite, bring the groceries into the kitchen. (*SARMITE picks up the bag and goes in the direction of the kitchen.*) Just put it there. I'll unpack it later on. You would do well by going upstairs and washing off the dust from the library. (*SARMITE goes into the kitchen, VELTA faces KARL.*) And you get hold of yourself! Don't start thundering and lightning before you find out how dark the storm clouds are! (*SARMITE comes out of the kitchen and looks at her parents.*) Go upstairs and freshen up. When you are ready come down so we can have a talk before the festivities start. (*SARMITE goes upstairs.*)

KARL (*throwing down his notes on the desk*): What more is there to talk about since it seems that you have forgiven her already for everything!

VELTA: I have not forgiven her for anything! We haven't even discussed yesterday.

KARL: Did you both have water in your mouths while walking home together?

VELTA: I told you to get hold of yourself! Even if something bad has happened, your anger will not change the situation. We did not have water in our mouths but Johnny from next door helped us carry the shopping bags, and he kept on talking about his new skis his father had given him for Christmas. (*Takes off her coat while talking and hands it to KARL.*) Here, be a gentleman! (*Karl takes the coat and goes to hang it up in the hallway. VELTA sits down at the desk and takes off her snowboots.*) I wonder if Santa Claus is going to bring me something nice this year.

KARL (*returning to his desk, falls back in his chair*): Velta, Velta, how can you make such small talk? Don't you see daily what is happening to our young people? And now Sarmite...

VELTA (*sharply*): Nothing has happened to her and nothing will.

KARL: How can you say that when only yesterday...

VELTA: And what did happen yesterday? As far as I can recall you were the only one who was fighting!

KARL (*as if in pain*): I was fighting because I was hurt!

VELTA (*stands up and walks up to KARL putting her arm around his shoulders*): Karl, don't you think I was hurt too? (*The moment of intimacy is very short. VELTA goes up to the window on the left and looks outside.*) It's beginning to snow again. The muddy streets are getting a festive white look. (*Quotes from a Latvian poet.*) And kissing tears from my eyes, you clad me in festive cloth...

KARL: Do you believe that nothing bad has happened?

VELTA: I don't believe, but I hope...please keep your anger! Let Sarmite tell us everything herself.

KARL: She even had the nerve to smile at me when she said hallo...

VELTA: And just because of that I hope nothing bad has happened. You had the same smile when you carried in my present. Was there something bad in it?

KARL (*having lost the battle*): There is a new coat for you...

VELTA: Aren't you something! Couldn't you have waited until I have opened the package?

KARL: You are not a small child; you only pretended not to know what's in the package...

VELTA: I knew, I knew. And thank you so much for it! (*Goes to KARL and kisses him. They stand there in an embrace for a few moments.*)

SARMITE (*having come downstairs stops on the last step when she sees her parents in an embrace*): If it were not snowing outside and if a nightingale were singing in a bird-cherry tree, one would think the merry month of May has arrived! (*Her parents pull apart.*) If the lovers could spare me a few minutes, I would like to talk to them.

KARL: Sarmite, I think your jokes are out of place here...

SARMITE: Jokes or not jokes, both of you should listen to me. Mother, please (*Makes VELTA sit down on the couch.*) Dad (*Makes him sit down in a chair.*) Do you want me to fix your pipe?

VELTA: Sarmite, stop fooling around. You'll only get your father angry at you.

SARMITE (*walks up to KARL'S desk, handles his pipe*): Dad is angry already and you are worried—so all my joking around can't cause any more trouble for me. (*With one hand she hands the pipe to her father, with the other hand a matchbox.*) I'm joking around because it is very difficult for me to say what I have to say to you. (*She places herself in front of them as if getting ready to deliver a speech.*) Ever since this morning I have tried to think how best I could explain everything to you ....Mommy, Daddy...I cannot find the right words! (*She kneels down and puts her head in her father's lap. KARL lifts his hand wanting to caress her hair, but his hand stops midway. SARMITE does not notice it, moves away from KARL and nestles up to her mother, then dutifully sits down between both.*) Let me be your little girl again and tell my woes.

KARL: Our little Sarmite had always made up all those tales of woe; we only pretended to believe in them. This time you seem to want to talk about real sins and wish that we pretend not to believe!

VELTA: Stop this, Karl! (*To SARMITE.*) Why did you do it?

KARL: Not why, but what did you do? Do you recall at all in what condition you were last night?

VELTA: Karl!

SARMITE: Please, Dad, before you pass judgement on me, let me speak. I do believe I can remember how I felt yesterday: there were moments I felt like I was in paradise, and then again moments as if I had descended into hell...

VELTA: But why Sarmite?

SARMITE: Mom, don't always ask *why*! It is not easy to explain. There are times I myself don't quite realize *why*.

KARL: In a few months you will be twenty-one. In half a year you

will graduate from college. But you are telling me that you
don't know why you did things about which your mother and I
tried to warn you!

SARMITE: Dad, I beg you! Let me first tell you what I have done,
or at least planned to do.... Then perhaps, with your help, I'll
be able to find out *why*.

VELTA: Well, then there is more to it! You planned to do something else?

SARMITE: Yes, Mother, but I did not do it!

KARL: God, help us! Wasn't that enough what you have done already? Don't you know right from wrong anymore?

SARMITE: What is good, what is bad, Dad? Haven't you noticed
that values change?

VELTA: About the change of values we have talked already in
the past. Don't rehash old things. Tell us what you did last night
at Peggy's and how did you become friends with her in the first
place?

SARMITE: Peggy is in my chemistry class and is a very good
student. You know that chemistry is not my best subject. She
has helped me many times with lab experiments. We did become friends, and that's the reason I was asked to her party.

KARL: The birthday party was probably only a cover-up for a
political cell meeting.

SARMITE: If you are referring to the presence of professor
Léger, then you are mistaken. He was invited by Peggy's boyfriend who is a political science student and is a member of
some political group.

VELTA: And being fully aware that there will be such activists
you went nevertheless?

SARMITE: Mom, I have to interact daily with such activists at
the college. In order to avoid them I would have to live in a
vacuum. Do you really think that my convictions can be
changed that easily?

KARL: Judging by what happened yesterday I do have my doubts.

SARMITE: We celebrated a birthday and decided not to discuss
politics. That's why Léger left so early. Someone later joked
that we had not provided the right social atmosphere for him.

VELTA: How did you celebrate her birthday?

SARMITE: First we had some hot dogs. There was enough wine
for everyone to drink a toast. Later the girls had coke and the
boys—beer. We told jokes, gossiped about the professors,
some tried to dance, but Peggy worried that dancing would not
sit well with her landlady and...

VELTA: Then someone just happened to have some pot that had to be tried.

SARMITE: Yes, there was pot, but no one forced it on anyone who did not want it. I did not even try it.

KARL: From what did you get then so 'high' last night?

SARMITE: I took some acid.

VELTA: Where did you get it? Are you sure it was LSD and not some other mixture of narcotics?

SARMITE: It was LSD. Our chemistry professor had it examined after some students had prepared it right there in the lab.

KARL: If it is the last thing I do, I'll inform the police about that professor!

VELTA: What are you saying, Karl! Didn't you yourself tell me that the campus is off limits to the police?

SARMITE: Dad, it is not the first time that LSD has been produced in the chemistry lab. The professor himself taught it to the students, convincing them that one of our constitutional rights in the United States is freedom of scientific experimentation.

VELTA: And you went to the party knowing there will be some using narcotics?

SARMITE: Yes, mother. But I did not go there to use drugs! I used them because I had lost the courage to do something I had already decided to do. (*KARL and VELTA want to say something.*) No, don't interrupt me now. I've almost answered the question *why*. (*Tries to find the right words, gets up and walks over to the desk and places herself between the far end of the desk and the public.*) Mother, Dad, I'm in love! Hopelessly in love! But my love is so tragic, I suffer because of it, because it is so hopeless.

KARL (*turns around in his seat towards SARMITE*): What is all that nonsense you are saying?

VELTA: Does it have something to do with what happened last night?

SARMITE: My unhappy love is the reason for what happened last night as well as for what I wanted to happen, but didn't.

KARL: Sarmite, are you losing your senses?

SARMITE: No, Dad, and especially not according to your values and criteria. My would-be love is just the opposite of any kind of madness. I'm hopelessly, unhappily in love with a very nice, intelligent, apolitical man who would pass your strictest scrutiny! He is a Latvian, and, though educated in America, he has remained Latvian to this very day. I'm in love with professor Lanka!

KARL (*exchanges glances with VELTA, gets up and walks behind his desk*): Sarmite, I truly think there is something wrong with you. And not because you are in love with Laimonis. That is something your mother and I can only be happy about. I'm thinking of your actions yesterday. Love makes a human being better; and it does not destruct.

SARMITE: But, Dad, I told you my love is a tragic one! Laimonis does not even notice me....When I go to his lectures, I'm always well dressed, I always sit in the front row, but he always looks away above me as if I did not exist. And when he comes here to see you, he does not even speak to me, except for the usual social niceties like 'hallo' and 'goodby'.

KARL: That still does not excuse your behavior yesterday.

VELTA: And because Laimonis ignores you, you decided to take revenge?

SARMITE (*walks towards the center of the room and stands between her father and her mother*): One could call it that. It had not occurred to me because I had not blamed him for ignoring me. This unhappy love for him is only a part of all my other misfortunes; one of those is the fact that I'm so very lonely. Forgive me, Mother, you are not only my mother, but also my friend. For that I thank you. But you are not of my generation. I have a need for a friend my own age. Peggy partially fills this need. I have had other American girl friends but no best friend with whom my philosophy of life and my interests would coincide completely. They were brought up in a completely different environment. I don't mean a better or worse environment—just different.

KARL: If you are accusing us for raising you in a Latvian environment—I plead guilty. Only remember one thing: your mother and I are Latvians. Even if we had wanted to, we could not have done it differently.

SARMITE: I'm not reproaching you. I'm thankful that you have given me a firm foundation in the still pure traditions and virtues which cannot be found in the melting pot of American culture. But my Latvian upbringing is my third problem! It is a paradox, but nevertheless it exists. This upbringing has prevented me from accepting the bad habits of this country and forced me to examine carefully the good ones.

VELTA: We had hoped to provide you with a cornerstone for the building of your life. You have that now and from now on you are responsible to construct it rightly. It is inevitable that you will have to acquire many American habits and we are not trying to prevent that.

SARMITE: In order to build my life I have to use two different types of material, and such a building often becomes an anachronism and almost the opposite of the builder's aesthetic expectations. One cannot empty two equal containers into a third one of the same volume.

KARL: You should be proud of your background and your origin. You tried to escape from them last night, didn't you?

SARMITE: I am proud of my origin, and this is my next complaint. For a Latvian to be proud boarders on vanity. We have been the best, the smartest! Be it farmer, soldier, politician, teacher! And we act that way everywhere, forgetting that other nations have smart if not smarter representatives in every field.

VELTA: This is a question you have discussed many times before with your father. From all I know, Laimonis is on your side in this dispute. You wanted to tell us what happened yesterday.

SARMITE: Yes, but I have already partially answered the question *why*.

KARL: Why didn't you go skiing with the others?

SARMITE: How did you know that they went skiing?

KARL: One of the guests—Léger said so.

SARMITE: Oh, that old gossip! No wonder the students call him a trouble-maker. (*After a short pause.*) Yes, the other guests of the party went skiing. I only accepted Peggy's invitation because such a trip was planned. (*With great difficulty.*) Mother, as a woman you should know that in the hearts of girls my age there are more than thoughts about platonic love. It does not matter if one's love is happy or unhappy, always it creates certain feelings which at times are labeled as animalistic. Not only the American boys but also the girls speak freely of their conquests in their love life. And one who does not have such adventures is regarded as somewhat strange. I decided that I would fit in better with my friends if I could talk about my love life too...

KARL: If you are going to tell me how far you have sunk, don't expect any sympathy from me! (*Gets up from his chair while saying this.*)

VELTA (*afraid of an outburst of anger from KARL, she gets up and walks over to him*): Karl, no one here has asked for your compassion. I beg of you to compose yourself! (*To SARMITE.*) And can you speak about any conquests now?

SARMITE: I don't know, Mother. (*KARL wants to say something*

to SARMITE but VELTA holds him back.) Mike, who is on the
Olympic swimming team, asked me to dance with him at the
senior prom. (*Begins speaking faster and faster in fear of losing courage to finish.*) Many girls had tried to conquer his body
and soul, as the old saying goes, but had failed. While dancing,
he held me very close and I was intoxicated by his sheer
presence. After the dance he took me home and kissed me
passionately saying he could no longer live without me and I
must belong to him.

VELTA: Did you agree?

SARMITE: Yes, Mother. (*KARL falls back into his chair and
cradles his head in his hands. Without thinking VELTA takes
her purse which she had left on the desk while taking off her
boots.*) Peggy invited Mike too. We had planned to remain
behind, alone, when the others went away on the skiing trip.

VELTA (*approaching SARMITE*): Sarmite, my dear!

SARMITE: Don't worry, Mother! Let me finish telling you all
about it. (*Both stand facing each other.*) During the party Mike
drank his glass of wine and Jackie gave him hers, and he asked
her to dance with him. While they were dancing they both became very loud and laughed a lot. Someone told me that Jackie
had put some LSD in the glass she handed to Mike. Peggy
wanted to know if I would hand Mike over to Jackie without a
fight. Could she rather let those two remain behind in her
room? Or would I like to get a little high? I said yes. And so I
got my portion of LSD. I was happy. I tried to get Mike away
from Jackie, but he became rude and told me he did not want
me anymore. He said he was going with Jackie on the skiing
trip.

VELTA (*puts her arms around SARMITE'S shoulders*): My dear
little girl!

SARMITE: I don't remember what happened next. As in a daze
I saw the others getting into the cars and driving away, leaving
me behind standing in a huge snowdrift.

VELTA (*takes the pill-dial from her purse*): Did you buy these so
you could remain alone with Mike in Peggy's room?

SARMITE: Yes, Mother. Please throw them away. I don't want
to see them!

VELTA: They are yours. Save them or give them to some of your
friends.

SARMITE (*snuggles up to her mother*): Mother, dear Mother!
(*VELTA makes SARMITE sit down on the couch.*) Last night
I woke up in this very place, when... (*Somewhat scared she*

looks up at KARL who gets up and approaches her.)

KARL: Sarmite, Sarmite.... My slap woke you up. Please forgive me, I lost my head. *(SARMITE snuggles up to her father.)*

SARMITE: Forgive me, Dad, for having been such a bad daughter!

VELTA *(patting SARMITE'S shoulder)*: You are not a bad daughter. *(The phone rings. VELTA goes to the desk and lifts the receiver.)*

SARMITE *(while VELTA goes to the phone)*: I wish all young people had fathers who could wake them up from the nightmares of today.

VELTA *(in the receiver)*: Hallo...yes...just a second, please.

KARL: And as for your unhappy love...

VELTA: Karl, the secretary of the college president wishes to speak to you. *(KARL goes to the phone. VELTA comes back to SARMITE.)*

KARL: Hallo...yes...yes... *(He appears somewhat confused as he replaces the receiver, turns towards both women.)* The college president wants to see me still this afternoon...

VELTA: What do you think he wants? If he himself does not care to celebrate Christmas Eve, at least he could let others do it.

KARL: Something urgent, I suppose. I'll have to go.

SARMITE: Don't forget we will be waiting for you with the Christmas dinner!

KARL *(getting his coat)*: Almost forgot to tell you that Lanka as well as the Légers—without the children—will be here tonight.

VELTA: In that case hurry home so that the two of us do not have to fight all the political battles alone! *(KARL leaves.)*

SARMITE: What do you think the president would want from Dad tonight?

VELTA: I would not know, dear...

CURTAIN

ACT THREE

(Stage setting the same as in second act. It is dark outside, and the stage is lit as in the first act; so are the electric candles on the Christmas tree. On the small table next to the couch are Christmas cookies. As the curtain opens VELTA and SARMITE, still in aprons, are getting ready for the guests.)

SARMITE (*comes from the kitchen carrying a vase with pine branches and goes to KARL'S desk*): I'm placing these branches on Dad's desk so that the manuscripts will have a festive feeling, too... (*Looks at the disorder on the desk.*) Mother, don't you think the desk should be cleaned up a bit? He is not going to work tonight anyway.

VELTA: For goodness sakes do not touch his papers! We will get scolded even on Christmas Eve. He will do it himself when he comes home. (*Places a tray with glasses on the small table next to the Christmas cookies; picks up a glass and checks if it is clean.*) It is time he came home. He's been gone for nearly two hours. He promised to fix the glow-punch.

SARMITE: It is almost seven and the guests will be here any minute now. Should I start warming the wine?

VELTA: I've done that already. Your father can mix the spices according to his recipe when he comes home.

SARMITE: I put some rolls in the oven; should I do the same with the cheese pastries?

VELTA: Just bring them out the way they are. If you warm them, they will fall flat, and Laimonis will not like them!

SARMITE (*walks towards the kitchen to fetch more food*): Don't tease me, Mother!

VELTA: Who is teasing? (*Looks where to seat her guests.*) Laimonis, both Légers, Dad, you and I. Altogether six of us. There will not be much sitting around while we exchange presents and have cookies and wine. Now when we eat supper...

SARMITE (*carries the baked goods in from the kitchen*): Shall I bring one more chair from the upstairs so that everyone can sit down for the buffet?

VELTA: We have five seating places here, and one of us will have to be running back and forth from the kitchen anyway. (*Notices the curlers in SARMITE'S hair.*) You better take the curlers from your hair, looking like this you will never catch a husband! And put on another dress!

SARMITE: I almost forgot about them. If you don't need me here any longer, I'll go and get ready.

VELTA: Go on. All I still need to do is to slice the roast. Then I'll go and get ready myself. (*Examines her nails.*) I wonder if at my age one still has to put on some nail polish?

SARMITE: You already have a husband, Mother, why do you need to worry? (*Someone at the outside door is shaking snow from his feet.*) Dad is finally home. I'll let him in. (*Goes to the outside door. VELTA goes into the kitchen. SARMITE opens the door.*) Where have you been so long? The guests will be arriving soon and you still have to shave! (*She comes back into the livingroom saying all this without having looked back.*)

LAIMONIS (*enters carrying three packages*): I was beyond twenty-seven mountains and seven seas to fetch some bird's milk for an angry spoiled girl. (*SARMITE turns around and does not know what to do or say. VELTA'S laughter coming from the kitchen door confuses her even more.*) And if this young lady did not have such terrible looking horns, I would kiss her on both cheeks just to prove that not only did I shave, but even have shaving lotion all over my face like someone who has come courting. (*He hands packages to SARMITE.*) Merry Christmas! (*SARMITE accepts the presents shyly and quickly disappears upstairs.*)

VELTA: Thank you, thank you! A fine suitor you turned out to be if girls fly from you like flies from insect repellent.

LAIMONIS: Not all will fly away! (*Looks around.*) Am I too early? Where is the Professor? Is he fixing his famous glow-punch?

VELTA: I really don't know where he could be. Two hours ago he had a phone call from the office of the college president; he wanted to speak with Karl. He went there and has not come back yet.

LAIMONIS: That is strange! An hour ago I saw the president going into the barber shop...

VELTA: Karl said something about having to pick up his mail. Maybe in the mail there was something that needed his immediate attention and he went over to his office. Isn't he something else...He knows very well we are having guests....Why don't you call him at his office while Sarmite and I get ready.

LAIMONIS: I'll do just that. Don't worry about me. I see the tape recorder has been used and the Professor has forgotten to turn it off. That can only mean the lecture I'm going to transcribe has been finished. I'll listen to it while you are getting dressed.

VELTA: Very well. I'll hurry up with getting the roast sliced. (*Goes into the kitchen.*)

LAIMONIS (*lifts the receiver and dials. When there is no answer, he replaces the receiver and walks into the direction of the kitchen*): Mrs. Abele, his office does not answer. He must be on his way home. (*The answer from the kitchen is not audible. LAIMONIS goes to the desk and unwinds the tape while looking at the manuscript. After getting to the place he remembers from last night, he starts listening and comparing it to the manuscript.*)

KARL'S VOICE FROM THE TAPE: ...theme for this lecture let us use a quote from Gaston Bachelard: "Things look at us as we look at them. They seem indifferent to us only because we look at them with indifference..." (*LAIMONIS stops the tape at this point and winds it fast forward; then listens again, trying to compare the script with what he hears. Instead of KARL'S voice he hears SARMITE'S voice. The tape recorder had recorded her conversation with her parents in the second act.*)

SARMITE'S VOICE: No, don't interrupt me now. I've almost answered the question **why**. (*A pause while SARMITE is taking several steps.*) Mother, Dad, I'm in love! Hopelessly in love! But my love is so tragic, I suffer because of it, because it is so hopeless.

THE VOICE OF KARL: What is all that nonsense you are saying?

THE VOICE OF VELTA (*not very audible since she was the farthest away from the recorder*): Does it have something to do with what happened last night?

THE VOICE OF SARMITE: My unhappy love is the reason for what happened last night as well as for what I wanted to happen, but didn't.

THE VOICE OF KARL: Sarmite, are you losing your senses?

THE VOICE OF SARMITE: No, Dad, and especially not according to your values and criteria. My would be love is just the opposite of any kind of madness. I'm hopelessly, unhappily in love with a very nice, intelligent, apolitical man who would pass your strictest scrutiny! He is a Latvian, and, though educated in America, he has remained Latvian to this very day. I'm in love with professor Lanka! (*Steps approaching the desk are heard. LAIMONIS stops the tape recorder unable to believe what he just heard. He wants to rewind the tape and listen to it once more, but when VELTA comes out of the kitchen, stops the recorder.*)

VELTA: So, now everything is ready for our guests. I still have to powder my nose. Isn't Karl back yet? I thought I heard his voice?

LAIMONIS: Mrs. Abele, did you have a chance to talk to Sarmite today?

VELTA: About yesterday? Yes, yes, nothing bad has happened.

LAIMONIS: Did she...

VELTA: Isn't she ready yet?

LAIMONIS: I wanted to know how she was feeling.

VELTA: Ask her yourself. (*Calling upstairs.*) Sarmite, how long is it going to take you? The guests are getting impatient.

(*SARMITE appears on the top of the stairs.*) Come down, keep our guest company until I powder my nose.

SARMITE: Isn't Dad home yet?

VELTA: We will have to start without him. (*Goes upstairs.*)

LAIMONIS (*standing at the desk*): Once again, Sarmite, merry Christmas!

SARMITE: Thank you, professor Lanka! Please do sit down. Would you like to taste some of our Christmas cookies?

LAIMONIS: We will get to that soon enough. I really wanted to have a talk with you before the others get here.

SARMITE (*puts back the dish with the cookies*): Very well, what shall we talk about?

LAIMONIS: First of all about grammar.

SARMITE: I thought you were a mathematician, not a linguist.

LAIMONIS: I'm mainly a teacher. Once a teacher finds a mistake, he wants to correct it.

SARMITE: And what mistake have I made?

LAIMONIS: You are using the wrong form of address. As far as I can remember at the summer camp last year we were on first name basis. Why again so formal?

SARMITE: You were not my professor at that time.

LAIMONIS: As soon as the semester ends and you have finished all the courses in mathematics, I will no longer be your professor.

SARMITE: Then I shall again call you by your first name.

LAIMONIS: Couldn't we start that with the New Year? Maybe with tonight? You don't have horns in your hair anymore and you look like a nice girl.

SARMITE: Only nice?

LAIMONIS: Let me see. If I examine you closer, you…the dress is very becoming. You know how to dress attractively.

SARMITE: How would you have to look at me in order to notice the thoughts in my mind?

LAIMONIS: You mean your stepping out of line last night?

SARMITE: That too.

LAIMONIS (*walks towards SARMITE*): Sarmite, forget about all that. You did not do anything really bad last night. At least nothing that would cause me to stop respecting you.

SARMITE: I was not aware that you respected me. Why should you?

LAIMONIS: You are like a princess sculpted in ice. (*SARMITE shrugs her shoulders.*) Do you know something? Let me melt that ice around you.

SARMITE: And what if there is also ice inside? You could destroy me completely by the melting process, professor Lanka!

LAIMONIS: Stop calling me by my last name! Sarmite, look at me and call me Laimonis...

SARMITE (*turns towards LAIMONIS, cooly*): Laimonis.

LAIMONIS: Just like an icicle. I don't understand how I could have fallen in love with such a girl?

SARMITE (*turns around quickly, almost defiantly*): What did you say? With whom have you fallen in love?

LAIMONIS: I just said I'm in love with you.

SARMITE (*moving away from LAIMONIS*): Please don't insult me!

LAIMONIS: What do you mean by that?

SARMITE: I understand now why Dad is not coming home. He went to you and sent you here to torture me. Thanks, but no thanks for your compassion. I don't need it. And everything Dad told you is sheer fantasy.

LAIMONIS: I have not seen your father today, and he has never told me anything. If the fact that I'm in love with you insults you, please forgive me. Being your professor, it is inappropriate to declare my love for you anyway.

SARMITE: Allright, I forgive you even though I don't believe my father has not told you about me.

LAIMONIS: Please do not blame your father for something he had nothing to do with. (*Glances at the tapes.*) And according to your logic, it turns out that you have insulted me too.

SARMITE: I insulted you? By doing what?

LAIMONIS: By talking about falling in love with me!

SARMITE: You must be silly! I cannot recall saying anything like that... (*LAIMONIS starts the taperecorder and SARMITE'S own voice is interrupting her.*)

THE VOICE OF SARMITE: ...even though he is educated in America, he is a Latvian to this very day. I'm in love with professor Lanka!

SARMITE (*in despair*): Oh, no! (*Runs to the tape recorder but LAIMONIS has stopped the tape already.*) Give it to me! (*When LAIMONIS places his hand on the tape in order to protect it, SARMITE starts hitting his hand.*) Give it back to me! All that is nothing but lies there!

LAIMONIS (*squeezing her hands in his own*): I'll give it back to you if you will admit that they were not lies you told your parents.

SARMITE (*suddenly very calm*): Let me go!

LAIMONIS: I'll let you go if you'll promise to tell me the truth.
SARMITE: Let me go! (*When LAIMONIS refuses to let her go.*)
   I promise! (*LAIMONIS lets go of her hands. SARMITE walks
   to the Christmas tree and touches an ornament.*)
LAIMONIS: Were you telling the truth or were you lying to your
   parents?
SARMITE (*facing LAIMONIS, quietly*): The truth.
LAIMONIS: Thank you, Sarmite. (*Works with the tape recorder.*)
   Let's erase it to the point where your father's lecture ends.
   (*Rewinds the tape, then starts it again listening to it.*)
VOICE OF KARL: ...If modern philosophy would not seek new
   ways, but would base its conclusions in traditions which...
   (*Noises are heard of VELTA and SARMITE entering the
   house.*)
VOICE OF SARMITE: Hallo, Dad!
LAIMONIS: Is this where your conversation started? (*SARMITE
   nods her head, LAIMONIS keeps on operating the recorder,
   pushing buttons and disconnecting the microphone.*) Let's dis-
   connect the microphone and keep it running on "record."
SARMITE: Did you hear the entire conversation? Did you also
   hear what I did at Peggy's place?
LAIMONIS: I only heard up to the point where you mentioned my
   name. The way you said it took me by surprise and I stopped
   the recorder. Did you go on speaking about your...Did you
   mention my name again?
SARMITE: Didn't you hear anything more?
LAIMONIS: I just told you so.
SARMITE: Well, that's nice.
LAIMONIS: Maybe I should have listened to it some more? Did
   you go on telling how many sheets and towels you have in your
   hope chest? And how foolish would be the man who's not able
   to appreciate it?
SARMITE (*walks over to the couch and sits down*): Now you are
   making fun of me...
LAIMONIS (*goes and sits down next to her*): No, Sarmite, I'm
   making fun of myself: while studying mathematics I have become a rather cold and calculating person.
SARMITE: You did not make that kind of an impression on me
   when we met at the summer camp last year. And listening to
   your lectures...
LAIMONIS: It was at the camp that I turned into a calculating
   person after I found out that our mothers had been good friends.
SARMITE: I don't see the connection.

LAIMONIS: When you told me that your father teaches at this college and you intend to get a degree in mathematics, I applied for a position here. In other words, just to be near you...

SARMITE: Now you are talking nonsense...

LAIMONIS: Don't interrupt me! Let me put all the cards on the table.... You know, I visited often in your home...

SARMITE (*getting an inkling of where the wind is blowing from, turns to teasing*): ...and discussed with my father esoteric questions of philosophy.

LAIMONIS: But all I saw was you. I noticed you during my lectures too, sitting in the front row always prim and attentive.

SARMITE: I sat in the front row because I was interested in mathematics!

LAIMONIS: It was also the best way to show the professor what beautiful legs you have!

SARMITE: Don't tease me, please!

LAIMONIS: Allright, let's go back to my calculations. Since you have expressed the desire of pursuing your studies in mathematics on graduate level, which cannot be done at this college, and since I have resigned here and accepted a job at a university where it's possible, how about...

SARMITE (*interrupts him*): ...about what?

LAIMONIS: I had planned on asking your parents to allow you to come and live with my mother and me in Florida while you continue your studies. I've perceived in your eyes something more than a simple respect for a professor. It might be still an unknown factor, but I hope that in time this respect—respect squared—will change into a definite quantity.

SARMITE: Into something like unhappy love, maybe?

LAIMONIS: Dear Sarmite, please understand my situation.

SARMITE: Any American professor would not give it a second thought if he were in love with one of his students. Don't you know how many professors at our college have affairs with their students even though they are married and have children at home?

LAIMONIS: Would you want me to follow their example?

SARMITE (*suddenly getting serious and kind*): No, Laimonis, I would not want you to be like that. Thanks for being you. (*Takes his hand.*) Thank you. See what has happened to us because of our upbringing!

VELTA (*enters during the last sentence*): Is that so? When the cat is gone the mice play.

SARMITE: But Laimonis has not even tasted the cookies.

(*LAIMONIS gets up, walks to the desk and turns off the recorder. SARMITE looks at him questioningly, and LAIMONIS gives her a nod that the tape is erased.*)

VELTA: I don't mean the cookies. What is the matter with Latvian upbringing? What harm has it done you both?

LAIMONIS: Same way you used the proverb, Mrs. Abele, meaning the opposite. The statement about Latvian upbringing was meant as a compliment.

SARMITE (*with great emotional feeling walks up to her mother, embraces her and kisses her on the cheek*): Thank you, Mother, for the way you raised me! Thank you! (*Looks at LAIMONIS.*) And thanks, squared.

VELTA: Well, what's gotten into you? And what's all the thanking in squared quantities?

SARMITE: Take one times one of 'thank you' and the result will be 'thank you' squared.

VELTA: What kind of arithmetic is that?

SARMITE: The kind my professor teaches me!

VELTA: I would let go of such a professor immediately!

LAIMONIS: That is easier said than done. Sarmite has even agreed to take courses in higher mathematics, where one and one makes three...or even more...

SARMITE: Laimonis, please not now!

VELTA: What's this all about? Wait a minute....One and one is ...That's how my grandmother figured when she tried to explain to me about birds and bees...

SARMITE: Laimonis thinks that I should continue my studies at a university. He said he would help me...We decided not to tell you just now, but (*With special emphasis towards LAIMONIS.*) like an old 'blabber-mouth' Laimonis himself gives it away immediately!

VELTA (*disappointed in her hopes that she has found a son-in-law*): Oh, that kind of higher mathematics. And I thought, maybe....Well, I see that the advice of grandmothers is not enough for these times....But where could Karl be?

SARMITE: Heavens! The glow-punch must be boiling over! I'll go and add sugar at least. What else does Dad mix in there?

LAIMONIS: Either cloves or cinnamon. Do you want me to help you?

VELTA: Why don't you both go. Two heads are better than one. I just hope that nothing has happened to him. (*Goes to the window and looks outside.*)

SARMITE (*in the kitchen*): Laimonis, what kind of spice is clove?

LAIMONIS: Don't worry, Mrs. Abele. If something had happened, the police or the hospital would have called. Maybe he has met a colleague...

SARMITE (*calling from the kitchen*): Laimonis, cloves please!

VELTA: A real snowstorm has started. One can hardly see the street anymore. (*Turns again towards LAIMONIS.*) Please, go and help Sarmite.

LAIMONIS: Very well. (*Goes into the kitchen.*) A clove is a spice that grows on myrtle trees...(*Disappears into the kitchen. VELTA looks at KARL'S desk, straightens a few things, then goes over to the Christmas tree and rearranges the packages. She breaks off a small branch, squeezes it between her fingers and smells it contemplating. There is a knock at the outside door. A heavy load seems to lift from her shoulders and she runs to answer.*)

VELTA: I was starting to think that... (*Stops when she sees both LÉGERS.*)

INA: Good evening, Mrs. Abele, and a merry Christmas!

VELTA: I was expecting my husband....But please do come in, don't stand there in the snowstorm.

SUDRABS (*entering*): Isn't the professor home yet?

VELTA: He was called to the president's office three hours ago.

SUDRABS: Yes, I know, but there he...I mean, that could have been settled in a few minutes.

VELTA (*noticing that INA stands still in her coat and SUDRABS is keeping his coat on too*): Please, let me have your coats!

INA : Thank you, Mrs. Abele! (*Takes off her coat and her headscarf.*) Sudrabs, please hang it up for me! (*SUDRABS takes the coat and goes out in the hall where he takes off his own coat, too. He is dressed formally.*) What a beautiful tree you have this year, Mrs. Abele!

VELTA: Yes, thank you. Please sit down!

INA: I just love to watch the snow flakes. Let me enjoy them for a while. (*Goes to the window.*)

VELTA (*becomes obviously nervous after the remark which SUDRABS made that he knew KARL was going to see the president*): Mr. Léger, you said you knew that Karl was going to see the president. Do you know why?

SUDRABS: I don't know the details...I assume some negotiations about the new contract.

VELTA: I thought the new contracts are discussed in the spring...

SUDRABS (*looks guiltily in INA'S direction*): The new president seems to have changed that custom...

VELTA (*becomes very nervous*): Please excuse me for a moment. There is something in the kitchen I must...there is Laimonis...(*Goes to the kitchen.*) Maybe he can help me...

INA (*when she is sure that VELTA is out of hearing distance*): Well, how do you like that?

SUDRABS: Where could the old fool be? The president said he was done with him in five minutes. And he had appeared to be very composed...how could one suspect him going to the forest to hang himself!

INA: Didn't I tell you we should not have come here at all? But you insisted. You wanted to see how the kulak gets cut down to size.

SUDRABS: Why don't you shut up! (*INA angrily turns around and looks out of the window.*) Just smile as sweetly as you did when we came in. I don't want to miss the spectacle.

VELTA (*returns with LAIMONIS from the kitchen*): Maybe you could go to his office...

LAIMONIS: I'll try to call first. (*Goes to the phone.*) Good evening Mrs. Léger, Professor! (*Turns his back towards the public and dials.*)

SUDRABS: Good evening, good evening and a merry Christmas to you! (*INA smiles.*)

VELTA (*to the LÉGERS*): Please do sit down. (*Helps them to take places on the couch, offers cookies, all the time observing LAIMONIS.*) Please have some of these too!

LAIMONIS: He is not in his office. There is no answer.

VELTA: Please call the small cafe where he sometimes sits reading the newspapers. (*LAIMONIS picks up the phone book and finds a number, talks to someone, then chooses another number and talks again with someone. All this is a silent play while the rest of the action continues.*)

SARMITE (*brings in from the kitchen cups with hot glow-punch*): Welcome to our home and a merry Christmas! If the guests are cold, this punch will warm up everyone with the first sip! (*Hands a glass to INA, SUDRABS, and her mother.*)

VELTA: Your father is not home yet, Sarmite.

SARMITE: Mother, he is a professor, and he might have forgotten to come home!

VELTA: How can you joke like that!

SUDRABS (*wanting to be sociable, he interrupts their conversation*): That's an old habit of professors: to be forgetful. At least that's how they are portrayed in the old Latvian plays.

SARMITE (*places a cup in front of LAIMONIS*): A cup full of nectar guaranteed to cure the sickness of forgetfulness! (*Teasing.*) Or maybe you are not playing a professor tonight?

SUDRABS: Yes, some of the professors play their roles very convincingly regardless of their forgetfulness! Did you know that professor Lanka is going to leave us?

VELTA (*to LAIMONIS*): Was he not at the cafe? (*Goes to the window.*)

LAIMONIS: No, and he has not been there. I just called the police. I remembered that most of the policemen in this town would know him because of his lectures to them during the 'law and order' week. They will find him; they promised to call us as soon as possible.

SUDRABS: Mr. Lanka, you did not answer Sarmite's question.

LAIMONIS: What question?

INA (*laughing loudly*): Good for you Sudrabs, that was a good joke!

SUDRABS: A good joke? Oh, I see. I caught professor Lanka being absentminded. (*LAIMONIS obviously still has not grasped the drift of the conversation.*) Sarmite asked if you were not playing a professor tonight.

LAIMONIS: No, Sarmite, I'm not playing a professor tonight. (*To SUDRABS.*) And I am not doing it any other day either. I cannot vouch for other professors, the present ones, of course, exempted!

INA: Aren't you conceited! Don't you see, my dear Sudrabs, how he is insulting you! Don't let him get the better of you!

VELTA (*standing at the window, turns to INA*): Your husband argues only with Karl. As far as I know, Laimonis is not interested in politics.

SUDRABS: Your husband is a worthy opponent. It is a joy to discourse with him. It's possible that Mr. Lanka is not bad either, but since he is planning to leave us, there is no use in instructing him in the art of dialectics.

LAIMONIS: I understand dialectics to be something more than talking in circles and using empty slogans.

SUDRABS: What is my esteemed colleague insinuating?

LAIMONIS: If you need examples, try to remember all your speeches and remarks at the faculty meetings. At one time you are supporting a point, in the next instance you oppose it. If that is not thrashing around with empty words... (*The phone rings, interrupting LAIMONIS.*)

VELTA (*lifts the receiver*): Hallo?...Yes, speaking...yes...

thank you…same to you! (*Replaces the receiver.*) It was the police. Karl is on his way home.

SARMITE: Did they say where Dad has been?

VELTA: They only said that he had just turned into our street. A police cruiser had recognized him. When the policeman told him that we had been looking for him, he said that he was on his way home.

LAIMONIS (*half to VELTA, half to LÉGERS*): See how nice it is to be good friends with the police! Can't ever get lost!

INA: Mr. Lanka, you do have a sharp tongue!

SARMITE (*innocently*): How would you know that?

SUDRABS: My wife means that his remarks might have offended me.

LAIMONIS: I beg your pardon if that is how it sounded. I had completely forgotten that during the anti-war demonstrations you had a little run-in with the police. Again my professional absentmindedness!

INA: You better get rid of that habit! As far as the police are concerned, I'll still show them. One ought to put all the blue gents into jail. (*To SARMITE.*) You don't know it, Sarmite, but the police in America are not much better than in Russia.

SARMITE (*pouring oil on hot coal*): Mr. Léger, in your lectures you often speak of Red China. Aren't there any policemen?

LAIMONIS (*before SUDRABS gets a chance to answer*): Three cheers to you, Sarmite. That is really funny. (*Bows to MRS. LÉGER.*) Pardon me for using your expression. (*Goes to the desk where he had left his cup of glow-punch.*) I'll turn into an actor if I keep on using expressions of others.

SUDRABS (*a little annoyed*): Or into a parrot. You must have heard of the fact, Sarmite, that parrots repeat what they hear.

LAIMONIS: Oh, parrots are those who repeat other people's words? And what do we call those who repeat slogans that are written, for example, in the red bible of Mao?

VELTA: I had misjudged you Laimonis. You are just as bad as Karl. (*To SARMITE.*) Daughter, please refill the punch. Maybe the tongues of our guests will turn sweeter. Fill one for your father too. He will be cold having been out for so long in the snowstorm.

SARMITE (*getting up from the easy chair goes into the kitchen*): Right away, Mother.

VELTA: And please don't eat each other, the sweet rolls are much tastier! (*She offers the baked goods to everyone.*) Since Karl will be home at any time now, I'll serve the cold supper in a minute. Excuse me, I'll go and set the table.

SARMITE (*her head in the kitchen door*): Please watch each other so that no one opens the presents without me!

VELTA (*pushes SARMITE back into the kitchen*): Won't you calm down, what has gotten into you tonight? (*Disappears into the kitchen.*)

SUDRABS (*gets up, listens at the kitchen door, then goes behind the couch and in a quiet voice warns LAIMONIS*): I advise you to watch what you are saying. My political convictions are of no concern to you.

LAIMONIS: Yes, but you force them on your students. They still do not know the difference between good and bad, especially when the professor praises the bad and slanders the good.

SUDRABS: The fact that our political system is corrupt is known to every schoolchild. I only point out to my students what is bad in our system and what we can learn from other political systems.

LAIMONIS: If Maoism is so superior to our system, what are you still doing here? The sooner you leave for Red China, the better.

INA: My dear Sudrabs, why are you arguing with this man? He has resigned already.

SUDRABS: That's his good fortune! Otherwise we would have taken care of him!

LAIMONIS: Same as you did with the history professor? The one who, upon your recommendation, will be released of his duties even before the end of the academic year?

SUDRABS: He is being dismissed because he teaches history without making it relevant to the present political change.

LAIMONIS: And what was it that the campus security chief could not make relevant when he was dismissed with a two week's notice?

SUDRABS: We cannot have people in our administration who are members of local political organizations. One cannot serve two masters at the same time.

LAIMONIS: Especially if one of the masters happens to be the local Veterans Organization which is unhappy about the activist behavior of our students and the faculty. (*He bows to INA.*)

INA (*stands up, angrily*): Sudrabs, this man is insulting me!

SUDRABS: Don't take him seriously, dear! (*In order to calm himself he moves down right. To LAIMONIS.*) If you were not a Latvian I could promise you something right after the holidays!

LAIMONIS: Oh, are Latvians immune to your dealings? Up till now in all revolutions brother was fighting against brother!

SUDRABS: And if the need arises, we will do it again!

SARMITE (*carries in more glow-punch*): Fighting already? Just like the historic Latvian Christmas battle! The one who wins will get the wine first! (*Offers the punch to her guests, and in order to hide the tension they all accept it. Everyone is quiet for a moment. Behind the door someone is coughing. All turn their attention to the door. INA is sitting on the couch, LAIMONIS stands next to the tree sipping his wine. SUDRABS still on the right side of the stage, SARMITE with the tray next to him.*)

SARMITE: Didn't someone cough behind the door? (*Puts the tray on the desk and goes to the door.*) Is Dad finally home or is Santa here already? (*Opens the door and sees her father sitting on the steps.*) Dad! What's the matter with you? Come inside!

KARL: Yes, my daughter, right away! (*Enters all white covered with snow and shivering. All his movements are stiff and slow, eyes staring distantly as if he had lost the sense of reality. While SARMITE is helping him with his coat, he stares at the Christmas tree. The outside door has remained open and snow blows in through them. Suddenly Christmas music as in Act One is heard over the loudspeakers.*) It must be eight o'clock. The music always starts at eight.

SARMITE: Dad, you must be cold! (*She goes and closes the door. The sound of music stops.*)

SUDRABS: Merry Christmas, professor!

KARL (*looks at SUDRABS but does not answer him. His eyes turn towards the Christmas tree.*) And the light of Christmas shines all night. (*Looks at INA who sits on the couch.*) Peace on earth and good will towards...

LAIMONIS (*supporting KARL leads him to a chair near the kitchen door*): Professor, you are frozen stiff! Come and sit down and drink something warm...(*When KARL approaches INA, she gets up in near disdain and walks over to SUDRABS.*)

SARMITE (*picks up a cup of the hot glow-punch and hands it to her father*): Here, Dad, this will warm you up. (*KARL clasps the cup with his trembling hands and drinks.*)

INA: The old one looks like he has lost his mind. Is this enough for you?

SUDRABS: Be quiet. The drama is not finished yet.

KARL (*having heard what SUDRABS said*): The drama is not over yet? Does the director of the play have another surprise

up his sleeve to heighten the suspense of this melodrama?
Don't hesitate....Give the directions to your actor now...he
will humbly carry them out...he will laugh and the audience
will adore him...he will cry and the audience will laugh at
him...

SUDRABS: I don't understand what you mean to imply by that?

INA: Please, do not start another discussion, don't you see he is
incoherent?

KARL: Well said, fair lady! It is a nightmare...for all of us.
Somewhere in the distance we see our ideals. We try to reach
out to them...as we sit in mud...we think we want to attain
our ideals, but that is only a mirage...at the same time we
muddy ourselves and others...

SARMITE (*touching her father's forehead*): Dad, do you feel alright?

KARL: Don't worry! No, I don't feel well, but I know what I'm
saying.

SUDRABS: You might think you know what you are saying but I
don't understand what you are thinking.

KARL: I did forget that you do not recognize symbols. (*Looks at
the Latvian pennant.*) Laimonis, please hand it to me.
(*LAIMONIS hesitates but complies with the wishes of KARL.*)
You may hand it to me without hesitation. It is not a knife nor
is it a gun. And it cannot hurt anyone in any way. (*He takes the
pennant from LAIMONIS.*) There might be a few of us who feel
a bit choked up and a few tears might come to some eyes...but
not because of pain....In the theatre we call it catharsis...it
is a word that Aristotle uses when he talks about the cleansing
of one's soul.

INA: Sudrabs, let's go home. I did not come here to listen to him
preach. (*Walks between the desk and the outside door.*) Are
you coming?

SUDRABS: But my dear, how can you say something like that!
This here is not a simple sermon...this here is the highest form
of philosophy of life and the distinguished Latvian philosopher
is sharing it with us.

KARL: No, I did not intend to preach. I just wanted to make sure
that I myself understood what symbols mean. And I wanted to
ask Mr. Léger to assist me in this.

SUDRABS: The symbol you are holding in your hand we already
discussed this morning. I don't want to repeat myself and talk
about it again.

INA: Then don't repeat yourself and let's go home! You can't be of any help here to anyone.

LAIMONIS (*grasping what KARL is trying to say*): Be patient, Mrs. Léger. You don't know who will need help here. If you don't believe in the virtues suggested in the Bible, please remember that one of our Latvian virtues is to help one's neighbor! It can happen that one day you or your husband might need help!

SUDRABS: The only help I need is an explanation of the double meanings in Mr. Abele's utterings. His comparisons escape me.

KARL (*sees that INA is putting on her coat*): I see Mrs. Léger is in a hurry, so let us not speak in parables but discuss concrete things. Let us assume this flag is not a symbol but a piece of cloth in two colors. I would think that you, Mr. Léger, remember that much of our history as to how these two colors came into existence?

SUDRABS (*moving towards INA*): Don't be childish! It is not history but a legend that at one time during the battle near Cesis a soldier was placed upon a sheet and his blood stained the sides of the sheet leaving the middle white.

KARL: If it is a legend, can we be sure that there was a battle at all?

SUDRABS: The general assumption is that the German Teutonic Knights were fighting a Latvian tribe.

KARL: But doesn't the same assumption tell us that with the German Knights members of other Latvian tribes were fighting on their side?

SUDRABS: I do not doubt that at all. Recent history also shows that Latvians have fought against each other under foreign war lords. (*Suddenly realizes that he is trapped in his own argument.*) I hope now your problem is solved. (*To SARMITE.*) Thank you for the wine and cookies!

VELTA (*comes in from the kitchen*): Supper is ready. Please, come into the kitchen...(*Sees INA in her coat.*) Are you cold, Mrs. Léger?

SUDRABS: We are going home, Mrs. Abele...right away.... Thank you!

VELTA: What's going on? Supper...and there are still the presents to be opened. We have some for your children, hoping that...(*Looks at SARMITE, LAIMONIS and KARL in utter confusion.*)

INA: We did not come here to receive presents for our children....They have everything they could want! Sudrabs only helped your husband to solve a problem...

KARL: One more question, Mr. Léger! (*SUDRABS turns around and looks suspiciously at KARL.*) Talking about the wounded soldier whose blood stained the sides of the sheet that later was to become our national flag...who do you think wounded the soldier?

SUDRABS: How should I know that?

KARL: It could have been another Latvian serving a foreign war lord.

SUDRABS (*not being able to contain himself any longer*): And if it were so? That Latvian serving the foreign war lord, as you like to express it, may have believed in the master he served!

KARL: Could be....Thank you, Mr. Léger! Thank you for everything...

SUDRABS (*to INA who is standing with his coat in her hands*): Why are we standing here? If you are ready, then let's go! (*Both leave, and the door stays wide open. Christmas music resounds and keeps playing until the curtain falls.*)

VELTA (*starts towards the outside door in order to close it but turns around in half way*): What happened here? Why did they run away like that?

SARMITE: Dad had been sitting on the doorstep...looked like a snowman.

LAIMONIS: Mr. Abele, what happened at the president's office?

VELTA: Karl, where have you been all this time?

KARL (*remembering what he had experienced in the last hours, suffering from chills, becomes incoherent*): I went to the forest...

VELTA: To the forest? You have not eaten all day long; what were you looking for in the forest?

KARL: In the forest? In the jungle...all around us is a jungle...

LAIMONIS: What did the president want from you?

KARL: The president? King of the jungle?...(*Takes an envelope from his pocket and hands it to LAIMONIS.*) I was handed a Christmas present...(*LAIMONIS takes out the letter and reads it fast.*)

SARMITE: Mother, I think Dad is getting sick...his head is burning hot.

VELTA (*walks over to KARL and touches his forehead, checks his pulse. LAIMONIS, having read the letter, throws it on the table*): You have a fever...and you are delirious! Sarmite, there is aspirin in the kitchen. Go get it! Karl, you go to bed! (*SARMITE runs out to the kitchen.*) What is the Christmas present he got from the president?

KARL: I forgot to thank Léger for it...the president's secretary told me that Léger had reminded her to give it to me still in the current calendar year...otherwise, according to the faculty handbook, it may not be valid...

VELTA: What are you talking about? (*SARMITE enters from the kitchen.*)

LAIMONIS: Mrs. Able, the professor has been dismissed as of the end of this semester. (*Reads from the letter.*) "In accordance with the decision of the faculty personnel committee chaired by professor Léger, according to the paragraph discussing incongruent educational philosophies, the college, in order to uphold the quality of its programs and to support the rights guaranteed by the Constitution of the United States, is forced to sever its contractual relationship with Associate Professor Karl Abele, granting him leave without pay beginning with..." etc., etc.

SARMITE (*hands the aspirin and the glass of water to VELTA*): Daddy, Daddy! (*Kneels in front of her father.*) Daddy, don't be sad! We...Laimonis and I...we will take you along with us to Florida! There is sunshine, warmth...

KARL (*tries to stand up*): Sun...warmth... (*Because of the warm room, the punch, lack of food, he becomes dizzy and falls back into the chair.*)

SARMITE: Dad! (*LAIMONIS hurries to his assistance, VELTA checks his pulse, lifts the lids of his eyes.*)

VELTA (*rushes to the phone, dials*): He is unconscious. (*In the receiver.*) Let me speak to doctor Thomas....This is Mrs. Abele...Yes...yes, emergency!

SARMITE: Dad, Dad...(*LAIMONIS takes SARMITE'S hand in his. SARMITE'S eyes fill with tears.*) Dad...please listen... Laimonis and I will take you away into the sunshine...Dad ....into the sunshine...Dad, do you hear me...into the sunshine...

CURTAIN

THE SCHOOL FOR LOVE

A comedy in three acts

by
Algirdas Landsbergis

From the original Lithuanian
Meilės mokykla
Translated by the author.

Introduction to
The School for Love

Algirdas Landsbergis was born 1924 in Kybartai, Lithuania. After graduating from high school in Kaunas, he studied Lithuanian literature at the University of Kaunas. During the German occupation of his native country he was forced to work in a wartime factory. As a refugee in post-war Germany, he continued his education at the University of Mainz where he studied English literature. At the same time he took courses in acting, as well as taught in the Lithuanian refugee high schools. He emigrated to the United States in 1949 and received a M.A. degree in comparative literature from Columbia University while working at the Public Library of Brooklyn and with the Assembly of Captive European Nations as a researcher and writer of modern East European history (1956-1966). Since 1965, Landsbergis is a professor of history and drama at Fairleigh Dickinson University.

Landsbergis' first poetry and stories were published in *Žvilgsniai,* 1946-1948 (Glances), an experimental "little magazine" of an avant-garde group of young Lithuanians in Germany. He achieved acclaim for his novel, *Kelionė,* 1954 (The Journey) depicting a young refugee's complex and traumatic war and exile experiences, presented through the prism of consciousness and revealing man's unceasing search for meaning of life and for new sets of meaningful human relationships. A collection of short stories, *Ilgoji naktis,* 1956 (The Long Night) deals with a series of often extreme human situations.

Landsbergis has translated Lithuanian poetry and folk songs into English, compiled and edited for the collections *The Green Oak,* 1961 and *The Green Linden,* 1964. He wrote the libretto for J. Kučinskas' opera *Juodas laivas,* 1972 (*The Black Boat*), as well as many articles and essays on theatre and literature scattered in Lithuanian and American magazines and anthologies.

Landsbergis is best known for his dramatic works. His first

play, *Penki stulpai turgaus aikštėje,* received a literary award in 1957 and has been performed repeatedly on Lithuanian immigrant stages, as well as in Latvian translation by Latvian theatres on the American continent. Its English version has been staged in Chicago (1961), New York (1961), Toronto (1966) and Carbondale, Illinois (1974). Successfully mixing realistic and theatrical styles and focusing on contradictory problems, such as duty and love, faith and despair, Landsbergis conveys a tragic and powerful vision of dehumanizing and demoralizing forces.

A writer of comedies must know that people are impossible. They are so often grotesque in their struggles with their unruly and demanding bodies. So often pathetic in their search for greatness or wisdom or happiness. They have too many illusions to protect themselves from cold reality and too many masks to protect themselves from others. The masks and illusions create the everlasting Vanity Fair that comedy writers offer us as a mirror of ourselves. They know our pretensions and explode them from within until we collapse in sympathetic laughter. It is not enough, however, to have a sharp perception of human foibles, not enough to recognize vice masquerading as virtue, to wield with grace and precision the analytical scalpel. A comedy writer must love the impossible people, difficult to love as they are. He must love their weaknesses. He must recognize the Beauty in the Beast and the Beast in the Beauty. Only then will he convince us of the marvellous and terrifying contradictions of human nature, the basis of all true comedy.

Algirdas Landsbergis is a writer who has dealt with ambiguities and illusions in all his plays. In "Wind in the Willows" and "Willows in the Wind," the first one lyrical, the second one farcical, he explores the theme of the strength and helplessness of love, from a love of a clown for a cook to that of a saint for his people. Love makes us undefeated in defeat and can even teach Heaven the truth that being human is to be rich beyond comprehension. In *Five Posts in the Market Place,* a play about the last days of Lithuanian guerrillas after World War II, he goes beyond the drama of an impossible fight against the Soviet giant to the inner tragedy of the protagonists—the fatal ambiguity of a sculptor-terrorist and a philosopher-executioner. It is, in a way, a tragedy of illusion. One cannot separate the man from his function. In the absurdist *The Beard*, he shows a young, fragile Everyman in search of his identity, trying to resist being made into an object by all-loving and all-destroying leaders. A common illusion to make someone happy against his wish. In *Goodbye, My King,* an old actor tries to create an illusion of grandeur in the bleak setting of gray poverty, loneliness and failing sense of reality. In *The Last Picnic*, two generations conflict since their illusions, concerned with the importance of ritual in the survival of social groups, are separated by the barrier of time.

All of these plays deal with the difficulty to see clearly into one's motivations, to recognize simple desires masked as principles and the inability to penetrate the sham personality. Landsbergis knows that it is terribly important to dream and that a dream is never ridiculous. It is the road to the dream that is sometimes tragic, often ridiculous.

The School for Love is the most exuberant of Landsbergis' plays. A mixture of fantasy and parody, with a dose of burlesque thrown in, it celebrates one of the oldest dreams of mankind — Eldorado. Here the image of Eldorado is concretized in the form of the American Dream: the literal meaning of the right to pursuit of happiness. Countless immigrants have been seduced by this dream, and the failure to reach it has been the subject of many writers. The stranger on the shore, wide-eyed in front of magic America does not know the rules of the game and falls prey to those who exploit his naivete. Or, he feels alienated and withdraws into his shell hugging to himself the remnants of his broken dream. *The School for Love* does not fit the familiar pattern. It is not about failure. It is about too much of success. It is not about lack of understanding. It is about understanding too well.

The play's center is a quest for wealth, which is a quest for power, which is, above all, a quest for revenge. The central character, Leo Leviathan, a man of gargantuan appetites and an absolute belief in himself, is ready to conquer the New World. He knows that instant gratification of desire is a promise that will allow him to manipulate the others. He knows that children of the Promised Land do not grow up, they live and die with malted milk on their lips. Still, greedy and uninhibited child that he is, Leviathan hides in himself the humble grocery clerk who wrapped up too many herrings in the small town in East Europe. Leviathan does not deny his past, his revenge on the past is to make those around him love herrings.

Two characters are instrumental in the rise and fall of Leviathan. One is Gabriel, a young poor immigrant in search of love which would give meaning to his life. Contrary to Leviathan who is a taker, he is continuously looking for someone to give himself to. Simple-hearted and full of generous thoughts he is also a poet at heart. The idea of starting a school for love is his, since people talk about love so much and know really so little about it. The other character is a small, gray, tightly buttoned-up man with dark thoughts of revenge. His quest is the destruction of Leviathan who has inadvertently caused the loss of the only pride and joy of this lonely man—his stamp collection. The Angel (a name given to him by Leviathan) once saved the hero from military police, now he endorses very enthusiastically the idea of the school, recognizing well that Leviathan's nature, knowing no half-measures, will become its own nemesis. The hero, as a true primitive, sees in The Angel a special providence watching over him. And so the school for love is born—for Leviathan a dream to erase the humiliations of the past and one day to see "a fleshy dream turning into fleshy flesh;" for The Angel a dream to exorcise a private demon ("I say—watch out for little men who discover what hells they have been carrying within"); for Gabriel a dream to make others' dreams come true. The last founder of the school is Diana, "a Pennsylvania girl, looks and brains, determined to make good in New York." In a sense, she too is looking for revenge—her father was a coal miner and she grew up looking at a postcard with a luxury liner on it. Her dream is freedom on the high seas of life. Leviathan's Girl Friday and the object of adoration of Gabriel, she is the most down-to-earth character of the four.

The search for personal Eldorado is also filled with illusion. Overwhelming in his desires and shrewd about vulnerability of people, Leviathan never manages to face the fact that it is impossible to wash the smell of herrings from his hands. Success makes his ego rise as a huge balloon. He sees himself as a true whale swallowing up all the small fish but love he cannot get. His Angel sabotages the school and Leviathan does not understand, even when the truth is revealed to him, what power has done to him.

Creating the school as an instrument to manipulate others he ended up being its instrument. A common enough illusion in too much success. The Angel who starts out with the idea of revenge for a very simple dream—he would have sold the stamp collection and bought a small green house with dark green shutters—ends up with the illusion of changing society through moral power. His vision of everyone put in a proper place and dressed in appropriate uniform finally resembles that of his enemy—happiness by decree. Diana realizes that luxury liners are worthless if one must travel on them with someone like Leviathan. Diana's practical sense was really an illusion. One cannot dissociate the child with his nose pressed against a show window full of toys from the grown-up who must pay the price. Diana is saved by Gabriel with whom she learns to abandon words and to read in him "lovely green and pale silver thoughts." The love story of Diana and Gabriel brings out the often forgotten fact that the material, concrete things in which we trust are very perishable and that only our illusions make them important. At the end of the play, they leave together to seek for Eldorado in each other. They leave behind a puzzled Leviathan who does not know that love is truth and power nothing but illusion.

The other characters belong to parody. *The School for Love* is a take off of society devoted to self-improvement. It is quite logical: we consume, after all, thousands and thousands of books telling us how to become healthy, beautiful, wealthy, important and loved. We embrace passionately every new fad. We trust our souls to prophets and psycho-analysts. *The School for Love* with all its teaching material (barns, hay, moon, mooing cows, wedding bells, etc.) is a practical application of the theory that one picture is worth a thousand words. As Libidstone, a reformed psychologist, puts it: "Listen, bookworms, wherever you are—one dark womb is worth more than forty thousand books."

The School for Love is rich in parodic detail. Pseudopsychology, mass media, marketing techniques, traditional view of man-woman relationship and the whole plastic world in which we live, serve Landsbergis' purpose. He does not, however, let his secondary characters become mere caricatures. They retain their humanity. The timid baker, who wants to become a masterful husband, offers cake and sympathy to a starved model. The model, Adenoid, whose shape has gone out of fashion, accepts the cake and starts longing for the shapes and smells of real life. She is tired of "living inside a deodorant tube." These two people are not just ridiculous. They come to the school in straitjackets that their minds created for them and in trying to acquire other qualities, even more fake, they manage to reach out for another human being.

Communication between people seems to lead to the real Eldorado. To reach it one must throw away the ready made formulas, the jargon, the fads and fetishes. Algirdas Landsbergis defines it through Gabriel to whom it is a place where words are "as chaste and new as newborn honeybees."

Ilona Gražytė-Maziliauskas

THE SCHOOL FOR LOVE

CHARACTERS

LEO LEVIATHAN: 50, a former grocery clerk in East Europe, black-market operator after the war in Central Europe, director of the School for Love in New York

DIANA: 20, a Pennsylvania girl, looks *and* brains, determined to make good in New York

GABRIEL: 23, a displaced person from Europe, newly arrived in the U.S., professionless

THE ANGEL: (Or is he?) 50, Leviathan's compatriot, former postal employee and stamp collector

JOSEPH OKEN: 35, New Yorker, lawyer for a Bakers' Union

GAIL ADENOID: 25, high fashion model, New Yorker

CARL LIBIDSTONE: 30, American, psychologist, unhappy despite talent and success

BUTLER: Ageless. Imported from England

MRS. OKEN: 35, as tough as they make 'em in New York

VOICE OF A WOMEN'S SLACKS MANUFACTURER

FAT BAKER

OLD PSYCHOLOGIST

FASHION EXECUTIVE: A woman

THE TOP MANUFACTURER OF KITCHEN APPLIANCES

DELIRIOUS WOMAN: Flesh and blood, or voices backstage

A DELEGATION OF LEADERS (Painted, not alive)

RADIO ANNOUNCER'S VOICE

CROWDS (Backstage, of course)

PLACE

New York, not so much of stone and glass as of dreams of those who watched its lights at night before disembarking for the first time.

TIME

A hot summer after the war (let us call it World War II), when crowds of immigrants went ashore and rubbed their eyes at America.

ACT ONE

(*The curtain opens on LEO LEVIATHAN'S office, a pocket mirror of his soul. It is crowded to the bursting point and reeks with opulence alleviated by confusion. The door stage-left leads to the foyer, while the door stage-right opens on the stairs leading to the second floor. A house-plant shoots up and disappears stage-left into infinity through a hole made especially for it in the ceiling. A solid safe, bought second-hand, stands beside the plant—a little fort in the shade of a palm tree. A folding advertising sign (to be carried on one's shoulders) leans against the safe. A huge painting dominates the wall and shows, in a popular turn-of-the-century manner, a life-size lady with a larger-than-life bosom, clad in a garment that might be a nightgown or an evening dress; the lady is embracing a (live) horse's head. File cabinets, ledgers are piled on a table and spill over onto the floor. A butterfly net is leaning against one of the chairs. In the very center of this farrago, LEO LEVIATHAN sprawls in a large soft chair, which he dwarfs anyway. His obesity has not much muscle but there is also nothing flabby about it—it is charged with energy. By jingo! He resembles a nineteenth-century colonial empire, reaching to absorb new lands, gay with greed, bursting with the lust to grab. His large appetites are written on his face—a grunt turned flesh. Opposite him, on the only normal-size chair, sits DIANA. She seems to have descended from one of the magazine color ads, but she is real! Honey-blond hair; a face that spells outdoor life, but also intelligence; a very feminine figure according to the requirements of the middle of the twentieth century. Although very much unlike LEVIATHAN, she resembles him in her restlessness and striving.*)

DIANA (*with a teacher's inflection and motions*): My—name—
   is...
LEVIATHAN: My-name-is-Leo-Leviathan!
DIANA: America...
LEVIATHAN: America-recieved-in-me-an-immigrant-of-distinc-
   tion...a-captain-of-industry-to-be...(*LEVIATHAN pro-*

nounces the second title automatically as they both perceive a large card with a drawing of an oil-well emerge from the top of the safe and slowly ascend. The ascension is accompanied by a loud sucking sound—a bath-tub drain in hi-fi, as it were. LEVIATHAN and DIANA follow the disappearance of the card with their eyes. A moment of silence, heavy with regret. Then DIANA opens a big ledger, makes a crossing-out motion, takes out a notebook from her pocketbook and does the same.)*

LEVIATHAN: What's left?

DIANA: Two oil-wells, one Cadillac, one ten-thousand-dollar account.

LEVIATHAN *(with horrified disbelief)*: No! *(Raising his arm in supplication.)* My Guardian Angel, wherever you fly, I know you know what you are doing, but please stop teasing me!

DIANA: Assuming I believe in his existence—which is a lot to ask from a modern girl...

LEVIATHAN *(still praying to his invisible ANGEL)*: Please come back home—three days without you is three years in hell...

DIANA: But what makes you think that an Angel would know how to handle stocks and bonds?

LEVIATHAN: That's American education for you—no history of heaven, no geography of hell. All you know is civilian war.

DIANA: Ci-vil. *(She smiles coquettishly and adjusts her skirt. He ogles her leg.)* Shall we go on? *(LEVIATHAN sighs and shrugs his shoulders. In a dictating tone.)* What are you doing now?

LEVIATHAN: I'm taking a curse in English.

DIANA *(shapes her lips with great care and, as she does so, begins to bend toward him, hinting that she would not mind being kissed)*: Course—course...

LEVIATHAN *(both tempted and frightened, he timidly looks around and, against his own desires, begins to lean away from her lips. But soon desire takes the upper hand, he stops leaning back and begins to incline toward her)*: Curse—curse— **Curse!** *(As LEVIATHAN'S lips almost touch DIANA'S, a card with a drawing of a Cadillac begins to ascend slowly from the top of the safe. LEVIATHAN jumps on his feet and reaches for it. The card vanishes very quickly, as if in response, with the same loud sucking sound. DIANA makes her ledger and note-book entries. LEVIATHAN slowly collapses in his chair.)*

DIANA: Cadillacs—none.

LEVIATHAN *(frightened and irritated)*: Curse—that's what my friend the Angel told me. You're for bigger things—he said— but if you touch a woman, a curse will fall on you so hard, you

won't know what hit you. You don't monkey with the supernatural.

DIANA: Will he tell you to fire me?

LEVIATHAN: I...hope not.

DIANA (*flirtatiously*): Why?

LEVIATHAN: We're both in New York—that elephant of a city—
and it makes me feel better to have a sort of an immigrant next
to me.

DIANA: No other reason?

LEVIATHAN (*evasively*): They say New York is not America;
tell me, Pennsylvania, where you come from, is that America?

DIANA: It's more America than New York, but it's not *America*.

LEVIATHAN: So Pennsylvania is not America, either. They say
Niagara Falls is not America—it's for tourists. What the hell
is America, then? *Where* is America? Maybe it will be *my* job
to find out and tell the Americans.

DIANA: But to do all that...

LEVIATHAN: I know, I know—I must learn good English. And I
will—I'm gon to learn millionaires' English—nice, fat, smoot
English!

DIANA: Smooth...

LEVIATHAN (*trying to pronounce it correctly*): Smoot...(*As
their lips purse to voice the word, they slowly incline toward
each other again. An oil-well card ascends from the safe.
LEVIATHAN sprints to the safe and then watches helplessly as
the card disappears above, with the same sucking sound.
DIANA makes her entries again.*)

DIANA: Oil wells—one. You still believe in his business know-
how?

LEVIATHAN: He'll explain! He's got no reason to punish me.
(*LEVIATHAN walks to the stairway door.*) Angel! Hey,
Guardian! (*Silence. LEVIATHAN crosses to the other door
and opens it. A touch of panic vibrates in his voice.*) Angel!
Damn!

DIANA: Worried?

LEVIATHAN: Me? I refuse to learn *that* word. (*With more hope
than conviction.*) The Angel would never leave me. (*The door
bell rings. Jubilantly.*) See! What did I tell you? (*The area
stage-right becomes visible. GABRIEL is pressing the button
and smilingly looking around. He is handsome, long-haired in
the European fashion. His face and behavior present a strange
mixture of naivete and experience. His clothes clash loudly;
his navy jacket is of an excellent cut and quality, but his olive*

green army work slacks show spots; he wears heavy army boots. In his hand he holds a small bundle wrapped in a newspaper.)

LEVIATHAN: Where's the damned butler?

DIANA: You sent him out for herrings; and it's the maid's day off.

LEVIATHAN: Let him in!

DIANA: I thought angels could walk through walls.

LEVIATHAN: They've got their whims like everybody else. Hurry, please!

DIANA: Yes, sir! (*As she rises, GABRIEL'S face, looking up, breaks into a big smile.*)

GABRIEL: Doves! Yoo-hoo! My first American birds! Hello, doves! (*Suddenly his expression changes and he gingerly wipes off the top of his head with a finger, while reproachfully addressing the birds.*) For Americans—they sing...(*More cheerfully.*) You'll sing for me, too!

DIANA (*opens the door at his last sentence and thinks that it is addressed to her*): That remains to be seen.

GABRIEL: I was talking to the birds. (*Looks her over thoroughly.*) Wasting my time. (*During GABRIEL'S and DIANA'S conversation LEVIATHAN takes a quick look inside the safe; opens one of the ledgers and holds it in his hand; suddenly remembering, dashes to the picture of the buxom lady and turns it against the wall.*)

DIANA: You must do a lot of talking to the birds—flying around all the time as you do.

GABRIEL: I took a boat across the Atlantic.

DIANA: A non-conformist? But come in, please, come in. You're expected. (*GABRIEL enters into the foyer.*) So you're it! I vaguely recall your pictures in a religion primer—never thought I'd meet you in the flesh: if I may use that word in your case.

GABRIEL: Please do! I wouldn't want it any other way—especially with girls like you around.

DIANA: Is that how you joked with the other secretaries before you got them fired?

LEVIATHAN (*backstage*): Angel, where are you?!

DIANA: One last word before you go in. You'll want to know why I took this job three days ago...

GABRIEL: Yes, doll, why did you?

DIANA: I'll be completely frank with you. You ever been to a Pennsylvania mining town?

GABRIEL: No.

DIANA: It's a pity. They could use you there much more than here on Park Avenue. And you'd understand why I came to New York—to succeed.

GABRIEL: Well did you?

DIANA: It's taking much longer than I expected. But when I saw Mr. Leviathan, I had a sudden feeling—mystical-like—that here outer space may open. I said to myself—if you want to go far, attach yourself to a rocket, not to a firecracker. And so I did. All right, now fire me!

GABRIEL (*jovially*): Let's be fired together. (*Softer, more to himself, reminiscing.*) Into a beech grove far away.

LEVIATHAN (*backstage*): Angel, what's keeping you?

DIANA: You'd better go in now, Mr. Angel.

GABRIEL: My name is Gabriel.

DIANA (*ushers him into the room*): Here is your transcendental business manager, Sir.

LEVIATHAN: What's **that**?

GABRIEL (*politely*): Good morning, Sir.

DIANA (*to GABRIEL*): You're not...?

LEVIATHAN: What's that, I asked.

DIANA (*her realization is followed by fury*): Oh! Throw him out! Out! Please!

LEVIATHAN (*looks GABRIEL over*): Lousy pants...

GABRIEL (*persistently*): Good morning, Sir.

LEVIATHAN: Lousy pants and good jacket.

GABRIEL: Four years savings. Enough for a jacket; not enough for pants. Good morning, Sir.

LEVIATHAN: You get no "good morning" from me.

GABRIEL: Why not?

LEVIATHAN: If I answer your "good morning," we start a conversation and you end by asking for my daughter's hand.

GABRIEL (*eyeing DIANA*): I wouldn't mind.

DIANA: Insolent!

LEVIATHAN: She's not my daughter, stupid. It's just an old story. And you don't talk—I talk.

DIANA: **Please** throw him out!

LEVIATHAN: Take it easy—this is not for you, an American woman, to understand. I lose most of my money, my Angel disappears, and this thing comes in—with his lousy pants. This must mean something—everything means something, understand? (*To GABRIEL.*) You're one of those displaced persons, immigrants...?

GABRIEL: Yes, Sir.

LEVIATHAN (*to DIANA*): Look at him. (*DIANA demonstratively turns away.*) I came here like him six months ago. Not in lousy pants—with a hundred thousand dollars in twenty-dollar pants pockets. (*To GABRIEL.*) You won the contest?

GABRIEL: Yes, Sir!

LEVIATHAN (*to DIANA*): I'm generous—I help these immigrant slobs. On each transport ship that comes with them they have a contest, they draw lots. The winner works a day for me. (*To GABRIEL.*) Put on that sign! (*GABRIEL takes the sign and puts it on. The front of the sign says;* **Mama, don't think I forgot you. Don't!**) She was a good mother—died at my birth—must have been good to bear me. (*Moment of silence.*) So what if I didn't know my father? (*Silence again.*) Nobody should forget nobody's mother!

DIANA (*still vehemently, but already returning to her teacher's role*): Anybody's!

LEVIATHAN: Or anybody's! (*To GABRIEL.*) Now turn around! (*GABRIEL turns around. The back of the sign reads: LEO LEVIATHAN—***You'd Better Remember the Name or Else!***) How about that! Very American, isn't it? It's called publicity. (*To GABRIEL.*) How much money you got much?

DIANA: You don't need the second "much."

LEVIATHAN: Listen to her. In America you need every "much" you can get! (*To GABRIEL again.*) How much?

GABRIEL: Fifty cents got much.

DIANA: The nerve.

LEVIATHAN: I'll give you five dollars much—I'll make you ten times much rich. And just after I lost my fortune. Plus a sandwich—all that for one day's work. O.K.?

GABRIEL: O.K. very much! (*LEVIATHAN goes to the safe.*)

DIANA (*hisses disdainfully, to GABRIEL*): Fifty cents—and a thousand dollar grin while I was confiding in you!

GABRIEL: I'm sorry. (*Seeing her disbelief.*) Honest—like you Americans say: "Cross my heart and knock on the wood." (*Seeing her turn away from him.*) But you confused me, too. Calling me Angel—I was sure you liked me.

DIANA (*mockingly*): "Girls-like-you, doll." Where did you learn such stuff—in the ship's boiler room?

GABRIEL: Hollywood movies—that's where. I was a dishwasher in a United States army canteen. There I learned my rough English. But at night, watching movies, I learned the real English, the dream American English. Like "Baby, you do things to me" or "Take off your glasses, pretty one." You're the first American girl to whom I talked that much.

LEVIATHAN (*back from the safe, a five-dollar bill in his hand*): You talk much too much. To work now! Park Avenue up, Madison Avenue down, Fifth Avenue up.

GABRIEL: That's much up and down.

LEVIATHAN: What do you think this is? America? (*BUTLER enters holding a herring wrapped in a newspaper.*)

BUTLER (*handing the herring to LEVIATHAN*): Your herring, Sir. I'm sorry it took so long. (*LEVIATHAN takes the herring. DIANA staggers, nearly fainting.*)

LEVIATHAN (*to DIANA*): What's the matter?

DIANA: Sorry, Mr. Leviathan, I know it's very silly of me, but I can't stand the smell of herring.

LEVIATHAN: That's much too bad, because I have a herring each day. Why? (*To GABRIEL.*) Listen before you leave, I give you a lesson for all life—free. When man stands on top of the mountain, his mountain is higher if he remembers how it was in the valley. Fifteen years ago I stood in my lowest valley—in an East European town the size of a midget's belch. I was wrapping herrings in newspapers and bowing and saying "Thank you," and "Please," and "Come again." And I could see the photographs of kings, receiving ambassadors, and ambassadors ogling at women with bosoms like heaps of snow, and busty women divorcing millionaires, and millionaires giving them heaps of money which they stuffed down their bosoms. And I said to myself—one day, one day I'll jam my belly at the very top, next to the kings and bosoms and million-aires—and I'm getting there, I can almost touch it. And each day here in America I have a herring wrapped in a news-paper, and it gives me one hell of a lot of joy when I touch the herring and sink my teeth into it because my every pore can still smell that other town—and, oh, how I wish all the town's people could see me now: the store owner, and the parish priest, and all these jokers who teased me about my weight, and the girls who refused to dance with me because my hands smelt of herring... (*At the peak of his excitement, LEVIATHAN suddenly realizes that they are watching him getting carried away and snaps out of it angrily. To DIANA.*) So you'd better get used to it, or else! (*He glances at the news-paper and explodes even louder at the BUTLER.*) But this is an American newspaper! Didn't I tell you to get a European paper? I didn't wrap no herrings in no American newspapers!

BUTLER: But, Sir, they were all out of them. I didn't want to be even more late.

LEVIATHAN (*his anger now turns to GABRIEL*): And you? You still here?

GABRIEL: May I help, Sir? Here's a European paper. (*As GABRIEL talks, he unwraps the newspaper from his bundle and reveals socks, a toothbrush in a cellophane container, and a shaving kit.*) I bought it six days ago, when they put us on the ship. Here it is. See the date?

LEVIATHAN (*still gruff, snatches the newspaper*): It's **European**, all right. (*He transfers the herring into the European newspaper. Less gruffly.*) Thanks.

GABRIEL: Please-welcome. Also, I like the way herring smells.

DIANA (*to GABRIEL*): Hypocrite! (*GABRIEL stealthily blows her a kiss. She pretends to study a ledger.*)

LEVIATHAN (*to GABRIEL*): Good for **you**. Without smells, life stinks. Trouble with women here is they smell of nothing.

GABRIEL: A woman must smell a little of woman.

LEVIATHAN: You're not completely stupid about women. You eat today?

GABRIEL: Not yet. I hurried here.

LEVIATHAN: Here. (*He tears the herring in two and gives one half to GABRIEL. They both begin chewing on it.*)

GABRIEL (*grinning*): Good morning.

LEVIATHAN (*shaking his finger good-naturedly*): **Good** morning. Hot, uh? Hot America.

GABRIEL: I like it when it's hot.

LEVIATHAN: Why so?

GABRIEL: When it's hot, girls wear less of a dress and I see more of the girls. Summer sort of undresses girls.

LEVIATHAN: A mind of one track, uh? Maybe that's how my mind is—one track and a train rushing on it, longer and longer, more dining cars, more gold chains on watches, more pearls on female skin....Take off that sign for a minute, will you? (*GABRIEL takes off the sign, manipulating the half-eaten herring.*) You may have holes in your pockets, but your brain is not all empty—so there's hope. I **can** stand you. You're not like these other immigrant beggars, these fools who get beaten even in the church. You know a little better, uh? And I know much better. I look at them like an earthquake looks at moles digging their little holes. (*He points at the floor, at the imaginary moles, with his chewed-off herring and accidentally points at GABRIEL'S meager bundle.*) All you own? (*GABRIEL*

nods.) Man must know how to live. Look at me. (*LEVIATHAN snaps his fingers at the BUTLER who hands him a snow-white batiste handkerchief.*) Imported from Switzerland. (*LEVIATHAN indicates GABRIEL, and BUTLER hands GABRIEL another batiste handkerchief. LEVIATHAN wipes his hands off with the handkerchief but GABRIEL catches his handkerchief on the back of his hand, presses it with his chin to his chest, takes out his crumpled one with another hand, cleans his hands with it, and puts the batiste handkerchief in his breast pocket. LEVIATHAN nods his head approvingly and snaps his fingers again. BUTLER hands toothpicks to him and GABRIEL*): Ivory—imported from Thailand. (*LEVIATHAN and GABRIEL pick their teeth. LEVIATHAN throws his toothpick over his shoulder. GABRIEL wipes his toothpick and carefully puts it into his pocket. Then LEVIATHAN takes the butler by the waist, like a ballerina, and whirls him around.*) Imported from England. (*BUTLER continues dutifully to turn around. The sucking sound is heard from the safe. LEVIATHAN freezes and tensely watches the safe. But no card comes up—the sucking sound ends with an abrupt belch. LEVIATHAN emits a deep sigh of relief and wipes the sweat off his forehead. He notices that the BUTLER is still turning around, snaps his fingers, and the BUTLER stops. Then LEVIATHAN gesticulates to GABRIEL to take the butterfly net which is leaning against one of the chairs. When GABRIEL does so, LEVIATHAN gesticulates to him to go to the safe and be ready to catch whatever comes up. GABRIEL nods understandingly. LEVIATHAN holds a finger to his lips. GABRIEL takes up his position. LEVIATHAN in a light conversational tone*): See that plant?
GABRIEL: Yes—big!
LEVIATHAN: It goes up for two more floors through holes in the ceilings. The richest man in my town had one. This one's three times bigger—at least.
GABRIEL (*points to the picture of the buxom lady*): This picture, Sir. Somebody in your town had one like that?
LEVIATHAN: Not stupid, quite not stupid. (*His memories again begin to carry him away on wings of lechery. He sits down on his chair, his eyes still on the picture.*) Yes, the postmaster had it on his living room wall. Mine is five times bigger. That woman—she caught my eye the first time I delivered herrings to the postmaster's house; she caught my eye and squeezed my heart. That's a woman for a man! Long hair, breasts, calves—

all woman! Can you imagine what a behind! Put her next to those over-showered, deodorized, dry-skinned, emaciated American women! (*During LEVIATHAN'S talk, GABRIEL is devouring DIANA with his eyes.*)

LEVIATHAN (*still looking at the picture. To GABRIEL*): What do you say?

GABRIEL (*ogling DIANA*): Delicious. (*Sucking sound. An oil well card ascends slowly. GABRIEL'S eyes are still riveted on DIANA.*)

LEVIATHAN: Grab it! (*GABRIEL wheels around and swings the butterfly net, but the card eludes him. As GABRIEL loses his balance, another card showing a bundle of banknotes, comes up with a sucking sound. LEVIATHAN hurriedly climbs on the safe to catch it. The card teasingly tickles his outstretched fingers, then quickly ascends and vanishes above. LEVIATHAN remains on his hands and knees on top of the safe gazing sadly in the direction where the rest of his fortune went.*) Gone—and cocks will still crow every morning. Why did the Angel drop me like an egg on a cobblestone?

DIANA: No oil wells, no Cadillacs, no bank accounts—no Angel.

LEVIATHAN: You don't believe it—about the Angel? (*DIANA shrugs her shoulders, looks into the mirror, adjusts her hair, checks her change purse.*) Call up the Mayor of the town in Germany, where I met the Angel! He'll tell you about the statue of the Angel there!

DIANA (*ironically*): What a pity I never learned German.

LEVIATHAN (*to GABRIEL*): **You** call!

DIANA: Transatlantic calls are very expensive, Mr. Leviathan.

LEVIATHAN (*To GABRIEL*): And you—you don't believe me neither. You think there are no miracles. What's a miracle, uh?

GABRIEL (*looking at DIANA*): If this roof would open, doves would come down, a girl with blue eyes would embrace me, and we would float toward the stars. That would be a miracle.

LEVIATHAN: Childish mind of one track. An Angel saved me and came to live with me—that's a miracle. (*GABRIEL smiles politely, shrugs his shoulders and puts the sign on again.*) I'll make you believe, or else! I'll show you! (*He slides down from the safe.*) We'll repeat the whole thing right here and that will bring the Angel to us—that type of magic always works. (*To GABRIEL.*) Take off that sign. (*GABRIEL takes off the sign.*) Climb on that chair! (*GABRIEL does, although reluctantly. To DIANA.*) Where d'you think you're going? (*He puts DIANA*

firmly down on another chair.) Now look and listen how I met
my supernatural friend, my sponsor, the Angel! (*Light in the
upper corner, stage-right, reveals the ANGEL about to speak
into a tape recorder. He is a small dry man, tightly buttoned
up, in a manner of speaking, to the top of his dirty grey head.
He flips on the tape recorder. His words are, of course, not
heard by the people on stage.*)

ANGEL: Leo, you dog... (*LEVIATHAN sneezes.*) You whale of a
crook...

LEVIATHAN (*sneezes again*): Someone must be mentioning me.

ANGEL: The Day of Judgment has come for you! I'll leave this
tape for you, and you won't have anybody to spit on in your
anger.

LEVIATHAN (*to GABRIEL*): You're a statue of an Angel, an
important Angel. It's night. It's a little town in Germany after
the war.

ANGEL: I'm dozing under the statue. I'm a little drunk, all broke
and mad angry! And what do I hear? Running steps, like a
hunted elephant. (*An enterprising director might play the
William Tell overture in the background for the next minute.*)

LEVIATHAN (*illustrates his tale with movements and, in no time
at all, begins to live it. His speech runs along with him, catches
breath, and gallops again*): I'm running for my life. The police
have just dug up my hiding place—two barrels of herrings, ten
cartons of cigarettes with the camel, five sacks of coffee. If
they catch me, all is over. They'll shut me in jail for black-
marketing. And when I'll get out, with a jail record, no immigration to America. (*GABRIEL taking advantage of
LEVIATHAN'S self-absorption, makes a motion of catching
DIANA with the butterfly net.*)

ANGEL: Why did I freeze my behind on that tombstone of a
statue when I could have been snoring in a warm bed? Because
of you, you monster-whale! (*LEVIATHAN sneezes.*) All had
been planned and safe and perfect. I had a suitcase crammed
with rare stamps—saved up over thirty years of mailroom
work in a post office. No big black market deals for me. Only
a small suitcase, and in it a little house, three meals a day, no
worry in America...

LEVIATHAN: Then I see this statue—must be an angel—wings
sharp in the full moon leading a horse. Angels love animals.
(*He turns to GABRIEL who stops flirting with DIANA and dutifully freezes into position.*) I fall on my knees and I pray from
the bottom of my heart! (*LEVIATHAN falls on his knees.*)

ANGEL: My suitcase!...now empty...What devil put you, Leo Leviathan, next to me on that train, with your sack of black market coffee? Why was the window open where I sat? Why did you have to point at me to save your own skin—me out of a train load of black market slobs? Why did the policeman rip my suitcase open by the open window? My stamps, like snow-flakes, windswept over the river. My stamps, my world, my life. Queen of England in maroon, triangle Graf Zeppelin in sepia...

LEVIATHAN: Angel of whatever name—I prayed. Angel Michael, Angel Gabriel...

ANGEL: Lenin Air Mail, Pope Pius XII in heavenly blue, brown American buffaloes...I wanted to jump after them—the police held me back. And they settled on the river and were cancelled forever.

LEVIATHAN: Help me, I begged! The police were clanking closer...Goodbye, America...

ANGEL: I almost yelled for the police. But then I slapped my hand over my mouth. That would've been too easy for you. They would've taken you out of my life. But I wanted your life because you had taken away my world! Revenge—I said— you'll be my America!

LEVIATHAN: And then—the Statue—the Angel—spoke!

ANGEL: Leo—I said, trying to sound like a priest—crawl into the stomach of this iron horse.

LEVIATHAN: A miracle! I almost fainted. But I'll take a miracle over a jail any time, and so I jumped in. The police rumbled by—I was safe! Hello, America!

ANGEL: I said, "Leo Leviathan, I saved you! Be prepared! Soon I'll come to you and guide your life."

LEVIATHAN: I mumbled my thanks and a thought struck me that now I'll be sure to achieve big things. And I waited.

ANGEL: And I came to you.

LEVIATHAN: And he took my money and said he'd make quin-tuplets for each couple of my dollars.

ANGEL (*triumphantly*): And now you're finished. (*He flips off the tape recorder, tucks it under his arm, and slides down the plant like a fireman. All present gasp in surprise.*)

LEVIATHAN: Angel...**Angel!** Salvation! (*To GABRIEL and DIANA.*) What did I tell you? He'll never leave me! (*Even GABRIEL and DIANA are impressed.*) I'm saved! Saved... (*ANGEL gives LEVIATHAN a nasty grin. LEVIATHAN be-gins to laugh dutifully; noticing that GABRIEL and DIANA are*

*not joining in the mirth, he motions to them and they, too, give
out dutiful little chuckles. LEVIATHAN'S eyes follow ANGEL
expectantly, like two hungry puppies. ANGEL opens the safe
door and points to its emptiness. LEVIATHAN shrugs his
shoulders and stretches his arms to ANGEL in question and in
supplication. ANGEL just stares at him, grinning.
LEVIATHAN slowly sinks on his knees, arms outstretched.)*
What happened?

ANGEL (*handing LEVIATHAN the tape and the recorder*): This
will tell you. (*LEVIATHAN, still kneeling and not taking his
eyes away from ANGEL, hands the tape recorder to DIANA.
She begins to put the tape on. ANGEL waves GABRIEL away.
GABRIEL steps from his imaginary pedestal and begins putting the sign on again.*)

LEVIATHAN (*suddenly embracing ANGEL'S legs*): You aren't
leaving me?

ANGEL (*viciously*): I may have to. You're all empty now, uh?

LEVIATHAN: Here, yes.

ANGEL: What d'you mean—"here?"

LEVIATHAN: There's a wine cellar—I forgot to mention it.

ANGEL: What?

LEVIATHAN (*as he begins to speak, a card with a picture of a
huge barrel of wine descends from the ceiling and disappears
in the safe*): I bought a wine cellar in Germany, before I left
for America. For a kind of insurance. Should be worth some
twenty thousand now... Tell me, you aren't leaving me! (*The
tape recorder begins playing.*)

ANGEL (*his voice comes from the tape recorder*): Leo, you
dog... (*ANGEL tries to get to the tape recorder, to shut it off,
but LEVIATHAN holds his legs locked firmly in his embrace.*)
Crook... (*ANGEL struggles frantically to free himself, and his
eyes alight on the word "MAMA" on the poster. Seeing that he
won't be able to free himself from LEVIATHAN'S bearish hug,
he starts singing at the top of his voice, to drown out the sound
of the recorder.*) Mamma, don't cry, don't cry, my dearest
mamma. Mamma, I shall return to you, my mamma. (*ANGEL
wildly gesticulates to everybody to join in the singing.
LEVIATHAN does so immediately, DIANA chimes in reluctantly, and GABRIEL responds by taking off his sign and adding his tenor. The sound of the tape recorder is drowned out
completely.*)

ALL: My life's a drama without your smile, my dearest mamma.
Oh, wait for mamma's sonny, mamma! (*LEVIATHAN lifts*

his hand to dry a tear, in overflow of emotion. ANGEL takes advantage of this and slips out from LEVIATHAN'S grip. Everybody stops singing. Several words still pour out of the tape recorder before ANGEL manages to reach it and turn it off.)

ANGEL (*voice from the tape recorder*): ...Zeppelin in sepia, Lenin Air Mail...(*ANGEL flips off the tape recorder.*)

LEVIATHAN: Was I wrong to buy that cellar? That was before I met you; before you promised me the greatest things. I thought I'd settle there in the cool darkness when I retire. I would stretch out there like a barrel among the moss-covered bottles and drink, and sleep, and drink...

ANGEL (*wiping the sweat off his forehead*): It's all right, it's all right...

LEVIATHAN (*joyfully*): You aren't leaving?

ANGEL: Who wants to leave; no, I'm staying.

LEVIATHAN: But what do we do now?

ANGEL: It's part of my big plans—yes, my big plans. We'll sell your wine cellar, right now. Then we'll invest the money in my new project. And that will take you to the top.

LEVIATHAN: Good! Invest in what?

ANGEL: In...

LEVIATHAN: Yes? Yes?

ANGEL: Of course, invest in...

GABRIEL (*steps forward*): Gentlemen, I beg your pardon, may I make a suggestion. I know it's not my business. You rich and wise and Angels and Americans and everything. But this seems to be my chance, and I'm going to take it. You can kick me out if my suggestion's very stupid. I've got to leave anyway.

ANGEL: Say it, for heaven's sake!

GABRIEL: If you plan investing money, something very good could be done—I think—with **love**.

LEVIATHAN (*to GABRIEL*): Love? Come on now! What's that—love?

ANGEL (*to GABRIEL*): Go on.

GABRIEL: Ever since I met my first American soldier in Europe, I saw it—Americans talk a lot about love but don't know very much, not at all...

LEVIATHAN: They don't know much about everything. They don't even know what is America.

GABRIEL: Well, I'm not interested in *everything*. The only thing I'm interested in is **love**.

LEVIATHAN: So?

GABRIEL: So if someone opens a school for love, like—you know
    —a school for dancing, wrestling, riding—that should be a
    sure thing.

LEVIATHAN: A school for **love**?

DIANA: Insane!

ANGEL (*breaks out in a broad vicious grin*): Yes! It's just what I
    myself had in mind! Yes—a **school for love**!

LEVIATHAN: School-for-Love...yes, I begin to see your point,
    Angel. To teach these women here who's lord and master.

DIANA: The idea is ridiculous, doomed in advance!

ANGEL: Woman, do you presume to contradict an angel?

LEVIATHAN: That shows they need a school here to teach them
    obedience!

ANGEL: You like it, eh? The real thing. We start right now.

LEVIATHAN: We'll be shameless rich! Eh? (*He nudges GABRIEL
    with his elbow.*) You'll work with us, you one-track-mind!
    We'll teach these American women to put on weight where it
    counts.

GABRIEL (*kicks the sign away, wistfully*): Love—we'll teach
    love.

LEVIATHAN (*to DIANA*): You with your pretty shape, you stay
    with us—no? (*In his excitement he slaps DIANA'S behind.
    Angel lifts his finger—both as a reproach and a warning.
    LEVIATHAN bows apologetically. To DIANA and GABRIEL.*)
    We three—with me as leader—we'll shake this town by its fat
    shoulders. (*Points to ANGEL.*) And with him on our side—
    we'll have no limits, no frontiers!

GABRIEL: America, here we come! (*They put their hands to-
    gether; DIANA somewhat reluctantly.*)

LEVIATHAN: I'll be shameless stinking rich!

ANGEL (*steps away from them and breaks the butterfly net in
    anger, aside*): You'll be shameless and stinking but not rich.
    In a month you'll be standing here penniless, in your under-
    wear, with a cold behind!

LEVIATHAN: Hooray for the School for Love! (*Lights fade, and
    as the stage is drowned in darkness, a rising clatter of type-
    writers and ticker tapes briefly precedes the outburst of a roar-
    ing anthem.*)

ANTHEM: Who has poured love into the world?
            Leo, Leo Leviathan!
            Life was dry, but now we're living high!
            Leo, Leo, Leo's our man!

(*As noise and the anthem rush to a crescendo, the stage bursts into light. There they all stand in exactly the same poses as before the blackout, but everything about them radiates smashing success — their beaming faces (except the ANGEL'S, exuding misery), hats on everybody's head, GABRIEL'S new dark pants, a new golden glow suffusing the stage. When the anthem expires, the noise of typewriters and ticker tapes changes into a background symphony of drills and hammers, punctuated with fanfares. They all stand frozen in the same pose for some 15 seconds and then suddenly erupt into excited movement. Almost to the end of the First Act they speak and move at a* staccato *speed, portraying a rush of events and days in the manner of a single vaudeville act.*)

BUTLER (*enters and hands a huge telegram to DIANA*): Telegram, Miss.

GABRIEL (*almost simultaneously hands LEVIATHAN a large scroll and a pen*): The contract, Sir, to rent the main auditorium for football in the fall.

DIANA (*glances at the telegram and rushes to LEVIATHAN*): Stop, Sir! (*LEVIATHAN'S pen freezes on the way to the scroll.*) "A sudden rush of new subscriptions....Every space jammed....Applicants camping in ten-block lines through the night."

LEVIATHAN: Rent gymnasiums, dance studios, church cellars.

ANGEL: All rented in the city.

LEVIATHAN: To hell with football, then. (*Tears up contract and scatters it.*) It's a stupid game anyway. (*BUTLER immediately sweeps up the shreds. To BUTLER.*) My binoculars! (*BUTLER hands LEVIATHAN the binoculars.*) I'm going on an inspection tour of the new building.

GABRIEL: You'd better take a car. It takes three days to cover the main building on foot.

LEVIATHAN: Butler, a car! What are the walls of the main building again?

ANGEL (*with disgust*): Pale green.

LEVIATHAN: Butler, my turquoise Cadillac! (*To all.*) See you tomorrow! (*LEVIATHAN exits. Powerful roar of an automobile engine, gradually dying away. BUTLER pushes in two mannequins — a corpulent woman and a beefy man with beard stubble. As the three cross the stage and go out on the other side, they pass entering LEVIATHAN, who is taking off his gloves. A mooing is heard, accompanied by church bells.*)

GABRIEL AND DIANA: Welcome back!

LEVIATHAN: The main building's too darn small. . . . What's that
noise?

ANGEL: The cows were just delivered. (*Sarcastically.*) You
know — the department on natural love: barns, hay, moon,
mooing.

LEVIATHAN: Are they wearing church bells?

ANGEL: No, Leo, no — that sound comes from the neighboring
department. (*Sarcastically again.*) Wedding Bells are
Ringing.

LEVIATHAN: Move the Wedding Bells Department farther
away. Otherwise, clients will think we have dinosaur cows with
church bells on their necks. D'you want to scare them away.
I'd say this is sabotage, if I didn't trust you all!

GABRIEL: Yes, Sir.

ANGEL: Well, you can trust me. (*Another flurry of movement.
BUTLER pushes in a four-poster and a bath tub equipped with
shower and curtain.*)

BUTLER: Telegram, Miss. (*DIANA takes the telegram, but suddenly screams and drops it, pointing to the ceiling. A pair of
women's slacks descends from above and stops, hanging in the
air. A large knife is stuck in them. The stage becomes a little
darker. A quivering shaft of light appears above the slacks.*)

VOICE OF THE TOP WOMEN'S SLACKS MANUFACTURER
(*ghostly*): Mr. Leviathan, you killed women's slacks!

LEVIATHAN: Serves them right!

VOICE: You're a murderer!

LEVIATHAN: May I see your admission ticket.

VOICE: I'm a ghost, Mr. Leviathan, a ghost of what has been the
top women's slacks manufacturer in this city — in the world.

LEVIATHAN (*contemptuously*): Women in slacks!

VOICE: Are you deaf to my tragedy?

LEVIATHAN: Sorry, Mac, but order means tragedy to disorder.
Now go home! Hey, Angel, can't you turn him off — he's down
your alley.

ANGEL: Mark this, Leviathan, it's not easy to run off a ghost bent
on revenge.

VOICE (*gleefully and maliciously*): You bet! D'you hear that
noise? (*Distant shouts back-stage.*) There they come, the
commandos of women's slacks manufacturers. Give them one
more hour and they'll be storming your palace walls. It's war,
Leviathan!

LEVIATHAN: War? I love war! (*To GABRIEL.*) We two know
why war's good. Because of war, Germans grabbed us for

work. And thanks to war, a black market came after the war, and everybody could make money. Without war the rich would stay rich and the poor would stay beggars. Hooray for war! (*A MANUFACTURER OF KITCHEN APPLIANCES appears in the door.*)

MANUFACTURER OF KITCHEN APPLIANCES: Hooray! (*His back to the audience, he is fencing with an invisible enemy back stage. He is wearing a tin pot on his head for a helmet and brandishing a pot cover as a shield. He speaks to LEVIATHAN between thrusts.*) Don't worry about them slack merchants!...Touche!...Glub!...We makers of kitchen appliances, we'll repel them....Wham!...We love you, Mr. Leviathan, honest we do!...En garde!...Glub!...Our sales are booming because the women have come back to the kitchens—thanks to your School for Love!...Yikes!...We repelled the commandos of them slacks merchants this morning....Touche!... Ugh! Our men are around your school now, armed with pots and pans....Zoom!...We'll repel them again and again!

SEVERAL VOICES OUTSIDE THE WINDOW: And again! (*Din and rattle of pots and pans in support.*)

LEVIATHAN: I appreciate it, pal. Could you do me a favor and kick out one of these slack big shots who snuck in here like a ghost.

MANUFACTURER OF KITCHEN APPLIANCES: Ghost? Nothing easier. (*Still fencing, he pulls out of his back pocket a pressurized spray can and hands it to LEVIATHAN.*) A squirt or two, just wipe it off afterwards! **Get rid of ghosts at no extra cost**!

LEVIATHAN: Gee, thanks!

ANGEL: Watch out, Leviathan! Don't monkey with the transcendental.

LEVIATHAN: Don't worry, Angel—I won't spray it on you.

VOICE OF THE TOP WOMEN'S SLACKS MANUFACTURER: I'll haunt you till your dying day, I'll...per...(*LEVIATHAN squirts at the quivering light above the pants. VOICE stops abruptly, emits a faint scream and is silent. Confetti-like white fluff flutters down. Lights go back to normal. BUTLER efficiently sweeps up the remains of the ghost.*)

GABRIEL (*fascinated*): Terrific.

LEVIATHAN (*to GABRIEL*): You like it, ah? (*To MANUFACTURER OF KITCHEN APPLIANCES.*) Thanks, pal—good stuff.

MANUFACTURER OF KITCHEN APPLIANCES: It gets where

bleach can't reach!...Zoom!...Don't mention it....Charge!...
Wham! (*He runs out, still fencing.*)

LEVIATHAN: They love me, eh? Let's distribute some coffee and
cake among our allies. It's been a long and busy morning for
them.

GABRIEL: Yes, Sir.

ANGEL: You'll have to wait till ovens bake cakes by themselves.
Most of the bakeries in the city have closed down.

LEVIATHAN: Why?

DIANA: Newspapers say the people have been eating so much
cake because they were unhappy.

GABRIEL (*looks at DIANA soulfully; in a whisper*): I still eat a
lot of cake.

DIANA (*also in a whisper*): And you will—for a long time.

GABRIEL: I believe in miracles. Tell me the truth—for you,
didn't I make a more believable angel than him? (*Beckons to
ANGEL.*)

DIANA (*takes one look at ANGEL*): That's not much of a compliment. (*To LEVIATHAN, loudly.*) The people have been eating
so much cake because their love life was confused. Psychologists have explained that now, with the School for Love, people
don't need cake anymore.

ANGEL (*menacingly*): Speaking about psychologists, most of
them are out of work. (*Mockingly.*) People now think the
School for Love solves all their problems.

LEVIATHAN: To hell with psychologists!

ANGEL: I warn you, Leviathan. War, chaos, hordes of unemployed....They'll stampede you! (*Outside the window—a
rising sound of thousands of feet on the asphalt, a veritable
stampede. All run to the window.*)

LEVIATHAN: Hordes and mobs!

DIANA: It looks like an exodus. They're leaving the city!

LEVIATHAN: Are they for or against me?

DIANA: Wait...each group is carrying a placard. Let me see...
**Sadists...Fetishists...Narcissists...Masochists...Homo-
sexuals...nymphomaniacs...**(*As she reads each placard, a
sorrowful wail rises from each of the groups mentioned.*)

LEVIATHAN: I've never heard of these organizations but if
they're afraid of me, they better run fast!

GABRIEL (*awe-struck*): And all because of the School for Love.

LEVIATHAN: Power is sweet, ah, my boy? Suck its breast as
it swells, and you'll grow big. Power and America! (*To
DIANA.*) Your cheeks are flushed too, ah?

DIANA: Things are happening—the rocket is off the pad. I wanted to be in the theatre, to turn a bare stage into an exploding star. Now it is happening.

LEVIATHAN: It's only the beginning. Let's distribute that coffee now. (*To GABRIEL.*) Get the press photographers on the scene. (*To the world outside.*) America, open your arms. Catch-as-catch-can. Your bridegroom is on the way. (*LEVIATHAN, DIANA, GABRIEL go out, leaving ANGEL alone.*)

ANGEL: Photographers! The dog—he's learned all the American tricks! (*ANGEL kicks the mannequin in anger. A sign descends slowly:* **If you love her, beat her.** *ANGEL throws a newspaper at the sign, and at the contact violin music erupts. ANGEL'S response to the music is a Bronx cheer, and the violin music, insulted, fizzles out. He picks up the newspaper and stands for a moment in deep thought. When he begins to speak, it is evident that a bold plan is being born.*) Sabotage... (*Scattered clapping of hands outside.*) Bakeries...(*Another spurt of clapping.*) Psychologists...(*Clapping.*) Models... (*Clapping. Outside a few shouts of "Bravo." Several voices break into "For he's a jolly good fellow... With a sudden determination, ANGEL steps to the telephone, quickly leafs in the telephone book, dials.*) Bakeries United?...No, I don't want to buy any cake—I know how things are. That's why I'm calling you....Please stop crying....I can't understand you....My message is...strike back!...No...no pie in the face...too obvious....Be like serpents. Infiltrate. Send your best man to the School for Love....Get him inside, and I'll help him out....It doesn't matter who I am....How will he recognize me? I'll introduce myself as a fellow-conspirator. I'll use the word h!a!t!e! (*His voice becomes inaudible. Another sprinkling of handclaps and "bravos" outside. As ANGEL dials again, a platform becomes visible in the background. OKEN and a fat old man in a baker's outfit are seen on it. OKEN kneels down, and the baker knights him with an oven-peel. OKEN stands up; they shake hands and kiss each other on both cheeks. Some flour gets on OKEN. The old man hands a cake box to OKEN. They wave to each other and are swallowed by darkness.*) Psychoanalysts Unlimit-ID?...No, I don't want to be analyzed. ...Thanks, I don't need a used sofa....Not even for nothing.... I know how things are....I want your most brilliant man. (*ANGEL goes on speaking but becomes inaudible. A platform again becomes visible in the background. A professorial type straight out of a turn-of-a-century Vienna University album—*

grey beard, a pince-nez, a hard collar — bids LIBIDSTONE to kneel. The professor knights LIBIDSTONE by slapping his shoulder with a note-pad. LIBIDSTONE stands up. They are about to embrace each other but the professor cautions LIBIDSTONE. They both smile and nod their heads understandingly. The professor gives LIBIDSTONE the notebook and as they wave goodbye the platform turns dark.)

ANGEL *(puts down the receiver, dials again)*: Models' Mart? No...yes... *(As his voice dies away, MISS ADENOID appears on the platform in the background. She shakes hands with a woman, executive type and executioner-size. ADENOID poses for a curtsy and the executive woman pats her shoulder with a camera tripod. ADENOID straightens herself. They strike several typical modeling poses of saying good-bye. Then they peck at each other posing again and are swallowed by darkness. ANGEL slams down the receiver and, with a determined grin on his face, shakes his fist toward the window.)* So you're higher now—so you'll fall harder. *(Mockingly.)* "Power, America"...we'll see who'll get it! You'll still have a cold behind! *(ANGEL smashes his fist on the table to emphasize his words. A statuette of a cupid descends from above, his chubby Rubenesque behind to the audience. The curtain follows the cupid, a bit more slowly.)*

CURTAIN

ACT TWO

(One of the many new offices of LEO LEVIATHAN. He sits behind an imposing desk and looks more grandiose than ever, in shirt-sleeves, a top-hat still perched on his head. His interest is absorbed by the large intercom board on the desk. ANGEL stands beside the table, but he is unaware of LEVIATHAN. He keeps staring downstage, as if expecting someone (which he is). Backstage, two partitions are visible behind gauze, dividing the area into three sections — instruction rooms. Stage-right, GABRIEL is sitting on a chair, beneath a pole-lamp, facing backstage, holding a book in one hand and a plastic female arm in another. He is reading intently, manipulating the plastic arm, gesticulating. Stage-left, DIANA is sitting on a chair, facing back-stage, under a pole-lamp. She is holding in her hand a large replica of a herring.

From time to time, she makes the extreme effort to bring it closer to her nose. Then she sighs and shakes her head. LEVIATHAN closes his eyes, circles the air with his finger, and hits one of the buttons.)

VOICE FROM INTERCOM: Reservations. All filled up for the night shift. (*LEVIATHAN presses a button to shut off the voice and aims blindly at another one.*) Research.

LEVIATHAN: Research, huh? Tell me—how many herrings a whale eats for one meal?

VOICE FROM INTERCOM (*worried*): Did you say herrings?

LEVIATHAN: Yeah!

VOICE FROM INTERCOM: One...moment—Sir...

LEVIATHAN: Stop! No books! Right now.

VOICE FROM INTERCOM (*panicky*): But, sir...(*LEVIATHAN'S answer is a malevolent laugh. He presses a button to shut off the voice. His laughter subsides to a bored silence. He speaks to ANGEL without looking at him.*)

LEVIATHAN: I need new buttons on this, Angel. These little guys, those squeaky voices—they're beginning to bore me. I want a button for—the President! (*Receiving no answer, he looks up.*) D'you hear? (*Turns around and notices that ANGEL is not listening to him.*) Hey, Angel, snap out of it! What are you staring at?

ANGEL: At heaven, you fool. Keeping in touch.

LEVIATHAN: Let me open the roof for you—you'll read the message more easily. (*LEVIATHAN presses a button and the vaulted roof high above slides open. Late afternoon sun gilds everything.*) Good old evening sun, kicking down a pail of gold paint—my Eldorado sun!

ANGEL: Close it, you materialist! You think that I need open roofs to speak to heaven? (*LEVIATHAN presses the button and the roof closes.*)

LEVIATHAN: Just trying to be helpful, that's all. (*Nodding upwards.*) What does heaven say? What's cooking for me?

ANGEL (*absent-mindedly*): Oh...big things, big things.

LEVIATHAN: The greatest, ah?

ANGEL: So you want a button for the President? And last week you were happy to have one installed for a millionaire.

LEVIATHAN: I'm growing, Angel!

ANGEL: Aren't you a bit scared? This thing is getting very big, like a huge clock—thousands of wheels turning on each other! Millions of screws! One little thing goes wrong—and all's screwed up. (*Looks toward the instruction rooms.*) One-two-three things.

LEVIATHAN: Little things—I'll squash them like lice! Even big things—with you at my side, with your connections. (*LEVIA-THAN'S tone changes to imploration.*) Your connections...you couldn't ask them for a little favor?

ANGEL (*waves his hand*): Look—all this is favor. You want more?

LEVIATHAN: One thing, very special.

ANGEL: Name it. (*LEVIATHAN'S lips, frustrated without end, are unable to pronounce the object of his desires, and his hands begin to form the shape of a woman in the air, making it bigger as they move and, finally, embracing that imaginary shape.*)

ANGEL (*with a sigh*): Of course, what else?

LEVIATHAN (*nods energetically*): They jam my dreams, like feather bedding. I look up, and there they crowd the sky—gorgeous clouds. I reach out—and pfft!...Just feathers and hot air...

ANGEL: So you'd like permission very much?

LEVIATHAN (*hopefully*): Yes!

ANGEL: Really much?

LEVIATHAN (*nods violently, presses all the buttons on the inter-com, and shouts at their joint noise*): Yes!!! (*He flips the inter-com buttons off and whispers.*) Yes...

ANGEL (*with a sudden cruel glint*): So, you won't get any permission! Isn't that shameful, a man getting all those favors and still so non-spiritual. Chosen for the greatest things—and he asks for a woman. I wonder if I haven't picked the wrong person...

LEVIATHAN: But, Angel! (*A red bulb starts blinking over the partition stage left, indicating the arrival of the first customer.*)

ANGEL: Shush, enough! (*To GABRIEL.*) Customer! (*To LEVIATHAN.*) You'll give the lesson.

LEVIATHAN (*gruffly*): Let someone else take it.

ANGEL: They paid for a lesson á la mode—with you. (*GABRIEL scurries to his feet, takes one more quick glance at his book and walks toward the partition stage-left. ANGEL exits stage-right.*)

LEVIATHAN: Angel...guardian...damn it! (*He angrily presses a button.*)

VOICE FROM THE INTERCOM: School for Love. Research.

LEVIATHAN: You're fired. (*LEVIATHAN flips off the button and rises in a huff. He takes a look at DIANA, who gets up, glances at her wristwatch and walks out holding the herring model*

*away from her. In anger, LEVIATHAN kicks his desk, which
moves stageright. LEVIATHAN sits at the desk in its new
position and adjusts a microphone. Meanwhile, the gauze
screen has opened, disclosing the three empty instruction
chambers. OKEN enters, still holding the cakebox in his hand.
He notices GABRIEL, waves to him and opens his mouth to
address him. At that moment, LEVIATHAN'S voice booms at
him magnified by a loudspeaker.)* United Bakeries?

OKEN: Right-o. Oken's my name. Are you people unionized?

LEVIATHAN: Love's Union, Mr. Oken, Love's Union. You are
married?

OKEN: Yep. *("On the Waves" waltz is heard softly in the background. GABRIEL steps out. BUTLER comes in down-stage-
left carrying the picture of the lady with the horse's head. He
is beckoned in by ANGEL whose head is sticking out up-stage-
right. LEVIATHAN rivets his eyes on the picture, forgetting
OKEN who follows it on its way across the stage.)*

ANGEL *(unseen by the others and taking advantage of GABRIEL'S
stepping out and LEVIATHAN'S absorption, talks in a not-to-
be-confused conspiratorial tone into a hand microphone)*:
Hate!

OKEN *(shivers with understanding and conspiratorial fervor)*:
Hate! *(GABRIEL pushes in a mannequin of a large woman;
BUTLER exits stage-right.)*

LEVIATHAN *(returning to the instructor's role)*: So, you're
married and unhappy.

OKEN *(surprised)*: Yes...

LEVIATHAN: And that mannequin's about your wife's size.

OKEN *(flabbergasted)*: Hey, how do you know all that?

GABRIEL *(mechanically)*: School for Love knows everything.

LEVIATHAN: Ever beat her?

OKEN: Are you kidding?

LEVIATHAN: How can she respect you, if you don't beat her?

OKEN: You should **see** my wife.

LEVIATHAN: She's a woman. If you beat a woman, she knows
that you care for her, that she does things to you.

GABRIEL: The School for Love knows everything.

OKEN: Hm. What about the neighbors, what would they say?

LEVIATHAN *(as he speaks, GABRIEL draws with chalk a
target on the mannequin's behind)*: You beat your wife privately and carefully. It inspires respect and it is healthy.
(OKEN slaps the mannequin more heartily. His eyes light up.)

OKEN: Hey, I like it!

LEVIATHAN: Atta boy! (*OKEN walks several steps back to have a better run-in and lowers his head. At that moment ADENOID comes in backward, gazing curiously at her surroundings. OKEN charges and slaps, by mistake, her behind instead of the mannequin's. ADENOID lets out a scream, drops her round case, wheels around and lands a slap on OKEN'S face. Startled, OKEN drops his cake box. He explains in emphatic gestures that he wanted to slap the mannequin and that he is very sorry. She gestures back, telling him that she accepts his explanation and is sorry, too. During this exchange they bend down to pick up their boxes, still looking at each other, pick up wrong ones and exchange them with friendly smiles.*)

LEVIATHAN (*interrupting their mute conversation*): Collision, confusion—that's what you get without the School for Love! Back to your places now! (*OKEN'S musical theme vanishes. He resumes his wife-beating exercises in his now dimmed partition. ADENOID enters the middle compartment on which light is concentrated.*)

LEVIATHAN (*rapidly*): Welcome! Female! Single!

ADENOID: By choice.

LEVIATHAN: Poor choice. Ten lessons, two hundred dollars on a deferred payment plan, and you make right choice.

GABRIEL: The School for Love knows everything. (*GABRIEL goes out, ANGEL waves in BUTLER with the picture again, LEVIATHAN'S eyes go astray as before.*)

ANGEL (*conspiratorially*): Hate!

ADENOID (*understandingly*): Hate! (*GABRIEL pushes in a four-poster.*) That's positively quaint! I posed in it once. I had pyjamas on with eyelet embroidery—and the daintiest lace...

LEVIATHAN: Skip the lace. Stand next to the bed. (*She does.*) Right. What's in your background now? A bed. Right? Now we must teach you to speak, to move in such a way that even when there's no bed next to you, men will see a bed in your background. You must, so to say...

GABRIEL (*automatically*): ...absorb it into your very being.

ADENOID: You mean, there's no bed in my background now?

LEVIATHAN: Sorry, no. An army cot, at most. You're much too thin for a woman. Also, you hit a man. Both mistakes fatal.

ADENOID: What should I have done?

LEVIATHAN: Watch closely. (*GABRIEL, automatically, slaps her behind. She lifts her hand to slap his face but realizes her error and covers her face bashfully instead.*)

LEVIATHAN: You're getting there! Blush a little, swoon a little.

Make him feel like a man! (*She takes her hands off her face.*) No, hold it! Keep your face covered! You have beautiful eyes, the rest is just so-so. Buy yourself a fan, buy a book. Keep your face covered; always, show your eyes! (*She covers her face up to her eyes with her left hand.*) And then—let him kiss your hand. (*She extends her right hand to GABRIEL. He kisses it and simultaneously sticks a plastic arm out to be kissed by OKEN.*) You've almost got it! Just keep your chief example before your eyes: the girls in the albums of our childhood—all sweetness, all obedience. (*With LEVIATHAN'S last sentence, light dims in ADENOID'S compartment and shifts to the third compartment which LIBIDSTONE enters.*)

LIBIDSTONE: Obedience? A forgotten word. Obedience to whom? To what? (*GABRIEL enters.*)

GABRIEL (*automatically*): The School for Love knows everything.

LIBIDSTONE: Omniscience—a grave delusion.

LEVIATHAN: We give explanations here. Married?

LIBIDSTONE: Single. Meaning alone. Which every modern man is.

LEVIATHAN: How are you making out with girls?

LIBIDSTONE: Frankly, not too well. (*LEVIATHAN switches on a sedate fox trot.*) You may say that many famous people didn't either. But then, what is fame? Ask one who tasted it at a very tender age. It's poisoned with loneliness. Why? Because we've lost the center of the world.

LEVIATHAN: We'll get you there in six lessons. Now, what picture comes to your mind when you think of a girl?

LIBIDSTONE: Amateur psychology...but, why not? Look where professionalism got us. All right—when I think of a girl, I see a fortress before me. A primitive fortress. Reason stands powerless before its closed gate.

LEVIATHAN: Peanuts! Eight lessons, and your fortresses will shrink to little bunkers. Assistant, exhibit fifty-nine! (*GABRIEL goes out, ANGEL waves in the BUTLER with the picture, etc. But this time BUTLER stops with his picture in the middle, holding LEVIATHAN'S attention longer, and ANGEL has more time for indoctrination.*)

ANGEL (*hissing*): Hate!

LIBIDSTONE: A neurosis.

ANGEL: I mean—hate!

LIBIDSTONE (*understanding*): Oh, yes, yes. **Hate**—the conspiracy.

ANGEL: Shhhh! Attention, everybody! (*ADENOID and OKEN stop their exercises. All three freeze attentively.*) We've gathered here an army of revenge!...Wait, this calls for a different music. (*Short pause. Then a rousing march blares out instead of the fox-trot.*) We'll strike tonight! When the lesson ends, you stay in your places. The night shift will be busy in the other part of the building but here the lights will go out. You'll wait in darkness, poised. The signal will be this march you hear now—I'll smash it on sweet violins. You'll jump out and start pressing every button like mad, pulling every puller like crazy. And this tower of Babel will collapse and will bury this whale, this elephant. Elephant... (*His voice trails off down memory lane, sinking to a sad complaining pitch.*) Siamese stamp, white elephant, purple, triangle, perforated... (*The martial music, as if keeping step with his voice, also fizzles away. The three conspirators begin to shift uneasily. Awakes suddenly from his reveries. Very loudly.*) To hell with stamps! To hell with memories! Stamp out memories! (*The conspirators again freeze in their attentive positions.*) You don't kill an elephant with peas. You smash him with all the buttons, levers, doors, walls, roofs, But before we smash him, we'll use a couple of peas to irritate him. (*GABRIEL pushes in a tub with a shower-spray and a curtain attached. BUTLER departs with picture.*)

LEVIATHAN (*follows the picture with his eyes*): What breasts...

LIBIDSTONE (*surprised*): I beg your pardon?

LEVIATHAN: Ahem...so, you have problems with girls, fortresses. First Lesson. (*Points to the tub.*) When you invite a young lady to your home, show her your little alligator.

LIBIDSTONE: My little what?

LEVIATHAN: Your little that! (*GABRIEL puts a little toy alligator into the tub.*) If the young lady is scared, she'll swoon into your arms. If not—she'll be aroused—and you'll be there!

LIBIDSTONE: But what happens if I'm scared?

LEVIATHAN: That—for the next lesson. (*Claps his hands.*) One more hand kiss! (*GABRIEL extends to LIBIDSTONE a plastic hand, while ADENOID extends her hand to be kissed by OKEN who kisses it a little longer than the rest. LEVIATHAN stands up and goes out stage-left.*)

ANGEL (*sneaks to the table microphone*): And don't forget. (*A bar of march music. A whisper.*) Hate. (*GABRIEL looks up. Loudly and cloyingly.*) Love! As the leader of our school, Leo Leviathan, said...(*LEVIATHAN briskly enters the students' area downstage-left. Fanfare music.*)

LEVIATHAN: Practice, practice, practice! (*Tension seizes the students. LEVIATHAN, like a general reviewing his troops, followed by GABRIEL, looks OKEN over. He removes a piece of lint from OKEN'S shoulder, autographs his own picture—which GABRIEL carries—and hands it to OKEN. Stepping over to ADENOID, LEVIATHAN shakes his head with sad disapproval at her waist and shows with his thumb and pinky how thin it is. Still sadly shaking his head, he gives her his autographed picture. She looks at his bulk, not unimpressed. LIBIDSTONE stares at LEVIATHAN with intense curiosity. They shake hands, but LIBIDSTONE gesticulates to LEVIA—THAN that he wants another handshake. LEVIATHAN obliges with a grin. LIBIDSTONE gratefully accepts the picture and makes a quick entry in his notebook. LEVIATHAN departs, followed by GABRIEL.*)

ANGEL (*into the table-microphone*): Fellow-conspirators... (*But their eyes are still riveted on LEVIATHAN'S trail.*) Hate! Revenge! (*They unglue their eyes from LEVIATHAN and turn their attention back to the ANGEL with some difficulty.*) You photographed the target in your minds, eh? And you, Miss Adenoid, will have the honor to shoot the first pea at the elephant. Here's how... (*The three compartments turn dark. Stage-right, DIANA emerges sitting on a chair, still absorbed in herring exercises. ANGEL strolls in with planned casualness.*)

ANGEL (*pointing to the herring model*): Any progress?

DIANA: I can stand a Norwegian herring two feet away.

ANGEL (*as if to himself*): On the big seas a herring, properly placed, may catch a whale. Ever think of it?

DIANA: When I think of the big seas, I think of a gleaming luxury liner...

ANGEL: You don't have to tell me—first time I met you, I saw two tiny luxury liners gleaming in the pupils of your eyes. Got your ship card yet?

DIANA: Got a herring in my hand and the buzz of the School in my ears.

ANGEL: Ah, but how your eyes were sparkling when the School had just started!

DIANA: It seemed like a rocket flashing into the blue. One moment more, I thought, and a light would burst into my eyes: the first glimpse of an angel's face—not yours but of the heaven I'd imagined.

ANGEL (*with sudden irritation*): I may not be the handsomest angel but why rub it in?

DIANA: Smelling herrings induces frankness. The blue of space, Mr. Angel, turned out to be the painted ceiling of the School.

ANGEL: I'll generously overhear the juvenile criticism of this institution. So, what's left for you?

DIANA: The luxury liner, I guess. It's either space or big seas for me.

ANGEL: A woman's mind—it's enough to give an angel a headache. I suspect half of the women in the school today—they're looking for their luxury cruises, hell-bent to snatch my Leviathan.

DIANA: Nobody will snatch him. (*Gloomily.*) He obeys you. Too well.

ANGEL: He'd better. I just hope they don't think of one way to snatch him. Such a simple, obvious way.

DIANA: I wonder if there is *any* way.

ANGEL: Obvious, like a drunkard's nose. (*BUTLER enters and hangs the woman-horse painting.*) Right. On this wall. His ideal woman—what does she look like? Yes—the picture! (*As ANGEL begins to describe the "obvious" way to snatch LEVIATHAN, a spotlight picks up ADENOID stage-left, dressed exactly as the woman in the picture whom ANGEL is describing. She is a little self-conscious and pulls her dress around.*) I hope no woman gets the idea of putting on a big wig and a grandmother's dress and taking a cardboard horse head in her arm...She wouldn't have to do anything, except just stand in the doorway and—bingo! He would wrap himself around her little finger and all the saints and angels wouldn't be able to tear him away...(*DIANA gets up. A faint smile appears on her lips.*)

DIANA: I still may catch that luxury liner. (*She puts down the herring and walks off with determination.*)

ANGEL (*as she is walking way*): I just hope no woman thinks of that...(*DIANA exits stage-right and, in her excitement, fails to notice GABRIEL who enters. He stops and looks at her longingly. ANGEL makes a leap of joy and begins to dance off stage-left.*) One pea will tickle, two peas will tease. (*When he sees LEVIATHAN entering—a herring in his hand—he stops his jig and song and switches to a dignified walk, his hands in a prayer position.*)

LEVIATHAN (*to GABRIEL, pointing to his slacks*): Nice pants! Hey, where's the smile, one-track mind? (*GABRIEL tries to smile.*) Bigger! Still bigger! Big business. Big life. Big future. The word "big" writes a smile on the lips.

GABRIEL: I'm a bit tired.

LEVIATHAN: Ah, girls! Too many girls. How many? Tell me all about it.

GABRIEL: One.

LEVIATHAN: No?

GABRIEL: And not even that one.

LEVIATHAN: You're kidding me—one track and not getting anywhere. Let me give you a lesson, free. Sit down. (*GABRIEL sits down under the light of the lamp and puts the instruction book on his knees.*) Now listen...(*A pause. LEVIATHAN looks at GABRIEL intently.*)

GABRIEL: Yes?

LEVIATHAN (*puts a finger to his lips. His voice is softer*): Sit still. I had a dream once. There was a lamp in it that gave light just like a sister to this light and under it a boy was sitting—just like you now—a boy who was somehow my own. And I knew in the dream—that was a family room. I never had a family room, you know, never—a son...(*He breaks off one half the herring and gives it to GABRIEL.*)

GABRIEL (*takes the herring encouraged by the unexpected softness in LEVIATHAN'S voice*): If you had a son and your son would want to confess something?

LEVIATHAN: He'd better confess fast.

GABRIEL: Well, I'm not very happy about...

LEVIATHAN: You want a raise? You got it.

GABRIEL: I've seen so little of America.

LEVIATHAN: Don't you get enough Americans here? And mind you—our job is not to see America—our job is to change America. Anything else?

GABRIEL: I'm tired of memorizing these lessons.

LEVIATHAN: Lazy, huh? Good life spoils. A kidney that swims in fat thinks the whole world swims in fat.

GABRIEL: Don't get me wrong, I never had it so good. Four meals a day and what a roof overhead. I **do** appreciate it.

LEVIATHAN: What's the matter then—you sick or something? Where's that bubbling milk of excitement of the first days: "America, here we come!" Something got sour?

GABRIEL: I thought—it was **my** dream—to put some of my own ideas into this School for Love, to see them work.

LEVIATHAN: Your—own? (*Ironically.*) And what would they be—these I?D?E?A?S?

GABRIEL: I saw the School something like a song, a lovely dance, a burst of light...

LEVIATHAN: Come now, one-track mind!

GABRIEL: I thought the Angel would bring in all these things — angels are supposed to — but he didn't. Why didn't he?

LEVIATHAN: Stop right there, boy! You're trying to jump higher than your navel! Mark this once and for all — you're not to think here, you're here to be happy! I think here, the Angel and I. Anything else bothering you?

GABRIEL: Aren't you fooling them a bit, the customers?

LEVIATHAN (*shakes his head*): You still gotta lot to learn. What's fooling — and what's truth? (*Shows around with a sweep of his arm.*) This is true, isn't it? So it is **truth**. And it belongs to me.

GABRIEL: I'm not against a little fooling. Who am I to give you advice? But when I have to keep saying "School for Love knows everything" — I blush. It just isn't so.

LEVIATHAN: Best business is with something that isn't. I'm not cheating them — they get more than their money's worth. Don't you read the papers? They have less ulcers now — thanks to me. America's today a better place to live — because of me! (*He pauses and takes a hard look at GABRIEL.*) Say, you're not one of those thankless...

GABRIEL: No, Sir! Not thankless — that's the greatest sin...

LEVIATHAN: These thankless curs who bit the hand... (*ANGEL sticks in a plastic woman's hand through a curtain right next to GABRIEL and some eight feet away from LEVIATHAN. A letter is stuck precariously between the fingers of the hand. LEVIATHAN notices the hand and gasps in surprise.*) The hand that feeds them...the hand...

GABRIEL (*who has not noticed the plastic hand*): Never, Mr. Leviathan!

LEVIATHAN (*hoarsely*): Grab that hand! (*GABRIEL steps to LEVIATHAN and grabs his hand in affirmation of his gratitude.*)

LEVIATHAN: The other one! (*GABRIEL grabs LEVIATHAN'S other hand.*) That one, stupid! (*GABRIEL at last notices the plastic hand, but as he tries to grab it, the hand releases the letter and vanishes behind the curtain. The letter flutters down, followed by their eyes. GABRIEL bends and picks it up.*)

GABRIEL: It's for you.

LEVIATHAN (*takes the letter and puts it to his nose*): That per-

fume? Just like the police chief wife's in our town! Did you see
that hand? Chubby, huh?

GABRIEL: And pink.

LEVIATHAN: Chubby and pink—best of hands. Oh, the rest of
her! (*He tears the letter open and pulls out a blond lock.*) I
could swear this was clipped from the head of the postmaster's
wife in my town! (*Reads hurriedly.*) "My big strong...man
of my life...I wait for you...by the bed...**Woman in the Picture.**"

GABRIEL: Mr. Leviathan, Sir, I meant it when I said I'd always
be thankful.

LEVIATHAN (*still enraptured*): Forget it. Run along. My heart is
pounding so! My fleshy dream is turning into fleshy flesh!...
Run! (*GABRIEL hastens out.*) Stop! (*GABRIEL stops.*) If you
see the Angel, keep him away from the four-poster.

GABRIEL: I will. Thanks again...

LEVIATHAN: Run! (*GABRIEL exits. LEVIATHAN opens the
background curtain revealing the section with the four-poster.
He takes the lock out from the envelope and fingers it. ADENOID
from behind the curtain, tickles his ear with a strand of
her wig-hair. LEVIATHAN gingerly touches it and compares it with the lock from his envelope, still not turning
back. He then reaches after more of her hair—she teasingly
withdraws it. LEVIATHAN turns around; ADENOID disappears behind the curtain. LEVIATHAN breaks out into a mis-
chievous grin and shows the audience how he will catch her
unawares; he will go around the bed in front and grab her from
behind. He starts tip-toing stage-right to round the bed. Meanwhile, ADENOID slips out from behind the curtain and crosses
the stage to the other side of the bed behind him—padded with
pillows, she is a faithful version of the picture. As LEVIATHAN
and ADENOID disappear behind the curtain on the other side
of the bed stage-right, DIANA enters stage-left, unseen by
LEVIATHAN and ADENOID, and stops by the bed. LEVIA-
THAN appears behind her mistaking her for the woman he
tried to outflank. He surveys her pillow-padded girth with en-
chantment, draws her shape with his hand in the air and then
gently squeezes her waist from behind. She opens her mouth
but refrains from screaming. He kisses her neck—her face
shows displeasure. He grows more persistent—her face clouds
with panic. Suddenly she stops struggling—an idea flashes
on her face. She wriggles flirtatiously, points to the bed and
beckons to LEVIATHAN to lie down on it indicating that she*

*will soon follow. LEVIATHAN jumps on the bed and stretches
out in an eager and trusting anticipation, his mouth open. She
stands still for a few seconds. This is her moment of decision—
luxury liner or Staten Island Ferry. Her eyes wander around
the place, stop at LEVIATHAN's prostrate bulk. LEVIATHAN
raises one hand invitingly, with his eyes still closed. She smells
the herring on his hand and, then, determinedly shakes her
head. The decision is made against the luxury liner. While
DIANA shakes her head facing the audience, ADENOID sticks
her head through the curtain at the other side of the stage and
peers straight at LEVIATHAN, without noticing DIANA.
Puzzled by the immobility of LEVIATHAN, ADENOID steps
nearer to him, bends down for a closer look, puts her ear to his
heart. He opens one eye slightly and grabs her hand. ADENOID
emits a squeak of surprise. DIANA turns toward the sound,
and at this instant, all three see each other. For a moment they
are all speechless but the shock is written largest on LEVIA-
THAN'S face who sees his fleshy dream split into two identical
halves. And then silence bursts—the two women scream;
LEVIATHAN slaps his hands over his face. Still screaming,
the women throw the horses' heads high in the air; ADENOID
faints and sinks down onto the bed; LEVIATHAN jumps up
from the bed; DIANA runs off stage-right. And ANGEL rushes
in stage-left, shouting, as though he was surprised by the noise.)*
ANGEL: Hey! What goes? *(LEVIATHAN,scared to the very
marrow that ANGEL will discover him in an amorous adven-
ture, quickly throws the blanket over prostrate ADENOID,
puts on one of the horses' heads to disguise himself and starts
tip-toeing away from the ANGEL. But the ANGEL overtakes
him and seizes him by the collar.)* Halt! Don't move! Who're
you? *(LEVIATHAN grunts in reply, trying to disguise his
voice.)* That's your name? It fits your face. Passport, ticket,
badge? *(LEVIATHAN shakes his head violently and emits a
grunting plea. ANGEL starts kicking LEVIATHAN.)* That's
for spying!...For bringing horse manure into our sparkling
school! *(Carried away, in a voice of genuine hysterical grief.)*
For my stamps, my life! *(LEVIATHAN emits a questioning
grunt and uses the moment of the ANGEL'S confusion to
wrench himself away and to dash off-stage. The ANGEL sends
him off with a loud laughter, clapping his knees. Then, as his
laughter subsides gradually, the other two instruction chambers open slowly. The lights begin to dim and stop at twilight.
OKEN is seen sitting by the mannequin, looking backstage;*

ADENOID awakes from her faint on the four-poster and begins taking off her wig; LIBIDSTONE sits inside the tub, meditating.) End of another day shift. Fake moonlight is about to rise over artificial lakes. Soon canned violins will sprinkle candied notes, trained cows will moo in unison, tinsel stars will blink and three thousand couples will be taught how to hold hands—for the last time! *(During his talk he checks and camouflages his fellow conspirators, unseen by them. He throws a drape over the mannequin to hide OKEN; he piles up pillows on the four-poster to conceal ADENOID; he pulls the shower-curtain around LIBIDSTONE. To audience.)* Listen! this morning I passed a small green house with dark green shutters. A house like that—that's all I wanted; a little house and peace. Didn't you all? You chuckle at me—a little man who collects pieces of paper. I say—watch out for little men who discover what hells they have been carrying within. You may return my stamps now, hand me my little house on a platter— it is too late. Even revenge, simple, sweet revenge is not enough anymore. In these spaces of America, now my hell, now my ambition has stretched far and wide. Now the prize is everything. This roof will open soon, the walls will crumble, the collapsing dome will bury the whale. And then I'll be on top, I'll turn this Babylonian tower into another school—for thrift, sobriety and strictest decency! And then, on top, perhaps you'll find me strong...and handsome. There will be no more chuckling! *(One more look and ANGEL goes out. An instant of complete silence which is punctured by a yawn from OKEN'S hiding place. His stretching arm becomes visible, then his face. Having established that the coast is clear, he opens his cake box, slices a piece with a pocket knife and begins to munch on it. Attracted by the rustling, ADENOID sticks out her inquisitive nose. Seeing the cake, she licks her lips, lifts her eyes and swallows deeply. She gives a conspiratorial cough and, remembering her lesson, covers her face up to her eyes. OKEN jumps back behind his drape and then peeks out.)*

OKEN *(whispers)*: What peepers! Wait a minute—I've seen them somewhere! *(They both drop curtains from their faces.)*

OKEN and ADENOID *(simultaneously)*: It's you! What are you doing here? *(Pause.)*

OKEN *(bows in mock-ceremony)*: Will you honor me by visiting my parlor?

ADENOID *(having already taken a couple of steps toward OKEN)*: Shall I?

OKEN: Feel at home. Late homework?

ADENOID: Not allowed to tell.

OKEN: Same here.

ADENOID: Any idea **who gives instructions**?

OKEN: Not the faintest!

ADENOID (*removing a long blond wig-hair from her shoulder*):
    All I can say is, he has some weird ideas on fashion.

OKEN: He didn't say we shouldn't have some fun while we wait.

ADENOID (*suspiciously*): How do you mean that?

OKEN: Join the picnic, have some cake.

ADENOID: Oh, cake...sorry.

OKEN: It's good—nine-layer.

ADENOID (*assuming the position for a VOGUE front cover*):
    I'm a model (*More militantly.*) That's why I'm here! (*The
    light switches to LIBIDSTONE'S section.*)

LIBIDSTONE: Why *am* I here? Conspiracy? That's only the
    uppermost layer. How many layers beneath? These strange
    noises, subliminal rumblings—will they tell me? Darkness is
    closer to the center of things—I'm in darkness—hence, I'm
    closer to the center of things. Is liberation in burial? A dazzling
    thought! (*The light switches to the middle section. DIANA
    walks in, bare-footed, weary and dazed. She is still in her
    "picture" costume and is carrying her 1919 shoes in her hand.
    She sits down on the four-poster and fingers a tress of her hair
    with skeptical fingers. Steps are heard. OKEN motions to
    ADENOID and they both quickly hide under the drape by the
    mannequin. LIBIDSTONE draws the shower curtain around
    himself. GABRIEL enters stage-left, a flashlight in his hand.
    The flashlight catches DIANA'S foot.*)

GABRIEL: Sorry, Miss...(*As his flashlight wanders over DIANA,
    with a voice full of disbelief.*) This section is closed for the
    night.... **Who** are you?

DIANA (*realizing that GABRIEL does not recognize her because
    of the darkness and her disguise—nonchalantly*): And who are
    you?

GABRIEL: I work here...wait—**you're** supposed to answer **my**
    question. (*His last sentence does not carry much authority. He
    studies her silhouette intently.*)

DIANA (*gets up*): Well, since you're closing up, I'd better be
    going. I wouldn't like to get a nice guy like you into trouble.

GABRIEL (*taking a long look at her*): No trouble. Could you stay
    a moment longer?

DIANA: Why?

GABRIEL: You remind me of someone. A photograph of a young woman dressed just like you in my godmother's album. A funny thing to remember, isn't it, when I remember so little from home?

DIANA: Do I look that old?

GABRIEL: No! Young and beautiful—that's how she looked. But you're right, by now she would be at least a hundred years old. Say, you're not some ball of mist, I mean, a spook; my boss has a spray against them.

DIANA (*beginning to enjoy the mix-up*): Thanks for the warning. I may be your fairy godmother. If you look behind the four-poster you'll find an album with one photograph missing— I've stepped out from it.

GABRIEL (*automatically makes a step toward the place she indicated, stops, wheels around, smiles*): You almost fooled me! (*DIANA begins to laugh and he joins her. More seriously.*) Your voice—I can swear I've heard it somewhere. Tell me about yourself. (*Light switches to OKEN and ADENOID.*)

OKEN: Tell me everything: your measurements, your bowling score, your social security number. Your measurements...

ADENOID: Ah, it was a lovely, lovely world I used to live in. A very gala world, a real Mecca for a young woman. It smelled nice, too. I lived luxuriously in my self-fitting bra. My filmy chiffons were pure flattery. And I was so smart to look my prettiest in fluid-line silk—blue mist, peach prelude, pool aqua, crystal pink. Nine out of ten top designers said I looked divine in my caftan coats. Yes, mine was the shape of three years ago, of two years ago, of one year ago...but **not** of this year!

OKEN: That's a dirty shame! Why not?

ADENOID: Someone has torn off my caftan coat, pulled off my sheath skirt, wrenched off my stiffened flirtatious petticoat and exposed my tiny natural waist to the world. (*Militantly.*) That's why I'm here!

OKEN: The man who did it should be shot. But I sort of envy him...

ADENOID (*with some indignation*): Mr. Oken, do you want me to leave? (*Light switches to LIBIDSTONE.*)

LIBIDSTONE: To leave this darkness will be like being born again. Oh, the pressure of the fat man's hand—power and confidence—like mother and father sublimated into a single palm. This dark, dark womb around me! Listen, bookworms, wherever you are—one dark womb is worth more than forty thousand books! (*Light switches to DIANA and GABRIEL.*)

DIANA: One fairy godmother knows more than all the books in the world. And they were made to be confided in.

GABRIEL: I will confide in you because you remind me of her.

DIANA: Of whom?

GABRIEL: The girl I love.

DIANA: Who is she?

GABRIEL: She works here. Diana's her name.

DIANA (*her voice loses its bantering tone*): How do you know, you —love her?

GABRIEL: That's all I know. War scorched the milk off my lips. War's rush, mud, smoke was unreal; but the short stops, warm touches, fast lips—these were, these are, the only real things I've ever known. What else *is* there?

DIANA: Is this now—another short stopover?

GABRIEL: No, no—this is quite different! Like a fresh wound. (*Searches for words.*) Did you ever see how a tree is grafted?

DIANA: Yes, in Pennsylvania...

GABRIEL: Back home, in East Europe, I was like a very young, ungrafted tree. Some girls had leaned against me and had left a hint of their perfume, a touch of their fingers. But ever since I've seen Diana, I'm like a tree that has been grafted.

DIANA: I understand you...

GABRIEL: Will she? She never seemed to listen.

DIANA: She may have been too busy watching for a luxury liner.

GABRIEL: But the School has no windows to the harbor.

DIANA: This fairy tale may explain it to you. Once upon a time, back in Pennsylvania, a little girl saw a postcard of a luxury liner—a gold-trimmed cloud of a ship. A former neighbor, who had struck it rich, mailed it to her family to make them envious. The little girl couldn't pull her eyes away from the ship. Her father pressed the postcard with his miner's fingers and his thumb-print remained on the white hull, indelible. It was then that the little girl vowed to herself she'd leave the mining town and get on that ship. And she's been carrying the postcard with her ever since.

GABRIEL: And then?

DIANA: The ship sank like soggy gingerbread. She took out her postcard. (*DIANA takes out a postcard from her 1919 dress pocket.*) She tore off the luxury liner. (*She tears off most of the postcard leaving only a small piece of it.*) And she will keep the only real part of it—an old miner's fingerprint.

GABRIEL: It's a beautiful fairy tale. But what should *I* do?

DIANA (*takes a long look at him, glances away from him, returns her eyes to him. Her voice caresses now*): Tell her.

GABRIEL: When?

DIANA: Right now. (*She slowly takes off the wig. Astonished recognition in GABRIEL'S eyes. Light switches to OKEN and ADENOID.*)

ADENOID (*with affection*): Tell me, pretty please.

OKEN: You can't be interested in Atlantic City conventions— you who had your pool aquas and pink crystals.

ADENOID: But I just **love** to hear you talk about it. The smoke- filled rooms, the men sweating in corridors, the convention nights. How exotic, exciting! Especially the sweat!

OKEN: What's so big about sweat?

ADENOID: I never had any, like I never had cake. I lived inside a deodorant tube! And you, you've led such an exciting life. Sweat!

OKEN: Your interest thrills me—imagine, it makes even perspir- ation inspiring. Will you believe me that I aimed much higher, that I didn't aim to stop in a union lawyer's shoes.

ADENOID: I'm sure you did. Through cigarette smoke, through sweat you reached higher.

OKEN: I used to get cakes on special occasions, with little figur- ines on top, a wedding that was called off, you know—and I always dreamt of getting one with a State Governor or a Senator on top—Big politics, that's where my secret heart is.

ADENOID: You should make good at it.

OKEN: Funny, coming from you, it doesn't sound so impossible. I haven't felt that confident since I was a law student. I was reaching for a Napoleon—you might say—and somehow I ended up with a doughnut. I woke up to see that I was sitting in somebody's palm and **that** somebody—in somebody else's, and so on. (*He takes her hand and puts his fist on it.*) There's only one way: you must be right next to the top guy. Like here. Whoever is next to the big guy here, has a whale of a luck. (*As he gazes into the distance, she puts her hand on his fist in her palm. He suddenly becomes aware of her motion and clasps his other hand over hers. The light switches to LIBID- STONE.*)

LIBIDSTONE: A whale! Could I be sitting in the entrails of a whale? To stay within the whale and to submit—is that the answer? Darkness and peace. No more need to strive, to search, to wade through footnotes—only to be, to be in the warm inside. (*Yawns.*) An unknown feeling floods my heart— gratitude. To that big, fat man. (*Yawns.*) To raise my hand

against him now? (*Yawns very deeply.*) No...inside the whale
...every grateful... (*Light to DIANA and GABRIEL. They hold
hands.*)

DIANA: Where are you taking me now?

GABRIEL: To a birch grove of my childhood. Step softly—some
angels are dozing against the trees. In the sun-drenched distance, my father is mowing the hay—he's very young.

DIANA: How do I look?

GABRIEL: Pig-tails, upturned nose, a smudge on your cheek.

DIANA (*raises her hand to strike him in mock indignation. He
catches her hand in the air. She fits her palm against his*):
Next to your childhood I'll place mine. A cluster of linden trees
in Pennsylvania.

GABRIEL: Your age?

DIANA: Early spring.

GABRIEL: The season?

DIANA: Fall.

GABRIEL: Let me watch you grow up.

DIANA: It's seven falls later. I've kicked through high school as a
drum majorette, May Queen, member of honor societies. The
baton and the crown decide my future. For me—it will be
acting fame; for father and mother—a husband with five
bathrooms and gilded faucets. The soot of the mines keeps
haunting them. I go to New York, immense New York. For
three years I storm the theatres and get tired. And now I'm
here.

GABRIEL: Do you love me?

DIANA (*she puts her head on his shoulder*): My head has found
its place. That is the greatest miracle. (*The roof opens slowly.
Pale moonlight colors the conspirators.*)

GABRIEL: A miracle!

DIANA: But it's not supposed to open now—they use the artificial
sky for the night shift.

GABRIEL: Whatever it is, it's right on time. (*He takes her ring
finger.*) From this moonlight I'll make you a ring... (*Light to
OKEN and ADENOID.*)

ADENOID (*notices in the moonlight the glitter of the ring on
OKEN'S finger*): A ring!

OKEN (*unsuccessfully trying to hide his ring*): Damn moonlight...

ADENOID (*shocked*): You're married!

OKEN: I guess a guy can't kick truth around too long.

ADNOID: You lied!

OKEN: No! Every word came straight from the middle of my

heart. My wife, she never gave a hoot about my work, my ambitions, as you do. She's a Sing-Sing and Siberia rolled into one, with a bit of Jersey City thrown in.

ADENOID: How horrible!

OKEN: I had even forgotten to try to get out. But here, I've got a new feeling, a feeling that everything is possible.

ADENOID: You, too? Oh, Joseph!

OKEN: You called me Joseph!

ADENOID: Yes—Joseph, Joseph, Joseph! (*A waltz of violins floats in.*)

OKEN: I've been liberated! Like I had gone to the head of the Statue of Liberty and, suddenly, the whole world is at my feet, laughing!

ADENOID: I'll share your liberty. (*She rips the cake box open, grabs a piece of cake and starts gobbling it up.*)

OKEN: I've seen oodles of mouths covered with cake crumbs but none can beat yours.

ADENOID: Oh, Joseph. (*Takes another slice.*) Love is—sweet.

OKEN: School for Love, I've an announcement to make. I thank you for bringing this woman into my life! To be fair and square —I thank you, big, fat man in charge. Without you—no school! Without school—Siberia. (*Suddenly, the sweet violin waltz veers into a blaring Sousa March.*)

OKEN and ADENOID: The signal! (*They look at each other and both shake their heads.*)

OKEN: I'm with you! We won't kick someone who brought us together. (*First faint rumblings and crashes in the distance. ADENOID and OKEN hide under the drape. More rumblings and crashes punctuated by ANGEL'S hysterical laughter. Light on DIANA and GABRIEL, holding hands.*)

DIANA: That noise! What can it be?

GABRIEL: Some new sound effect.

DIANA: They've never used it before.

GABRIEL: All things are new—because we're in love. (*Lights dim. Noises multiply, become louder. Light on ANGEL in the background, standing on the steps.*)

ANGEL (*softly*): Friends. (*Getting no response, louder.*) Allies! (*Losing patience.*) It's on! Out, out, to work! (*Hearing no answer, ANGEL dashes downstage-left. He tears off the drape from the mannequin: OKEN and ADENOID are kissing each other, oblivious of him or anything else. ANGEL clutches his head with his hands in despair and runs forward. He collides with the four-poster and notices GABRIEL and DIANA in an embrace. ANGEL raises his arms in rising despair and dashes to the next section. He tears open the closed shower curtain— LIBIDSTONE is sound asleep. ANGEL emits a yell of accumulated rage and turns on the water.)*

LIBIDSTONE (*jumps out blinded, half-awake*): Water! The whale has swallowed water! (*ANGEL stares at him in surprise.*)

ANGEL: He's nuts—they've all gone nuts! But even if the whole world goes crazy—I'll do it alone!! (*ANGEL dashes out stage-right. Then pandemonium erupts. Several musical scores blare out trying to drown each other. Petals of flowers flutter down gently, interrupted by bursts of confetti. A violinist descends from the ceiling, serious and engrossed in his music. Doves glide by, cows moo and rumble across the stage, shadows of love students flit by in panic, bicycles—built-for-two collide and fall apart, little cupids ascend and descend together with signs proclaiming the slogans of the School for Love.*)

LIBIDSTONE (*dripping wet, runs to the front of the stage and falls on his knees*): Praised be the whale!

CURTAIN

ACT THREE

(Through the still open roof, pale dawn falls on a scene of destruction as a clock strikes five. The only sign of life is LIBIDSTONE, sitting on the edge of the bathtub and furiously writing in his notebook. The clock strikes six—more light. OKEN crawls out from under a heap of mannequins and reveals ADENOID, peacefully asleep. OKEN bends to wake her but then changes his mind, covers her and tucks her in. He peeks into the cake box only to find to his regret that it is empty. He stretches, yawns, does a couple of knee-bends. Meanwhile, LIBIDSTONE gets up, holds his notebook proudly before himself, gives it a spontaneous kiss, and presses it to his chest. After a yawn and a stretch, LIBIDSTONE sets out to walk stage-right, just as OKEN begins marching stage-left, still yawning and stretching. They bump into each other, and their first impulse is to run away but then they recognize each other as fellow students. They exchange views—in pantomime—and their gestures bespeak swift initial agreement. As the clock strikes

seven, they march off stage-right, their agreement cemented. More morning light filters through. Stirring is visible on the four-poster. A feminine hand removes pieces of colored plastic and torn slogans. DIANA sits up in bed and stares into the chaos, at first not understanding. She turns to her left and lifts a torn piece of a slogan [which says **Love Is . . .** *] and looks down on the face of GABRIEL who is still asleep. Her face breaks into a loving smile, but then she looks around once more and returns her gaze to him clouded with worry. As if feeling a chill, she clasps her arms around herself. He turns his face in sleep, and she notices a bruise on his temple. She bends down to him — all concern and tenderness now. As soon as GABRIEL, not quite awake yet, feels her touch, he pulls her down to him. She shakes him by the shoulder and, as he wakes up, he half-releases her from his embrace to look at her. She turns his chin toward the surroundings. He absorbs the shock, turns back to her and clasps her hands.)*

GABRIEL (*worried*): You all right?

DIANA: Yes. (*Touches his temple.*) Your bruise?

GABRIEL: Nothing.

DIANA: An earthquake — and we felt nothing.

GABRIEL: I wouldn't have felt the end of the world. Tell me you love me. (*Silence.*) Why don't you?

DIANA: Not now, Gabriel! Not here! I'm afraid!

GABRIEL: Of what? Daylight?

DIANA: All I need is to whisper the word and each wall will echo it back at me quoting the page in the instruction book.

GABRIEL: Don't we have words that are ours, ours alone? We can go back to them, start from the very beginning.

DIANA: Your name? Gabriel . . .

GABRIEL: Wait! It's not quite mine — I didn't choose it, it was given to me.

DIANA: Your turn to try.

GABRIEL: Dear.

DIANA: No! The school crawls with this word. Take a step and you'll squash one.

GABRIEL: We can still be quiet together. We can hold hands and read thoughts in each other's eyes.

DIANA (*takes his head in her hands; watches his eyes; smiles*): What a lovely green thought. Here comes one of pale silver. (*Slaps his hand.*) This one's too purple. But wait, what's that? (*Pause. Sadly.*) A quote from a School textbook . . .

GABRIEL: I'll tear it out.

DIANA: Why not tear the School out? (*Looks around again.*) The

School—maybe it's destroyed. We could just walk out!

LEVIATHAN (*backstage gaily*): Who has poured love into the World? Leo, Leo, Leviathan!

GABRIEL: The School's alive! He wouldn't be singing!

DIANA (*reproachfully*): You seem to be glad.

GABRIEL: Can't you understand? That's a lifetime job for me.

DIANA: But we must go away from here.

GABRIEL: I've got no other trade.

DIANA: To stay here with Leviathan forever?

GABRIEL: The School—it may change. There was a moment yesterday; you should have seen Leviathan's eyes; his voice was like a father's.

DIANA: When he embraced me yesterday—his hairy hands, his folds of flesh—I touched the bottom of his soul. Gabriel, it is a stockyard, and it can change only into more greed, more stench.

GABRIEL: He embraced you?

DIANA: But worst of all, that moment I saw my own soul reflected in his—and a part of my soul was drawn to him, as yours is. We must leave before it's too late.

GABRIEL: You let him embrace you?

DIANA: We have no time for explanations now! He's coming!

GABRIEL: Explain! Did you let others, too?

DIANA: You dare to question me and you submit to him and let him wipe his greasy thoughts on you.

GABRIEL: Damn the daylight!

DIANA: If you can't face the daylight, you can have him! (*DIANA runs out.*)

GABRIEL: Diana!

LEVIATHAN (*backstage—very close*): Angel! (*LEVIATHAN enters stage-left in surprisingly good spirits. GABRIEL wheels around to face him, hostile.*) Ah, boy! What a daylight! Remember the air raids!

GABRIEL: Mr. Leviathan, did you embrace a woman yesterday?

LEVIATHAN: One-track mind...

GABRIEL: I'm very serious.

LEVIATHAN (*pulls GABRIEL to himself, confidentially*): I did and I did not. Remember, when I went to rendez-vous the lady of my dreams? She comes, I squeeze her, and she screams and splits in two and disappears. (*GABRIEL'S face lights up and he breaks into laughter.*) We'll see how you'll laugh when you see a whole woman split.

GABRIEL (*still laughing*): So that's how it was.

LEVIATHAN: The Angel played some magic trick on me. But he still likes me. (*Shows around.*) Look at this mess. The eggs are broken—the Angel's planning some extra special omelette. There'll be great changes, boy. I have a feeling way down in my guts—this may be my giant step.

GABRIEL (*happily*): Changes! There will be changes! And you thought it was the woman in the picture!

LEVIATHAN: Did you get knocked over by a beam? Stop babbling and help me find the Angel.

GABRIEL: Changes...Diana! (*GABRIEL runs out.*)

LEVIATHAN (*laughing affectionately*): One-track mind... (*Turns around.*) Come on, Angel. You playing hide-and-seek? (*Faint whining from extreme stage-right*) Is that you? (*Whining affirmative. LEVIATHAN starts unearthing a pile of cross-beams, wigs, false moons. Midway, he finds a violin and plucks at its strings. Whining desperate.*) O.K. O.K. (*He removes the last piece of trash and—lo!—there is the ANGEL. A female wig is perched crooked on his head. LEVIATHAN pulls him out.*) That is you! (*ANGEL finally gets on his feet and dusts himself violently. Helpful, LEVIATHAN pats him forcefully. ANGEL pushes away his hand. LEVIATHAN takes another look at the wig, of which ANGEL is still unaware, and doubles over from laughter. ANGEL realizes the reason for LEVIATHAN'S mirth, tears the wig off and throws it away.*) How did you get there, and you an Angel?

ANGEL: A damn cow knocked me off last night.

LEVIATHAN: A cow? A measly rented city cow that gives milk powder knocking off an angel?

ANGEL: She couldn't've been a simple cow, stupid! She must've come from India with a special mission to knock me off. (*Furiously.*) If not the cow, I might have completed...(*Stops, realizing that he is giving himself away.*)

LEVIATHAN: Completed what?

ANGEL: Completed—saving your blasted palace. But someone, someone messed things up and I just couldn't do it alone.

LEVIATHAN: Oh, that's O.K. That's O.K. fine.

ANGEL: Leviathan, how come you're so gay, so devil-may-care? After all...(*Shows around with his hand.*) Just look at this mess...

LEVIATHAN: Come on, Angel. Quit joking. One of your tricks, eh?

ANGEL: What?

LEVIATHAN: We two know, don't we? The giant step! (*ANGEL*

raises his arms in despair. Knocking is heard stage-left.) Come in. (*The door opens and ANGEL'S raised hands clench themselves into fists. LIBIDSTONE and OKEN enter. Both, in their own different ways, are filled with premonitions of great events to come and are trembling with eagerness to impart their important tidings.*)

LIBIDSTONE: Sir...

OKEN: Mr. Director...

LEVIATHAN (*to ANGEL*): Who are they? (*ANGEL tries to speak. He opens his mouth a couple of times but the rage at his former allies paralyzes him and no sound comes out.*)

LIBIDSTONE: Your students, Sir; we happened to be here last night.

OKEN: Under the rubble.

LIBIDSTONE: As the night ended, we had become so absorbed with your exciting enterprise that we felt completely identified with it.

OKEN: He means, we want to join you.

LEVIATHAN: Ah! (*Nudges the ANGEL jovially. To LIBIDSTONE.*) Go on.

LIBIDSTONE: I spent the entire night trying to sketch, at least in broad outline, some of the ramifications of your project. Would you care to look at my notes? (*Pulls out his notebook and hands it to LEVIATHAN.*)

LEVIATHAN (*takes the notebook, flips the pages over once*): Good! Nothing like work for a young man! (*He gives the notebook to ANGEL who takes it as if it were a frog. Very loudly.*) Hey, Gabriel, d'you hear that? Work brings joy! (*Moment of silence as LEVIATHAN waits for GABRIEL'S answer.*) He acts like some cow knocked him out. (*LIBIDSTONE sneezes.*) If you caught that cold here, you get free aspirins.

LIBIDSTONE: Sir, this is the first meaningful cold of my life. (*ANGEL flips the notebook, which seems to soil his hands, to OKEN, who, not to be upstaged by LIBIDSTONE, also sneezes.*)

LEVIATHAN: And you—you worked all night, too, all uncovered?

OKEN (*passes the notebook to LIBIDSTONE*): Um, in a manner of speaking, I was sort of mulling over my lesson of yesterday. I caught a cold, too! But this morning I got out and spread the good word for a few minutes. Have you been out yet? Have you seen the crowds?

LEVIATHAN: Crowds? Is that the noise outside, like a sea swell?

LIBIDSTONE: A sea that is ready to welcome a whale—the

royal whale. (*He hands the notebook back to LEVIATHAN.*)

LEVIATHAN (*accepting the notebook and thrusting it into his pocket*): It sounds crazy but I get you.

OKEN (*competing for attention*): They've come here from all over to say how much they like you. A lot of them are just dying to help out. I took the liberty of suggesting to some of your men to go outside with sacks—to accept their donations.

LEVIATHAN (*to OKEN and LIBIDSTONE*): Good work! Smart boys! (*To ANGEL.*) You supernatural rascal, confess you have a finger in that holy pie.

ANGEL (*killing OKEN and LIBIDSTONE with his eyes*): And how I do! (*His arms rise to strangle OKEN and LIBIDSTONE but then drop helplessly—he cannot give himself away.*) When that sneaky traitor started pushing all those buttons last night, I was on the way to stop him. But then I held my hand back. I had a sudden vision that he was a godsend—he thought he was destroying us and really he was a tool of good—a fool of a tool.

LEVIATHAN: I knew it. It's your cleverest yet, my dear Angel! A crash, an explosion. To cover me with a debris of sympathy, of admiration. To catapult me to the greatest things!

OKEN: Mr. Director, excuse me for saying it, but how can you do it when a screw is loose?

LEVIATHAN (*angrily*): Now what d'you mean by that?

OKEN: Oh no, not what you think I meant! I mean the traitor. Let's face it. Someone tried to destroy the works here last night. A rotten apple is at the bottom of your basket, Mr. Director!

LEVIATHAN: Go on. What d'you suggest I do about that rotten screw?

OKEN: With your permission, I suggest we need something like secret police.

LIBIDSTONE: Sir, let us not be sidetracked by petty details. Our main task is calling—the healing of society!

ANGEL (*nods to OKEN*): He's got something there. Perhaps I...

LEVIATHAN: Now wait here, Angel. Secret police and heaven just don't seem to mix.

ANGEL: And who d'you think wiretaps all the conversations in the world? (*To OKEN.*) You take that over, eh?

OKEN: I'd sure appreciate it, Mr. Angel. (*Softly.*) Imagine— Herbert Oken, chief of Secret Police. (*He gives everybody a piercing glance.*)

LIBIDSTONE (*to LEVIATHAN*): Sir, when you will come to

things that matter—mind, spirit—you will keep me in mind.

LEVIATHAN: Spirit? It's all yours. (*To ANGEL.*) I like people who work for nothing.

ANGEL (*to OKEN*): Chief, I've got a clue for you. I caught an intruder here yesterday, disguised with a plastic horse's head. (*OKEN writes it down.*)

LEVIATHAN (*to OKEN*): Give me that notebook. (*OKEN obliges. LEVIATHAN tears out a page and sticks it into his pocket.*) I know as sure as I'm standing here that it wasn't him who done it. So I'm saving you work.

OKEN (*with a military bow*): Much obliged.

LEVIATHAN: It must be someone else. (*His look wanders around.*)

ANGEL (*uneasy*): Drop that, Leviathan. The crowds are waiting!

LIBIDSTONE: He's right, Sir. The mob is now in the pre-orgasmic stage of affection for you.

OKEN: Let's put it more simply.

LIBIDSTONE: Let's not!

LEVIATHAN: Let it be the crowds! Butler! (*BUTLER enters.*) Get the junk out of the way, clear the road to the balcony! We need space! (*BUTLER begins to clear away the rubble and pushes the bed out. All present give him a hand. The backstage curtain opens revealing a large glass door through which a balcony is visible. The noise of the CROWD outside surges louder. Brass bands oompah in the distance. LEVIATHAN stares at the door and then turns to his followers with a triumphant expression. They nod and point to the door. LEVIATHAN opens the glass door and steps onto the balcony. The roar of the CROWD engulfs him. He begins to make a deep bow, but halfway, changes his mind, straightens himself out and gives a proud, curt Caesarean nod instead to which the CROWD reacts with a hush of awe and admiration. He points his finger up and the roar rises; he points the finger down and the roar decreases. LEVIATHAN enjoys this and indulges in a few variations of sound in various speeds. Then he lifts both arms, conductor-like, and the voices break out into the "**Love Anthem**".*)

CROWD (*backstage*): Who has poured love into the world?
                Leo, Leo Leviathan!
                Life was dry but now we're living high—
                Leo, Leo, Leo's our man!

(*After the first words of the anthem, the door stage-right bursts open and BUTLER is seen trying to hold back several chubby, middle-aged, flower-hatted WOMEN over whose*

ample bosoms pink sashes taper with "LEVIATHAN" em-
broidered on them in gold.)

WOMEN (*piercing the anthem*): Leviathan, we want Leviathan!
To touch him! I've come from North Dakota! Louisiana!
Alaska! (*DIANA appears down-stage-left, out of breath and
bewildered. Almost simultaneously, GABRIEL enters down-
stage-right, still searching for her. At the moment they perceive each other, the noise of the CROWD and of the WOMEN
dies away. All, except DIANA and GABRIEL, continue their
motions in silence.)*

GABRIEL & DIANA (*excitedly, almost simultaneously*): Diana!
Gabriel! Forgive me for accusing you....If you'll forgive me
for trying to run away. (*A brief pause.*)

GABRIEL: I searched for you everywhere.

DIANA: I tried to get out. Some doors were locked; when I opened
others, a wall of people stood outside shouting for Leviathan.
As I slammed the door against their shouts, my mind turned
coal-black for a moment. My father had been trapped in a coal-
mine once. I felt I was in that mine—looking through his eyes.
Gabriel, I'll need your strength to leave here!

GABRIEL: We may not have to leave. Leviathan mistook you for
someone else when he embraced you.

DIANA: I've seen the bottom of his soul.

GABRIEL: You said, a part of your soul was drawn to him; well,
a part of his soul is drawn to us and it's winning. I have tremendous news for you! Big changes are on the way! He told me
himself—a giant step! The angel with his dreary ways is losing
out, I'm sure!

DIANA: I've still seen the bottom of his soul!

GABRIEL (*takes her hand*): Please, once more—come with me
and hear what the changes are. (*The CROWD noises resume
gradually.*)

DIANA (*folllowing him reluctantly*): It cannot, it cannot change...

GABRIEL: Only once more... (*As they turn downstage, the noises
resume fully. BUTLER finally manages to close and lock the
door, panting and wiping his sweat off, the anthem expires.
The CROWD roars again. LEVIATHAN turns back to his followers proudly beaming and notices the BUTLER who straightens his disheveled livery and bows.*)

LEVIATHAN: Brought my herring, eh? We'll need more!
Herrings for Gabriel there! Herrings for everybody! On the
house!

BUTLER: It is not the herring, Sir—I'll be leaving for it present-

ly—it's a delegation of leaders to see you. These wild women
have delayed me...

LEVIATHAN: Wild women? How can you afford wild women on
your salary? One wild woman per servant per month—that's
my policy.

BUTLER: Sir, I meant the female trespassers! A delegation of
leaders is now waiting to see you. Shall I announce them?

LEVIATHAN: Leaders of what?

BUTLER: Organizations, Institutions—everything.

LEVIATHAN: "Leaders." I don't like that word in plural. Make
a note. The plural of the word "leader" to be abolished. (*OKEN
makes the note. To BUTLER.*) Let them in—I'm in a generous
mood today.

OKEN: Wait, Mr. Director! (*Stops BUTLER with a sign of his
hand. To LEVIATHAN.*) I'm sorry, but now you're smack in
the middle of a real electoral campaign. Now, this needs planning; nothing can be left to chance.

LEVIATHAN: Are you saying that I could make a mistake?

OKEN: God forbid! But these visitors might.

LIBIDSTONE: Their vision may not stretch far enough to reach
you. What they need is a bridge. Sir, I offer myself. I'll serve
as a living bridge.

OKEN: What you need is honest-to-goodness experience, not
fancy talk. And I've got it.

LEVIATHAN (*lifts his arms in a pacifier's gesture*): You'll take
turns, like two good boys. (*A large canvas descends stage-
left representing the front page of a newspaper. It is topped by
a large headline:* **Leaders Meet Leviathan.** *Under the headline
is a large photograph of a representative group of American
public figures, including an Indian in full regalia.*) Come-in-
come-in-feel-at-home-nice-meeting-you-come-in-hi-there...

MAN-IN-A-MAYOR'S-TOP-HAT: Let me say on behalf of all the
delegates how glad we all are that you and your worthy institution have weathered this unfortunate storm...

LEVIATHAN: I'm glad you're glad.

OKEN (*upstaging LIBIDSTONE*): Mr. Leviathan appreciates it.

MAYOR: I must confess that I was a bit disturbed about your
school at first. Didn't you teach women that if they wanted to
win a man's heart, they should dig out his footprints...

LEVIATHAN: Yes, and put them in a pot and plant marigolds in
it...

MAYOR: Well, women in our city started tearing up sidewalks
for footprints—no soil in the city, you know. But then, it

dawned on me that our sidewalks were quite in disrepair. We put in new ones; and now we're famous all over the world for our sidewalks.

OKEN: Terrific civic sense Mr. Leviathan has.

LIBIDSTONE: Sense for the organic—buried beneath the asphalt and cement of our civilization.

MAN-WITH-A-LABOR-REPRESENTATIVE'S-COUNTENANCE: Labor wants to know...

OKEN: Look for yourself. Unemployment is down, down, down. Women have stopped clogging the labor market and have returned to clogged sinks.

BALD MAN: The question is discussed in academic circles: what makes Mr. Leviathan run? What is his motivation? What force does he represent?

LEVIATHAN: A lot of force, let me tell you.

LIBIDSTONE (*quickly taking over*): Ultimately, Mr. Leviathan represents the unconscious at its most creative; the unconscious that has set out to heal the disruption of society by creating values of order and meaningfulness. (*Awed hush runs through the listeners.*)

MAN-IN-A-CLERGYMAN'S-OUTFIT: And how is Mr. Leviathan disposed toward religion?

OKEN: Have you checked up on virginity lately? It's spreading like wildfire. Who reduced divorce rates? Who brought stability back into marriage?

FAT MAN: We Americans of conservative beliefs...

LIBIDSTONE: Back to the older, more secure patterns, back to the fountainhead of tradition—these are his guiding thoughts.

THIN-MAN-WITH-GLASSES: Allegations have been made about Mr. Leviathan's reactionary leanings. We, liberal radicals and moderately radical liberals...

OKEN: Just look around—what does everything spell here? C-H-A-N-G-E—change! That's what he believes in. That's what he brought to America!

A-ROSY-CHEEKED-LADY-WITH-A-FLOWER-HAT: The gentlemen here have all asked very pertinent questions, I'm sure, but I guess it takes a lady with her feminine sensitivity to ask the central question which must be asked and asked again if the United States are to survive and to flourish. Is Mister—I have difficulty in pronouncing his name—is he American born? We would be very relieved to hear that he at least comes from Anglo-Saxon stock. Is there any truth to the rumors that he has come from Eastern Europe? My organization has always regarded with utmost concern such a concentration of power in the hands of the un-American-born...

LEVIATHAN (*menacingly*): Now, listen, you...

OKEN (*hurriedly taking over, he stalls with the real answer while he is putting a record on the phonograph*): An excellent question! We're glad you asked it. American-born you said? (*The record begins playing "Going Home."*) Yes, he **was** born. And d'you know when he first opened his eyes? You'll never guess. On April 21, 1898! What bell does that ring, Americans—compatriots—patriots? The Liberty Bell, of course! Hardly had he opened his eyes when he had to blink from the first shot of the Spanish-American War. How many of us, ladies and gentlemen—how **many**—can claim **that**? And what was the first thing he saw when he first opened his eyes? The face of the midwife, a woman, whose brother spent almost all his life in Pi—Pi—Pittsburgh. (*He sneezes. The record stops.*)

LIBIDSTONE (*takes advantage of the sneeze pause and takes over*): It's obvious that in his deepest subconscious he was genuinely American.

LEVIATHAN (*whispers to LIBIDSTONE*): The newspapers with pictures from America, where I wrapped my herrings.

LIBIDSTONE: Oh, yes! And each day he read American newspapers, learned them by heart! He was a little island of America abroad, waiting to rejoin the mainland, waiting for his destiny to whisper to him: Go West, ever-young Leviathan. And he came—ladies and gentlemen—he came when the womb of America was crying out for him. He came when we were about to drown in stratification, departmentalization, auto-auto-mation... (*He sneezes.*)

OKEN (*taking advantage of LIBIDSTONE'S sneeze*): When we're getting lazy and flabby...

LIBIDSTONE (*cuts in*): When we're beginning to lose the qualities of our forefathers who built up this country, here he emerges before us: with American history engraved in his infant's eyes, with American headlines emblazoned on his boyish looks, with America's destiny grafted onto the core of his heart. The bearer of the American pluck and stout courage, the only remaining true pioneer left...

OKEN (*jumps into the breach when LIBIDSTONE takes a breath*): All-American Leviathan! (*Ovation drowns out their words as the page lights up and starts blinking like a pinball machine after a full hit.*)

LEVIATHAN (*raises his hand; ovation subsides*): So that's that for who's American!

INDIAN: And who here can say he's really American? How?

LEVIATHAN: You said it, brother!

THIN-MAN-WITH-GLASSES: He called the Indian "brother"! This removes my last doubt! Hurrah for Leviathan! (*Ovation again as the newspaper page vanishes upstairs. Another large front-page comes down, its headline screaming:* **Meeting Huge Success. Presidential Timber Mentioned.** *LEVIATHAN and his followers read the headline. Brief silence, as all realize the magnitude of the event.*)

OKEN (*his voice trembling*): Mr. Director, you already had the masses in your pocket—now you've put the bosses into the other one. If you go on the balcony now and face this crowd and lift your little finger, by God, they'll fall on their knees—they'll elect you President!

LEVIATHAN: President? No...not President. President's too mushy—like cereal, children's stuff.

OKEN: King?

LEVIATHAN: King? There must be a stronger word.

LIBIDSTONE: High Priest, Sir!

LEVIATHAN: I plan to do some unpriestly things.

ANGEL: What about "tsar"?

LEVIATHAN: Shaggy beard, bullet holes? No thanks.

OKEN: **Emperor?**

LEVIATHAN: **Em-Pe-Ror?** That's it! Yes! I'll be **emperor!**

LIBIDSTONE: Sir, you just made yourself an Emperor. You took the crown and put it on your head. Like Napoleon.

LEVIATHAN: Did I? I did, uh?

LIBIDSTONE (*softly*): But you won't stop here, you'll go beyond it—one day you'll be **High** Priest. (*Carried away by his vision, LIBIDSTONE kneels on one knee. OKEN follows him—not to lose ground in the race. GABRIEL, DIANA and ANGEL remain standing. LEVIATHAN'S eyes are staring at glorious distances.*)

OKEN: Napoleon, he had the—watchamacallit—the old guard, the guys with beaver hats. I saw them in the movie; they stuck with him from the beginning all the way down the wire. Mr. Director, I mean Emperor, will you let me...us...be that guard for you?

LEVIATHAN: Order your beaver hats right now. (*LIBIDSTONE and OKEN get up.*) We gonna move! We're gonna play no more; no more dilly-dally; no more School for Love!

GABRIEL (*in disbelief*): No more School for Love?

LEVIATHAN: Right you are!

GABRIEL: But the change, you said you'd change it!

LEVIATHAN: Change all the way!

GABRIEL: But love...

LEVIATHAN: Listen like mad now, boy: **There ain't no love!**
Put that in your pipe if you want to stay ahead! Itch, hunger,
appetite, heat—yes, heat! But no love!

GABRIEL: No love?

LEVIATHAN: Stop playing echo to me! We've got no time for we
must march, march all across America while I make clear like
hell to those Americans what is America. Yes, sirree, this
country begs and screams for order and I'm got to jam order
down its throat. Uniforms first—uniforms for all: too much
confusing civilian clothes here.

GABRIEL: Leviathan, you can't!

ANGEL: Dark for kindergarten, inky for high school, raven for
university and jet-black with a thin white stripe for the clergy.

LEVIATHAN: Gold, blue and purple plumes for the police—the
peacocks of my power. Grey pullovers for common people,
with names and numbers on their jackets...

OKEN: Like baseball players?

LEVIATHAN: Don't use that word! Baseball will be forbidden
by law. We shall erase these crazy lines and put in soccer
markings, straight and sensible. Why? I played soccer as a
boy, that's why!

ANGEL: Boys—they'll click their heels when facing elders,
they'll stay away from dirty books...

LIBIDSTONE: What's dirty books?

ANGEL: I will decide! We'll gather all the dirty books, pour
gasoline on them and burn them.

LEVIATHAN: Gasoline tanks all over the United States will be in
my shape—practical statues to remind the people of the order
and happiness I've brought them.

GABRIEL (*hopelessly and sorrowfully*): Leviathan...

LEVIATHAN: And what parades we'll have; officers only from
major up, all on horses, lances in the sun, and I sky-high up in
the podium, and little girls in folk costumes will hand me flowers—buttercups—and millions of children will cheer me in the
stands; and when I say children, I mean Americans, 'cause
they are children, brats all of them, with malted milk on their
lips from cradle to grave!

ANGEL: Grave I will be and very strict. The rod they need; the
rod I will not spare. I'll be the rod through which the lightning

will strike them.

LEVIATHAN: Strike, yes, strike, because the iron's hot, the iron is America, the hammer—me... (*To GABRIEL, hoarsely.*) A glass of water, fast! (*GABRIEL does not move. OKEN quickly pours a glass of water and gives it to LEVIATHAN. LEVIATHAN gulps the water greedily.*)

DIANA: Gabriel...

GABRIEL: Yes. Yes! Wait for me. (*With determined steps, GABRIEL walks off stage-right. LEVIATHAN throws the glass away.*)

LEVIATHAN: And when I'm through with America, the world comes next!

ANGEL: Sick world, rotten globe...

LEVIATHAN: It must obey one man...

ANGEL: Obey me!

LEVIATHAN: You hear, world? Obey me! You hear, all herrings in the world? Big fish eat little fish but the whale eats a whole school, a university of fish—five thousand herrings for a meal. I, I who used to wrap herrings, I will have my picture in all the newspapers in the world, and'll swallow all the herrings in the world. All! (*He stops to draw a breath.*)

LIBIDSTONE: Don't leave us, please!

LEVIATHAN: All!... (*He sputters the last word of his monologue and inhales. To LIBIDSTONE.*) Why d'you say that?

LIBIDSTONE: As you spoke, you kept rising like a huge balloon, resplendent, magnificent, higher and higher—please, don't leave us when such horizons are opening!

LEVIATHAN: If I rise, you rise with me. Leviathan crushes treason but rewards loyalty. You'll be around me always, my satellites, rich, fat and tanned in my sunshine. (*GABRIEL enters stage-right. He is wearing the same clothes as during his first appearance: the jacket, the army slacks, the heavy boots.*) Like children you will be around me! (*Points to them, one by one.*) You, and you, and you... (*His finger stops at GABRIEL.*) You... what d'you think you are doing. Masquerade?

GABRIEL: I'm leaving.

LEVIATHAN: Leaving? Ha! Ha, ha! Leaving! Always trying to be funny! First time he opened my door, he was telling jokes.

GABRIEL: I mean it, Leviathan!

LEVIATHAN: That's enough, now!

DIANA: He means it, Mr. Leviathan! (*She scatters a batch of pamphlets high in the air.*) He means it!

LEVIATHAN: No!

GABRIEL: I want to leave in peace. I thank you for all the good you've done me. Let's part friends.

LEVIATHAN (*now convinced of GABRIEL'S seriousness*): Friends, he says. Like one of those juvenile criminals—whom I'm going to liquidate—he kicks his father's teeth and says: **Friends!**

OKEN (*to LEVIATHAN*): You want me to take care of him?

LEVIATHAN (*waves OKEN off*): This case is my baby! (*To GABRIEL.*) You hear—a juvenile who spits into his mother's face!

GABRIEL: I'm grateful to you, Leviathan, I said it, but you're not my father and mother!

LEVIATHAN: Oh, no? Who made you? When you opened my door, you were nothing! I made you! And what plans I had for you!

GABRIEL: You're killing the School for Love! It was my idea, my very own. I said it first: "Let us build a school for love!"

LEVIATHAN: We're out to change the world and he's babbling about love! The School—that was a local station on the Brooklyn El. We're shooting for the stars now. We're going to bring order into the world and teach people happiness!

GABRIEL: Leviathan, you're playing God!

LEVIATHAN: God alone can tell me to stop playing God, and I'm pretty sure He won't; He'd better not!

GABRIEL: But if the School is gone, if love's no more, what, in heaven, can you give the people?

LEVIATHAN: You don't need to love people to show them the right way!

GABRIEL: You're a tyrant then, that's what you are!

OKEN: Emperor, I can't let this go unanswered! (*To GABRIEL.*) You've got a lot to learn, you fresh young man. Tyrant means slavery. Now let me tell you, I felt free for the first time in my life when I faced this great man. (*Points to LEVIATHAN.*) I should know, I've dealt with law. Our life is tied to the ground like a Gulliver with hundreds of laws, big and little. I joined him, and I can brush them all away like a bunch of cobwebs!

LEVIATHAN (*to GABRIEL*): You hear that?

LIBIDSTONE (*to GABRIEL*): To make it short, hothead— Leviathan liberates. And that applies not only to the average citizen (*Points to OKEN.*) but to individuals like me as well. When we, Americans, joined him, we embraced America! (*The door stage-left bursts open and MRS. OKEN, her hair in curlers, storms inside. BUTLER tries to drag her back but she knocks him down with one clean swoop.)*

MRS. OKEN *(to JOSEPH OKEN)*: Joseph! What's the meaning of this? Here I'm watching TV with my hair dryer on and there you are with your guilty face behind some strange balcony.

LEVIATHAN: Throw her out!

MRS. OKEN *(disregarding him. To OKEN)*: Love school, huh? When I called you at work, they said you were out on business. *(OKEN smacks her cheek loudly. She stands flabbergasted. Then he pulls her to the next chair, throws her over his knee and gives her a brief but thorough spanking. MRS. OKEN gets up, looks at him, breaks into a huge smile, suddenly embraces him. Then she steps to LEVIATHAN, kneels and kisses his hand.)*

LEVIATHAN: What can I do for you, my friend?

MRS. OKEN: You've done it already. You're in charge here, aren't you? I saw you on TV.

LEVIATHAN: Yes, I'm in charge. *(Triumphantly, with a side glance to GABRIEL.)* And what have I done for you, my dear?

MRS. OKEN *(points to JOSEPH OKEN)*: You made a man out of him! I'm basically very feminine, you know, but his lack of spine forced me out into the world. I acquired a career, read books—oh, what a waste—because all the time I was just longing for a clear picture of what my duties are as a woman— for security. And now, all of a sudden, he is a man and I can be a woman. Now I'll be able to stay home and clean his shoes and iron his socks and be humble and feminine. And all this thanks to you!

LEVIATHAN: Get up!

MRS. OKEN *(jumps to her feet)*: Yes, Sir! You are a very manly man, just as I imagined you.

LEVIATHAN: Go to your lord and master...I have some unfinished business here!

MRS. OKEN: I go...in happiness. *(She walks to her husband swaying happily.)*

LEVIATHAN *(to GABRIEL, mimicking him)*: "What-can-you-give-the-people?" I give them what they need and make them happy. What else is there?

GABRIEL: The rings of moonlight, the graft marks in the trees...

LEVIATHAN *(to others)*: His mind is off the track.

GABRIEL: Don't speak of tracks to me, Leviathan. **You** are a freight train wild on a wrong track, crushing all in your way!

LEVIATHAN *(to GABRIEL)*: Last chance, and I mean *last!*

GABRIEL: If I know anything, it's that someone must say "no" to all you do. NO. (*BUTLER enters holding a herring wrapped in a newspaper. GABRIEL and LEVIATHAN look at it and then at each other. There is a flash of reminiscence in their eyes, a touch of sadness. LEVIATHAN takes the herring from BUTLER and, in a hopeful and not ungentle gesture, offers it to GABRIEL. But GABRIEL answers with a determined head-shake. Then, with a sudden motion, LEVIATHAN throws the herring out of the balcony window. A shout of surprise and ex-hilaration wells up from the crowd.*)

RADIO ANNOUNCER (*backstage. During his rapid and excited account of the goings-on outside, LEVIATHAN and GABRIEL stand facing each other motionlessly, but anger keeps rising in LEVIATHAN'S face and puffing up his body. His huge frame suggests more and more a whale poised for a jump on a lone harpoonist*): There it goes! A small object! It's landing. Look at them run toward it. A fight, a fight! Everybody wants to have a Leviathan souvenir. And here's the winner. Here's the lucky guy. He holds the object high above his head! What? A herring! How original! The luckiest man in the country today is at the microphones! Will you say a few words to our listeners? He's all choked up—he cannot speak! Isn't that touching? What? He's whispering to us—he won't wash his hands till the end of the year! What about that folks? Special bulletin! He's just been offered a holiday for two in Miami! He's getting married right now. After two weeks at the School for Love, of course!

LEVIATHAN (*through his teeth*): Why did you betray me?

GABRIEL: To do what's right.

LEVIATHAN: A phony word! You must be loyal to people who do you good. That's right and just and nothing else!

GABRIEL: There's a world of things you don't know, Leviathan.

LEVIATHAN: Traitor! (*He looks around for words to wound, breathing heavily.*) It's you! It's you who tried to blow this place to bits last night!

OKEN: Yea! Every time he'd leave the instruction booth, we'd hear a voice through some mike telling us how the place must be destroyed!

LEVIATHAN: Filthy, puny, stinking traitor!

GABRIEL: I'm not! You must believe me, Leviathan!

ANGEL (*seizing upon the opportunity to establish a complete alibi for himself*): Yes, he did it! Now I recognize his face, his shape! He tried to explode the school and you and I just managed to save everything by a hair!

LEVIATHAN (*to GABRIEL, mockingly*): "To do what's right."
Deny **that**, you piece of ingrate filth! Dare to say "no" to an
Angel!

GABRIEL: The Angel lies!

LEVIATHAN: I'll pull your tongue out!

GABRIEL: The Angel lies...but Angels never lie! Something is
foul here, something stinks up to heaven! I know! He's not an
Angel! He never acted like an Angel! He's done this whole
mess himself!

LEVIATHAN: He? (*Laughs briefly and ferociously.*) You'll get a
lightning on your head now!

GABRIEL: Get rid of the Angel, Leviathan! Then I will stay!

ANGEL: I **am** very generous but if he goes on like that, I can't
guarantee that I won't let some lightning loose!

GABRIEL: Then...let it loose! Let all hell loose! You've made
me mad, Leviathan, and I'm not going to leave here in peace.
I'm going to prove the Angel's done it!

LEVIATHAN: Get out of here!

GABRIEL: Afraid of my proof?

LEVIATHAN: Prove it or you'll fly down after the herring!

GABRIEL: O.K., I will! Where's **your** proof, Angel? Where's your
angelic passport?

LEVIATHAN: The miracle's his proof!

GABRIEL (*to ANGEL*): From what hell did you come to make
the miracle?

LEVIATHAN: Prove it or...

GABRIEL: Germany? Somewhere in Germany must be a trap-
door through which you came from hell.

ANGEL: The joker has confused heaven with hell.

LIBIDSTONE: Common delusion.

GABRIEL: Yes, trap-door! (*To LEVIATHAN.*) What's the name
of that town in Germany where you met the Angel?

LEVIATHAN: Niederzwehren-Oberzwehren, punk! Want to telephone for a ticket on a luxury liner to Germany?

GABRIEL: Not necessary. (*Points at the telephone.*) Will you pay
for a call across the ocean?

LEVIATHAN: To the moon, if you wish! And then I'll send your
bits and pieces after it! (*OKEN, LIBIDSTONE, ANGEL laugh
dutifully.*)

GABRIEL (*lifts the telephone receiver, dials*): Operator, please.
Europe, Germany, the Mayor of Niederzwehren-Oberzwehren.

ANGEL (*a bit concerned, to LEVIATHAN*): Why waste time with
him? Kick him out!

OKEN: My kicking foot is at your disposal, Emperor. Twelve field goals for Brooklyn College, 1939!

LEVIATHAN: I wanta see him strangle himself with a telephone wire—transatlantic! (*To GABRIEL.*) The proof!

GABRIEL (*into the receiver*): Mr. Mayor? This is America.... Yes, I understand your English...America...New York... School for Love. (*A distant brass band blares out from the receiver, followed by a chorus intoning the School for Love anthem in German.*)

CHORUS (*backstage, across the ocean*):
>	Wer hat Liebe wiedereingegossen?
>	Leo, Leo, Leo Leviathan!

GABRIEL (*the blast of sound forces him to hold the receiver away from his ear. Then he shouts back into the receiver*): Schoen! Nice band! Nice town! Mr. Mayor, I have an important question. (*The noise recedes.*) Listen carefully—have you got a statue of an Angel in your town? What is the Angel's name? Has anybody seen the Angel alive?...Very important! ....What?...Only one?...Yes....Yes... (*As he is listening, his eyes fasten on the Angel.*) Beard...Wart....Rubber?...Oh, *robber.* Thank you, Mr. Mayor. You've done a great service. Yes—to the School for Love...(*He replaces the receiver. Silence. All stare at him.*) One! One single statue in Niederzwehren-Oberzwehren! And it's not an Angel. It's a statue of a robber-baron; the Mayor said it's like a Middle Age gangster. The gangster-statue's got a beard and a big wart. Now, Angel, how come you came from a gangster-baron's statue? (*LEVIATHAN glances at ANGEL.*)

ANGEL: Fresh hooligan! (*Milder.*) He's joking. (*Fiercely again.*) He's bluffing! Don't you see? He spoke to no Mayor...he spoke to the telephone operator!

GABRIEL (*to LEVIATHAN*): Want to call the Mayor yourself?

LEVIATHAN (*to ANGEL*): Say, it's not true.

ANGEL: It's not true.

LEVIATHAN: Prove it! Prove him apart, prove him to pieces! You know how! (*The crowd outside bursts out in a roar. GABRIEL flings the balcony door open. Another roar and multi-colored confetti, in dusk, covers the horizon outside the balcony like a sudden snow-storm.*)

ANGEL (*he stares at the confetti, as if hypnotized, and whispers automatically and absent-mindedly*): It's not true...it's not... They look like stamps...my stamps...my world! (*His control collapses. He turns to LEVIATHAN with a violent motion, hate screaming from his entire body.*) It's true! Yes—true, true, true! The hooligan is right! There is no Angel, Leviathan! You killed my stamps, my life! I'll tear your life like you tore my stamps!

LEVIATHAN (*softly*): The world's gone crazy... (*Pauses, points to GABRIEL absent-mindedly*). What lousy pants... (*Sits down heavily. Softly.*) The cocks—the cocks will crow each morning... (*ADENOID enters, rubbing her eyes. She is surprised seeing all the people but controls herself and immediately assumes a modelling pose as befits the occasion.*)

ADENOID: Oh, I beg your pardon... I must have overslept. (*To OKEN, with conspiratorial affection.*) Joseph, you rascal, you let me sleep all day. (*OKEN gestures frantically to her to keep quiet and points at his wife. He stops the display but MRS. OKEN has already noticed it.*) You don't have to tell me. I know it was affection. (*MRS. OKEN makes an angry questioning motion at her husband. He replies to her by indicating that ADENOID must be slightly nuts. ADENOID turns to the others.*) You people simply must hear about the dream I had. There I was modelling again, abroad I'm sure, on a sandy beach. I was leaning against an honest antique column, in a sheath skirt, fully lined with its own wide straw belt. A Cary Grant type was handing binoculars to me. And then I laughed out loud, threw the binoculars on the sand and said: "Sir, I'm through with this life! Take me to the pastry shop where I'll join Joseph on the wedding cake. We shall honeymoon in Atlantic City where convention is on and people talk loud and sweat..." (*MRS. OKEN puts her heavy hand on her husband's shoulder. He tries to flip it off with a nonchalant masterly gesture but is not able to.*)

OKEN (*casting a fearful glance at his wife, to ADENOID*): I'm sorry, Miss, but there must be some mistake! I don't think we have been introduced.

ADENOID: Joseph! Mistake? (*Sits down.*) Have I sleepwalked from dream to dream?

LEVIATHAN (*still not moving, staring before himself, whispering plaintively*): Dream... all the women I could have had... a thousand belly buttons lost forever...

ADENOID: Lost...

LEVIATHAN (*jumps to his feet with a ferocious scream and seizes ANGEL by the collar*): I'll tear you to pieces like your stamps! (*ANGEL, no less militant, manages to get hold of LEVIATHAN'S collar. They stand thus entwined, breathing their hot hate into each other's face.)*

ANGEL: Gorilla! I'll tear your hair out—a hair for a stamp and I had eighty thousand!

GABRIEL: Goodbye, Leviathan.

LEVIATHAN (*to GABRIEL*): And you—you'll starve by the roadside! You are a nobody and you ain't got nothing and no-one!

DIANA: Your grammar is falling apart, Mr. Leviathan, and your sense is collapsing. He has me. (*LEVIATHAN pushes away ANGEL, who bounces into LIBIDSTONE, who pushes him into OKEN'S arms, who tries to seize him but ANGEL slips away and bumps into ADENOID who starts bawling louder.*)

LEVIATHAN (*grabs DIANA by the hand*): You stay with me, Diana, baby. I'm still rich, rich and powerful.

DIANA (*shaking off his hand*): You'll have to get another teacher.

LEVIATHAN: Don't take up with a beggar and a traitor!

ANGEL (to DIANA): He'll become fat and greedy like Leviathan. (*To DIANA and Gabriel.*) And you two will end up by hating each other...and will die!

LEVIATHAN (*grabs ANGEL by the collar again*): You'll die first!

OKEN: I'm with you, Emperor, remember! Want me to handle all those traitors?

MRS. OKEN (*to OKEN*): You stay out of this! (*The door swings open revealing a panel crowded with photographers and cameras.*)

LIBIDSTONE: Emperor—photographers! Your pose!

OKEN: Change your pose, Emperor! Hold it for them!

LEVIATHAN: Throw the photographers out!

OKEN: No, Emperor, no! If you want to get anywhere, you must hold it for the photographers—and smile! (*LEVIATHAN and ANGEL still holding fast to each other's collars, put on frozen smiles and turn their faces toward the door. Several flashbulbs. As OKEN shuts the door, LEVIATHAN'S and ANGEL'S faces turn grim again and they resume shaking each other. GABRIEL'S and DIANA'S hands find each other and they nod their agreement to leave.*)

LEVIATHAN (*seeing GABRIEL and DIANA about to leave*): You'll rot!

OKEN: Mr. Leviathan...pardon—Emperor—let them rot...we can't lose any more time! The mob needs your speech right now.

LIBIDSTONE (*looks out the window*): I see in the distance a young man with giant sideburns strumming a guitar. Some people are walking over to him. What could that mean?

OKEN: Five more minutes and they'll start cooling off. Speak to them now and they'll make you anything you want!

LIBIDSTONE: Not anything—high priest! Formulate it clearly—"high priest."

OKEN: Baloney!

LIBIDSTONE (*to OKEN*): Primitive, power-grabbing simpleton!

MRS. OKEN (*to LIBIDSTONE*): Watch your language! (*To OKEN.*) We're leaving right now! Trust me to see when something starts to fall apart. (*OKEN tries to slap her behind but she catches his hand in midair and deals an uxorial blow on his neck. Then she proceeds to pull him out of the room against his resistance.*)

LEVIATHAN (*despairingly*): Gabriel? Where are you? (*GABRIEL stops for a moment but does not turn around to LEVIATHAN.*) I don't understand this no more!

ANGEL (*with triumphant hostility*): You understand me and I understand you, and so it will be...

LEVIATHAN: Stop it! I order you to stop it!

ANGEL (*persistently*): For bad or for worse, until death will us part! Angel and Leviathan will burst like bubbles and Babylon will remain Babylon!

OKEN (*resisting his wife, to LEVIATHAN*): Emperor—the crowds....It's now or never!

LEVIATHAN (*glances around, confused, no more dead-certain. There is genuine grief in his voice*): Not today...tomorrow, maybe...

LIBIDSTONE: Tomorrow I must explore the phenomenon of the young man with the giant sideburns. Magnetism of power—fascinating...

ADENOID: Tomorrow—another name for a dream!...

LEVIATHAN: Gabriel...(*With LEVIATHAN'S outcry, all present—except GABRIEL and DIANA who have reached the edge of the stage—freeze in their positions. A brown gauze curtain and dimmed light separate them from the young lovers.*)

DIANA (*stretches out her hand to catch an invisible falling leaf. She regards it in her hand*): I had stopped to catch a falling leaf when I left Pennsylvania. Now the summer's gone again.

GABRIEL (*takes the invisible leaf from her hand; then suddenly raises his hand*): Listen...(*Lets his hand sink slowly.*) I thought I heard him call me again...(*The group in LEVIA—*

*THAN'S office become black silhouettes in almost total dark-
ness.)*

DIANA (*whispers*): I'm cold.

GABRIEL (*takes off his jacket and puts it on her shoulders*):
We have reached winter.

DIANA: My feet are swollen... (*With a sudden outburst of doubt
and despair.*) Gabriel, will we do better than they? Doesn't
everybody learn hate, grow old and die?

GABRIEL: Just keep repeating to yourself: we will, we **will** get
there.

DIANA: Where?

GABRIEL: Seven more mountain ranges. And then—a valley
ringed with the proudest of trees; the beat of angels' wings;
and words as chaste and new as newborn honeybees.

DIANA: Eldorado?

GABRIEL: Yes.

DIANA: America?

GABRIEL: America.

CURTAIN

ATARAXIA

A play in one act

by
Antanas Škėma

Translated from Lithuanian by
Kristina Škėma-Snyder

Introduction to
Ataraxia

Ataraxia, meaning "calmness of the mind and emotions," implies a state of being dependent upon a certain quality of existence. Such qualified dependence, in turn, suggests adherence to the strain in philosophy known as existentialism which sees existence as prior to essence—a major concern of other philosophical trends. Thus, it seems that by choosing this specific Greek word for the title of his play, the author, Antanas Škėma, indicates his alignment with the existentialist school of thought which persists in asking the question, "what does it mean 'to be' or 'to exist'?" and which argues that each man must define his own values if he is "to exist" as a human being. Škėma's alignment with the existentialists, who sought to liberate the individual from external impositions and to make him discover internally the conditions for choosing and acting, is evidenced by pronouncements found in his writings as well as in descriptions of his actions and life style by his contemporaries.

Antanas Škėma was born 1911 in Lòdż, Poland. During World War I he lived in Russia but returned with his parents to Lithuania in 1921. From 1929-1931 he studied medicine and from 1931-1935 law at the University of Kaunas. In 1935, Škėma started his career in theatre at the State Theatre in Kaunas, first as a student, then as an actor. In 1940, he moved to Vilnius State Theatre where he acted and directed until the Soviet occupation of Lithuania in 1944.

The next five years Škėma spent in Germany acting and directing for several Lithuanian theatre groups in the displaced persons' camps. He emigrated to the United States in 1949 and for a while worked as an elevator operator in New York. As an actor and director, he participated in Lithuanian productions in Chicago, Boston, New York, and Montreal. From 1960 to his death in an automobile accident on Pennsylvania Turnpike in 1961, he was on the editorial staff of the newspaper *Vienybe* (Unity).

Škėma began his literary career in 1941 writing scripts for

radio. He completed his first play, *Julijana,* a three-act drama with a prologue, in 1943. A collection of his short stories and sketches, including a one-act play, *Vieną vakarą* (One Night), was published 1947 in Germany under the title, *Nuodėguliai ir kibirkštys* (Charred Stumps and Sparks). A persistence to understand war and oppression is demonstrated throughout the volume by various protagonists, although Škėma's heroes seem more puzzled than shocked seeing that the forces of evil apparently have the upper hand. A collection of short stories, *Šventoji Inga* (Saint Inga) and a collection of poetry in prose, *Celesta,* followed in 1952 and 1960 respectively. In both, attention is focused on the integrity of man in the moment of defeat or even of death. In his novel, *Balta drobulė,* 1958 (The White Shroud) Škėma deals with man's dualistic existence—the past and the present, his intimate inner life and his need to communicate with the outside world— neither of which can be reconciled: an exile poet goes insane, thus ending his agonizing efforts in asserting personal identity and finding the meaning of life.

Even in his apparently realistic plays, such as *Pabudimas* (The Awakening) and *Žvakidė* (The Candlestick), Škėma is more concerned with the protagonist's inner life and the search for identity than with the plot. It would be wrong to say that Škėma is not concerned with structure in his plays: the structure, however, develops out of the motivations of the play's characters, instead of being a causal or episodic arrangement of events involving the characters. It can be construed as a combination of leitmotifs of the separate characters that advance the dramatic action, at the same time remaining static in a symphonic whole. Such a recurrence of leitmotifs is best demonstrated in Škėma's dramatic legend, *Zivile,* 1948, where two characters, Gluosnis and Živile, reappear in three scenes, each happening in a different time period and setting. Both characters are unavoidably caught by different historical events, each time reincarnated to live in another. The first scene is set in medieval Lithuania with Gluosnis, victorious in a battle with the Russians, seeking the hand of Živile. Her father, the duke, refuses and Gluosnis must betray him and kill his rival Ašautas in order to win Živile. When Živile hears about Gluosnis' deeds, she kills him. The second scene is set during the peasant uprising of 1863 where Gluosnis is a revolutinary and Živile the daughter of a land baron. The third scene takes place during the Russian invasion of Lithuania in 1941 where Živile, Gluosnis and Ašautas are all part of the underground. Ašautas turns out to be a Bolshevik agent, and Živile and

Gluosnis choose suicide rather than betray their comrades in the movement.

There is no doubt that Škėma was influenced by the existential-ist school of thought: one is constantly reminded of Jean-Paul Sartre, Albert Camus, and James Joyce during the perusal of Škėma's works. As a matter of fact, Škėma—the artist and the man—seems to have been the embodiment of Sartre's "ideal man" depicted as Orestes in *The Flies*. Sartre's Orestes asserts his independence both of Jupiter (god) and Egistus (state)—the symbols of externally imposed order. He rids himself of the sense of guilt, traditionally induced by defying authority, and he is willing to correct the errors of the past through active "engage-ment." Sartre's Orestes differs from his prototype in Aeschylus' *Oresteia*; so does Antanas Skema from other Lithuanian writers in exile who, though aware of their condition, are still able to return, albeit only in memory, to the green earth of their native Lithuania. Škėma's creative urge and his unceasing questioning of his condition as an exile, seemed to have closed the gates to the past. He was a true exile fitting the description in an essay on Skema by Professor Rimvydas Šilbajoris: "A man is an exile be-cause his spark of divinity alienates him from the earth, his mother."

There are similarities between Škema, the artist, and most of the protagonists in his prose writings as well as dramas. It would be impossible to determine, however, if the fictional characters in Skėma's works were molded after the artist himself or if they were composites of his contemporary Lithuanian exiles. Škėma may well have created them according to a universal model that is not a rarity in our century of exile guided by the thought that "…in a universe suddenly divested of illusions and lights, man feels an alien, a stranger. His exile is without remedy since he is deprived of the memory of a lost home or the hope of a promised land," as expressed by Albert Camus in "The Myth of Sisyphus."

Gluosnis, the protagonist in *Ataraxia*, fits the parameters of an exile as delineated by Camus: his universe is dark, without illu-sions, he has no friends and he is forced to name complete strangers as witnesses to his recent activities and whereabouts. There seems to be no remedy for his present condition as he is unable to return to the past even in memory, and the way to the promised land is blocked by a "no exit" situation he has chosen voluntarily, though without an option for reversal of his action. Sartre's *No Exit* comes to mind, because also there the results of failing to choose properly are depicted. While in both plays torture

—something one would expect in Hell—constitutes the main action, in *No Exit* it occurs in the minds of the characters as opposed to the need to reenact physically torturous deeds of the past in *Ataraxia*. Hell in *No Exit* is depicted according to the Judeo-Christian concept and is possible anywhere, whereas in *Ataraxia*, as the names of the three establishment representatives —Messrs. Smith, John, and Brown—and their eager servants, Madam and the Attendant, the latter stereotyped as belonging to the Black race, suggest, it cannot be anywhere else but in America—the land of the free. Still, not the locale but, as Garcin at the very end in *No Exit* discovers, "Hell is—other people." The difference between the two plays is in the fact that Sartre's "other people" are inside the "no exit" locale while Škėma's "others" are imposing pressure upon Gluosnis and Isaac from the outside and through their servants are urging conformity—another aspect of existentialists' Hell.

It is interesting to note that definite parallels exist also between Sartre's *Dirty Hands* and Škėma's *Ataraxia*. While *Dirty Hands* treats the necessity and danger of engagement in a roundabout fashion, in *Ataraxia* it is part of the direct action: Gluosnis actively seeks the engagement with Isaac, though unaware that it will be the repetition of their previous encounter. *Dirty Hands* suggests that the social or political choices a man might face are not always ideal and that most of them are sometimes completely unacceptable. It means that participation in a political action without doubt will dirty, even bloody, one's hands. In *Ataraxia* we learn how and why Gluosnis and Isaac made their choices first from Madam's report and later through direct action. While Sartre in his play seems to suggest that refusal to participate— to become engaged—because of fear that one's hands may get dirty would be merely letting others make the choices which determine man's fate, Škėma plays out the moment of choosing in a climactic scene between two former antagonists, Gluosnis and Isaac, who, having made their choice to kill the Attendant, stand united against the external pressures. If love can exist between people, even between former enemies, their "Hell is other people" has been abolished. Gluosnis and Isaac, because they were able to make the proper choice, are free to leave.

Ataraxia thus ends with an optimistic turn which seems to include a message. Such a turn also removes the play from purely existentialist drama whose general purpose is only to explore a condition. *Ataraxia*, besides exploring Gluosnis' condition, also tells a story as well as advocates peaceful coexistence between former enemies.

While a notion of peaceful coexistence might be acceptable to a reader or spectator who has not experienced the conditions of exile, it seems unthinkable to those who were forced into exile as a result of philosophical and political differences in their homelands. The first generation Lithuanian immigrants in the U.S.A., in most part, think of their exile as temporary, and they do everything possible to fight the existing order in their former country. Therefore, the ending of *Ataraxia* is unacceptable to them.

The existentialist thought quite often deals with the sense of guilt. Gluosnis in *Ataraxia* exhibits feelings that can be associated with culpability, with a recognition of having done something wrong. The action of the play revolves around an attempt to right this wrong or, at least, to atone for one's sins. In the opinion of the Lithuanian exiles, they have not committed a sin. Then why should Skema invent an action that suggests a sense of guilt? Did he want to mollify his own conscience or did he detect such a need in his fellow exiles? Whatever the reason, *Ataraxia* remained in manuscript form at the time of its author's death. To this day it has not been produced in its original Lithuanian version, although it was included in Škema's Collected Works, published 1970.

The English version was first produced in 1976 by the SIUC Theatre Department at Carbondale, Illinois and advertised as "an experiment in subconscious drama." A twenty minutes long reminiscing about the author by his daughter and translator of his plays preceeded each performance in the theatre's auditorium. Then the curtain opened slightly in order to let the audience onto the stage where tiers of seats were arranged completely surrounding the acting area which could be reached by the actors only through a trap door in the stage floor. The performance lasted one hour, and an additional time period was allotted to audience discussion of the play and performance. The imaginative scenography by a doctoral candidate in theatre and the production concept by a professional Jewish-American guest director were praised profusely by the audience—mostly university faculty and students. There were, though, voices that proclaimed the subject matter too daring and too painful to be presented in public. They suggested that the artist must make certain compromises in order not to offend his public.

Antanas Škėma was not a man of compromises. He might have agreed wholeheartedly with his compatriot, Jonas Jurašas, the former Chief Artistic director of the State Drama Theatre at

Kaunas (he also attended the above described performances) and a recent exile himself with such Broadway credits as Nikolai Erdman's *The Suicide*, when he wrote in an open letter to the world's artistic community: "Compromises....They are convenient for accidental drifters who are looking for peaceful backwaters in the sphere of art."

Alfreds Straumanis

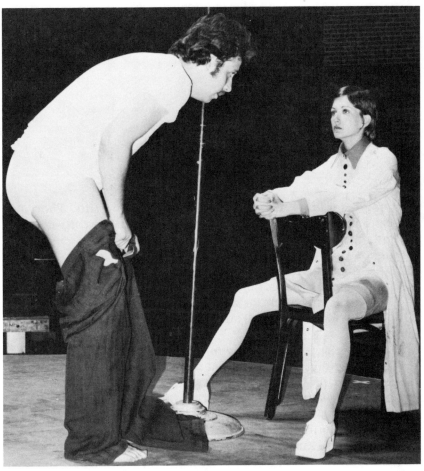

Ataraxia. Southern Illinois University Theatre, 1975. Director: Arnold Kendall   Scenographer: Jim Utterback   Costume Design: Mary E. Rose Gluosnis: Peter Zopp   Madam: LaVetta Zopp

ATARAXIA

CHARACTERS

(in order of appearance)

ANDRIUS GLUOSNIS
MADAM
ATTENDANT
MR. SMITH
MR. JOHN
MR. BROWN
ISAAC

(*On stage is a table, chairs, and a window with grills. There are posters on the walls of pretty but unhappy people, mostly children resting against mothers, wearing decorative rags, marching through a sign:* **Help!** *It is dusk. Enters a pleasant, gray-haired MADAM and ANDRIUS GLUOSNIS, a middle-aged man.*)

MADAM (*places a sheaf of papers on the table and sits down*): This will be more comfortable. Please sit.

GLUOSNIS (*still standing*): I don't know if this is really comfortable.

MADAM (*writes while talking to GLUOSNIS*): We're very sorry. Unfortunately, this is the most pleasant room. Anyway, please sit. (*GLUOSNIS sits.*) Well now, how can I be of help? (*She smiles an institutional smile and speaks in a kindly institutional tone.*)

GLUOSNIS (*imitating MADAM'S tone and smile*): Well now, I myself, don't know very well why I came here.

MADAM: Don't worry. You're not the first. But, I trust, you have some awareness of your situation?

GLUOSNIS: Approximately. Still, I don't especially trust the authenticity of my awareness. I came here, because I asked an

348

old man for advice; we spent many hours sitting in a little park near Halsey Street, drinking a lot of bad whiskey. When we drank up the last of our money, that old esteemed gentleman gave this address and I got on a bus.

MADAM: Fine. So then, you came voluntarily?

GLUOSNIS: So it seems.

MADAM: That's fine. Really fine.

GLUOSNIS: Thank you. In that case, I allow myself a partial explanation of this, let us say, rather strange situation. Here— we are separated by a table, nevertheless, we are able to communicate. Do you, dear Madam, understand at least partially what I wanted, however inadequately, to express?

MADAM: But of course.

GLUOSNIS: Thank you again. The name, Isaac, is no doubt familiar to you? Oh yes, I understand, it's not up to me to remind you of the simplest events in the Bible. At any rate, I think, calculating in the New Testament, these Anno Domini years and this magnificent spring day....How sticky green the trees are in your park! At any rate, any search, let's say my search, can always be supported by old books, just like that always old and young spring! (*He pathetically stretches out his hand toward the window.*)

MADAM: Your introduction is almost mathematically precise. You successfully tied it in with a cosmic timetable. Could I ask for a few facts, details, so that your petition could gain a more symmetrical construction? Like the ancient Greeks, for example.

GLUOSNIS: Of course, of course. That's right. Like the ancient Greeks. Isn't it amazing the way they ordered the universe? (*He takes out a long envelope from his pocket, waves it under MADAM'S nose, puts it back.*) This is the most important. And besides, I have witnesses in New York. The last were....One moment! Oh yes, two Metropolitan Museum guards, a liquor store owner, greatly resembling an amoeba, I would almost dare to venture that he is a reincarnation of an amoeba, for you see, Indians were not only confused with Buddha, but with Western winds....Further....So, also a kindly citizen from the third floor who yelled, goddam bastard, when I fell on the stairs. Finally, a woman or girl in a white robe, but I don't remember if she said anything to me or if I said anything to her. Well, I guess, that's all.

MADAM: My deepest thanks. Stay a moment while I inform my superiors.

GLUOSNIS: Of course, of course. I'll gladly wait.

MADAM (*gathers the papers preparing to leave*): Make yourself at home. (*Exits. GLUOSNIS sits a while, goes to the window, gazes out for a moment, walks around. Finally he stops and starts doing gymnastics. The ATTENDANT enters, a heavy black man in a gray uniform, bringing a small plate with currant jam on it.*)

ATTENDANT (*putting the plate on the table*): Eat.

GLUOSNIS (*stops exercising*): Excuse me?

ATTENDANT: Eat.

GLUOSNIS (*looking at the jam*): I don't like currant jam. Even when I was small, it made me shudder.

ATTENDANT: You were told—make yourself at home. Eat, I don't have time. (*GLUOSNIS obeys, sits and with disgust quickly eats the jam. The ATTENDANT stands next to him. As soon as GLUOSNIS finishes, the ATTENDANT grabs the plate and spoon from him and leaves.*)

GLUOSNIS: A stupid business. What a stupid business. (*Wipes his mouth with his hand.*) And the taste is a mess. What should I do till they come...who comes? I don't even know who is coming. (*Sings.*)

> Laugh, clown, your love is lost,
> Laugh, though you're torn with pain....

Sounds awful. This isn't the bathroom. Maybe something folksy? (*Sings.*)

> My mother sent me
> To the sea waters,
> To the sea waters,
> Drawing the water,
> A black ship sailed in,
> A black...

ATTENDANT (*entering with a phonograph, puts it on the table*): Shut up! (*GLUOSNIS quiets down.*) Now listen to the music. (*Plugs in the phonograph, a very war-like march can be heard. ATTENDANT listens contentedly, waving his hands. Suddenly he unplugs the phonograph.*) Enough. (*Taking the phonograph, he leaves. MR. SMITH enters. He is well-dressed, with a pleasant look.*)

MR. SMITH: Good day. I am Mr. Smith. (*Shakes hands.*)

GLUOSNIS: My pleasure. And I am Andrius Gluosnis. In English—Andrew Gluosnis. G, L, U, O, S, N, I, S. Gluosnis—a willow tree in Lithuanian. Willows grow hanging over weedy ponds and young girls tell them their sorrows. At least that's

how it used to be. A willow evokes elegiac sadness and other
exalted visions. (*Pause.*) Why...was I forced to eat currant
jam? I hate it.

MR. SMITH (*smiling*): Oh, forgive us. Our attendant is rather
strange, I would say, innocently strange. We forgive him his
tiny lapses because he is useful to us in other matters. I hope,
Mr. Gluosnis, that you forgive him also?

GLUOSNIS: Oh yes, yes. I already did.

MR. SMITH: Many thanks. (*Enter MR. JOHN and MR. BROWN.
MR. JOHN is gray-haired with professorial appearance. MR.
BROWN has sharp, uneasy features, horn-rimmed glasses.
They, like, MR. SMITH are elegantly dressed.*)

MR. JOHN (*shaking GLUOSNIS' hand*): Hello. I am Mister John.

GLUOSNIS: Andrew Gluosnis—G, L, U, O, S, N, I, S.

MR. BROWN (*not shaking GLUOSNIS' hand*): I am Mr. Brown.

GLUOSNIS: A pleasure. Andrew Gluosnis—G, L, U, O, S, N, I, S.

MR. JOHN: Very fine. Let's sit. (*Everyone sits.*) I think, we can
begin. (*His colleagues nod.*)

MR. SMITH: We are very glad that you came. We read your
petition and, to your deep pleasure, it is intelligent and
original. Our chief colleague, Mr. John, will introduce you to
what is called the intellectual aspect of the situation. Please,
Mr. John.

MR. JOHN (*takes out a silk handkerchief from the small side-
pocket of his jacket, elegantly wipes his lips, and puts it back.
The talk is accented on logical strokes*): As you know, various
surprises lose their meaning, if they are repeated at
meaningful intervals. That is an abstract statement, only...
we can always find enough examples to illustrate. If you experience a fear of space twenty times a day, you finally get tired,
and the twenty-first time, I repeat—first, no longer tires you.
Or, twenty times shot in a bunker, you want to return to the
past and deliver a fiery speech at the Reichstag, remembering
that the world war has not started yet. I don't mean to tire you
with long conclusions and a myriad of examples. I just want to
emphasize that our system is based on the method of artificial
repetition. Didn't La Fontaine, upon hearing someone lament
the fate of those condemned to be sunk into the flames of hell,
say: "I believe, they will get used to it and finally feel like fish
in water." You are an intelligent person and understand that
the finale of this witicism is convincing, unavoidable and very
hopeful. Needless to say, you may not be able to, perhaps not
want to, perhaps will get tired of, repeating over and over that

which affects you unpleasantly. In other words, you will be tired of trying hard to feel that in that hopeful finale you will be truly and hopelessly tired. Here is where we come in to help and with your help we will try to lead you towards an epicurean ataraxia, if one can call the ancient Greek a priori solutions a mature invention of western civilization. Not wanting to tire you with the depth and consequence of this thoroughly tested and experienced method—I trust, my colleagues will agree (MR. SMITH *nods.*)—thank you—I would like to emphasize the final finale or the endless non-end, yes plus yes are only one yes, similarly no plus no are only one no; for in our opinion, free will always plays a favorable part in any determination. If any one be a genius, or if he be an idiot, or a two-year old child, or a hundred year old man, who has already lost his faculties for some time....Free will lurks in every individual from birth to death. So, dear sir, I ask you to believe and trust us. This is a fateful hour for you. In the beginning, the statutes of our method require that you are asked to answer a few questions. By the way, realize that the general aim for all of us is to return you to a primary, I would even say, embryonic state, or, to explain more visually, to return you from the bunker to the Reichstag. (*As the monologue ends, the ATTENDANT enters the room. He straightens MR. JOHN'S handkerchief, combs MR. SMITH'S hair, takes off MR. BROWN'S glasses, wipes them, puts them back on and before leaving, slaps GLUOSNIS on the behind.*)

GLUOSNIS: Excuse me...excuse me, I don't have a Hitler complex.

MR. JOHN: Why do you mention proper names?

GLUOSNIS (*mutters*): Just like you.

MR. JOHN: I used them as examples.

MR. BROWN: He thinks he is also an example. (*All three laugh. GLUOSNIS gets up suddenly.*)

GLUOSNIS: Forgive me, sirs, but...I suddenly feel...how to explain this to you...I confess, I made a mistake and came to the wrong place. Thanks for everything. Good-bye. (*Starts to leave. The ATTENDANT pops out.*)

ATTENDANT: Get back. And don't try a second time. I'll break your bones. (*Disappears.*)

GLUOSNIS: You talked of free will. But...I'm forbidden to leave.

MR. JOHN: You came here alone, Mr. Gluosnis?

GLUOSNIS: Yes, but...

MR. JOHN: You appealed to our employee for help?

GLUOSNIS: Yes, but...

MR. JOHN: You began an association with us?

GLUOSNIS: Yes, but...

MR. JOHN: So, be kind enough to continue the association. You volunteered for confinement. You chose of your own free will. Please sit. (*GLUOSNIS stands silently. MR. JOHN orders.*) Please sit!

GLUOSNIS (*walking to the chair*): What a shitty business.

MR. JOHN: Excuse me?

GLUOSNIS: Oh, nothing special. Just a native expression useful for various occasions.

MR. JOHN: Is it obscene?

GLUOSNIS: It's real. (*MR. SMITH gently puts his arms around GLUOSNIS' shoulders and seats him.*)

MR. SMITH: So. I trust you feel comfortable?

GLUOSNIS: Like home.

MR. SMITH: I'm glad. (*Pause.*)

GLUOSNIS: Could I get a glass of water? (*Mr. Smith looks at his colleagues. They shake their heads no.*)

MR. BROWN: You ate currant jam. Is that so?

GLUOSNIS: That's why I'm thirsty.

MR. BROWN: True. And that's why you can't have a drink. Because you ate currant jam. Water and currant jam—a dangerous combination.

GLUOSNIS: Splendid. I'm not thirsty.

MR. BROWN: That's a lie. You are thirsty.

GLUOSNIS: Forgive me. I am thirsty.

MR. BROWN: We already told you; you can't have a drink.

GLUOSNIS: True. You said, I can't have a drink.

MR. BROWN: But you want one anyway?

GLUOSNIS (*screams*): Yes! Yes! I want and I can't!

ATTENDANT (*sticks out his head*): Shut up! (*Disappears.*)

MR. JOHN (*gently*): Mr. Gluosnis! Why are you trying to disagree with yourself? If you act this way, you will never return to the embryonic state, you will never attain epicurean ataraxia. You will never embrace satori, if eastern resignation is closer to your heart. Very true. Resignation. You are required to be resigned, Mr. Gluosnis. That's the initial way out to the final way out. Your "I" will melt into cosmic consciousness and—I don't know...I don't like to predict—but it's possible, you will succeed, and you will attain that blessed state which in the whole world, at all times, all philosophical systems, and all religions, at least theoretically, have attained a long time ago. (*Sighs.*) Will you now be kind enough to answer a few questions, Mr. Gluosnis?

GLUOSNIS: Oh yes!

MR. JOHN (*to MR. SMITH*): You continue.

MR. SMITH: Your first and last name?

GLUOSNIS: I already said it.

MR. SMITH: Mister...

GLUOSNIS: Yes, yes, forgive me. I am Andrius Gluosnis. In English—Andrew Gluosnis. G, L, U, O, S, N, I, S. Gluosnis— a Lithuanian willow tree. Willows grow hanging over weedy ponds and... (*Grows silent.*)

MR. SMITH: Why did you stop?

MR. JOHN: Good. He's already trying. Continue.

MR. SMITH: In your petition Isaac's name is mentioned. Why?

GLUOSNIS: I got a letter from Isaac.

MR. SMITH: Where is it?

GLUOSNIS: In my pocket.

MR. SMITH (*puts out his hand*): If you please.

GLUOSNIS: In the letter there's only Isaac's name, printed.

MR. JOHN (*reaches out his hand*): If you please.

GLUOSNIS: You'll return it? (*MR. BROWN reaches out his hand.*) My intuition...instinct...no matter which...tells me not to give it to you. (*MR. BROWN claps his hands. ATTENDANT enters. He lifts GLUOSNIS like a baby and starts to carry him out.*)

GLUOSNIS: Where are you taking me?

ATTENDANT (*stops*): You asked for water, huh? We have cold, cold water here. Lots and lots of water.

GLUOSNIS: Let go.

ATTENDANT: Will you talk?

GLUOSNIS: I'll talk. (*The ATTENDANT carries GLUOSNIS back and carefully seats him in the chair. He leaves.*) That's coercion!

MR. JOHN: Is it? Why didn't you resist? (*Pause.*) The letter, please. (*GLUOSNIS hands the letter to MR. JOHN. He takes it out of the envelope, reads it, and hands it to his colleagues. They, having read it, return it to MR. JOHN. The latter puts it in the envelope and stuffs it in his pocket.*)

MR. SMITH: Is Isaac persecuting you?

GLUOSNIS: I don't know which one is persecuting which. Probably I am looking for him.

MR. SMITH: What is your relationship with him?

GLUOSNIS: Our relationship ended. A long time ago. Suddenly, with this letter, he reminded me that it still exists.

MR. SMITH: In your opinion Isaac no longer exists?

GLUOSNIS: I'm not sure. I already killed him with a soldier's spade but...maybe he's alive. I snuck out of the garage very quickly and went to Vytautas Prospect without looking back.

MR. SMITH: Would you like to kill him again?

GLUOSNIS: I haven't thought about it. First, I would like to find him.

MR. SMITH: It's possible, he's looking for you.

GLUOSNIS: It's possible. (*The ATTENDANT enters. In his hand he's holding three crumpled cigarettes. He puts a cigarette into each Mister's mouth, lights them and they smoke. ATTENDANT leaves.*) I would like a cigarette, too. (*The Misters exchange glances.*)

MR. SMITH: We'll leave you a few puffs.

GLUOSNIS: Thanks.

MR. SMITH: Not at all. (*All three smoke intensely. MADAM enters with a clapboard and a paper attached to it.*)

MADAM: Escuse me, I just received Andrius Gluosnis' report. Should I read it?

MR. JOHN: Please.

MADAM (*reads*): Andrius Gluosnis, born in 1920, in Lithuania. Parents were townspeople. Childhood facts incomplete. It has been determined that he was vaccinated against smallpox, didn't like currant jam and beat up younger kids. He was an average student and during classes he scratched his behind. Tried to attend the University and in his free time drank and had sexual relations with seamstresses and factory workers. Belonged to a branch of a nationalistic Lithuanian movement whose aim he believed was to return to the age of Vytautas the Great. In 1940, during the bolshevik occupation of Lithuania he was put in jail in Kaunas where he was tortured. The torture was executed by a Jew named Isaac who belonged to a branch of a nationalistic Jewish movement, whose aim, he believed, was to return to the age of Moses. Isaac's nationalism allowed him to choose communism. In 1941 during the German occupation in Lithuania, Isaac was caught in the garage courtyard and Andrius Gluosnis found himself there at the same time. His nationalism allowed him to choose Nazism. With the approval of the SS, he killed, or tried to kill, Isaac with a small soldier's spade. Further events are of a purely historical nature. He escaped to Germany, and later came to America. Having avoided death in a concentration camp,

Isaac came to America also. And that's all.

MR. JOHN: Thank you. You may go. (*MADAM leaves.*) The matter is clear. I would say, even banal. There are a million like him. (*To MR. SMITH.*) I don't think we're needed here. That's your department, Mr. Brown.

MR. BROWN: Every banality is assigned to my department.

MR. JOHN: You are renowned for your imagination, Mr. Brown. Good luck! (*Both put out their cigarettes in the ashtray and start to leave.*)

GLUOSNIS: One minute! (*Both stop.*) You didn't leave a few puffs for me. You cheated me.

MR. JOHN: We cheated?

GLUOSNIS: You promised me a few puffs and...

MR. JOHN: And you lost a few puffs. I underline—lost. It was your affair and your duty to stop us, when we still held the cigarettes in our hands. (*MR. JOHN and MR. SMITH leave. During this exchange MR. BROWN also puts out his cigarette in an ashtray. GLUOSNIS tries to reach the butt. The ATTENDANT enters, slaps GLUOSNIS on the hand and takes out the ashtray.*)

MR. BROWN: Your first and last name?

GLUOSNIS (*quiet for a moment*): Andrius Gluosnis. In English Andrew Gluosnis. G, L, U, O, S, N, I, S. A willow tree in Lith...

MR. BROWN (*interrupts*): I'm not interested in your explanations. I'm interested in answers. So. **Don't throw stones at a glass house.** What does that mean?

GLUOSNIS (*quiet for a moment*): I don't really know....Perhaps your question should be understood in a figurative sense. In that case...

MR. BROWN (*interrupts*): Questions are not answered by questions. One moment. Let me explain. Simply. For example. Question: what is love? Answer: a physiological and spiritual act. What is a physiological and spiritual act? Love. Or death, if the latter is more acceptable to you. Simple, or not? So, I repeat. **Don't throw stones at a glass house.** What does that mean?

GLUOSNIS (*like a student*): What does that mean? Answer: don't throw stones at a glass house.

MR. BROWN: Listen, Mr. Gluosnis. Your stubborness is really fantastic. And furthermore, pay attention. I'm not as kind as my colleagues. What's more, in your case any kindness might even be harmful. So, be good enough to answer. (*GLUOSNIS is silent.*) I'm waiting. (*GLUOSNIS is silent.*) I am bored waiting. (*GLUOSNIS is silent.*) Passive resistance? Sit-down strike? Fine. (*Claps his hands. The ATTENDANT enters.*) Ask...

ATTENDANT (*interrupts*): I know. (*Leaves.*)

GLUOSNIS: Who is coming?

MR. BROWN: Not your affair.

GLUOSNIS: All right. I'll try... I'll really answer your question.

MR. BROWN: Too late. (*MADAM enters. She is dressed in a white coat and with a stethoscope around her neck.*) He's yours. (*Leaves.*)

MADAM (*with authoritative strictness*): Get undressed.

GLUOSNIS: Completely?

MADAM: And how else? (*GLUOSNIS smiles foolishly.*) Don't grin like an idiot. Hurry up. (*GLUOSNIS starts undressing clumsily. He takes off his jacket. Unties his necktie. ATTENDANT enters with a white tablecloth, tidies the table, puts on the tablecloth, leaves. GLUOSNIS takes off his shirt and with some apprehension, his undershirt. ATTENDANT re-enters with a vase of red roses, puts it on the table, leaves. GLUOSNIS waits.*) Take off your shoes. (*GLUOSNIS, hopping on one foot, takes off his shoes.*) Socks. (*GLUOSNIS takes off his socks. ATTENDANT enters with two black candlesticks and red candles in them, puts them on either side of the vase, leaves.*) Pants. (*GLUOSNIS obediently takes off his pants, leaving bathing trunks on. ATTENDANT enters with an oblong box, puts it on the table, leaves.*) Why are you wearing bathing trunks?

GLUOSNIS: It's a nostalgic matter.

MADAM: Sit in this chair. (*She takes a chair and places it in front of him. GLUOSNIS sits. MADAM puts the stethoscope on his forehead, listens.*)

GLUOSNIS: Should I breathe?

MADAM: As you like. (*She walks around him, puts the stethoscope on the back of GLUOSNIS' head, listens again.*) It's a clear case. You won't hold out. Get dressed.

GLUOSNIS (*surprised*): Finished?

MADAM: Finished. (*Leaves.*)

GLUOSNIS: What is this comedy?

MADAM (*stops, turns around*): What comedy?

GLUOSNIS: I mean... candles, flowers, stethoscope, examination...

MADAM: It's an illusion. Get dressed quickly. It's cold here. You'll last longer. (*Leaves. GLUOSNIS dresses quickly. ATTENDANT enters with an atomizer, perfumes the room, starts leaving.*)

GLUOSNIS: Listen, friend...

ATTENDANT: Be kind enough to shut up for once. (*Leaves. GLUOSNIS walks to the window, looks quietly at the bars for a while. Looks at his fingers. ISAAC enters the room — a heavy set, dark man. Same age as GLUOSNIS. GLUOSNIS keeps standing with his back to him. ISAAC sits at the table. Smells the roses. Looks distrustingly at GLUOSNIS a few times. Finally coughs.*)

GLUOSNIS (*turning around*): Excuse me?

ISAAC: Please.

GLUOSNIS: You...are you with them?

ISAAC: So it seems. (*Pause.*)

GLUOSNIS: Those roses suit your face.

ISAAC: Thank you!

GLUOSNIS: So do the candles.

ISAAC: Thank you!

GLUOSNIS: Do these things symbolize something?

ISAAC: I don't answer those questions. (*Smells the roses.*)

GLUOSNIS: Did you order them brought in?

ISAAC: I don't order.

GLUOSNIS: Ah! Is that so?

ISAAC: That is so. (*Smells the roses.*)

GLUOSNIS: Forgive me. One more question.

ISAAC: Please!

GLUOSNIS: Are you smelling artificial roses?

ISAAC: An accurate observation.

GLUOSNIS: Why?

ISAAC: It is because they are artificial that I smell them. I am familiar with the smell of real roses. (*Smiles.*) What I just said doesn't symbolize anything either.

GLUOSNIS: What shall we do?

ISAAC: Why are you always asking questions?

GLUOSNIS: I have no idea. Perhaps because you don't ask me questions. (*ISAAC takes out matches.*) You have your own matches?

ISAAC: I am somewhat privileged. (*Lights both candles.*) Please sit.

GLUOSNIS: I think, or so it would seem to me, it really would be nice, in other words — let's introduce ourselves.

ISAAC: We already know each other.

GLUOSNIS: Forgive me...

ISAAC: I am Isaac.

GLUOSNIS (*puts out his hand*): And I am Gluosnis. In English, G, L, ... (*His hand falls.*) You — Isaac?

ISAAC: Remember?

GLUOSNIS: I'll always remember.

ISAAC: And you forgot on sight.

GLUOSNIS: A stupid thing. It's really a stupid thing. (*Looks through his pocket.*)

ISAAC: Don't bother to look. They took the letter.

GLUOSNIS: Yes. They took it. In any case — we finally met. (*Walks around the room.*) Twenty years, just think, twenty years, hang it all! Believe me, Isaac, I had never forgotten! A sudden meeting... confused me. When you're waiting all the time, it seems like you find it a million times, and when you really find it, it seems — you have to keep on waiting. I still wasn't completely sure if you were alive. Yes, yes, I know, even with the letter, I thought: and now I am still mistaken.

ISAAC: Come here. (*GLUOSNIS comes closer. ISAAC bows down and parts his hair.*) You see?

GLUOSNIS: I see. A scar.

ISAAC: Correct. A scar.

GLUOSNIS (*holds out both hands*): I'm very sorry, but I can't present any proof. Those needles you stuck under my nails left no signs. And those pincers. Only a memory left. For example, during the night. Suddenly I jump out of bed with a sharp, stabbing sensation. I think — you stabbed my brains. (*ISAAC'S fingers gently caress the box lid.*) What's in that box?

ISAAC: Your memories. (*Silent for a moment.*) And mine.

GLUOSNIS: You think... (*Quiets down.*)

ISAAC: What?

GLUOSNIS: You think — we'll have to repeat?

ISAAC: That's up to us.

GLUOSNIS: I don't think so.

ISAAC: Why?

GLUOSNIS: The attendant brought that box. Unless... no, that's absurd!

ISAAC: What's absurd?

GLUOSNIS: Unless you are in charge.

ISAAC: Now we are both in charge.

GLUOSNIS: As I recall, you remarked at first that it's possible you are with them. Now you maintain we are both in charge. In that case...

ISAAC (*interrupts*): I don't think the dialectical method suits us.

(*The ATTENDANT enters and remains standing respectfully.*)

GLUOSNIS (*to ISAAC*): What does he want?

ATTENDANT (*especially polite*): Perhaps, sirs, you need anything?

ISAAC: Ask him. (*Points at GLUOSNIS.*)

GLUOSNIS: Me?

ISAAC: But, of course.

ATTENDANT (*to GLUOSNIS*): How can I serve you? (*Bows.*)

GLUOSNIS: Look at that! How can I serve? One moment! (*ATTENDANT bows.*) Fantastic! I would like a bottle of Chianti; for some reason I want something sour, and a few sandwiches, with ham, let's say and... oh yes, do you have a cigarette?

ATTENDANT: Just a moment. (*Takes out a box from his pocket, taps it on the bottom and a cigarette pops out.*)

GLUOSNIS: Amazing! Thanks. (*Takes the cigarette.*)

ATTENDANT: Please. (*Lifts one candle stick and GLUOSNIS lights up. ATTENDANT puts it down again.*)

GLUOSNIS: Once again—thanks.

ATTENDANT: It's a pleasure to serve you. I'll bring your order momentarily. (*Bows and leaves.*)

GLUOSNIS: What happened?

ISAAC: Excuse me? Oh! You mean the change in the attendant? (*GLUOSNIS nods.*) He hasn't changed. His manner has changed. Temporarily. This type of familiarity is part of the method. The attendant is very well trained. That is all. (*Pause.*) You waited for me twenty years? (*GLUOSNIS nods.*) I think we have chatted enough. (*Caresses the box.*) Let's start.

GLUOSNIS: From the beginning?

ISAAC: From the beginning.

GLUOSNIS: What wretched tobacco! (*Throws the cigarette on the floor, steps on it.*) I don't want it.

ISAAC: You waited for me twenty years?

GLUOSNIS: And you wrote me a letter only twenty years later. Is that so?

ISAAC: Well then we finally agree. Let's start.

GLUOSNIS: What if I... refuse?

ISAAC: Impossible. You came here voluntarily. Three misters decided. The gray-haired Madam checked your health. The attendant is strong enough. The window is covered with bars. Impossible.

GLUOSNIS: And what if... I ignore it?

ISAAC: You're not one of those. You better sit. And... we'll start. (*GLUOSNIS circles the table indecisively.*) Sit! (*GLUOSNIS falls in the chair, ISAAC carefully opens the box and takes out a few instruments.*) I'm not sure, after all this time, if I'm capable of such precision and can slowly...I always liked surgery. (*Takes out a handkerchief and cleans the instruments.*) Unfortunately, I only had a short time to experiment. (*Selects instruments.*) Which one is first here? Oh yes, it's this one, absolutely right, I started with this one.

GLUOSNIS: You know what you are? (*Pause.*) A horrid, sadistic, shitty Jew! That's what you are!

ISAAC (*quietly*): That could be. I have my own collection of curses. By the way, there's something left for you in this box.

GLUOSNIS: For me?

ISAAC: Glance at it. (*GLUOSNIS leans over the table and takes out a soldier's spade.*)

GLUOSNIS: My God! The same spade!

ISAAC (*smiling*): The same. Put it back. For now. (*GLUOSNIS puts the spade in the box, collapses in the chair. ATTENDANT enters with a tray, on it a bottle of Chianti and attractively arranged sandwiches.*)

ATTENDANT: Your order, sir.

GLUOSNIS (*looks at the tray for a long time; suddenly*): Go to hell!

ATTENDANT (*bows*): As you wish. (*Leaves.*)

GLUOSNIS: Hold it. (*ATTENDANT stops, GLUOSNIS walks over to him, takes the bottle and glass.*) Now quickly, go to the devil!

ATTENDANT: My heartfelt thanks. (*Bows and leaves.*)

GLUOSNIS (*tastes the wine*): Loathsome!

ISAAC: Sit!

GLUOSNIS (*waters the roses with wine, puts the bottle on the table, sits*): Now the flowers will smell of wine at least.

ISAAC (*warming up the instruments on the candle flame*): And how will the candles smell?

GLUOSNIS: Listen, Isaac!

ISAAC: Don't interrupt. (*Pause.*) Enough. Put out your hands.

GLUOSNIS: You have definitely decided to torture me.

ISAAC: My God, how tiresome you are! Be good and put out your hands. (*GLUOSNIS puts out his hands. ISAAC looks at them like a professional manicurist.*) Your nails are clipped short. Oh well, we'll manage somehow. I'll just have to go under more....Put your hands on the table. (*GLUOSNIS obeys.*) Excuse me. At first, I need only one hand. Which one do I need? Left, right?

GLUOSNIS: I don't care.

ISAAC: But I care. We are obliged to be accurate. And I can't remember which hand I started with twenty years ago.

GLUOSNIS: I don't remember either.

ISAAC: Let's both try. (*Pause.*) The doors were on the left, is that so?

GLUOSNIS: I think so.

ISAAC: Left. The table stood in the middle. The lamp...the lamp is unimportant. You came in...

GLUOSNIS (*obligingly*): I was brought in by two NKVD's. Sort of heavy boys, about six feet tall.

ISAAC: True, my dear. Thanks. I was sitting...where was I sitting?

GLUOSNIS: Behind the table, of course.

ISAAC: Behind the table is behind the table. But on which side?

GLUOSNIS: I don't remember.

ISAAC: Nor do I...and there is the whole secret. If the doors were on the left and I was sitting on that side of the table...

GLUOSNIS: Which is **that** side of the table?

ISAAC (*silent*): That's it. Which is **that**?

GLUOSNIS: What I recall from childhood, **that** side is the opposite of the **other**.

ISAAC: And vice versa, I would think.

GLUOSNIS: It's possible. (*Pause.*) Perhaps we should start with the pain? (*ISAAC looks questioningly.*) When I screamed like an animal, they held me by the shoulders, and I tried to escape. For a moment I freed one hand...(*Grows silent.*)

ISAAC (*jumps up*): Which hand? (*GLUOSNIS shrugs his shoulders.*) Andrius, dearest! (*ISAAC walks toward Gluosnis.*) Remember, I beg of you, remember, which hand you managed to free. Understand, if you remember which was freed, then it will be clear which one lay on the table. (*Kneels in front of GLUOSNIS, takes his hands in his.*) Your hands are alive, your hands are warm. I have never forgotten them. When I looked for you...but no, I looked for your hands. I always saw their yellowish skin, bluish veins, pink nails. I saw their trembling on the worn table. Your hands didn't belong to you. They had a separate life. You didn't scream — your hands screamed. you didn't beg for mercy — it was your fingers writhing in agony. (*Kisses GLUOSNIS' hands.*) I can still feel the blood pulsing... life pulsing. The same as twenty years ago. You know, Andrius, I want to weep like a small child. Such joyous weeping, like my forefather who wanted to sacrifice his son on the stone altar.

Andrius, dearest, remember. I beg of you, which hand did you succeed in freeing?

ATTENDANT (*enters and, seeing this sensitive mis-en-scene, coughs in his fist*): Excuse me. They're waiting. (*GLUOSNIS cries and shakes his head.*)

ISAAC (*gets up in a daze*): What is it? Who is waiting?

ATTENDANT: Mister John, Mister Brown, and Mister Smith. They are waiting for the results.

ISAAC: I haven't started yet.

ATTENDANT: That's the whole problem. According to their calculations, you should be half way. Therefore, they ask urgently, they are reluctant to order, they ask you to finally start. (*Pause.*) What can I report?

ISAAC: Say...we can't remember several details. In principle— the matter is solved.

ATTENDANT: I am ordered to inform you to please hurry. (*Bows and leaves.*)

GLUOSNIS: Well, we're finally caught!

ISAAC: Frigging business! (*Paces nervously. Suddenly stops.*) What if we started from the other end? What do you think?

GLUOSNIS: I don't understand.

ISAAC: You don't understand? You yourself showed the solution. If it's unclear to us both, which is **that** side, perhaps it will become clearer if we start from the **other** side. Clear?

GLUOSNIS: A little bit. You think...

ISAAC: Yes. It's the only way out.

GLUOSNIS (*goes to the box and takes out the spade, turning it in his hands*): In this case I'm sure. I grabbed the spade with both hands and smashed it on your head.

ISAAC (*clapping his hands and hopping around like a small child*): Bravo! Bravo! (*He starts to laugh. The laughter becomes louder. He grabs GLUOSNIS by the hands and they both dance a pseudo-Indian dance. GLUOSNIS waves his spade like a tomahawk. In between, they shout "ugh" and laugh loudly. Finally, tired, they fall on the chairs. GLUOSNIS throws the spade on the table.*) What lunacy! How simple! God, how simple!

GLUOSNIS: It really is simple!

ISAAC: Don't delay Andrius. Don't delay, while I'm in this blessed frenzy.

GLUOSNIS: Fine, Isaac. (*Takes the spade, walks towards ISAAC.*) Will you kneel? Like twenty years ago? My aim will be better. (*ISAAC kneels. GLUOSNIS parts ISAAC'S hair, puts*

the spade on the scar to aim better, raises it, and freezes.
Pause.) I can't.

ISAAC: Why?

GLUOSNIS: I'm afraid I'll miss.

ISAAC: If you raise it correctly, you'll hit it right.

GLUOSNIS: It's possible. But it's only a possibility, understand
Isaac, just a possibility. (*Kneels before ISAAC.*) A possible
thing, a possible possibility, but...how can you know...if I hit
on the side—then it's very possible I'll split your head a second
time. If a second wound opens up, then it won't be the first.
In that case the other side will not be the new side and you and
I, not having found the other side, will not be able to find that
one.

ISAAC: Damnation! You are hellishly logical.

GLUOSNIS: What shall we both do now?

ISAAC: I don't know, I really don't know. (*Both fall to the floor.*)

GLUOSNIS: I think...

ISAAC (*suddenly*): What do you think?

GLUOSNIS (*longingly*): I think, we are lacking inspiration.

ISAAC (*doubtfully*): Oh! (*Quiet for a moment.*) We have flowers,
candles, posters.

GLUOSNIS: The flowers are artificial, candles smouldering, the
people in the posters too pretty. We need real inspiration.
(*Suddenly jumps up.*) Listen! I already know!

ISAAC (*jumps up*): What?

GLUOSNIS: We need... (*Stops.*) Is there a microphone hidden in
the walls, or anywhere else?

ISAAC: I don't know. Perhaps. (*GLUOSNIS walks to the window
and gestures for ISAAC. He comes closer. They start a sound-
less conversation. GLUOSNIS persuading, ISAAC resisting.
Slowly he starts agreeing. Finally, they cheer up and shake
each other's hand. During this silent conversation a word or
two can be heard and each partner silences it by raising his
finger and whispering "shh". Having finished their conversation, both go to the table and blow out the candles. The room
gets darker. They sit across from each other, dead-pan faces.
For a moment complete silence. ATTENDANT enters.*)

ATTENDANT: Excuse me, honorable sirs! Why did you blow
out the candles? I can't see what you are doing at the table. Oh
yes, I know, I've been ordered not to interrupt, but nevertheless I have to report to my supervisors if you are doing anything at all. (*They sit quietly and don't move.*) Don't think it's
easy for me to be polite. I don't know what my supervisors

think, but politeness is the most idiotic means. (*They sit quietly and don't move.*) O.K. That's enough stinking at the table! Up! (*They sit quietly and don't move.*) Your case isn't the first or last. I've fixed quite a few. Even passive resistance didn't help. Up, animals! (*They sit quietly and don't move.*) All right. You want a box on the ears. (*ATTENDANT walks to the table. When he stops behind ISAAC'S back, ISAAC grabs the spade on the table and turning around hits the ATTENDANT on the head. ATTENDANT moans and falls. Tries to get up. GLUOS-NIS grabs the spade from ISAAC'S hand and hits the ATTENDANT a second time on the head. He quietly stretches out flat on the floor and doesn't move. The spade falls out of GLUOSNIS' hand. Suddenly both fall into each others arms and kiss passionately.*)

ISAAC: Beloved! Your hands were the key to a deep secret, a voice from heaven, a voice of eternal love. Not understanding that I love you, I tortured your hands. Now we don't need a stone altar, dearest!

GLUOSNIS: Forever yours! (*They kiss each other.*)

ISAAC: Your lips are like honey!

GLUOSNIS: And yours! (*Finally they come to their senses.*) What will we do with him?

ISAAC (*pressing GLUOSNIS to his heart*): This is the year of peace. We should honor him.

GLUOSNIS: We really should. (*Removes himself from the embrace.*) In some opera I saw...I think "Tosca"....Light the candles. (*ISAAC kisses GLUOSNIS gently on the cheek, takes out a match and lights the candles. GLUOSNIS takes the candlesticks and places them on either side of the ATTENDANT'S head.*) Pretty, isn't it?

ISAAC: Very. He suits the flowers, the candles, the posters. Our love.

GLUOSNIS: We solved the problem, Isaac. That side and the other side—united.

ISAAC: We have united after twenty years. (*They embrace and walk to the window dreamily.*)

BLACKOUT

CONTRIBUTORS

ILONA GRAŽYTĖ-MAZILIAUSKAS is a Professor of English language and literature at College Ahuntsic in Montrèal, Canada. She received her Ph.D. degree from Université de Montrèal. Her essays and review articles have appeared in Lithuanian and English magazines and journals, such as *Metmenys, Aidai, Akinačiai, Lituanus,* and *World Literature Today.*

HEIN KÕVAMEES received his BA degree in Comparative Literature from Indiana University at Bloomington. He is in Canadian Government employment.

JUTA KÕVAMEES-KITCHING, formerly an Assistant Professor at Laurentian University, is a staff member of Simon Fraser University Library. She received her Ph.D. degree in Uralic Linguistics from Indiana University at Bloomington. Her review articles and essays have appeared in various Estonian newspapers and in *World Literature Today;* she is a coauthor of *Canadian Estonians;* and a book by Ivar Paulson, *The Old Estonian Folk Religion,* in her translation has been published by the Indiana University Press.

HILJA KUKK is a reference librarian at the Hoover Institution, Stanford University. She received her BA degree in Slavic Languages and her M.L.S. degree from the University of California at Los Angeles. Besides participating in research projects of the Association for the Advancement of Baltic Studies and the Estonian Learned Society of America, Ms. Kukk has translated five Estonian plays into English. Her original and translated articles have appeared in scholarly journals, such as *Journal of Baltic Studies,* among others.

JĀNIS PENIĶIS is an Associate Professor of Political Science, Indiana University at South Bend and a visiting professor of Latvian Studies at Western Michigan University. He received his Ph.D. degree in Political Science and Sociology from the University of Wisconsin at Madison. He has lectured extensively on topics, such as international politics, immigration, ethnicity and economics, among others. His articles have appeared in Latvian ethnic press, e.g., *Jaunā Gaita*; and he is coauthor of the book, *Nationalism in the U.S.S.R. and Eastern Europe,* published by the University of Detroit Press. Dr. Penikis has served as Director of Latvian Studies seminars in the U.S.A. and Venezuela, as well as consultant on projects supported by state and federal agencies.

HILJA PIKAT is a Ph.D. candidate in German Literature at the University of Illinois, Champaign. She has published articles on ethnic drama in *Bridging the Gap*, a monograph of a project supported by the Illinois Humanities Council for which she served as a consultant.

ANDRÉ ŠEDRIKS is an Assistant Professor of Theatre at Trinity University. He received his Ph.D. in Speech/Theatre from Southern Illinois University at Carbondale. Dr. Šedriks has acted and directed in off-Broadway, resident, and university theatres; he has been Director in Residence of the Kansas Arts Council at Wichita, as well as taught acting at HB Studio in New York. His essays on Latvian drama and translations have appeared in *Confrontations with Tyranny* and *The Golden Steed,* two anthologies of Baltic drama. He has been awarded a NEH fellowship for a summer seminar on Eastern European drama in 1980.

KRISTINA ŠKĖMA-SNYDER, after receiving her B.A. degree in English, considers raising a family her main duty. She specializes in translating her late father's works; recently she finished translating *The White Shroud,* last of her father's novels. Her translation of *Pabudimas* has appeared in *Confrontations with Tyranny.*

BRIGITA STEFFEN received her MA degree in German Language and Literature with a minor in Russian from the University of Nebraska. She has taught at the University of Nebraska, Thiel College, and SUNY—Albany where she held the rank of Assistant Professor. The translation in this volume is her first major work to be published.

ALFREDS STRAUMANIS is Professor of Theatre at Southern
Illinois University—Carbondale where he also directs the
Baltic Drama project. He received his Ph.D. in Drama from
Carnegie Institute of Technology (now Carnegie-Mellon Uni-
versity) as an Andrew Mellon Fellow. His plays—original and
translated—have been produced in the U.S.A., Australia, and
Canada. He is the author of a novel, short stories, and theatre
reviews published in French and German newspapers as well
as in Latvian ethnic publications. He is a coauthor of books,
In the World of Mārtiņš Zīverts and *Ethnic Theatre in the
U.S.A.;* editor of Baltic drama anthologies, *Confrontations
with Tyranny* and *The Golden Steed*; and the editor of *Baltic
Drama: A Handbook and Bibliography.* His essays on drama
and theatre have appeared in journals such as *Jaunā Gaita,
Journal of Baltic Studies, The Nationalities Papers,* and
Southern Theatre, among others.

JURIS VALTERS is a visiting director of the Latvian American
theatre ensembles. He received his MA in Theatre from
Southern Illinois University at Carbondale. He has translated
plays by Anšlavs Eglītis and Mārtinš Ziverts, the two major
Latvian dramatists in exile, and his essays on drama have
appeared in *Archivs* (Australia) and in *Bridging the Gap,* a
monograph of a project supported by the Illinois Humanities
Council.

A CONCISE GUIDE TO IMPROVING
STUDENT LEARNING

A CONCISE GUIDE TO IMPROVING STUDENT LEARNING

Six Evidence-Based Principles and
How to Apply Them

Diane Cummings Persellin and

Mary Blythe Daniels

Foreword by Michael Reder

STERLING, VIRGINIA

Published by Stylus Publishing, LLC
22883 Quicksilver Drive
Sterling, Virginia 20166-2102

Library of Congress Cataloging-in-Publication Data

Persellin, Diane.
A concise guide to improving student learning : six evidence-based
principles and how to apply them / Diane Cummings Persellin and
Mary Blythe Daniels.—First Edition.
  pages cm
Includes bibliographical references and index.
ISBN 978-1-62036-091-0 (cloth : alk. paper)—
ISBN 978-1-62036-092-7 (pbk. : alk. paper)—
ISBN 978-1-62036-093-4 (library networkable e-edition)—
ISBN 978-1-62036-094-1 (consumer e-edition)
1. College teaching—Handbooks, manuals, etc.
I. Daniels, Mary Blythe. II. Title.

LB2331.P425 2014
378.1'25—dc23
                                        2013049706

13-digit ISBN: 978-1-62036-091-0 (cloth)
13-digit ISBN: 978-1-62036-092-7 (paperback)
13-digit ISBN: 978-1-62036-093-4 (library networkable e-edition)
13-digit ISBN: 978-1-62036-094-1 (consumer e-edition)

Printed in the United States of America

All first editions printed on acid-free paper
that meets the American National Standards Institute
Z39-48 Standard.

Bulk Purchases

Quantity discounts are available for use in workshops and for
staff development.
Call 1-800-232-0223

First Edition, 2014

10 9 8 7 6 5 4 3 2 1

To my parents, Floyce and Kent Cummings; my favorite teacher,
Carole Flatau; and my husband, Robert Persellin,
for their inspiration and encouragement.

DCP

For my mother, Rachel Daniels, who inspired me to teach.
In memory of my brother-in-law, Patrick Mulholland,
who inspired so many to learn.

MBD

CONTENTS

FOREWORD

Brevity is the soul of wit.

—Hamlet, William Shakespeare

You have in your hand, in one compact package, a primer, a detailed guidebook to becoming a more effective teacher. In just 60 pages of main text you will find rich morsels, insights, and wisdom about approaches to improving student learning. Professors Persellin and Daniels have combed through the best ideas about effective teaching and learning, straining them down to six straightforward principles. The most recent literature on how learning works—such as James Zull on the neuropsychology of learning, Susan Ambrose and colleagues on research-based teaching, Dee Fink on course design—shape these principles. The authors also take into account contemporary theories of student intellectual development, as well as the current larger conversations taking place about higher education. It will aid you in making educated, intentional decisions about your teaching and course design—decisions based not only on hunches or feelings or previous experiences, but on research and theory.

Informed by research, the approaches and examples in this book are real-world, rooted not just in theory but also in practice. Each of the six principles has clear instructional applications, and is illustrated by a series of brief suggestions for assignments or techniques, enabling you to easily apply these ideas to your own courses and teaching. Following each principle, the authors include a short annotated bibliography of the research studies that inform these practices, allowing you to delve deeper into the literature.

The book also includes a series of written workshops on best practices, offering more in-depth examinations of key approaches to improving student learning. Rich in examples and resources, these workshops both offer insights into some of the most powerful curricular learning experiences—such as writing and community learning—as well as elaborate on more specific, classroom-based teaching techniques—such as how to develop and use rubrics, approach formative assessment and foster student self-reflection, and offer effective feedback on essays and exams.

Like good teaching, the book is constructed to actively engage the learner. This brief but powerful work does not lecture you; *it invites you to learn.* It provides opportunities for readers to engage with these ideas and approaches and then to reflect upon them. It asks you to stop and think about your own practices, your own teaching.

Toward an Intentional, Critically Self-Reflective Practice

There is an assortment of effective approaches to teaching, and how a faculty member constructs her or his course and runs her or his classroom (or lab or studio) should accurately reflect both the variety of disciplinary styles and the individual personality and identity of that teacher. There is no single "right" or effective way to teach. This book not only acknowledges the diversity of approaches to improving student learning, but also reveals a wide range of options that allow us to make those informed choices about our teaching practices.

Whether you are an experienced teacher or a relative neophyte, the information in *A Concise Guide to Improving Student Learning* will allow you to become a more knowledgeable practitioner and approach your teaching—as we do our disciplinary scholarship and creative work—in an informed, critically reflective manner.

Why Another Book About Effective Teaching and Learning?

When I first learned about *A Concise Guide to Improving Student Learning,* the question that first came to my mind was, Why? What does this book do that is different from the other books about teaching and learning? What does this work contribute to the already substantial body of research and theory about learning, of works that address approaches to and techniques for teaching?

Those of us who have ventured into the literature on teaching and learning know that, over the past two decades, it has become a discipline unto itself. The options and resources for improving one's teaching sometimes feel limitless and overwhelming, especially for faculty members who are busily engaged not only in teaching and service, but also in research and creative work. So even though this book is focused on improving student learning, it is written by and for faculty—it is written for us. The authors are well aware of their audience, all of whom live very busy professional lives.

As a director of a faculty center for teaching and learning, a large part of my work is to take the myriad ideas about teaching and learning, separate the wheat from the chaff, and share those ideas with my colleagues. *A Concise Guide to Improving Student Learning* reviews, condenses, and explains those theories and practices—allowing you, the reader, to efficiently and effectively engage with those ideas.

Michael Reder
Director
Joy Shechtman Mankoff Center for Teaching & Learning
Connecticut College

PREFACE

This concise guidebook was designed to be a resource for academics who are interested in engaging students according to the findings of peer-reviewed literature and best practices but who do not have the time to immerse themselves in the scholarship of teaching and learning. In the last decade alone, many research studies about the process of learning have emerged at the K–12 level. Such scholarship has great potential to dramatically affect teaching. Although it seems obvious that an understanding of how learning works could transform our teaching, in higher education we have been slower to engage with this growing body of scholarship. Our book, intentionally brief, is intended to (a) summarize recent research on six of the most compelling principles in learning and teaching, (b) provide applications to the college classroom based on this research, (c) include special sections about teaching strategies that are based on best practices, and (d) offer annotated bibliographies and important citations for faculty who want to pursue additional study.

The field of teaching and learning is developing rapidly, and we have endeavored to keep up with the newly emerging body of scholarship. Many excellent books are available, and we have included recent leading research as well as seminal texts in the field. We based our six principles on research studies, most of which have been replicated in multiple settings. The six principles were chosen because, in our judgment, they are the most solidly grounded in evidence-based scholarship. Annotated bibliographies of research studies are included in the chapters as examples that illustrate the principles. The bibliography at the end of the book is broader and also includes articles and resources for teaching that are not necessarily based on research.

In the sections devoted to teaching applications, we have included a diverse range of disciplines, including sciences, humanities, arts, and pre-professional programs. Most of these applications can be implemented without extensive preparation. We encourage instructors to adapt these strategies according to specific needs, interests, disciplines, and classroom contexts.

Although the book emphasizes research-based learning, we as practitioners appreciate the need for pragmatic pedagogies. For that reason we have also included special sections dedicated to best practices, rather than research-based principles. The workshops, shaded in gray, elucidate topics such as problem-based learning, assessment strategies, concept mapping, and community-based learning.

The introduction, "Knowing About Learning Informs Our Teaching," provides an overview of how we learn that includes important topics such as the definition of *expert* and *novice learners*, memory, prior learning, and metacognition. The body of the book is divided into three chapters, each of which includes teaching principles, applications, and related strategies.

Chapter 1, "Deeper Learning and Better Retention," is divided into three research-based principles: Desirable Difficulties Increase Long-Term Retention, Meaningful and Spaced Repetition Increases Retention, and Emotion and Relevance Deepen Learning.

Chapter 2, "Actively Engaged Learning," synthesizes recent studies documenting that students who are actively engaged in meaningful and challenging activities learn more deeply. The two research-based principles presented in this chapter are Multisensory Instruction Deepens Learning and Small Groups Engage Students.

Chapter 3, "Assessment," presents one research principle: Formative Assessment or Low-Stakes Evaluation Strengthens Retention. This chapter focuses on how good assessment techniques ask students to review, apply, analyze, and evaluate current and prior learning. We also include a section on assessment resources, such as rubrics and grading strategies. The appendices address aspects of course design such as creating a syllabus, presenting a successful lecture, and leading a meaningful in-class discussion.

Owing to the scope of this book, these sections are necessarily short; we have not delved into the complexities of how each of these principles is interrelated. However, we have cross-referenced as much as possible, and we hope that the bibliographies and other resources provided will guide the interested reader to a fuller understanding of each principle. Finally, we, of course, realize not every principle or strategy in the book is suitable for everyone. Moreover, there is no one teaching strategy that will provide the silver bullet for student engagement. Our goal is to provide a foundation that will assist instructors in making good choices for their pedagogical needs.

ACKNOWLEDGMENTS

W e thank the Associated Colleges of the South (ACS) Faculty Renewal Grant for supporting us in writing the pilot version of this book (Persellin & Daniels, 2012), which was distributed in celebration of the 20th anniversary of the ACS Teaching and Learning Workshop. We also are indebted to an ACS Mellon Grant for helping us substantially revise the manuscript for publication. Many people have helped us on this journey: early readers of the manuscript, Sarah Goodrum (University of Colorado, Boulder), Barbara Lom (Davidson College), Barbara MacAlpine (Trinity University), and Elizabeth Osland (Monte Esperança, Lisbon, Portugal); focus groups at Trinity University and Centre College; and the ACS Teaching and Learning Workshop staff. We appreciate the time and energy of Kent Anderson (Birmingham-Southern College), Sean Connin (Trinity University), Emily Gravett (Trinity University), Sarah Lashley (Centre College), and Harry Wallace (Trinity University), who read and commented on our final draft. A very special thanks to Robert Persellin and Laurie Davison for their support and encouragement during the writing of this book.

INTRODUCTION

Knowing About Learning Informs Our Teaching

I never try to teach my pupils anything,
I only try to create an environment in
which they can learn.
—Albert Einstein

Expert learners consider the knowledge explicitly and
separate from the present task. There is consideration
for when and where that knowledge can be used
in the future. They negotiate meaning with their
peers. They ask questions. They seek
answers and construct solutions.
—Peter Skillen (n.d.)

How can we as educators help our students remember and process information for long-term memory rather than short-term responses on an exam? How do we help students transfer their newly acquired knowledge and skills to other contexts and problems? How can we support students who are still working as novices in our more complex disciplines? In other words, how do we help our students learn? As instructors, we need to remember that our students do not think like we do, and we need to help them develop as learners.

When instructors have an understanding of the cognitive development of their students, they may be able to plan their teaching strategies more effectively. In this introduction we present a brief summary of a model for understanding student learning that contrasts novice and expert learners. To help students move along the continuum from novice to expert learners, it is important for instructors to have a framework of how memory works as well as an understanding of the importance of prior knowledge and metacognitive skills. Our intention is to provide an introduction to these topics rather than a comprehensive study of neuroscience or intellectual development, which is beyond the scope of this project. For more thorough discussions and resources related to learning and cognitive development, we refer the reader to the bibliography on page 79.

Expert and Novice Learners

Students who are new to our subject areas or lack a background in the topic think differently from students who have more experience when solving problems and learning new material. Understanding the differences between how novices in our fields think about new problems and how students who have more expertise approach them can help us teach better. Bransford, Brown, and Cocking's (2000) model of expert and novice learners, even in its most basic form as presented here, is an excellent means to help instructors think about both the challenges of developing expertise and its implications for teaching. The following list of differences between expert and novice learners was adapted from Vanderbilt University (n.d.):

1. The expert learner is able to establish meaningful patterns and organize information around content, whereas novices do not necessarily recognize these patterns.
2. Experts are fluent at retrieving information, whereas novices have to apply significant effort to retrieve information. An expert's knowledge is organized to support understanding, not just memorization.
3. Experts' knowledge is not a list of isolated facts. Their knowledge is organized around broader concepts that guide their thinking. Experts frame their knowledge within a context.
4. There are both routine experts and adaptive experts. Routine experts function well in one setting but encounter difficulty in a different setting. Adaptive experts, owing to their metacognitive skills, are able to transfer knowledge to different circumstances.

Ironically, our expertise as instructors can pose pedagogical challenges when we assume our students have our level of fluency in organizing and interpreting information. It is, therefore, important for instructors to make explicit the strategies for moving from a novice learner to an independent and sophisticated thinker. That is, instructors must help students learn both to organize and integrate new information and to think critically about their own thought processes.

Memory

A widely respected theory of how memory works was first proposed by Atkinson and Shiffrin in 1968. Their model proposes that memory consists of three separate and distinct storage systems: sensory memory, short-term memory, and long-term memory. For this reason the model is called the multistore model. According to the model, new information is received by our senses. If a student is paying attention to the input, this information is quickly converted into a type of code that is stored in a working memory. Working memory, however, has a fast turnover (up to 15 seconds) and limited capacity for new information (Baddeley, 1986). Information is more likely to move from working memory to long-term memory if it is relevant to the learner, who can then place the material into a framework developed by prior knowledge. This new information is then available to be located and retrieved when needed; however, it is more easily retrieved if the information has been reinforced. Strategies that cognitive neuroscientists and other experts (Braun & Bock, 2007; Caine, Caine, McClintic, & Klimek, 2005; Kember, Ho, & Hong, 2008) have identified as being critical to committing information to long-term memory include the following:

1. *Repeating and rehearsing new information.* An entire section of this book is devoted to this important topic (see Principle 2: Meaningful and Spaced Repetition Increases Retention, p. 12). Instructors can aid students with the process of remembering by showing them connections between new information and what they already know to help make the material relevant.
2. *Establishing meaningful patterns to organize learning.* People tend to remember patterns and meaning before remembering specific details (Medina, 2008).
3. *Allowing students time to process information.* Processing is a critical component to integrating new information into long-term memory structures.
4. *Finding relevance in the learning* (see Principle 3: Emotion and Relevance Deepen Learning, p. 15). When a new topic is relevant to learners, they are better able to anchor it in their long-term memory.

A novice learner often remembers less information than an expert learner because retention is closely linked to the relationship between the new material one is learning and material one already knows. Prior knowledge is central to a learner's capacity to make meaning from new information. Students come to our courses with beliefs and attitudes gained in other courses and through daily life. Using this knowledge, students filter and interpret what they are learning. If what they already know is factually accurate, it provides a strong foundation for the construction of knowledge. However, when prior knowledge leads to misconceptions, the latter can be remarkably resistant to correction. A professor can activate prior knowledge and pave the way for new learning by asking students to make connections and to see patterns between new information and information they already know (Squire, 2004; Zull, 2002). This also allows instructors to gauge students' understanding and correct inaccurate perceptions. A teacher can then help students determine when it is appropriate to apply prior knowledge and when it is not.

Metacognition is an important part of cognitive theory and is defined as "the process of reflecting on and directing one's own thinking" (National Research Council, 2001, p. 78). In other words, students must be able both to monitor their own process and to adapt their strategies as needed (Ambrose, Bridges, DiPietro, Lovett, & Norman, 2010). To fully develop as expert learners, students must be self-aware, be responsible, and take initiative. Instructors can help students develop these traits by explicitly asking students to evaluate their own skills, encouraging them to predict outcomes, and helping them learn from their successes and failures. When students analyze how they think, deeper learning can take place (Chin & Brown, 2000). As William Perry (1970) explained, when students move from a black-and-white level of dualism as first-year students to a more discerning relativist perspective as they mature and gain more expertise and comfort with multiple perspectives, they then start to understand that most knowledge is dependent upon context. Increasingly, instructors can encourage students to think independently and analytically and to begin to view the instructor as a facilitator in the process of learning (Moore, 1989).

I

DEEPER LEARNING AND BETTER RETENTION

Great teachers [are] those people with considerable success in fostering deep approaches and results among their students.
—Ken Bain and James Zimmerman (2009)

Deep learning involves the critical analysis of new ideas, linking them to already known concepts and principles so that this understanding can be used for problem solving in new, unfamiliar contexts.
—Julian Hermida (n.d.)

Chapter 1 examines three research-based principles for teaching and learning: (a) desirable difficulties, or requiring students to work harder in the initial learning period; (b) repetition; and (c) emotion in teaching and learning. In each section we share teaching applications. The workshops, or best practices, shaded in gray address concept maps and community-based learning (CBL).

Principle 1: Desirable Difficulties Increase Long-Term Retention

---

We often seek to eliminate difficulties in learning, to our own detriment.
—Jeff Bye (2011)

According to the pain is the gain.
—Ben Hei Hei, *Ethics of the Fathers*, 5:21 (220 CE)

5

Requiring students to organize new information and to work harder in the initial learning period can lead to greater and deeper learning. Although this struggle, dubbed a *desirable difficulty* by investigator R. A. Bjork (1994), may at first be frustrating to learner and teacher alike, ultimately it improves long-term retention. For example, the research of Rohrer and Taylor (2007) revealed that increased challenges during a math class produced better long-term performance. The authors instructed subjects how to find the volume of four geometric figures. Group 1 was taught how to find the volume of only one figure, while group 2 was taught several different types of problems. Although initially the second group performed worse in practice sessions, after a week delay they outperformed the first group on tests, answering 63% of the questions correctly compared to only a 20% correct response rate from group 1.

In the short term, conditions that make learning more challenging—such as generating words instead of passively reading them, varying conditions of practice, transferring knowledge to new situations, or learning to solve multiple types of math problems at once—might slow down performance. However, there is a yield in long-term retention. At first the learner may make more errors or forget an important process,

> but it is this forgetting that actually benefits the learner in the long term; relearning forgotten material takes demonstrably less time with each iteration. The subjective difficulty of processing disfluent information can actually lead learners to engage in deeper processing strategies, which then results in higher recall for those items. (Bye, 2011)

By forcing the brain to create multiple retrieval paths, a desirable difficulty makes the information more accessible. If we can use information in multiple ways and multiple contexts, we build many pathways to memory; thus, if one pathway is blocked, we can use another.

These difficulties invite "a deeper processing of material than people would normally engage in without explicit instruction to do so" (Bjork, 1994). However, teaching with desirable difficulties can be challenging. Learners, of course, are gratified when they feel that they are processing information easily. Instructors understandably want learning to come quickly for students and may choose the method that produces immediate results. However, as Bye (2011) states, when "instructors facilitate learning by making it easier, it may increase short-term performance, but it may decrease long-term retention." Bjork (2013) suggests that once instructors decide what they want students to remember a year after their course is over, they then think about how to implement desirable difficulties into their course. This may mean introducing an important concept multiple times in different ways through-out the semester, making the important class concepts relevant to other course material (see Principle 3: Emotion and Relevance Deepen Learning, p. 15), and asking students to analyze and produce knowledge, rather than listen to the instructor present it (see chapter 2, "Actively Engaged Learning," p. 23).

Instructional Applications

Quiz Students

Quiz students on material rather than having them simply restudy or reread it (Karpicke & Blunt, 2011; Roediger & Karpicke, 2006). Even if quizzes are low-stakes assessments, they force students to generate information rather than passively read (see Principle 6: Formative Assessment or Low-Stakes Evaluation Strengthens Retention, p. 43).

Generate Knowledge

Ask learners to generate target material through an active, creative process, rather than simply by reading passively. This could involve role playing, structured debates, puzzles, or scientific study (McDaniel & Butler, 2010; see chapter 2, "Actively Engaged Learning," p. 23).

Space Practice Sessions

Have students rehearse or practice important skills during different sessions. Dempster and Farris (1990) and Cepeda, Pashler, Vul, Wixted, and Rohrer (2006) found that when sessions were spaced further apart, students were more likely to retain material (see Principle 2: Meaningful and Spaced Repetition Increases Retention, p. 12).

Allow for Confusion

When a concept is difficult, allow students to experience and work their way through their frustration. When students are able to resolve their initial confusion themselves, deeper learning takes place.

Challenge the Reader

When learners perceive that material is more difficult to read, they tend to read it with more care and process it more deeply (McNamara, Kintsch, Songer, & Kintsch, 1996). Studies suggest that even using fonts that are slightly more difficult to read affects engagement and processing (Alter, Oppenheimer, Epley, & Eyre, 2007; Diemand-Yauman, Oppenheimer, & Vaughan, 2011; Yue, Castel, & Bjork, 2013).

Wait for an Answer

Allowing time to think between asking a question and requiring an answer gives students the opportunity to better formulate their answers and, therefore, increases the depth of answers. It also lets students know the instructor will not be answering his or her own questions.

Interleave Material

Teach several skills or concepts in the same class rather than focusing on only one specific idea.

Create Concept Maps

Ask students to create a concept map. This requires them to generate relationships based on the class discussions or readings (see Workshop 1.1: Concept Maps).

Annotated Research Studies

Dempster, F., & Farris, R. (1990). The spacing effect: Research and practice. *Journal of Research and Development in Education, 23*(2), 97–101.

In this study investigators found that spaced instruction yielded significantly better learning than massed presentations. Two spaced presentations were nearly twice as effective as two massed presentations. In many cases effectiveness increased as the frequency of the presentations increased.

Diemand-Yauman, C., Oppenheimer, D., & Vaughan, E. (2011). Fortune favors the bold (and the italicized): Effects of disfluency on educational outcomes. *Cognition, 118*(1), 111–115. doi:10.1016/j.cognition.2010.09.012

This article reports the results of two studies examining the impact on learning of a font that is slightly more difficult to read. Both studies found that information in harder-to-read fonts was better remembered than information shared in easier-to-read fonts. The struggle to read the material was thought to contribute to deeper processing.

Karpicke, J., & Blunt, J. (2011). Retrieval practice produces more learning than elaborative studying with concept mapping. *Science, 331*(6018), 772–775. doi:10.1126/science.1199327

Two hundred college students were divided into four groups and asked to read several paragraphs about a scientific topic. Each group performed one of the following learning strategies: (a) reading the text for 5 minutes, (b) reading the text in four consecutive 5-minute sessions, (c) drawing diagrams about information from the excerpt they were reading, and (d) reading the passage once and taking a "retrieval practice test" that required them to write down what they recalled. A week later all four groups took a quiz asking them to recall facts from the passage they had read and to draw conclusions on the basis of those facts. The students in the fourth group, who took the practice test, recalled 50% more of the material than those in the other three groups. The investigators concluded that by organizing and creating meaningful connections, struggling to remember information, and identifying areas of weakness, students were able to better recall information.

McDaniel, M., Hines, R., Waddill, P., & Einstein, G. (1994). What makes folk tales unique: Content familiarity, causal structure, scripts, or superstructures? *Journal of Experimental Psychology: Learning, Memory, and Cognition, 20*(1), 169–184.

Investigators asked students to generate new material by creating puzzles and other active processes related to the literature to be learned. Students who were actively involved in creating the new material remembered the material significantly better than students who had passively read the material.

McNamara, D. S., Kintsch, E., Songer, N. B., & Kintsch, W. (1996). Are good texts always better? Interactions of text coherence, background knowledge, and levels of understanding in learning from text. *Cognition and Instruction, 14*(1), 1–43. doi:10.1207/s1532690xci1401_1

The investigators examined students' comprehension of one of four versions of a text. They found that readers who knew little about the topic of the text benefited from a strong, coherent text, whereas high-knowledge readers benefitted from a weak, minimally coherent text. The investigators argued that the poorly written text forced the knowledgeable readers to work harder to understand the unstated relationships in the text.

Workshop 1.1
Concept Maps

A map does not just chart, it unlocks and formulates meaning; it forms bridges between here and there, between disparate ideas that we did not know were previously connected.

—Reif Larsen,
The Selected Works of T. S. Spivet (2010)

Concept maps were initially created to improve learning in the sciences but are now also used as graphic organizers that illustrate relationships among ideas, images, or words. These maps function as visual displays of the hierarchal organization of ideas. They could also illustrate a process or a sequence of events similar to a flow chart. By establishing relationships and demonstrating how discrete ideas form a larger whole, the maps are a way to develop logical thinking and study skills.

Nilson (2010) notes that by asking students to fill in missing sections of an incomplete concept map, these maps can serve as assessment tools (see also Clark, 2011). If students are not familiar with creating a map, demonstrate the process to the class and then ask students to work in small groups to create a simple model. If a more colorful and less structured tool fits instructional needs, a mind map can work well. Mind maps and concept maps differ in that the first focuses on subtopics of one idea whereas the second connects relationships among multiple ideas. Both types of maps can be used to enhance motivation, attention, understanding, and recall through reflecting on connections between ideas.

Several good tutorials on creating concept maps are available on YouTube:

iMindMap. (2007, January 8). Maximise the power of your brain: Tony Buzan Mind Mapping [YouTube video]. Retrieved from http://www.youtube.com/watch?v=MlabrWv25qQ
Penn State University Libraries. (2013, January 17). How to create a concept map [YouTube video]. Retrieved from http://www.youtube.com/watch?v=eYtoZRmWLBc
University of Ontario Institute of Technology, Academic Success Centre. (2011, August 30). Concept maps—A visual study tool [YouTube video]. Retrieved from http://www.youtube.com/watch?v=vuBLI6ijHHg
University of Waterloo. (2011, May 3). Three concept map tools: CmapTools, VUE, and Mindmeister [YouTube video]. Retrieved from http://www.youtube.com/watch?v=PODBS-YbRc0&list=TLaeCperJK3vA
Western Washington University, Center for Instructional Innovation and Assessment. (2008, October 7). Classroom assessment technique: Concept maps [YouTube video]. Retrieved from http://www.youtube.com/watch?v=Gm1owf0uGFM

Uses of Concept Maps

Concept maps can be used in a variety of ways in the classroom:

1. To evaluate prior knowledge. Ask students to create a visual representation of what they know about an idea or concept.
2. To demonstrate how experts organize knowledge. Build a map that shows students how an expert learner thinks. (This exercise could also help in the course-design process.)
3. To summarize reading. Ask students to map ideas about an article, the main points of a chapter, or the theme of a novel in order to see relationships.

4. To plan a task. Have student groups visualize a project or lab assignment with a concept map in order to create an overview of the steps that are involved.
5. To assess learning. At the end of a unit or course, ask students to create a map to show what they have learned.

Instructional Applications

The following are some strategies for constructing concept maps (Clark, 2011; Nilson, 2010):

1. Identify the key concepts from the lecture or reading and put each one on a sticky note on a whiteboard. Place the main concept in the center. Then order concepts with the broadest ideas closest to the main topic. Circle concepts that have a relationship to each other. Draw dotted lines to indicate links or connections between concepts. (Maps can also be transferred to paper or software.)
2. Give students a partially constructed map to complete.
3. Create several maps over time, allowing students to see how their understanding changes.
4. Construct maps with reference to a "focus question" that specifies the problem or issue as a class.

Software programs such as CmapTools, MindManager, and Inspiration allow multiple users to work on a map at the same time.

Figure 1.1 A concept map on concept maps. Created by J. Novak on Cmaps, courtesy of the Institute for Human and Machine Cognition. Used with permission.

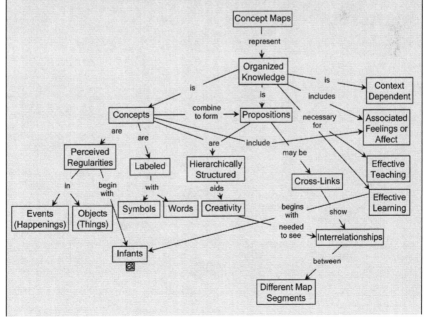

Annotated Research Studies

Daly, B. (2004). Using concept maps with adult students in higher education. In A. J. Cañas, J. D. Novak, & F. M. González (Eds.), *Concept maps: Theory, methodology, technology: Proceedings of the first international Conference on Concept Mapping* (Vol. 1, pp. 183–190). Retrieved from http://cmc.ihmc.us/cmc2004Proceedings/cmc2004%20-%20Vol%201.pdf

Two groups of graduate students were taught to use concept maps as a constructivist learning strategy. They were followed over the course of a year to see the impact concept mapping had on their learning. Results indicated that these students became significantly more aware of their own learning processes as well as their learning strategies than the control group.

Horton, P. B., McConney, A., Gallo, M., Woods, A., Senn, G., & Hamelin, D. (1993). An investigation of the effectiveness of concept mapping as an instructional tool. *Science Education, 77*(1), 95–111.

Nineteen studies were analyzed for the effect on test scores and student attitude. Test scores increased from the 50th percentile to the 68th percentile in classes using concept maps. Student attitudes toward classes when using concept maps were also significantly higher.

Zelik, M., Schau, C., Mattern, N., Hall, S., Teague, K., & Bisard, W. (1997). Conceptual astronomy: A novel model for teaching postsecondary science courses. *American Journal of Physics, 6*(10), 987–996. doi:10.1119/1.18702

In this experimental study, the astronomy students who developed concept maps scored higher than the control group on three kinds of conceptual examinations: the ability to relate concepts, a multiple-choice test of facts, and a fill-in-the-blank concept map.

Principle 2: Meaningful and Spaced Repetition Increases Retention

Repetitio mater memoriae.
[Repetition is the mother of memory.]
—Latin proverb

We are what we repeatedly do. Excellence,
then, is not an act, but habit.
—Aristotle

Repetition is essential to learning because, as noted by Zull (2002), it is one way that short-term learning is converted into long-term memory (see

p. 3, this volume). When a memory is formed, a pathway is created between neurons. Just as a well-worn path becomes a road from continued use, the pathway between neurons is cultivated by reiterating and replicating ideas or skills (Reiser & Dempsey, 2007). By repeating deliberately, wisely, and (to avoid boredom) differently, educators increase the probability that learners will store information in their long-term memory, where it can be retrieved and applied when needed. Differences, or twists, in repetition could include reviewing new concepts by playing a game, working in pairs or small groups, or writing a 1-minute paper.

Learners acquire new information more effectively if it is introduced gradually and repeated in timed intervals (Kornell, 2009; Squire, 2004). This "distributed practice" benefits long-term retention more than learning material in close succession. Although students may achieve high scores on tests taken shortly after new material is presented, this is not an indicator of long-term retention. In fact, without sustained practice over time, new material is forgotten because it loses its meaning and there is no longer reason for it to be stored in long-term memory (Sousa, 2006). As current research has shown (Cepeda et al., 2006; Delaney, Verkoeijen, & Spirgel, 2010; Medina, 2008), spaced schedules of testing are key to long-term retention. Distributed practice "sustains meaning and consolidates the learning into long-term storage in a form that will ensure accurate recall and applications in the future" (Sousa, 2006, p. 99).

Instructional Applications

Encourage Distributed Practice Through Distributed Testing

Instructors can nudge students toward distributing their practice by distributing testing. Frequent testing can provide a strong incentive for regular review. Begin or end each class session with a review exercise. Student response instruments (clickers) can also be implemented for regular assessments (see Principle 6: Formative Assessment or Low-Stakes Evaluation Strengthens Retention, p. 43).

Break Down a Skill Into Parts Before Repeating and Practicing It

When a course involves learning a particular skill, such as giving an oral presentation, interviewing, or performing a piece on a musical instrument, divide the skill into its component parts. This allows students to know which parts of the skill need their attention, and they can then design ways to practice the skill through repetition. The famous golfer Tiger Woods practiced one skill, such as hitting golf balls out of sand traps, hundreds of times in one session to hone his technique (Medina, 2008).

Schedule Daily Study Sessions
Encourage students to schedule a 50-minute study session each day for every course. Once the semester gets rolling, adjustments may have to be made since courses demand different amounts of study time. By planning ahead, students will become accustomed to thinking in terms of distributed practice rather than cramming before an exam.

Use Student-Created Learning Tools
Encourage students to review by creating their own learning tools, such as flash cards, outlines, PowerPoint slides, or MP3s. These tools allow students to repeat, self-test, and review outside class material that they will need to recall on a quiz or exam. Interactive web-based sources are listed for these tools under Principle 6: Formative Assessment or Low-Stakes Evaluation Strengthens Retention (p. 43).

Annotated Research Studies

Bahrick, H. P. (1979). Maintenance of knowledge: Questions about memory we forgot to ask. *Journal of Experimental Psychology: General, 108*(3), 296–308.

In this classic study, students learned translations of Spanish words in one session and then participated in six additional sessions in which they retrieved and relearned (with feedback) the translations. Spaced practice was more effective than massed practice, and the longer the lag time the greater the benefit.

Cepeda, N. J., Pashler, H., Vul, E., Wixted, J. T., & Rohrer, D. (2006). Distributed practice in verbal recall tasks: A review and quantitative synthesis. *Psychological Bulletin, 132*, 354–380.

This meta-analysis of the distributed practice effect examined the findings of 317 experiments. Spaced learning events, as opposed to massed learning events, consistently showed benefits.

Dunlosky, J., Rawson, K., Marsh, E., Nathan, M., & Willingham, D. (2013). Improving students' learning with effective learning techniques: Promising directions from cognitive and educational psychology. *Psychological Science in the Public Interest, 14*(1), 4–58. doi:10.1177/1529100612453266

In this metastudy Dunlosky et al. summarize studies of distributed practice with multiple variables. The overall assessment is that spaced practice is effective and works in a wide variety of teaching and learning situations. Spaced practice is easy to implement and has been used successfully in a number of classroom studies. The optimal number of days between teaching sessions varies from student to student and from task to task, but the teaching strategy of distributed practice is strong.

Principle 3: Emotion and Relevance Deepen Learning

By actively solving relevant problems, exploring current case studies, and discussing local and newsworthy events through peer interaction, debate and dialogue, relevance can bring theory to life, and provide the motivation necessary to inspire deep and sustained learning in higher education.

—Natasha Kenny (2010)

Emotion is the on/off switch for learning. . . . The emotional brain, the limbic system, has the power to open or close access to learning, memory, and the ability to make connections.

—Priscilla Vail (2010)

The link between learning and emotion is powerful; emotion gets our attention. Our memories retain charged events for long periods. In a 2011 webinar, Nilson made this connection explicit when she asked participants to recall where they were a week ago Tuesday, a year ago on June 21, the evening of their previous birthday, and the day of the 9/11 tragedy. Of course, attendees were much more likely to remember their birthdays and the 9/11 tragedy. When we have learning experiences that involve emotion—whether it is fear, anger, excitement, drama, humor, or empathy—those experiences are more likely to be remembered. What is happening in the brain to trigger this memory? When the brain detects emotion, neurons release the chemical dopamine, which is like a "chemical Post-it note that says 'remember this'" (Medina, 2008, p. 81). That Post-it note ensures that the memory will be processed more deeply.

One way to make courses emotionally meaningful is to give students opportunities to connect course material to the world around them. For a 2008 article, Kember, Ho, and Hong interviewed students in nine undergraduate programs at three different universities in Hong Kong. The authors found that relevance of course material was the most prominent component for student motivation. Indeed, students were more eager to learn new material when professors established relevance by "showing how theory can be applied in practice, establishing relevance to local cases, relating material to everyday applications, or finding applications in current newsworthy issues" (p. 249).

Creating challenging assignments that allow students to be successful can have a powerful impact in the classroom. Positive and successful learning activities stimulate the brain to reward itself through the release of neurotransmitters such as dopamine and serotonin (Medina, 2008). When positive feelings are associated with new learning, additional synaptic connections are formed. These connections create additional circuits that help place new information into a framework of existing knowledge, which allows for greater recall (Medina, 2008; Rogan, Stäubli, & LeDoux, 1997; Zull, 2002).

We know from recent research (Braun & Bock, 2007; Caine, Caine, McClintic, & Klimek, 2005) that relevant learning experiences not only motivate students but also enhance student comprehension. When students can connect new information with a larger body of knowledge, they are better able to anchor the information into their long-term memory. Having multiple connections between what they are learning and what they already know also makes it easier for students to access new information when they need it (Nilson, 2010; Zull, 2002).

Instructional Applications

Create a Positive Environment

This may seem obvious, but work toward creating a positive environment in class. Take an interest in students, learn their names, and explain the purpose of the various teaching strategies to create relevance. A positive teacher attitude and passion for the topic go a long way in making learning pleasant and successful (see Workshop A.1: The Syllabus, p. 61).

Cultivate Emotion as an Instructor

Nilson (2010) invites educators to be "dramatic, humorous, surprising, maddening" and encourages them to allow students to reflect on and write down their responses to the material. "Any emotion will aid learning by inducing more enduring changes—that is, the generation of new, lasting synapses—in the brain" (p. 5).

Recognize Where Students Are Developmentally and Cognitively

As Ambrose, Bridges, DiPietro, Lovett, and Norman (2010) point out,

> As educators, we are primarily concerned with fostering intellectual and creative skills in our students, but we must recognize that students are not only intellectual, but also social and emotional beings, and that these dimensions interact within the classroom climate to influence learning and performance. (p. 156)

When we understand our students developmentally and cognitively, we can then find strategies to shape our classroom climate in appropriate ways.

Use Role Playing

A dry text can come to life when students are asked to take on the roles. This can easily work in a history class—students could become the characters they read about—but it also may work well in a science class. For example, in a biology class students could become atoms and interact with one another.

Increase Opportunities for Student Success
Give frequent low-stakes feedback to help foster an environment where it is safe to learn from one's errors.

Remember the Power of the Spoken Word
Students can read a poem but never really hear the poem. Read excerpts of powerful texts out loud and let students hear the emotion behind the words.

Lower Student Anxiety
Reminding learners of what they already know makes them feel less anxious and gives them a positive feeling about what they are learning.

Bait the Hook
"Bait the hook" throughout the class with concise narratives related to the topic. These examples could be humorous, moving, or provocative to (re)capture the students' attention.

Develop Review Games
Create a game that will review the concepts learned and simultaneously allow learners to feel successful. User-friendly templates for *Jeopardy!* and other games can be found in Overstreet (2007).

Tell a Story
Storytelling is often used as an attention grabber that can evoke positive emotions. There is good reason why telling an engaging story is a part of nearly every culture as a means of entertainment and education. Uses of storytelling include sharing history, personal narratives, political commentary, and evolving cultural norms.

Make It Relevant
Share a photo or a newspaper or magazine clipping that connects the topic to current events, pop culture, or student interests in order to increase student motivation. Create learning activities based on topics that are highly engaging and relevant to your students' lives and that activate prior knowledge. Ask them to provide relevant examples from their experiences.

Annotated Research Studies

Ainley, M. (2006). Connecting with learning: Motivation, affect and cognition in interest processes. *Educational Psychological Review, 18*, 391–405.

Using interactive software, the researcher monitored dynamic states and behaviors while subjects learned tasks. This study demonstrates the possible relationship between student interest and alertness, attention, and concentration.

Dolan, R. J. (2002). Emotion, cognition, and behavior. *Science, 298*(5596), 1191–1194. doi:10.1126/science.1076358

This article explores the neurobiological substrates of emotion and interrogates the ways in which emotion interacts with cognition. It describes the broad outline of the brain structures that regulate emotion. Educators may find the sections on "Emotions Perception and Attention" and "Emotion, Memory and Learning" useful.

Kember, D., Ho, A., & Hong, C. (2008). The importance of establishing relevance in motivating student learning. *Active Learning in Higher Education, 9*(3), 249–263.

In this study 36 students were interviewed about motivation, and the authors found that students had less motivation if a course was based on theory alone. When students understood how the theory could be applied to the discipline or profession, they became more motivated. Guest speakers, field trips, CBL, and problem-based learning can all establish relevance and motivate student learning.

Pekrun, R., Goetz, T., Titz, W., & Perry, R. (2002). Academic emotions in students' self-regulated learning and achievement: A program of qualitative and quantitative research. *Educational Psychologist, 37*(2), 91–106.

This study demonstrates that there is a rich diversity of academic emotions. To date, most research has centered on text anxiety. The authors use a self-report instrument called the Academic Emotions Questionnaire to measure students' emotions of enjoyment, hope, pride, relief, anger, anxiety, shame, hopelessness, and boredom. The results indicate a significant relationship between students' academic emotions and their "motivation, learning strategies, cognitive resources, self-regulation, and academic achievement" (p. 91).

Shultz, P., & Pekrun, R. (Eds.). (2007). *Emotion in education.* Burlington, MA: Academic Press.

Scholars from around the world contributed chapters on aspects of emotion and learning for this book. The authors describe the current state of research on emotion and learning and posit questions for future study. The book is divided into three sections: the first integrates current theory, questions, and methodologies regarding emotion and learning; the second focuses on students' emotions; and the third focuses on the importance of professors' emotions in an academic context. Contributors have different perspectives, but in most chapters the authors have described specific emotions and their potential outcomes. The final chapter explores future directions for the field.

Workshop 3.1
Community-Based Learning

Community-based learning is experiential education in which students engage in activities that address human and community needs together with structured opportunities intentionally designed to promote student learning and development. Reflection and reciprocity are key concepts of [community-based] learning.

—Barbara Jacoby (1996)

CBL, also known as service-learning, is a powerful strategy to make the classroom come alive. It is important to remember that CBL differs from both volunteerism (which focuses on community benefit) and internships (which focus on student benefits). Ideally, CBL should be equally beneficial to the student and the community. CBL works best in the context of a rigorous academic experience. Instructors are encouraged to include a strong academic component that incorporates guiding and challenging the students to process the material and relate it to course content.

Instructors often regard community experiences in the same way they do a traditional text. CBL can function as a primary, supplementary, or optional text. In a traditional course, students are not normally graded on having completed the reading; instead, they are graded on how they demonstrate the knowledge via tests, papers, and presentations. CBL can work in a similar way—students are graded not for time they spend in the community, but rather for the quality of their academic experience.

Implementing Community-Based Learning

Instructors who are planning to implement CBL are encouraged to consider the following (Howard, 2013–2014):

- *Learning objectives.* Whether creating a new course or revising one, CBL needs to match learning objectives.
- *Role in the course.* Decide what role CBL will play in the course. Will CBL act as a supplemental activity in your course, or will it play a central role? Best practices indicate that CBL is most rewarding when it is a significant component in the course.
- *Community.* Speak with leaders in the community that will be served. Make sure the project will benefit the community in a meaningful way.
- *Time frame.* Allow ample time for planning and executing the project. Generally, it is best to have planned the project and contacted the partnering organization before the semester starts.

- *Student needs.* Students need training and orientation before they begin their project. Also, students need to understand why they are participating in CBL.
- *Paperwork.* Before students start their projects, they may need to have background checks or other paperwork done. Make sure they are informed about what paperwork they will need and can begin the process early in the semester.
- *Plan for assessment.* Have a clear plan for how students will be assessed in the academic component of the CBL project.

Instructional Applications

Sociology

In a sociology class at Colby College, teams of students met with community leaders, executives, development directors, and boards of nonprofits to get an insider's view of nonprofits. These student teams then took on the challenge of writing fundable grants for their partnering agency. The entire class also acted as a foundation, with a mission statement and parameters for giving grants. Finally, the class reviewed the grant applications and voted on a fundable grant. Through the Learn by Giving and the Sunshine Lady Foundation, the class had $10,000 of real money to be divided among the best proposals. Students were able not only to identify needs in the community and partner with nonprofits but also to understand how funding for worthy causes is given or denied. For more information see Meader (2011).

Environmental Studies

As a capstone experience, students partner with a local agency involved with environmental issues to determine a question of interest. They then collect and analyze data and present their findings to the community. The community members themselves ultimately decide how they want to proceed.

Spanish

In a Spanish conversation class, students work with children in a local Hispanic community—in an afterschool program, as tutors, or as mentors. For their culminating activity, they reflect on their service and what they learned by producing videos about the experience. They then watch their peers' videos and have a class discussion as a final reflection.

Annotated Resources

Boyer, E. (1996). The scholarship of engagement. *Bulletin of the American Academy of Arts and Sciences, 1*(1), 18–33.

Boyer makes a powerful argument for engaged learning, stating that "scholarship has to prove its worth not on its own terms, but in its service to the nation and the world." Excerpts from this article may help students understand why they are being assigned a service project and its importance in the classroom.

Bringle, R., Philips, M., & Hudson, M. (2004). *The measure of service learning: Research scales to assess student experiences.* Washington, DC: American Psychological Association.

This book provides scales to measure the impact of service-learning. It offers scales to measure such things as critical thinking, moral development, and attitudes.

Campus Compact. (2003). *Introduction to service learning toolkit: Readings and resources for faculty.* Boston, MA: Author.

This is an invaluable book for those interested in service-learning. It offers information on learning theory and the pedagogy of CBL, as well as practical guidance for those interested in implementing service-learning in their classes.

Correia, M., & Bleicher, R. (2008). Making connections to teach reflection. *Michigan Journal of Community Service Learning, 14*(12), 41–49.

The authors discuss ways in which effective reflection can be taught and offer detailed guidelines for teachers to help their students get the most out of the process.

Felten, P., Gilchrist, L. Z., & Darby, A. (2006). Emotion and learning: Feeling our way toward a new theory of reflection in service-learning. *Michigan Journal of Community Service Learning, 12*(2), 38–46.

This article stresses the importance of recognizing how dialogue between the emotional and the intellectual form the experience and methodology of service-learning.

Hatcher, J. A., Bringle, R. G., & Muthiah, R. (2004). Designing effective reflection: What matters to service-learning? *Michigan Journal of Community Service Learning, 11*(1), 38–46.

This study reports on a multicampus research survey that asked students how emotion and reflection were implemented in their service-learning courses. The results indicated that integrating an academic component with a structured reflective component significantly improved the quality of the course.

Howard, K. (2013–2014). *Community based learning at Centre College: Faculty handbook.* Retrieved from Centre College Center for Teaching and Learning website: http://ctl.centre.edu/assets/cblhandbook.pdf

This handbook is an excellent resource for professors and students who want to engage in service-learning. It also offers examples of CBL across the disciplines and has links to sample syllabi. Although the handbook offers sound pedagogical reasons to implement service-learning, it also offers practical tips—including forms students need to complete and sample contracts with partner organizations.

Jacoby, B. (Ed.). (1996). *Service-learning in higher education.* San Francisco, CA: Jossey-Bass.

This book of fourteen essays analyzes the theoretical approaches to service-learning and provides practical means of implementation.

Videos

The following are brief videos illustrating examples of CBL:

Mount Holyoke College. (2010, March 17). Community-based learning at MHC [YouTube video]. Retrieved from http://www.youtube.com/watch?v=wB5_5X4w_-8

University of Notre Dame, Center for Social Concerns. (2012, October 30). ROLL and CSC community-based learning [YouTube video]. Retrieved from http://www.youtube.com/watch?v=i4YbxoOICwA

Online Resources

Generator School Network's National Service-Learning Clearinghouse, http://gsn.nylc.org/clearinghouse

This database offers syllabi, lesson plans, and project ideas for those who want to include CBL as a component of their course.

Learning by Giving Foundation, www.learningbygivingfoundation.org

This foundation promotes "the teaching of effective charitable giving." It supports rigorous, full-credit courses with grants of $10,000 that can be distributed to local nonprofits.

Michigan Journal of Community Service Learning, http://ginsberg.umich.edu/mjcsl/

This link gives access to past and present articles from the Michigan Journal of Community Service Learning. The journal is peer-reviewed and focuses on the research, theory, pedagogy, and practice of service-learning.

2

ACTIVELY ENGAGED
LEARNING

Learning is not a spectator sport. Students do not learn by sitting in class listening to teachers, memorizing prepackaged assignments, or spitting out answers. They must talk about what they are learning, write about it, relate it to past experiences, and apply it to their daily lives. They must make what they learn a part of themselves.

—Joseph R. Codde (2006)

The one who does the work is the one who does the learning.

—Terry Doyle (2008)

Chapter 2 synthesizes research about active learning and offers ways to engage students both inside and outside class time. We pay special attention to multisensory teaching and group learning. Workshops in this section present strategies to flip the classroom, asking students to view mini-lectures before class, and provide guidelines for using both problem-based learning (PBL) and process-oriented guided-inquiry learning (POGIL).

Engaged Learning

People learn most effectively when they are engaged in a meaningful and challenging activity. As Nilson (2010) points out, "The human brain can't focus for long when it is in a passive state" (p. 4). Students need to work to solve problems so that they can both teach themselves and construct a new understanding of the material. By being challenged and actively grappling with the subject, students learn more deeply (see Principle 1: Desirable Difficulties Increase Long-Term Retention, p. 5). Recent research indicates that the benefits of using interactive engagement strategies are considerable. Hake (1998) found that test scores evaluating conceptual understanding were almost twice as high for students in classes that used engaged learning methods than for those in traditional classes. Prince (2004) concluded that the "magnitude of improvements resulting from active-engagement methods" (p. 28) is significant. In addition, Brewer and Burgess (2005) found that students are more motivated to attend classes when active-learning strategies are used as opposed to classes that are solely lecture based.

In the last few decades, educators have become aware of many active-learning strategies (e.g., role playing, group work). It is important to remember, however, that *active learning* can be defined as "any instructional method that engages students in the learning process" (Prince, 2004, p. 28). That means that tried and true methods such as asking questions, taking notes, drawing, writing, and testing are actively engaging students. Indeed, using several of these methods to teach the same material activates different areas of the brain, giving students the opportunity to learn more deeply (Nilson, 2010).

One of the keys to engaged learning is to help students realize they are not solely looking for an answer but instead are discovering a process. Discovery occurs when learners act and take control of their own learning. Initially, this process may feel uncomfortable to some students. To address possible student resistance, instructors are encouraged to make their goals for using active-learning strategies explicit. When students understand that instructors value both process and product, they may be more comfortable exploring and executing new ideas.

Annotated Research Studies

Hake, R. (1998). Interactive-engagement vs. traditional methods: A six-thousand-student survey of mechanics test data for introductory physics courses. *American Journal of Physics, 66*(1), 64–74. doi:10.1119/1.18809

Pre- and posttest data for more than 6,000 students in introductory physics courses were analyzed. Students in classes where engaged learning techniques were used scored twice as high on tests measuring concepts than those in traditional classes.

Pascarella, E. T., & Terenzini, P. T. (2005). *How college affects students: Vol. 2. A third decade of research.* San Francisco, CA: Jossey-Bass.

Conducting a meta-analysis of hundreds of empirical studies, authors found that active-learning approaches provided a significant advantage over passive-learning approaches in terms of acquiring subject matter knowledge and academic skills.

Prince, M. (2004). Does active learning work? A review of the research. *Journal of Engineering Education, 93*(3), 223–231.

In this review of literature on active learning, the author found that students remember more content if lectures include brief activities rather than focus on covering the most material. He found that although the results vary in strength, there is broad support for active, collaborative, cooperative, and problem-based learning.

Wood, W. B., & Gentile, J. M. (2003). Teaching in a research context. *Science, 302*(5650), 1510. doi:10.1126/science.1091803

Physics, chemistry, and biology educators developed and used objective tests to compare student learning gains in traditional courses and in courses that used active engagement methods. The results provided substantial evidence that students acquired and integrated new knowledge more effectively in courses that included active, inquiry-based, and cooperative learning and courses that incorporated information technology, rather than in traditional courses.

Principle 4: Multisensory Instruction Deepens Learning

Our senses evolved to work together—vision influencing hearing, for example—which means that we learn best if we stimulate several senses at once.
—John Medina (2008)

A picture is worth a thousand words.
—Unknown

Investigators in large metastudies have concluded that multisensory teaching and learning can be more effective than traditional, unimodal teaching and learning (Fadel, 2008; Kress, Jewitt, Ogborn, & Charalampos, 2006; Medina, 2008; Tindall-Ford, Chandler, & Sweller, 1997). According to Nilson (2010), "Students learn new material best when they encounter it multiple times and through multiple teaching and learning strategies and multiple input modes" (p. 4). Learners cannot focus for long in a passive state (Jones-Wilson, 2005; Svinicki, 2004). Multisensory teaching activates different parts of the brain, which allows the brain to encode a memory more deeply. The more elaborately a memory is developed, the more meaningful the learning will be because the learner has to work harder to process information.

Teaching using multiple senses is different from teaching to "learning preferences" or "learning styles." Teaching to learning styles matches instruction to the students' supposed learning style (e.g., visual, auditory, read/write, or kinesthetic). In recent years a number of studies have shown this practice to be ineffective (Delahoussaye, 2002; Pashler, McDaniel, Rohrer, & Bjork, 2008).

Approaching a concept from multiple angles and asking students to use more than one of their senses strengthen their overall understanding. Our senses evolved to work together, so we learn best if we involve several senses. For example, adding visuals to text or auditory input can lead to considerable improvements in learning (Fadel, 2008; Medina, 2008). Several studies have demonstrated that after three days participants remembered only 10% of information received via auditory input. However, when a picture was added to this input, participants remembered 65% of the information (Kalyuga, 2000; Mayer & Gallini, 1990).

Functional magnetic resonance imaging (fMRI) scans demonstrate that our brains process visual, textual, and auditory input in separate channels, allowing for "simultaneous reinforcement of learning" (Fadel, 2008, p. 13). Teaching using the visual sense leads to deeper, more conceptual learning because visuals can provide cues to better understand how concepts are related. Visuals help learners both retain information for longer periods and retrieve it more easily (Medina, 2008; Pieters & Wedel, 2004; Stenberg, 2006; Vekiri, 2002).

When engaging students in complex multisensory tasks, instructors are encouraged to give students time to reflect and process in order to avoid cognitive overload (Kalyuga, 2000). In-class writing exercises or group work or simply turning to write on the board gives students a moment to review and assimilate new learning. Moreover, the senses do not need to be simultaneously stimulated; they can be sequentially stimulated. For example, an instructor may decide to begin with a lecture and then follow with discussion or an activity. In this way, students use more than one of their senses to reinforce their learning.

Instructional Applications

Create Opportunities to Hear, Read, Write About, See, Talk About, Act Out, Think About, and Touch New Material

Involve as many senses as possible when planning teaching for enhanced student learning. Encourage students to create concept maps or mind maps (see Workshop 1.1: Concept Maps, p. 9), work in pairs or groups, free-write, take a practice quiz, or solve a problem (Nilson, 2010). Introduce a concept with one modality and then reinforce student learning by using a different modality. For example, begin class with a discussion and then reinforce student learning by adding a visual or a kinesthetic element.

Use PowerPoint Effectively
Keep in mind when creating a PowerPoint presentation that a picture really is worth 1,000 words. Instructors are encouraged to use more images and less text to make these presentations memorable and to increase retention (Mayer & Gallini, 1990; Medina, 2008; Pieters & Wedel, 2004; Stenberg, 2006; Vekiri, 2002).

Create a Barometer or Human Graph
After students have read a text or have heard a short lecture, ask them to move their desks out of the way (this exercise will require use of the whole room). Designate one end of the room as the "agree" area and the opposite end as the "disagree" area. Tell students that they will hear a series of statements and will need to decide whether they agree with them or not. To indicate that they agree with a statement, the students should stand in the "agree" area; if they disagree, they should stand in the "disagree" area. The students may also stand anywhere between the two extremes. Students must defend their position, but they can also move if they are convinced by their peers' arguments. Have students respond in this way to several statements before they return to their seats for a more in-depth discussion. This exercise requires not only that students have read the text before class but also that they listen to their peers' opinions during discussion.

Create Posters
By creating paper or virtual posters, students are encouraged to both synthesize material and use more than one of their senses. Have students examine a number of posters and then select criteria for making their own. Next, either as individuals or in small groups, they can design their posters. Once students have a basic design, allow them time to get peer feedback on their work via a gallery walk around the room. Students can then present their posters either for the class or for other students in their discipline (National Council of Teachers of English, 2004).

Reenact Material
Encourage students to bring costumes and props to class to reenact scenes from historical or literary texts or ethnographies. For example, students can wear costumes, introduce themselves as a historical figure, and take questions

about their contributions to a particular historical movement. Or, as an alternative, students can hold a debate, but they must base their arguments on their character's beliefs or writings. This requires that students have a firm grasp of the writings or actions of their character before arriving in class.

Use PechaKucha

PechaKucha, pronounced "pe/chahk/cha," is Japanese for "chit chat." The concept was developed in Tokyo in 2003 by two architects as a new way to deliver PowerPoint presentations. In PechaKucha 20 slides, each shown for 20 seconds—for a total of 6 minutes 40 seconds—are advanced automatically as the speaker presents. This practice follows the brain-friendly guideline of grouping or chunking information into short learning segments. It also requires that the presenter work to distill content to the most important points. PechaKucha is most effective when one uses more graphics and very few words on each slide. Short discussion periods should follow each presentation. Encourage students to talk with one another about the information, not just ask the presenter questions. The discussion period helps students to process the new information and connect it to prior knowledge. For more information see Jung (n.d.). To watch successful PechaKucha presentations, see www.pechakucha.org/watch.

Ask Students to Give Micro-TED Talks

Invite students to give short TED talks on assigned topics. A suggested length of time is 4 minutes. Setting a time limit requires students to prioritize their points. Encourage students to illustrate their talk with a poster that can be displayed in the room and shared via a gallery walk to review the topics. Instructors may wish to have students record a practice session of their talks and evaluate their performance before their talk is to be given. In this way students are required to practice, and they can also determine what still needs rehearsal before they give their talk to the class. (Also see strategies included in Principle 3: Emotion and Relevance Deepen Learning, p. 15; Principle 5: Small Groups Engage Students, p. 32; and Principle 6: Formative Assessment or Low-Stakes Evaluation Strengthens Retention, p. 43.)

Annotated Research Studies

Ginns, P. (2005). Meta-analysis of the modality effect. *Learning and Instruction, 15,* 313–331.

Ginns reviewed 43 experimental studies and found that students who learned from instructional materials that combined graphics and spoken texts performed significantly better than students who learned from graphics with printed text.

Mayer, R. E. (2005). Cognitive theory of multimedia learning. In R. E. Mayer (Ed.), *Cambridge handbook of multimedia learning* (pp. 31–48). New York, NY: Cambridge University Press.

Mayer presents rules for more effective use of multimedia presentations. He also advocates using both pictures and text close together on the screen, but without extraneous information.

Pashler, H., McDaniel, M., Rohrer, D., & Bjork, R. (2008). Learning styles: Concepts and evidence. *Psychological Science in the Public Interest, 9*(3), 105–119. doi:10.1111/j.1539-6053.2009.01038.x

This metareport did not find sufficient evidence to justify matching teaching to specific learning style assessments.

Tindall-Ford, S., Chandler, P., & Sweller, J. (1997). When two sensory modes are better than one. *Journal of Experimental Psychology: Applied, 3*(4), 257–287. doi:10.1037/1076-898X.3.4.257

The results of this study indicate that when participants incorporated audio text and visual diagrams into their study, they performed better than those who studied using only visual tools.

Workshop 4.1
The Flipped Classroom

The flipped classroom is a pedagogical model in which the typical lecture and homework elements of a course are reversed. Short video lectures are viewed by students at home before the class session, while in-class time is devoted to exercises, projects, or discussions.

—EDUCAUSE (2013)

In a flipped class, students watch a brief, 10-minute screencast or short narrated video—usually created by their instructor—posted on a college course management website, such as Moodle or Blackboard. During class time, rather than listening to a content-heavy lecture, students work as a class or in small groups analyzing and applying key concepts. Their preparation outside class gives more time to interact with their peers and their instructor during class. In other words, the flipped classroom promotes hands-on, inquiry-based learning and gets students actively engaged in content-rich courses. Students both contribute to and assess their own learning in a meaningful way. This pedagogical model can be used either occasionally or on a regular basis throughout the semester, depending on the needs of the instructor and the class. An additional advantage of the flipped classroom is it allows the opportunity to have students approach a concept from multiple angles, which promotes deeper learning (see Principle 4: Multisensory Instruction Deepens Learning, p. 25).

Experienced "flippers" say that the assessment step is key to the success of this strategy. Asking students to take a short quiz either before class (electronically) or at the beginning of class allows instructors to quickly gather information about student understanding and tailor activities to meet students' learning needs (see Principle 6: Formative Assessment or Low-Stakes Evaluation Strengthens Retention, p. 43). The instructor then has the choice of giving a mini-lecture in class focusing on the most difficult parts of the material, making connections, or helping students conceptualize the material when they need guidance.

Some instructors assign homework related to the video due at the beginning of class. If students get a question wrong, they must rewatch that segment of the video. In fact, one advantage to a flipped class is students can view the professor's lecture as many times as needed in order to grasp complex concepts. Students can also engage in active-learning activities that require them to apply new information. For example, they could be asked to participate in a "Numbered Heads Together" activity (see p. 35) and then journal about how they reached their answers.

Although the flipped or reversed classroom has received a lot of attention in the past few years as an exciting new teaching and learning strategy, the basic premise of preparing before class is not new. What is new is that the technology that students are already using enables instructors to create short narrated videos for students to observe and study prior to attending class. (Some examples of this technology and software are provided at the end of this chapter.)

Annotated Research Studies

Bodie, G., Powers, W., & Fitch-Hauser, M. (2006, August). Chunking, priming and active learning: Toward an innovative and blended approach to teaching communication-related skills. *Interactive Learning Environments, 14*(2), 119–135.

The research on priming and memory indicates that when students have received direct instruction before class, they are "primed" for active-learning activities that will take place in a flipped classroom and will then have better recall of facts. The prior experience with the stimuli increases learning.

Finkel, E. (2012). Flipping the script in K12. Retrieved from District Administration website: http://www.districtadministration.com/article/flipping-script-k12

In this study the failure rate of students in a high school mathematics class in Michigan dropped from 44% to 13% after adopting flipped classrooms.

Flipped Learning Network. (2012). Improve student learning and teacher satisfaction with one flip of the classroom. Retrieved from http://flippedlearning1.files.wordpress.com/2012/07/classroomwindowinfographic7-12.pdf

This article indicates that currently there is not strong scientific data indicating the effectiveness of the flipped classroom. However, 453 instructors who had flipped their classes were surveyed, and 67% found that their students' test scores were higher and 80% reported improved student attitudes. Ninety percent of the instructors said they would flip their classrooms again.

Videos

Crowder College. (2013, April 24). The flipped classroom—Crowder College [YouTube video]. Retrieved from http://www.youtube.com/watch?v=r8mMiO-u2lw

Durley, C., Janke, P., & Johnson, G. (2012, May 14). The flipped classroom as a vehicle to the future [YouTube video]. Retrieved from http://www.youtube.com/watch?v=ZpHfTO8SW7U

Wilmot, J. (2013, January 16). How to flip the classroom [YouTube video]. Retrieved from http://www.youtube.com/watch?v=IjUtSvGvB-0&feature=endscreen

Online Resources

Aune, S. P. (2008, February 21). 12 screencasting tools for creating video tutorials. Retrieved from Mashable: http://mashable.com/2008/02/21/screencasting-video-tutorials/

EDUCAUSE. (2013). 7 things you should know about flipped classrooms. Retrieved from http://www.educause.edu/library/resources/7-things-you-should-know-about-flipped-classrooms

Software

Jing from Techsmith (limited to 5 minutes), http://www.techsmith.com/jing.html

Panopto, http://panopto.com

Screenr, http://www.screenr.com/

Screencast-o-matic, http://www.screencast-o-matic.com/

Principle 5: Small Groups Engage Students

*In the long history of humankind (and animal kind, too)
those who learned to collaborate and improvise
most effectively have prevailed.*

—Charles Darwin

*Individual commitment to a group effort—that is
what makes a team work, a company work,
a society work, a civilization work.*

—Vince Lombardi, head coach of the 1959–1967
Green Bay Packers

Hundreds of studies have found that students who were engaged in group work displayed deeper learning, higher academic achievement with difficult assignments, and increased student responsibility than students who worked alone (Johnson, Johnson, & Smith, 1991, p. 98; Millis, 2010; Nilson, 2010, p. 156; Prince, 2004; Wenzel, 2000). These studies used different methodologies and included participants from different socioeconomic classes, ethnicities, and cultural backgrounds. Although the results varied in statistical strength, the studies indicated that when compared with students exposed to traditional means of instruction, students who learned in small groups "exhibited better reasoning and critical thinking skills, proposed more new ideas and solutions when presented with problems, and transferred more of what they learned in prior situations to new problems" (Wenzel, 2000, p. 295A). Moreover, engaged learning in group work has been found to be successful in motivating female and minority students to become involved in math and science (Johnson et al., 1991; Wenzel, 2000).

Group work is also called collaborative learning, cooperative learning, and peer instruction. Since the late 1990s, medical schools and the sciences have been using carefully designed team-learning methods, such as PBL and POGIL. These structured methods are devised to teach both content and writing skills through collaboration, using an inquiry-based learning approach (Farrell, Moog, & Spencer, 1999). We have devoted Workshops 5.1 and 5.2 to exploring these topics because of their complexity.

Strategies for working in small groups do not have to be highly structured to be effective. Students can play a variety of roles in group work from having specific responsibilities in more complex group assignments to simply partnering in a think-pair-share exercise. Think-pair-share (see p. 34, this volume) is easy to implement and can quickly change the energy in the room by getting everyone talking; moreover, it primes the pump for a productive discussion. To break up a lecture, instructors can divide students into groups to solve a challenging problem.

Group work can serve as a major semester assignment, a lecture break, or an assessment tool. However instructors decide to use group work, it is helpful to the students if they understand the goal. When students understand the reason behind working in groups and the instructor's expectations, they are less likely to resist these activities. (See the annotated resources for Principle 5, p. 37, for strategies for assessing group work.) In this way instructors remind students of course content, establish expectations for active learning, and help students understand why professors aren't lecturing for the entire class period. With thoughtful implementation, cooperative learning can be a powerful tool in the professor's toolbox.

Instructor-Created Groups

Heller and Hollabaugh (1992) found that instructor-created groups that were heterogeneous in ability and gender promoted better learning and development of social skills. Long-term groups, in particular, performed better with fewer issues of cronyism when instructors created the groups. Weimer (2010) suggests that instructors take into account student skills, previous experiences, and background knowledge when creating groups. One means of gathering this information is through a prior knowledge survey.

Conversely, Chapman, Meuter, Toy, and Wright (2006) found that self-selection of groups in an accounting class fostered better group dynamics, more positive attitudes toward the group experience, and better group outcomes. Hilton and Phillips (2010) found that "although student-selected groups perceived they produced higher-quality work, the actual grades assigned to the group projects did not differ between group formation conditions" (p. 26). In summary, instructors are encouraged to invite students to form their own groups for short-term assignments intended to energize the class but to create instructor-created groups for longer-term projects.

For more information about forming groups, see Weimer (2011).

Instructional Applications

Fishbowl
With this exercise students respond to a controversial claim made by the instructor, but only students sitting inside the "fishbowl" may talk. Students outside the fishbowl listen to arguments and prepare to enter. To set up the exercise, place several chairs (two to six, depending on the size of the class) in a circle in the middle of a classroom with one to three empty chairs just outside the circle. The rest of the class sits in a larger circle around the fishbowl.

When students outside the fishbowl want to talk, they must go to one of the empty ("on-deck") chairs just outside the circle. Several variations on this exercise are possible: (a) all students can be required to take a turn in the fishbowl by the end of the exercise; (b) students can be asked to prepare for the activity by writing a response to the initial claim before the fishbowl begins; and (c) students observing the fishbowl can be required to take notes for a post-fishbowl discussion.

Jigsaw

In a jigsaw exercise, students are divided into groups of four to six. During the first phase of the activity, each group reads or researches a different topic in order to become experts on that topic. During the second phase, the experts on a single topic are separated. New groups comprising students who have researched other areas of interest are formed, and students coach one another on their assigned topics. For example, in a literature class, the instructor might divide the class into five groups. One group might be assigned symbolism in the reading while another group works on imagery. Each group refines and researches one concept, and every group member is expected to become an "expert." It is helpful to have the groups devise ways of presenting their content area to others. In the second phase, each of the new groups now has an "expert" on one of the assigned topics. All students in each group are then responsible for teaching their concept.

Think-Pair-Share

The instructor poses a question requiring reflection and gives students time to think through and possibly write an appropriate response. Each student then turns to a partner and shares his or her reflections. Finally, students share their responses (and possibly the responses of their partners) with the class. A variation on this strategy is "think-pair-scare," in which students take a short quiz after reviewing with a partner.

Deck of Cards

Students enter the classroom and take a card from the deck. All students who have the same number will be in a group together that day. When group work is first used in a class, students are often relieved to be assigned to a group rather than having to find their own partners. Also, randomly assigning groups eliminates the tendency for students to work with the same people.

Case Studies or Case-Based Learning

Cases introduce students to challenging, real-world situations. Students are asked to apply what they have learned in class in order to analyze the case and to devise workable solutions. The cases should be well structured but lack an obvious or clear solution. Case-based learning is similar to PBL (see Workshop 5.1, p. 38), but PBL problems tend to be "messier and fuzzier" (Nilson, 2010, p. 187) and course material alone cannot provide viable solutions.

Numbered Heads Together
Divide students into groups of four and assign each student a number. Ask a question or pose a problem and allow the students time for discussion. Call out a number. The students with that number summarize what their group has discussed. This exercise demands that everyone in the group participate and be ready to speak (Nilson, 2010).

Send a Problem
For this exercise instructors divide the class into groups containing four or five students. Each group receives an envelope with a different problem attached. The groups discuss their problem, and at the end of the allotted time, they put their solutions into the envelope and give it to another group. The next group tries to solve the problem without looking at the solution in the envelope. After time is called, the groups again pass their problems to another group. The last group opens the envelope and then analyzes, evaluates, and synthesizes the proposed solutions in order to present their peers with best approaches and answers.

Document Sharing
Use document sharing in a program such as Google Docs to have students edit one another's writing. Document sharing also allows the instructor to track student work.

Heterogeneous Skill Groups
Mix up the skill levels in groups so that students can teach and learn from one another. For example, in a calculus class a professor assigns groups based on the amount of math students have taken prior to the class. Four or five weeks into the semester, she makes new heterogeneous groups based on students' performance in the class, and five weeks later she changes the groups again. This helps students learn to work with many of their classmates and also allows groups to change, avoiding difficult group dynamics.

Round
Form groups of four to six students. Each student has a limited amount of time—for example, 2 or 3 minutes—to express his or her point of view on a given topic. A group scribe records responses and then reports these to the class. This strategy is used to elicit a range of viewpoints and to build a sense of safe participation (Angelo & Cross, 1993).

Peer Writing in Groups
Students read and respond to one another's drafts for a writing assignment. For these groups to be productive, the instructor needs to help students set up specific procedures and objectives. For example, students need to know what they must prepare, how the groups will be organized, and what their group's goal will be. For a good resource on peer writing group guidelines, see George Mason University (n.d.).

Inkshedding
This is a technique for peer review in which students write a response to a question, news event, or class discussion. They then pass their text to another student who highlights the most striking or intriguing passages. The most often marked passages are then transcribed and distributed in the next class for discussion. See Sargent (n.d.).

Speed Dating
Form two concentric circles with chairs in the outer circle facing the chairs in the inner circle in pairs. Once they are seated, students are given a topic to discuss, and the instructor sets a timer, usually for 2–8 minutes. When the timer sounds, those seated in the outer circle move clockwise. This continues until every person in the outer circle has spoken with every person in the inner circle. This activity is especially useful at the beginning of class, as it allows students to generate ideas with their peers before discussing them in a more complex way with the entire class.

Team-Based Learning
Team-based learning (TBL) is a strategy that uses long-term and instructor-assigned groups of five to seven students with diverse skill sets and backgrounds. Students complete assigned reading and homework before taking a quiz in class (a "readiness assurance process"). Immediately afterward, students take the same quiz again with members of their group, this time working on a single answer sheet. Students can appeal answers that their team missed citing statements in the reading to support their arguments. While most of the class is devoted to small-group activities, the instructor can also build on questions raised during class discussion. Teams are awarded points for working well together. Points are withheld when a team member does not contribute. Learning how to work, interact, and collaborate in a team is essential for success in this kind of environment. The instructor's role changes from being the "expert" to facilitating the learning process. For more information on TBL, see Plank (2011) and www .teambasedlearning.org.

Annotated Resources

Johnson, D. W., Johnson, R. T., & Smith, K. A. (1998). Cooperative learning returns to college: What evidence is there that it works? *Change, 20*(4), 26–35.

The investigators examined 168 studies of cooperative learning conducted over 73 years. They found that group learning is almost 150% as effective as individual or competitive learning in acquisition and retention of knowledge, problem-solving skills, higher-level reasoning, and verbal tasks. Moreover, when engaged in cooperative learning, students demonstrate persistence, a willingness to take on difficult tasks, and higher motivation. They are also better able to transfer learning from one situation to another.

Lord, T. R. (2001). 101 reasons for using cooperative learning in biology teaching. *American Biology Teacher, 6*(1), 30–38.

This article elucidates the reasons for incorporating peer learning in classes and backs up assertions with citations from research on group learning. For example, the author cites a study published in Richard Light's 1990 Harvard Assessment Seminars report in which it was shown that students in teams did significantly better in all measures of their biology course than students who studied alone. Light also reported that students in teams spoke more often, asked more questions, and were more engaged in biology than those in nongrouped, teacher-directed classes.

Slavin, R. (1991). Synthesis of research on cooperative learning. *Educational Leadership, 48*(5), 71–82. Retrieved from http://www.ascd.org/ASCD/pdf/journals/ed_lead/el_199102_slavin.pdf

Seventy studies that compared classes taught using cooperative learning with classes using traditional methods for more than 4 weeks were reviewed. Forty-one of the studies, or 61%, found that students in classes using cooperative-learning approaches significantly outperformed students in traditional classes. This study also found that the most successful cooperative-learning teaching strategies involved group goals and individual accountability.

Williamson, V. M., & Rowe, M. W. (2002). Group problem-solving versus lecture in college-level quantitative analysis: The good, the bad, and the ugly. *Journal of Chemical Education, 79*(9), 1131–1134.

In this study one section of a chemistry course was taught using traditional lecture methods, while students in another section were asked to problem solve in groups. The two sections were given the same final exam, and the grade distribution was similar in both sections. However, 33.3% of the students in the lecture section dropped the course, and only 17.3% of the students dropped the class in the section using cooperative learning. Moreover, the students who were asked to work in groups came to office hours more frequently and asked more questions in class.

Videos

The following are brief videos of examples of group work can be found on these sites:

Chasteen, S. (2010, June 29). Effective group work in college science class-rooms: Part 1 [YouTube video]. Retrieved from http://www.youtube.com/watch?v=TzMei8KDkGI
Chasteen, S. (2010, July 1). Effective group work in college science class-rooms: Part 2 [YouTube video]. Retrieved from http://www.youtube.com/watch?v=rUSN8vHRB-A

IDEA Papers

Barbara J. Millis provides a series of resources on learning in small groups in her IDEA papers:

Active learning strategies in face-to-face courses (IDEA Paper No. 53). (2012). Retrieved from Idea Center website: http://www.theideacenter.org/sites/default/files/paperidea_53.pdf
Enhancing learning—and more!—through cooperative learning (IDEA Paper No. 38). (2002). Retrieved from Idea Center website: http://www.theideacenter.org/sites/default/files/IDEA_Paper_38.pdf
Promoting deep learning (IDEA Paper No. 47). (2010). Retrieved from Idea Center website: http://www.theideacenter.org/sites/default/files/IDEA_Paper_47.pdf

Workshop 5.1
Problem-Based Learning

Complex, real-world problems are used to motivate students to identify and research the concepts and principles they need to know to work through those problems. Students work in small learning teams, bringing together collective skills at acquiring, communicating, and integrating information.

—Stanford University (n.d.)

We only think when we are confronted with problems.

—John Dewey (1906)

A PBL model is a type of group-oriented, engaged learning in which students participate in solving complex problems and work together to find a solution. Students who are working in small groups identify (a) what they already know about the topic, (b) what they need to know to solve the problem, and (c) what steps they will have to take to solve the problem. The instructor (known as the tutor in PBL) is responsible for enhancing learning by guiding students through the learning process (Schmidt, Rotgans, & Yew, 2011).

PBL encourages students to connect disciplinary knowledge to real-world problems—and in the process, motivates students to learn. Although it originated in medical schools, PBL is now also used widely in undergraduate education. The goals of PBL are to foster effective problem-solving and collaboration skills (Hmelo-Silver, 2004).

Studies have demonstrated that PBL boosts long-term retention of knowledge; increases library use, textbook reading, and class attendance; and promotes better study habits (Major & Palmer, 2001; Strobel & van Barneveld, 2009). PBL also encourages studying for meaning rather than simply memorizing facts. Strobel and van Barneveld (2009) found that PBL was more effective than traditional approaches for development of skills, long-term retention, and teacher and student satisfaction. Short-term retention was higher in students who studied using more traditional approaches.

Creating Problem-Based Learning Strategies Within Teams

The following list provides instructors with step-by-step guidelines for using PBL in their classes (Study Guides and Strategies, n.d.):

1. Give each team an "ill-structured" problem and ask them to discuss it. Having the team reach a consensus about the issues in each of the following steps is essential.
2. Create lists of what is known about the problem and what strengths and capabilities each team member has.
3. Create a written explanation of the problem based on the group's analysis of what is known and what is still needed to reach a solution.
4. List possible solutions, ordering them from strongest to weakest.
5. Choose the best solution.
6. List actions to be taken to solve the problem using a time line.
7. Create a list of what is still needed in order to solve the problem, as well as a list of possible resources. Determine if students will need to work individually or in teams to solve the problem. If the research supports the solution and if there is general agreement, go to step 8. If not, return to step 4.
8. Have teams write the solution with supporting documentation outside class and present their findings by summarizing the problem, the process, and the solution.
9. Review the performance.

Annotated Research Studies

Major, C. H., & Palmer, B. (2001). Assessing the effectiveness of problem-based learning in higher education: Lessons from the literature. *Academic Exchange Quarterly, 5*(1), 4–9.

According to this meta-analysis of students in the sciences, there is no significant difference between the knowledge acquired by PBL students and nonPBL students. However, students who learned by solving problems in PBL classrooms were more likely to transfer their knowledge to solve new and different problems. Moreover, PBL students were more likely to perceive that their communication skills, sense of responsibility, and critical-thinking skills were strong.

Strobel, J., & van Barneveld, A. (2009). When is PBL more effective? A meta-synthesis of meta-analyses comparing PBL to conventional classrooms. *Interdisciplinary Journal of Problem-Based Learning, 3*(1), 44–58.

This meta-analysis compared the effects of PBL to those of traditional forms of instruction. Although traditional approaches were more effective for students studying for short-term retention in standardized board exams, PBL was found to be more effective for long-term retention, skill development, class attendance, studying for meaning rather than recall, and satisfaction of students and teachers.

Videos

Short videos that demonstrate PBL classrooms can be found on YouTube:

Erasmus University. (2012, December 13). Erasmus University College—Problem based learning [YouTube video]. Retrieved from http://www.youtube.com/watch?v=ITjZqK_zhcl

Hoffman, C. (2011, February 16). Project-based learning explained by Westminster College [YouTube video]. Retrieved from http://www.youtube.com/watch?v=2KzWu8mQSZo

Online Resource

Bessant, S., Bailey, P., Robinson, Z., Tomkinson, C., Tomkinson, R., Ormerod, R., & Boast, R. (2013). *Problem-based learning: Case study of sustainability education: A toolkit for university educators.* Retrieved from http://www.heacademy.ac.uk/assets/documents/ntfs/Problem_Based_Learning_Toolkit.pdf

An online toolkit for introducing PBL in sustainability education.

Workshop 5.2
Process-Oriented Guided-Inquiry Learning

POGIL is a classroom and laboratory technique that seeks to simultaneously teach content and key process skills such as the ability to think analytically and work effectively as part of a collaborative team. Students work in small groups with individual roles to ensure that everyone is fully engaged in the learning process.

—POGIL Project (2013)

In POGIL students use class time to work in learning teams on specially designed activities. Students are divided into teams of three or four, and each student is assigned a role, such as manager, recorder, spokesperson, or reflector. During a POGIL activity, students are given a piece of data and then asked questions that require them to analyze that data. Once the students have drawn conclusions about their material, they are asked to apply this knowledge to a new situation. Students must reach consensus.

The group structure requires that students both listen to and learn from one another (POGIL Project, 2013). Students take on greater responsibility for their education; they learn to rely on thinking skills rather than memorization; they improve performance skills while learning subject content; and they develop positive relationships with other students and faculty (Hansen, 2006).

Annotated Research Studies

The POGIL Project website (www.pogil.org/about/effectiveness) summarizes the effectiveness of POGIL, citing the following research studies:

Farrell, J. J., Moog, R. S., & Spencer, J. N. (1999). A guided inquiry general chemistry course. *Journal of Chemical Education, 76*(4), 570–574. doi:10.1021/ed076p570

This study compares the performance of general chemistry students who were taught using traditional methods with those who were taught using the POGIL method over a 4-year period. The attrition rate for traditionally taught students was 21.9%. Fifty-two percent of those students who finished the course earned an A or B. The attrition rate for students taught using the POGIL method was only 9.6%, and 64% of those who finished the course earned an A or B.

Hanson, D. M., & Wolfskill, T. (2000). Process workshops—A new model for instruction. *Journal of Chemical Education, 77*(1), 120–130. doi:10.1021/ed077p120

Both high- and low-achieving students uniformly performed better on examinations after the implementation of the POGIL method in recitation sessions for general chemistry.

Lewis, J. E., & Lewis, S. E. (2005). Departing from lectures: An evaluation of a peer-led guided inquiry alternative. *Journal of Chemical Education, 82*(1), 135–139. doi:10.1021/ed082p135

Investigators analyzed the effect of replacing one of three general chemistry lectures each week with a POGIL session. Students who attended the team-learning sessions achieved above-average scores on the common examinations.

Straumanis, A., & Simons, E. A. (2008). A multi-institutional assessment of the use of POGIL in organic chemistry. In R. S. Moog & J. N. Spencer (Eds.), *Process-oriented guided inquiry learning* (pp. 224–237). New York, NY: Oxford University Press.

Complementary methods were used to compare POGIL and organic chemistry lecture courses in a multi-institutional study. The studies provide strong evidence of the effectiveness of POGIL. At each institution there were twice as many unsuccessful students in traditional sections as in POGIL sections.

Videos

Jensen, M. (2013). POGIL 01–07 [YouTube videos]. Retrieved from http://www.youtube.com/watch?v=OohcFS8CmXM&list=PLHfUqastpusvJBQmabvAcaiyD72EXRdm6&index=1

The following are brief videos demonstrating various aspects of a POGIL process:

POGIL Project. (2010, September 23). Pogil Web.mov [YouTube video]. Retrieved from http://www.youtube.com/watch?v=UkH1USXy8FO

A video demonstrating how POGIL works in a chemistry class at Franklin and Marshall College.

TED. (2011, January 10). Andrei Straumanis, TEDxSanMigueldeAllende [YouTube video]. Retrieved from http://www.youtube.com/watch?v=XFYVmJYGJe8

Andrei Straumanis presents a TED talk on POGIL.

Online Resource

POGIL Project, http://www.pogil.org/about

3

ASSESSMENT

*Any time a learner tests out her ideas, she does it through action,
and that action generates learning.*
—James Zull (2002)

*Without continuous assessment, student learning is limited to a
one-shot, hit-or-miss event—maybe they get it, maybe they don't.*
—Jay McTighe and Marcella Emberger (2006)

Chapter 3 focuses on assessment of learning. We share research that documents that students demonstrate higher achievement when frequent low-stakes formative assessment practices are implemented. In our workshops we also discuss summative assessment, or graded, high-stakes work that evaluates a student's competency at the end of a unit or the course. In addition we will examine assessment tools such as creating rubrics and developing grading practices.

Principle 6: Formative Assessment or Low-Stakes Evaluation Strengthens Retention

*When the cook tastes the soup, that's formative; when
the guests taste the soup, that's summative.*
—Robert Stake (2004)

*[Good assessment techniques make] your students review, retrieve,
apply, analyze, synthesize or evaluate the material in your lectures,
classroom activities, and reading assignments as well as
their prior learning experiences.*
—Linda Nilson (2010)

Formative assessment is a range of formal and informal evaluation strategies used by instructors to modify teaching and learning activities to improve retention (Shepard, 2005). These low-stakes evaluative strategies are based on the concept that when pressure to perform is minimal, students feel free to explore ideas or admit confusion. Formative assessment focuses on student learning early in the process, before the student receives a major grade (summative assessment), after which it may be more difficult to revise teaching and learning strategies. Additionally, formative assessments are effective for creating active lecture breaks, preparing students to engage in the material at the beginning of a class, or closing the day's class session.

Professors can help promote long-term recall by regularly asking students to apply and evaluate newly presented material. For example, after explaining a concept, an instructor can ask students to transfer this idea to a new situation. When instructors require students to put additional effort into organizing and retrieving information, they foster deeper learning (see Principle 1: Desirable Difficulties Increase Long-Term Retention, p. 5).

Recent research indicates that formative assessment may be more important than summative in terms of student learning. In two projects Black, Harrison, Lee, Marshall, and William (2003, 2004) determined that high-stakes grading tends to stress competition instead of personal improvement. Moreover, feedback from summative assessments can have an adverse effect on low-achieving students who believe that they lack ability and, therefore, cannot learn. Feedback from a final exam may not be provided or may be offered too late to improve learning. However, student achievement increases with the use of practice testing or repeated retrieval and other formative assessment techniques (Black et al., 2003).

In fact, Karpicke and Roediger (2007) found "repeated retrieval to be the key to enhancing later retention" (p. 159). Practice testing does not have to be complicated or a time-consuming in-class activity: students can answer questions at the end of a lecture or take online quizzes outside class time. However, according to recent studies, to fully benefit from practice testing, students need to take these assessments during different sessions over time. The longer the intervals between practice sessions the greater the benefits (Carpenter, Pashler, & Cepeda, 2009; Rohrer, 2009; Rohrer & Taylor, 2006). (See Principle 2: Meaningful and Spaced Repetition Increases Retention, p. 12.)

Studies also indicate that both writing better test questions and asking better questions in class result in deeper learning (Anderson & Krathwohl, 2001; Black et al., 2003, 2004). Lower-level questions deal solely with recalling and remembering (Bloom, 1956), whereas higher-level questions involve evaluating and creating. Bloom (1956) designed a tiered model of classifying thinking and questioning, which was later revised by Anderson and Krathwohl (2001). This hierarchy can apply to both formative and summative assessments.

The categories of Bloom's revised taxonomy (Anderson & Krathwohl, 2001), with examples of key verbs, are as follows:

- Remembering (lowest level): Recalling, defining, listing, describing
- Understanding: Interpreting, summarizing, inferring, paraphrasing, classifying
- Applying: Implementing, using, executing
- Analyzing: Comparing, organizing, deconstructing, attributing, outlining
- Evaluating: Checking, critiquing, judging, testing
- Creating (highest level): Designing, constructing, planning, producing

Asking strong questions in class is a basic formative assessment strategy to assess retention, understanding, and application. Nilson (2010) suggests opening a discussion with a few *remembering*-stage questions (who, what, where, and when) as a mental warm-up, although she cautions instructors to avoid questions that call for one- or two-word answers. Follow these questions by moving to the *understanding* stage, which checks for comprehension and allows time to clarify misconceptions. Students should then be ready to respond to *application* questions, which require problem solving. Finally, they can *evaluate*, or critique, the strengths and shortcomings of the argument and then *create* their own model. (See also Appendix C, "Workshop on Classroom Discussions," p. 73.)

Following are a few resources for creating learning objectives, teaching strategies, and sample questions using Bloom's revised taxonomy:

Educational Origami. (n.d.). Bloom's digital taxonomy. Retrieved from http://edorigami.wikispaces.com/Bloom%27s+Digital+Taxonomy
Iowa State University, Center for Learning and Teaching. (2011). A model of learning objectives. Retrieved from http://www.celt.iastate.edu/teaching/Revised-Blooms1.html
University of North Carolina–Charlotte, Center for Teaching and Learning. (2004). Writing objectives using Bloom's taxonomy. Retrieved from http://teaching.uncc.edu/articles-books/best-practice-articles/goals-objectives/writing-objectives-using-blooms-taxonomy

Effective formative assessment must be coupled with feedback that provides information to help students progress to meet established criteria. This feedback is balanced between reinforcing positive attributes that should be maintained and constructive feedback indicating what should be modified. Feedback should be offered frequently and given to both individual students and the class. Peer feedback may also be valuable when used with a rubric or with clear guidance about how to assess and be constructive with one's classmates.

Instructional Applications

Minute Paper or Muddiest Point
In the last 5 or 10 minutes of class, ask students to write either the most important thing learned in the day's class or one to two important questions about the lecture or reading assignment. These responses can be used to start the next class in order to connect discussions between days and can also motivate students to be punctual.

Just-in-Time Teaching
Just-in-Time Teaching (JiTT) asks students to respond to web-based questions that they receive before class as warm-up exercises (Novak, Patterson, Gavrin, Christian, & Forinash, 1999). Two questions usually focus on key principles with the third question addressing more open-ended topics. Answers are due before class begins. The instructor reviews student responses and develops classroom activities based on the trouble spots.

Note Sharing
Periodically pause for a few moments and allow groups of two to three students to compare notes. This allows the students to write down information they may have missed and double-check to see that they understand the most important points in the lecture.

Student-Created Flash Cards
Ask students to create their own flash cards to test themselves and others when working in small groups. Websites and apps—such as Evernote Peek (http://evernote.com/peek), Study Blue (www.studyblue.com/study-tools), and Flashcard Machine (www.flashcardmachine.com)—are also available to create digital flash cards on computers, tablets, and cell phones.

Think-Pair-Share
This strategy can serve as an excellent in-class questioning technique to encourage discussion and to assess learning. Students reflect on a question (think), discuss possible answers with another student (pair), and share responses with the class (share) (see p. 34). Think-pair-share can alternately

be presented as "think-pair-scare," with the "scare" being a quiz. Variations on this strategy include asking students to reach a consensus, which they either turn in or share with the class.

Pre- and Post-Assessment
Devise questions for students to answer at the beginning of the unit (or class) that will inform instructors about student knowledge and skill level as well as reveal their underlying assumptions about the material. Ask the same questions at the end of the unit so that student and instructor alike can determine how their knowledge and perceptions have changed.

Scratch-Off Sheets
The immediate feedback assessment technique (IF-AT) uses a multiple-choice form much like a lottery ticket. Students scratch off their answer to a question on the form. If the response is correct, a star appears within the scratched-off rectangle. Students can also work in small groups to come to a consensus on the correct answer. (For more information about IF-AT, see www.epsteineducation.com/home/about/.)

Background Knowledge Probe
Students' prior knowledge can be evaluated on the first day of class or before introducing a new unit by using a few short-answer or multiple-choice questions. In the next class, share the results with students and explain how their current knowledge can affect them as learners.

Knowledge Survey
Instead of asking students to answer questions, a knowledge survey measures students' confidence in their ability to answer questions accurately. The Cornell University Center for Teaching Excellence provides a valuable website on knowledge surveys (see Cornell University, 2013).

Misconception/Preconception Check
Checking student misconceptions or preconceptions is useful in classes that deal with potentially contentious or sensitive material. Create a brief questionnaire to determine problematic assumptions that may interfere with student learning.

Pick Your Poison
Ask students to write test questions for their next exam. Share the questions with the class. Let students know the best questions will be included on the next exam.

Peer- and Self-Assessment

For group assignments, ask students to complete and submit a confidential form used to assess how well they and other members of their group met particular expectations (that are clearly noted in the assignment). Examples include meeting deadlines, providing feedback, and dividing the workload. The information provided does not have to be part of the students' grades, but be sure to give out these forms at the start of the project in order to preempt common problems that can arise during group work, such as poor division of labor.

What You Know, What You Want to Know, and What You Learned

A "what you know, what you want to know, and what you learned" (KWL) chart helps activate prior knowledge and prime the pump for student learning. The chart has three columns. Before beginning a reading assignment, the students fill out the first two columns of the chart (*K*, for what the students already know, and *W*, for what the students want to know). After reading the assignment, students fill in the third column, *L*, for what they learned on completion of the assignment. A fourth column, *C*, can be added to address what students still find confusing (KWLC). The KWL(C) chart both motivates students and gives the instructor insight into students' prior and developing knowledge (University of Illinois Online Network, n.d.).

Classroom Response Systems

Use electronic classroom response systems, such as iClickers, or the students' own smartphones to assess how well students understand the reading at the beginning of class or the material discussed at the middle or end of class. For more information about classroom response systems, see *Agile Learning* (http://derekbruff.org/?cat=122).

Low-Tech Clickers

Create large flash cards by folding a piece of paper into four quadrants, each with a unique color or letter that corresponds to an answer to a question. Students are instructed to answer a question by displaying the appropriate color or letter under their chin. This allows the instructor to quickly scan the room to assess understanding of the concept. As a simple alternative, students can display 1, 2, 3, or 4 fingers under their chin to correspond to A, B, C, or D of a multiple-choice question.

Four-Question Technique

Dietz-Uhler and Lanter (2009) found students' quiz scores improved when they were asked the following four questions about an in-class activity:

1. What is one important concept, research finding, theory, or idea in psychology that you learned while completing this activity?
2. Why do you believe that this concept, research finding, theory, or idea in psychology is important?
3. Can you apply what you have learned from this activity to some aspect of your life?
4. What question(s) has the activity raised for you, and what are you still wondering about?

Waiting for an Answer

While not a specific assessment technique, waiting for an answer after posing a question can strengthen the assessment process. Given time to think about their response, students can better formulate answers. In addition, they are more likely to participate in classroom discussions when given adequate time to think about responses.

ConcepTests

Eric Mazur (1997) developed ConcepTests to introduce active-learning strategies into a physics lecture without having to significantly restructure his classes. These tests, a variation of think-pair-share, ask students to individually answer multiple-choice questions. After they have formulated their answers, students work in groups following a protocol that can be adapted to the needs of the professor. For further details and videos, see McConnell (2012).

Critical Incident Questionnaire

A critical incident questionnaire (CIQ) is a one-page form distributed to students at the end of class each week. It is composed of five questions asking students to recall details about events that happened in the class that week. The CIQ encourages students to focus on specific, concrete discussions and events. For more information about CIQs, see Brookfield (2013).

Annotated Research Studies

Gier, V. S., & Kriener, D. S. (2009). Incorporating active learning with Power-Point–based lectures using content-based questions. *Teaching of Psychology, 36*(2), 134–139.

An experimental group of psychology students received handouts of slides from PowerPoint lectures plus practice test questions generated from these presentations. The control group, a second section of the same class taught by the same instructor, received the PowerPoint lecture slides and the hand-outs and then met in small groups for 30-minute discussions but were not provided the practice test questions. Results indicated that the experimental group with the practice test questions performed significantly better on the unit and final exams than the control group.

Higgins, R., Hartley, P., & Skelton, P. (2002). The conscientious consumer: Reconsidering the role of assessment feedback in student learning. *Studies in Higher Education, 27*(1), 53–64.

This article reports the findings of a 3-year research project that investigated the impact of student assessment and feedback in higher education. Findings indicated that formative assessment feedback was key in students' learning deeply.

Karpicke, J., & Blunt, J. (2011). Retrieval practice produces more learning than elaborative studying with concept mapping. *Science, 331*(6018), 772–775. doi:10.1126/science.1199327

This study involving 200 college students found that taking a practice test before an exam better prepared students than other methods of studying—including repetition and concept mapping. Students were divided into four groups and asked to read several paragraphs about a scientific topic. Each group performed one of the following learning strategies: (a) reading the text for 5 minutes, (b) reading the text in four consecutive 5-minute sessions, (c) drawing diagrams about information from the excerpt they were reading, and (d) reading the passage once and taking a "retrieval practice test" that required them to write down what they recalled. A week later all four groups took a quiz asking them to recall facts from the passage they had read and to draw conclusions on the basis of those facts. Students in the fourth group, who took the practice test, recalled 50% more of the material than those in the other three groups. Investigators concluded that by organizing and creating meaningful connections, struggling to remember information, and identifying areas of weakness, students were able to better recall information.

Lyle, K. B., & Crawford, N. A. (2011). Retrieving essential material at the end of lectures improves performance on statistics exams. *Teaching of Psychology, 38*(2), 94–97.

The authors explored what they call the PUREMEM (pronounced "pure mem," pure memory, or practicing unassisted retrieval to enhance memory for essential material) technique. They found that students had higher exam scores when they were asked to respond to questions on new material at the end of their stats class. Exam scores were significantly higher in the course section that was taught using the PUREMEM strategies than in the section taught without them.

McDaniel, M. A., Howard, D. C., & Einstein, G. O. (2009). The read-recite-review study strategy: Effective and portable. *Psychological Science, 20*(4), 516–522.

Two groups of engineering students were tested on recall of reading materials immediately and then again after a one-week delay. The first group reviewed the material by taking multiple-choice and short-answer practice tests. The second group reread the material and took notes on the information. The members of the first group, who had taken the practice tests, performed better both immediately and after the one-week delay.

McDaniel, M. A., Wildman, K. M., & Anderson, J. L. (2012). Using quizzes to enhance summative-assessment performance in a web-based class: An experimental study. *Journal of Applied Research in Memory and Cognition, 1*, 18–26.

In a web-based college class, core concepts were quizzed in practice tests with multiple-choice and short-answer questions, while other concepts were not. Multiple attempts on each practice test were encouraged, and feedback was available after each. The practice tests enhanced exam performance significantly when the questions were worded identically but also nominally when worded differently.

Roediger, H. L., Agarwal, P. K., McDaniel, M. A., & McDermott, K. B. (2011). Test-enhanced learning in the classroom: Long-term benefits from quizzing. *Journal of Experimental Psychology: Applied, 17*(4), 382–395. doi:10.1037/a0026252

The authors incorporated online practice tests into a cognitive psychology undergraduate lecture course. With the addition of these tests to the course, class performance improved according to several criteria relative to prior semesters when practice tests were not used. Practice tests were found to be a practical way to help students learn and retain the course material, without taking class time.

Videos

Western Washington University, Center for Instructional Innovation. (2008, April 17). Using assessment to improve instruction [YouTube video]. Retrieved from http://www.youtube.com/watch?v=BZ3USs16J3Y

Xeriland, T. (2012, March 12). Formative assessment/evaluation [YouTube video]. Retrieved from http://www.youtube.com/watch?v=cvXS2x3UhQU

Workshop 6.1
Grading, Summative Assessment, and High-Stakes Evaluation

---

*Let us not judge our students simply on what they know.
Rather let them be judged on what they can generate
from what they know—how well they can leap
the barrier from learning to thinking.*

—Jerome Bruner (1961)

Feedback or knowledge of results is the lifeblood of learning.

—Derek Rowntree (1987)

Summative assessments are recorded judgments about student performance. Techniques for summative assessment include papers, exams, portfolios, projects, laboratory notebooks, artistic performances, in-class demonstrations, journals, homework, problem sets, reports, clinical experiences, research projects, case studies, posters, and exhibits. Some of these techniques can also be used as formative or low-stakes assessment, but the focus in this workshop is on summative assessment. Instructors are encouraged to vary their assessment strategies, allowing students to demonstrate learning in multiple ways over time (Wiggins & McTighe, 2005).

When considering summative assessment strategies, Wiggins and McTighe (2005) advocate backward design or planning the learning outcomes before developing assessment techniques. The backward design model focuses on beginning the planning process by identifying the results desired at the end of the course. The instructor then works backward "to develop instruction rather than the traditional approach, which begins with defining what topics need to be covered" (Wiggins, 2005) and creating a syllabus from these topics.

As instructors are planning evaluation of learning in a course, Wiggins and McTighe (2005, p. 146) encourage them to consider the following:

1. What do they want students to learn by the conclusion of this course?
2. What would count as evidence of successful learning?
3. What specific characteristics in student responses, products, or performances demonstrate successful learning?
4. Do results give a clear picture of the students' understanding of the course goals?

Assessments of learning should be made early and often and should include both formative and summative assessments to give students more feedback about their learning. Myers and Myers (2007) compared two sections of statistics with the same content and instructor. The control group had only a midterm and final, whereas the experimental section had biweekly exams and the same final. At the end of the semester, the experimental section, which received regular feedback via multiple summative assessments throughout the semester, scored 15% higher on the final exam. Moreover, this group had significantly fewer withdrawals and ranked the course and instructor significantly higher than the control group did.

Workshop 6.1A
Creating Assessment Tools

Developing criteria for assessment can do the following:

- Help determine what to teach and how to teach it
- Communicate early expectations to students about how their work will be evaluated
- Save the instructor time
- Make grading more uniform and fair

To minimize student confusion about grades remember the following:

- Include grading policies and procedures in your syllabus (see Workshop A.1: The Syllabus, p. 61)
- Remind students of grading criteria when both assigning work and returning graded work
- Minimize in-class discussion of grades and instead concentrate on the course's learning objectives (Vanderbilt University, n.d.)

Writing Test Questions

Ideally, some of the test questions will be written before the course begins while determining what students need to learn and what evidence will be needed to demonstrate knowledge has been attained. Include both formative and summative assessments when planning courses. Most formative preparatory assignments, quizzes, or homework may be ungraded, pass/fail, or check/check-plus (see Principle 6: Formative Assessment or Low-Stakes Evaluation Strengthens Retention, p. 43).

Immediately after teaching material in class, review the test questions created before the course began. This is an excellent time to edit previously designed questions for clarity and emphasis. Then write additional questions based on recent instruction and course objectives. Consider including a variety of types of questions based on course objectives, such as true/false, matching, multiple-choice, fill-in-the-blank, and essay questions. In addition to assessing factual information, multiple-choice test questions can also assess higher-order thinking skills (Bloom, 1956; see the categories of Bloom's revised taxonomy, p. 45) if based on a realistic stimulus, such as a new scenario, table, graph, or quotation. The following are excellent resources about creating multiple-choice questions:

Brigham Young University, Faculty Center. (2001). 14 rules for writing multiple-choice questions. Retrieved from http://testing.byu.edu/info/handbooks/14%20Rules%20 for%20Writing%20Multiple-Choice%20Questions.pdf
Burton, S. J., Sudweeks, R. R., Merrill, P. F., & Wood, B. (1991). *How to prepare better multiple-choice test items: Guidelines for university faculty.* Retrieved from Brigham

Young University Testing Center website: http://testing.byu.edu/info/handbooks/betteritems.pdf

Vanderbilt University, Center for Teaching. (n.d.). Writing good multiple choice test questions. Retrieved from http://cft.vanderbilt.edu/teaching-guides/assessment/writing-good-multiple-choice-test-questions/

Using Portfolio Assessments

When using student portfolios for assessment purposes, remember the following:

- Student portfolios are collections of their work that represent their progress in a class or program.
- Examples of students' work can show their range of skills and abilities and can be used to show development and growth.
- Effective portfolios can be electronic or hard copy.

Online Resources

Bruff, D. (2009–2010). Multiple-choice questions you wouldn't put on a test: Promoting deep learning using clickers. *Essays on Teaching Excellence, 21*(3). Retrieved from http://podnetwork.org/content/uploads/V21-N3-Bruff.pdf

Harvard University, Derek Bok Center for Teaching and Learning. (2006). Grading papers. Retrieved from http://isites.harvard.edu/fs/html/icb.topic58474/GradingPapers.html

Jacobs, L. (n.d.). *How to write better tests: A handbook for improving test construction skills.* Retrieved from Indiana University–Bloomington website: http://www.indiana.edu/~best/pdf_docs/better_tests.pdf

Reiner, C., Bothell, T., Sudweeks, R., & Wood, B. (2002). *Preparing effective essay questions: A self-directed workbook for educators.* Stillwater, OK: New Forums Press. Retrieved from Brigham Young University Testing Center website: http://testing.byu.edu/info/handbooks/WritingEffectiveEssayQuestions.pdf

Teaching Effectiveness Program. (2013, May 16). Writing multiple-choice questions that demand critical thinking. Retrieved from University of Oregon Teaching and Learning Center website: http://tep.uoregon.edu/resources/assessment/multiplechoicequestions/mc4critthink.html

University of Washington, Center for Teaching and Learning. (n.d.). Constructing tests: Essay questions. Retrieved from http://www.washington.edu/teaching/constructing-tests/#essayquestions

Vanderbilt University, Center for Teaching. (n.d.). Grading student work. Retrieved from http://cft.vanderbilt.edu/teaching-guides/assessment/grading-student-work/

Workshop 6.1B
Constructing Rubrics

One way to measure student performance against a predetermined set of criteria is to create a rubric—a scoring scale that contains criteria for a task and appropriate levels of performance. "A rubric allows for standardized evaluation according to specified criteria to make evaluating simpler and more transparent in a reliable, fair, and valid manner. It can give students clear feedback about their performance" (Kappa Omicron Nu Honor Society, 2013). A rubric can also save the instructor time in grading. While it is a summative assessment, it can also be used as a formative assessment during revision of a project or document (Mueller, 2012).

An online tutorial for creating a rubric is available from University of Colorado–Denver (2006). This resource presents a step-by-step process for creating rubrics, criteria for judging rubrics, and examples of different types of rubrics.

Steps for Developing a Rubric

When developing effective rubrics, instructors are encouraged to consider the following steps (University of Colorado–Denver, 2006):

1. Determine the purpose of the assignment and what students should learn. Will students receive a grade based on the rubric, or will the feedback be formative only?
2. Determine what type of rubric will be created. An analytic rubric breaks down a complex project into individual components with each skill or component scored separately. A holistic rubric, on the other hand, is used to make an overall judgment on a minor assignment with feedback about a learning task with a single score.
3. Create criteria for the project by determining what students should learn from the task. How will they demonstrate that they have learned the task? What are characteristics of the final product? Are the criteria observable and measurable?
4. Design the rating scale for the rubric. A 2-point, or all-or-nothing, checklist simply indicates whether the project met or did not meet standards. To provide more detailed feedback, use a 4- or 5-point rating scale.
5. Write performance descriptors for each scale point. These descriptors should be observable and measurable behaviors, should use parallel language with each point, and should indicate the degree to which standards are met.
6. Double-check the new rubric for consistency and effective assessment of the task. After using the rubric with student projects, refine it to make it even more effective.

Undergraduate Research Paper Rubric

Undergraduate research is becoming more important in higher education. Clear, inquiry-based learning and scholarship promote student learning. The standards listed in Table 3.1 describe effective research papers.

TABLE 3.1
Rubric for Evaluating Undergraduate Research Papers

Standards	5–4 Exemplary	3–2 Satisfactory	1–0 Unacceptable	Score	Weight	Total Score
Abstract	Clearly states problem and question to be resolved; clearly summarizes method, results, and conclusions	Summarizes problem, method, results, and conclusions but lacks some details	Is vague about the problem; does not provide a summary of the whole project		X 2	
Introduction	Provides background research on the topic and summarizes important findings from the review of the literature; describes problem to be solved; justifies the study; explains the significance of the problem to an audience of nonspecialists	Provides background research into the topic and describes the problem to be solved	Provides background research on the topic but does not describe the problem to be solved; insufficient or nonexistent explanation of details for nonspecialists		X 1	
Discussion	Addresses the topic with clarity; organizes and synthesizes information; draws conclusions	Addresses the topic; lacks sub-stantive conclusions; sometimes digresses from topic of focus	Presents little to no clarity in formulating conclusions or organization		X 2	
Summary	Presents clear recommendations or implications for future research	Presents a logical explanation for findings	Does not adequately explain findings		X 2	
Mechanics and Documentation	Examines paper for accuracy of grammar, spelling, and writing mechanics; compares text with documentation to ensure accuracy of sources	Demonstrates an understanding of grammar, spelling, writing mechanics, and appropriate documentation.	Has errors that obscure meaning of content or add confusion; neglects important sources or documents few to no resources		X 1	

Note. We gratefully acknowledge permission to share this rubric, created by Dorothy I. Mitstifer, Kappa Omicron Nu Honor Society, www.kon.org/contact.html.

Online Resources

General Education Critical Thinking Rubric (Northeastern Illinois University), http://cft
.vanderbilt.edu/files/Rubric-Critical-Thinking-NE-Illinois.pdf

Georgia State University, Center for Instructional Innovation, http://cii.gsu.edu/writing-
across-the-curriculum/resources/assignments-syllabi-rubrics/

Indiana University–Purdue University Indianapolis, https://sites.google.com/site/iupuinca
2012/Home/creating-rubrics

iRubric, http://www.rcampus.com/indexrubric.cfm

National Institute for Learning Outcomes Assessment, http://www.learningoutcomeassess
ment.org/Rubrics.htm

Rubric for Opinion Paper (Derek Bruff), http://cft.vanderbilt.edu/files/Rubric-Opinion-
Paper-DB.pdf

Rubric for Research Paper (Winona State), http://cft.vanderbilt.edu/files/Rubric-Research-
Paper-Winona-State.pdf

Rubric Samples for Higher Education (Kappa Omicron Nu Honor Society). http://rubrics
.kappaomicronnu.org/contact.html

Valid Assessment of Learning in Undergraduate Education (VALUE), http://www.aacu.org/
value/rubrics/index_p.cfm?CFID=47221224&CFTOKEN=21204686

Workshop 6.1C
Tips for Grading Papers and Essay Exams

The following suggestions may be helpful when reading essays and grading papers:

Create assignments that have well-defined objectives for assessment so students understand what they are asked to do.

Grade in a pleasant place, free from distraction. If grading is a semipleasant activity done in comfortable surroundings, it will not be quite as painful.

Read 5 or 10 papers or exams before making any marks at all. Assign preliminary grades on sticky notes. Place these notes in order from best to worst and determine grading scheme from there.

Establish a grading schedule. Determine an overall schedule and set a timer for each paper. Use a time limit as an average because some papers and exams may take longer than others. Grade no more than 20 pieces of student work at a time to avoid burnout and lack of attention to detail.

Put potentially plagiarized papers in a pile and check them all at once. Checking for plagiarism can be time consuming. Put suspicious papers in a pile to be examined later. When dealing with these papers, check Google or Google Scholar first. Take the oddest phrase and put it in quotes.

Restrict comments to those that students can use for future improvement. Spend more time on providing guidance for students for future work rather than on grading itself.

Devote time to important issues—such as the thesis statement and the paper's strengths and weaknesses—first. Final comments should prompt further inquiry by students instead of providing them with answers (Vanderbilt University, n.d.).

Do not correct grammar/spelling on each page. Trying to fix mistakes or to highlight the errors on each page can be time consuming. Circle and fix offending words in the first paragraph or on the first page. Then write a note in the margin encouraging the student to make similar changes in the paper and resubmit. Students do not tend to learn from comments made on written work after they have completed the paper and have received a grade (Semke, 1984).

Have students give feedback to each other. This practice will save the instructor time commenting on mistakes that could have been caught by a peer. A rubric can be particularly helpful when peer editing as students may initially be reluctant to give less than positive feedback to a peer.

Don't waste time on careless student work. Ask students to complete a checklist and attach it to their papers before submission for grading. Items on the checklist could include revising, proofreading, and asking for peer feedback. This checklist can serve as a good reminder that basic issues should be addressed before a student submits a paper (Walvoord & Anderson, 1998).

Provide students with a guide for grading. Shaw (1984), for example, states that students should know that if they can answer no to any of the following four questions, the grade for their paper will be lowered significantly:

- Does the paper have a thesis?
- Does the thesis address itself to an appropriate question or topic?
- Is the paper free from long stretches of quotations and summaries that exist only for their own sakes and remain unanalyzed?
- Is the paper largely free of basic grammatical errors?

Ask students to correct their tests (perhaps to increase their grade) so that they can learn from their mistakes. Allowing test corrections may save time grading because the professor need give only a little feedback for wrong answers. The corrections may not take much time to grade since there is a higher likelihood that the answers will be mostly correct.

Provide video feedback on grading. Personalized feedback using video can also be helpful. It can be more personal to view an instructor discussing a paper rather than reading notes in the margin. It can also save the instructor time. Instructors can take a digital picture of a student paper, convert it to a PDF, write comments on it, and then record a video with verbal comments. Before meeting with students, ask them to view their personalized feedback video. Several apps are available to create these videos, including ScreenChomp (www.techsmith.com/screenchomp.html) and Camtasia (www.techsmith.com/camtasia.html). A short explanatory video is available on YouTube:

Spencer, D. (2012, March 30). Personalized feedback with ScreenChomp [YouTube video.] Retrieved from http://www.youtube.com/watch?v=igp7rHZRg4M&feature=youtu.be

Workshop 6.2
Soliciting Midsemester Student Feedback to Improve a Course

---

*While knowing thyself is useful, it's also useful to
know what your students are thinking.*
—Brian Croxall (2012)

Instructors are encouraged to solicit student feedback about the course during the semester. This process can either be informal and individual or involve the institution's teaching center. Students take more seriously the opportunity to give their instructors midterm feedback than they do opportunities for end-of-the-semester feedback because they stand to benefit more from the earlier requests (Nilson, 2010). Instructors then have the opportunity to explain why they are making some requested changes and not others. Instructors who provide reasons for their decisions demonstrate that they are listening to student concerns and can often make a difference in class climate and the learning environment (Lewis, 2001). (See Principle 3: Emotion and Relevance Deepen Learning, p. 15.) Moreover, research has found that these evaluations have resulted in significantly higher student evaluations at the end of the term (Cohen, 1980).

Instructional Applications

Midcourse Evaluation
After the fourth or fifth week of classes, ask students what is working and what improvements need to be made in the course to help them learn more effectively. The response rate will be higher if this evaluation takes place during class. Of course, these student evaluations should be anonymous. Students will be able to provide better feedback if they have specific questions to answer, for example, "What do you think is going well in this course?" or "What changes would you like to see to facilitate your learning?" After reading the evaluations, summarize them for the students and discuss plans for implementing or not implementing their suggestions. Finally, talking with a colleague about these evaluations can also be helpful and can provide another perspective.

Small-Group Instructional Diagnosis
Small-group instructional diagnosis (SGID) "generates feedback from midterm small-group discussion among students about a course. Students offer suggestions to solving problems in instruction for the instructor's consideration" (Clark & Redmond, 1982, p. 2). This technique allows the instructor to gather impartial feedback from students. SGIDs are most effective if they are conducted before the middle of the semester, allowing the instructor time to make necessary changes. This process requires asking a facilitator to meet with students to collect honest feedback. Teaching and learning centers can be an excellent resource, but colleagues from outside the department or institution can also serve as

outside interviewers. The interviewer should divide students into groups and ask groups to respond to questions such as, What is working in the class? What is not working? What suggestions can be offered to improve the class? The outsider then polls the group as a whole and focuses on consensus and solutions rather than concerns (Cook-Sather, 2009; Sorenson, 2001). Later, the facilitator discusses students' suggestions and concerns with the professor. However, for this protocol to work, students must be assured that their anonymity will be preserved.

Public Midterm Evaluations Using Google Docs

Midsemester, Croxall (2012) modified settings in a Google doc to allow students to edit the document and view one another's edits. He then asked them to respond anonymously to two brief prompts in the document in class: "What is working?" and "What could be done better?" He wanted students to know what their peers thought were strengths and weaknesses of the class. Because the comments were "public," the students could then hold him accountable to respond to them. Croxall also found that students wrote more in response to open-ended questions when they could use a keyboard than when they had to write by hand.

Focus/Advisory Groups

In a large class, the instructor meets every few weeks with 6–10 randomly chosen students to talk about how the course is going. Do more listening than talking in these meetings. Some colleges and universities have teaching and learning centers that can facilitate these meetings.

Appendix A

COURSE DESIGN WORKSHOPS

Workshop A.1
The Syllabus

If you don't know where you are goin',
you will probably not wind up there.
—Forrest Gump, *Gumpisms* (Groom, 1994)

A syllabus can be many things, but faculty should not neglect its
power to communicate important messages and motivate and
set high standards. In addition to serving as a contract with
students and a way to clarify goals of the course, a syllabus
is students' first contact with you and the course material.
—José Bowen (2012)

The syllabus may be the first statement that students encounter in a class. It gives students a message not only about the professor but also about the goals of the course. For example, when Ken Bain (2004), author of *What the Best College Teachers Do*, is planning a syllabus, he asks himself the following questions:

- What big questions will my course help students answer?
- What skills, abilities, or qualities will my course help them develop?
- How will I encourage my students' interest in these questions and abilities?
- What reasoning abilities must students have or develop to answer the questions that the course raises?
- What mental models are students likely to bring with them that I will want them to challenge?
- What information will my students need to understand in order to answer the important question of the course? How will they best obtain that information?

- How will I share the intellectual and professional standards I will be using in assessing students' work? Why do I use those standards? How will I help students learn to assess their own work using those standards?

Bain develops his syllabus from the answers to these questions. Instead of designing a syllabus solely around content topics, he uses the syllabus as a tool to determine how he can achieve his course goals.

Bain's questions are congruent with Wiggins and McTighe's (2005) method of backward design. They advocate creating a syllabus, as well as a course, in three phases, using the following backward design process:

1. Identify desired results. At the end of the term, what should students know, understand, and be able to do?
2. Determine assessment evidence. What projects or other assessment methods will be used for students to demonstrate their progress in meeting learning objectives?
3. Plan learning experiences and instruction. What assignments, questions, and strategies will be used to help students develop their abilities?

Whether or not an instructor chooses to use backward design, it is important to create a thoughtful syllabus. Recently, educators have begun to focus not only on the information conveyed in a syllabus but also on the tone of the information communicated. Harnish et al. (2011) define a *warm syllabus* as one that "removes unnecessary and unhelpful barriers between instructors and students, making the classroom a comfortable and safe place for discovery." Wasley (2008b) notes that in classes with syllabi with a less punitive tone—for example, those with fewer bolded statements with exclamation points regarding consequences—students are more likely to approach their professor. In "Creating the Foundation for a Warm Classroom Climate," Harnish et al. (2011) include the following components for a positive tone that may help build class community:

- Positive or friendly language
- Rationale for assignments
- Humor
- Compassion (While instructors should have clear policies, they may want to acknowledge that unforeseen events do occur.)
- Enthusiasm for the topic

In fact, Singham (2007) and Wasley (2008b) advocate abandoning the traditional, rule-laden syllabus for a less legalistic and more learner-friendly syllabus. Singham (2007) goes so far as to advocate that students build their own syllabus. He suggests that professors go to class the first day with a tentative time line for reading and writing assignments. When students and professors know one another better, they discuss and decide together the criteria for a good paper, define good participation, and create rubrics for assessing student performance. In Singham's experience, the students are more invested in the class when they collaborate on developing the syllabus.

To create a thoughtful and effective syllabus, instructors should include the following components (Lowther, Stark, & Martens, 1989; Nilson, 2010, pp. 33–36):

- Instructor contact information, office hours, and communication information, such as Twitter, e-mail response time, and network requests
- Course requirements, grading scale, and criteria
- Required and optional materials
- Course purpose and learning outcomes
- Policies on attendance and missed or late assignments
- Academic integrity policy
- Organization of the course with calendar
- Statement that the syllabus may be subject to change by mutual agreement

Syllabi are frequently reviewed in the promotion and tenure process. Instructors are encouraged to check with their institutions on the role the syllabi will play in assessment processes.

Annotated Resources

Fink, L. D. (2005, August). *A self-directed guide to designing courses for significant learning.* Retrieved from http://www.deefinkandassociates.com/GuidetoCourseDesignAug05.pdf

This brief free online workbook helps instructors design courses that include such components as active learning, significant learning, and educative assessment.

Fink, L. D. (2013). *Creating significant learning experiences: An integrated approach to designing college courses* (Rev. ed.). San Francisco, CA: Jossey-Bass.

This newly updated edition helps instructors with the design process. It combines current research-based practices with learning-centered strategies. The author asks educators to think about learning objectives and to create learning strategies that maximize student achievement.

Harnish, R., McElwee, R., Slattery, J., Frantz, S., Haney, M., Shore, C., & Penley, J. (2011). Creating the foundation for a warm classroom climate: Best practices in syllabus tone. *Observer, 24*(1). Retrieved from http://www.psychologicalscience.org/index.php/publications/observer/2011/january-11/creating-the-foundation-for-a-warm-classroom-climate.html

This article discusses the implications and importance the syllabus has on creating tone in the classroom and lists ideas that instructors might implement to help create a warm classroom climate.

Hara, B. (2010, October 19). Graphic display of student learning objectives [web log post]. *ProfHacker.* Retrieved from http://chronicle.com/blogs/profhacker/graphic-display-of-student-learning-objectives/27863

Hara shares three examples of graphic displays of course objectives used in syllabi.

Nilson, L. B. (2007). *The graphic syllabus and the outcomes map: Communicating your course.* San Francisco, CA: Jossey-Bass.

Nilson advocates creating a graphic syllabus and an outcomes map, which may look like a diagram, flow chart, or concept map. The strength of a graphic syllabus is that it can show relationships among topics and the learning process to achieve understanding of those topics.

O'Brien, J. G., Millis, B. J., & Cohen, M. W. (2008). *The course syllabus: A learning centered approach* (2nd ed.). San Francisco, CA: Jossey-Bass.

The authors present eight principles for designing a course that promote critical thinking. The book also advocates changing the focus of the syllabus from material to be covered to student learning tools.

Slattery, J. M., & Carlson, J. (2005). Preparing an effective syllabus: Current best practices. *College Teaching, 53*(4), 159–164.

This article suggests that the tone of a syllabus (friendly or punitive) sets the tone for class and cites studies that indicate students perform better in classrooms where there is a friendly tone. The authors also suggest that a syllabus should be the product of a strongly articulated teaching philosophy.

Wasley, P. (2008a). Research yields tips on crafting better syllabi. *Chronicle of Higher Education, 54*(27), A11–A12.

This article reviews several studies on the relationship between the tone of a syllabus and student engagement. The findings indicate that students are significantly less likely to approach a professor who gives students a rule-laden syllabus.

Wasley, P. (2008b). The syllabus becomes a repository of legalese. *Chronicle of Higher Education, 54*(27), A1–A10.

The author interviews professors on the goals of a syllabus: Is it meant to prevent conflict, or is it meant to be learner centered? She discusses a learner-centered syllabus created collaboratively by a professor who comes to class with a tentative time line of readings and written assignments and his or her students.

Wiggins, G., & McTighe, J. (2005). *Understanding by design.* Alexandria, VA: Association for Supervision and Curriculum Development.

This book shares an excellent overview and step-by-step process for creating a syllabus using backward design, as well as templates and other tools. See the Jay McTighe and Associates website (http://jaymctighe.com/resources/) for extensive online resources for creating syllabi.

Workshop A.2
Strategies for the First and Last Days of Class

By giving students an interesting and inviting introduction, I was able to reduce anxiety about the course and help students view the class as a collaborative learning process. Every field has its own exciting research or striking examples, and it is a good idea to present a few of these up front. The teaching challenge is to find special ideas within your own field. Your class will thank you.

—Kevin L. Bennett (2004)

The first day of class is a terrific opportunity to motivate students, demonstrate why your subject matters, create a greater sense of wonder, and surprise students with how your class might change how they look at the world.

—José Bowen (2012)

Strategies for the First Day of Class

The first day of class sets the tone for the rest of the course. It is an opportunity to engage students and to trigger prior knowledge about course material. The level of participation on the first day of class will send students a strong message about expectations for the rest of the semester. Prepare students for the semester by employing relevant classroom strategies from day one; ask them to participate in a discussion, write a brief passage, give a short oral presentation, or work in groups. These activities will promote community building, which is important to help students begin to feel more connected to the instructor and to the class (Pascarella & Terenzini, 2005). Students will leave a successful first day of class interested in taking the course and in learning the topics presented.

The following are some strategies for creating a learning environment on the first day of class:

- *Predicting class topics based on prior knowledge.* Lyons, McIntosh, and Kysilka (2003) suggest the following exercise:
  - Ask each student to create a list of topics that he or she hopes or predicts will be included in the class.
  - Have students share their ideas with another student and then create categories of ideas based on the discussion. They should give these categories names.
  - Have the pairs join another pair of students and combine ideas. The groups should arrange their categories into a logical sequence on a sheet of chart paper, a laptop, or a tablet to share with the class.

    ○ Use this information to structure a general course outline. Explain to students that while their ideas will be incorporated into the course, instructors have a responsibility to ensure that the course conforms to university guidelines. Assure students that many of their ideas line up with a rough draft of an agenda that has already been created by the instructor. Before the next class meeting, create the formal syllabus and course agenda to meet the stated description and course objectives, including student input (see Workshop A.1: The Syllabus, p. 61).

- *Writing and sharing basic introductions.* Distribute to each student a half sheet of paper with questions such as, (a) What is your name? (b) What is your hometown? (c) What is your favorite book? (d) What is your favorite film? (e) What is a little known but interesting fact about yourself? Then go around the room and read from these sheets. Even the shyest student is able to read the prepared responses.

Instructional Applications

Weimer (2013) shares some first-day-of-class activities that ask students to think about how they best learn and that stress student responsibilities in creating a positive classroom environment:

Best and Worst Classes
On the first day of class, instructors ask students to recall the best and worst classes they have taken. The students are then asked to go to the board and respond to the prompts "what the teacher did" and "what the students did" in their best and worst classes. When the students read what their classmates have shared, it quickly becomes apparent that student effort is a key ingredient to have a "best class experience" (Weimer, 2013).

First Day Graffiti
This is an adaptation of an activity proposed by Barbara Goza (1993; as cited in Weimer, 2013). Place flip charts with markers or tablets around the classroom. On each chart the instructor writes the beginning of a sentence the students must complete. Some examples are as follows:

    "I have trouble participating in class when . . . "
    "I feel most comfortable contributing to class discussion when . . . "
    "I have had successful learning experiences when . . . "

As students walk around the room and write their answers, they are encouraged to talk about their responses with their peers and their instructor. Once there are comments on each flip chart, the instructor can talk about several of the responses and tell the students what they can expect during the semester.

Syllabus Speed Dating
This first-day-of-class activity was created by Karen Eifler (as cited in Weimer, 2013), a University of Portland education professor. Two rows of chairs face each other so that students can sit across from one another. The instructor asks the students, working in pairs,

to discuss two questions. One question is a personal interest question, and the other is about the syllabus. The questions allow the students to get to know each other and discuss important aspects of the course. Once students have had a few minutes to chat about the first two questions, those in one row move down a seat to form new pairs. The instructor then asks a different set of questions.

Online Resources

Cox, K. J. (2005). Group introductions—Get-acquainted team building activity. Retrieved from http://www.docstoc.com/docs/34260610/Group-Introductions-Get-Acquainted-Team-Building

This document, which includes questions for reflection, presents a method for student introductions for group work or small classes.

Fleming, N. (2003). *Establishing rapport: Personal interaction and learning* (IDEA Paper No. 39). Retrieved from Idea Center website: http://www.theideacenter.org/sites/default/files/IDEA_Paper_39.pdf

This paper discusses the relationship between rapport and motivation. It also notes the importance of rapport as a predictor of outcomes.

Iowa State University, Center for Excellence in Learning and Teaching. (2011). Welcoming students on the first day [Video]. Retrieved from http://www.celt.iastate.edu/teaching/video/welcoming.html

This video is part of a series about creating a positive learning environment.

Palmer, M. (n.d.). Not quite 101 ways to learn students' names. Retrieved from University of Virginia Teaching Resource Center website: http://trc.virginia.edu/teaching-tips/not-quite-101-ways-to-learning-students-names/

This resource provides many tips for remembering student names. It includes standard methods, such as flash cards and memorization, and more inventive strategies, such as scavenger hunts.

Strategies for the Last Day of Class

The last day of class can serve as a culminating experience or as a transition to continued learning by the student.
—Endicott College Center for Teaching Excellence

The last day of class can be a transformative and exciting experience for both professors and students. It is a moment when students can reflect on what they have accomplished, how much they have learned, and how their new knowledge will be relevant to their future.

Strategies for inviting reflection and providing closure include the following:

- Ask students to write three of the most important ideas they learned in class. After 10 minutes of writing, invite students to share what they have written. Participating in this discussion helps students develop a better understanding of what they have learned (Lang, 2006).
- On the first day of class, ask students to complete an information sheet about what they hope to learn in class. On the last day of class, return those sheets and asks them to discuss "whether they fulfilled their hopes or learned something new" (Lang, 2006).
- Ask students to write a letter to future students, giving them advice about how to succeed in the class. This can be a good way for students to reflect on how much they have learned during the semester.
- Ask the class as a whole to construct a concept map of the course, demonstrating their understanding of how the course worked. Appoint three students, each with a different color marker, to be the artists and invite the rest of the students to make suggestions. Alternatively, have groups of five to six students create posters using self-sticking posters. (See Workshop 1.1: Concept Maps, p. 9.)
- Ask students to think about how course material might be pertinent to their future. This can help give learning more meaning and can close the course on a positive note.
- Invite students to review the syllabus to reaffirm that learning outcomes have been met and to remind them of the material that has been covered. Ask them what they think they will remember or use the longest. Ask them what will make the greatest and least impact on their learning goals and personal life.
- If you assessed student knowledge in the first few days of class via a pretest, use the pretest again on the last day as a type of posttest. This will help students recognize how much they have learned during the semester.

Appendix B

WORKSHOP ON LECTURES AND MINI-LECTURES

A lecture is much more of a dialogue than many of you probably realize.

—George Wald (1969)

Workshop B.1
Planning and Delivery

For many instructors lectures are part and parcel of their teaching. Hoyt and Perera (2000) reported that 45% of faculty sampled in a study listed lecture as their primary method of teaching. Well-crafted lectures that include active-learning strategies tend to be the most effective (Nilson, 2010). Bligh (2000) and McKeachie and Svinicki (2013) provide several situations in which the lecture is the most effective teaching method, including giving students a personal viewpoint on the reading, updating students on new material not yet available, modeling a problem-solving approach, and clarifying a complex concept in the reading. Note the absence of lecturing on material that duplicates what students have read. Active-learning activities are more beneficial to students' learning than listening to a lecture on material that they were assigned to read (Nilson, 2010).

Planning

First, you will need to establish learning goals. Often the act of creating learning goals brings a course into sharper focus, thus reducing the amount of material to be studied. Although scaling back on the amount of content can be challenging for many college instructors, the result can be that students focus on the primary goals of the course rather than on the superficial.

Rather than using lectures to convey factual information, use them as a means for posing problems and raising issues. Students can be held accountable for finding facts in their reading, leaving instructors free to devote lectures to synthesis and analysis.

Delivery

Opening Strategies

Students tend to best remember information or experiences presented first; they remember second best what is presented at the end of class. Their recall of skills and concepts taught just past the middle of class is weakest. These findings are known respectively as "primacy" and "recency" in the serial position effect (Burns, 1985; Reed, 2006; Terry, 2005). Capitalize on the primacy/recency effect by introducing the most important information at the beginning of class, when retention tends to be best. Following are some opening strategies:

- Begin with a high-level question or quotation from the day's reading that will be further developed in class. Ask students to discuss the question or quotation with a partner, write about it, or respond to it verbally (see Think-Pair-Share, pp. 34 and 46).
- Open with a story, anecdote, question-and-answer session, or demonstration related to the lecture.
- Ask students to spend a few minutes writing about the readings for the day.
- Briefly share the broad goals of the day's class before moving to the specifics. Connect these goals to the previous class material to reinforce their importance.

The Interactive Lecture

For an effective interactive lecture, divide the material into 10–15 minute chunks, or mini-lectures (Medina, 2008). Separate these chunks with active-learning activities. These activities can range from 2 to 15 minutes in length and will serve to reboot the lecture, give students a break, and encourage students to interact with the lecture content, their notes, and each other. Alternating between mini-lectures, discussion, and activities allows students time to assimilate what they've learned. In addition, students know that the pace will change often, so they are more apt to stay engaged in class. Some strategies to keep students engaged during lectures include the following:

- Do not overload students. Students lose sight of the main ideas when too many details are given or when too many ideas are presented and not developed. Engage students more fully with less material. If the material is well developed, students will learn better.
- Help students relate new material to something they already know. Build on their past experience and coursework to help connect new material to old. The human brain is constantly seeking meaning and pattern in facts, memories, and emotions (Davis, 2008). (See Principle 3: Emotion and Relevance Deepen Learning, p. 15.)
- Connect information with values and feelings so that it will be more readily learned. Students should be encouraged to develop passionate stances on issues so that they will retain information more efficiently. (See Principle 3: Emotion and Relevance Deepen Learning, p. 15.)
- Organize material in a logical order, such as cause-effect, chronological, contrast and comparison, problem-solution, pro-con, or importance.

- Most students learn best from a combination of aural, visual, and verbal presentations. Use visuals to increase understanding and impact. (See Principle 4: Multisensory Instruction Deepens Learning, p. 25.)
- For projected text, use a large font in a dark color and leave some lights on in the room to allow students to take notes.
- A good lecture involves a dialogue between the instructor and students, even if the instructor delivers longer prepared remarks before inviting responses. Interactive exercises help students learn and retain more details than does passive listening for extended periods.

Focus on Speaking Skills

To maintain student engagement, it is important to consider these speaking skills:

- Vary speech from loud to soft, quick to slow, excited to calm.
- Pause to get students' attention and to give them time to take notes.
- Enunciate clearly.
- Be expressive with face and hands.
- Move freely away from class notes while lecturing. Walk around in front of the class rather than staying anchored to lecture notes. The more audience members are encouraged to pay attention to movement and change, the less likely they are to lose interest.
- Be encouraging and welcoming.
- Speak from an outline that will allow organization of thoughts in a coherent manner. Do not write out the lecture, as this will lead to reading from notes and a poor delivery; instead, provide general topic headings and a few key details or sentences that should be included.
- Keep text to a minimum in projected slides, such as a PowerPoint presentation, and focus more on images (see Principle 4: Multisensory Instruction Deepens Learning, p. 25).

Closure

A strong conclusion to the class is important as it can solidify learning of new skills and concepts presented that day. Plan to use the last few minutes of class to have students summarize key points and make connections to past and future topics. A short in-class practice test or 1-minute paper can be invaluable to help students review and retain the material discussed in class (Karpicke & Blunt, 2011; Roediger & Karpicke, 2006). (See Principle 6: Formative Assessment or Low-Stakes Evaluation Strengthens Retention, p. 43.)

Annotated Research Studies

Huxham, M. (2005). Learning in lectures: Do "interactive windows" help? *Active Learning in Higher Education, 6*(1), 17–31.

"Interactive windows" are activities embedded in a lecture, such as discussions, problem-solving exercises, and think-pair-share. Huxham examined the use of these short interactive windows in lectures over a 5-year period. Teaching evaluations involving more than 500 responses showed that the "interactive windows" were the most popular aspect of the courses. The classes that were taught interactively showed strong evidence of their positive influence on recall and learning.

Terry, W. (2005). Serial position effects in recall of television commercials. *Journal of General Psychology, 132*(2), 151–163.

College students viewed lists of 15 commercials and were asked to recall the product brand names. When tested, they easily remembered the first commercials (a primacy effect) and the last (a recency effect). Their ability to remember the products from commercials viewed in the middle, however, was significantly lower. In a test administered at the end of the term, recall of the first items persisted, whereas recall of the middle and last items disappeared.

Online Resources

Denman, M. (2005). How to create memorable lectures. *Speaking of Teaching, 14*(1), 1–5. Retrieved from http://www.stanford.edu/dept/CTL/Newsletter/memorable_lectures.pdf

Drummond, T. (1995). A brief summary of the best practices in college teaching. Retrieved from University of North Carolina–Charlotte Center for Teaching and Learning website: http://teaching.uncc.edu/articles-books/best-practice-articles/course-development/best-practices

Hamm, P. H. (2006). *Teaching and persuasive communication: Class presentation skills.* Retrieved from Brown University Harriet W. Sheridan Center for Teaching and Learning website: http://brown.edu/about/administration/sheridan-center/sites/brown.edu.about.administration.sheridan-center/files/uploads/Teaching%20and%20Persuasive%20Communication.pdf

University of California–Berkeley, Center for Teaching and Learning. (n.d.). Large lecture classes: Six ways to make lectures in a large enrollment course more manageable and effective. Retrieved from http://teaching.berkeley.edu/large-lecture-classes

University of Minnesota, Center for Teaching and Learning. (2010). Planning lectures. Retrieved from http://www1.umn.edu/ohr/teachlearn/tutorials/lectures/planning/index.html

Appendix C

WORKSHOP ON CLASSROOM DISCUSSIONS

The exceptional teachers did not just want to get students speaking; they wanted them to think and learn how to engage in an exchange of ideas.

—Ken Bain (2004)

The classroom ought to be a place where things are said seriously—not without pleasure, not without joy—but seriously, and for serious consideration. . . . I see it as a fundamental responsibility of the teacher to show by example the ability to listen to others seriously.

—bell hooks (1994)

Workshop C.1
Classroom Discussions

The purpose of class discussion is to enrich the understanding of a topic or text. Professors can also use discussions to generate interaction following a section of a lecture. In-class discussions engage students with a topic, encourage student participation, and help develop important speaking and listening skills. Brookfield and Preskill (2005) point out that discussion promotes habits of good discourse, helps students learn to synthesize and integrate new information, permits students to test out their ideas against the opinions of others, and allows different perspectives to be heard. Moreover, discussion is a crucial process for students to learn how to construct knowledge through grappling with complex ideas and raising questions. However, these goals are achieved only if the discussion is a success. Brookfield and Preskill (2005, pp. 37–39) suggest that the primary reasons discussions fail are unrealistic expectations, lack of ground rules, perceived unwelcoming classroom environment, unprepared students, and no teacher modeling. This workshop is designed to offer some techniques for inspiring successful class discussions.

Guidelines for Good Discussions

Define *Participation*

- Instructors are encouraged to define what they mean by *participation*. Students need to understand that class discussions are about developing good habits of discourse, that is, both speaking and listening. Extroverted students must understand that part of their role in creating a constructive discussion is to leave room for the shy students to speak, while introverted students must make an effort to contribute. It is essential that students know that they are not having a dialogue with the professor but instead with their peers. They must listen and respond to one another. Motivate students to pay attention by making it explicit that they need to take notes on what their classmates say.

Be Transparent

Students are more willing to participate if they recognize the value of class discussion. When they understand that they are developing skills that will help them in the future, they are more likely to take class discussion seriously.

Give Participation a Value

Make it clear early that participation is expected. Instructors are encouraged to inform students that participation will be a component of their grade.

Get Students Involved

Bain (2004) believes that the longer students sit without entering the discussion the harder it will be for them to participate. Early in the term, it is especially important to devise ways for each student to have something to say. (See the following instructional applications for specific suggestions.) Allowing students time to collect their thoughts is one of the surest ways to get students to engage in the discussion. If instructors give students time to write about a topic before beginning a discussion, students will be more likely to have something useful to offer. Highly structured group work can also foster a safe environment for students to participate in discussions (see Principle 5: Small Groups Engage Students, p. 32). When students have a clear understanding of their role in a conversation, they often feel more comfortable critiquing, questioning, and challenging. Group work has the added benefit of allowing students to practice articulating their ideas with a few peers before sharing them with the entire class. If students are resisting participating in class discussion, it may be wise to invite them to contribute.

Encourage Student Preparation

To participate, students must be prepared for class. Bain (2004) advocates treating readings as sources for solving problems or raising issues. Nilson (2010) suggests having students take notes on readings or write reactions or summaries; then allow students to use their summaries in class. Instructors can also send students study questions and permit them to use their answers during in-class discussion. This both prepares students and gives them confidence to speak.

Choose Relevant Topics

If topics are relevant and important to the students, they are more likely to participate. Bain (2004) suggests that students are more willing to ask questions about something that perplexes, stirs, frustrates, or outrages them. It is also important for instructors to press students for evidence substantiating their ideas. Instructors can encourage students to question and challenge one another and the instructors themselves.

Pose Good Questions

Ross (1860) wrote, "To question well is to teach well." Some approaches to encourage students to think critically through effective questioning include the following:

- Pose questions that require analysis and synthesis. This aids students in formulating their thoughts and constructing solid arguments rather than encouraging simple recall. (See Bloom's taxonomy, p. 45.)
- Consider using a question-based structure, such as the Socratic method, for class discussion (see Stanford University, 2003).
- Create questions by working backward from the course goals. Such questions require instructors to think about the primary "take-away message" of their class and then to create questions that will guide students to grapple with thought-provoking issues (Nilson, 2010).

Model Listening

Students must feel that they are heard, respected, and taken seriously for discussion to work well, and they must see that their professors listen to them and their peers. When students are asked to engage their imaginations and articulate their thoughts, instructors may hear wrong answers. Rather than correcting a wrong response, instructors can ask students questions that help them articulate their thought process and explore new ideas. By asking students to reflect on their own thinking, instructors model important metacognitive skills. (See metacognition, p. 4.)

Wrap Up

Students may find it difficult to know the objective of a discussion class (another reason to make it explicit that in-class discussion is meant to develop their speaking, listening, and critical-thinking skills). To alleviate student anxiety, provide a wrap-up of the day's discussion. Nilson (2010) suggests randomly selecting a student to summarize the major points made in class and then asking others to contribute their opinions. Professors may also want to ask concluding questions about what was learned and what else students should know.

Instructional Applications

Bring Quotes to Class

Ask students to bring a meaningful quote from the reading to class on an index card. Have students read their quotes at the beginning of class to generate discussion. A variation of this activity is to have students anonymously drop their quotes into a box as they enter the class. Then choose a student (perhaps a quiet one) to select a quote to read and have the class discuss the passage.

Generate Questions

Invite students to prepare questions before class and to turn in these questions at the beginning of class. Ask a student to select a question to discuss. Students may also be asked to write one or more questions before class and then lead discussion of their questions. They can also work in small groups and determine a question for the class to answer, and then the groups can lead discussion about their questions.

Recall Concrete Images

This strategy is especially helpful for getting quieter students to talk. Invite each student to recall an important event or image from the text. List these images on the board. Remembering concrete scenes often prompts further recollections. The instructor can then ask follow-up questions, such as, "What themes emerge from this list?"

Shift Points of View

After discussing a text or question from one viewpoint, ask students to consider another perspective. Compare and contrast the strengths and weaknesses, or benefits and disadvantages, of different views.

Take a Poll

Prepare students for the day's topic by polling them before the discussion. This can be done prior to or at the beginning of class using student response instruments (clickers) or Twitter. A poll will provide a picture of where the class stands and allow students to see they are not alone in their opinions. This will make them more comfortable sharing their views.

Generate Truth Statements

To develop critical skills and generate "friendly rivalry" among groups, divide students into groups and instruct each group to choose three statements that are true about a particular issue. Frederick (1981) gives these examples:

"It is true about slavery that . . ."
"We have agreed that it is true about the welfare system that . . ."
"It is true about international politics in the 1950s that . . ."
"We know it to be true about the theory of relativity that . . ."

This strategy generates discussion not only inside the groups as they have to agree what is "true" but also in the class as a whole. It also reveals student assumptions about an issue while demanding that they analyze their own assumptions. (For additional strategies on leading discussions, see Frederick, 1981.)

Lead a Circular Response Discussion
Brookfield and Preskill (2005) suggest a circular response discussion for honing student listening skills. For this exercise students sit in a circle and are given a prompt to discuss. Each speaker has 1 minute to address the prompt, but the speaker must incorporate the comments of the preceding speaker. The speakers do not have to agree with the comments that have already been made, but they do have to use them as a springboard for their own comments. This exercise encourages both respectful listening and respectful disagreement. The rules that Brookfield and Preskill (2005, p. 80) outline are as follows:

- No one interrupts the speaker.
- No one speaks out of turn.
- Each person is allowed 1 minute (or so, to be determined by the size of the class and the goals of the professor).
- Each person strives to show how his or her comments respond to the comments of the previous speaker.

Assign Conversational Roles
Brookfield (2006, pp. 146–147) suggests that to have a fruitful discussion, students can be assigned roles for the discussion. It is important that if instructors use this technique on a regular basis, they must have students alternate roles. Some of the suggested roles are as follows:

- Theme poser: This person posits the problem or issue to be discussed.
- Reflective analyst: This person occasionally summarizes what he or she hears during the conversation.
- Devil's advocate: When there seems to be a consensus, this person offers another view.
- Detective: This person challenges unchecked or unchallenged biases.
- Textual focuser: This person requires that the discussants back up their assertions with text.

Videos

Harvard University, Derek Bok Center for Teaching and Learning. (2007, September 4). Derek Bok Center: The art of discussion leading [YouTube video]. Retrieved from http://www.youtube.com/watch?v=G53os5becKU

Professor Roland Christenson from the Harvard Business School demonstrates and shares tips on how to lead a good discussion.

Otis College of Art and Design. (2009, July 18). Otis teaching tips: Leading classroom discussions [YouTube video]. Retrieved from http://www.youtube.com/watch?v=T_BAN-RJZedU

Heather Joseph-Witham from the Otis College of Art and Design shares ideas and examples for leading class discussions.

Online Resources

For definitions and examples of discussion protocols see the following sources:

Looking at Student Work. (n.d.) Protocols. Retrieved from http://www.lasw.org/protocols.html
McDonald, J. P., Zydney, J. M., Dichter, A., & McDonald, E. C. (2012). Abbreviated protocols. Retrieved from Teachers College Press website: http://www.tcpress.com/pdfs/mcdonaldprot.pdf

BIBLIOGRAPHY

Preface

Persellin, D., & Daniels, M. (2012). *Strengthening undergraduate learning: Six research-based principles for teaching and applications.* Atlanta, GA: Associated Colleges of the South.

Introduction

Ambrose, S. A., Bridges, M. W., DiPietro, M., Lovett, M. C., & Norman, M. K. (2010). *How learning works: Seven research-based principles for smart teaching* (pp. 10–39). San Francisco, CA: Jossey-Bass.

Argyris, C. (2002). Teaching smart people how to learn. *Reflections, 4*(2), 4–15.

Atkinson, R. C., & Shiffrin, R. M. (1968). Human memory: A proposed system and its control processes. In K. W. Spence & J. T. Spence (Eds.), *The psychology of learning and motivation* (Vol. 2, pp. 89–195). New York, NY: Academic Press.

Baddeley, A. D. (1986). *Working memory* (Oxford Psychology Series No. 11). Oxford, UK: Clarendon Press.

Baxter-Magolda, M. (1992). *Knowing and reasoning in college: Gender-related patterns in students' intellectual development.* San Francisco, CA: Jossey-Bass.

Belenky, M. F., Clinchy, B. M., Goldberger, N. R., & Tarule, J. R. (1986). *Women's ways of knowing.* New York, NY: Basic Books.

Bransford, J. D., Brown, A. L., & Cocking, R. R. (Eds.). (2000). *How people learn: Brain, mind, experience, and school.* Washington DC: National Academies Press.

Bransford, J. D., & Schwartz, D. (1999). Rethinking transfer: A simple proposal with multiple implications. *Review of Research in Education, 24,* 61–100.

Braun, A., & Bock, J. (2007). Born to learn: Early learning optimizes brain function. In W. Gruhn & F. Rauscher (Eds.), *Neurosciences and music pedagogy* (pp. 27–51). New York, NY: Nova Science.

Caine, G., Caine, R. N., McClintic, C., & Klimek, K. (2005). *12 brain/mind learning principles in action.* Thousand Oaks, CA: Corwin Press.

Chin, C., & Brown, D. (2000). Learning in science: A comparison of deep and surface approaches. *Journal of Research in Science Teaching, 37*(2), 136.

Deutsch, J. (2004). Memory: Experimental approaches. In R. Gregory (Ed.), *Oxford companion to the mind* (2nd ed., pp. 568–571). New York, NY: Oxford University Press.

Doyle, T., & Zakrajsek, T. (2013). *The new science of learning: How to learn in harmony with your brain.* Sterling, VA: Stylus.

Kember, D., Ho, A., & Hong, C. (2008). The importance of establishing relevance in motivating student learning. *Active Learning in Higher Education, 9*(3), 249–263.

King, P. M., & Kitchener, K. S. (2004). Reflective judgment: Theory and research on the development of epistemic assumptions through adulthood. *Educational Psychologist, 39*(1), 5–18.

Kloss, R. J. (1994). A nudge is best: Helping students through the Perry scheme of intellectual development. *College Teaching, 42*(4), 151–158.

McLeod, S. A. (2007). Multi store model of memory—Atkinson and Shiffrin, 1968. Retrieved from Simply Psychology website: http://www.simplypsychology.org/multi-store.html

Medina, J. (2008). *Brain rules* (pp. 95–119). Seattle, WA: Pear Press.

Moore, W. S. (1989). The learning environment preferences: Exploring the construct validity of an objective measure of the Perry scheme of intellectual development. *Journal of College Student Development, 30,* 504–514.

National Research Council. (2001). *Knowing what students know: The science and design of educational assessment.* Washington DC: National Academies Press.

Nilson, L. B. (2013). *Creating self-regulated learners: Strategies to strengthen students' self-awareness and learning skills.* Sterling, VA: Stylus.

Overstreet, K. (2007). PowerPoint activities. Retrieved from http://teach.fcps.net/trt10/PowerPoint.htm

Perry, W. G. (1970). *Forms of ethical and intellectual development in the college years: A scheme.* San Francisco, CA: Jossey-Bass.

Perry Network. (n.d.). Retrieved from http://www.perrynetwork.org/

Skillen, P. (n.d.). Expert learners. Retrieved from Construction Zone website: http://theconstructionzone.wordpress.com/the-construction-zone/expert-learners/

Sousa, D. (2006). *How the brain learns.* Thousand Oaks, CA: Corwin Press.

Squire, L. (2004). Memory systems of the brain: A brief history and current perspective. *Neurobiology of Learning and Memory, 82*(3), 171–177.

Squire, L., Berg, D., Bloom, F., du Lac, S., & Ghosh, A. (2008). *Fundamental neuroscience* (3rd ed.). Burlington, MA: Academic Press.

Sviniki, M. (2004). *Learning and motivation in the postsecondary classroom.* Bolton, MA: Anker.

Vanderbilt University, Center for Teaching. (n.d.). How people learn. Retrieved from http://cft.vanderbilt.edu/teaching-guides/pedagogical/how-people-learn/

Wirth, K., & Perkins, D. (2007). Learning to learn. Retrieved from http://cgiss.boisestate.edu/~billc/Teaching/Items/learningtolearn.pdf

Zull, J. E. (2002). *The art of changing the brain: Enriching the practice of teaching by exploring the biology of learning* (pp. 13–29). Sterling, VA: Stylus.

Chapter 1

Principle 1

Alter, A., Oppenheimer, D., Epley, N., & Eyre, R. (2007). Overcoming intuition: Metacognitive difficulty activates analytic reasoning. *Journal of Experimental Psychology: General, 136*(4), 569–576.

Bain, R., & Zimmerman, J. (2009). Understanding great teaching. *Peer Review, 11*(2). Retrieved from http://www.aacu.org/peerreview/pr-sp09/pr-sp09_bain-zimmerman.cfm

Bjork, E. L., & Bjork, R. A. (2011). Making things hard on yourself, but in a good way: Creating desirable difficulties to enhance learning. In M. A. Gernsbacher, R. W. Pew, L. M. Hough, & J. R. Pomerantz (Eds.), *Psychology and the real world: Essays illustrating fundamental contributions to society* (pp. 56–64). New York, NY: Worth Publishers.

Bjork, R. A. (1994). Memory and metamemory considerations in the training of human beings. In J. Metcalfe & A. Shimamura (Eds.), *Metacognition: Knowing about knowing* (pp. 185–205). Cambridge, MA: MIT Press.

Bjork, R. A. (2013). Applying cognitive psychology to enhance educational practice. Retrieved from University of California–Los Angeles Bjork Learning and Forgetting Lab website: http://bjorklab.psych.ucla.edu/research.html

Bye, J. (2011, May 5). Desirable difficulties in the classroom [web log post]. *Psychology Today.* Retrieved from http://www.psychologytoday.com/blog/all-about-addiction/201105/desirable-difficulties-in-the-classroom

Cepeda, N. J., Pashler, H., Vul, E., Wixted, J. T., & Rohrer, D. (2006). Distributed practice in verbal recall tasks: A review and quantitative synthesis. *Psychological Bulletin, 132*, 354–380.

Dempster, F., & Farris, R. (1990). The spacing effect: Research and practice. *Journal of Research and Development in Education, 23*(2), 97–101.

Didau, D. (2013, June 10). Deliberately difficult—Why it's better to make learning harder [web log post]. *Learning Spy.* Retrieved from http://www.learningspy.co.uk/featured/deliberately-difficult-focussing-on-learning-rather-than-progress/

Diemand-Yauman, C., Oppenheimer, D., & Vaughan, E. (2011). Fortune favors the Bold (and the Italicized): Effects of disfluency on educational outcomes. *Cognition, 118*(1), 111–115. doi:10.1016/j.cognition.2010.09.012

Hermida, J. (n.d.). Deep learning. Retrieved from http://www.julianhermida.com/algoma/law1scotldeeplearning.htm

Karpicke, J., & Blunt, J. (2011). Retrieval practice produces more learning than elaborative studying with concept mapping. *Science, 331*(6018), 772–775. doi:10.1126/science.1199327

Linn, M. C., & Bjork, R. A. (2006). The science of learning and the learning of science: Introducing desirable difficulties. *Observer, 19*(3). Retrieved from http://www.psychologicalscience.org/index.php/publications/observer/2006/march-06/the-science-of-learning-and-the-learning-of-science.html

McDaniel, M., & Butler, A. C. (2010). A contextual framework for understanding when difficulties are desirable. In A. S. Benjamin (Ed.), *Successful remembering and successful forgetting: Essays in honor of Robert A. Bjork* (pp. 175–199). New York, NY: Psychology Press.

McDaniel, M., Hines, R., Waddill, P., & Einstein, G. (1994). What makes folk tales unique: Content familiarity, causal structure, scripts, or superstructures? *Journal of Experimental Psychology: Learning, Memory, and Cognition, 20*(1), 169–184.

McNamara, D. S., Kintsch, E., Songer, N. B., & Kintsch, W. (1996). Are good texts always better? Interactions of text coherence, background knowledge, and levels of understanding in learning from text. *Cognition and Instruction, 14*(1), 1–43. doi:10.1207/s1532690xci1401_1

Roediger, H., & Karpicke, J. (2006). Test-enhanced learning taking memory tests improves long-term retention. *Psychological Science, 17*(3), 249–255.

Rohrer, D., & Taylor, K. (2007). The shuffling of mathematics practice problems improves learning. *Instructional Science, 35*, 481–498.

Yue, C. L., Castel, A. D., & Bjork, R. A. (2013). When disfluency is—and is not—a desirable difficulty: The influence of typeface clarity on metacognitive judgments and memory. *Memory and Cognition, 41*(2), 229–241.

Workshop 1.1

Baume, D., & Baume, C. (2008). *Powerful ideas in teaching and learning*. Wheatley, UK: Oxford Brookes University.

Beissner, K. L. (1991). Use of *concept mapping* to improve problem solving. *Journal of Physical Therapy, 6*(1), 22–27.

Budd, J. W. (2004). Mind maps as classroom exercises. *Journal of Economic Education, 35*(1), 35–46.

Buzan, T. (1995). *The mind map book* (2nd ed.). London, UK: BBC Books.

Clark, C. (2011, May 10). Best tools and practices for concept mapping [web log post]. *NspireD²*. Retrieved from http://ltlatnd.wordpress.com/2011/05/10/best-tools-and-practices-for-concept-mapping/

Daly, B. (2004). Using concept maps with adult students in higher education. In A. J. Cañas, J. D. Novak, & F. M. González (Eds.), *Concept maps: Theory, methodology, technology: Proceedings of the First International Conference on Concept Mapping* (Vol. 1, pp. 183–190). Retrieved from http://cmc.ihmc.us/cmc2004 Proceedings/cmc2004%20-%20Vol%201.pdf

Eppler, M. (2006). A comparison between concept maps, mind maps, conceptual diagrams, and visual metaphors as complementary tools for knowledge construction and sharing. *Information and Visualization, 5*, 202–210.

Horton, P. B., McConney, A., Gallo, M., Woods, A., Senn, G., & Hamelin, D. (1993). An investigation of the effectiveness of concept mapping as an instructional tool. *Science Education, 77*(1), 95–111.

Llewellyn, D. (2007). Making the most of the concept maps. *Science Scope, 30*(5), 74–77.

Morse, D., & Jutras, F. (2008). Implementing concept-based learning in a large undergraduate classroom. *Life Sciences Education, 7*(2), 243–253. doi:10.1187/cbe.07-09-0071

Nilson, L. B. (2010). *Teaching at its best: A research-based resource for college instructors* (3rd ed., pp. 243–245). San Francisco, CA: Jossey-Bass.

Novak, J., & Canas, A. (2008). *The theory underlying concept maps and how to construct and use them* (Technical Report IHMC CmapTools 2006-01 Rev 01-2008). Retrieved from Institute for Human and Machine Cognition website: http://cmap.ihmc.us/publications/researchpapers/theorycmaps/theoryunderlying conceptmaps.htm

Zelik, M., Schau, C., Mattern, N., Hall, S., Teague, K., & Bisard, W. (1997). Conceptual astronomy: A novel model for teaching postsecondary science courses. *American Journal of Physics, 6*(10), 987–996. doi:10.1119/1.18702

Principle 2

Bahrick, H. P. (1979). Maintenance of knowledge: Questions about memory we forgot to ask. *Journal of Experimental Psychology: General, 108*(3), 296–308.

Cepeda, N. J., Pashler, H., Vul, E., Wixted, J. T., & Rohrer, D. (2006). Distributed practice in verbal recall tasks: A review and quantitative synthesis. *Psychological Bulletin, 132,* 354–380.

Cull, W. L. (2000). Untangling the benefits of multiple study opportunities and repeated testing for cured recall. *Applied Cognitive Psychology, 14,* 215–223.

Delaney, P. F., Verkoeijen, P. J., & Spirgel, A. (2010). Spacing and testing effects: A deeply critical, lengthy, and at times discursive review of the literature. *Psychology of Learning and Motivation: Advances in Research and Theory, 53,* 63–147.

Dunlosky, J., Rawson, K., Marsh, E., Nathan, M., & Willingham, D. (2013). Improving students' learning with effective learning techniques: Promising directions from cognitive and educational psychology. *Psychological Science in the Public Interest, 14*(1), 4–58. doi:10.1177/1529100612453266

Karpicke, J., & Roediger, H. (2008). The critical importance of retrieval for learning. *Science, 319*(5865), 966. doi:10.1126/science.1152408

Kornell, N. (2009). Optimizing learning using flashcards: Spacing is more effective than cramming. *Applied Cognitive Psychology, 23,* 1297–1317.

Medina, J. (2008). *Brain rules* (pp. 95–119). Seattle, WA: Pear Press.

Meltzoff, A., Kuhl, P., Movellan, J., & Sejnowski, S. (2009). Foundations for a new science of learning. *Science, 325*(5938), 284–288.

Reiser, R. A., & Dempsey, J. V. (2007). *Trends and issues in instructional design* (2nd ed.). Upper Saddle River, NJ: Pearson Education.

Sousa, D. (2006). *How the brain learns.* Thousand Oaks, CA: Corwin Press.

Squire, L. (2004). Memory systems of the brain: A brief history and current perspective. *Neurobiology of Learning and Memory, 82*(3), 171–177.

Zull, J. E. (2002). *The art of changing the brain: Enriching the practice of teaching by exploring the biology of learning* (p. 129). Sterling, VA: Stylus.

Principle 3

Ainley, M. (2006). Connecting with learning: Motivation, affect and cognition in interest processes. *Educational Psychological Review, 18*, 391–405.

Ambrose, S. A., Bridges, M. W., DiPietro, M., Lovett, M. C., & Norman, M. K. (2010). *How learning works: Seven research-based principles for smart teaching* (pp. 153–187). San Francisco, CA: Jossey-Bass.

Braun, A., & Bock, J. (2007). Born to learn: Early learning optimizes brain function. In W. Gruhn & F. Rauscher (Eds.), *Neurosciences and music pedagogy* (pp. 27–51). New York, NY: Nova Science.

Caine, G., Caine, R. N., McClintic, C., & Klimek, K. (2005). *12 brain/mind learning principles in action*. Thousand Oaks, CA: Corwin Press.

Dolan, R. J. (2002). Emotion, cognition, and behavior. *Science, 298*(5596), 1191–1194. doi:10.1126/science.1076358

Hodges, D. (2010). Can neuroscience help us do a better job of teaching music? *General Music Today, 23*(3), 3–12.

Kember, D., Ho, A., & Hong, C. (2008). The importance of establishing relevance in motivating student learning. *Active Learning in Higher Education, 9*(3), 249–263.

Kenny, N. (2010, April 30). Relevance: The secret to motivating student learning [web log post]. *Natasha Kenny's Blog*. Retrieved from http://natashakenny.wordpress.com/2010/04/30/relevance-the-secret-to-motivating-student-learning/

Lattuca, L., & Stark, J. (2009). *Shaping the college curriculum: Academic plans in context*. San Francisco, CA: Jossey-Bass.

Lawson, C. (2012). The connections between emotions and learning. Retrieved from Center for Development and Learning website: http://www.cdl.org/resource-library/articles/connect_emotions.php

Medina, J. (2008). *Brain rules* (pp. 79–82, 215–221). Seattle, WA: Pear Press.

Nilson, L. B. (2010). *Teaching at its best: A research-based resource for college instructors* (3rd ed., pp. 243–245). San Francisco, CA: Jossey-Bass.

Nilson, L. B. (2011). *The mind has a mind of its own: Teaching and learning that's in sync with the mind* [webinar]. Retrieved from Emphasis on Excellence website: http://www.meggin.com/classes/previous-classes/the-mind-has-a-mind-of-its-own/

Pekrun, R. (1992). The impact of emotions on learning and achievement: Towards a theory of cognitive/motivational mediators. *Applied Psychology, 41*(4), 359–376.

Pekrun, R., Goetz, T., Titz, W., & Perry, R. (2002). Academic emotions in students' self-regulated learning and achievement: A program of qualitative and quantitative research. *Educational Psychologist, 37*(2), 91–106.

Rogan, M. T., Stäubli, U. V., & LeDoux, J. E. (1997). Fear conditioning induces long-term potentiation in the amygdala. *Nature, 390*, 604–607.

Shultz, P., & Pekrun, R. (Eds.). (2007). *Emotion in education*. Burlington, MA: Academic Press.

Sylwester, R. (1994). How emotions affect learning. *Educational Leadership, 52*, 60–65.

Turk-Browne, N. B., Yi, D. J., & Chun, M. M. (2006). Linking implicit and explicit memory: Common encoding factors and shared representations. *Neuron, 49*, 917–927.

Vail, P. L. (2010). The role of emotions in learning. Retrieved from Great Schools website: http://www.greatschools.org/parenting/teaching-values/the-role-of-emotions-in-learning.gs?content=751&page=2

Wieman, C. (2007, September-October). Why not try a scientific approach to science education? *Change*, 9–15. Retrieved from http://www.changemag.org/Archives/Back%20Issues/September-October%202007/full-scientific-approach.html

Willis, J. (2006). *Research-based strategies to ignite student learning: Insights from a neurologist and a classroom teacher*. Alexandria, VA: Association for Supervision and Curriculum.

Zull, J. E. (2002). *The art of changing the brain: Enriching the practice of teaching by exploring the biology of learning* (pp. 69–87). Sterling, VA: Stylus.

Workshop 3.1

Boyer, E. (1996). The scholarship of engagement. *Bulletin of the American Academy of Arts and Sciences, 1*(1), 18–33.

Bringle, R., Philips, M., & Hudson, M. (2004). *The measure of service learning: Research scales to assess student experiences*. Washington DC: American Psychological Association.

Campus Compact. (2003). *Introduction to service learning toolkit: Readings and resources for faculty.* Boston, MA: Author.

Correia, M., & Bleicher, R. (2008). Making connections to teach reflection. *Michigan Journal of Community Service Learning, 14*(12), 41–49.

Felten, P., Gilchrist, L. Z., & Darby, A. (2006). Emotion and learning: Feeling our way toward a new theory of reflection in service-learning. *Michigan Journal of Community Service Learning, 12*(2), 38–46.

Hatcher, J. A., Bringle, R. G., & Muthiah, R. (2004). Designing effective reflection: What matters to service-learning? *Michigan Journal of Community Service Learning, 11*(1), 38–46.

Howard, K. (2010–2011). *Community based learning at Centre College: Faculty handbook*. Retrieved from Centre College Center for Teaching and Learning website: http://ctl.centre.edu/assets/cblhandbook.pdf

Jacoby, B. (Ed.). (1996). *Service-learning in higher education*. San Francisco, CA: Jossey-Bass.

Meader, L. (2011). Real money, real lessons. *Colby Magazine, 100*(2). Retrieved from http://www.colby.edu/colby.mag/issues/58/article/1266/real-money-real-lessons/

Chapter 2

Bonwell, C. C., & Eison, J. A. (1991). *Active learning: Creating excitement in the classroom* (ASHE-ERIC Higher Education Report No. 1). Washington DC: George Washington University, School of Education and Human Development.

Brewer, E. W., & Burgess, D. N. (2005). Professor's role in motivating students to attend class. *Journal of Industrial Teacher Education, 42*(23), 23–47.

Codde, J. R. (2006). Applying the seven principles for good practice in undergraduate education. Retrieved from https://www.msu.edu/user/coddejos/seven.htm

Doyle, T. (2008). *Helping students learn in a learner centered environment: A guide to teaching in higher education.* Sterling, VA: Stylus.

Hake, R. (1998). Interactive-engagement vs. traditional methods: A six-thousand-student survey of mechanics test data for introductory physics courses. *American Journal of Physics, 66*(1), 64–74. doi:10.1119/1.18809

Hodara, M. (2011). *Reforming mathematics classroom pedagogy: Evidence-based findings and recommendations for the developmental math classroom* (Working Paper No. 27). New York, NY: Community College Research Center.

Jones-Wilson, T. (2005). Teaching problem-solving skills without sacrificing course content: Marrying traditional lecture and active learning in an organic chemistry class. *Journal of College Science Teaching, 35*(1), 42–46.

Kuh, G. D., Cruce, T. M., Shoup, R., Kinzie, J., & Gonyea, R. M. (2008). Unmasking the effects of student engagement on first-year college grades and persistence. *Journal of Higher Education, 79*, 540–563.

Millis, B. (2010). *Promoting deep learning* (IDEA Paper No. 47). Retrieved from Idea Center website: http://www.theideacenter.org/sites/default/files/IDEA_Paper_47.pdf

Nilson, L. B. (2010). *Teaching at its best: A research-based resource for college instructors* (3rd ed., p. 7). San Francisco, CA: Jossey-Bass.

Pascarella, E. T., & Terenzini, P. T. (2005). *How college affects students: Vol. 2. A third decade of research.* San Francisco, CA: Jossey-Bass.

Prince, M. (2004). Does active learning work? A review of the research. *Journal of Engineering Education, 93*(3), 223–231.

Wood, W. B., & Gentile, J. M. (2003). Teaching in a research context. *Science, 302*(5650), 1510. doi:10.1126/science.1091803

Zull, J. E. (2002). *The art of changing the brain: Enriching the practice of teaching by exploring the biology of learning* (pp. 135–152). Sterling, VA: Stylus.

Principle 4

Delahoussaye, M. (2002). The perfect learner: An expert debate on learning styles. *Training, 39*(5), 28–36.

Fadel, C. (2008). *Multimodal learning through media: What the research says.* Retrieved from Cisco Systems website: http://www.cisco.com/web/strategy/docs/education/Multimodal-Learning-Through-Media.pdf

Gazzaniga, M. (2008). *Learning, arts, and the brain.* Retrieved from Dana Foundation website: http://www.dana.org/uploadedfiles/news_and_publications/special_publications/learning,%20arts%20and%20the%20brain_artsandcognition_compl.pdf

Ginns, P. (2005). Meta-analysis of the modality effect. *Learning and Instruction, 15*, 313–331.

Jones, J. (2009, November 2). Challenging the presentation paradigm (in 6 minutes, 40 seconds): Pecha kucha [web log post]. *ProfHacker.* Retrieved from http://

chronicle.com/blogs/profhacker/challenging-the-presentation-paradigm-in-6-minutes-40-seconds-pecha-kucha/22807

Jones-Wilson, T. (2005). Teaching problem-solving skills without sacrificing course content: Marrying traditional lecture and active learning in an organic chemistry class. *Journal of College Science Teaching, 35*(1), 42–46.

Jung, F. (n.d.). Guide to making a PechaKucha presentation: Overview. Retrieved from http://avoision.com/pechakucha

Kalyuga, S. (2000). When using sound with a text or picture is not beneficial for learning. *Australian Journal of Educational Technology, 16*(2), 161–172.

Kress, G., Jewitt, C., Ogborn, J., & Charalampos, T. (2006). *Multimodal teaching and learning: The rhetorics of the science classroom.* London, UK: Continuum.

Kress, G., & Van Leeuwen, T. (2006). *Reading images: The grammar of visual design.* New York, NY: Routledge.

Mayer, R. E. (2005). Cognitive theory of multimedia learning. In R. E. Mayer (Ed.), *Cambridge handbook of multimedia learning* (pp. 31–48). New York, NY: Cambridge University Press.

Mayer, R. E., & Gallini, J. K. (1990). When is a picture worth a thousand words? *Journal of Educational Psychology, 82,* 715–726.

McKeachie, W. J., & Svinicki, M. D. (2013). *McKeachie's teaching tips:* Strategies, *research and theory for college and university teachers* (14th ed.). Belmont, CA: Wadsworth.

Medina, J. (2008). *Brain rules* (pp. 197–219). Seattle, WA: Pear Press.

National Council of Teachers of English. (2004). NCTE beliefs about the teaching of writing. Retrieved from http://www.readwritethink.org/classroom-resources/lesson-plans/designing-effective-poster-presentations-1076.html

Nilson, L. B. (2010). *Teaching at its best: A research-based resource for college instructors* (3rd ed., pp. 113–125). San Francisco, CA: Jossey-Bass.

Pashler, H., McDaniel, M., Rohrer, D., & Bjork, R. (2008). Learning styles: Concepts and evidence. *Psychological Science in the Public Interest, 9*(3), 105–119. doi:10.1111/j.1539-6053.2009.01038.x

Pieters, R., & Wedel, M. (2004). Attention capture and transfer in advertising: Brand, pictorial, and text-size effects. *Journal of Marketing, 68*(2), 36–50.

Pink, D. (2007). Pecha kucha: Get to the PowerPoint in 20 slides then sit the hell down. *Wired, 15*(9). Retrieved from http://www.wired.com/techbiz/media/magazine/15-09/st_pechakucha

Stenberg, G. (2006). Conceptual and perceptual factors in the picture superiority effect. *European Journal of Cognitive Psychology, 18*(6), 813–847.

Svinicki, M. (2004). *Learning and motivation in the postsecondary classroom.* Bolton, MA: Anker.

Tindall-Ford, S., Chandler, P., & Sweller, J. (1997). When two sensory modes are better than one. *Journal of Experimental Psychology: Applied, 3*(4), 257–287. doi:10.1037/1076-898X.3.4.257

Vekiri, I. (2002). What is the value of graphical displays in learning? *Educational Psychology Review, 14*(3), 261–312.

Workshop 4.1

Aune, S. P. (2008, February 21). 12 screencasting tools for creating video tutorials. Retrieved from Mashable: http://mashable.com/2008/02/21/screencasting-video-tutorials/

Bergmann, J., & Sams, A. (2012). *Flip your classroom: Reach every student in every class every day.* Washington DC: International Society for Technology in Education.

Bodie, G., Powers, W., & Fitch-Hauser, M. (2006, August). Chunking, priming and active learning: Toward an innovative and blended approach to teaching communication-related skills. *Interactive Learning Environments, 14*(2), 119–135.

EDUCAUSE. (2013). 7 things you should know about flipped classrooms. Retrieved from http://www.educause.edu/library/resources/7-things-you-should-know-about-flipped-classrooms

Finkel, E. (2012). Flipping the script in K12. Retrieved from District Administration website: www.districtadministration.com/article/flipping-script-k12

Flipped Learning Network. (2012). Improve student learning and teacher satisfaction with one flip of the classroom. Retrieved from http://flippedlearning1.files.wordpress.com/2012/07/classroomwindowinfographic7-12.pdf

Hamden, N., McKnight, P., McKnight, K., & Arfstrom, K. (2013). *A review of flipped learning.* Retrieved from Flipped Learning Network website: http://www.flippedlearning.org/cms/lib07/VA01923112/Centricity/Domain/41/LitReview_FlippedLearning.pdf

Musallam, R. (2011, October 26). Should you flip your classroom? [web log post]. *Edutopia.* Retrieved from http://www.edutopia.org/blog/flipped-classroom-ramsey-musallam

Nagel, D. (2013, June 18). Report: The 4 pillars of the flipped classroom. *The Journal.* Retrieved from http://thejournal.com/articles/2013/06/18/report-the-4-pillars-of-the-flipped-classroom.aspx?=THENU

Pacansky-Brock, M. (2012). *Best practices for teaching with emerging technology.* New York, NY: Routledge.

Talbert, R. (2013, April 4). Data on whether and how students watch screencasts [web log post]. *Casting Out Nines.* Retrieved from http://chronicle.com/blognetwork/castingoutnines/2013/04/04/data-on-whether-and-how-students-watch-screencasts/?cid=wc&utm_source=wc&utm_medium=en

TED. (2011, March). Salman Khan: Let's use video to reinvent education [TED video]. Retrieved from http://www.ted.com/talks/salman_khan_let_s_use_video_to_reinvent_education.html

University of Texas–Austin, Center for Teaching and Learning. (2013). "Flipping" a class. Retrieved from http://ctl.utexas.edu/teaching/flipping_a_class

Principle 5

Angelo, T., & Cross, P. (1993). *Classroom assessment techniques: A handbook for faculty* (2nd ed.). San Francisco, CA: Jossey-Bass.

Barkley, E. F., Cross, K. P., & Major, C. H. (2004). *Collaborative learning techniques: A handbook for college faculty.* San Francisco, CA: Jossey-Bass.

Bransford, J. D., Brown, A. L., & Cocking, R. R. (Eds.). (2000). *How people learn: Brain, mind, experience, and school.* Washington DC: National Academies Press.

Centre for the Study of Higher Education. (2002). Assessing group work. Retrieved from http://www.cshe.unimelb.edu.au/assessinglearning/03/group.html

Chapman, K., Meuter, M., Toy, D., & Wright, L. (2006). Can't we pick our own groups? The influence of group dynamics and outcomes. *Journal of Management Education, 30,* 557.

DeHaan, R. L. (2005). The impending revolution in undergraduate science education. *Journal of Science Education and Technology, 14*(2), 253–269.

Farrell, J. J., Moog, R. S., & Spencer, J. N. (1999). A guided inquiry general chemistry course. *Journal of Chemical Education, 76*(4), 570–574. doi:10.1021/ed076p570

Felton, P. (2008). Resource review: Visual literacy. *Change, 40*(6), 60–63.

George Mason University, Writing Across the Curriculum. (n.d.). *Peer response groups.* Retrieved from http://wac.gmu.edu/supporting/peer_response.php

Heller, P., & Hollabaugh, M. (1992). Teaching problem solving through cooperative grouping. Part 2: Designing problems and structuring groups. *American Journal of Physics, 60*(7), 637–644.

Hilton, S., & Phillips, F. (2010). Instructor-assigned and student-selected groups: A view from the inside. *Issues in Accounting Education, 25*(1), 15–33.

Jassawalla, A. R., Malshe, A., & Sashittal, H. (2008). Student perceptions of social loafing in undergraduate business classroom teams. *Decision Sciences Journal of Innovative Education, 6*(2), 403–426.

Johnson, D. W., Johnson, R. T., & Smith, K. A. (1991). *Active learning: Cooperation in the college classroom* (pp. 89–100). Edina, MN: Interaction Book.

Johnson, D. W., Johnson, R. T., & Smith, K. A. (1998). Cooperative learning returns to college: What evidence is there that it works? *Change, 20*(4), 26–35.

Kalman, C., Rohar, S., & Wells, D. (2004). Enhancing conceptual change using argumentative essays. *American Journal of Physics, 72*(5), 715–717. doi:10.1119/1.1645285

Levine, A., & Dean, D. R. (2012). *Generation on a tightrope: A portrait of today's college students.* San Francisco, CA: Jossey-Bass.

Lord, T. R. (2001). 101 reasons for using cooperative learning in biology teaching. *American Biology Teacher, 6*(1), 30–38.

Michaelson, L., Knight, A. B., & Fink, L. D. (Eds.). (2002). *Team-based learning: A transformative use of small groups.* Westport, CT: Praeger.

Millis, B. (2002). *Enhancing learning—and more!—through cooperative learning* (IDEA Paper No. 38). Retrieved from Idea Center website: http://www.theidea-center.org/sites/default/files/IDEA_Paper_38.pdf

Millis, B. (2010). *Promoting deep learning* (IDEA Paper No. 47). Retrieved from Idea Center website: http://www.theideacenter.org/sites/default/files/IDEA_Paper_47.pdf

Millis, B. (Ed.). (2010). *Cooperative learning in higher education across the disciplines, across the academy.* Sterling, VA: Stylus.

Millis, B. (2012). *Active learning strategies in face-to-face courses* (IDEA Paper No. 53). Retrieved from Idea Center website: http://www.theideacenter.org/sites/default/files/paperidea_53.pdf

Nilson, L. B. (2002–2003). Helping students help each other: Making peer feedback more valuable. *Essays in Teaching Excellence, 14*(8), 1–2. Retrieved from http://podnetwork.org/content/uploads/V14-N5-Nilson.pdf

Nilson, L. B. (2010). *Teaching at its best: A research-based resource for college instructors* (3rd ed., pp. 155–165). San Francisco, CA: Jossey-Bass.

Plank, K. (Ed.). (2011). *Team teaching: Across the disciplines, across the academy.* Sterling, VA: Stylus.

Plank, K. (2013). *Team teaching* (IDEA Paper No. 55). Retrieved from Idea Center website: http://theideacenter.org/sites/default/files/paperidea55.pdf

Pratt, S. (2003). Cooperative learning strategies. *Science Teacher, 4,* 25–29.

Prince, M. (2004). Does active learning work? A review of the research. *Journal of Engineering Education, 93*(3), 223–231.

Sargent, E. (n.d.). Connecting reading and writing: Inkshedding-to-learn. Retrieved from http://www.mhhe.com/socscience/english/tc/pt/sarg/mginkshd_final.html

Slavin, R. (1991). Synthesis of research on cooperative learning. *Educational Leadership, 48*(5), 71–82. Retrieved from http://www.ascd.org/ASCD/pdf/journals/ed_lead/el_199102_slavin.pdf

Sweet, M. (2012). *Team-based learning in the social sciences and humanities: Group work that works to generate critical thinking and engagement.* Sterling, VA: Stylus.

Weimer, M. (2010). Student-formed or instructor-assigned groups? *Teaching Professor, 24*(4), 2–4.

Weimer, M. (2011, June 10). Group work: Are student-selected groups more effective? Retrieved from Faculty Focus website: http://www.facultyfocus.com/articles/teaching-and-learning/group-work-are-student-selected-groups-more-effective/#sthash.ff5mkxah.dpuf

Weimer, M. (2013). *Learner-centered teaching: Five key changes to teaching* (2nd ed.). San Francisco, CA: Jossey-Bass.

Wenzel, T. (2000). Cooperative student activities as learning devices. *Analytical Chemistry, 72,* 293A–296A.

Williamson, V. M., & Rowe, M. W. (2002). Group problem-solving versus lecture in college-level quantitative analysis: The good, the bad, and the ugly. *Journal of Chemical Education, 79*(9), 1131–1134.

Workshop 5.1

Barron, B., Schwartz, D., Vyer, N., Moore, A., Petrosino, A., Zech, L., & Bransford, J. (1998). Doing with understanding: Lessons from research on problem- and project-based learning. *Journal of the Learning Sciences, 7*(3/4), 271–311.

Bessant, S., Bailey, P., Robinson, Z., Tomkinson, C., Tomkinson, R., Ormerod, R., & Boast, R. (2013). *Problem-based learning: Case study of sustainability education: A toolkit for university educators.* Retrieved from http://www.heacademy.ac.uk/assets/documents/ntfs/Problem_Based_Learning_Toolkit.pdf

Dewey, J. (1906). *The child and the curriculum.* Chicago, IL: University of Chicago Press.

Duch, B. J., Groh, S., & Allen, D. E. (2001). *The power of problem-based learning: A practical "how to" for teaching undergraduate courses in any discipline.* Sterling, VA: Stylus.

Eberlein, T., Kampmeier, J., Minderhout, V., Moog, R., Platt, T., Varma-Nelson, P., & White, H. (2008). Pedagogies of engagement in science: A comparison of PBL, POGIL, and PLTL. *Biochemistry and Molecular Biology Education, 36*(4), 262–273.

Hanson, D. (2006). *Instructor's guide to process-oriented guided-inquiry learning.* Lisle, IL: Pacific Crest. Retrieved from http://pogil.org/uploads/media_items/pogil-instructor-s-guide-1.original.pdf

Hmelo-Silver, C. E. (2004). Problem-based learning: What and how do students learn? *Educational Psychology Review, 16*(3), 235–266. doi:10.1023/B:EDPR.0000034022.16470.f3

Hung, W. (2011). Theory to reality: A few issues in implementing problem-based learning. *Educational Technology Research and Development, 59*(4), 529–552. doi:10.1007/s11423-011-9198-1

Illinois Mathematics and Science Academy, PBL Network. (2013) Retrieved from http://pbln.imsa.edu/

Kuh, G. D., Cruce, T. M., & Shoup, R. (2008). Unmasking the effects of student engagement on first-year college grades and persistence. *Journal of Higher Education, 79*, 540–563.

Kuh, G. D., Kinzie, J., Schuh, J. H., & Whitt, E. J. (2005). *Student success in college: Creating conditions that matter.* San Francisco, CA: Jossey-Bass.

Major, C. H., & Palmer, B. (2001). Assessing the effectiveness of problem-based learning in higher education: Lessons from the literature. *Academic Exchange Quarterly, 5*(1), 4–9.

Rangachari, P. K. (2002). Prolegomena to problem writing. In *Writing problems: A personal casebook.* Retrieved from http://fhs.mcmaster.ca/pbls/writing/intro.htm

Schmidt, H., Rotgans, J., & Yew, E. (2011). The process of problem-based learning: What works and why. *Medical Education, 45*(8), 792–806. doi:10.1111/j.1365-2923.2011.04035.x

Stanford University. (n.d.). *Problem-based learning: Examples of PBL problems.* Retrieved from http://ldt.stanford.edu/~jeepark/jeepark+portfolio/PBL/example2.htm

Strobel, J., & van Barneveld, A. (2009). When is PBL more effective? A meta-synthesis of meta-analyses comparing PBL to conventional classrooms. *Interdisciplinary Journal of Problem-Based Learning, 3*(1), 44–58.

Study Guides and Strategies. (n.d.). *Problem-based learning.* Retrieved from http://www.studygs.net/pbl.htm

Technology for Learning Consortium. (n.d.). *Problem-based learning resources.* Retrieved from http://www.techforlearning.org/PBLresources.html

University of Delaware. (2005). *Problem-based learning at the University of Delaware.* Retrieved from http://www.udel.edu/pbl/problems/

Williamson, V. M., & Rowe, M. W. (2002). Group problem-solving versus lecture in college-level quantitative analysis: The good, the bad, and the ugly. *Journal of Chemical Education, 79*(9), 1131–1134.

Workshop 5.2

Brown, P. (2010, September). Process-oriented guided-inquiry learning in an introductory anatomy and physiology course with a diverse student population. *Advances in Physiology Education, 34,* 150–155.

Eberlein, T., Kampmeier, J., Minderhout, V., Moog, R. S., Platt, T., Varma-Nelson, P., & White, H. B. (2008). Pedagogies of engagement in science: A comparison of PBL, POGIL, and PLTL. *Biochemistry and Molecular Biology Education, 36,* 262–273.

Farrell, J. J., Moog, R. S., & Spencer, J. N. (1999). A guided inquiry general chemistry course. *Journal of Chemical Education, 76*(4), 570–574. doi:10.1021/ed076p570

Hale, D., & Mullen, L. G. (2009). Designing process-oriented guided-inquiry activities: A new innovation for marketing class. *Marketing Education Review, 19,* 73–80.

Hanson, D. M. (2006). *Instructor's guide to process-oriented guided-inquiry learning.* Lisle, IL: Pacific Crest. Retrieved from http://pogil.org/resources/implementation/instructors-guide

Hanson, D. M., & Moog, R. S. (n.d.). *Introduction to POGIL.* Retrieved from http://www.pcrest.com/PC/pub/POGIL.htm

Hanson, D. M., & Wolfskill, T. (2000). Process workshops—A new model for instruction. *Journal of Chemical Education, 77*(1), 120–130. doi:10.1021/ed077p120

Lewis, J. E., & Lewis, S. E. (2005). Departing from lectures: An evaluation of a peer-led guided inquiry alternative. *Journal of Chemical Education, 82*(1), 135–139. doi:10.1021/ed082p135

Moog, R. S., Creegan, F. J., Hanson, D. M., Spencer, J. N., Straumanis, A., Bunce, D. M., & Wolfskill, T. (2009). POGIL: Process-oriented guided-inquiry learning. In N. J. Pienta, M. M. Cooper, & T. J. Greenbowe (Eds.), *Chemists' guide to effective teaching* (Vol. 2, pp. 90–107). Upper Saddle River, NJ: Prentice Hall.

POGIL Project. (2013). Retrieved from http://www.pogil.org/

Straumanis, A., & Simons, E. A. (2008). A multi-institutional assessment of the use of POGIL in organic chemistry. In R. S. Moog & J. N. Spencer (Eds.), *Process-oriented guided inquiry learning* (pp. 224–237). New York, NY: Oxford University Press.

Chapter 3

Principle 6

Anderson, L., & Krathwohl, D. (Ed.). (2001). *A taxonomy for learning, teaching, and assessing: A revision of Bloom's Taxonomy of Educational Objectives* (Complete ed.). New York, NY: Longman.

Andrade, H., & Du, Y. (2007). Student responses to criteria-referenced self-assessment. *Assessment and Evaluation in Higher Education, 32*(2), 159–181. Summarized in *Teaching Professor, 23*, 1.

Angelo, T., & Cross, P. (1993). *Classroom assessment techniques: A handbook for faculty* (2nd ed.). San Francisco, CA: Jossey-Bass.

Black, P., Harrison, C., Lee, C., Marshall, B., & William, D. (2003). *Assessment for learning: Putting it into practice.* Buckingham, UK: Open University Press. Retrieved from http://www.canterbury.ac.uk/education/protected/ppss/docs/gtc-afl.pdf

Black, P., Harrison, C., Lee, C., Marshall, B., & William, D. (2004). Working inside the black box: Assessment for learning in the classroom. *Phi Delta Kappan, 86*, 1–8.

Bloom, B. (1956). *Taxonomy of educational objectives: The classification of educational goals, by a committee of college and university examiners: Handbook 1. Cognitive domain.* New York, NY: Longmans.

Boud, D., Cohen, R., & Sampson, J. (1999). Peer learning assessment. *Assessment and Evaluation in Higher Education, 24*(4), 413–426.

Brookfield, S. D. (1995). *Becoming a critically reflective teacher.* San Francisco, CA: Jossey-Bass.

Brookfield, S. D. (2013). Critical incident questionnaire. Retrieved from http://stephenbrookfield.com/Dr._Stephen_D._Brookfield/Critical_Incident_Questionnaire.html

Butler, A., & Roediger, H. (2008). Feedback enhances the positive effects and reduces the negative effects of multiple-choice testing. *Memory and Cognition, 36*(3), 604–616. Retrieved from http://commonsenseatheism.com/wp-content/uploads/2011/01/Butler-Feedback-enhances-the-positive-effects.pdf

Carpenter, S., Pashler, H., & Cepeda, N. (2009). Using tests to enhance 8th grade students' retention of U.S. history facts. *Applied Cognitive Psychology, 23*, 760–771.

Cauley, K., & McMillan, J. (2010). Formative assessment techniques to support student motivation and achievement. *Clearing House, 83*(1), 1–6.

Cornell University, Center for Teaching Excellence. (2013). What do students already know? Retrieved from http://www.cte.cornell.edu/teaching-ideas/assessing-student-learning/what-do-students-already-know.html

Dietz-Uhler, B., & Lanter, J. R. (2009). Using the four-questions technique to enhance learning. *Teaching of Psychology, 36*(1), 38–41.

Dunlosky, J., Rawson, K., Marsh, E., Nathan, M., & Willingham, D. (2013). Improving students' learning with effective learning techniques: Promising directions from cognitive and educational psychology. *Psychological Science in the Public Interest, 14*(1), 4–58. doi:10.1177/1529100612453266

Educational Origami. (n.d.). Bloom's digital taxonomy. Retrieved from http://edori-gami.wikispaces.com/Bloom%27s+Digital+Taxonomy

Fisher, P., Zeligman, D., & Fairweather, J. (2005). Self-assessed student learning outcomes in an engineering service course. *International Journal of Engineering Education, 21*, 446–456.

Gier, V. S., & Kriener, D. S. (2009). Incorporating active learning with Power-Point–based lectures using content-based questions. *Teaching of Psychology, 36*(2), 134–139.

Greenstein, L. (2010). *What teachers really need to know about formative assessment.* Alexandria, VA: Association for Supervision and Curriculum Development.

Hargreaves, D. (2005). *About learning: Report of the Learning Working Group.* Retrieved from Demos website: http://www.demos.co.uk/publications/about-learning

Higgins, R., Hartley, P., & Skelton, P. (2002). The conscientious consumer: Recon-sidering the role of assessment feedback in student learning. *Studies in Higher Education, 27*(1), 53–64.

Hill, J., & Flynn, K. (2006). *Classroom instruction that works with English language learners.* Alexandria, VA: Association for Supervision and Curricular Develop-ment.

Iowa State University, Center for Learning and Teaching. (2011). A model of learn-ing objectives. Retrieved from http://www.celt.iastate.edu/teaching/Revised-Blooms1.html

Karpicke, J., & Blunt, J. (2011). Retrieval practice produces more learning than elaborative studying with concept mapping. *Science, 331*(6018), 772–775. doi:10.1126/science.1199327

Karpicke, J., & Roediger, H. (2007). Repeated retrieval during learning is the key to long-term retention. *Journal of Memory and Language, 57*, 151–162.

Lord, T., & Baviskar, S. (2007). Moving students from information recitation to information understanding: Exploiting Bloom's taxonomy in creating science questions. *Journal of College Science Teaching, 36*(5), 40–44. Retrieved from http://www.eos.ubc.ca/research/cwsei/resources/Lord%26Baviskar-Blooms.pdf

Lyle, K. B., & Crawford, N. A. (2011). Retrieving essential material at the end of lectures improves performance on statistics exams. *Teaching of Psychology, 38*(2), 94–97.

Mazur, E. (1997). *Peer instruction: A user's manual.* Upper Saddle River, NJ: Prentice Hall.

McConnell, D. (2012). ConcepTests. Retrieved from Carleton College Science Edu-cation Resource Center website: http://serc.carleton.edu/introgeo/conceptests/index.html

McDaniel, M. A., Howard, D. C., & Einstein, G. O. (2009). The read-recite-review study strategy: Effective and portable. *Psychological Science, 20*(4), 516–522.

McDaniel, M. A., Wildman, K. M., & Anderson, J. L. (2012). Using quizzes to enhance summative-assessment performance in a web-based class: An experimental study. *Journal of Applied Research in Memory and Cognition, 1*, 18–26.

McKeachie, W., & Svinicki, M. (2013). *McKeachie's teaching tips: Strategies, research, and theory for college and university teachers* (14th ed.). Belmont, CA: Wadsworth.

McTighe, J., & Emberger, M. (2006). Teamwork on assessments creates powerful professional development. *Journal of Staff Development, 27*(1), 38–44.

Morton, J. P. (2007, June). The active review: One final task to end the lecture. *Advances in Physiology Education, 31*, 236–237.

Nilson, L. B. (2010). *Teaching at its best: A research-based resource for college instructors* (3rd ed., pp. 273–294). San Francisco, CA: Jossey-Bass.

Novak, G., Patterson, E., Gavrin, A., Christian, W., & Forinash, K. (1999). Just in Time Teaching. *American Journal of Physics, 67*(10), 937. doi:10.1119/1.19159

Pyc, M. A., & Rawson, K. A. (2010). Why testing improves memory: Mediator effectiveness hypothesis. *Science, 330*(6002), 335. *doi:*10.1126/science.1191465

Roediger, H. L., Agarwal, P. K., McDaniel, M. A., & McDermott, K. B. (2011). Test-enhanced learning in the classroom: Long-term benefits from quizzing. *Journal of Experimental Psychology: Applied, 17*(4), 382–395. doi:10.1037/a0026252

Roediger, H., & Karpicke, J. D. (2006). Test-enhanced learning: Taking memory tests improves long-term retention. *Psychological Science, 17*(3), 249–255.

Rohrer, D. (2009). The effects of spacing and mixing practice problems. *Journal for Research in Mathematics Education, 40*, 4–17.

Rohrer, D., & Taylor, K. (2006). The effects of overlearning and distributed practice on the retention of mathematics knowledge. *Applied Cognitive Psychology, 20*, 1209–1224.

Shepard, L. A. (2005). *Formative assessment: Caveat emptor.* Retrieved from http://www.cpre.org/ccii/images/stories/ccii_pdfs/shepard%20formative%20assessment%20caveat%20emptor.pdf

Stake, R. (2004). *Standards-based and responsive evaluation.* Thousand Oaks, CA: Sage Publications.

University of Illinois Online Network. (n.d.). Online teaching activity index: KWL. Retrieved from http://www.ion.uillinois.edu/resources/otai/KWL.asp

University of Massachusetts–Amherst, Office of Academic Planning and Assessment. (n.d.). *Course-based review and assessment methods for understanding student learning.* Retrieved from http://www.umass.edu/oapa/oapa/publications/online_handbooks/course_based.pdf

University of North Carolina–Charlotte, Center for Teaching and Learning. (2004). Writing objectives using Bloom's taxonomy. Retrieved from http://teaching.uncc.edu/articles-books/best-practice-articles/goals-objectives/writing-objectives-using-blooms-taxonomy

Vanderbilt University, Center for Teaching. (n.d.). Classroom assessment techniques. Retrieved from http://cft.vanderbilt.edu/teaching-guides/assessment/cats/

Zull, J. E. (2002). *The art of changing the brain: Enriching the practice of teaching by exploring the biology of learning* (pp. 203–220). Sterling, VA: Stylus.

Workshop 6.1

Bailey, R., & Garner, M. (2010). Is the feedback in higher education assessment worth the paper it is written on? Teachers' reflections on their practices. *Teaching in Higher Education, 15*(2), 187–198.

Bean, J. C. (2011). *Engaging ideas: The professor's guide to integrating writing, critical thinking, and active learning in the classroom* (2nd ed., pp. 267–289). San Francisco, CA: Jossey-Bass.

Bean, J. C., & Peterson, D. (1998). Grading classroom participation. *New directions for teaching and learning, 74*, 33–40.

Bloom, B. (1956). *Taxonomy of educational objectives: The classification of educational goals, by a committee of college and university examiners: Handbook 1. Cognitive domain.* New York, NY: Longmans.

Brigham Young University, Faculty Center. (2001). 14 rules for writing multiple-choice questions. Retrieved from http://testing.byu.edu/info/handbooks/14%20Rules%20for%20Writing%20Multiple-Choice%20Questions.pdf

Brown, E., & Glover, C. (2006). Evaluating written feedback. In C. Bryan & K. Clegg (Eds.), *Innovative assessment in higher education* (pp. 81–91). New York, NY: Routledge.

Bruner, J. (1961). The act of discovery. *Harvard Educational Review, 31*, 21–32.

Burke, D. (2009). Strategies for using feedback students bring to higher education. *Assessment and Evaluation in Higher Education, 34*(1), 41–50.

Burton, S. J., Sudweeks, R. R., Merrill, P. F., & Wood, B. (1991). *How to prepare better multiple-choice test items: Guidelines for university faculty.* Retrieved from Brigham Young University Testing Center website: http://testing.byu.edu/info/handbooks/betteritems.pdf

Carless, D. (2006). Differing perceptions in the feedback process. *Studies in Higher Education, 31*(2), 219–233.

Coleman, L. (2002). *Grading student papers: Some guidelines for commenting on and grading students' written work in any discipline.* Retrieved from University of Maryland Center for Teaching Excellence website: http://www.cte.umd.edu/teaching/resources/GradingHandbook.pdf

Cornell University, Center for Teaching Excellence. (n.d.). Course-level assessment methods. Retrieved from http://www.cte.cornell.edu/teaching-ideas/assessing-student-learning/course-level-assessment-guide.html#assessmentmethods

Crisp, B. R. (2007). Is it worth the effort? How feedback influences students' subsequent submission of assessable work. *Assessment and Evaluation in Higher Education, 32*(5), 571–581.

Myers, C. B., & Myers, S. M. (2007). Assessing assessments: The effects of two exam formats on course achievement and evaluation. *Innovative Higher Education, 31*, 227–236.

Nilson, L. B. (2010). *Teaching at its best: A research-based resource for college instructors* (3rd ed., pp. 273–280). San Francisco, CA: Jossey-Bass.

Rowntree, D. (1987). *Assessing students: How shall we know them?* New York, NY: Taylor & Francis.

Schechter, E. (Ed.). (2011). *Internet resources for higher education outcomes assessment.* Retrieved from http://www2.acs.ncsu.edu/UPA/archives/assmt/resource.htm

Suskie, L. (2009). *Assessing student learning: A commonsense guide* (2nd ed.). Bolton, MA: Anker.

Vanderbilt University, Center for Teaching. (n.d.). Classroom assessment techniques. Retrieved from http://cft.vanderbilt.edu/teaching-guides/assessment/cats/

Vanderbilt University, Center for Teaching. (n.d.) Writing good multiple choice test questions. Retrieved from http://cft.vanderbilt.edu/teaching-guides/assessment/writing-good-multiple-choice-test-questions/

Wiggins, G., & McTighe, J. (2005). *Understanding by design* (pp. 146–171). Alexandria, VA: Association for Supervision and Curricular Development.

Workshop 6.1A

Bloom, B. (1956). *Taxonomy of educational objectives: The classification of educational goals, by a committee of college and university examiners: Handbook 1. Cognitive domain.* New York, NY: Longmans.

Brigham Young University, Faculty Center. (2001). 14 rules for writing multiple-choice questions. Retrieved from http://testing.byu.edu/info/handbooks/14%20Rules%20for%20Writing%20Multiple-Choice%20Questions.pdf

Bruff, D. (2009–2010). Multiple-choice questions you wouldn't put on a test: Promoting deep learning using clickers. *Essays on Teaching Excellence, 21*(3). Retrieved from http://podnetwork.org/content/uploads/V21-N3-Bruff.pdf

Burton, S. J., Sudweeks, R. R., Merrill, P. F., & Wood, B. (1991). *How to prepare better multiple-choice test items: Guidelines for university faculty.* Retrieved from Brigham Young University Testing Center website: http://testing.byu.edu/info/handbooks/betteritems.pdf

Harvard University, Derek Bok Center for Teaching and Learning. (2006). Grading papers. Retrieved from http://isites.harvard.edu/fs/html/icb.topic58474/GradingPapers.html

Jacobs, L. (n.d.). *How to write better tests: A handbook for improving test construction skills.* Retrieved from Indiana University–Bloomington website: http://www.indiana.edu/~best/pdf_docs/better_tests.pdf

Reiner, C., Bothell, T., Sudweeks, R., & Wood, B. (2002). *Preparing effective essay questions: A self-directed workbook for educators.* Stillwater, OK: New Forums Press. Retrieved from *Brigham Young University Testing Center website:* http://testing.byu.edu/info/handbooks/WritingEffectiveEssayQuestions.pdf

Teaching Effectiveness Program. (2013, May 16). Writing multiple-choice questions that demand critical thinking. Retrieved from University of Oregon Teaching and Learning Center website: http://tep.uoregon.edu/resources/assessment/multiplechoicequestions/mc4critthink.html

University of Washington, Center for Teaching and Learning. (n.d.). Constructing tests: Essay questions. Retrieved from http://www.washington.edu/teaching/constructing-tests/#essayquestions

Vanderbilt University, Center for Teaching. (n.d.). Grading student work. Retrieved from http://cft.vanderbilt.edu/teaching-guides/assessment/grading-student-work/

Vanderbilt University, Center for Teaching. (n.d.). Writing good multiple choice test questions. Retrieved from http://cft.vanderbilt.edu/teaching-guides/assessment/writing-good-multiple-choice-test-questions/

Workshop 6.1B

Kappa Omicron Nu Honor Society. (2013). Rubric samples for higher education. Retrieved from http://rubrics.kappaomicronnu.org/contact.html

Mitstifer, D. (2013). Undergraduate research paper rubric. Retrieved from Kappa Omicron Nu Honor Society website: http://rubrics.kappaomicronnu.org/rubric-documents/Undergraduate-Research-Paper-Rubric4.pdf

Mueller, J. F. (2012). *Authentic assessment toolbox.* Retrieved from http://jfmueller.faculty.noctrl.edu/toolbox/rubrics.htm

Pickett, N. (1999). Guidelines for rubric development. Retrieved from http://edweb.sdsu.edu/triton/july/rubrics/rubric_guidelines.html

Stevens, D. (2004). *Introduction to rubrics: An assessment tool to save grading time, convey effective feedback, and promote student learning.* Sterling, VA: Stylus.

Stevens, D., & Levi, A. (2013). *Introduction to rubrics: An assessment tool to save grading time, convey effective feedback and promote student learning* (2nd ed.). Sterling, VA: Stylus.

University of Colorado–Denver, Center for Faculty Development. (2006). Creating a rubric. Retrieved from http://www.ucdenver.edu/faculty_staff/faculty/center-for-faculty-development/Documents/Tutorials/Rubrics/index.htm

University of Massachusetts–Amherst, Office of Academic Planning and Assessment. (n.d.) *Course-based review and assessment methods for understanding student learning.* Retrieved from http://www.umass.edu/oapa/oapa/publications/online_handbooks/course_based.pdf

Wiggins, G., & McTighe, J. (2005). *Understanding by design* (pp. 146–171). Alexandria, VA: Association for Supervision and Curricular Development.

Workshop 6.1C

Harvard University, Derek Bok Center for Teaching and Learning. (2006). Grading papers. Retrieved from http://isites.harvard.edu/fs/html/icb.topic58474/GradingPapers.html

Orsmond, P., Merry, S., & Reitch, K. (1996). The importance of marking criteria in the use of peer assessment. *Assessment and Evaluation in Higher Education, 21*(3), 239–249.

Rae, A., & Cochrane, D. (2008). Listening to students: How to make written assessment feedback useful. *Active Learning in Higher Education, 9*(3), 217–230.

Ruszkiewicz, R. (2009). *How to write anything: A guide and reference.* New York, NY: Bedford/St. Martin.

Semke, H. D. (1984). Effects of the red pen. *Foreign Language Annals, 17*(3), 195–202. Retrieved from http://www.annenbergmedia.org/workshops/tfl/resources/s3_redpen.pdf

Shaw, H. (1984). Responding to student essays. In F. V. Bogel & K. Gottschalk (Eds.), *Teaching prose: A guide for writing instructors.* New York, NY: Norton. Retrieved from https://my.hamilton.edu/writing/writing-resources/how-i-assign-letter-grades

Vanderbilt University, Center for Teaching. (n.d.). Grading student work. Retrieved from http://cft.vanderbilt.edu/teaching-guides/assessment/grading-student-work/

Walvoord, B., & Anderson, V. (1998). *Effective grading* (pp. 128–129). San Francisco, CA: Jossey-Bass.

Walvoord, B., & Banta, T. (2010). *Assessment clear and simple: A practical guide for institutions, departments, and general education.* San Francisco, CA: Jossey-Bass.

Workshop 6.2

Brigham Young University, Center for Teaching and Learning. (n.d.). Using midcourse evaluations. Retrieved from http://ctl.byu.edu/collections/using-midcourse-evaluations

Clark, D. J., & Redmond, M. (1982). *Small group instructional diagnosis: Final report.* Available from ERIC Document Reproduction Service. (No. ED217954)

Coconino Community College. (2010). *Mid-course evaluations.* Retrieved from http://www.coconino.edu/research/Pages/MidCourseEvaluations.aspx

Cohen, P. (1980). Effectiveness of student-rating feedback for improving college instruction: A meta-analysis of findings. *Research in Higher Education, 13*(4), 321–341.

Cook-Sather, A. (2009). From traditional accountability to shared responsibility: The benefits and challenges of student consultants gathering midcourse feedback in college classrooms. *Assessment and Evaluation in Higher Education, 34*(2), 231–241.

Croxall, B. (2012, February 21). Conducting your midterm evaluations publicly with Google docs [web log post]. *ProfHacker.* Retrieved from http://chronicle.com/blogs/profhacker/make-your-midterm-evaluations-public-with-google-docs/38680

Diamond, R. (2004). The usefulness of structured mid-term feedback as a catalyst for change in higher education classes. *Active Learning in Higher Education, 5*(3), 217–231.

Lewis, K. G. (2001). Using midsemester student feedback and responding to it. *New Directions in Teaching and Learning, 87,* 33–44.

Millis, B., & Vazquez, M. (2010). Quick course diagnosis (QCD) and the structured focus groups. Retrieved from California State University–Channel Islands website: http://facultydevelopment.csuci.edu/on_line_resources.htm

Millis, B., & Vazquez, J. (2010–2011). Down with the SGID! Long live the QCD! *Essays on Teaching Excellence, 22*(4). Retrieved from http://podnetwork.org/content/uploads/V22_N4_Millis_Vasquez.pdf

Nilson, L. B. (2010). *Teaching at its best: A research-based resource for college instructors* (3rd ed., pp. 315–328). San Francisco, CA: Jossey-Bass.

Sorenson, D. L. (2001). College teachers and student consultants: Collaborating about teaching and learning. In D. Miller, J. Groccia, & M. Miller (Eds.), *Student-assisted teaching: A guide to faculty-student teamwork* (pp. 228–239). San Francisco, CA: Jossey-Bass.

Appendix A

Workshop A.1

Bain, K. (2004). *What the best college teachers do* (pp. 48–67). Cambridge, MA: Harvard University Press.

Bowen, J. (2012). *Teaching naked: How moving technology out of your college classroom will improve student learning.* San Francisco, CA: Jossey-Bass.

Concepción, D. W. (2009–2010). Transparent alignment and integrated course design. *Essays on Teaching Excellence, 21*(2). Retrieved from http://podnetwork.org/content/uploads/V21-N2-Concepcion.pdf

Diamond, R. (2008). *Designing and assessing courses and curricula* (3rd ed.). San Francisco, CA: Jossey-Bass.

Fink, L. D. (2005, August). *A self-directed guide to designing courses for significant learning.* Retrieved from http://www.deefinkandassociates.com/GuidetoCourseDesignAug05.pdf

Fink, L. D. (2013). *Creating significant learning experiences: An integrated approach to designing college courses* (Rev. ed.). San Francisco, CA: Jossey-Bass.

Groom, W. (1994). *Gumpisms: The wit and wisdom of Forrest Gump.* New York, NY: Pocket Books.

Harnish, R., McElwee, R., Slattery, J., Frantz, S., Haney, M., Shore, C., & Penley, J. (2011). Creating the foundation for a warm classroom climate: Best practices in syllabus tone. *Observer, 24*(1). Retrieved from http://www.psychologicalscience.org/index.php/publications/observer/2011/january-11/creating-the-foundation-for-a-warm-classroom-climate.html

Hara, B. (2010, October 19). Graphic display of student learning objectives [web log post]. *ProfHacker.* Retrieved from http://chronicle.com/blogs/profhacker/graphic-display-of-student-learning-objectives/27863

Huxham, M. (2005). Learning in lectures: Do "interactive windows" help? *Active Learning in Higher Education, 6*(1), 17–31.

Lattuca, L., & Stark, J. (2009). *Shaping the college curriculum: Academic plans in context.* Hoboken, NJ: Wiley & Sons.

Lowther, M. A., Stark, J. S., & Martens, G. G. (1989). *Preparing course syllabi for improved communication*. Washington DC: Office of Educational Research and Improvement.

Nilson, L. B. (2007). *The graphic syllabus and the outcomes map: Communicating your course*. San Francisco, CA: Jossey-Bass.

Nilson, L. B. (2010). *Teaching at its best: A research-based resource for college instructors* (3rd ed., pp. 33–37). San Francisco, CA: Jossey-Bass.

O'Brien, J. G., Millis, B. J., & Cohen, M. W. (2008). *The course syllabus: A learning centered approach* (2nd ed.). San Francisco, CA: Jossey-Bass.

Singham, M. (2007). Death to the syllabus! *Liberal Education, 93*(4), 52–56. Retrieved from http://www.aacu.org/liberaleducation/le-fa07/le_fa07_myview.cfm

Slattery, J. M., & Carlson, J. (2005). Preparing an effective syllabus: Current best practices. *College Teaching, 53*(4), 159–164.

Terry, W. (2005). Serial position effects in recall of television commercials. *Journal of General Psychology, 132*(2), 151–163.

University of Minnesota, Center for Teaching and Learning. (2008). Student roles. Retrieved from http://www1.umn.edu/ohr/teachlearn/tutorials/syllabus/expectations/student/index.html

Wasley, P. (2008a). Research yields tips on crafting better syllabi. *Chronicle of Higher Education, 54*(27), A11–A12.

Wasley, P. (2008b). The syllabus becomes a repository of legalese. *Chronicle of Higher Education, 54*(27), A1–A10.

Wiggins, G., & McTighe, J. (2005). *Understanding by design* (pp. 13–34). Alexandria, VA: Association for Supervision and Curricular Development.

Workshop A.2

Ambrose, S. A., Bridges, M. W., DiPietro, M., Lovett, M. C., & Norman, M. K. (2010). *How learning works: Seven research-based principles for smart teaching* (p. 84). San Francisco, CA: Jossey-Bass.

Bennett, K. L. (2004). How to start teaching a tough course: Dry organization versus excitement on the first day of class. *College Teaching, 52*(3), 106.

Bowen, J. (2012). *Teaching naked: How moving technology out of your college classroom will improve student learning*. San Francisco, CA: Jossey-Bass.

Carnegie Mellon University, Eberly Center. (n.d.). Make the most of the first day of class. Retrieved from http://www.cmu.edu/teaching/designteach/teach/firstday.html

Cox, K. J. (2005). Group introductions—Get-acquainted team building activity. Retrieved from http://www.docstoc.com/docs/34260610/Group-Introductions-Get-Acquainted-Team-Building

Douglas, C. (2013). Wrap-up activities for training professionals. Retrieved from Leadership Strategies website: http://www.leadstrat.com/component/content/article/12-forfacilitators/122-wrap-up-activities-for-training-professionals

Fleming, N. (2003). *Establishing rapport: Personal interaction and learning* (IDEA Paper No. 39). Retrieved from Idea Center website: http://www.theideacenter.org/sites/default/files/IDEA_Paper_39.pdf

Goza, B. K. (1993). Graffiti needs assessment: Involving students in the first class session. *Journal of Management Education, 17*(1), 99–106.

Grimes, J., & Desrochers, C. (2010). Making your first class session really first class [Video]. Retrieved from http://elixr.merlot.org/case-stories/course-preparation--design/first-day-of-class/goals-for-first-day-of-class7

Harnish, R., McElwee R., Slattery, J., Frantz, S., Haney, M., Shore, C., & Penley, J. (2011). Creating the foundation for a warm classroom climate: Best practices in syllabus tone. *Observer, 24*(1). Retrieved from http://www.psychologicalscience.org/index.php/publications/observer/2011/january-11/creating-the-foundation-for-a-warm-classroom-climate.html

Iowa State University, Center for Excellence in Teaching and Learning. (2011). Welcoming students on the first day [Video]. Retrieved from http://www.celt.iastate.edu/teaching/video/welcoming.html

Lang, J. M. (2006). Finishing strong. *Chronicle of Higher Education, 53*(9), C2. Retrieved from http://chronicle.com/article/Finishing-Strong/46812/

Lyons, R., McIntosh, M., & Kysilka, M. (2003). *Teaching college in an age of accountability* (p. 87). Boston, MA: Allyn and Bacon.

Maier, M. H., & Panitz, T. (1996). Ending on a high note: Better endings for classes and courses. Retrieved from http://home.capecod.net/~tpanitz/tedsarticles/endingcourses.htm

Nilson, L. B. (2010). *Teaching at its best: A research-based resource for college instructors* (3rd ed., pp. 26–27). San Francisco, CA: Jossey-Bass.

Palmer, M. (n.d.). Not quite 101 ways to learning students' names. Retrieved from University of Virginia Teaching Resource Center website: http://trc.virginia.edu/teaching-tips/not-quite-101-ways-to-learning-students-names/

Pascarella, E. T., & Terenzini, P. T. (2005). *How college affects students.* San Francisco, CA: Jossey-Bass.

Provitera McGlynn, A. (2001). *Successful beginnings for college teaching: Engaging students from the first day.* Madison, WI: Atwood.

Uhl, C. (2005). The last class. *College Teaching, 53*(4), 165–166.

Weimer, M. (2013, January 9). First day of class activities that create a climate for learning [web log post]. *Teaching Professor Blog.* Retrieved from http://www.facultyfocus.com/articles/teaching-professor-blog/first-day-of-class-activities-that-create-a-climate-for-learning/

Appendix B

Workshop B.1

Bask, K., & Bailey, E. (2002). Are faculty role models? *Journal of Economic Education, 33*(2), 99–124.

Bligh, D. A. (2000). *What's the use of lectures?* San Francisco, CA: Jossey-Bass.

Bodie, G., Powers, W., & Fitch-Hauser, M. (2006, August). Chunking, priming and active learning: Toward an innovative and blended approach to teaching communication-related skills. *Interactive Learning Environments, 14*(2), 119–135.

Burns, R. A. (1985, May). *Information impact and factors affecting recall.* Paper presented at the Annual National Conference on Teaching Excellence and Conference of Administrators, Austin, TX. Available from ERIC Document Reproduction Service. (No. ED258639)

Davis, D. (2008). A brain-friendly environment for learning. Retrieved from Faculty Focus website: http://www.facultyfocus.com/articles/instructional-design/a-brain-friendly-environment-for-learning/

Denman, M. (2005). How to create memorable lectures. *Speaking of Teaching, 14*(1), 1–5. Retrieved from http://www.stanford.edu/dept/CTL/Newsletter/memorable_lectures.pdf

Drummond, T. (1995). A brief summary of the best practices in college teaching. Retrieved from University of North Carolina–Charlotte Center for Teaching and Learning website: http://teaching.uncc.edu/articles-books/best-practice-articles/course-development/best-practices

Graesser, A. C., Olde, B., & Klettke, B. (2002). How does the mind construct and represent stories? In M. C. Green, J. J. Strange, & T. C. Brock (Eds.), *Narrative impact: Social and cognitive foundations* (pp. 231–263). Mahwah, NJ: Lawrence Erlbaum Associates.

Halpern, D., & Hakel, M. (2003). Applying the science of learning. *Change, 35*(4), 36–41.

Hamm, P. H. (2006). *Teaching and persuasive communication: Class presentation skills.* Retrieved from Brown University Harriet W. Sheridan Center for Teaching and Learning website: http://brown.edu/about/administration/sheridan-center/sites/brown.edu.about.administration.sheridan-center/files/uploads/Teaching%20and%20Persuasive%20Communication.pdf

Heath, C., & Heath, D. (2010). *Teaching that sticks.* Retrieved from http://groups.haas.berkeley.edu/CTE/documents/Teaching%20That%20Sticks.pdf

Hoyt, D., & Perera, S. (2000). *Teaching approach, instructional objectives, and learning* (IDEA Research Report No. 1). Retrieved from Idea Center website: http://www.theideacenter.org/sites/default/files/research1.pdf

Huxham, M. (2005). Learning in lectures: Do "interactive windows" help? *Active Learning in Higher Education, 6*(1), 17–31.

Karpicke, J., & Blunt, J. (2011). Retrieval practice produces more learning than elaborative studying with concept mapping. *Science, 331*(6018), 772–775. doi:10.1126/science.1199327

King, A. (1993). From sage on the stage to guide on the side. *College Teaching, 41*(1), 30–35.

McKeachie, W. J., & Svinicki, M. (2013). *Teaching tips: Strategies, research, and theory for college and university teachers* (14th ed.). Belmont, CA: Wadsworth.

Medina, J. (2008). *Brain rules* (pp. 73–93). Seattle, WA: Pear Press.

Nilson, L. B. (2010). *Teaching at its best: A research-based resource for college instructors* (3rd ed., pp. 113–125). San Francisco, CA: Jossey-Bass.

Reed, S. K. (2006). *Cognition: Theory and applications* (7th ed). Belmont, CA: Wadsworth.

Roediger, H., & Karpicke, J. (2006). Test-enhanced learning taking memory tests improves long-term retention. *Psychological Science, 17*(3), 249–255.

Ruhl, K. L., Hughes, C. A., & Schloss, P. J. (1987). Using the pause procedure to enhance lecture recall. *Teacher Education and Special Education, 10,* 14.

Terry, W. (2005). Serial position effects in recall of television commercials. *Journal of General Psychology, 132*(2), 151–163.

University of California–Berkeley, Center for Teaching and Learning. (n.d.). Large lecture classes: Six ways to make lectures in a large enrollment course more manageable and effective. Retrieved from http://teaching.berkeley.edu/large-lecture-classes

University of Minnesota, Center for Teaching and Learning. (2010). Planning lectures. Retrieved from http://www1.umn.edu/ohr/teachlearn/tutorials/lectures/planning/index.html

Wald, G. (1969). A generation in search of a future [Lecture]. Retrieved from http://www.elijahwald.com/generation.html

Appendix C

Workshop C.1

Bain, K. (2004). *What the best college teachers do* (pp. 48–67). Cambridge, MA: Harvard University Press.

Baxter, J., & Bush, R. T. (2010). Classroom discussion as a skill, not a technique. Retrieved from DePaul University Teaching Commons website: http://teaching-commons.depaul.edu/Classroom_Activities/discussion.html

Brookfield, S. (2006). *The skillful teacher* (pp. 115–131). San Francisco, CA: Jossey-Bass.

Brookfield, S., & Preskill, S. (2005). *Discussion as a way of teaching: Tools and techniques for democratic classrooms.* San Francisco, CA: Jossey-Bass.

Dawes, J. (2007). Ten strategies for effective discussion leading. Retrieved from Harvard University Derek Bok Center for Teaching and Learning website: http://isites.harvard.edu/fs/html/icb.topic58474/Dawes_DL.html

Duquesne University, Center for Teaching Excellence. (2004). *Facilitating classroom discussions.* Retrieved from http://www.duq.edu/Documents/cte/_pdf/classroom-discussions.pdf

Frederick, P. (1981). The dreaded discussion: Ten ways to start. *Improving College and University Teaching, 29*(3), 109–114. Retrieved from http://www.indiana.edu/~tchsotl/part%201/part1%20materials/The_Dreaded_Discussion.pdf

Henning, J. E. (2005). Leading discussions: Opening up the conversation. *College Teaching, 53*(3), 90–95.

hooks, b. (1994). *Teaching to transgress: Education as the practice of freedom.* New York, NY: Routledge.

Huston, T. (2009). *Teaching what you don't know* (pp. 144–165). Cambridge, MA: Harvard University Press.

Looking at Student Work. (n.d.) Protocols. Retrieved from http://www.lasw.org/protocols.html

McDonald, J. P., Mohr, N., Dichter, A., & McDonald, E. C. (2007). *The power of protocols: An educator's guide to better practice* (2nd ed.). New York, NY: Teacher's College Press.

McDonald, J. P., Zydney, J. M., Dichter, A., & McDonald, E. C. (2012). Abbreviated protocols. Retrieved from Teachers College Press website: http://www.tcpress.com/pdfs/mcdonaldprot.pdf

Nilson, L. B. (2010). *Teaching at its best: A research-based resource for college instructors* (3rd ed., pp. 113–125). San Francisco, CA: Jossey-Bass.

Nunn, C. E. (1996). Discussion in the college classroom: Triangulating observational and survey results. *Journal of Higher Education, 67*(3), 243–266.

Pennsylvania State University, Schreyer Institute for Teaching Excellence. (2013). Using discussion in the classroom. Retrieved from http://www.schreyerinstitute.psu.edu/tools/Discuss/

Ross, W. (1860). Methods of instruction. *Barnard's American Journal of Education, 9,* 367–379.

Rotenberg, R. (2005). The discussion classroom. In R. Rotenberg (Ed.), *The art and craft of college teaching: A guide for new professors and graduate students* (pp. 131–143). Chicago, IL: Active Learning Books.

Smith, M., Wood, W., Adams, W., Wieman, C., Knight J., Guild, N., & Su, T. (2009). Why peer discussion improves student performance on in-class concept questions. *Science, 323*(5910), 122–124.

Stanford University, Center for Teaching and Learning. (2003). The Socratic method: What is it and how to use it in the classroom. *Speaking of Teaching, 13*(1). Retrieved from https://www.stanford.edu/dept/CTL/Newsletter/socratic_method.pdf

INDEX

Idea-Based Learning
A Course Design Process to Promote Conceptual Understanding
Edmund J. Hansen

"*Idea-Based Learning* has much to commend it. It is not directed toward any specific discipline; instead, Hansen has included examples from across the curriculum. Hansen's book is readable and thought-provoking. It does not bog down the reader with excessive theory or debate, but rather seeks to be a concise guidebook for course design. It is an excellent starting point for new teachers, while also offering something to those more seasoned in the classroom. Finally, his work provides enough context that the reader is encouraged to move beyond this particular work in order to gain further depth into one's own reflection on teaching."

—*Forrest Clingerman*,
Ohio Northern University, in Teaching Theology & Religion

Sty/us

22883 Quicksilver Drive
Sterling, VA 20166-2102

Subscribe to our e-mail alerts: www.Styluspub.com

Also available from Stylus

Facilitating Seven Ways of Learning
A Resource for More Purposeful, Effective, and Enjoyable College Teaching
James R. Davis and Bridget D. Arend
Foreword by L. Dee Fink

"In a crowded marketplace of snake oil cure-alls for higher education comes this refreshingly straight-forward, sensible, and practical guide for college teachers. As Davis and Arend point out, learning is not just one thing, but many. Learning a skill is different from learning information, which is different form learning to think critically or creatively. It follows that there cannot be one way to teach it all. With careful attention to the research about multiple types of learning, Davis and Arend have provided a treasure trove of tips and techniques, from low-tech engaging discussions to high-tech virtual reality simulations, to help college teachers create learning environments that work."

—Michael Wesch,
2008 US Professor of the Year, University Distinguished Teaching Scholar, Kansas State University

"Slam dunk, touchdown, goal, grand slam, ace!!! This book is fabulous. Davis and Arend have pulled together an exceptional resource for better understanding effective teaching strategies by demonstrating how to adjust teaching based on what students need to learn. As faculty, we expect students to learn a wide variety of concepts, processes, and applications. To accomplish this, research clearly suggests using a variety of strategies. This book not only explains that research, but also gives concrete examples and a solid rationale for each learning approach.

While the authors note this material is not intended for those brand new to teaching, and although I believe just about anyone teaching at the postsecondary level could learn from this book, the primary audience really is faculty who are looking to rethink what they are currently doing. This book will result in seriously reassessing how to best facilitate learning.

This is the perfect book for groups and reading circles of experienced teachers. I will certainly add to my faculty development collection."

—Todd Zakrajsek,
Associate Professor, School of Medicine, University of North Carolina at Chapel Hill